SMITHSONIAN INSTITUTION
BUREAU OF AMERICAN ETHNOLOGY
BULLETIN 59

KUTENAI TALES

BY

FRANZ BOAS

TOGETHER WITH TEXTS COLLECTED BY

ALEXANDER FRANCIS CHAMBERLAIN

WASHINGTON
GOVERNMENT PRINTING OFFICE
1918

LETTER OF TRANSMITTAL

Smithsonian Institution,
Bureau of American Ethnology,
Washington, D. C., March 3, 1915.

Sir: I respectfully submit herewith for your consideration the manuscript of a work entitled "Kutenai Tales," by Franz Boas, "together with texts collected by Alexander Francis Chamberlain," with the recommendation that this material be published, with your approval, as Bulletin 59 of this Bureau.

Yours, very respectfully,

F. W. Hodge,
Ethnologist-in-Charge.

Dr. Charles D. Walcott,
Secretary of the Smithsonian Institution.

PREFACE

THE following collection of Kutenai tales embraces a series of texts collected by the late Alexander F. Chamberlain in 1891, and another one collected by me in the summer of 1914. The texts collected by Dr. Chamberlain were told by two men— Paul, who, according to information received in 1914, lived near St. Eugène Mission, and who had spent some time among the Blackfeet; and Michel, who belonged to the same region. The name of the narrator of the Lower Kutenai tales is given in "The International Congress of Anthropology" (Chicago, 1894) as Angi McLaughlin. The texts recorded by Chamberlain are brief. It should be remembered that these were recorded on the first field expedition ever undertaken by Dr. Chamberlain, and that it requires a considerable amount of practice to record long tales. This accounts to a great extent for the fragmentary character of his notes.

Among the texts collected by me, one was told by Pierre Andrew, a man about 33 years of age, who has a good command of English. He is not able, however, to interpret with any considerable degree of accuracy the grammatical forms of Kutenai, so that his own translation is always a rather free rendering of the Indian sentences. Two tales were told by Pierre Numa, an older man, who, however, spoke so rapidly that the tales had to be redictated by Pierre Andrew, who served as interpreter. Three other tales were told in the same way by Mission Joe, a man about 60 years old, whose dictation was repeated by Felix Andrew, a young man who speaks English very well, but whose ability to interpret the Indian texts word by word was even less than that of Pierre Andrew. One tale was told by Felix Andrew himself and was recorded by Mr. Robert T. Aitken. The rest of the stories were told by Barnaby, a man about 60 years of age, who, after very short practice, learned to speak slowly and distinctly, and whose dictation was perfectly satisfactory. All these tales were recorded without translation; and the translation was made later on, in part with the assistance of Pierre Andrew, in part with that of Felix Andrew. All my informants were Upper Kutenai, and the revision of Chamberlain's tales was also made by Upper Kutenai; so that the dialectic forms of the Lower Kutenai have probably disappeared.

It is interesting to note that Barnaby refused to tell the Mosquito story (p. 25), because, as he said, it was proper for children, not for adults.

I wish to express my sincere thanks for much kindly assistance rendered to me in the course of my work by Rev. F. E. Lambot, O. M. I., and the Sisters in charge of the Government School of St. Eugène.

FRANZ BOAS

COLUMBIA UNIVERSITY
New York

CONTENTS

CONTENTS

CONTENTS

III. ABSTRACTS AND COMPARATIVE NOTES

IV. VOCABULARY

^a, ⁱ, ^u vocalic resonance of consonants.

a, e, i, u short weak vowels, very slightly voiced.

E very weak vowel of indeterminate timber, lips, palate, and tongue almost in rest position, larynx not raised.

a_a, e_i, i_i, o_u diphthongized vowels, ending with a decided glottal stricture, so as to be set off from the following consonants, without, however, forming a complete glottal stop.

p, t, ts, k, k^u, q strongly aspirated surd stops (k^u labialized, q velar). *ts* is pronounced by many individuals as *tc;* but careful speakers, particularly old men, pronounced a clear *ts*. When followed by *w* or *y*, the stops lose some of the strength of their aspiration. Terminal *k* is somewhat palatalized, except when it follows a *u*.

p!, t!, ts!, k!, q! very strong glottalized consonants (fortis). *ts!* has in its continuant part a pure *s* character.

s as in English.

x̣ velar spirant.

ł voiceless *l*.

dl voiced affricative, only in the word *kudlidlus* ("butterfly").

m, n often strongly sonant, with sonancy beginning suddenly before complete labial or lingual closure.

' glottal stop.

' aspiration. All surd stops are strongly aspirated, but the aspiration has been indicated only in words beginning with a_a'.

The primary accent is always on the penultima, the weak vowels, a, i, u, not being counted.

KUTENAI TALES

By Franz Boas

TOGETHER WITH TEXTS

Collected by Alexander Francis Chamberlain

I. TEXTS COLLECTED BY ALEXANDER F. CHAMBERLAIN IN 1891 (Nos. 1–44)

[Nos. 1–23. Told by Paul]

1. Coyote and Fox

Coyote started. He saw Fox. Coyote said: "Give me your blanket. Let us be friends." Coyote said: "Let us go." Fox said: "Yes, let us be friends." Then he started. He went along. He saw people. There were many tents. Then they had a race.

2. Coyote and Locust[1]

Coyote went along. He saw Locust. He said to him: "Give me your shirt. If you give it to me, you will be my younger brother.

---

1. Coyote and Fox

Ts!ɑnaʾxeˑ skɛʾnˑkuˑts. nʾuʾpxₐneˑ naˑʾk!ₑyoʾs. qakeʾᵢneˑ skɛʾnˑkuˑts
He started   Coyote.   He saw   Fox.   He said   Coyote:

hamatɛʾktsu sɛʾt!neˑs. huts!ɛnʾɑłaʾₐneˑ swoʾtᵢmo. taʾxas qakeʾᵢneˑ
"Give me   your blanket.   We shall be   friends."   Then   said

skɛʾnˑkuˑts hułts!ɛnaxaʾₐła. qakeʾᵢneˑ naˑʾk!ₑyo heˑ taʾxas
Coyote: "Let us go."   He said   Fox: "Yes,   now

huts!ɛnałaʾₐneˑ swoʾtᵢmo. taʾxas ts!ɛnaʾxeˑ. qaˑnaʾxeˑ. nʾuʾpxₐneˑ
we shall be   friends."   Then   he started.   He went along.   He saw

aˑʾqłsmaʾkₑnɛk!s. yuˑnaqaʾₐneˑ aₐˑkɛtˑłaʾeˑs. taʾxas nʾɛtkɛʾnˑeˑ   5
people.   Many were   their tents.   Then   he made

kałnuxuʾknaˑm.
a race.

2. Coyote and Locust

Qaˑnaʾxeˑ skɛʾnˑkuˑts. nʾuʾpxₐneˑ aₐˑkukˑłakoʾwumʾs. qakɛʾineˑ
He went along   Coyote.   He saw   Locust.   He said to him:

hamatɛʾktsu aₐˑqaˑtwumłaʾₐtᵢnis. hɛnaˑmatɛʾktsaˑp hɛntsxałɛʾnˑeˑ
"Give me   your shirt.   If you give it to me   you will be

---

[1] See No. 57, p. 140.

I shall carry you." He said to him: "Don't, we shall be brothers." Coyote started. He carried Locust. The two went. He saw Grizzly Bear coming. Locust said: "Put me off." He was put off. There was a cliff, on the edge of which he staid. (Grizzly Bear Woman) arrived, and (Locust) scared her, and (Grizzly Bear) fell down. Coyote went back. He went around. He reached the place where Grizzly Bear lay. He ate her. He took her out of the fire. He took the meat and the fat. He ate. He tied it up. Coyote started. He carried Locust. He went along. He saw Grizzly Bear (Man) coming. Locust said: "Put me off." Coyote said: "It is my turn. Let me scare him." (Grizzly Bear) arrived. Coyote became a stump. Grizzly Bear arrived. He said: "Let me bite him." He saw it was Coyote. Coyote said: "I am Coyote. Let us start." He knew where Locust was. Coyote said to Grizzly Bear: "Will you eat grease?" Grizzly Bear said: "Yes, I'll eat it." Coyote untied

---

ka'tsa·. a'tutsxałxon⸍'s₁ne·. qak.ła'pse· ma_ats huts!n·ała'_ane·
my younger brother. I shall carry you." He said to him: "Don't! we shall be

tsa'_at₁mo. ts!na'xe· sk⸍'n·ku·ts. nałxo'_une· a_a'kuk.łako'wum's.
brothers." He started Coyote. He carried the Locust.

qa·nak⸍'k₁ne·. n'u'px_ane· k.ła'włas ska'se·. qake'₁ne· a_a'kuk.łako'wum
The two went. He saw Grizzly Bear coming. He said Locust:

p⸍sxo'_unu. p⸍sxo'hne· s₁n·umu'k!se· ⸍'nta·s. qaosaqa'_ane·. wa'xe·.
"Put me off!" He was put off where was a cliff, at edge. There he staid. He arrived.

5 naq!maxo'_une·ts wa't!m⸍ta·ktse'₁te·. ła·qanxa'xe· sk⸍'n·ku·ts.
He scared her and made her fall down. He went back Coyote.

qakxałaka'menqa·'tse·. qaoxa'xe· qa·kqa'pse· k.ła'włas. n'⸍'k₁ne·.
He went around. He reached where lay Grizzly Bear. He ate it.

ła·upkak!o'_une·. tsuk^ua'te· a_a'ku'ła_aks a_a'q!u'ta_als. n'⸍'k₁ne·.
He took it out of fire. He took meat fat. He ate.

n'⸍tuk!sa'_ane·. ts!na'xe· sk⸍'n·ku·ts. nałxo'_une· a_a'kuk.łako'wum's.
He fried it. He started Coyote. He carried Locust.

qa·na'xe·. n'u'px_ane· ska'se· k.ła'włas. qake'₁ne· a_a'kuk.łako'wum
He went along. He saw coming Grizzly Bear. He said Locust:

10 p⸍sxo'_unu. qake'₁ne· sk⸍'n·ku·ts ła·ts ka'min huts!⸍'s₁nl-
"Put me off." He said Coyote: "In turn I I myself shall

haq!maxo'_une·. qaoxa'xe· sk⸍'n·ku·ts. n'₁nqa'pte·k a_a'qułu'k!pko.
scare him." He arrived Coyote. He became a stump.

qawaka'xe· k.ła'wła. qake'₁ne· hul⸍'t!xa. n'u'px_ane·
He arrived Grizzly Bear. He said: "Let me bite him." He saw

n'⸍'nse· sk⸍'n·ku·ts·. qake'₁ne· sk⸍'n·ku·ts hun'⸍'n·e· sk⸍'n·ku·ts.
it was Coyote. He said Coyote: "I am Coyote.

huts!naxa'_ała. n'u'px_ane· sa·usaqa'pse· a_a'kuk.łako'wum's. qa-
Let us start." He knew where was Locust. He said

15 k⸍'ine· k.ła'włas sk⸍'n·ku·ts k₁ntsxa'l'e·k a_a'q!u'tał. qake'₁ne·
to him to Grizzly Bear Coyote: "Will you eat grease?" He said

k.ła'wła he· hutsxał⸍'k₁ne·. n'aqte'₁te· ka'łxo᷄ sk⸍'n·ku·ts.
Grizzly Bear: "Yes, I will eat it." He untied what carried Coyote.

what he was carrying. He gave it to him. (Grizzly Bear) saw it.
Grizzly Bear said: "Did you not see an old woman? She must have
passed here." Coyote said that he had not seen anything. Coyote
said: "It is Beaver, therefore it is fat." Grizzly Bear said: "It is
not Beaver." Coyote said: "You ought to have said, 'It is the old
woman.'" Coyote started to run. Coyote was going along. (Grizzly
Bear) pursued him. Grizzly Bear thought: "First let me bite the little
one." Grizzly Bear thought he was on the right trail. "Later on,
after I have bitten him, I will bite (this one)." Grizzly Bear
started. He pursued Coyote. Coyote went along. He was tired.
He chased him around the tree. He fell down and thrust his hand
into a (buffalo) horn. Coyote pursued Grizzly Bear. He overtook
him. He struck him. Coyote turned back.

3. COYOTE AND LOCUST

Coyote went along. He saw Locust. He (Locust) carried his leg.
Coyote saw it. Coyote thought: "Let me also break my leg."

---

namatɛ́ktseˑ. tseᵢkaʹteˑ. qakeʹᵢneˑ k.łaʹwła kɛnqa.upxaʹkeˑł tɛʹłna
He gave it to him.　　He saw it.　　He said　　Grizzly　　"Did you not see　　an old
　　　　　　　　　　　　　　　　　　　　　　　　Bear:　　　　　　　　　　　　woman?

nas qaʹkiłqahaʹxeˑ. qakeʹᵢncˑ skɛʹnˑkuˑts łuʹneˑ łaˑtseᵢkaʹteˑ. qakeʹᵢneˑ
Here she must have passed."　He said　　Coyote　　nothing　　he saw.　　He said

skɛʹnˑkuˑts nɛʹnˑeˑ sɛʹnˑa słaqałsɛʹkᵢneˑ. qakeʹᵢne k.łaʹwła qa.ɛʹnˑeˑ
Coyote:　　"It is　　beaver,　therefore it is fat."　He said　　Grizzly　　"It is not
　　　　　　　　　　　　　　　　　　　　　　　　　　Bear:

sɛʹnˑa. qakeʹᵢneˑ skɛʹnˑkuˑts xmanqakeʹᵢneˑ nɛʹnˑeˑ tɛʹłna. noˑtsɛnqku-
beaver."　He said　　Coyote:　　"Ought you to have　'It is　　old　　He started
　　　　　　　　　　　　　　　　said,　　　　　　woman.'"

pekɛʹmeˑk skɛʹnˑkuˑts. qanaʹxeˑ skɛʹnˑkuˑts. mɛtyaxnaʹpseˑ. qałwiʹyneˑ   5
to run　　　Coyote.　　He went along　　Coyote.　　He pursued him.　　He thought

k.łaʹwła huʹpaₐks hułsłɛʹtǃxa na ktsaquʹna. qałwiʹyneˑ k.łaʹwła
Grizzly Bear:　"First　　let me bite　this　little one."　　He thought　　Grizzly Bear

ksuˑkqanmɛʹteˑk. taʹxta hunułɛtǃxaʹmiˑł kutsxałɛʹtǃxa. tsǃɛnaʹxeˑ
he was on right trail.　"Later on　after I have bitten him　I'll bite him."　He started

k.łaʹwła. mɛtyaʹxₐneˑ skɛʹnˑkuˑtsˑ. qanaʹxeˑ skɛʹnˑkuˑts. nukᵘłuʹkᵤneˑ.
Grizzly Bear.　He pursued　　Coyote.　　He went along　　Coyote.　　He was tired.

aₐʹkɛtsǃłaʹeˑns naʹkamɛnłaˑtnotaʹpseˑ. qanaxuʹneˑ qanaqǃałeᵢxoʹmeˑk
A tree　　　he chased him around it.　　He fell down;　　he thrust his hand into

aₐʹkuʹqłeˑʹs. mɛtyaʹxₐneˑ skɛʹnˑkuˑts k.łaʹwłas. łaxanxoʹᵤneˑ.   10
a horn.　　He pursued　　Coyote (subj.)　Grizzly Bear (obj.).　He overtook him.

qanłaʹłteˑ. łaˑłuqᵘałqaʹtseˑ skɛʹnˑkuˑts.
He struck him.　He turned back　　Coyote.

3. COYOTE AND LOCUST

Qanaʹxeˑ skɛʹnˑkuˑts. nʼuʹpxₐneˑ aₐʹkuk.łakoʹwumʼs. nałxoʹᵤneˑ
He went along　　Coyote.　　He saw　　Locust.　　　He carried

aₐʹksaʹqǃeˑs. nʼuʹpxₐneˑ skɛʹnˑkuˑts. qałwiʹyneˑ skɛʹnˑkuˑts aₐʹkeˑ
his leg.　　He saw it　　Coyote.　　He thought　　Coyote:　　"Also

Then Coyote broke his leg. He carried it. Then Coyote started. Coyote carried his leg. He saw Locust. Locust said: "Is there any one similar to me?" Coyote said: "I am that way, too." Locust said: "We shall be friends." Then Locust said: "Now, go ahead. You go first." Then Coyote started ahead. Behind him was Locust. He went along. He thought: "I shall kill Coyote." Then Coyote ran. He went way around. He caught up with him and went ahead. He went along. He was tired. Locust reached him. He kicked him. Locust killed Coyote. Locust started. He went along. Coyote lay there for several days. Magpie flew along. He saw Coyote lying there. He thought: "Let me eat Coyote's eyes; he is dead." Then Magpie ate Coyote's eyes. Coyote came back to life. Coyote said: "A manitou passed by here. He carried

---

ka′min huɫ′umɛtskɛn kaa′ₐksaq!.   ta′xas n′umɛtskɛ′nˑe· aₐ′ksa′q!eˑs
  I   let me break   my leg."   Then   he broke   his leg

skɛ′nˑku·ts.   naɫxo′ᵤneˑ.   ta′xas   tsɛna′xe·   skɛ′nˑku·ts.   naɫxo′ᵤneˑ
   Coyote.   He carried it.   Then   he started   Coyote. ·   He carried

aₐ′ksa′q!eˑs   skɛ′nˑku·ts.   n′u′pxₐne·   aₐ′kuk.ɫako′wum′s.   qake′ineˑ
   his leg   Coyote.   He saw   Locust.   He said

a′ₐkuk.ɫako′wum   a′ₐ·keˑ   k.ɫqa′qa   qa′psin   huyaˋₐqaqapmɛ′lke·.
     Locust: "Also   is there   something   that is like me?"

5 qake′ineˑ   skɛ′nˑku·ts   a′ₐ·keˑ   ka′min   huqaqa′ₐneˑ.   qake′ineˑ
   He said   Coyote: "Also   I   am that way."   He said

aₐ′kuk.ɫako′wum   huts!ɛnˑala′ₐneˑ   swᵘ′țmo.   ta′xas   qake′ineˑ
   Locust: "We shall be   friends."   Then   said

aₐ′kuk.ɫako′wum   ta′xa   ɫu′nˑu   nɛ′nko   u′s′meˑk.   ta′xas   tsɛna′xe·
   Locust: "Now   go ahead   you   first."   Then,   started

n′ɛ′nˑe·   u′s′meˑks   skɛ′nˑku·ts.   iɫna′haˑks   aₐ′kuk.ɫako′wum.   qaˑna′xe·.
   he   first   Coyote.   Behind   Locust.   He went along.

qalwi′yneˑ   huɫ′u′pi·ɫ   skɛ′nˑku·ts.   ta′xas   tsɛna′k̦neˑ   skɛ′nˑku·ts.
  He thought: "Let me kill   Coyote!"   Then   he ran   Coyote.

10 n′ɛtkɛkqɫaˋɫaɫqaˑ′tseˑ.   la·ɫaxanxo′ᵤneˑ.   qa′yaqaˑna′xe·.   qaˑna′xe·.
    He went way around.   He caught up with him   he went ahead.   He went along.

nuk.ɫu′kᵤneˑ.   laˑxa′xe·   aₐ′kuk.ɫako′wum.   qanaqlɛ′kxₐneˑ.   n′ipɛ′lneˑ
  He was tired.   He reached him   Locust.   He kicked him.   He killed
                                                                              him.

skɛ′nˑku·ts·   aₐ′kuk.ɫako′wum.   tsɛna′xe·   aₐ′kuk.ɫako′wum.   qaˑna′xe·.
   Coyote (obj.)   Locust (subj.).   He started   Locust.   He went along.

naˑqsanmi′yet.s   qakqa′ₐneˑ   skɛ′nˑku·ts.   qaˑnaˋnˑoxo′ᵤneˑ   a′nˑan.
   Several days   he lay there   Coyote.   He flew along   Magpie.

n′u′pxₐneˑ   sakqa′pseˑ   skɛ′nˑku·ts·.   qalwi′yneˑ   huɫ′ɛ′k̦miˑɫ   aₐ′kaqlɛ′lˑeˑs
   He saw him   lying there   Coyote.   He thought: "Let me eat   his eyes

15 skɛ′nˑku·ts   pa·ɫ   ksɛ′lˑeˑp.   ta′xas   n′ɛ′k̦neˑ   a′nˑan   aₐ′kaqlɛ′lˑ·seˑs
    Coyote's,   he has been   Then   he ate   ·Magpie   his eyes
                    dead."

skɛ′nˑku·ts·.   skɛ′nˑku·ts   lạtq!aˋnxa′mˑneˑ.   qake′ine   skɛ′nˑku·ts
   Coyote's.   Coyote   came back to life.   He said   Coyote:

his leg and killed me." Coyote started and went back. He saw Locust. He slapped himself. Out came his corpses.[1] He said to them: "Tell me, how shall I kill him?" He was told by one of them: "He is always carrying his leg." He was told by the other one: "I shall be a knife. I shall be on the sole of your foot. When you overtake him and he says, 'You shall go ahead,' you shall say, 'You go ahead.'" Locust started. Coyote was behind. Coyote ran. He overtook Locust. He kicked him. Coyote killed Locust. Enough.

4. COYOTE AND GRIZZLY BEAR

Coyote went along. He saw Grizzly Bear's dung, unchewed wild rhubarb. Coyote laughed. Coyote took Grizzly Bear's dung. Coyote hung Grizzly Bear's dung on a pole in a line. He laughed. Coyote started. Grizzly Bear was staying there. He thought: "Let

---

na$_a$s qaha′xe·	nüp′k!a.	naɫxo′une·	a$_a$′ksa′q!e·s	n′upɫa′pine·	tsknа′xe·
"Here passed	a manitou.	He carried	his leg	and killed me."	He started

sk′n·ku·ts	ɫaxa′xe·.	n′u′px$_a$ne·	a$_a$′kuk.ɫako′wum's.	qanɫa′ɫte·k·
Coyote	and went back.	He saw	Locust.	He slapped himself.

n′akaxo′se·	a$_a$′kuq!ɫayet′k′n′e·s.	qak′ɫne·	tsxanata′pkiɫ	ka$_a$s
Out came	his corpses (dung).	He said to them:	"Tell me,	how

kutsa$_a$qaɫ′u′pe·ɫ.	k!o′k!we·'s	qak.ɫa′pse·	pe′k!a·ks	n′upɫa·′t$_i$yi·ɫqaɫ-
shall I kill him?"	By one	he was told:	"Already	always he carries

xo′une·	a$_a$′ksa′q!e·s.	k!o′k!we·'s	qak.ɫa′pse·	ka′min	hutsxaɫ′′n·e·	5
his leg."	By the other	he was told:	"I	shall be	

a$_a$′ktsa′ma·ɫ.	a$_a$′k.ɫ′k$_i$ne·s	hutsqa′kɫq!a′$_a$ne·.	hкn′i·naɫaxa′me·ɫ
a knife.	The sole of your foot	I shall hang at it.	When you overtake him

qa′k.ɫe·s	n′nko	u′s′me·k	′n·en′	hкnts!qak′ɫne·	n′nko	′n·en′	u′s′me·k·
if he says,	'You	first	be,'	you will say to him,	'You	be	first.'"

ts!кna′xe·	a$_a$′kuk.ɫako′wum	iɫna′ha·ks	n′′n·e·	sk′n·ku·ts.	ts!кna·′k$_i$ne·
He started	Locust.	behind	was he	Coyote.	He ran

sk′n·ku·ts.	ɫaxa′xe·	a$_a$′kuk.ɫako′wum's.	qa·nak.ɫ′kx$_a$ne·.	n′ip′ɫne·
Coyote.	He overtook	Locust.	He kicked him.	He killed him

a$_a$′kuk.ɫako′wum's	sk′n·ku·ts.	ta′xas.	10
Locust (obj.)	Coyote (subj.).	Enough.	

4. COYOTE AND GRIZZLY BEAR

Qa·na′xe·	sk′n·ku·ts.	n′u′px$_a$ne·	a$_a$′q!uɫ′′se·s	k.ɫa′wɫas	qaa′qtsx$_a$ne·
He went along	Coyote.	He saw	his dung	Grizzly Bear's,	not chewed

wu′m′a·ɫs.	n′uma′tsine·	sk′n·ku·ts.	tsuk^{u}a′te·	a$_a$′q!uɫ′′se·s	k.ɫa′wɫas
wild rhubarb.	He laughed	Coyote.	He took	his dung	Grizzly Bear's

sk′n·ku·ts.	ne′liɫqa·h·tsxomu′n·e·	k.ɫa′wɫas	a$_a$′q!uɫ′′se·s	sk′n·ku·ts·.
Coyote.	He hung it on a pole in a line	Grizzly Bear's	dung	Coyote.

n′uma′tsine·.	ts!кna′xe·	sk′n·ku·ts.	qaosaqa′$_a$ne·	k.ɫa′wɫa.	qaɫwi′yne·
He laughed.	He started	Coyote.	There staid	Grizzly Bear.	He thought:

---

[1] Two pieces of dung.

me go (and see) why Coyote is always laughing." Grizzly Bear went there. He saw his dung hanging there. Grizzly Bear became angry. He thought: "Let me go and kill Coyote." Grizzly Bear started. He saw Coyote coming. He thought: "What does Coyote like?" Grizzly Bear thought: "Let me make sisketoon[1] berries." He made sisketoon berries. He staid there. He thought: "I shall bite him right here." Coyote went along. He saw many sisketoon berries. He went there; he ate and spit them out again. Coyote said: "If Grizzly Bear had seen this, what an amount of dung there would be!" Coyote started. Grizzly Bear was angry. He thought: "If I don't bite you!" Coyote went along ahead. Grizzly Bear made choke cherries just at that place. Coyote went there. He ate and spit them out again. Then Coyote started. Then (Grizzly Bear thought): "I shall bite you." Coyote went along ahead. Just there Grizzly Bear made large rose hips. Coyote went there. He saw many rose hips. Then

---

hułts!ɛna′meįł   qa′psins   sła′qała′tįyił′u′mats   skɛ′nˑkuˑts.   qaoχa′χeˑ
"Let me go"   what   long time laughs   Coyote."   He went there

k.ła′wła.   n′u′pχₐneˑ   aₐ′q!uˑ′łˑeˑs   sakiłq!a′nseˑ.   saˑnⁱłwi′yneˑ   k.ła′wła.
Grizzly Bear.   He saw   his dung   hanging.   He became angry   Grizzly Bear.

qałwi′yneˑ   hułts!ɛna′meįł   huł′u′peįł   skɛ′nˑkuˑts.   ts!ɛna′χeˑ   k.ławła.
He thought: "Let me go   let me kill   Coyote."   He started   Grizzly Bear.

n′u′pχₐneˑ   ska′seˑ   skɛ′nˑkuˑtsˑ.   qałwi′yneˑ   qa′psins   nɛ′nˑeˑus   ktsła′keįł
He saw   coming   Coyote.   He thought: "What   does he   like

5   skɛ′nˑkuˑts.   qałwiˑ′yneˑ   k.ła′wła   huł′eˑįtkɛn   sq!ʋ′mˑo.   nɛ′tkɛˑneˑsq!ʋ′mˑos.
    Coyote?"   He thought   Grizzly   "Let me   sisketoon   He made   sisketoon
                                 Bear: make   berries."   berries.

qaosaqa′ₐneˑ.   qałwi′yneˑ   naₐsts   kutsqaₐkil′i′t!χa.   qaˑna′χeˑ   skɛ′n-
He staid there.   He thought: "Here   I shall bite him."   He went along   Coy-

kuˑts.   n′u′pχₐneˑ   yuˑnaqa′pseˑs   sq!ʋ′mˑo′s.   qaoχa′χeˑ   nɛ′kįneˑts
ote.   He saw   many   sisketoon berries.   He went there;   he ate and

ła′matqłaχwa′ₐteˑ.   qake′įneˑ   skɛ′nˑkuˑts   łaⁱsnakatni′kteˑt   k.ła′wła
he spit them out again.   He said   Coyote: "If he had seen this   Grizzly Bear,

χma   ła′akasqantsłaq!uχne′įłeˑk.   ts!ɛna′χe skɛ′nˑkuˑts.   saˑnⁱłwi′yneˑ
how big he would have defecated."   He started   Coyote.   He was angry

10   k.ła′wła.   qałwi′yneˑ   hułɛntsχałqa′ɛt!χₐnɛ′sįneˑ.   qaˑna′χeˑ   skɛ′nˑkuˑts
    Grizzly Bear.   He thought: "If I do not bite you."   He went along   Coyote

u′s′meˑks.   qaoχał′itkɛ′neˑ   aₐ′keˑ′lmaˑk!s   k.ła′wła.   qaoχa′χeˑ   skɛn-
first.   Just there he made   choke cherries   Grizzly Bear.   He went there   Coy-

kuˑts.   nɛ′kįneˑ   łamatqłaχwa′ₐteˑ.   ta′χas   ts!ɛna′χeˑ   skɛ′nˑkuˑts.
ote.   He ate   he spit it out again.   Then   he started   Coyote.

ta′χas   huts′ɛt!χₐnɛ′sįneˑ.   qaˑna′χeˑ   skɛ′nˑkuˑts   u′s′meˑks.   qaoχał′ɛt-
Then   "I shall bite you."   He went along   Coyote   first.   There

kɛ′nˑeˑ   wuq!o′′peˑs[2]   k.ła′wła.   qaoχa′χeˑ   skɛ′nˑkuˑts.   n′u′pχₐneˑ
he made   large rose hips (?)   Grizzly Bear.   He went there   Coyote.   He saw

---

[1] Service berries.   [2] Similar to rose hips (q!u′lwa), but larger.

he ate. He stood there eating. He saw many rose hips in the bushes. He went to the place where there were many rose hips. There was Grizzly Bear. Then Coyote shut his eyes and chewed rose hips. He did not see Grizzly Bear. [He was lying there.] He went there to pick and eat them. Grizzly Bear took hold of him together with the bushes. Grizzly Bear said: "What did you say?" Coyote said: "I said, 'I wonder whether Grizzly Bear is hungry.'" Grizzly Bear said: "No, you said something else."—"No, I said, 'I wonder whether Grizzly Bear is hungry.'"—"No, I didn't mean that first; I said that before ??." He hit him while saying so; Coyote hit Grizzly Bear with his elbow. Coyote ran off quickly. Nothing runs so fast as he was running. Coyote started. Coyote was pursued by Grizzly Bear. Coyote went along. Grizzly Bear made many turns. Grizzly Bear caught up with him. Coyote went ahead.

---

yuˑnaqa′pseˑ　q!u′łwaₐs.　　taˑ′ɣas　　n′ɛ′kinɛˑ.　　ya′wɛtsi′nɛt!ɣa′meˑk.
many　　　　rose hips.　　　Then　　　he ate.　　　　He stood eating.

n′u′pɣₐneˑ　　ɫoˑqtsqaˑ′haks　yuˑnaqa′pseˑ　wuq!o′′peˑs.　　qaoɣa′ɣeˑ
He saw　　　in the thick (bushes)　many　　　　rose hips (?).　　He went there

ya′kɫyuˑnaqa′pskeˑ　　wuq!o′′peˑs.　　saosaqa′ₐneˑ　　k.ła′wła.　　taˑ′ɣas
to where there were many　rose hips (?).　　There was　　　Grizzly Bear.　　Then

ts!oˑpɛnłaˑte′qłɛɣa′meˑk　skɛ′nˑkuˑts　wuq!o′′peˑs.　　qa.u′pɣₐneˑ　k.ła′w-
he shut his eyes and chewed　　Coyote　　　rose hips (?).　　Not he saw　　　Grizzly

ła′s.　　[sɫqa′oɣakqa′pseˑ.]　qa′oɣ′′ałhałq!at!eˑɣa′meˑk.　　nɛt!qaoɣa-　5
Bear.　　[He was lying there.]　　He went there to pick and eat them.　　He took

q!oˑnawoˑkɛnmunˑa′pse　k.ła′wła.　　qakeˑ′ine　k.ła′wła qaˑ kɛ′nskił′a-
hold of him with the bushes　　Grizzly Bear.　He said　Grizzly "What　　did you
　　　　　　　　　　　　　　　　　　　　　　Bear:

qakeˑ′ikił.　qakeˑ′ine　skɛ′nˑkuˑts　ma koqᵘa′keˑ　łaaˑ′qak.łaˑ′tɛnkɛkino′ᵤk-
say?"　　　He said　Coyote:　　"I said,　　　'I wonder whether he may be

tseˑk k.ła′wła.　　qakeˑ′ine　k.ła′wła wa′ha ma kɛn′ak!łana′keˑ.　wa′ha
hungry　Grizzly　　He said　Grizzly Bear: "No,　　you said differently." — "No,
　　　Bear.'"

ma koqᵘa′keˑ　łaaˑ′qak.łaˑ′tɛnkɛkino′ᵤktseˑk　k.ła′wła.　　wa′ha hoqa.eˑ-
　I said,　　　'I wonder whether he may be hungry　Grizzly Bear.'"　　"No,　I did not.

kɛ′kteˑ qo hoˑ′′paˑk qo taˑɣ ma huˑskiłqakeˑ′ineˑ.　nałatke′kɛłq!anłuk-　10
mean　that　first　　that then　　I said before."　　　He hit him while saying

ɣo′ᵤmeˑk neᵢs qaqkupnu′qtaptsek!aneˑya′ɣₐneˑ　k.ławłas skɛ′nˑkuˑts.
so,　　　that　he hit him　　with his elbow　　Grizzly Bear (obj.) Coyote.

noˑtsɛnqkupeˑkɛ′meˑk skɛ′nˑkuˑts.　ɣaˑtsqa′nuɣuˑnekɛ′meˑk　kts!ɛn-
He ran off quickly　　Coyote.　　　Nothing runs as fast　　　running

ma′łqa.　ts!ɛna′ɣeˑ skɛ′nˑkuˑts. mitɛyaɣna′pseˑ k.ła′wła skɛ′nˑkuˑtsˑ.
together(?).　He started　Coyote.　He was pursued by　Grizzly Bear　Coyote.

qaˑna′ɣeˑ skɛ′nˑkuˑts.　n′ɛtkɛkqłaˑ′łałqaˑ′tseˑ skɛ′nˑkuˑts.　łaˑ′łaɣan-
He went along　Coyote.　He made many turns　　　　Coyote.　　　He caught

ɣo′ᵤneˑ k.ła′wła.　qa′yaqaˑna′ɣeˑ.　qaˑna′ɣeˑ skɛ′nˑkuˑts. n′ɛtkɛkqłaˑ′-　15
up　　Grizzly Bear.　He went ahead.　He went along　Coyote.　　He made

He went along. Coyote made many turns. Then Coyote became tired. He asked for the help of the manitous. He said to them: "Tell me, what shall I do? Grizzly Bear is pursuing me." He was told by one of them: "I shall be a river." He was told by another one: "I shall be a tree." He was told by another one: "I shall be a tent. Then when Grizzly Bear comes, you will come out, you will say to him, 'Dead![1] you wish you could bite me.'" A tree was bobbing up and down. He said to him: "I shall hold the tree with my feet." He held it with his foot. (The Bear) walked across the water. He just came to the middle. He was in the middle over the water. Coyote let go of the tree [with his foot]. Then it bobbed up and down again. Grizzly Bear fell into the water. He was drowned. Enough.

5. COYOTE GOES VISITING

Coyote had a tent and was married to Dog. He told his children: "Over there is the tent of your uncles; they are never hungry; you

---

łałqaˑ'tse· skɛ'nˑkuˑts.   ta'xas nuk.łu'kune· skɛ'nˑkuˑts.   n'akmɛ''nte·.
many turns   Coyote.   Then   became tired   Coyote.   He asked for the help of the manitous.

qakɛ'lne· tsxa'nata'pkeᵢl kaₐs kuł'aqa'ke·n skanuta'pine· k.ła'wła.
He said to them: "Tell me,   what   shall I do?   he pursues me   Grizzly Bear."

k!o'k!we·s qak.ła'pse· ka'min hutsxał'ɛ'n·e· aₐ'kɛnmi'tuk. k!o'k!we·s
By one   he was told: "I   shall be   a river."   By one

qak.ła'pse· ka'min hutsxał'ɛ'n·e· aₐ'kɛts!ła'e·n. k!o'k!we·s qak.ła'pse·
he was told: "I   shall be   a tree."   By one   he was told:

5 ka'min   hutsxał'ɛ'n·e·   aₐ'kit.ła·'nam.   ta'xas   hɛ'n'waˑm k.ła'wła
"I   shall be   a tent.   Then   when he comes, Grizzly Bear

hɛn·tsł'aˑkaxa''mne·. hɛntsqakɛ'lne· n'ɛpna'mne· kɛnqa'łwiy kɛnts!-
you will come out.   You will say to him,   'some one dead   you wish   you will

ɛ't!xₐnap. wane'ᵢse· aₐ'kɛts!ła'e·ns. qakɛ'lne· hu'tsawi'tsɛkɛ'n·e· ɛn
bite me.'"   Moved up and down   a tree.   He said to him: "I shall hold with my feet   the

aₐ'kɛts!ła'e·n. naˑwɛtsɛkɛ'n·e·. nuˑlqanka·qoq!ʷnu'ne·. qa'ł'ɛn qaya-
tree."   He held it with the foot.   He climbed across water.   Just   in

qa'woᵤs qa'skaqo·qunu'ne·. pɛsɛkɛ'n·e· skɛ'nˑkuˑts aₐ'kɛts!ła'e·ns.
the·middle   he was on the middle of it on the water.   He let go with the foot   Coyote   the tree.

10 ta'xas ła'wane'ᵢne·. nonaqʷ'n·e· k.ła'wła. n'upʷ'qune·. ta'xas.
Then   it moved again.   He fell into the water   Grizzly Bear.   He was drowned.   Enough.

5. COYOTE GOES VISITING

Kqaˑni't.ła   skɛ'nˑkuˑts.   ksałe'ᵢte·t   xa'ₐltsins.   kqaˑ'keˑł
There being a tent   Coyote.   He was married to   Dog.   He told

ałaqa'łt!e·s   neᵢs   saˑnit.la'ₐne·   ałhatsanɛ'skeᵢl   at qahuwa's ₐne·
his children: "That   there is the tent   your uncles,   they are never hungry,

---

[1] An exclamation similar to "Confound it!"

ought to visit them." At night Coyote slept. Early the next morning Coyote said to his wife: "Where are my clothes?" Coyote was
given his clothing. Coyote dressed himself. Coyote started. He
went along. He saw the tent of Kingfisher. Coyote went there.
Coyote entered the tent of Kingfisher. He sat down. Kingfisher
said: "Where is my sharp horn?" He stretched his hand back.
He brought it forward. He put it down in front of himself. Kingfisher took it. He said to his children: "Go and get a switch."
His two children went out. They brought in two switches. Kingfisher took them. He tied up his hair over his forehead. Kingfisher
hopped about. He made noise when he started. He jumped and
stopped on the smoke hole. He jumped down. The two children
thought they would look out. Their mother said to them: "Don't
look out! He might not find the hole in the ice where he went in."

---

xma hɑnqe·na'milkɛ'łne·.   ktsɛmi'yɛt   q!u'mne'ɪne·   skɛ'n·ku·ts
ought   you to visit them."   At night   he slept   Coyote.

kkanmi'yɛt.ts   wo'łna·ms   qakɛ'łne·   tɛłnamu''e·sts   skɛ'n·ku·ts
The next morning   early   he said to   his wife   Coyote:

ka_as   ka·ku'qła'nt!.   namatɛkts'ɛ'łne·   a_a'kuqła''nt!e·s   skɛ'n·ku·ts.
"Where   are my clothes?"   He was given them   his clothes   Coyote.

n'ituqla'ntɛ'le·k   skɛ'n·ku·ts.   ts!na'xe·   skɛ'n·ku·ts.   qa·na'xe·.
He dressed himself   Coyote.   He started   Coyote.   He went along.

n'u'pxₐne·   sa·nit.ła'_ase·   q!a'pqa·łs.   qaoxa'xe·   skɛ'n·ku·ts.   5
He saw   there was the   Kingfisher.   He went there   Coyote.
                tent of

t‗inaxa''mne·   skɛ'n·ku·ts   a_a'kɛt.łaɛ'se·s   q!a'pqa·ł.   qa_ₐnqa'me·k.
He entered   Coyote   the tent of   Kingfisher.   He sat down.

qake'ɪne·   q!a'pqa·ł   ka_as   ke''e·n   kuł·aɛ'sɪnq!a'k.le·.   ła'ntaqahe'ɪne·.
He said   Kingfisher: "Where   is   my sharp horn?"   He put backward his
                                                                    hand.

ło·'nquwa'ₐkakɛ'n·e·.   qaoxakiɪnɛkts'ɛ'łne·.   tsuk·u·a'te·   q!a'pqa·ł.
He put it before himself.   It was put there.   He took it   Kingfisher.

qakɛ'łne·   ałaqa'ɪt!e·s   a'nyaxa'keɪł   ła·m'.   n'anakɛɛxa''mne·
He said to   his children: "Go out and get   a switch!"   They two went out

ne_ɪ   łkamuk·u_ɛ'ste·k.   ła'tkaki's_ɛkɛ'n·e·   ła·m's.   tsuk·u·a'te·   10
the   two children.   They brought in two   switches.   He took them

q!a'pqa·ł.   n'ɛtuk!·u·a'tsɪnk!o·nɛ'le·k.   qakqanmɛ'tinqa'me·k   q!a'pqa·ł.
Kingfisher.   He tied his hair in front.   He hopped about   Kingfisher.

n'a·'qkupkiłq!a'nło·k·u·akɛ'me·k.   a_a'k!ɑnqo·'t!e·s   qaowaxmɛt'wɛtsq!-
He made noise when starting.   To the smoke hole   he jumped and stopped

nu'ne·.   n'o·'nmeno'xunqa'_ₐne·.   qałwi'yne·   ne_ɪ   łkamuk·u_ɛ'ste·k
there.   He jumped down.   They thought   the   two children

kɪn'a'n'awɛtskɛ'ki_ɪne·.   qak.la'pse·   ma'e·s   ma_ats   an'awɛtske'_ɪ-
they would look out.   She told them   their   "Don't   look out!
                                            mother:

keɪł.   ła'qa·i·'ktsk!a·'qonɛ'le·k.   qaosaqa'_ₐne·   skɛ'n·ku·ts.   ła·t-   15
He might not find the hole in the ice   He staid there   Coyote.   He
where he went in."

Coyote staid there. Kingfisher re-entered carrying two switches.
He boiled them. Coyote ate. After eating, Coyote left for his tent.
He got back at night. Coyote slept that night.

Dog said to her children: "To-morrow you ought to visit your
uncles. There is their tent." Coyote slept. Early next day Coyote
started. He went along. He arrived at the tent of Moose. He
entered the tent of Moose. He sat down. (Moose) said to his wife:
"Look this way." She looked at her husband. Moose took a knife.
He cut off her nose. He took ashes. He threw them on, and it was
whole again. He threw it into the fire. He rolled it in the fire. He
took it out of the fire again. He said to his children: "Go and get
the roots of a tree." They brought them in. He threw these roots
into the fire. He rolled them in the fire. They became guts. He

---

kaxa"mse·	q!a'pqa·ɫs	ɫaa'se·	ɫa·m's.	na·nmukuɫɛ'sɪne·.	n'ɛ'kɪne·
re-entered	Kingfisher	with two	switches.	He boiled them.	He ate

skɛ'n·ku·ts.	ku'ɫe·kts	ɫa·ts!ɛna'xe·	skɛ'n·ku·ts	aₐ'kɛt.ɫa'e·s.
Coyote.	After eating	he left again	Coyote	for his tent.

ɫaɫaxa'xe·	ktsɛlmi·'yɛt.s.	q!u'mne'ɪne·	skɛ'n·ku·ts	neᵢs	ktsɛlmi·'yɛt.s.
He got back	at night.	He slept	Coyote	that	night.

Qakɛ'lne·	xa'ₐltsin	aɫaqa'lt!e·s	kkanmi·'yɛt.s	xma	hɪnqona·miɫkɛ'lne·
She said	Dog	to her children:	"To-morrow	ought	you to visit

5
aɫhatsanɛ'ske·ɫ.	neᵢs	sa·nɛt.ɫa'ₐne·.	neᵢs	kq!u"mne·	skɛ'n·ku·ts.
your uncles.	That	there is their tent."		He slept	Coyote.

kkanmi·'yɛt	wʊ'ɫna·ms	ts!ɛna'xe·	skɛ'n·ku·ts.	qa·na'xe·.	ɫaxa'xe·
Next day	early	he started	Coyote.	He went along.	He arrived

sa·nɛt.ɫa'ₐse·	nɛtsna'pko·ᵤs.	tɪnaxa"mne·	aₐ'kɛt.ɫa·ɛ'se·s	nɛtsna'pko·ᵤs.
where was the tent of	Moose.	He entered	the tent of	Moose.

qa·nqa'mek.	qakɛ'lne·	tɪnamu"e·s	ɫa'n·a	qa'kawɛtskɛ'ke·n'.	tseᵢka'te·
He sat down.	He said to	his wife:	"This way	look."	She looked at

nu·ɫaqₐna'e·s.	tsukᵘa'te·	aₐ'ktsa'ma·ɫs	nɛtsna'pku.	ɫuqsaɫa'ₐte·.
her husband.	He took	a knife	Moose.	He cut off her nose.

10
tsukᵘa'te·	aₐ'koq!mo·'ko·ps.[1]	qawaxmɛ'te·.	ɫaq!ape'ᵢse·.	xunmɛ'te·.
He took	ashes.	He threw them on.	It was whole again.	He threw it into the fire.

qa·kqayk!o'ᵤne·.	ɫa·upkakɛ'n·e·.	qakɛ'lne·	aɫaqa'lt!e·s	a'nyaxa'keᵢɫ
He rolled it about.	He took it out of the fire again.	He said to	his children:	"Go and get

aₐ'kuk!pʊ'ka·m.	ɫa'tka·kɛ'sɛlkɛ'n·e·.	xunmɛ'te·	neᵢs	aₐ'kuk!pʊ'ka·ms.
the root of a tree."	They two brought one in.	He threw into the fire	those	roots.

qa·kqayk!o'ᵤne·.	n'ɛn·qapta'kse·	aₐ'ku'qt!e·s.	ɫa·u'pkak!o'ᵤne·.
He rolled them about.	They became	its guts.	He took them out of the fire.

---

[1] Also aₐkuq!mʊ'ko·ps.

took them out of the fire. He arose. He slapped his backside, and camas came out. They put it into the kettle. It was given to Coyote. He ate. He finished eating. Coyote said: "To-morrow you will visit my tent." Coyote started back. Coyote arrived back at his tent. On the following day Moose arrived at the tent of Coyote. Coyote was seated. He said to his wife: "Look this way!" His wife looked at him. At once he cut off her nose. At once Dog ran out howling. Dog re-entered. He threw ashes on her, but her nose was not restored. Moose took ashes. He put them on her nose and it was whole again. He said to the two children: "Bring a root." They two went out. They brought it in. He took it. He threw it into the fire. He took it out of the fire. It turned into guts. He rolled them in the fire and gave them to (Coyote). Moose said to him: "Eat." Moose started back. Enough.

---

n'uwu'kₙneˑ.	t!akpuk!xo'ₙmeˑk	n'ananɛtsk!a'seˑ	xa'peᵢs.
He arose.	He slapped his backside,	it came out	camas.

n'o'qoˑxa'nt.ɫ'sᵢneˑ	a'tsoᵤs.	qaoxakinɛktsɛ'lneˑ	skɛ'n·kuˑts.	n'ɛ'kᵢneˑ.
They put it into	the kettle.	It was given to	Coyote.	He ate.

ku'l'eˑk.	qake'ineˑ	skɛ'n·kuˑts	kkanmi'yɛt	hɛntsqona'xeˑ	kakɛ't.ɫa.
He finished eating.	He said	Coyote:	"To-morrow	you will visit	my tent."

ɫatsⱡna'xeˑ	skɛ'n·kuˑts.	ɫaˑɫaxa'xeˑ	aₐ'kɛt.ɫa'eˑs	skɛ'n·kuˑts·.
He started back	Coyote.	He arrived back	at his tent	Coyote.

kkanmi'yɛt.s	ɫaxa'xeˑ	nɛtsna'pku	aₐ'kɛt.ɫa.ɛ'seˑs	skɛ'n·kuˑts·.	5
Next day	arrived	Moose	at the tent of	Coyote.	

qa'nqa'meˑk	skɛ'n·kuˑts.	qa'kɛ'lneˑ	tɛⱡnamu''eˑs	ɫa'n·a
He sat down	Coyote.	He said to	his wife:	"This way

qa'kawɛtskɛ'ke·n'.	tseᵢkata'pseˑ	tɛⱡnamu'eˑs.	ɫuqkupqsaɫa'ₐteˑ.
look!"	She looked at him	his wife.	Quickly he cut off her nose.

n'anmuqkupnoxo·'ne·ɫkɛkwakɛ'me·k	xa'ₐltsin.	ɫatkaxa''mneˑ
Quickly she ran out howling	Dog.	She re-entered

xa'ₐltsin.	qawaxmɛ'teˑ	aₐ'kuq!mʋ'ko·ps	qa'qaɫha·k!anu'qsaɫa'aseˑ.
Dog.	He threw on her	ashes	her nose was not restored.

tsukᵘa'teˑ	aₐ'kuq!mʋ'ko·ps	nɛtsna'pku.	qawaxmɛ'teˑ	10
He took	ashes	Moose.	He threw them on	

aₐ'kuqsa'ɫa.ɛ'seˑs.	ɫaq!ape'ᵢseˑ.	qakɛ'lneˑ	neᵢs	ⱡkamukᵘɛsta'ke·s
her nose.	It was whole again.	He said to	those	two children:

a'nya·xa'keᵢɫ	aₐ'kuk!pʋ'kam.	n'a'nakɛsxa''mneˑ.	ɫatkakɛ'sɛlkɛ'n·eˑ.
"Fetch	a root."	They two went out.	They brought it in.

tsukᵘa'teˑ.	xunmɛ'teˑ.	ɫa.upkakɛsk!o'ₙneˑ.	n'ɛnqapta'kseˑ
He took it.	He threw it into the fire.	He took two out of the fire.	They turned into

aₐ'ku'qt!eˑs.	ɫa.upkak!o'ₙneˑ.	qaoxakinɛ'ktseˑ.	qakɛ'lneˑ	e'ᵢkeᵢɫ.
guts.	He rolled them about	and gave them to him.	He said to him:	"Eat!"

ɫatsⱡna'xeˑ	nɛtsna'pku.	ta'xas.		15
He started back	Moose.	Enough.		

6. COYOTE AND BUFFALO [1]

Coyote went along. There was a bull's skull lying there, and he knocked it about. He started off. He went along. There was a hill. He went up the hill. Coyote staid there. There was noise of running. He raised his head quickly, but there was nothing. He sat down again (??). Again there was noise of running. He saw a Buffalo Bull coming. He started to run away quickly. He went along. Then they met again. He went along. Coyote said: "Oh, where are you staying, manitous?" He said: "Nephew, come, our(?)." Coyote saw burnt trees standing there. Coyote arrived, and sat down on top of them. Bull butted the tree. He broke it. Coyote started to run quickly. Coyote went along. He was tired. He said: "Where are you staying, manitous?" He was told: "Nephew, come, our (?)." Coyote went. There lay a stone. He entered it. Bull butted the stone. He broke it. Coyote

---

6. COYOTE AND BUFFALO

Qa·na'xe· sk⸃n·ku·ts.   sk⸃k.ła"m·ala'kse· ni'lsiks ts!⸃naqa'ylik⸃'n·e·.
He went along Coyote.   A skull lying there   a bull's   he knocked it about.

ts!⸃na'xe·.   qa·na'xe·   sw⸃tsłe⸃'t.se·.   qa·ox^uałyuxa'xe·.   qaosaqa'ₐne·
He started off.   He went along   where was a hill.   He went up hill.   There staid

sk⸃'n·ku·ts.   nałukm⸃'se·.   nuknuqkupq!ala"mne·   ło'ᵤse·
Coyote.   There was noise of   He raised his head quickly,   not there
              running.

qa'psins.   łaqa'ₐtstakqa'ₐne·.   łaha·'łukm⸃'se·.   n·u'pxₐne·   ska·'se·
was anything.   Again (?).   Again there was noise of   He saw   coming
                              running.

5 ni'lsiks.   no·ts⸃nqku·pek⸃'me·k.   qa·na'xe·.   ta'xas   ła·xan·xona'pse·.
a bull.   He started to run away quickly.   He went along.   Then   again they met.

qa·na'xe·.   qake'ₐne·   sk⸃'n·ku·ts   hał·ya·   k⸃n·aqasaqa·'łqa
He went along.   He said   Coyote: "Oh,   where are you staying,

nöp⸃'k!an⸃'nte·k.   tsxa'se·   pa·t!   qaowakaxa"me·n'   kaquxma'ła.
manitous?"   He said: "Nephew,   come   our (?)."

tse₍ka'te·   sk⸃'n·ku·ts   s⸃nq!o·mkaki'łioqaku'pse·.   qaoxa'xe·   sk⸃'n-
He saw   Coyote   burnt trees standing there.   He arrived   Coyote

ku·ts   naqo_ᵤsaq!maxo'ᵤme·k.   nako'ᵤne·   a_a'k⸃ts!ła'ens   ni'lsik.   ts⸃k!-
he sat down on top of them.   He butted   the tree   the bull.   He

10 k!o'ᵤne·.   no·ts⸃nqkupek⸃'me·k   sk⸃'n·ku·ts.   qa·na'xe·   sk⸃'n·ku·ts.
broke it.   He started to run away quickly   Coyote.   He went along   Coyote.

nuk^ułu'k_ᵤne·.   qake'ₐne·   k⸃n·aqasaqa·'łqa nöp⸃'k!an⸃'nte·k.   qak.la'pse·
He was tired.   He said: "Where are you staying,   manitous?"   He was told:

pa·t! qaowakaxa"me·n'   kaquxma'ła.   qaoxa'xe·   sk⸃'n·ku·ts   sk⸃knu'k-
"Nephew,   come   our (?)."   He went   Coyote   where lay a

se·.   nukwaq!ma·k⸃kqa'ₐne·.   nako'ᵤne·   nu'kwe·s   ni'lsik.   ts⸃k!k!o'ᵤ-
stone.   He entered it.   He butted   the stone   the bull.   He broke it.

started to run away quickly. Coyote went along. There was a
(body of) water. Coyote jumped into the water. He dived. The
Bull came to the water and drank. He stood there drinking. He
drank it all. Coyote started. He went along. He said: "Where are
you, manitous?" He heard speaking, and was told: "Nephew, come,
our (?)." The two went. There was a little rosebush. Coyote
went. He sat down on top of it. The Bull arrived. He butted it.
He couldn't break it. Again he butted it. He tore it into shreds.
Coyote said: "Now let me go; I will fill a pipe for you." The Bull said:
"I don't smoke." Coyote said: "I will fill a pipe; I don't know what
the Bull likes to smoke." Coyote was told: "I smoke tobacco.
When I finish filling the pipe, I hold it up to the sun. It catches fire.
It catches fire by means of the sun." (Coyote) was afraid. (The
Bull) smoked. He continued to smoke. The Bull said: "I had a wife

ne·. no·tsknqkupekⁱ'me·k skⁱ'n·ku·ts. qa·na'xe· skⁱ'n·ku·ts skⁱk-
He started to run away quickly   Coyote.   He went along   Coyote   where lay

q!nu'kse·. nuluⁱnnⁱtqu'ie·k skⁱ'n·ku·ts. k!anwa'ts!ne·. xuna'xe·
a lake.   He jumped into the water   Coyote.   He dived.   He came to
                                                                           the water

ni'łsik neⁱqu'łne·. qa·wⁱtsku'xune·. n'oko_uku'xune·. ts!ⁱna'xe· skⁱ'n-
the bull   and drank.   He stood drinking water.   He drank it all.   , He started   Coy-

ku·ts. qa·na'xe·. qake'ⁱne· kⁱn'aqasaqa·'łqa nöpⁱ'k!anⁱ''nte·k. nuł-
ote.   He went along.   He said: " Where are you,   manitous?"   He

pa'łne· tsxa'se· qak.ła'pse· pa·t! qaowakaxa''me·n' kaquxma'ła. 5
heard   speaking   and was told: "Nephew,   come   our (?)."

qawⁱtskⁱ'k_ine· sⁱn·qa'pse· sq!o·mowokna'nas. qaoxa'xe· skⁱ'n·ku·ts.
They went   where was   a little rosebush.   He went   Coyote.

nuqo_usaq!maxo'_ume·k.   łaxa'xe· ni'łsik.   qo·nanoxo·n łamaneya'-
He sat down on top of it.   He arrived   the bull.   He hit it with his head (?).

xane·. qata'ł'ak!o'_une·. łaqonaxo·n łamaneya'xane·. nⁱta'mk!o'_une·
He could not break it.   Again he hit it with his head (?).   He tore it into

ła_ɐm's. qake'ⁱne· skⁱ'n·ku·ts ta'xas qa·qaskⁱ'n·u. hutsku'łnak!uk-
shreds.   He said   Coyote: "Now   let me go.   I'll fill a pipe for

tsⁱ's_ine·. qake'ⁱne· ni'łsik atuqaⁱknoqʋ'k_une·. qake'ⁱne· skⁱ'n- 10
you."   He said   the bull: "I do not smoke."   He said   Coy-

ku·ts hutskułnak!o'_une·. hoqa·u'pxami'łne· qa'psinsts ł'e·kⁱnoqʋ'ko·
ote: "I'll fill a pipe.   I do not know   what   he may smoke

ni'łsik. qakiłⁱ'łne· skⁱ'n·ku·ts wasa'q_an·a·n huts!ⁱknoqʋ'k_une·.
the bull."   He was told   Coyote: "Tobacco (?)   I smoke.

nułkułnak!o'_une· qaoxawⁱ'tsx_ane· nata·'nⁱk!s. tsukʋ'px_ane·. sⁱtsu-
When I finish filling the   I hold it up toward   the sun.   It catches fire.   It catches
pipe

kʋpxanʋ'n·e· nata·'nⁱk!s. n'onⁱ'łne·. n'ⁱknoqʋ'k_une·. qa·kⁱ'ⁱkno-
fire by means of   the sun."   He was afraid.   He smoked.   He continued

qʋ'k_une·. qake'ⁱne· ni'łsik. hunała·'łtⁱ'tⁱne· husł'a·qak.łⁱm·ała'- 15
to smoke.   He said   the bull: "I had a wife   where my head

where my head lay. Let us be friends." Coyote said: "We will go
to your wife." The two started. The two went along, and he saw
his wife among a crowd. Coyote sharpened his friend's horns.
Coyote said: "Now go ahead. When you run along, turn this way."
The Bull went there. The Bull was seen running toward the place
where Coyote was. He went past. Another Bull arrived. He shot
him. Coyote killed him. The other Bull came back. He said:
"Let us go to my wives." The two went. Coyote was told: "Which
one will you take?" Coyote said: "Let me take the larger one."
Coyote started with his wife. The two went along. He said to his
wife: "Now go ahead; go up the valley and go across." Coyote
started. He went to the valley. He staid there. He saw his wife
coming. He broke a stick when his wife was coming. He hit her.
It did not enter her body. He laughed at his wife. He said to her:

---

kᵢneꞏ.   huts!nꞏala'neꞏ   swʊ'tᵢmoꞏ.   qake'ᵢneꞏ   skɛ'nꞏkuꞏts   hults!na'-
lay.   We shall be   friends."   He said   Coyote: "We will

xala'eꞏs   tɬnamu''neꞏs.   ts!nakɛ'kᵢneꞏ.   qaꞏnakɛ'kᵢneꞏts   n'ʊ'px̣aneꞏ
go to   thy wife."   They two started.   They two went along and he saw

sakɛmnaɬiɬ's ᵢneꞏ   tɬnamu''eꞏs.   laɛ'sɛnq!aqleꞏ'x̣aneꞏ   swʊ''eꞏs   skɛ'nꞏ-
among a crowd   his wife.   He sharpened his horns again   his friend's   Coy-

kuꞏts.   qake'ᵢneꞏ   skɛ'nꞏkuꞏts   taꞏ'x̣a   bⁿ'nꞏu   naꞏ   hɛnsɬaqakax̣a''mk-
ote.   He said   Coyote: "Now   go ahead   here   when you turn."

5 tseꞏk.   qaox̣a'x̣eꞏ   ni'lseꞏk.   n'upx̣ana'pseꞏ   ni'lseꞏksts   mityax̣ana'pseꞏ
He went   the bull.   He was seen   the bull   running

ɬaqaka'x̣eꞏ   yaqaosaqa'pskeꞏ   skɛ'nꞏkuꞏts.   ɬaqayaqaha'x̣eꞏ.   wa'x̣eꞏ
coming toward   where was   Coyote.   He went past.   He arrived

nao'k!weꞏ   ni'lseꞏk.   mi'tx̣aneꞏ.   n'ɬwa'nꞏeꞏ   skɛ'nꞏkuꞏts.   ɬawa'x̣eꞏ
one   bull.   He shot it.   He killed it   Coyote.   He went back

nao'k!weꞏ   ni'lseꞏk.   qake'ᵢneꞏ   hults!ina'x̣ala'eꞏs   katɬna'mu.   qao-
one   bull.   He said: "Let us go   my wife."   They

x̣akɛ'kᵢneꞏ.   qakiɬɛ'lneꞏ   skɛ'nꞏkuꞏts   kaₐ   kɛ'ntsɬtso'ᵤkᵘaꞏt.   qa-
two went.   He was told   Coyote: "Which   will you take?"   He

10 ke'ᵢneꞏ   skɛ'nꞏkuꞏts   naꞏ   kwi'ɬqa   hutsɛtsukᵘa'teꞏ.   ts!na'x̣eꞏ
said   Coyote: "This   large one   let me take!"   He started

skɛ'nꞏkuꞏts   n'asma'lneꞏ   tɬnamu''eꞏs.   qaꞏnakɛ'kᵢneꞏ.   qakɛ'lneꞏ   tɬ-
Coyote   two together   his wife.   They two went along.   He said to   his

namu''eꞏs   taꞏx̣a   bⁿ'nꞏu   qoꞏ   hank!aꞏmⁿ'na'keꞏ   hɛntsqanalwat!a'x̣eꞏ.
wife: "Now   go ahead,   that   the valley   you will go through across."

ts!na'x̣eꞏ   skɛ'nꞏkuꞏts.   qaox̣a'x̣eꞏ   qoₙs   aₐ'k!aꞏmɛ'na's.   qaosa-
He started   Coyote.   He went   there to   the valley.   He staid

qa'aneꞏ.   n'ʊ'px̣aneꞏ   ska'seꞏ   tɬnamu''eꞏs.   yɛqe'ᵢteꞏ   a'ₐkɛts   wa'seꞏ
there.   He saw   .coming   his wife.   He broke   a stick   coming

15 tɬnamu''eꞏs.   mi'tx̣aneꞏ.   qatak!o'ᵤneꞏ.   n'umatsna'ateꞏ   tɬnamu''eꞏs.
his wife.   He shot her.   It did not go in.   He laughed at her   his wife.

"Now go ahead." She started, and he said to her: "Go up the valley and go across there." Coyote started. He ran. He got there. He stopped there. His wife came. He shot her and killed her. He butchered her and skinned her. There was a flat stone, and he sat down on it. He saw Wolf coming. He thought he would hit it. He was going to get up. He couldn't get up. He shot at that Wolf. He had no more arrows. He took off his bowstring and struck him with his bow stave. The Wolf ate that game. He ate it all. Coyote got up again. He went and took the bones. He thought he would break them up. He was told by (a bird): "Don't strike them." Coyote stood there holding an ax. Then Badger pounded them. He finished breaking the bones and put the marrow into the tripe. Coyote was told: "Take hold of my tail." Coyote took hold of (Badger's) tail. (Badger) finished putting in the marrow. Badger started to run away. Coyote followed him. He

---

qakɛ′lneˑ ta′xa ɫ′n·u. ts!ᴧna′se·. qakɛ′lneˑ qoᵤ hank!a′m′na′ke·
He said to her: "Now go ahead." She started. He said to her: "There up the valley

qo·tax hᴧntsqanaɫwat!a′xe·. ts!ᴧna′xe· skɛ′n·ku·ts. ts!ᴧn·a′kᵢne·.
there then you will go through across." He started Coyote. He ran.

ɫa·xa′xe·. qaosaqa′ₐne· wa′se· tᴧlnamu′′e·s. mi′txₐne· n′ɫwa′n·e·.
He got there. He stopped there. She came his wife. He shot her, he killed her.

nu·mitse′ᵢte· konu′q!me·. qa·kts!lanu′kse· qaoxaɫ′ᴣsakₐnu′ne·.
He butchered her, he skinned her. There was a flat stone; he sat down on it.

n′ʋ′pxₐne· ska′se· ka′ₐke·ns. qaɫwi′yne· ktsqanɫa′le·t. ktsxaɫ′o′ᵤwuk. 5
He saw coming the wolf. He thought he would hit it. He was going to rise.

qataɫ′uwu′kᵤne·. mi′txₐne· neᵢs ka′ₐke·ns. ɫa·′ɫitka′ₐne·. ɫukᵘɛ′n·e·
He could not rise. He shot at that wolf. He was without arrows. He took off

t!awᵘm′ka′e·s qanɫaltᴣmu′n·e· aₐk.ɫa·kwo′ᵤte·s. n′ɛ′kᵢne· ka′ₐke·n
his bowstring he struck with it his bow stave. He ate the wolf

neᵢs iya′mu′s. q!a′pxₐne·. ɫa·uwu′kᵤne· skɛ′n·ku·ts. qaoxa′xe·
that game. He ate it all. He got up again Coyote. He went and

tsukᵘa′te· ma·k!ɛ′se·s. qaɫwi′yne· ktsaqtsa′kxo·. qak.ɫa′pse·
took its bones. He thought he would break them up. He was told by

wa′ku·ks maₐts qanɫa′lte·n′. qa·qawᴣtskᴣnɛ′le·k aₐ′qu·ta·ls skɛ′n- 10
(a bird with "Don't strike it." He stood holding an ax Coy-
white spot on
head):

ku·ts. ta′xa tsᴣn qoᵤs n′aqtsaxo′ᵤne· na′ɫme·t!. kuɫya′q!a·
ote. Then only there he pounded Badger. Having finished
breaking

qana′′nte· aₐk.ɫaqpɛ′sqaps aₐ′kinu′ɫmak. qakiɫɛ′lneˑ skɛ′n·ku·ts
he put them into tripe the marrow. He was told Coyote:

hawᴣtsqatkɛ′nu. nawᴣtsqatkᴣnka′ₐne· skɛ′n·ku·ts. kuɫqana·′′ne·t
"Take hold of my tail." He took hold of the tail Coyote. He finished putting
it inside

aₐ′kᴣnu′ɫma·ks. nu·tsᴣnqkupekɛ′′me·k na′ɫme·t!. mᴣteᵢxa·′mʋmu- 15
the marrow. He started to run away Badger. He followed

kᵘa′ₐne· skɛ′n·ku·ts. n′upsɫatnu·tmʋ′nukᵘa′ₐne·. ɫa·ileᵢqa′ninmitk-
him Coyote. He continued to run. It is thrown backward

continued to run. The tripe was thrown back at him. Coyote licked the tripe. He thought: "I will break it." He was told by (a bird): "I will break it." Coyote was told: "Start for the place where there is a plain on the hill, Coyote." Coyote started. He was told: "Come back when you see smoke; then you shall eat grease." (The bird) was pounding it. He finished pounding it, and put green boughs on the fire. Coyote saw the smoke. He started to come back. Coyote came back. He stood there and looked about. There was nothing there. Here (the bird) dropped a little grease. He looked up. He saw (the bird) flying off. Coyote was standing there helplessly. Coyote was without even a mouthful of (the meat of) his wife.

7. COYOTE AND BUTTERFLY

Coyote went along. He heard some one singing. Coyote reached there. He saw Butterfly. Coyote thought he would steal Butterfly. He said to him: "I don't steal men." Coyote started.

---

tsɛ'łneˑ   aₐ'k.łaqpɛ'sqaps.   n'łta'xₐneˑ   aₐ'k.łaqpɛ'sqaps   skɛ'nˑkuˑts.
to him   the tripe.   He licked   the tripe   Coyote.

qałwi'yneˑ   kuts!aqtsa'kxoˑ.   qak.ła'pseˑ   wa'kuks   hutsłɛ'sᵢniła'qtsa-
He thought: "I will break them."   He was told by   (a bird):   "I will break

kxo'ₓneˑ.   qakiłɛ'łne   skɛ'nˑkuˑts   ts!ɛ'n·an'   qoₓ   haq!an·uqłe.ɛ'tkeˑ
them."   He was told   Coyote: "Start for   there   where is a plain on a hill,

skɛ'nˑkuˑts.   ts!ɛna'xeˑ   skɛ'nˑkuˑts.   qakiłɛ'łne   hɛn'u'pxa   ya'm·uts
Coyote!"   He started   Coyote.   He was told: "When you see   smoke

5 hɛntsła·tska'xeˑ   ta'xas   hɛntsxałɛ'kᵢneˑ   t!ɛna'mu.   qa·kłaqtsa-
   then come back,   then   you will eat   grease."   Along he pounded

kxo'ₓneˑ   wa'kuks.   koₓłaqtsa'kxoˑ   xunakɛ'n·eˑ   aₐku'ła·łs.   n'u'p-
it   (the bird).   Having finished   he put on fire   green boughs.   He
                                    pounding it

xₐneˑ   ya'm·u's   skɛ'nˑkuˑts.   ła·ts!ɛna'xeˑ.   ła·łaxa'xeˑ   skɛ'nˑkuˑtsˑ.
saw   the smoke   Coyote.   He started back.   He got back   Coyote.

qaₐkqa·'nwɛsqa'ₐneˑ   łoₓ·seˑ   qa'psins.   naₐs   qa'waₐkał'okɪnɛ·tseˑ
He stood and looked about;   not there was   anything.   Here   she dropped a little

t!ɛna'mu's.   wa·wɛtskɛ'kᵢneˑ.   n'u'pxₐneˑ   wa'kuks   nułnuxu'seˑ.
grease.   He looked up.   He saw   (the bird)   flew towards water

10 qakuqkatwɛsqa'ₐneˑ   skɛ'nˑkuˑts.   pał   słɛ'tkɛk.łɛ'lqutmɛ'n·eˑ   tłɛna-
   In vain he stood there   Coyote.   He was without even a mouthful of   his wife

mu''e·s   skɛ'nˑkuˑts.
                  Coyote.

7. COYOTE AND BUTTERFLY

Qa·na'xeˑ   skɛ'nˑkuˑts.   nułpałnitɛ'tᵢneˑ   ka·wasxoneya'm·eˑs.   qao-
He went along   Coyote.   He heard   singing.   He reached

xa'xeˑ   skɛ'nˑkuˑts.   n'u'pxₐneˑ   ko·dli'dlus   pał   nilkɛ'lseˑ.   qałwi'yneˑ
there   Coyote.   He saw   Butterfly   it was he.   He thought

skɛ'nˑkuˑts   ktsxa'łay   ko·dli'dlus.   qak.ła'pseˑ   atu'qaa'yneˑ   tɛ'tqa·t!.
Coyote   he would steal   Butterfly.   He said to him: "I do not steal   men."

15 ts!ɛna'xeˑ   skɛ'nˑkuˑts.
   He started   Coyote.

8. Coyote and Grouse

Grouse was living in a tent and had many children. They were in her tent. Grouse started with her husband. They two were going along. Coyote was going along. He saw the tent of Grouse. Coyote reached there. He entered. There were many children. He took a bag, put them into it, and carried them along. He started. He went along. They broke the bag by scratching it, and went right through the hole. Coyote was going along. He thought: "Now I'll eat." He looked, and there was nothing. Coyote started.

9. Coyote and Star

Star was going along. He saw a child eating earth. It was Goose. He started. He saw a Golden Eagle sitting on a tree. He saw him, and he was screeching. Star also said . . . (??) He went up. He reached the place where the bird was, and killed it (?).

---

8. Coyote and Grouse

Qanɛt.la'ₐne kia'wats yunaqa'pse· aɫaqa'lt!e·s. qaqa'pse· aₐ'kɛt.-
She lived in tent   Grouse   many   her children.   They were in   her

ɫa'e·s.   ts!ɛna'xe·   kia'wats   n'asma'lne·   nuɫaqₐna'e·s.   qa·nakɛ'kne·.
tent.   She started   Grouse   two together   her husband.   They two went
                                                                                        along.

qa·na'xe·   skɛ'n·ku·ts.   n'u'pxₐne·   sanɛt.la'ₐse·   kia'wats.   qaoxa'xe·
He went along   Coyote.   He saw   the tent there of   Grouse.   He arrived

skɛ'n·ku·ts.   tᵢnaxa''mne·.   yunaqa'pse·   ɫkamnɛ'nta'ke's.   tsukⁿa'te·
Coyote.   He entered.   Many were   the children.   He took

aₐ'tsu·'ɫa·'s   qana''nte·   naɫaxo'ᵤne·.   ts!ɛna'xe·.   qa·na'xe·.   n'umɛts-   5
a bag,   he put them   he carried them.   He started.   He went along.   They
               into it

kɛ'n·e·   neᵢs   aₐ'tsu·'ɫa·'s   sukqa'naɫtᵢnaxa'mne·.   qa·na'xe·   skɛ'n·ku·ts.
broke by   that   bag,   they went right there through   He went along   Coyote.
scratching   a hole.

qaɫwi'yne·   ta'xas   huɫ'e·'ek.   tseᵢka'te·ts   ɫo'ᵤse·.   ts!ɛna'xe·
He thought: "Then   let me eat."   He looked,   there was nothing.   He started

skɛ'n·ku·ts.
Coyote.

9. Coyote and Star

Qa·na'xe·   aₐ'kɛno'hos.   n'u'pxₐne·   ɫka'm·u's   n'ɛ'kse·   a'm·aks paɫ
He went along   Star.   He saw   a child   eating   earth,

n'ɛ'nse·   kaxu'lo·ks.   ts!ɛna'xe·.   n'u'pxₐne·   qawɛtsq!nu'se·   kiaq!nu'-   10
who was   Goose.   He started.   He saw   standing on a tree   Golden

kⁿats.   n'u'pxₐne·   t!aɫo'ᵤkse·.   a'ₐke   qake'ᵢne   aₐ'kɛno'hos.
Eagle.   He saw it   screeching.   Also   said   Star.

n'iktka'xe·.   ɫaxa'xe·   neᵢs   toq!tsqa'mnas   yaₐqaosaqa'pske·
He went up.   He reached   there   the bird   where it was

n'upɫa'pse·.
(and) killed it.

10. Coyote and the Woman

Coyote went along. There was a hill. He arrived on top. He saw a woman. Then the woman saw Coyote. She was afraid. Then she lay down. Then Coyote started. He saw the woman lying there. He thought she was dead. Coyote said: "Why is she dead? Let me see what killed her." Then he looked. He did not know what had killed her. Then Coyote started toward the back-side of the woman. Coyote looked. He saw her backside. He tore it. He put his finger in. He smelled of it. He said: "It stinks. She has been dead for a long time." Then Coyote went on. The woman lay there. She thought: "Let me go to Coyote; let me marry him." Then the woman started. She got there. She said to Coyote: "Let us go to my tent." She started; she got to her tent. She staid there.

---

10. Coyote and the Woman

Qa·na′xe·   skɛ′n·ku·ts.   swɛtslɛɛ′t.se·.   youxa′xe·.   n′u′pxₐne·
He went along   Coyote.   There was a hill.   He got on top.   He saw

pa·′łkeᵢs.   ta′xas neᵢ pa·′łkeᵢ n′u′pxₐne· skɛ′n·ku·ts·.   n′oni′łne·.   ta′xas
a woman.   Then   that   woman   saw   Coyote.   She was afraid.   Then

n′itxo′ᵤlne·k.   ta′xas   ts!ɛna′xe·   skɛ′n·ku·ts.   n′u′pxₐne·   pa·′łkeᵢs
she lay down.   Then   he started   Coyote.   He saw   the woman

sakqa′pse·.   qałwi′yne·   ksɛ′ɬ′e·ps.   qake′ᵢne·   skɛ′n·ku·ts   qa′psins
lying there.   He thought   she was dead.   He said   Coyote: "What

5 ksɛ′ɬ′e·p.   hułtseᵢka′tmił   qa′psins   ksɛ′ɬ′e·p."   ta′xas   tseᵢka′te·.
is she dead?   Let me see   what   killed her."   Then   he looked.

qa.u′pxₐne·   qa′psins   ksɛ′ɬ′e·ps.   ta′xas   ts!ɛna′xe·   skɛ′n·ku·ts
Not he knew   what   killed her.   Then   he started   Coyote

aₐ′kɛkpukk′se·s   pa·′łkeᵢs.   tseᵢka′te·   skɛ′n·ku·ts.   n′u′pxₐne·   aₐ′kɛkpu-
to her backside   the   He looked   Coyote.   He saw   her back-
the woman's.

kk′se·s.   n′u·mitse′ᵢse·.   tsaqa·natsq!ahe′ᵢne·.   nakumsɛke′ᵢte·.   qake′ᵢne·
side.   He tore it.   He put his finger into it.   He smelled of it.   He said:

ksłuktu′kᵘe·s   peɛ′k!aks   k.łsɬ′upɛ′łe·k.   ta′xas   ts!ɛna′xe·   skɛ′n·ku·ts.
"It stinks,   long ago   she has been   Then   started   Coyote.
killed."

10 qa·kqa′ₐne·   neᵢ   pa·′łkeᵢ.   qałwi′yne·   hułts!ɛna′mi·ɬ   skɛ′n·ku·ts
She lay there   that   woman.   She thought: "Let me go to   Coyote,

kułsałɛ′te·t.   ta′xas ts!ɛna′xe·   pa·′łkeᵢ.   łaxa′xe·.   qakɛ′łne·   skɛ′n·ku·ts·
let me marry him."   Then   she started   the   She got   She said to   Coyote:
woman.   there.

hułts!ɛnaxa′ła   kaₐ′kɛ′t.ła.   ts!ɛna′xe·   łaxa′xe·   aₐ′kɛt.ła′e·s.
"Let us go to   my tent."   She started,   she got to   her tent.

qaosaqa′ₐne·.
She staid there.

11. Coyote and the Manitou with the Hat

Coyote went along. He saw a manitou having a hat made of belly fat. He touched it. He took a piece off. He ate it. Again he broke a piece off. Again he ate it. He was told: "Go away." He was told: "You hurt me." Coyote went off.

12. Coyote and the Ducks [1]

Coyote with his two children went along. There was a lake. He saw many ducks. He said to his children: "Cry!" The children cried. They cried thus: "My father's brothers-in-law!" Coyote cried thus: "My brothers-in-law!" One Mallard Duck said to his children: "Listen! a manitou is crying." Mallard Duck said: "Go to him (and listen to) what he is talking about." One of them went ashore. He came to Coyote. He said to him: "What do you refer to when you cry?" Coyote said: "Come ashore, all of you!" All the ducks came ashore. He pulled out their feathers. Enough.

---

11. Coyote and the Manitou with the Hat

Qa·na'xe·   sk⏑'n·ku·ts.   n'u'px̣ₐne·   nöp⏑'k!as   k!ayukᵘa'ₐse·
He went along   Coyote.   He saw   a manitou   having a hat

aₐ'kowuma'łqaₐps.   qunya'x̣ₐne·.   qasɟ·ukᵘ⏑'n·e·.   n'⏑'k̨ine·.
made of belly fat.   He touched it.   He took a piece off.   He ate it.

łaqasɟ·ukᵘ⏑'n·e·.   ła·⏑'k̨ine·.   qak.ła'pse·   yu'wa.   qak.ła'pse·
Again he took a   Again he   He was told: "Go away."   He was told:
piece off.   ate it.

hₐn'upła'pₐne·.   ts!ₐna'xe·   sk⏑'n·ku·ts.
"You hurt me."   He went off   Coyote.

12. Coyote and the Ducks

Qa·na'xe·   sk⏑'n·ku·ts   n'asma'łne·   x̣ałe'es   sk⏑kq!nu'kse·.   5
He went along   Coyote   with two   his children   to where was a lake.

n'u'px̣ₐne·   yunaqa'pse·   kia'qła's.   qak⏑'łne·   x̣ałe'e·s   e'łan'.
He saw   many   ducks.   He said to   his child: "Cry!"

n'⏝a'n·e·   neᵢ   łka'm·u.   qało'ᵤkᵤne·   ałska·t!e·s   kat⏑'tu.   sk⏑'n·ku·ts
He cried   that   child.   He cried thus: "His brothers-   my father!"   Coyote
                                              in-law

qało'ᵤkᵤne·   ałka'skat.   n'ok!we'ine·   kanq!usqwe'ᵢkak   qak⏑'łne·
cried thus: "My brothers-in-   One   Mallard Duck   said to
              law!"

ałaqa'łt!e·s   tsₐn   k!a'pałtₑᵢx̣a'keᵢł.   nöp⏑'k!a   s⏝'eła'n·e.   qake'ₐne·
his children: "Only   listen ye!   A manitou   is crying."   He said

kanq!usqwe'ᵢkak   qunam⏑'łkeᵢł   qa'psins   k!u'pske·.   k!o'k!we·   10
Mallard Duck: "Go to him   what   he talks about."   One

tsinał'upa'xe·.   łax̣a'xe·   sk⏑'n·ku·ts·.   qak⏑'łne·   qa'psin   kₐn'u'pske·
went ashore.   He came to   Coyote.   He said to him: "What   do you say

kₐn'e'ła.   qake'ₐne·   sk⏑'n·ku·ts   q!a'pe·   upka'keᵢł.   q!a'pe·   n'upka'xe·
do you cry?"   He said   Coyote: "All   come ye ashore."   All   came ashore

kia'qła.   q!a'pe·'s   łu'nte·   aₐ'kₐnqoa·⏑'se·s.   ta'x̣as.
the ducks.   All   he removed   their feathers.   Enough.

---

13. COYOTE AND OWL[1]

There was a town. A child was crying. It was told: "Don't cry, Owl will take you." The child cried. Owl took it. He put it into a birch-bark basket. Then there were no more children. Coyote said: "I shall cry." At night Coyote cried. He was told: "Don't cry, else Owl will take you." Coyote cried aloud. Owl arrived. He said: "Give me the child." (Coyote) was given to him. (Owl) put him into the birch-bark basket. He carried him away. Owl arrived at his tent. Coyote saw many children dancing. He took gum. He rubbed it on Owl's eyes, and (Owl) was blind. He threw him into the fire. (Owl) was burned entirely. All the children started back to the tents of their parents.

---

13. COYOTE AND OWL

Qa·k.łuna′mne·.	n'iła′n·e·	łka′m·u.	qakeł′łne·	ma̱ts	e·′łan′
There was a town.	It cried	a child.	It was told:	"Don't	cry;

tsxałtsukᵘatℰ′sₐne·	ku′pi.	n'iła′n·e·	łka′m·u.	tsukᵘa′te·	ku′pi.
he will take you	Owl."	It cried	the child.	He took it	Owl.

n'oqoxᵘakℰ′n·e·	na′he·ks.	ta′xas	łało′ₐne·	łka′m·u.	qake′ₐne·	skℰ·n·-
He put it into	a birch-bark basket.	Then	no more	children.	He said	Coy-

ku·ts	ka′min	hutsxał'iła′n·e·.	ktsℰmi′yℰt.s	n'iła′n·e·	skℰ·n·ku·ts.
·ote:	"I	I shall cry."	At night	he cried	Coyote.

5
qakeł′łne·	ma̱ts	e·łan′,	to′xwa	ku′pi	tsxałtsukᵘatℰ′sₐne·.	wℰłke′ₐne·
He was told:	"Don't	cry,	else	Owl	will take you."	He cried aloud

skℰ·n·ku·ts.	wa′xe·	ku′pi.	qake′ₐne·	ts!ka·kℰ′nkeₐł	łka′m·u.
Coyote.	He arrived	Owl.	He said:	"Give me	the child."

namatℰktsℰ′łne·.	n'oqoxᵘakℰ′n·e	na′he·ks.	ts!ℰnałkℰ′n·e·.	łaxa′xe·
He was given to him.	He put him into	the birch-bark basket.	He carried him away.	He arrived at

a̱·kℰt.ła′e·s	ku′pi.	n'u′pxₐne·	skℰ·n·ku·ts	yunaqa′pse·	łkamnℰ′nta′-
his tent	Owl.	He saw	Coyote	many	children

ke·s	naqwℰ′łse·.	tsukᵘa′te	ℰ′łwa·s.	yu·hakℰ′n·e·	a̱·kakaqłℰ′se·s
dancing.	He took	gum.	He rubbed it on	his (Owl's) eyes,

10
łałtqłℰ′łse·.	xunmℰ′te·.	q!apku′ₐne·.	łats!ℰna′xe·	q!a′pe·	łkamnℰ′n-
and he was blind.	He threw him into the fire.	He was burnt entirely.	They started back	all	the children

te·k	a̱·kℰt.łaℰ′se·s	ała̱kℰnℰ′k!e·s.
to the tents of	their parents.

[1] See pp. 37, 50.

14. CHICKADEE AND ELK

Chickadee went along a river. On the other side he saw Elk. Chickadee said: "There is a good place on the other side; I wish I could get across." Elk said he would take him across. He went across in the water. (Chickadee) was riding. Elk walked in the water. He just got ashore and (Chickadee) stabbed him. Chickadee killed Elk.

15. FROG AND PARTRIDGE

Frog was going along. She saw Partridge. She said to him: "You shall be my husband." He went to her tent. He arrived. He always went hunting. He killed much (game). Frog said: "Now look for your wife." Partridge started. He found his wife. He said to her: "Where are the children?" That woman said: "They are where you come from." The two started. He arrived at his tent. He staid there again.

---

14. CHICKADEE AND ELK

Qa·na'xe· mɛts!qa'qas aₐ'kɐmi'tuks. łe'ₑne·s n'u'pxₐne· ła'wo's.
He went along Chickadee   river.   On the   he saw   Elk.
                                          other side

qake'ₑne· mɛts!qa'qas: ksɐlsuk.łe'ɛt qo łe'ₑne· huł·e·ni'nam.
He said   Chickadee: "A good place there on the other side if I could get across."

qake'ₑne· ła'wo ałqanyaxaqo'ₙkił. n'ałqananu'qₙne· youxal'isuk-
He said   Elk   he would take him across. He went across in the he was riding,
                                              water,

nu'n·e· ts!ɐmanu'qₙne·. qałɐn n'üpanu'qₙne· naₐk!o'ₙne·. n'ipɛ'łne·
he walked in the water.   Just   reaching the shore, he stabbed him. He killed

ła'wo's mɛts!qa'qas.   5
Elk   Chickadee.

15. FROG AND PARTRIDGE

Qa·na'xe· wa'tak. n'u'pxₐne· t!a'n·qu·ts. qakɛ'ₑne· hₐntsxal'ɛ'n·e
She went   Frog.   She saw   Partridge.   She said to   "You will be
along   him:

kanuł'a'qₐna. ts!ɐna'xe· aₐ'kɛt.ła'e·s. łaxa'xe·. at n'upsła'tiyił'ana'xe·.
my husband."   He started for   his tent.   He arrived.   He always went hunting.

ta'xas yunaqa'pse· k!ɛ'łwa. qake'ₑne· wa'tak ta'xa b'n·u itskɛ'łen'
Then   many   he killed. She said   Frog: "Now   go   look for

tɛłnamu''ne·s. ts!ɐna'xe· t!a'n·qu·ts. n'u'pxₐne· tɛłnamu''e·s. qakɛ'ₑne·
your wife."   He started   Partridge.   He found   his wife.   He said to
                                                                          her:

kaₐs łkamnɛ''nte·k. qake'ₑne· nei pa'łkei qo ta'xa hₐn·yaqakei- 10
"Where the children?"   She said   that woman: "Then now   where you

ka'ɷ̃nke·¹ saosaqa'ₐne·. ts!ɐnakɛ'k̲ₑne·. łaxa'xe· aₐ'kɛt.ła'e·s.
come from   they are."   They two started.   He arrived at his tent.

łaₐtsxanit.ła'ₐne·.
He staid there again.

---

¹ Barnaby prefers qo·sɛnła'yaqa·keₑkami'łke·.

16. BEAVER AND TURTLE

Beaver and Turtle were living together in a tent. (Turtle) started. There was a town. He went there. He entered the tent of the chief. The chief was asleep. Turtle cut off the chief's head. He went out again; he passed outside to the rear of the tent. He crawled under the cover. He staid there. In the morning the chief was lying down. His food had been prepared. He did not arise; and the chief was shaken. He was told: "Rise, I have finished your food." He did not arise. He was shaken again. He was told: "Arise." He was looked at. He was dead. They searched for tracks (to discover) who had done it. Tracks were seen. The tracks did not go out again. They were looked at. (Turtle) was seen. He was there. He was brought out. He was carrying the head of the chief. Some one said: "Where is a knife?" Turtle said: "I do not fear a knife." Some one said: "Where is a bow?" Turtle said: "I do not fear a bow." Some one said: "Where is

---

16. BEAVER AND TURTLE

Qaˑnɛt.łaˊₐneˑ sɛˊnˑa n'asqunamaˊlneˑ kaˊχaχs. ts!ɛnaˊχe qaˑk.łu-
He lived in a tent Beaver, they were two together Turtle. He started to where was a

namɛˊsɪneˑ. qaoχaˊχeˑ. tɛnaxaˊmneˑ aₐˑkɛt.łaɛˊseˑs nasoˊᵤkᵘeˑns.
town. He went there. He entered the tent of the chief.

qaˑk.łeˊɪtseˑ nasoˊᵤkᵘeˑns. łułaˊmaₐneˑ nasoˊᵤkᵘeˑns kaˊχaχ.
Was asleep the chief. He cut off his head (of) the chief Turtle.

łaanaxaˊmneˑ nas qahaˊχeˑ aˊpkoˑk!s. qanał'oᵤnɛlnaxaˊmneˑ.
Again out he went; here he passed outside, oppo- He crawled under the cover.
                                        site the door (be-
                                        hind the tent).

5 qaosaqaˊₐneˑ. kkanmiˊyɛt.s qakqaˊₐneˑ nasoˊᵤkᵘeˑn. n'ɛtkɛnłˊsɪneˑ
He staid there. In the morning lay down the chief. It was prepared

ki'ek. qao'knoχaˊˊmneˑ wanˑkinɛˊlneˑ nasoˊᵤkᵘeˑn. qakiłɛˊlneˑ
food. Not he arose; he was shaken the chief. He was told:

oknoχaˊmen' hunokᵘɛˊn'eˑ kɛˊn'eˑk. qao'knoχaˊˊmneˑ. ławanˑkinɛˊlneˑ.
"Arise, I have finished your food." Not he arose. Again he was shaken.

qakiłɛˊlneˑ oknoχaˊmen'. tseₗkatɛˊlneˑ pał n'ɛˊn'eˑ ʋpnaˊmu.
He was told: "Arise." He was looked at he was dead.

tseₗkat.łkinɛˊlneˑ qaˊpsin no'ła. n'upχałkinɛˊlneˑ. łaqaanałɛˊkɪneˑ.
It was looked for tracks what did it. Tracks were seen. Again not out went tracks.

10 tseₗkatɛˊlneˑ. n'upχaˊlneˑ. saosaqaˊₐneˑ. tunwaₐkaˊnulkɪniˊlneˑ.
It was looked at. He was seen. He was there. He was brought out.

nałˑamkɛˊn'eˑ nasoˊᵤkᵘeˑns. qakiyaˊmneˑ kaₐs aₐˊktsaˊmał. qakeˊɪneˑ
He held the head (of) the chief. Some one said: "Where is the knife?" He said

kaˊχaχ huqa.onɛˊlneˑ aₐˊktsaˊmał. qakiyaˊmneˑ kaₐs t!aˊwu.
Turtle: "I do not fear knife." Some one said: "Where is the bow?"

qakeₗˊneˑ kaˊχaχ huqa.onɛˊlneˑ t!aˊwu. qakiyaˊmneˑ kaₐs aₐˊu'tał.
He said Turtle: "I do not fear bow." Some one said: "Where is ax?"

an ax?" Turtle said: "I do not fear an ax." Some one said: "Pour water on him." Turtle said: "Don't." Some one said: "Throw him into the water." Turtle lied when he said he was not afraid of ax, knife, and bow. He lied when he said that he was afraid of water, for that was the place from which he had come ashore. He was taken to the water. He carried the chief's head. He was thrown into the water. He sank. After a while there in the middle he emerged. He shook the chief's head in the water. Some one said: "It is Turtle." Turtle started for his tent. Turtle came home. Then Beaver made holes in all directions. He bit them off (the bows), he dragged them into his hole, then the manitous went back. (Their bows) were broken. (They said:) "My bow is bad."

17. SKUNK AND PANTHER [1]

Skunk went along. He saw Panther. Panther was afraid of Skunk. Panther pretended to be dead. Skunk went there. He

---

qake′ₗne· ka′ẋaẋ huqa.onɛ′łne· aqu′tał. qakiya′mne· yuᵤẋakułẋa′kił.
He said   Turtle: "I do not fear   ax."   Some one said: "Pour ye water on him."

qake′ₗne· ka′ẋaẋ maₐts. qakiya′mne· ẋunmitqu′lkił. słutske′ₗne·
He said   Turtle: "Don't."   Some one said: "Throw him into the water."   He lied

ka′ẋaẋ neₗs kqa′ke· kqa.o′nił aqu′talsts aₐktsa′malsts t!a′wu′s.
Turtle   that   saying   not afraid of   ax   and knife and   bow.

słutske′ₗne· neₗs kqa′ke· k!o′ne·ł wu′o·s pa·ł ne·sts· kqakeₗkału′pkam.
He lied   that   saying   being afraid   of water   that   where he came ashore from.

qa′oẋałẋu′nanulkinɛ′łne·.   nał′amkɛ′n·e·   naso′ᵤkᵘe·ns.   ẋunmitqu- 5
He was taken to the water.   He carried the head   the chief's.   He was thrown

ł′łne·. niktsnoqu′n·e· qawunikɛ′t.se· qo′s qayaₐqa′wo·s łaqaₐ-
into the water.   He sank.   After a while   there   in the middle   he

kał′awa′ₐkawa′ts!ne·. wan·qoᵤk.ła′mkɛ′n·e· naso′ᵤkᵘe·ns. qakiya′m-
emerged.   He shook the head in the water   the chief's.   Some one

ne· pa·ł n′ɛ′ne· ka′ẋaẋ. ts!namɛ′łkił aₐkɛt.ła′e·s ka′ẋaẋ.
said: "It is he   Turtle.   Start for   his tent   Turtle."

ła·łaẋa′ẋe· aₐkɛt.ła′e·s ka′ẋaẋ. ta′ẋas sɛ′n·a n′ɛtqanłɛłq!aqo′ᵤk!a-
He got home to   his tent   Turtle.   Then   Beaver   he made holes in all

mekɛɛ′łe·k. q!aₐnina′ẋₐne·. aₐqo·k!ame′es qa·nałtsa′qanawɛs·nuk- 10
directions.   He bit them off.   His hole   he dragged them into it.

qu′ẋᵤne·. łaẋa′ẋe· nöpɛ′k!a. n′umɛtskinłɛ′s·ₗne·. saha′n·e· kat!a′wu.
They went back   the manitous.   It was broken for them.   "Bad is   my bow."

17. SKUNK AND PANTHER

Qa·na′ẋe· ẋa′ẋas. n′u′pẋₐne· swa′s. swa′ n′onɛ′łne· ẋa′ẋas·.
He went along   Skunk.   He saw   Panther.   Panther   was afraid of   Skunk.

n′ʋ′pse·k swa′. qaoẋa′ẋe· ẋa′ẋas. tsukᵘa′te· swa′s nałẋo′ᵤne·.
He pretended to be dead   Panther.   He went there   Skunk.   He took   Panther and carried him on his back.

---

[1] See pp. 40, 48.

took Panther. He carried him on his back. Skunk went along.
Panther thought: "What shall I do with him?" He thought: "He
shall put me down." He put him down. Skunk let out his fluid.
Panther arose. Panther kicked Skunk's bucket. He broke his
bucket. Panther started away. He went along, going in a circle.
Skunk arrived. He saw the bucket there. He was angry. He
started. He looked for Panther. He saw his tracks. Panther went
along and came back to the same place. Skunk started. He saw the
tracks where (Panther) had been going. He made tracks. He knew
it was the same one. He followed the tracks. He tracked him. He
saw the tracks were still there. He followed the tracks. He tracked
him. There was a lake. There were tracks. He drank. Skunk
looked into the water. There he was. He thought he saw him.
Then he broke wind. Many times he broke wind. He looked again.
There he was. He broke wind again. He looked again. There he
was. Then he was tired. He lay down on his back. He saw

---

qa·na′xe· xa′xas. qałwi′yne· swa′ ka‚as huł′aqa′ke·n? qałwi′yne·
He went   *Skunk.*   *He thought*   *Panther:*   *"How*   *shall I do?"*   *He thought:*
along

łpɛsxo′ᵤnap.   pɛsxo′ᵤne·.   n′u′xte·k   xa′xas.   n′owu′kᵤne·   swa′.
"He shall put me   *He put him*   *He defecated*   *Skunk.*   *He arose*   *Panther.*
down."   *down.*

qanaqłⵯ′kxₐne·   yɛtskᵢmeⵯ′se′s   swa′   xa′xas·.   n umɛtskⵯ′n·e·
He kicked   *the bucket*   *Panther*   *Skunk's.*   *He broke it*

yɛtskᵢmeⵯ′se′s.   ts!na′xe· swa′.   qa·na′xe· n′uk!qałqa′ₐtse·.   qaoxa′xe·
his kettle.   *He started*   *Panther.*   *He went along*   *he went about in a circle.*   *He arrived*

5   xa′xas. n′u′pxₐne· saoqa·ᵛqa′pse· yɛtskⵯ′me·s. sa·nⴰłwi′yne·. ts!na′xe·.
    Skunk.   *He saw*   *there was*   *his kettle.*   *He was angry.*   *He started.*

n′itskⵯ′łne·   swa′s.   n′u′pxₐne· aₐk.łⵯk!′se·s.   qa·na′xe· swa′ a′ₐ′ke
He looked for   *Panther.*   *He saw*   *his tracks.*   *He went along*   *Panther*   *and*

ła·uk!qak.łati·ᵛqa′ₐtse·.   ts!na′xe·   xa′xas.   n′u′pxₐne· sakiłałⵯ′kse·.
he went around in a circle.   *He started*   *Skunk.*   *He saw*   *tracks being there.*

kaₐs n′aₐqo′nas n′ɛtkⵯ′n·e· aₐk.łⵯk!′se·s.   n′u′pxₐne· o·k!ᵘina′mus
Where   *he went*   *he made*   *his tracks.*   *He saw*   *the same as*

pał   n′ⵯ′nse·.   ta′xas   n′aq!as·litⵯ′tᵢne·.   ts!nan·uqkᵘanxo′ᵤne·.
he.   *Then*   *he followed the tracks.*   *He pursued him.*

10 n′u′pxₐne·   sakiłałⵯ′kse·.   n′aq!as·litⵯ′tᵢne·.   ts!nan·uqkᵘanxo′ᵤne·
    He saw   *tracks being there.*   *He followed the tracks.*   *He pursued him*

skⵯkq!nu′kse· qaoxałⵯ′kse·. n′ⵯku′łne·. n′u′pxₐne· xa′xas neᵢs wu′os.
to where was a lake   *where were tracks.*   *He drank.*   *He saw*   *Skunk*   *the water.*

saosaqa′pse·. qałwi′yne· ksi·łⵯu′pxa. ta′xas n′atsu′kpᵢne· yunaqa′pse·
It was there.   *He thought*   *he saw him.*   *Then*   *he broke wind;*   *many (times)*

k!a′tsu·kp.   łatseᵢka′te· saosaqa′pse·.   łaatsu′kpᵢne·.   łatseᵢka′te·
breaking wind.   *He looked again*   *where he was.*   *Again he broke wind.*   *Again he looked*

saosaqa′pse·.   ta′xas   nuk.łu′kᵤne·.   tuwuł′itxo′ᵤmek.   n′u′pxₐne·
where he was.   *Then*   *he got tired.*   *He lay down on back.*   *He saw*

Panther. He thought: "I will break wind against him." Then he
turned his backside to him. Panther took off his last finger-nail and
put it on his arrow. He shot Skunk. Panther killed Skunk.

18. THE MOSQUITO

Mosquito went along. He saw a town. He was told: "Come, eat
choke cherries." Mosquito said: "I don't eat choke cherries." Mosquito went along. He saw a town. He was told: "Come, you shall
eat service berries." Mosquito said: "I don't eat service berries."
Mosquito went on. Mosquito was going along. He saw a town.
He was told: "Come, you shall eat blood." Mosquito went there.
He ate blood. He ate much. His belly became big. He went out
again. He broke sticks and all (?). Mosquito died. Little birds
flew out of him. Those were mosquitoes. "Wuu, wuu! you are a
manitou; you shall be mosquitoes."

---

swa's.   qałwi'yne·   ktslaatsukpu'ꭓa.   ta'ꭓas   qaoꭓak!ałaꭓe'kpₗne·.
Panther.   He thought   he would break wind again.   Then he turned his backside up.

ło·kᵘʹne·   kiapt!aha'nłukp   swa'.   qaoꭓak!o'ᵤne·   a'ₐ'k!e·s.
He broke off   the claws   Panther.   He pointed   his arrow.

mɛ'tꭓₐne·   ꭓa'ꭓas·.   n'upɛ'łne·   ꭓa'ꭓas·   swa'.
He shot   Skunk.   He killed   Skunk   Panther.

18. THE MOSQUITO

Qa·na'ꭓe·   qatsts!a'ła.   n'u'pꭓₐne·   sak.łunamɛ'sₗne·.   qakiłɛ'łne·
He went   Mosquito.   He saw   a village was there.   He was told:

ła'n·a   ɛ'ke·n'   aₐ'ke'łma·k!."   qake'ₗne·   qatsts!a'ła   hutsqa.ɛ'kₗne·   5
"Come,   eat   choke cherries."   He said   Mosquito: "I do not eat

aₐ'ke'łma·k!.   ts!ɛna'ꭓe·   qatsts!a'ła.   n'u'pꭓₐne·   sak.łunamɛ'sₗne·.
choke cherries."   He started   Mosquito.   He saw   a village was there.

qakiłɛ'łne·   ła'n·a   hɛntsꭓal'ɛ'kₗne·   sq!u'm·o.   qake'ₗne·   qatsts!a'ła
He was told: "Come,   you shall eat   service berries."   He said   Mosquito:

hutsqa.ɛ'kₗne·   sq!u'm·o.   ts!ɛna'ꭓe·   qatsts!a'ła.   qana'ꭓe·.   n'u'pꭓₐne·
"I do not eat   service berries."   He started   Mosquito.   He went along.   He saw

sak.łunamɛ'sₗne·.   qakełɛ'łne·   ła'n·a   hɛntsꭓal'ɛ'kₗne·   wa''nmo.
there was a village.   He was told: "Come,   you shall eat   blood."

qaoꭓa'ꭓe·   qatsts!a'ła.   n'ɛ'kₗn·e·   wa''nmo's.   yunaqa'pse·   n'ɛ'kₗne·.   10
He went there   Mosquito.   He ate   blood.   Much   he ate.

wɛłwụ'mne·.   łaanaꭓa'mne·   n'upła'pse·   łoᵤk!s   ła.uk!eł'anaꭓo'se·ts.
His belly was big.   He went out again,   he was killed   stick   broke him (?).

n'ɛ'pₗne·   qatsts!a'ła.   tsaqona'ne·   tuq!wɛtsqa'mna   qakꭓa·ł'anano-
He died   Mosquito.   Little   birds   flew

ꭓu'n·e· pał n'ɛ'n·e· qatsts!a'ła.   wu'u, wu'u nöpɛ'k!a nɛ'nko.   kɛ'nłeₗn
out,   those were Mosquitoes.   "Wu'u, wu'u!   a manitou   you.   You shall be

qatsts!a'ła.
mosquitoes."

19. The Man and the Wasps

An old man went along. He defecated. Wasps stung his anus. He put his hand in. He soiled his hand. He shook his hand. There was a stone. He hurt his hand. He put his hand into his mouth. He tasted his excrement.

20. Lame Knee

There was a town. The chief said they would break camp in order to plant.[1] They broke camp. The chief's wives went to draw water. There were the friends of Lame Knee. His friends said: "You ought to steal the chief's wife." Lame Knee started. He went there limping. The chief's wife came back carrying water. He seized her. She said to him: "Let me go; the chief wants to drink." Lame Knee said: "I will not let you go." The woman said: "Let me go;

---

19. The Man and the Wasps

Qa·na′xe·   nu·ła′qₐna.   qaoxał′u′xte·k.   n′itk!ona′pse·   yu·′wat!s
He went along   an old man.   He defecated.   They stung him   wasps

aₐ·k!ałaxe′kp!ēs.   qa′naq!ałe′ᵢne·   mats!e′ᵢne·.   neᵢs qaqₐna′ₐne·   aₐ·ke′es
his anus.   He put his hand in,   he soiled his hand.   That   he did   his hand
                                                                    (he shook)

sw⟨et⟩tsnu′kse·.   t!aqtseyxo′ᵤme·k.   naqtuq!waq!ałe·′ne.   n′u′ktukᵘe′ᵢse·
where was a stone.   He hurt his hand.   He put his hand into his mouth.   It smelled his
                                                                    hand of

aₐ‛q!u·′łe·′s.
his excrement.

20. Lame Knee

5   Qa·k.łuna′mne·.   qake′ᵢne·   naso′ᵤkᵘe·n   tsu′qnaneya′mne·ts   ts!⟨et⟩t-
There was a town.   He said   the chief   they would break camp   to sow

mo·k!o·′łne·.   ta′xas   n′um⟨et⟩tsk.łuna′mne·.   xunyaxak!o′ᵤse·   t⟨el⟩łna-
ᵢn the ground.   Then   they broke camp.   They went and dipped   the
                                                            water

mu′′e·s   naso′ᵤkᵘe·n.   qahaqa′ₐne·   ałswⱷ′tᵢmo   q!o·małq!a′n·k!o.
wives of   the chief.   There were   friends   Lame Knee.

qak.ła′pse·   ałswu′e·s   xma·′nhaw⟨et⟩tsnutɛm⟨e⟩′łne·   t⟨el⟩łnamu′′e·s
They said   his friends: "You ought to steal   the wife of

naso′ᵤkᵘe·n.   ts!⟨en⟩na′xe·   q!o·małq!a′n·k!o.   qaoxᵘaq!ank!o′ᵤte·k.
the chief."   He started   Lame Knee.   He went there limping.

10   łaₐpskałko′łse·   t⟨el⟩łnamu·⟨e⟩′se·s   naso′ᵤkᵘe·ns.   ts⟨en⟩k⟨e⟩′n·e·.   qak.ła′pse·
She came back carry-   his wife   the chief's.   He took hold of   She said to him:
ing water   she.

p⟨es⟩sk⟨e⟩′n·u   ma kts!e′ᵢko·ł   naso′ᵤkᵘe·n.   qake′ᵢne·   q!o·małq!a′n·k!o
"Let me go,   he wants to drink   the chief."   He said   Lame Knee:

hutsłaqa′p⟨es⟩sk⟨en⟩⟨e⟩′sᵢne·.   qak.ła′pse·   neᵢs   pa·′łkeᵢs   p⟨es⟩sk⟨e⟩′n·u tu′xwa
"I will not let you go."   She said   that   woman: "Let me go,   almost

---

[1] The planting of tobacco is meant.

the chief might be angry; the chief wants to drink." Then they
broke camp. They went to the chief. The chief was told: "Lame
Knee is holding your wife." The chief said: "Go to him. Tell him
to let her go because I am thirsty." They went to him. He
was told: "The chief says he wants you to let her go because he
wants to drink." Lame Knee said: "Go to the chief; tell him that
I shall not let her go." They went to the chief. He was told:
"Lame Knee says that he will not let her go." The chief said, being
now angry: "Ha, ha, hoya!"—"Tell him I shall not let the chief's
wife go." (The chief) took a knife. He went there. He arrived at
the place where his wife was. Lame Knee was holding the wife of the
chief. (The chief) said to him: "Let go of her." Lame Knee said:
"I shall not let go of her." The chief went there. He cut off his head.
He threw it away. The head turned over; it smiled while it was rolling

---

łsanℓ'łwey   naso'ₐkᵘeˑn.   ma ktsℓe'ᵢkoˑł   naso'ₐkᵘeˑn.   ta'xas
may be angry   the chief.   He wants to drink   the chief."   Then

n'umℓtsk.łuna'mneˑ.   qaoxaxamℓ'sᵢneˑ   naso'ₐkᵘeˑn.   qakiłℓ'łneˑ
they broke camp.   They went to   the chief.   He was told

naso'ₐkᵘeˑn saˑwℓtskℓ'nˑeˑ q!oˑmałq!a'nˑk!o tℓlnamunℓ's'meᵢł. qa-
the chief: "He holds her   Lame Knee   your wife."

ke'ᵢneˑ naso'ₐkᵘeˑn qoˑnamℓ'łkeᵢł qakℓ'łkeᵢł kℓlpℓ'skeᵢn ma kohokᵘ-
He said   the chief: "Go to him   tell him   he shall let her go   because

nuq!luma'meᵢł. qoˑnaxamℓ'sᵢneˑ. qakiłℓ'łneˑ qake'ᵢneˑ naso'ₐkᵘeˑn 5
I am thirsty."   They went to him.   He was told: "He says   the chief

kℓlpℓskℓ'nmeᵢł ma ktsℓe'ᵢkoˑł. qake'ᵢneˑ q!oˑmałq!a'nˑk!o qoˑnamℓ'ł-
you shall let her go   he wants to drink." He said   Lame Knee: "Go

keᵢł naso'ₐkᵘeˑn. kℓlłqakℓ'łkeᵢł kuˑsłaqa'pℓskℓ'nmeᵢł. qoˑnaxamℓ'sᵢ-
to   the chief.   Tell him   I shall not let her go."   They went to

neˑ naso'ₐkᵘeˑn. qakiłℓ'łneˑ qake'ᵢneˑ q!oˑmałq!a'nˑk!o ksℓłaqapℓ'skℓn.
the chief.   He was told: "He said   Lame Knee   he will not let her go."

qake'ᵢneˑ naso'ₐkᵘeˑn ta'xas ksanℓ'łwey haˑhaˑhoˑya. kℓlłqa-
He said   the chief   now   being angry: "hā hā hōya." —   "Tell

kℓ'łkeᵢł kuˑsłaqa'pℓskℓ'nmeᵢł tℓlnamu'eˑs naso'ₐkᵘeˑn. tsukᵘa'teˑ 10
him   I shall not let go   the wife of   the chief."   He took

aₐ'ktsa'maˑłs. qaoxa'xeˑ. łaxa'xeˑ saˑwℓsqa'pseˑ tℓlnamu'eˑs.
a knife.   He went there.   He arrived   where was   his wife.

q!oˑmałq!a'nˑk!o saˑwℓtskℓ'nˑeˑ tℓlnamuℓ'seˑs naso'ₐkᵘeˑns. qa-
Lame Knee   held   the wife of   the chief.

k.ła'pseˑ pℓskℓ'neˑn'. qake'ᵢneˑ q!oˑmałq!a'nˑk!o hutsła'qapℓskℓ'nˑeˑ.
He said to him: "Let go of her." He said   Lame Knee: "I shall not let go of her."

qaoxa'xeˑ naso'ₐkᵘeˑn. łulama'ₐneˑ. n'ℓlqanmℓ'teˑ. łuqa'q!makℓk.-
He went there   the chief.   He cut off his   He threw it away.   The head
                                         head.

ła''mneˑ   qoₐs yaˑqaˑoxaqa'yeˑxome'ᵢkeˑ łaˑtuwitsłiłnu'kᵘena'nˑeˑ. 15
turned over; there   the place where it rolled   he was smiling.
                to

along. He cut off his arm. It remained hanging down. He cut off
the other arm. It was thrown away. Then both arms were off.
One leg was cut off. It was thrown away. The other leg was cut
off. The body fell down. Then it was cut to pieces. Then the
people went away and put up the tents at Where-they-used-to-sow-
Tobacco. At night the people were asleep. Some one was heard
singing. The people said: "It sounds like Lame Knee, who is
dead." Lame Knee arrived. He killed the chief. He married his
two wives. He took both of them.

21. THE YOUTH WHO KILLED THE CHIEFS [1]

An old man who had a daughter lived in a tent. A man arrived.
He kept his daughter.[2] She had another child. It was a male.
He killed him. The woman lived in the tent. She had another child.

łu·qᵘałɛ'sᵢne·   aₐ'k.ła't!e·s.   qa·qaq!ma'wɛsłatxo'ᵤne·.   nao'k!ᵘe's   aₐ'k.-
<small>It was cut off.   his arm.   It remained hanging down.   The other</small>

ła't!e·s   łuqᵘałɛ'sᵢne·.   n'dqanmɛt.łɛ's ᵢne·.   ta'xas   xatsɛndałɛt.ła·'t!ne·.
<small>arm   he cut off.   It was thrown away.   Then   both arms were off.</small>

nao·k!ᵘsa'q!e·s   łu·saq!qa'łne·.   n'dqanmɛt.łɛ's ᵢne.   nao·k!ᵘsa'q!e·s
<small>One leg   was cut off.   It was thrown away.   The other leg</small>

łuqᵘałɛ'sᵢne·.   n'o'naxo'ᵤne·.   ta'xas   na'n·oqᵘe·qa'łne·.   ta'xas
<small>was cut off.   The body fell down.   Then   it was cut to pieces.   Then</small>

5   no'q!naneya'mne·   qaoxᵘat.łana'mne·   aₐ'qa·nak!ałamu'k!o.
<small>people went away   and put up the tents at   Where-they-used-to-sow-
                                                                                                Tobacco.</small>

ktsdmi·'yɛt   kq!u'mne·''na·m.   nułpałnɛ'łne·   na·wasxoneya'mne·.
<small>At night   people were asleep.   It was heard   some one singing.</small>

qakeya'mne·   ndke'ᵢne·   q!o·małq!a'n·k!o.   ma·ki'ip.   sł·axa'xe·
<small>People said: "It must be   Lame Knee   who is dead."   He arrived</small>

q!o·małq!a'n·k!o.   n'ipɛ'łne·   neᵢs   naso'ᵤkᵘe·ns.   n'asa·łtɛ't.se·.
<small>Lame Knee.   He killed   that   chief.   He married them.</small>

xa'tsɛndtsukᵘa'te·.
<small>Both he took.</small>

21. THE YOUTH WHO KILLED THE CHIEFS

10   Qanɛt.ła'ₐne·   nuł'a'qₐna   naqa'łte·   pa'łkeᵢs.   wa'xe·   tɛ'tqa·t!.
<small>There lived in a   an old man   had a child   a woman.   He arrived   a man.
tent</small>

tsukᵘa'te·swɛnɛ'se·s.   łahaqa'łte·   n'ɛ'nse·   tɛ'tqa·t!s.   q!akpakitxo'ᵤne·.
<small>He took   his daughter.   She also had a   it was   a male.   He killed him.
                                                child,</small>

qanɛt.ła'ₐne·   neᵢ   tdna'mu.   łahaqa'łte·   n'ɛ'nse·   na·utena'nas.
<small>She lived in a tent   that   old woman.   Again she had a   it was   a girl.
                                                                        child;</small>

---

[1] According to Barnaby, a Blackfoot tale.
[2] Evidently he had married the girl, and he was in the habit of preserving the lives of his daughters,
but killing his sons.

It was a girl. He kept her. The chief lived there, driving game.
He skinned a buffalo cow. He started to go back. He took a travois.
He started off. He put the meat into it. He started to go back.
He came back. That chief did not give any meat to his parents-in-
law. The old woman was hungry. The old man's son-in-law did
not give him anything to eat. She had another child, a male. She
said: "Do not tell the chief that I have given birth." She said to
her father: "Early to-morrow shoot a buffalo cow. Don't be afraid
of the chief." Early the next day the old man shot a buffalo cow.
He killed a cow. (The chief) went out early. He saw the old man
skinning. He went in again. He took a bow. He thought: "I will
kill that old man." The chief started. He arrived. He said to him:
"Did you kill a cow?" The old man said: "Yes, it is mine." The
chief said: "No; it is not yours, it is mine." The chief took his bow.

---

tsuk\u{u}a'te·. qaosa˘qa'˔ane· ne₁ naso'ₐk\u{u}e·n naqₐn˔'le·k. n'umitse'₁te·
He took her. *He staid* *the* *chief* *driving game.* *He skinne·.*

łu'kpu·s. łats!ₐna'xe·. tsuk\u{u}a'te· aₐ'q!ₐkamał˔'se·s. ts!ₐna'xe·. n'o-
a cow. *He started back.* *He took* *a travois.* *He started.*

qoxa''nte· aₐ'ku'la·ks·. łats!ₐna'xe·. łałaxa'xe·. qah˔'se· nawaspa'l'e·s
He put into it *the meat.* *He started back.* *He got back.* *Not he gave meat to* *his parents-in-law*

ne₁ naso'ₐk\u{u}e·n. nuwa'si₍ne· ne₁ tₐłna'mu. qah˔sa'pse· nawaspa'l'e·s
that *chief.* *She was hungry* *the* *old woman.* *Not he gave him to eat* *his son-in-law*

ne· nuł'a'qₐna. łahaqa'łte· t˔'tqa·t!s. qak.ła'pse· maₐts tsxana''te·n' 5
the *old man.* *She had a child again* *a male.* *She said:* *"Don't* *talk about it to*

naso'ₐk\u{u}e·n ne₁s kohaqa'pmił. qak˔'łne· t˔tu'e·s kanmi'yit w\u{o}'łna·m
the chief *that* *I have given birth."* *She said to* *her father:* *"To-morrow* *early*

hₐntsm˔'tx̱ₐne· ·łu'kpu·. maₐts hₐnts!on˔'łne· naso'ₐk\u{u}e·n.
you will shoot *a cow.* *Don't* *be afraid of* *the chief."*

kkanmi'y˔t.s w\u{o}'łna·ms m˔'tx̱ₐne· łu'kpu·s ne₁ nuł'a'qₐna.
The following day *early* *he shot* *a cow* *that* *old man.*

n'uk!\u{u}ił'łwa'ne· łu'kpu·s. w\u{o}'łna·ms n'anaxa'mne· n'u'px̱ₐne· sak-
One he killed *cow.* *Early* *he went out.* *He saw*

nu·q!me'₁se· ne₁s nuł'a'qₐnas. ła·tₐnaxa'mne·. tsuk\u{u}a'te· t!a'wu·s. 10
skinning *that* *old man.* *He went in again.* *He took* *a bow.*

qałwi'yne· huł'u'pił ne₁ nuł'a'qₐna. ts!ₐna'xe· ne₁ naso'ₐk\u{u}e·n.
He thought: *"Let me kill* *that* *old man."* *He started* *that* *chief.*

łaxa'xe·. qak˔'łne· ke'ₐn n˔'nko łu'kpu· kinsł˔'łwa. qake'₁ne·
He arrived. *He said to him:* *"Is it* *yours* *a cow* *did you kill?"* *He said*

ne₁ nuł'a'qₐna he· n'˔'ne· ka'min. qake'₁ne· ne₁ naso'ₐk\u{u}e·n
that *old man:* *"Yes,* *it is* *mine."* *He said* *that* *chief:*

wa'ha qa˔'ne· n˔'nko. n'˔'ne· ka'min. tsuk\u{u}a'te· t!awu''e·s
"No, *not it is* *yours.* *It is* *mine."* *He took* *his bow*

He did not see the youth who was there.[1]   He thought he would kill the old man.   The youth arose.   He took his bow.   He shot the chief.   He killed him.   He said to his father: "Now take the meat and go back home."   He took it.   He arrived at home.   The youth entered the chief's tent.   At once he killed the chief's wives.   He threw them outside.   He said to his father: "Go in, it shall be your tent."

He said to his mother: "Are there no people?"   He was told: "There is a town down the river."   He was told: "The chief there is like this one was.   He does not give away any food."   The youth said: "I will start."   The youth started.   He arrived there. He entered an old woman's tent.   He said to her: "I am hungry." He was told: "We are hungry."   She took a dish.   She put something into it.   She gave it to him.   She was told: "I said I am hungry."   The old woman said: "We are hungry.   There is much

---

naso′ₐkᵘe·n.   qa.u′pχₐne·   nɛtsta′haɫs   saosaqa′pse·.   qaɫwi′yne·
the chief.   Not he saw   the youth   being there.   He thought

kɛtsu′piɫ ne·s   nuɫ′a′qₐnas.   n′owo′kₐne·   neᵢ nɛtsta′haɫ.   tsukᵘa′te·
he would kill   the   old man.   He arose   that   youth.   He took

t!awu′′e·s.   mɛ′txₐne·   naso′ₐkᵘe·ns.   n′ipɛ′ɫne·.   qakɛ′ɫne·   tɛtu′e·s
his bow.   He shot   the chief.   He killed him.   He said to   his father:

ta′χas   tsukᵘa′te·n′   aₐku′ɫa·k   kɛnɫats!ɛ′n·am.   tsukᵘa′te·.   ɫaɫaχa′-
"Now   take   the meat   and go back home."   He took it.   He arrived at home.

5 χe·.   tᵢnaχa′mne·   aₐ′kɛt.laɛ′se·s   neᵢs   naso′ₐkᵘe·ns   neᵢ   nɛtsta′haɫ.
He entered   his tent   that   chief's   that   youth.

tɛlnamuɛ′se·s   n′uk!ᵘiɫq!akpakitχo′ₐne·.   n′anaqanmɛ′te·.   qakɛ′ɫne·
His wives   at once he killed them.   He threw them outside.   He said to

tɛtu′′e·s   nɛ′nko   tɛnaχa′me·n′.   tsχaɫ′ɛ′n·e·   aₐ′kit.ɫa′′ne·s.
his father: "You   enter.   It will be   your tent."

Qakɛ′ɫne·   ma′e·s   ke′ɫu   aqɫsma′kinɛk!.   qak.la′pse·   neᵢ   k!unanmi′tuk
He said to his mother: "No   people?"   He was told: "That   down river

saₐk.ɫuna′mne·.   qak.ɫa′pse·   yaₐqaqa′ₐke·   na·   aₐ′′ke   qaqa′ₐne·
is a town."   He was told: "The way as was   this one   also   is

10 naso′ₐkᵘe·n.   at qahɛska′ₐne·.   qakɛ′ᵢne·   neᵢ   nɛtsta′haɫ   huts!ɛna′χe·.
the chief.   Not he gives to eat to any one."   He said   that   youth: "I'll start."

ts!ɛna′χe·   neᵢ   nɛtsta′haɫ.   ɫaχa′χe·.   tᵢnaχa′mne·   aₐ′kɛt.ɫaɛ′se·s
He started   that   youth.   He arrived there.   He entered   her tent.

tɛlna′mu′s.   qakɛ′ɫne·   hunuwa′sᵢne·.   qak.ɫa′pse·   hunuwas′naɫa′ₐne·.
an old woman's.   He said to her: "I am hungry."   He was told: "We are hungry."

tsukᵘa′te·   a′tsus.   n′oqoχa′′nte·.   namatɛ′ktse·.   qak.ɫa′pse·
She took   a dish.   She put it in.   She gave it to him.   She was told:

hoqᵘake′ᵢne· hunuwa′sᵢne·.   qakɛ′ᵢne·   neᵢ tɛlna′mu hunuwas′naɫa′ₐne·.
"I said   I am hungry."   She said   that old woman: "We are hungry.

---

[1] Evidently this is the son, who had grown up meanwhile.

food in the chief's tent, but nobody goes in there." The youth said:
"I'll go." He was told by the old woman: "Don't go." The youth
arose. He went there. He entered the chief's tent. (The chief)
was asleep. (The youth) said to him: "I have entered your tent."
(The chief) got up from his bed. He became a rattlesnake. (The
youth) took his arrow. He struck him. He knocked him down. His
wives at once became rattlesnakes, and he knocked them down. He
went out again. He said: "Come in, all of you, and get meat."

The youth said: "Are there no other people?" He was told: "There
is a town down the river." The youth said: "I will start." He was
told: "The chief is bad." He started. He arrived at the town.
There an old woman was living in a tent. He entered. He said to
her: "I am hungry." He was told: "We are hungry." She took
a dish. She put something into it. She gave it to him. He said
to her: "I said I am hungry." He was told: "There is no food."
He was told: "There is much food in that tent, but nobody goes in

---

naso'ᵤkᵘe·n aₐ'kɛt.ła'e·s yunaqa'ₐne· k!i'keɨł at qaₐtᵢnaxamna'mne·.
The chief   his tent   much   food,   but   not any one goes in."

qake'ᵢne· neᵢ nɛtsta'hał huts!ɛna'xe·. qak.ła'pse neᵢs tɛlna'mu's
He said   that   youth: "I'll go."   He was told by   that   old woman:

maₐts ts!ɛ'nan'. n'owo'kᵤne· neᵢ nɛtsta'hał. qaoxa'xe·. tɛnaxa'mne·
"Don't   go!"   He arose   that youth.   He went there.   He entered

aₐ'kɛt.łaɛ'se·s naso'ᵤkᵘe·ns. sak.łe'ᵢtse·. qakɛ'łne· husɛłtkaxa'mne·
the tent of   the chief.   He was asleep.   He said to   "I have entered
                                                    him:

aₐ'kɛt.ła''ne·s. n'ukᵤnoxa'mne·. n'ɛnqa'pte·k wɛ'łma·ł. tsukᵘa'te· 5
your tent."   He got up from his bed. He became a rattlesnake. He took

a'ₐ'k!e·s. qanła'łte·. q!akpakitxo'ᵤne·. neᵢs ałtɛłnamu''e·s
his arrow. He struck him. He knocked him down. Then   his wives

n'uk!ᵘił'ɛn'qapta'kse· wɛ'łma·ɨs. n'uk!ᵘiłq!akpakitxo'ᵤne. ła·ana-
at once became   rattlesnakes. One at a time he knocked them down. He went

xa'mne·. qake'ᵢne· q!a'pe· qokᵘayaxa'keɨł aₐ'ku'la·k.
out again. He said: "All   come and get   meat."

Qake'ᵢne· nɛtsta'hał ki'łu aq!sma'kᵢnɛk! łaa'k!ła·k. qakilɛ'łne· neᵢ
He said   the youth: "Are   people   others?"   He was told: "That
           there no

k!unanmɛ'tuk saₐk.łuna'mne·. qake'ᵢne· neᵢ nɛtsta'hał hults!ɛna'xe·. 10
down river   is a town."   He said   that   youth: "I'll start."

qakilɛ'łne· saha'n·e·ᵢ naso'ᵤkᵘe·n. ts!ɛna'xe·. łaxa'xe· saₐk.łunamɛ's_ᵢ
He was told: "Bad is   the chief."   He started. He arrived   where was a town

ne·. sanɛt.ła'ₐse· tɛlna'mu's. tɛnaxa'mne·. qakɛ'łne· hunuwa'sᵢne·.
Where lived in a tent   an old woman.   He entered.   He said to   "I am hungry."
                                                         her:

qak.ła'pse· hunuwas'nała'ₐne·. tsukᵘa't.se· a'tsu·s. n'oqoᵤxakɛ'nse·
He was told: "We are hungry."   She took   a dish.   She put it into it,

namatiktsa'pse·. qakɛ'łne· hoqᵘake'ᵢne· hunuwa'sᵢne·. qak.ła'pse·
she gave it to him. He said to   "I said   I am hungry."   He was told:
                     her:

ło'ᵤne· ku.ikᵢna'ła. qak.ła'pse· neᵢ hant.łana'mke· yunaqa'ₐne· 15
"There is   our food."   He was told: "That   where tent is   is much
none

there." The youth said: "I'll go." He went out. He got there. He entered, and the chief was asleep. He said to him: "Get up." The chief got up from his bed. He became a grizzly bear. The youth took his arrow and struck him. He knocked him down. At once (the chief's) wives became grizzly bears. He knocked them down. He threw them outside. The youth went out again. He said: "Take the meat." They took the meat.

The youth said: "Are there no other people?" He was told: "There is a town down the river." The youth started. He arrived at the town. He entered the tent of an old woman. He said to her: "I am hungry." He was told: "We have no food." She took a dish and put something into the dish. She gave it to him. He spoke to her, he said: "I am hungry." He was told: "There is much food in that tent, but nobody goes in there." The youth said: "I'll

---

k!ɛ'ke·ɫ at qatɛnaxamna'mne·. qake'ɪne· neɪ nɛtsta'haɫ huts!ɛna'xe·.
food   but   not any one goes in."   He said   that   youth: "I'll go."

n'anaxa'mne·.   qaoxa'xe·.   tɛnaxa'mne·.   sak.ɫe'ɪtse·   naso'ukue·n.
He went out.   He got there.   He entered.   He was asleep   the chief.

qakɛ'ɫne·   o·kunoxa'men'.   n'okunxa'mne·   neɪ   naso'ukue·n.
He said to   "Arise."   He got up from the bed   that   chief.
him:

n'ɛnqa'pte·k k.ɫa'wɫa's. tsukua'te· a'ak!e·s neɪ nɛtsta'haɫ. qanɫa'ɫte·.
He became a   grizzly bear.   He took   his arrow   that   youth.   He struck it.

5 q!akpakitxo'une·.   neɪs   aɫtɛnamu.ɛ'se·s   no'k!uɫ'ɛnqapta'kse·
He knocked it down.   Then   his wives   each became

k.ɫa'wɫa's no'k!uiɫq!akpakitxo'une·. n'anaqanmɛ'te·.   ɫaanaxa'mne·
grizzly bear   he knocked them down.   He threw them outside.   He went out again

neɪ   nɛtsta'haɫ.   qake'ɪne·   qokuayaxa'keɫ   aa·ku'ɫa·k.
that   youth.   He said: "Take ye   the meat."

qokuayaxa'ɫne· aa·ku'ɫa·k.
They took   the meat.

Qake'ɪne· neɪ nɛtsta'haɫ ki'ɫu aqɫsma'kɪnɛk! ɫaa'k!ɫa·k. qakiɫɛ'ɫne·
He said   that   youth: "Are   people   others?"   He was told:
                        there no

10 neɪ k!unanmi'tuk saak.ɫuna'mne·. ts!ɛna'xe· neɪ nɛtsta'haɫ. ɫaxa'xe·
"That   down river   there is a town."   He started   that   youth.   He arrived;

saak.ɫunamɛ'sɪne·. tɛnaxa'mne· aa·kɛt.ɫa.ɛ'se·s tɛna'mu's. qakɛ'ɫne·
there was a town.   He entered   the tent of   an old woman.   He said to
                                                                         her:

hunuwa'sɪne·. qak.ɫa'pse· ɫo'une· kuɛkna'ɫa. tsukua't.se· a'tsus n'oqou-
" I am hungry."   He was told: "There   our food."   She took   a dish;   she put
                        is none

xa''nt.se· a'tsus. namatiktsa'pse·. qakɛ'ɫne· hoquake'ɪne· hunuwa'sɪne·.
it into it   the dish.   She gave it to him.   He said to   " I said   I am hungry."
                                                  her:

qak.ɫa'pse· neɪ hanɛt.ɫan·a'mke· yunaqa'ane· k!ɛ'ke·ɫ at qatɛnaxam-
He was told: "That   where tent is   is much   food,   but   not any one

go." He was told by the old woman: "Don't go there." He arose. He went out. He went there. He entered. He sat down. He said to (the chief): "Arise." The chief got up from his bed. He became a buffalo bull. (The youth) took his arrow and struck him with it. He knocked him down. (The chief's) wives at once became buffalo cows. He knocked them down. He threw them outside. He said: "Come and take the meat."

22. The White Man

A white man went along. He saw (another) white man on the branch of a tree. He was chopping off the limb close to the trunk. The white man was told: "You will fall." The white man said: "I shall not fall." He said no more. This one started. (The other one) was chopping along. He chopped it off. He fell down.

---

na′mne·. qake′ₗne· neᵢ nɛtsta′haɫ huɫts!ɛna′xe·. qak.la′pse· neᵢs
goes in."   He said   that   youth: "I'll go."   He was told by   that

tɛlna′mu's maₐts ts!ɛ′nan′. n′owo′kᵤne·. n′anaxa′mne·. qaoxa′xe·.
old woman: "Don't   go there."   He arose.   He went out.   He went there

tɛnaxa′mne·. n′ɛsakᵤnu′n·e·. qakɛ′lne· oknoxa′men′. n′oknoxa′mne·
He entered.   He sat down.   He said to   "Arise."   He got up from his.
            him: bed

neᵢ naso′ᵤkᵘe·n. n′ɛnqa′ptse·k nɛ′ɫseᵢks. tsukᵘa′te· a′ₐk!e·s
that   chief.   He became   a bull.   He took   his arrow;

qanɫaltimu′n·e·. q!akpakitxo′ᵤne·. neᵢs alt ɛlnamu.ɛ′se·s n′ok!ᵘiɫ′ɛn-   5
he struck it with it.   He knocked it down.   Then   his wives   at once

qapta′kse· ɫu′kpu·s n′ok!ᵘiɫq!akpakitxo′ᵤne·. n′anaqanmɛ′te·.
became   cows   at once he knocked them down.   He threw them outside.

qake′ₗne· qo·kawɛsyaxa′keᵢɫ aₐku′la·k.
He said: "Come and take   the meat."

22. The White Man

Qa·na′xe· soya′pe·. n′u′pxₐne· soya′pe·s aₐ′kɛts!la′e·ns qawɛtsq!-
He went along   a white man.   He saw   a white man   a tree   standing on

nu′se· aₐ′kɛts!k!a′ɫaks. n′ɛntaₐkitsxo′ᵤne·. qak.la′pse· soya′pe·s
a branch.   He chopped off the limb   He was told   the white man:
            close to the trunk.

hɛnts!onaxu′n·e·. qake′ₗne· neᵢ soya′pe· at huqa′onaxu′n·e. la′qats-   10
"You will fall."   He said   the white   "I (shall) not fall."   He said no
            man:

xa′n·e·. na· ts!ɛna′xe·. qaₐnkitsxo′ᵤne·. k!axo′ᵤne·. n′onaxu′n·e·.
more.   This one started.   He chopped along.   He chopped it   He fell down.
                                                 off.

23. THE FRENCHMAN AND HIS DAUGHTERS

There lived a Frenchman and his three daughters. He said to them: "You shall do whatever I tell you." The Frenchman went away. There was a stump. He arrived and struck it. It opened, and it was a door. Grizzly Bear came to look, and (the Frenchman) was told: "Come!" The Frenchman entered. He took food. He ate, and after eating he was told: "You will give me your child. I shall marry her." The Frenchman said to the Grizzly Bear: "I will give you my daughter." He went back. He arrived at home. He said to his eldest daughter, he said to her: "I told you, 'Whatever I tell you, that you must do.'" The girl said: "You said so." Her father said to her: "Let us go to-morrow." On the following day the Frenchman went with his daughter. He arrived at the stump. The Frenchman knocked at the stump. The door opened. The Grizzly Bear came out and said to him: "Come in!" The two entered.

---

23. THE FRENCHMAN AND HIS DAUGHTERS

Qa·nɛt.ła′ₐne· nu·ɬa′qₐna qałsaqa′łte· na.u′tē′s. qakɛ′łne· ka· hu′-
There lived   an old man   three children   girls.   He said to "Whatever
(Frenchman)   them:

n'aqak.łɛ′ke·łts qa′łɛn a′tɛntsqa′qₐnapkɛ′łne·. ts!ɛna′xe· neᵢ nu·ɬ-
I tell you   just,   however, you shall do."   He started that

a′qₐna sɛnqʊłukpku′pse· łaxa′xe· qanła′łte·. nuk!ᵘɛnɛnmuxu′se·
Frenchman to where was a stump. He arrived, he struck it. It opened,

pa·ł sɛnk!ała·xwe.ɛ′ts·e·. nakaₐwɛtskɛ′kse· k.ła′włas qak.ła′pse· ła′n·a.
it was a door.   Came out to look Grizzly Bear, he was told: "Come!"

5 tᵢnaxa′mne· neᵢ nu·ɬa′qₐna. n'itkɛ′nse· ki′ek. n'i′kne· ku′ɬe·k.
He entered the   Frenchman.   He took   food.   He ate; he finished
                                                          eating.

qak.ła′pse· hɛntsa'matɛktsa′pne· aₐqa′łtne·'s huts·alitɛ′tne·. qakɛ′łne·
He was told: "You will give me   your child, I shall marry her." He said to him

neᵢ nu·ɬa′qₐna k.ła′włas hutsa'matɛktsɛ′sᵢne· ka′swɛn. łats!ɛna′xe·.
that Frenchman Grizzly Bear: "I'll give her to you my daughter." He went back.

ła·łaxa′xe· aₐ′kit.ła′e·s. qakɛ′łne· neᵢs kwɛ′łqaps swɛ′ne·s. qakɛ′łne·
He arrived at his tent. He said to that eldest his daughter. He said to her:

ma koqa′k.łe·s ka· hun'aqa′k.łe·s qa′łɛn at kɛntsqa′qₐna. qake′ᵢne·
"I told you whatever I tell you just, however, you must do." She said

10 neᵢ na.u′te· ma koqa′ke·. qak.ła′pse· su′'ēs kkanmi·′yɛt hutsts!ɛ-
that girl: "I said so." She was told by her father: "To-morrow we

naxała′ₐne·. kkanmi·′yɛt.s ts!ɛnakɛ′kᵢne· swɛ′ntmo neᵢ nu·ɬa′qₐna.
shall go." Next day they two went with his daughter that Frenchman.

łaxa′xe· sɛnqʊłukpku′pse·. qanła′łte· neᵢ nu·ɬa′qₐna neᵢs
He arrived at the stump. He knocked that Frenchman that

aₐ′qʊłu′kpkoᵤp's. nuk!ᵘɛnɛnmoxo′ᵤne· łak!anxo′ᵤna·ł. n'akaxa′mse·
stump. It opened. the door. He came out

k.ła′włas. qak.ła′psc· tkaₐxa′mkeᵢł. tɛna·kɛsxa′mne·. n'itkɛ′nse·
the Grizzly Bear. He said to him: "Come in." The two entered. He prepared

He prepared food. They ate. After he had finished eating, he said to his daughter: "You shall marry him." The Frenchman went back. At night his daughter came back. He said to her: "Why did you come back?" His daughter said to him: "I was afraid; he is a Grizzly Bear." The Frenchman said: "He will bite us." He said to his (next) daughter: "To-morrow we shall go to him. You shall marry him." On the following day he went with his daughter. The two went there. He knocked at the door. (The Grizzly Bear) opened it. They entered. He prepared food. After they had eaten, the Frenchman went back. In the evening his daughter came back. He said to her: "Why did you come back? The Grizzly Bear will bite us." He said to the youngest daughter, he said to her: "To-morrow we shall go to the Grizzly Bear. You shall marry him." The following day they two went together. They went there together. He arrived. He knocked at the door. The Grizzly Bear opened it. They entered. He prepared the food. After they had eaten, the Frenchman went back. In the evening the woman went

---

ke'e·k.   n'ɛ'kᵢne·.   ku'l'e·k.   qakɛ'lne·   swɛ'ne·s   hɛnts·alitɛ'tne·.
food.   They ate.   They finished eating.   He said to   his daughter: "You will marry him."

la·tslɛna'xe·   neᵢ   nu·l'a'qₐna.   ktsɛlmi'yɛt.s   la·wa'se·   swɛ'ne·s.
He started back   that   Frenchman.   At night   came back   his daughter.

qakɛ'lne·   qa'psin   kɛnsɛd·ats!ɛ'ka·m.   qak.la'pse·   swɛ'ne·s   hun'onɛ'lne·
He said to her: "Why   do you come back?"   She said to him   his daughter: "I was afraid;

pal   ke'en   k.la'wla.   qake'ine·   neᵢ   nu·l'a'qₐna   tsxa·'lit!xana-
he   is a   Grizzly Bear."   Said   that   Frenchman: "He will bite

wa'sᵢne·.   qakɛ'lne·   swɛ'ne·s   kkanmi'yɛt   hutsqona'xala·ɛ'sᵢne·   hɛn-   5
us."   He said to   his daughter: "To-morrow   we shall go to him,   you

ts·alitɛ'tᵢne·.   kkanmi'yɛt.s   qo·nakɛkma'lne·   swɛ'ne·s.   laxa'kɛkma'lne·.
!will marry him."   Next day   they two went together   his daughter.   They two went back.

qanla'lte·   laq!anxō'na·ls.   nuk!ᵘɛn·kɛ'n·e·.   tɛnaxa'mne·.   n'ɛtkɛ'nse·
He knocked at   the door.   He opened it.   They entered.   He prepared

ke'e·k.   ku'l'ek   la·ts!ɛna'xe·   neᵢ   nu·l'a'qₐna.   ktsɛlmi'yɛt.s   la·wa'se·
food.   When they fin-ished eating,   he went back   the   Frenchman.   In the evening   came back

swɛ'ne·s.   qakɛ'lne·   qa'psin   kɛnsɛd·a·ts!ɛ'ka·m.   tsɛt!xanawa'sᵢne·
his daughter.   He said to her: "Why   did you come back?   He will bite us

k.la'wla.   qakɛ'lne·   neᵢs   ktsaqu'nas   swɛ'ne·s.   qakɛ'lne·   kkanmi·'yɛt   10
the Grizzly Bear."   He said to her   that   youngest one   his daugher·   He said to her: "To-morrow

hutsqona'xala·ɛ'sᵢne·   k.lawla.   hɛnts·a·litɛ'tne.   kkanmi'yɛt.s   ts!ɛna-
we shall go to him   the Grizzly Bear.   You will marry him."   Next day   they two

kɛkma'lne·.   qao·xwakɛkma'lne·.   laxa'xe·.   t!axo'ₐne·   laq!anxo·'nals.
went together.   They went there together.   He arrived.   He knocked at   the door.

nuk!ᵘɛn·kɛ'n·e·   k.la'wla.   tɛnaxa'mne·.   n'ɛtkɛ'nse·   ke'e·k.   ku'l'ek
He opened   the Grizzly Bear.   They entered.   He prepared   food.   When they fin-ished eating,

la·tsɛlna'xe·   neᵢ   nu·l'a'qₐna.   ktsɛlmi'yɛt.s   q!u'mne'ᵢne·   neᵢ   pa·'lkeᵢ.
he started back   that   Frenchman.   In the evening   she slept   that   woman.

to sleep. She did not see where her husband slept. Early the next morning she saw her husband. He was walking about. The Frenchman thought: "I might go to my daughter to see whether he bit her." He started. He arrived. He knocked at the door; he opened; he entered. There was his daughter; Grizzly Bear had not bitten her. He went back. He came back. He said to his wife: "Go to the Grizzly Bear." The old woman started. She arrived at her daughter's tent. She knocked at the door. The Grizzly Bear opened it. He said to her: "Come in!" The old woman entered. Food was prepared for her. She ate. After she had eaten in the evening, she staid there over night. At night she wanted to see how the Grizzly Bear slept. The old woman went to sleep. She did not see where he slept. In the morning she saw him walking about.

---

qa.u'pxₐne·　ka·s　naₐqałq!u''mneᵢs　nu·łaqₐna'ēs.　kkanmi'yɛt.s
Not she saw　how　slept　her husband.　Next day

wɛ'łna·ms　n'u'pxₐne·　nu·łaqₐna'e·s　sła·tɛqa'atse·.　qałwi'yne·　neᵢ
early　she saw　her husband　he walked about.　He thought　that

nu·ł'a'qₐna　hułts!ɛna'mi·ł　ka'swin　naₐqanqa.ɛ't!xₐnaps.　ts!ɛna'xe·.
Frenchman:　"I might go to　my daughter　whether he did not bite her."　He started.

łaxa'xe·.　t!axo'ᵤne·　łaq!anxo·''nałs.　nuk!ᶦᵘɛnkɛ'n·e·.　tɛnaxa'mne·.
He arrived.　He knocked at　the door.　He opened.　He entered.

5 sa'osaqa'pse·　swɛ'ne·s　pa·ł　qae't!xₐna·psɛ'sne·　k.ła'włas.　ła·ts!-
She staid there　his daughter;　he had not bitten her　the Grizzly Bear.　He started

ɛna'xe·.　ła·łaxa'xe·.　qakɛ'łne·　tɛnamu''e·s　ts!ɛnamɛ'łe·n'　k.ła'wła.
back.　He went back.　He said to　his wife:　"Go to him　the Grizzly Bear."

ts!ɛna'xe·　neᵢ　tɛlna'mu.　łaxa'xe·　aₐk·ɛt.ła.ɛ'ses　swɛ'ne·s.　t!axo'ᵤne·
She started　that　old woman.　She arrived at　her tent　her daughter's.　She knocked at

ła·q!anxo·''na·ls.　nuk!ᶦᵘɛn·kɛ'n·e·　k.ła'wła.　qakɛ'łne·　tkaxa'men'.
the door.　He opened　the Grizzly Bear.　He said to her:　"Come in!"

tkaxa'mne·　neᵢ　tɛlna'mu.　n'ɛtkɛnłɛ'sne·　ke'e·k.　n'ɛ'kᵢne·.　ku'ł'e·k
She entered　that　old woman.　It was prepared　food.　She ate.　When she finished eating

10 wałkwa.iyɛ't.se·　łaqa·'kiyiksɛ'łek.　ktsɛlmi'yɛt.s　qałwi'yne·　ktsu'pxa
in the evening,　she staid over night.　At night　she wanted　to see

k.ła'włas　ka·s　tsa·qałq!u''mne's.　q!u'mneᵢne·　neᵢ　tɛlna'mu.
the Grizzly Bear　how　he would sleep.　She slept　that　old woman.

qa.u'pxₐne·　ka·s　na·qałq!u''mne's.　kkanmi'yɛt　n'u'pxₐne·
Not she saw　how　he slept.　In the morning　she saw him

sła·tɛqa'ₐtse·.
walking about.

[Nos. 24–31. Told by Michel]

24. COYOTE AND OWL[1]

There was a tent far away. Owl was there. When a child cried, its mother said: "Don't cry. Owl may take you!" At night, however, Owl came to the tent and took many children in his bark basket in which awls were standing. With these he killed them. Coyote said: "I shall become a child." Then Coyote became a child. Coyote said: "At night you shall throw me out." At night Coyote was taken and thrown out. He was taken by Owl. Owl started back to his tent. There were many children. They were there in the tent of Owl. At night Coyote said: "To-morrow you will get gum." The following day gum was taken. At night they danced. First Owl danced there. He perspired. Coyote said: "Later on I shall speak." Coyote said: "Throw the gum into the fire." The gum was thrown into the fire. It became hot. Coyote took

---

24. COYOTE AND OWL

Qaₐt.ɫana′mneˑ iɫqa′haˑk. ku′pi saosaqa′ₐneˑ. n′e′ɫa ɫka′mˑu ma′es
There was a tent   far.   Owl   was there.   When   a child   its mother   cried

qak.ɫa′pseˑ maₐts e′ɫan′ ɫtsukᵘa′teˑs ku′pi. tsɛɫmi′yɛt.sts at
said: "Don't   cry,   he may take you   Owl."   At night   however

notsa′xeˑ ku′pi at tsukᵘa′teˑ yunaqa′pseˑ ɫka′mˑu′s na′hi′k!eˑs
came to tent   Owl   but   took   many   children   his bark basket

nakiɫwɛtsqa′pseˑ ɫo′o′s. at n′upɛɫmu′nˑeˑ. qake′ineˑ skɛ′nˑkuˑts
stood in it   awls.   But   he killed them with them.   He said   Coyote:

ka′min hutsxaɫ′ɛ′neˑ ɫka′mˑu. ta′xas skɛ′nˑkuˑts n′ɛnqa′pteˑk 5
"I   shall be it   a child."   Then   Coyote   became

ɫka′mˑu′s. qake′ineˑ skɛ′nˑkuˑts tsɛɫmi′yɛt hɛnts!anˑmitapkɛ′lneˑ.
a child.   He said   Coyote: "At night   you shall throw me out."

tsɛɫmiyɛ′t.seˑ tsukᵘatɛ′lneˑ skɛ′nˑkuˑts. n′anˑmitɛ′lneˑ tsukᵘata′pseˑ
At night   he was taken   Coyote   he was thrown out,   he was taken by

ku′pis. ɫats!na′xeˑ ku′pi aₐ′kɛt.ɫa′e′s. yunaqa′ₐneˑ ɫka′mˑu
Owl.   He started back   Owl   to his tent.   There were many   children

saosaqa′ₐneˑ aₐ′kɛt.ɫaɛ′seˑs ku′pis. ktsɛɫmi′yɛt.s qake′ineˑ skɛ′nˑkuˑts
they were there   the tent of   Owl.   At night   said   Coyote:

kanmi′yɛt hɛnts!tsukᵘa′teˑ i′ɫwas. kkanmi′yɛt.s tsukᵘatɛ′lneˑ i′ɫwas. 10
"To-morrow   you will take   gum."   The next day   it was taken   gum.

ktsɛɫmi′yɛt naqwɛɫna′mneˑ. u′smeˑks ku′pi qaosaqwɛ′lneˑ. naq!ako′ᵤ-
At night   they danced.   First   Owl   there danced.   He perspired.

neˑ. qake′ineˑ skɛ′nˑkuˑts ma′qak hutsxa′nˑeˑ. qake′ineˑ skɛ′nˑkuˑts
He said   Coyote: "Later on   I shall speak."   He said   Coyote:

xunakɛ′nkiɫ i′ɫwas. xunakinɛ′lneˑ i′ɫwas. n′utineˑineˑ. tsukᵘa′teˑ
"Throw ye into the fire   gum."   It was thrown into the fire   the gum.   It became hot.   He took

---

[1] See pp. 20, 50.

the gum. Coyote said: "Later on Owl (shall do so)." He closed Owl's eyes with the gum. Owl had no eyesight. He could not see. Owl was taken. Coyote himself took Owl. He threw him into the fire. Owl died. Small ones flew out. Coyote said: "You shall be owls."

25. COYOTE AND TROUT

There was Coyote. It was winter. Coyote went along. Some one said to Coyote: "Coyote, come, come!" He went there. He saw a woman. He stole her and slept with her. He was told: "We shall start for a water hole in the ice." The woman started. Coyote went with that woman, his wife. Then Coyote staid in the water. His wife was Trout. On the following day he was told: "We shall start to where many people are fishing; there is much food." Then they started. There were many trout. Coyote went along. They came to a fish line. All the people were fishing. They

---

i′ɫwas· skɛ′n·ku·ts.   qake′ine· skɛ′n·ku·ts ma′qak ku′pi.   n′itkɛ′n·e·
the gum   Coyote.   He said   Coyote: "Later on   Owl."   He made

ku′pis aₐ′kaqɫɛ′′ɑse·s neis i′ɫwas·.   ɫo′use· aₐ′kaqɫɛ′l′e·s ku′pi.   qa.-
Owl   his eyes   the   gum.   None   his eyes   Owl.   Not

u′pxₐne·.   tsukᵘatɛ′ɪne· ku′pi.   skɛ′n·ku·ts n′ɛsniɫtsukᵘa′te· ku′pis.
he saw.   He was taken   Owl.   Coyote   himself took him   Owl.

xunmɛ′te· aₐ′kɛnqꜜu′ko·s.   n′ɛ′pine· ku′pi.   tsaquna′n·e·· nuɫnoxo′ne·.
He threw him   fire.   He was dead   Owl.   They were small.   They flew out.
into the fire

5 qake′ine· skɛ′n·ku·ts nɛ′nko kɛnɫe′en ku′pi.
He said   Coyote: "You   shall be   an owl."

25. COYOTE AND TROUT

Qaosaqa′ₐne· skɛ′n·ku·ts.   wanuyɛ′t.se·.   qa·na′xe·   skɛ′n·ku·ts.
There was   Coyote.   It was winter.   He went along   Coyote.

qakyamɛ′sine· skɛ′n·ku·ts skɛ′n·ku·ts ɫa′n·a ɫa′n·a.   qaoxa′xe·.
They said to   Coyote: "Coyote,   come,   come!"   He went there.

n′u′pxₐne· pa′ɫkeis. n′a′yne· qꜜu′mnema′ɪne·. qak.ɫa′pse· hutstsꜜkna-
He saw   a woman.   He stole   he slept with her.   He was told: "We shall start
             her,   for

xa′ɫa a′ₐ′ka·k. tsꜜkna′xe· nei pa′ɫkei. skɛ′n·ku·ts qsama′ɪne· neis
the water hole."   She started   that   woman.   Coyote   went with her   that

10 pa′ɫkeis n′ɛ′nse· tɛnamu′′e·s.   taxas qaosaqa′ₐne· skɛ′n·ku·ts wu′us
woman,   that   his wife.   Then   staid   Coyote (at the)   water,

n′ɛ′nse· tɛnamu′′e·s qu′stɛt!s.   kanmi′yɛt.s qak.ɫa′pse· hutstsꜜknaxa′-
that   his wife   Trout.   Next day   he was told: "We shall start

ɫa neis yunaqa′pse· at naɫuqɫawu′te· aₐ′qɫsma′kinɛk! yunaqa′ₐne·
that   where many   are fishing   people;   much

kꜜlikeiɫ. taxas tsꜜkna′xe·.   yunaqa′ₐne· qu′stɛt!. qsama′ɪne·
food."   Then   they started.   Many   trout.   He went with them

skɛ′n·ku·ts. ɫaxa′xe· aₐ′kuqɫa′wo·s. naɫuk.ɫawu′te· qꜜa′pe· aₐ′qɫs-
Coyote.   He came to   a hook with line.   They were fishing   all

killed trout, many trout. Coyote alone broke the hook. The people made a fish hook, a thick and big fish hook. The people were fishing. The (fish) ate the bait. Coyote was pulled out of the water. Then Coyote was taken. Then Trout was no longer Coyote's wife. Coyote staid among the Indians.[1]

---

ma'kᵢnɛk!.   n'upɛ'łne·   qu'stɛt!s.   yunaqa'ₐne·   qu'stɛt!.   n'ok!ᵘe'ᵢne·
people.   They killed   trout.   Many were   trout.   Only one

skɛ'n·ku·ts at n'umitskɛ'n·e·   aₐ'kuqła'wo·s.   n'itkɛ'n·e·   aₐ'kuqła'wo·s
Coyote   broke   the hook.   They made   fish hook

aₐ'qłsma'kᵢnɛk!   n'ałe'ᵢse·   wɛłqa'pse·   tsu'wak!s.   nałuqławu'te·
the people,   thick   large   fish hook.   They fished

aₐ'qłsma'kᵢnɛk!.   n'uq!ᵘyun·ko'x̱une·.   n'öpkaqo·x̱a'łne·   skɛ'n·ku·ts.
the people.   They took the bait.   He was pulled out of water   Coyote.

ta'x̱as   tsukᵘatɛ'łne·   skɛ'n·ku·ts.   łaqa.ɛ'n·e·   skɛ'n·ku·ts   tɛłna-   5
Then   he was taken   Coyote.   No more   Coyote   his wife

mu''e·s qu'stɛt!s.   łaqaosaqa'ₐne·   aₐ'qłsma'kᵢnɛk!   skɛ'n·ku·ts.
Trout.   He staid (among)   the Indians   Coyote.

---

[1] It was explained to me that when Coyote was caught, he was clubbed, and shouted: "I am no trout, I am Coyote!"

26. Skunk and Panther

Qaosaqaʼₐneˑ x̣aʼx̣as. qa.onɛʼlneˑ q!aʼpeˑs qaʼpsin. qaˑnaʼx̣eˑ.
n'uʼpx̱aneˑ swaʼs. n'onɛʼlneˑ x̣aʼx̣asˑ. qałwiʼyneˑ: "ksaʼhanˑ x̣aʼx̣as;
kłts!ɛʼpłap x̣aʼx̣as." n'ɛtx̣oʼᵤmek. qaˑnaʼx̣eˑ x̣aʼx̣as, n'uʼpx̱aneˑ
swaʼs. tseᵢkaʼteˑ. qałwiʼyneˑ: "kqasts!uʼmqaʼqa swaʼ; qaʼpsins
5 ksłʼpłaps?" tsukᵘaʼteˑ x̣aʼx̣as swaʼs. n'oqoᵤx̣akɛʼn·e yɛtskɛmeʼeˑs.
n'ałax̣oʼᵤneˑ. ts!ɛnaʼx̣eˑ. qaˑnaʼx̣eˑ. qałwiʼyneˑ swaʼ: "qaʼpsins
n'oʼneˑł x̣aʼx̣as?" qakeʼᵢneˑ x̣aʼx̣as: "n'ok!weʼᵢne kooʼnił aₐʼkiˑʼ-
łukwax̣niʼyam." qaˑnaʼx̣eˑ; pɛskɛʼn·eˑ. skanaʼx̣eˑ. nuʼx̣te·k x̣aʼx̣as.
qaosaqaʼₐneˑ. nałʼukwax̣niyamɛʼsᵢneˑ. n'onɛʼlneˑ x̣aʼx̣as. ts!ɛnaʼx̣eˑ
10 x̣aʼx̣as. swaʼ n'ömitskɛʼn·eˑ[1] yɛtskɛmeɛʼse·s. ts!ɛnaʼx̣eˑ swaʼ qałwiʼyneˑ
ma ksaʼhan x̣aʼx̣as. ts!ɛnaʼx̣eˑ swaʼ. n'onɛʼlneˑ x̣aʼx̣as. qaˑnaʼx̣eˑ
swaʼ. skikiłats!łɛʼnseˑ neᵢs skanaʼx̣eˑ. nas łaqakaʼx̣eˑ. neᵢs
łaqanaʼx̣eˑ. łaqawaₐkaʼx̣eˑ yunaqaʼpseˑ aₐʼk.łɛʼk!e·s. ts!ɛnaʼx̣eˑ
x̣aʼx̣as. qałwiʼyneˑ naqałsłɛʼtskeˑ swaʼ. łqaʼe·p. łats!ɛnaʼx̣eˑ.
15 łaˑłax̣aʼx̣eˑ yɛtskɛmeʼʼeˑs n'ömitseʼᵢseˑ yɛtskɛʼme·s. n'uʼpx̱aneˑ łoʼᵤseˑ
swaʼs. n'uʼpx̱aneˑ paˑł qaɛʼpseˑ. n'uʼpx̱aneˑ aₐʼk.łɛk!ɛʼse·s. ts!ɛnaʼx̣eˑ
aₐʼk.łɛk!ɛʼse·s. qaˑnaʼx̣eˑ x̣aʼx̣as yunaqaʼpseˑ aₐʼk.łɛk!ɛʼse·s. qa.uʼp-
x̱aneˑ kaₐs naₐqaʼnas swaʼs. n'itskɛʼlneˑ yunaqaʼpseˑ aₐʼk.łɛk!ɛʼse·s.
n'uʼpx̱aneˑ aₐʼk.łɛk!ɛʼse·s. snałʼkseˑ. ts!ɛnaʼx̣eˑ. ts!ɛnaʼk!ᵢneˑ.
20 qałwiʼyneˑ: "kots!uʼpił swaʼs." łax̣aʼx̣eˑ aₐʼkɛnmiʼtuks swaʼ.
waₐq!nuʼneˑ aₐkɛts!łaʼens. łax̣aʼx̣eˑ x̣aʼx̣as. n'ekuʼlneˑ. n'uʼpx̱aneˑ
swaʼs aₐʼkɛnmɛʼtuks saosaqaʼpseˑ. mɛʼtx̱aneˑ. yunaqaʼpseˑ k!aʼₐtsukp.
łałoʼᵤseˑ aₐq!ułuʼkp!e·s. at łatsukᵘaʼteˑ aₐʼq!ułuʼkp!e·s, at n'itkɛʼ-
n·eˑ at łaatsuʼkpaneˑ. nuk.łuʼkᵤneˑ, n'itx̣oʼᵤmek. n'uʼpx̱aneˑ swaʼs
25 aₐʼkts!łaʼens qaosaqaʼpseˑ. mɛʼtx̱aneˑ. n'ɛpɛʼlneˑ swaʼs x̣aʼx̣as.

27. The Deluge

Qaₐt.łanaʼmneˑ. at yunaqaʼₐneˑ kałq!aʼt!eᵢ ławiʼyałs. naqaʼpseˑ tɛnamuʼʼe·s ɛʼnła·k. nałq!at!eʼᵢseˑ ławiʼyałs. ts!ɛnaʼx̣eˑ
ɛʼnła·k. n'uʼpx̱aneˑ tɛnamuʼʼe·s. qa.uʼpx̱aneˑ tɛnamuʼʼe·s
yawoʼʼnɛk! tɛnamuʼʼe·s tsukᵘat.łɛʼsᵢneˑ. tsukᵘaʼt.seˑ yawoʼ-
30 nɛk!s. saˑnɛłwiʼyneˑ. mɛʼtx̱ₐneˑ. n'ɛsk!oʼᵘneˑ. n'ekuʼlneˑ
yawoʼʼnɛk!. łałoʼᵤneˑ. łatsukᵘaʼteˑ łałoʼᵤneˑ q!aʼpeˑ wuʼuˑ.
n'ekuʼlneˑ yawoʼʼnɛk!. łatsukᵘaʼteˑ ɛʼnła·k aʼₐk!e·s. łakx̣aʼmneˑ
wuʼu. nutsuʼkᵤneˑ. q!aʼpeˑ aₐʼqłsmaʼkinɛk! notsₐnqaʼₐtseˑ.
taʼx̣as łax̣aʼx̣eˑ wuʼu. qałwiʼyneˑ q!aʼpeˑ aₐʼqłsmaʼkinɛk!
35 kɛtsx̣aʼłep. łukᵘɛʼn·eˑ aₐʼkɛnuq!manaʼeˑs ɛʼnła·k. n'eyakɛʼn·eˑ.
qakeᵢʼneˑ: "łaʼłu aₐkɛnuq!maʼₐnam taʼx̣as hutsłałʼunałaʼₐneˑ."
taʼx̣as x̣aₐtsanmaˑʼq!łiłnoq!manaʼₐneˑ. taʼx̣as n'uk!qapeʼᵢseˑ.
qakeʼᵢneˑ "łaʼłu kaₐko·ʼq!łiłnoq!maʼₐna taʼx̣as q!aʼpeˑ huts!-
upnałaʼₐneˑ." taʼx̣as łax̣aʼx̣eˑ. ts!ɛnekɛʼme·k wuʼu. taʼx̣as
40 łakiłuʼkᵤneˑ. ła.unaʼx̣eˑ aₐʼqłsmaʼkinɛk!.

---

26. SKUNK AND PANTHER[1]

There was Skunk. He was not afraid of anything. He went
along. | He saw Panther. He was afraid of Skunk. He thought:
"Skunk is bad; | Skunk may kill me." He lay down. Skunk went
along, he saw | Panther. He looked at him. He thought: "Panther
is smart; what || may have killed him?" Skunk took Panther. He 5
put him into his bucket. | He carried him on his back. He started.
He went along. Panther thought: "What | may frighten Skunk?"
Skunk said: "I am afraid of one thing— | whistling." He went along.
He put him down. He went along. Skunk squirted out his fluid. |
He stopped there. Somebody whistled, and Skunk was scared.
Skunk started. || Panther broke his bucket. Panther started. He 10
thought | Skunk was bad. Panther started. Skunk was afraid.
Panther went along. | There were trees where he went. He came
back here. | When he went along, he came back where there were
many tracks. Skunk went along. | He thought Panther had lied
and that he was not dead. (Skunk) started again. || He got back to 15
his bucket. His bucket was broken. He saw no | Panther. He knew.
that he was not dead. He saw his tracks. He started | (following)
his tracks. Skunk went. There were many tracks. He did not | see
where Panther was. He looked for him. His tracks were many. |
He saw his tracks. There were tracks. He went. He went quickly. ||
He thought: "I'll kill Panther." Panther came to a river. | He 20
climbed a tree. Skunk arrived. He drank. He saw | Panther
in the river. He shot him. He broke much wind. | He had
no more fluid. He took back his fluid. He did it | and he broke
wind again. He was tired. He lay down. Then he saw Panther || in 25
the tree. He shot him. Skunk killed Panther. |

27. THE DELUGE[2]

There was a camp. There were many who picked huckleberries. |
Chicken Hawk had a wife. She picked huckleberries. Chicken
Hawk went. | He saw his wife. He did not know that | Yawo'nik!
had taken his wife. Yawo'nik! had taken her. || He was angry. He 30
shot him. He hit him. Yawo'nik! drank water. | There was no
more (water). He took it again. There was no more water. |
Yawo'nik! drank. Then Chicken Hawk took (pulled out) his arrow.
Out came | the water. There was a flood. All the people went up
the mountains. | The water reached there. All the people thought ||
they would die. Chicken Hawk took off his tail. He put it up. | He 35
said: "If there is no more tail, then we shall all be lost." | The tail
had four stripes. Then there was one left. | He said: "If there is no
stripe on my tail, then we shall all die." | It reached there. The
water stopped. Then || it went down. The people went down.[3] | 40

[1] See pp. 23, 48.
[2] See p. 218.
[3] Chicken Hawk put up his tail, and said that if the water should cover the four stripes on the tail,
then the people would all die.

28. Chicken Hawk and Toad

Qaosaqa′ₐne· ko′ᵤko n′asma′ɬne· kiaq!nu′kᵘa·ts. qakɛ′ɬne·
qake′ine ko′ᵤko: "Huɬts!ɩna′xaɬa′e·s; kanuɬaqₐnana′ɬa ɛ′nɬa·kts
kiaqka′loᵤk." ɩaxa′xe· ta′xas n′ɛ′nse· nuɬaqₐna′e·s. qastsu′m-
qaqa′ₐne·. tsukᵘa′te· tsu′pqa′s. kanmi′yɛt.s n′ɛtskɛ′ɬne·
5 tsu′pqa′s. kanmi′yɛt.s qake′ine· ko′ᵤko: "huɬqsana′ɬa." ta′xas
ts!ɩna′xe·. n′ɛtskɛ′ɬne· tsu′pqa′s, q!a′pe·s qa′psins kwi′ɬqɬe·s.
qa·na′xe· ɛ′nɬa·kts ko′ᵤko. tsɛmak!ɛ′·se· no′kwe·s. ɛ′nɬa·k
qaɬwi′yne·: "huɬ′ɛ′pe·ɬ." n′ipɛ′ɬne· ko′ᵤko′s ɩats!ɩna′xe· aₐ′kɛt.-
ɬa′e·s ɛ′nɬa·k. aɬaₐ′kɩɛ′k!e·s ko′ᵤko n′upxₐna′pse· tsukᵘata′pse·.
10 ɩats!ɩnaɬkna′pse· aₐ′kɛt.ɬa′e·s. saniɬwi′yne· ma′e·s ko′ᵤko·
qake′ine· ma′e·s ko′ᵤko: "huɬts!ɩnaxa′ɬa." ts!ɩna′xe·. qake′ine·:
"na·s at kaha′xe· ɛ′nɬa·k." qaosaqa′ₐne· ki′as ma′timo ko′ᵤko
na·kɛɩwɛtskɛ′ɬne· ɛ′nɬa·k. n′u′pxₐne·; ska′xe· ɛ′nɬa·k. n′ɛt.ɩatsu′n·e·
ko′ᵤko ma′timo. wa′xe· ɛ′nɬa·k. tsukᵘatɛ′ɬne·. ɩatsinamnaɬɛ′ɬne·
15 ɛ′nɬa·k aₐ′kɛt.ɩana′me·s. k!umnaqaqa′ₐne·. aₐ′kɩnq!o′kops atwɛ-
seya′mne· noko′ᵤne·.[1] k!umnaqaqa′ₐne·. n′u′pxₐne· kiaqka′ɩoᵤk
k!umnaqa′qaps tsa′′e·s. ts!ɩna′xe·. tsukwa′te· tsa′′e·s. ɩats-
kaɬkɛ′n·e. n′ɛtkɛ′n·e ɩasoᵤ′kse· tsa′′e·s. kiaqka′ɩoᵤk. kanmi′yɛt.s
n′ɛtskɛ′ɬne· q!a′pe·s qa′psins. so′ᵤkse· qak!umnaqaqa′ₐne· ɛ′n-
20 ɬa·kts kiaqka′ɩoᵤk. ta′xas.

29. Race of Frog and Antelope

Qaqa′ₐne· wa′tak. qake′ine·: "huɬts!ɩnaxa′ɬa nɛ′ɬtuk!p
aₐ′kɛt.ɬa′e·s hutsaɬnuxonaqnemaɬnaɬa′ₐne·." naɬnukupqa′ₐne·
nɛ′ɬtuk!p. qamatɛ′ɬne· naɬnukupqa′ₐne·. ɩaxaxe· wa′tak.
qakɛ′ɬne· q!a′pe·s wa′taks: "ne· qakna′pkeiɬ." n′ɛtxo′ᵤme·k
25 q!a′pe· wa′tak. pɛskɛ′n·e· q!a′pe·′s aₐ′kuqɬa′′nte·s. pɛskɛ′n·e·
nɛ′ɬtuk!p aₐ′kuqɬa′′nte·s. ta′xas na′ɬnuxonaqna′mne·. n′itkɛs-
wisqa′ₐne·. ts!ɩna′xe·. qa·ts!ɩna′kne· nɛ′ɬtuk!p. ta′xas wa′tak
ts!ɩna′kne·. matɛ′ɬne· nɛ′ɬtuk!p. tsukᵘat.ɩɛ′sine· aₐ′kuqɬa′′nte·s.
ɩats!ɩna′xe·. wa′takq!a′pe· sakqa′ₐne·. nuwa′sine· nok!nuqɬu-
30 ma′n·e·. kwaɬkwa′yit.s ɩats!ɩna′xe· q!a′pe· wa′tak. matɛ′ɬne·
nɛ′ɬtuk!p.

30. The Woman and the Giant

Qaosaqa′ₐne· aₐ′qɩsma′kinɛk!. ts!ɩna′xe·. qa·na′xe·. n′u′pxₐne·
e′′ka·s; n′ipɬa′pse·. ɩaqawa′xe· aₐ′kɛt.ɬa′e·s. ts!ɩna′xe· n′ok!ᵘe′ine·
pa·′ɬkei. naqa′pse· aₐ′qa′ɬt!e·s. qa·na′xe·. n′u′pxₐne· e·′′ka·s.
35 qak.ɩa′pse·: "qa′psin?" qake′ine· e·′′ka: "ka·s kɩn·aqa′ki·n."
qak.ɩa′pse· neis pa·′ɬkeis: "n′ɛ′n·e tsa′′ne·s." qake′ine·: "ka·s
kɩn·aqa′ki·n ksɩaqts!ɛxmaɬa′ɬa." qak.ɩa′pse·: "hukᵘe·′kine·ts sɩaqts-
ts!ɛxmaɬa′ₐne·." qake′ine·: "kɛ·′kinu." qak.ɩa′pse· neis pa·′ɬkeis:

---
[1] This sentence is unintelligible.

28. Chicken Hawk and Toad

There was the Toad. With him was Golden Eagle. Toad said | [he said to him]: "Let us go! Chicken Hawk and Blue Hawk (?) shall be our husbands." | Then he was her husband. He was skillful. | He caught Deer. One morning he was watching ‖ the Deer. In the 5 morning Toad said: "I'll go with you." Then | he started. He watched the Deer and everything—mountain sheep, rams.[1] | Chicken Hawk and Toad went along. His stone was hard (?). Chicken Hawk | thought: "I'll kill her." He killed Toad. Chicken Hawk started back | to his tent. Toad was seen by her parents. She was taken. ‖ They went to their tent. The mother of Toad was angry. | 10 The mother of Toad said: "Let us go!" They started. She said: | "Chicken Hawk passes by here." The two, Toad and her mother, staid there. | Chicken Hawk was watched for. They saw Chicken Hawk coming along. | Toad and her mother were in hiding. Chicken Hawk arrived. He was taken. ‖ Chicken Hawk 15 was carried back to the tent. He was poor. He was made to perspire over the fire (?). | He was poor. Blue Hawk (?) knew | that his younger brother was poor. He went. He took his younger brother. | He went to take him. Blue Hawk (?) restored his younger brother. On the following day | he looked for all kinds (of animals). He was well. ‖ Chicken Hawk and Blue Hawk were no 20 longer poor. |

29. Race of Frog and Antelope[2]

There was Frog. He said: "Let us go to Antelope's | tent! We will race with him." Antelope was a fast runner. | He was never beaten in racing. Frog arrived there. | He said to all the Frogs: "Do this." ‖ All the Frogs lay down. (Frog) put down all her clothes. | 25 Antelope put down his clothes. Then he ran fast. | They two stood together. He started. Antelope did not run fast. Then Frog | went fast, got ahead of Antelope, and took her clothes. | She started again. All the Frogs were lying there. (Antelope) was hungry and thirsty. ‖ In the evening all the Frogs started. They got ahead of | Antelope. | 30

30. The Woman and the Giant

There were the Indians. They started. They went along. They saw | a Giant, who killed them. They did not return to their tents. One | woman started. She had a child. She went along. She saw the Giant. ‖ She said to him: "What is it?" The Giant said: "What 35 are you doing?" | The woman said to him: "This is your younger brother." He said: "What | did you do to make him so white?" She said to him: "I cooked him | to make him white." He said:

---

[1] That means he was hunting deer, mountain sheep, and other animals.   [2] See p. 241.

"tsukᵘa'ten' łuk!." tsukᵘa'te· łoᵤk!s. ta'xas n'itkɛ'ne··
aₐ'k.ła'xwe·k!s (skɛk.łaxwɛ'k!ᵢne·). łu'ᵤnte· tsa'hałs neᵢ pa'łkeᵢ.
tsukᵘa'te· no'kᵘe·s. tsukᵘa'te· łoᵤk!s. ta'xas n'itxo'mek
e·'ka. ta'xas n'ɛtkɛnłɛ'sᵢne· a'm·a·ks. yunamok!o'ᵤne· neᵢ
5 pa'łkeᵢ. n'ɛłko'xᵤne·. ta'xas qake'ᵢne· e·'ka: "ɛskuku' ɛskuku'
ɛskuku'." ta'xas łaqatsxa'n·e· e·'ka. ta'xas n'ɛ'pᵢne·. łats!ɛna'-
xe· neᵢ pa'łkiᵢ. qake'ᵢne·: "tseᵢka'tkeᵢł hun'ɛpɛ'łne· e·'ka." ta'xas.

31. THE TWO TSA'KAP [1]

Qaosaqa'ₐne· tsa'kaps asma'łne· ałɛtskɛ'ł'e·s. qak.ła'pse·:
"maₐts ałqa'nam."[2] qałwi'yne· neᵢ: "ho'yas neᵢ hułqa'nam."
10 ts!ɛna'xe·. qa·na'xe·. qaₐwɛtsq!nu'se· aₐ'kɛts!ła'e·ns ta'k!ats.
mɛ'txₐne·, qaₐłak!o'ᵤne·. tsukᵘa'te· nᵥpɛ'k!as a'ₐk!e·s. mɛ'txₐne·.
n'ɛsk!o'ᵤne·. n'ipɛ'łne·. n'ɛtskɛ'łne· sakq!nu'kse· qa'hₐłin qayaₐqa'wos łoᵤkwɛ'n·e aₐ'koqła"nt!e·s. ts!ɛna'qne: qaoxa'xe· k!uł-
łe·etnana'se· to'hołs. n'onoq!oyata'pse·.
15 Qaosaqaₐ'ne· ałɛtskɛ'ł'e·s. ło'ᵤne· tsa'kaps. qałwi'yne· neᵢ
pa'łkeᵢ: "qa'psin kseᵢ'ł·o· tsa'kaps?" ts!ɛna'xe· neᵢ pa'łkeᵢ neᵢs
aₐ'ko'q!noᵤks. tseᵢka'te· aₐ'kuqławu't!e·s. nakunkɛ'n·e·. n'ᵥpka-
qu'xₐne· to'hołs. tsɛ'k!qₐne·. tsxa'ne· tsa'kaps. qake'ᵢne·:
"tsɛk!kɛ'ne·n'." ta'xas tsɛ'k!qₐne·. tsɛ'k!qₐne· aₐ"kwums. n'ukᵤ-
20 noxa'mne· tsa'kaps. łats!ɛnakɛkma'łne· ałɛtskɛ'łe·s tsa'kaps
aₐ'k.ɛt.ła'e·s. qak.ła'pse·: "maₐts neᵢ qa'nam." qałwi'yne·:
"hułts!ɛ'nam." ts!ɛna'xe·. swɛtsq!nu'se· ta'k!ats. mɛ'txₐne·.
qałak!o'ᵤne·. tsukᵘa'te· nᵥpk!aka'e·s. mɛ'txₐne·. n'ɛsk!o'ᵤne·.
n'ɛtskɛ'łne· aₐ'k!e·s. qa·na'xe·. snit.łanamɛ'sne·. tɛnaxa'mne·.
25 snakna'kse· pa'łkiᵢs. qak.ła'pse·: "qa'psin." qakɛ'łne·: "hus-
łitskɛ'łne· kaₐk!." qak.ła'pse·: "hułts!ɛnaxa'ła hułha'wɛskaxuk-
tsiu'ła." qak.ła'pse·: "ho'ya." qakɛ'łne·:"ho'pak nɛ'nko." n'ɛsak-
mu'n·e·. qakɛ'łne·: "ho'pak nɛ'nko." qak.ła'pse·: "nɛ'nko
ho'pak." ta'xas nawɛskaxo'ᵤktsek tsa'kaps. qaomitse'ᵢse·.
30 ła.unaxa'mne· tsa'kaps. qakɛ'łne· neᵢs pa'łkeᵢs:. "ła·ts nɛ'nko
nawɛskaxo'ᵤktsek." n'omitse'ᵢse·. n'ɛ'pᵢne· neᵢ pa'łkeᵢ łats!ɛ-
na'xe· tsa'kaps. łałaxa'xe· aₐ'kɛt.ła'e·s.
Qak.ła'pse· ałɛtskɛ'ł'e·s: "maₐts at na słqa'nam." ts!ɛna'xe·.
n'u'pxₐne· nᵥpɛ'k!a·s. słɛtski'łse· sɛ'n·as. yunaqa'pse· aₐ'qłsma'kᵢ-
35 nɛk! nᵥpɛ'k!as. qake'ᵢne·: "hułtsu'kᵘat sɛ'n·a." n'ipiłɛ'sᵢne·,
tsukᵘa'te·. łats!ɛna'xe·. mɛtyaxna'pse· tsa'kaps. qak.ła'pse·:
"pɛskɛ'nen', ka'min n'ɛ'n·e·. hɛnsł'ayniła'pin." qake'ᵢne·: "maₐts
ka'min n'ɛ'n·e·." łałaxa'xe· aₐ'kɛt.ła'e·s. qakɛ'łne· ałɛtskɛ'ł'e·s:
"ke'łoᵤ's katitunała'e·s.?" qak.ła'pse·: "ło'ᵤse·." qałwi'yne·:
40 "ła'kakati'tu." kanmi'yɛt.s qakɛ'łne· ałɛtskɛ'ł'e·s: "słutske'ᵢne·.

---
[1] Chamberlain translates this word by "ghost." My informant did not know the word.
[2] Throughout this story the forms used by a man talking to his sister, and *vice versa*, are used.

"Cook me." The woman said: | "Bring wood." He gathered wood. Then she made | a pit (it was a pit for cooking). The woman pulled out grass. | She took stones. She took wood. Then the Giant lay down. | Then soil was taken. The woman threw it on top. ‖ She set fire to it. Then the Giant said: "Iskuku′, iskuku′, | iskuku′!" Then the Giant spoke no more. Then he was dead. The woman | started to go back. She said: "Look! I killed the Giant." Enough. |

31. THE TWO TSA′KAP

There were two Tsa′kap, brother and sister. (The brother) was told: | "Don't go there!" He thought: "I will go there." ‖ He started. He went along. There was a squirrel sitting on a tree. | He shot at it. He did not hit it. He took his manitou arrow and shot | and hit it. He killed it. He watched. There was a lake. Just | in the middle he took off his clothing. He swam. | A little ways out in the water there was a charr. It swallowed him. ‖

There was his sister. The Tsa′kap had disappeared. That woman thought: | "Why is there no Tsa′kap?" The woman started to | the lake. She looked at the fish-line. She pulled it up. | She pulled the charr out of the water. She cut it open. The Tsa′kap spoke (inside). He said: | "Split it." Then she split it. She split the belly. ‖ The Tsa′kap arose. They two, the Tsa′kap brother and sister, went back together | to their tent. She said to him: "Don't go there." He thought: | "I will go." He went. There was a squirrel on a tree. He shot at it. | He did not hit it. He took his manitou arrow and shot. He hit it. | He looked for his arrow. He went along. There was a tent. He entered. ‖ A woman was sitting there. She said to him: "What is it?" He said to her: "I am | looking for my arrow." She said to him: "Let us go! We'll go swinging." | He said to her: "Well." She said to him: "You first." | He sat down. He said to her: "You first." She said to him: "You | first." Then the Tsa′kap swung. (The rope) did not break. ‖ The Tsa′kap went down again. He said to that woman: "Now you | swing!" (The rope) broke, and the woman was dead. | The Tsa′kap went on and arrived at his tent. |

He was told by his sister: "Don't go that way." He started. | He saw a manitou looking for beaver. There were many ‖ manitou people. He said: "Let me take a beaver." He killed it. | He took it. He started back. The Tsa′kap was pursued. He was told: | "Put it down, it belongs to me; you stole it from me." He said: "No; | it is mine." He went home to his tent. He said to his sister: | "Have we no father?" She said to him: "No." He thought: ‖ "Oh, if I had a father!" On the following day he said

5

10

15

20

25

30

35

40

ɬɛnaqa′pseˑ katitu′miɬ.″ qak.ɬa′pseˑ: ″naqa′pseˑ tɛtu′eˑs.
n′ɛpɬapsɛ′sᵢneˑ k.ɬa′wɬas tɛtu′eˑs qoˑs sakq!yuɬɛ.ɛ′t.seˑ.″ kanmi′yɛt
ts!ɛna′xeˑ tsa′kaps. ɬaxa′xeˑ. tsxa′nˑeˑ: ″ɬa′nˑa, huts!upɬɛ′sᵢneˑ.″
ɬaxa′xeˑ k.ɬa′wɬa. qakɛ′lneˑ: ″kaₐ kinaqa′keˑ?″ qakeᵢne′:
5 ″huts!upɬɛ′sᵢneˑ.″ qakeᵢne′: ″mɛ′txan′!″ ·mɛ′txₐneˑ tsa′kaps
aₐ′kɛts!ɬa′eˑns. snaxu′se: qakɛ′lneˑ: ″ts!ɛ′nan.″ ts!ɛna′xeˑ k.ɬa′wɬa
aₐ′koq!yuɬe′et.s. ɬaxa′xeˑ. n′ɛtwɛsqa′ₐneˑ k.ɬa′wɬa. wɛ·eˑ.ɛ′t.seˑ
mɛtxa′lneˑ k.ɬa′wɬa. n′ipiɬɛ′lneˑ. qaoxa′xeˑ tsa′kaps. n′omɛ′tsqₐneˑ.
tsukᵘa′teˑ tɛtu′eˑs aₐ′kuq!ɬamɛ′seˑs. ts!ɛna′xeˑ ɬaxa′xeˑ aₐ′koq!-
10 yuɬe′et.s. qakeᵢne′: ″k.ɬa′wɬa, ɬa′nˑa, huts!upɬɛ′sᵢneˑ.″ ts!ɛna′xeˑ
k.ɬa′wɬa. ɬaxa′xeˑ. qakeᵢne′: ″qa′psin?″ qakeᵢneˑ tsa′kaps:
″huts!upɬɛ′sᵢneˑ.″ qakeᵢneˑ k.ɬa′wɬa: ″mɛ′txan′ aₐ′kɛts!ɬa′eˑn.″
mɛ′txₐneˑ·; snaxu′neˑ aₐ′kɛts!ɬa′en. qakeᵢneˑ k.ɬa′wɬa: ″maₐts
huts!upɬɛ′sᵢneˑ tsa′kaps.″ qakeᵢne′: ″huts!upɬɛ′sᵢneˑ.″ qakɛ′lneˑ
15 k.ɬa′wɬas: ″ɬu′nˑu.″ ts!ɛna′xeˑ k.ɬa′wɬa aₐ′koq!yuɬe′et.s.
n′itwɛsqa′ₐneˑ. mitxa′lneˑ. n′ipiɬɛ′lneˑ. ts!ɛna′xeˑ tsa′kaps.
tsi′k!qₐne. tsukᵘa′teˑ aₐ′koq!ɬamɛ′seˑs. ɬats!ɛna′xeˑ aₐ′kɛt.ɬa′eˑs.
qaosaqaₐ′neˑ. kanmi′yɛt.s qakɛ′lneˑ aɬɛtskɛ′lˑeˑs: ″huɬuqᵤnan-
yaɬa′eˑs.″ taxas ts!ɛna′xeˑ. wat!a′xeˑ.

[Nos. 32–37. Lower Kutenai. Toĭd by Angi McLaughlin]

32. CHIPMUNK AND OWL

20 Qaosaqa′ₐneˑ wa′tak. tɛte′eˑs q!u′tsats. n′iɬa′neˑ q!u′tsaˑts,
nuwa′sᵢneˑ. qak.ɬa′pseˑ tɛte′eˑs: ″aₐ′kɛnuxo′ᵤnuk ts!ɛ′nan′ ɬeˑ″-
neˑ.″ k.ɬa′xam q!u′tsaˑts naqa′pseˑ q!u′lwa. naɬxo′ᵤneˑ na″heks.
ta′xas tsukᵘa′teˑ. n′uk!ᵘniɬoqoᵤxa″nteˑ. ta′xas n′ɛt!qa′pseˑ
aₐq!ᵤna′ₐwoᵤk. qaosaqa′ₐneˑ q!u′tsaˑts. nuɬpa′lneˑ ku′pis, t!a-
25 ɬo′kseˑ: ″ɬa′nˑa.″ ta′xas ts!ɛna′seˑ aₐqa′t!aks q!u′tsaˑts yaₐ-
qaosaqa′ₐkeˑ. qakeᵢneˑ ku′pi: ″hutsxaɬts!ɛnaxaɬa.ɛ′sᵢneˑ ma″-
neˑs.″ qakeᵢneˑ q!u′tsaˑts: ″wa′ha, pɛ′k!aks ɛ′pᵢneˑ ka′ma.″
n′onɛ′lneˑ q!u′tsaˑts. qaɬwi′yneˑ: ″ktsxaɬ′ɛ′pɬaps.″[1] qakeᵢneˑ
q!u′tsaˑts: ″manwitsi′yin′.″ k!okᵘina′ₐneˑ (?) ku′pi: ″ts!up-
30 naqɬɛ′len′.″ ɬaqanaɬts!ɛna′xeˑ q!u′tsaˑts. neᵢs qaqna′ₐneˑ ku′-
pi. yuˑk!kaka′teˑ ta′xa neᵢ q!u′tsaˑts paɬ k.ɬats!ɛ′nam aₐ′kɛt.-
ɬa.ɛ′seˑs tɛte′eˑs. ta′xas ɬatɛnaxa″mneˑ. qakɛ′lneˑ tɛtu′eˑs: ″tsxaɬ′-
ɛpɬa′pneˑ. ɛt.ɬatsu′to.″ qakeᵢneˑ wa′tak. qakeᵢneˑ: ″qa′psin
kuɬ′ɛ′tkin?″ qanaɬtsukᵘa′teˑ neᵢ wa′tak tɛte′eˑs. n′oqoᵤnaq-
35 kɛ′nˑeˑ wo′q!kaˑ′s. n′ɛ′pᵢneˑ q!u′tsaˑts.

---

[1] Or ktsxaɬ′ö′plaps.

to his sister: "You told a lie. | I ought to have a father." She said to him: "You have a father. | Your father was killed by Grizzly Bear. There is a mountain over there." The following day | the Tsa'kap started. He arrived. He said: "Come, I'll kill you!" | The Grizzly Bear came. He said to the two (the Tsa'kap): "What did you say?" The Bear said: ‖ "I'll kill you!" He said: "Shoot at it!" The Tsa'kap shot at | a tree. It fell down. (The Tsa'kap) said to (the Grizzly Bear): "Go!" The Grizzly Bear went | to the mountain. He got there. The Grizzly Bear stopped. From far away | he was shot and was killed. The Tsa'kap went there. He skinned it. | He took his father's hair. He started. He arrived at ‖ the mountain. He said: "Come, Grizzly Bear, I'll kill you!" Grizzly Bear started. | He got there. He said: "What is it?" The Tsa'kap said: | "I'll kill you!" The Grizzly Bear said: "Shoot that tree!" | He shot at it. The tree fell. The Grizzly Bear said: "I will not | kill you, Tsa'kap." (The Tsa'kap) said: "I will kill you." He said to ‖ the Grizzly Bear: "Go on!" The Grizzly Bear started for the mountain. | He stopped. He was shot and was killed. The Tsa'kap started. | He cut him open. He took his hair. He went back to his tent. | He staid there. The following day he said to his sister: | "Let us move camp." Then he started. He went across the mountains. ‖

[Nos. 32–37. Lower Kutenaï. Told by Angi McLaughlin]

32. CHIPMUNK AND OWL[1]

There was Frog. His grandmother was Chipmunk. Chipmunk was crying. | He was hungry. He was told by his grandmother: "Go to the river; go to the other side." | When Chipmunk arrived, there were rose hips. He carried a bark basket. | Then he took it. He filled it at once. Then it was full. | There were willows. Chipmunk heard Owl making a noise. ‖ "Come here!" Then he started. (Owl) went to where Chipmunk | was sitting. Owl said: "Let us go home to your mother." | Chipmunk said: "No; my mother died long ago." | Chipmunk was afraid. He thought: "He will kill me." Chipmunk said: | "Cover your eyes with your hand." Owl did so. He shut his eyes. ‖ Then Chipmunk started, going along. Owl did thus.[2] | He could not get him. Then Chipmunk got home to the tent of | his grandmother. Then he entered. He said to his grandmother: "He will | kill me. Hide me!" Frog said: "What | shall I do?" Frog took her grandson and put him into ‖ the soup. Chipmunk died. |

---

[1] See p. 58.

[2] Owl stretched out his hand to catch Chipmunk, and scratched him.

33. The Sun

Qaᵃna′xe· skɛ′n·ku·ts n′asmaʼine· ɛ′nɫa·k. qake′ɪne· skɛ′n·ku·ts:
"huɫts!ɪnaxaʼɫa   qo   iɫkaʼhak   aₐ′q!sma′knɛk!   sakɛ̓′ɛtkɛ′n·e·
nata′n·ɛk!s."   u′s′meks skɛ′n·ku·ts qake′ɪne·: "hutsxaɫ′ɛ′n·e·
nata′nɛk!."   qake′ɪne· ɛ′nɫa·k: "u′s′mek ka′min."   qake′ɪne·
5 skɛ′n·ku·ts: "waʼha."   taʼxas ts!ɪna′xe·.   qaᵃna′xe· qake′ɪne·
ɛ′nɫa·k: "hɛntsxaɫhuɫpaɫnaʼpne·."   qake′ɪne·   skɛ′n·ku·ts:
"qaʼpsin?"   qake′ɪne· ɛ′nɫa·k: "ne̞ᵢ hutsyaₐqanaxaɫaₐ′ake·."
qake′ɪne· skɛ′n·ku·ts: "qaʼpsin?"—"taʼxa ne̞ᵢ hutsqaosaʼqo-
waɫaʼₐne· ne̞ᵢ anɫonik.le′ɛt. tsaqaʼₐne· t!ɪna′m·u; at qahaʼxam
10 aₐ′q!sma′knɛk! at qaʼsxₐne·."   taʼxas ɫaxaʼxe·.   qaʼsxₐne·
ɛ′nɫa·k·.   "taʼxa nɛ′nko," qake′ɪne· ɛ′nɫa·k.   taʼxas qayaₐ-
qahaʼxe· ɛ′nɫa·k.   taʼxas tsukⁿaʼte· skɛ′n·ku·ts· n′onaxu′n·e·
ne̞ᵢ t!ɪna′m·u.   ne̞ᵢs qanaqayaqaʼₐne· skɛ′n·ku·ts.   taʼxas
ts!ɪna′xe· skɛ′n·ku·ts taʼxas ts!ɪna′k̵ine· ɫaxa′nxo′ₐne· ɛ′nɫa·k.
15 qake′ɪne· ɛ′nɫa·k. "huɫpaʼɫnu kaₐ huts!aₐqaʼk.ɫe̞ᵢs."   taʼxas
qatsxaʼn·e·. ɫaxaʼxe·.   taʼxas tsɛmiyɛ′t̞ɪne· qake′ɪne· skɛ′n·ku·ts:
"u′s′mek ka′min."   qake′ɪne·   ɛ′nɫa·k: "maₐts."   taʼxas
ts!ɪna′xe·.   wɛ′ɫna·m qawunikɛ′t̞ɪne·.   waɫkwayɛ′t̞ɪne· ɫawaʼxe·
skɛ′n·ku·ts. qake′ɪne· aₐ′q!sma′knɛk!: "sahaʼn·e· skɛ′n·ku·ts."   qa-
20 wunikɛ′t.se· qake′ɪne· ɛ′nɫa·k: "taʼxa ka′min. taʼxa hutsxaɫɛ̓′s-
niɫts!ɪna′xe·."   qake′ɪne· ɛ′nɫa·k. taʼxas yuwaₐk!mɛnuqkaʼn·e·.
so′ₐkⁿe· nata′nɛk! ɛ′nɫa·k.   saₐnɫwi′yne· skɛ′n·ku·ts.   qaɫwi′yne·
kinmɛ′txₐne· ɛ′nɫa·ks.   naq!aku′pse· aₐ″k!e̞·s   skɛ′n·ku·ts·
q!apiɫaq!aku′pse· aₐ″k!e̞·sts t!awu′e·s. pɛskɛ′n·e·. q!apiɫ-
25 aq!aku′pse· aʼm·a·ks. ts!ɪna′xe· hanɫukpqaʼₐne· q!apiɫ′aq!-
ako′ₐne·. qa.u′pxₐne· qaʼpsins ɫ̓ɛ′tkin. qaosaʼxe· aₐ′k̞ɪma-
na′me·s.   qanaɫ′itxo·′mek.   qahaq!aku′pse· aₐ′k̞ɪmana′me·s.
taʼxas qake′ɪne· skɛ′n·ku·ts: "Husukⁿiɫq!o′kₐne· ne̞ᵢ kuqaʼe·p."
taʼxas.

34. Fox and Skunk

30   Qana′xe· xaxastai′ya. qaqaʼₐne· naʼk!ᵢyu. naɫxo′ₐne· yɛts-
kme′e·s. qaɫwi′yne· kts!isaʼknu. pɛsxo′ₐne· yɛtskme′e·s. qana′-
xe·. qake′ɪne·: "ɫu′ₐne· qaʼpsin kuo′niɫ xaxastai′ya." qake′ɪ-
ne·: "qaqaɫ′uk!ᵘe′′ne· kuo′niɫ ne̞ᵢ kaɫukwaxni′yam." taʼxas
n′isak̞ɪnu′n·e·. qanaɫ′uknoxa′′mne· naʼk!ᵢyu. qaoxaɫhaɫukwax-
35 ni′ɫe·k. nosanoxunqaʼₐne· xaxastai′ya. n′umɛtskɛ′n·e· yɛts-
kmɛ′se·s naʼk!ᵢyu. ts!ɪna′xe· naʼk!ᵢyu. ɫawa′xe· xaxastai′ya.
n′u′pxₐne· ne̞ᵢs k!umɛ′tse̞ᵢs yɛtskme′e·s. n′iɫaʼne. qaɫwi′yne·
ktsxaɫ′ɛ′piɫ naʼk!ᵢyu. taʼxas ts!ɪna′xe· xaxastai′ya. n′u′pxₐne·
aₐ′kɛnmi′tuks. n′eku′ɫne· xaxasta′ya. n′u′pxₐne· naʼk!ᵢyu yaʼwo′s
40 wu′os. taʼxas n′atsu′kpne·. n′uk.ɫu′kₐne· n′itxo·′me·k ne̞ᵢsqaɫwaₐ-
kiɫwitskɛ′k̞ɪne· n′u′pxₐne· naʼk!ᵢyus qo′s naʼₐtas qaosaqaʼpse·
ne̞ᵢs qaɫ′ukaxo·′mek. qaɫwi′yne· tsxaɫaxaq!u′ɫukp, mɛtxna′pse·
naʼk!ᵢyus. taʼxas.

33. THE SUN[1]

Coyote went along with Chicken Hawk.   Coyote said: | "Let us go there far away, where the people are making | the sun."   Coyote said first: "I'll be | the sun."   (Chicken Hawk said:) "I first." || Coyote said: "No."   Then they started.   They went along.   Chicken 5 Hawk said: | "You shall listen to me."   Coyote said: | "What is it?"   Chicken Hawk said: "It is where we are going." | Coyote said: "What is it?"   (Chicken Hawk said:) "Then we'll stay | over there.   There will be grease.   When people pass, || they bite off a 10 piece."   They arrived there.   Chicken Hawk bit off a piece. | "Now you," said Chicken Hawk.   Then Chicken Hawk passed. | Then Coyote took it.   The grease fell down. | Coyote went rolling along.   Then | Coyote started.   He went quickly.   Chicken Hawk overtook him. || Chicken Hawk said: "Listen to me, what I tell you."[2]   Then | 15 he did not speak.   They arrived there.   Then in the evening Coyote said: | "I first."   Chicken Hawk said: "No."   Then | they started early.   After a little while it was evening.   Coyote arrived. | The people said: "Coyote is bad." || After a little while Chicken 20 Hawk said: "Now I, now I myself shall | start."   Thus spoke Chicken Hawk.   Then the sun rose. | Chicken Hawk was a good sun.   Coyote was angry.   He thought | he would shoot Chicken Hawk.   Coyote's arrow burned. | His arrow and his bow were all burned.   He put it down. || The earth was all burned.   He started running, and 25 everything was on fire. | He did not know what to do.   He came to a trail | and lay down there.   The trail did not burn. | Then Coyote said: "I am glad that I am not dead." | Enough. ||

34. FOX AND SKUNK[3]

Skunk was going along.   There was Fox.   He carried a | pot.[4] 30 He wanted to sit down.   He put down his pot.   He went along. | (Skunk) said: "There is nothing I am afraid of."   He said: | "The only thing I am afraid of is whistling."   Then | he sat down.   Fox arose.   There was the sound of whistling. || Skunk ran away.   Fox 35 broke the pot. | Fox started.   Skunk arrived. | He saw that his pot was broken.   He cried.   He thought | he would kill Fox.   Then Skunk started.   He saw | a river.   He was going to drink.   He saw Fox inside || the water.   Then he squirted his fluid at him.   He be- 40 came tired.   He lay down and | looked up.   He saw Fox, being above.   Then | he turned around.   He thought he would squirt his fluid at him, but Fox shot him. | Enough. |

---

[1] See pp. 66, 116.   [2] See p. 110.   [3] See pp. 23, 40.
[4] That is, Fox was in the pot that Skunk was carrying.

35. COYOTE AND CARIBOU

N'asma'ɬne· na'ẋane·. at ts!ɜna'ẋe· na'ẋane·. sa·nⱡwi'yne· skɜ'n·-
ku·ts. qaⱡwi'yne· tsẋaⱡ'u'piⱡ neᵢs na'ẋanc·s. qake'ᵢne· skɜ'n·ku·ts:
"qa'psin at skiⱡwunikɜ't·ne·?" qake'ᵢne· na'ẋane·: "at husiⱡ'ɜ'kᵢne·
ktsaqu'na tsa'haⱡ at husⱡaqaⱡwa·sⱡsɜ'kᵢne·." n'ipɜ'ⱡne· skɜ'n·ku·ts
5 neᵢs na'ẋane·'s. ⱡaska'ẋe· skɜ'n·ku·ts· qaoẋaⱡtɜnaẋa'mne· neᵢs
aₐ'kit.ⱡa.ɜ'se·s. n'ɜ'pᵢne· na'ẋane·. n'iⱡa'n·e· skɜ'n·ku·ts. qake'ᵢne· "ma
kutsⱡa'keᵢⱡ ka'swu." ta'ẋas.

36. COYOTE AND OWL

Ku'pi sakiⱡa'ync· ⱡkamnɜ'nta'ke·s. qake'ᵢne· skɜ'n·ku·ts: "huts-
ẋaⱡ'ɜ'n·e· ⱡka'm·u." n'ⱡa'n·e· skɜ'n·ku·ts tsiⱡmiyɜ't.se·. qakiⱡɜ'ⱡne·:
10 "hɜnsa·nⱡuẋⱡitɜ't·ne·, to'ẋwaⱡɜntkayaẋni'sᵢne· ku'pi." qanaⱡqunyaẋa'ⱡ-
ne· skɜ'n·ku·ts. qa·waẋmitɜ'ⱡne· aₐ'k!aⱡaẋwe'et.s. qanaⱡtsukᵘata'pse·
ku'pi's, ts!ɜnaⱡkna'pse·. qake'ᵢne·: "hun'ɜ'n·e· skɜ'n·ku·ts." qakɜ'ⱡne·
ku'pi's: "huⱡa'qwiⱡna'ⱡa." naqwi'ⱡne· skɜ'n·ku·ts a'ₐ'ke ku'pi. skɜ'n·-
ku·ts n'ipɜ'ⱡne· neᵢs ku'pis. k.ⱡaa'yne· ⱡkamnɜ'nta'ke·s. ⱡats!ɜna'ẋe·.
15 qake'ᵢne·: "hun'ipɜ'ⱡne· ku'pi." ta'ẋa.

37. COYOTE AND DEER

Qa·na'ẋe·. n'u'pẋₐne· tsu'pqa's. qaⱡwi'yne· ktsẋaⱡmi'tẋa.
naⱡomi'se·, sⱡ'oneⱡa'pse· neᵢs qakɜ'n·e·. ⱡats!ɜna'ẋe· qawɜsqa'pse·
n'ɜsqawitsⱡa''mse·. qake'ᵢne· skɜ'n·ku·ts: "k!ɜsɜnyu'kᵘa¹ tɜtu''ne·s?"
qake'ᵢne· neᵢ qa'psin: "qa'psin? kinq!akpa'mek neᵢ kinɜ'pⱡap?"
20 qake'ᵢne· skɜ'n·ku·ts: "huqᵘaⱡwi'yne· paⱡ ke'ⱡo· qa'psin." ta'ẋas.

[Nos. 38–44. Description of Dances, Games, and Hunting]

38. KISSING DANCE

Kt!amu'ẋo·ⱡ ka'qwɜ tɜ'tqa·t!ts pa'ⱡkeᵢ kaⱡqok!aⱡma'ẋnam. nama-
 Drum dance men and women   kiss.   They

tɜktsɜ'ⱡne· sɜ·'ɜt!s. ⱡaa'k!ⱡaₐk naⱡqok!aⱡmaẋa'ⱡne·. namatɜktsɜ'ⱡ-
 are given blankets. Another one   is kissed.   They are

ne· yunaqa'ₐne· qa'psin.
 given many things.

39. SUN DANCE

N'itɜt.ⱡana'mne· tsẋaⱡhanquẋo'ᵤⱡne·   ts!ɜsɜn·ɜnquẋonaⱡka''ne·
 They build a tent will be Sun dance.   The Sun-dance leader

25 na'ksaq.
 is master.

_____

¹ Or aₐ·'kiyuka''nam.

35. Coyote and Caribou

There were two—(Coyote and) Caribou. Caribou started. Coyote was angry. | He thought he would kill Caribou. Coyote said: | "Why does it take you so long?" Caribou said: "I eat | small grass and I quickly get fat." Coyote killed || Caribou. Coyote 5
came along. He entered | (Caribou's) tent. Caribou was dead. Coyote cried. He said: | "I loved my friend." Enough. |

36. Coyote and Owl [1]

Owl stole children. Coyote said: | "I'll be a child." Coyote cried in the evening. He was told: || "You make a bad noise. Owl may al- 10
most take you away." | Coyote was taken. He was thrown out of the doorway. Owl took him along. | He carried him along. He said: "I am Coyote." Owl was told: | "Let us dance!" Coyote and Owl danced. Coyote | killed Owl, who had stolen the children. They started back. || He said: "I killed Owl." Enough. | 15

37. Coyote and Deer

He went along. He saw Deer. He thought he would kill him. | The wind was blowing and frightened him. He did thus to it. He went on. He stood there holding (in the hand) | his head thus. Coyote said: "Is that your father's war bonnet?" | The thing said: "What is it? Do you forget that you killed me?" || Coyote said: 20
"I thought it was nothing." Enough. [2] |

[Nos. 38–44. Description of Dances, Games, and Hunting]

38. Kissing Dance

The drum is beaten. Men and women dance and kiss one another. In return blankets are given. Another person is kissed and many things are given.

39. Sun Dance

They build a tent to have a Sun dance. The Sun-dance leader is master.   25

---

[1] See pp. 20, 37.

[2] This story was not known to my informants. It seems to mean that Coyote intended to kill Deer and in pursuing him was frightened by the wind. It seems that then he shot Deer, and Deer was standing there holding his own head in his hands. He did not recognize it, and asked the Deer: "Is that your father's war bonnet?"

40. Manitou Performance

Kq!axna'mnam.   n'ɛsin'wisχa'ɩnc·   Na'qₐne·.   qakɛ'kse·   nöpɛk!a'e·s
They tie up some one.   He is behind a screen   "He Swims."[1]   He says   his manitou

ɩatikmi'tiɩ.   qakɛ'kse·   nöpɛk!a'e·s   tsχalhaqayeqa'mek.
when he is   He says   his manitou   he will roll himself.
thrown back.

41. Medicine Performance

T!amoχo'ᵤɩne·   sɛɩwanaqₐnanuq!namna'mne·   yunaqa'pse·   qa'psins
The drum is beaten   they practice medicine performances   many   things

ktso'ᵤkᵘaₐt   χatknoᵤkᵘɛ'ne·.
who take   save him.

42. Gambling

5   Kaɩuwa'ts!nam   yunaqa'ₐne·   k!ɛskaχₐmɛ'tiɩ   qa'psin;   kq!a'ɩaχa'ₐɩ-
     Gambling   many   are lost   things;   horses,

tsin,   se·'ɛt!,   aₐ'qatwu'mɩa,   t!a'wu,   aₐ'ktsa'maɩ,   nɛ'ɩko;   q!a'pe·
blankets,   shirts,   bows,   knives,   money;   all

qa'psin   n'ɛskaχₐmetɛ'ɩne·.
things   are lost.

43. Games

K!ɛtkɛ'niɩ   kene'he,   ɩaa'k!ɩaₐk   .kawɛsk!akana'nam,   k!iktsikna'm-
It is done   dancing in circle   other one   down squatting,   blind man's
             hand in hand,

nam.   at sɩɛtkinɛ'ɩne·   kk.ɩɛnq!o'yam,   at sɩɛtkinɛ'ɩne·   qa'ɩa   ɩka'm·u
buff.   It is made   a toy,   it is made   some   child,

10   n'iktsi'kiɩ   ɛ'n·e·n   nɛtsta'haɩna'na   at swu'ᵤte·   aₐ'kɛnu'ɩa·ms,   na.ut-
     if he is caught,   if he is   a boy,   he is given as   a snake;   a
                                                    a bow

na'na   at   n'ɛ'nse·   kiyukmu'ɩ'e·s   at   n'ɛ'nse·   aₐ'kɛnu'ɩa·ms.
girl,   however,   she   her digging-stick,   however,   it is   a snake.

44. Hunting on the Plains

Neᵢ   ɩawat!ɛ'nak   ninaɩhuɩ'unɛ's¡nam   at   n'oᵤniɩɛ'ɩne·
Those   across the moun-   when they went out on   however,   were feared
         tains   the prairie,

sa'nɩa.   at   q!untkaɩhawasχuneya'mne·   at   sɩ'oᵤniɩɛ'ɩne·   sa'nɩa
the   How-   around they sing,   but   they were feared   the Pie-
Piegans.   ever,   gans

ktsχaɩ'a'y   kq!aɩ'aχa'ₐɩtsins.   at   n'upsɩa'tiyiɩqanikɛ't¡ne·   ninaɩ-
they would steal   horses.   But   they did this always   when

15   huɩ'unɛ's¡nam   ɩa.upkaɩonɛ'snam   no·qanki'kiɩ'akni'yam.   ta'χas
     they were on the prairie   when they went out on   they rounded up buffaloes.   Then
                                 the prairie

at   qaₐqaskᵢnɛ'ɩne·.
they stopped.

---

[1] Name of a man, known under the French name Louis.

40. MANITOU PERFORMANCE

Some one was tied up. Louis was sitting behind the blanket. His manitou spoke when he was thrown back. His manitou spoke when he would roll himself about.

41. MEDICINE PERFORMANCE

The drum is beaten, and somebody does medicine work. They take many things. They save (the patient).

42. GAMBLING

In gambling many things are lost—horses, blankets, shirts, bows, knives, money—everything is lost.

43. GAMES

Children play, dancing hand in hand in a circle, swinging their hands. Other games are dancing about squatting, and playing blind-man's buff. Toys are made. Some child is caught: if it is a boy, a snake is given to·him for a bow; if it is a girl, a snake is given to her for a digging-stick.

44. HUNTING ON THE PLAINS

Across the mountains they went out on the prairie, but they were afraid of the Piegans. They sang, traveling around there. They were afraid that the Piegans would steal their horses. They did that always when they went on the prairie. They came back when they finished rounding up the buffaloes. Then they stopped.

[No. 45. Told by Pierre Andrew]

45. RABBIT, COYOTE, WOLF, AND GRIZZLY BEAR

There was Coyote. All at once he saw Rabbit coming. He said to him: "Why are you running?" Rabbit said: "I am running away." He went past and went on. Coyote was sitting there. He thought: "Oh, something must have happened, and I might almost have been in trouble myself!" Coyote started to run. He went along and went along. There was a little prairie. There was Wolf. Wolf was there, and saw Coyote coming. Coyote arrived, and said to Wolf: "Why are you running?"—"I am running away." Coyote went past. Wolf was sitting there. He thought: "Oh, some-

---

45. RABBIT, COYOTE, WOLF, AND GRIZZLY BEAR

Qawɛsaqa'ane· skɛ'n·ku·ts. n'uk!ᵘɛnł'ʋ'pxₐne· kianuqłu'mnas
He staid   Coyote.   All at once he saw   Rabbit

ska'se·. qakɛ'łne· qa'psin kɛnsɛlts!ɛ'na·k. qake'ᵢne· kianuq-
coming.   He said to him: "Why   are you running?"   He said   Rab- bit:

łu'mna husxa''mktse·k. qayaxa'xe· neᵢ skana'xe·. qaₐnka'-
"I am running away."   He went past;   that   one went on.   He was

me·k skɛ'n·ku·ts. qałwi'yne· a·· at ktsɛnma'łqa tu'xwa kuł'isɛn-
sitting   Coyote.   He thought: "Oh, something happened   almost   I might have

qapwɛtska'ₐxa. sqa·łwuts!ɛ'n·qkupekɛ'me·k skɛ'n·ku·ts. qa·n a'xe·   5
been in trouble in   He also started to run   Coyote.   He went
his place!"   along,

qa·na'xe·. skɛknu'qłe.itnana'n·e·. saosaqa'ane· ka'ₐke·n. qa-
went along.   There was a little prairie.   There was   Wolf.   There

osaqa'ₐne· ka'ₐke·nts n'ʋ'pxₐne· ska'ₐse· skɛ'n·ku·ts·. wa'se·ts
was   Wolf   he saw   coming   Coyote.   He arrived

qakɛ'łne· qa'psin kɛnsɛlts!ɛ'na·k. huxxa''mktxi·k.[1] qayaqa·'xe·
and he said   "Why   are you running?" —   "I am running away."   He went past
to him:

---

[1] Coyote uses x̱ (palatalized x) instead of s.

thing must have happened, and I might almost have been in trouble myself!" Wolf started to run. He went along and went along. There was a little prairie. There was Grizzly Bear. He saw Wolf coming. When he was coming along and when he arrived, he said to him: "Now, why are you running?" He was told: "I am running away." Wolf went past. Grizzly Bear staid there, and thought: "Oh, something must have happened, and I might almost have been in trouble myself!" Grizzly Bear started to run. Grizzly Bear went along and went along. There was a prairie. There he saw the three friends. He went on, and arrived there. He saw Wolf sitting there, a little farther along Coyote, a little farther along Rabbit. Grizzly Bear said to Wolf: "Now, why did you run away? There is hardly anything to run away from." Wolf said: "I was staying there, and saw Coyote coming. When he arrived, I said to him, 'Now, why are you running?' He said to me, 'I am running

---

skɛ′nˑkuˑts.   qaˑnqa′meˑk   kaˈₐkeˑn.   qałwiˈyneˑ at   ktsɛnma′łqa
Coyote.   He was sitting   Wolf.   He thought: "Something happened,

tu′χwa   atułɛˈsɛnqapwɛtskaˈₐχₐneˑ.   nutsɛnqkupekɛ′meˑk
almost   I might be in trouble myself in his place."   He started to run

kaˈₐkeˑn.   qaˑna′χeˑ   qaˑna′χeˑ.   skiknuˈqłe.itnana′seˑ.   saosa-
Wolf.   He went along,   went along.   There was a little prairie.   There

qaˈₐneˑ   k.łaˈwła.   nˈʊ′pχₐneˑ   ska′seˑ   kaˈₐkeˑns   qaˑwaka′seˑ.
was   Grizzly Bear.   He saw   coming   Wolf.   He was coming.

5   kiˑ′wasts   qakɛ′łneˑ   taˈχa   qa′psin   kɛnsɛlts!ɛ′naˑk.   qak.ła′pseˑ
When he   he said to   "Now,   why   are you running?"   He was told:
arrived   him:

husχaˈ″mktseˑk.   qayaqa′χeˑ   kaˈₐkeˑn.   qaosaqaˈₐneˑ   k.łaˈwłats
"I am running away."   He went past   Wolf.   He staid   Grizzly Bear,

qałwiˈyneˑ   at   ktsɛnmałnɛ′keˑt.   tu′χwa   atułnɛˈsɛnqapwɛts-
and he thought: "Something happened to him.   Almost   I might be in trouble myself in

kaˈₐχₐneˑ.   nutsɛnqkupekɛ′meˑk   k.łaˈwła.   qaˑna′χeˑ   k.łaˈwła.
his place."   He started to run   Grizzly Bear.   He went along   Grizzly Bear.

qaˑna′χeˑ.   skɛknuqłeɛˈt.seˑ.   nˈʊ′pχₐneˑ   saqa′pseˑ   ałswʊ′tⁱmos.
He went along.   There was a prairie.   He saw   those there   friends.

10   qaˑoχa′χeˑts   łaχa′χeˑ.   nˈʊ′pχₐneˑ   qoᵤ   naqna′kseˑ   kaˈₐkeˑns   anłʊˈ′-
He went on   and arrived.   He saw   there sitting down   Wolf;   a little

nˑoˑ′sts   skɛˈnˑkuˑts   aˑnłʊˈnˑoˑ′sts   kianuqłuˈmna.   k.łaˈwła   qakɛ′łneˑ
farther   Coyote;   a little farther   Rabbit.   Grizzly Bear   said to

kaˈₐkeˑns   ˈtaˈχa   qa′psin   kɛnsχaˑ′mktsaˈkeⁱl   maˑnqaˈnekaχaˈ″mk-
Wolf: "Now,   why   did you run away?   There is hardly anything to run away from."

tseˑk.   qakeˈⁱneˑ   kaˈₐkeˑn.   huqaˑosaqaˈₐneˑ   hunˈʊ′pχₐneˑ   skɛˈnˑ-
     He said   Wolf: "I was staying,   I saw   Coyote

kuˑts   ska′χeˑ.   kiˑ′wamts   huqakɛ′łneˑ   taˈχa   qa′psin   kɛnsɛlts!ɛ′naˑk.
coming.   When he   I said to him: 'Now,   why   are you running?'
         arrived,

away.'" Coyote was told: "And why did you run away?" He said: "I was staying there, and Rabbit came. When he arrived, I said to him, 'Now, why?' He said, 'I am running away.' I thought, 'Oh, something must have happened, and I myself might almost have been in trouble!' Then I ran away." Then Rabbit was told: "Now, why did you run away?"—"I was eating branches, the wind was blowing, the snow fell from the trees, and a branch broke off the tree; it almost fell on me. Then it made me run away. That is what I meant when I said, 'I am running away.'" Then they laughed and separated. Now it is ended.

---

qak.ła′pne·	huχχa″mktχe·k.	qakiłɛ′łne·	skɛ′n·ku·tsts	nɛ′nko·
He said to me:	'I am running away.'"	He was told	Coyote:	"And you,

qa′psin	kɛnsła′qakałts!ɛ′na·k.	qake′ine·	huqaᶜosaqa′ₐne·	ska′χe·
why	were you running?"	He said:	"I was staying there;	he came

kianuqłu′mnats	ki·′wamts	huqⁿakɛ′łne·	ta′χa	qa′psints	qake′ine·
Rabbit,	when he arrived	I said to him:	'Now,	why?'	and he said:

husχa″mktse·k.	huqⁿałwi′yne·	at	ktsɛnma′łqa	tu′χwa	at huł′ɛ-
'I am running away.'	I thought:		'Something happened	almost	I myself

sɛnqapwɛtsqa′ₐχa	ta′χa	ma	kusłaqakałts!ɛ′na·k.	Qakiłɛ′łne·	5
might be in trouble in his place,'	then,	however,	therefore I ran away."	He was told	

kianuqłu′mnats	nɛ′nko	ta′χa	qa′psin	kɛnsł′aqakaχa″mktse·k.
Rabbit:	"Now you,	now,	why	did you run away?'

qake′ine·.	huqⁿa′ₐkił′ikuła′t!ne·	n′uk!ᵘɛnłhałumɛ′n·e·	nupuma′k-
He said:	"I was eating branches,	at once the wind was blowing,	snow fell from

ne·ts	qake′ikał′yaqɛtsk!ała′ₐkine·,	tu′χwa	ma	ksɛł′yuwitsχo′ᵤ-
the trees and	a branch broke off a tree,	almost		it fell on me.

na·p.	ta′χa	husłhutsqankaqkupekɛ′me·k.	ta′χa	ma	kuɛ′łki·t
Then		towards it made me run.	Then	however	I meant that when I said

kusχa″mktse·k.	ta′χas	numats′na′m·ne·ts	łapaₐtsqa·tsa′m·ne·.	10
'I am running away.'"	Then	they laughed and	separated again.	

ta′χas	qaqa·′sₐne·.
Then	it is ended.

[Nos. 46 and 47.   Told by Pierre Numa and Pierre Andrew]

46. FROG AND CHIPMUNK

Qaˑnit.la′ₐneˑ wa′tak n′ɛˑnseˑ t́ɛte′eˑs q!u′tsaₐts. q!u′tsaₐts
at qqa′ₐtseˑ, at n′ɛtsḱɛ′lneˑ qaˑ′psɛns. qaḱɛ′lneˑ t́ɛte′eˑs wa′tak:
"maₐts neᵢ at qa′naˑn′." ta′χas at łaqqa′ₐtseˑ q!u′tsaₐts. qałwi′y-
neˑ: "qaˑ′psɛns sɛ′k.laˑp, maₐts neᵢs at kułqana′meᵢł?" qałwi′y-
5 neˑ q!u′tsaₐts: "neᵢ hułqa′naˑm neᵢs yaˑqanałqake′ᵢkeˑ maₐts
at kuˑłqana′meᵢł." ta′χas ts!ɛna′χeˑ. ta′χas n′u′pχₐneˑ ku′peᵢs.
ta′χas ku′peᵢ tsχa′nˑeˑ; qake′ᵢneˑ: "kutsḱɛ′t!χa łka′mˑu."
sɛłałq!atχa′meˑk tsa′qaˑs, q!u′łwaˑs. ta′χas neᵢsts k!aqaḱɛ′leᵢł
słaqawanχa′mneˑ. qake′ᵢneˑ ku′peᵢ: "qake′ᵢneˑ maˑ″nis kułˑats!-
10 maχała″eˑs."—"peɛ′k!aks n′ɛ′pıneˑ ka′maˑ." qake′ᵢneˑ: "tso″-
nis kułˑats!maχała″eˑs." qake′ᵢneˑ: "peɛ′k!aks n′ɛ′pıneˑ ka′tsu."
qake′ᵢneˑ: "koˑ′kt,nis kułˑats!maχała″eˑs."—"peɛ′k!aks n′ɛ′pıneˑ
ka′koᵤkt."—"qak.ɛ′sᵢneˑ t́ɛt′t!neˑs kułˑats!maχała″eˑs."—
"peɛ′k!aks n′ɛ′pıneˑ kat́ɛ′tteˑt!."—"qak.ɛ′sᵢneˑ nana′ₐneˑs ku-
15 łˑats!maχała″eˑs."—"peɛ′k!aks n′ɛ′pıneˑ kana′na." qake′ᵢneˑ q!u′-
tsaₐts; qaḱɛ′lneˑ ku′peᵢs: "hɛnˑ′ɛseᵢkate′ᵢneˑ; hɛnwɛłkɛsqł́ɛ′lneˑ. ma
ne′yɛn′ aₐ′kaqł́ɛ′lneˑs, ta′χas hutsłats!ɛna′χeˑ." mane′ᵢneˑ ku′peᵢ
aₐ′kaqł́ɛ′Īeᵢs. ta′χas neᵢsts kɛna′neˑ aₐ′kaqł́ɛ′Īeˑs ku′pi, łahutsɛn-
qkupeḱɛ′meˑk q!u′tsaₐts. ɛaqkupq!ałe′ᵢneˑ ku′pi. nɛksiat́ɛ′lneˑ
20 q!u′tsaₐts. tseᵢka′teˑ aₐku′kp!eˑs ku′peᵢ, nakumału′kpıneˑts
n′ɛłtaˑ′χaneˑ. ta′χas łaˑłaχa′χeˑ aₐ′kɛt.łaɛ′seˑs t́ɛte′eˑs. qaḱɛ′lneˑ:
"kat́ɛ′te, s′nuta′pıneˑ koˑ′ᵤpi." qak.łaˑ′pseˑ t́ɛte′eˑs; "hoqᵘaˑ′ało-
qałtił′ɛ′sᵢneˑ." tsukᵘa′te t́ɛte′eˑs wa′tak, ts!ɛn′oqoˑχaḱɛ′nˑeˑ
naˑ′h́ɛ′k!eˑs. qaˑatsḱɛk.łɛknat́ɛ′tne q!u′tsaₐts qoᵤs ʋ′qoᵤks
25 naˑ″heˑks. wa′tak qałwi′yneˑ ktsχalhawɛtsqo′ᵤχᵘats paˑł saˑ-
haˑ′nseˑ. ta′χas łaˑaqtuq!ᵘiqaqḱɛ′nˑeˑ. qaₐku′kseˑ naˑ′qpoᵤks
huˑ′q!ᵘkaˑ′s qanał′o′qonaqḱɛ′nˑeˑ. ta′χas tsɛn sanqa′mik wa′tak.
ta′χas tkaχa″mneˑ ku′pi. qake′ᵢneˑ ku′pi; qaḱɛ′lneˑ wa′taˑks;[1]
"kqa.u′pχa łka′mˑu′s?" ˑwa′tak qake′ᵢneˑ: "kusaˑ′kqanq!ał-
30 saˑ″meᵢł, hoqa.upχańɛ′lneˑ." qake′ᵢneˑ ku′pi; "naₐ sɛłqaˑwaˑ-
kałɛ′kseˑ." qake′ᵢneˑ wa′tak: "hoqa.upχańɛ′lneˑ łka′mˑu′s."
qake′ᵢneˑ ku′pi: "k.łɛ′tuks? humuk!nuˑ′q!łumaḿɛ′lneˑ."
qake′ᵢneˑ wa′tak: "łɛtu′kseˑ." ta′χas qake′ᵢneˑ ku′pi:
"k.łɛ′tuks naˑ′qpoᵤks?" qake′ᵢneˑ wa′tak: "łɛtu′kseˑ; ɛs nɛˑ′nseˑ
35 huˑ′q!ᵘkaˑ′s." qake′ᵢneˑ ku′pi: "hutsekułḿɛ′lneˑ." qake′ᵢneˑ
wa′tak: "tsχałq!atskuχaktsa′pₐneˑ." taχas n′eˑku′lneˑ ku′pi.
n′u′pχₐneˑ paˑł nasˑwɛsu′qseˑ neᵢs łkamˑuˑ′s. qake′ᵢneˑ ku′pi:
"nasˑwɛsu′qseˑ; paˑł słutske′ᵢneˑ neᵢs kqa′keˑ kqa.u′pχa." tsχa′-
nˑeˑ wa′tak, qaḱɛ′lneˑ: "tsχałsoᵤḱɛ′nˑeˑ maˑk!ɛ′seˑs." ta′χas
40 n′ɛ′t!χₐneˑ ku′pi neᵢs łka′mˑu′s. ta′χas n′ɛ′kıneˑ. neᵢsts kuˑ′Īeᵢks
ta′χas łaˑakaχa″mneˑ. ta′χas n′iła′neˑ wa′tak neᵢs ke′ips t́ɛte′eˑs.

---

[1] The following is in the form of speech used between sister and brother.

[Nos. 46 and 47. Told by Pierre Numa and Pierre Andrew]

46. FROG AND CHIPMUNK[1]

Frog was living in a tent, and her granddaughter was Chipmunk. Chipmunk | went around. She looked for everything. Frog said to her granddaughter: | "Don't go that way." Then Chipmunk went about again. She thought: | "What did she mean me to do, that I should not walk there?" Chipmunk ‖ thought: "I will go that way 5 where she told me not | to go." Then she went. She saw Owl. | Owl spoke, and said: "I shall bite the child." | (Chipmunk) was picking partridge berries and rose hips. On account of what had been said she did not move. Owl spoke, and said: "Your mother says we shall go ‖ home."— "My mother died long ago." He said: "Your 10 sister (says) | we shall go home." She said: "My sister died long ago." | He said: "Your mother's sister (says) we shall go home."— | "My mother's sister died long ago." He said to her: "Your father's sister says we shall go home."— | "My father's sister died long ago."— "Your younger sister ‖ says we shall go home."—"My younger 15 sister died long ago." Chipmunk spoke, | and said to Owl: "You look terrible; you have big eyes. | Cover your eyes with your hands, then I'll go along." Owl covered his eyes with his hands. | When Owl had covered his eyes with his hands, Chipmunk began | to run. Owl tried to kill her, and scratched ‖ Chipmunk. Owl looked at his 20 claws, and he licked off the blood that was on his claws. | Then she got back to her grandmother. She said: | "Grandmother, Owl is pursuing me." She said to her granddaughter: "There is no place where I can hide you." | Frog took her granddaughter and put her | in a birch-bark basket. Chipmunk made a noise inside ‖ that 25 basket. Frog thought she would hold her in her mouth, but it was very bad. | Then she took her out of her mouth. There was soup of | rotten bones. She dipped her into it. Then Frog just sat down. | Owl came in. Owl spoke, and said to Frog:[2] | "Did you see the child?" Frog said: "I did not look around. ‖ I did not see her." Owl 30 said: "There are her tracks." | Frog said: "I did not see the child." | Owl said: "Is there no water? I am thirsty." | Frog said: "There is no water." Then Owl said: | "Is there no soup?" Frog said: "There is no fluid. This is ‖ rotten bone." Owl said: "I'll drink 35 of it." Frog said: | "Leave some fluid for me." Then Owl began to drink. | He saw the child was inside. Owl said: | "She is inside; you told me a lie; you said that you had not seen her." Frog spoke, | and said to him: "You shall preserve her bones." Then ‖ Owl bit 40 the child. Then he ate her. After he had eaten, | he went out of the house. Then Frog began to cry because her granddaughter was

---

[1] See p. 46. [2] Frog is Owl's sister.

ko‸ľe′₁la wa′tak tsukⁿa′te· ma·kǃ′se·s. ne₁s ɣaqawutsiknakℇ′ske·
n′ℇ!qa.oxakℇ′n·e·. ta′xas tsǃɲalkℇ′n·e· wuu′′e·s. qaoxaɫpℇsuq-
kℇ′n·e·. ta′xas ɫat.tsǃɲa′xe· wa′tak aₐ′kℇt.ɫa′e·s. ɫat₁naxa′′mne·ts
45 n′ℇsaknu′′ne·. qawun·ekℇ′t.se· ɫatℇnmoqkupnoxunqa′mek qǃu′-
tsaₐts. ne₁sts ma ɣa·′qaqa′pske·ts o·kǃuna′mu′s ɫa.ℇ′nse·. su-
kwℇɫqǃo′‸k‸ne·. mℇtia′xₐne·, nakam′nwutskℇ′n·e·. qakℇ′ne·: "hu-
sukwℇɫ′qo′‸k‸ne· katℇ′te· kuɫa·′upxₐnamna·′ɫa." ta′xas
sɫqa·qa′sₐne·.

47. COYOTE AND BUFFALO

Kqa·′nam skℇ′n·ku·ts. n′u′pxₐne· sak.ɫa′m·se· nℇ′ɫse·ks. qun-
ɣa′xₐne·ts n′ɫqanmℇ′te·. ta′xas ɫa·ts!ℇna′xe·. qa·na′xe·ts, ne₁s
qaɫqa′tse·ts ɫa·man·qa′ₐtse· ne₁s ma ɣaₐqana′mke·. qa·na′xe·
sɫaɫaxa·′xe· ne₁s ma ɣaqa·k.ɫa′mske·. qaɫao·′qǃⁿkⁿa qa′pse· ne₁s
5 a′ₐk.ɫa·ms nℇ′ɫse·ks. qaɫsaq.ǃa′ɫe·ɫqana′xe·. ta′xas qakℇ′ɫne·:
"qa′psin pℇ′kǃak na huqa′xe·ts nanqa·kqa′ₐne·ts kℇnɫao·′kǃqwa·′-
qka." tsukⁿa′te· no′‸kwe·ts n′aqtsxo′‸ne·. ne₁ tsukⁿa′te·ts
paₐtsℇnmℇ′te·. ta′xas tsǃɲa′xe· qa·na′xe·ts skℇkts!ɫanu′kse·.
qaoxaɫit!nam ℇ′te· sℇ′tǃe·s. n′ℇtxo′‸mek′. ne₁sts haqa′ₐke·ts
10 n′ℇɫa′′ne·. qake′₁ne·, qaɫo′‸k₁ne·:

> "Haɫma′′t₁mu xa′‸ɫtsℇn qǃuta′ptse₁k mℇs·quɫo′‸wo·m
> ha·haho′ya; we·s, wℇs, wℇs."

Nuɫpaɫnℇtℇ′t₁ne· naɫo·kmℇ′se·. nuk‸ninmℇ′tek. tse₁kaɫitℇ′t₁ne·ts
ɫo′‸se· qa′psins. "ha·, ko·qa′ɫ‸wey ksɫo′k‸me·ts tsℇn ksɫ′aka′qa
15 o·′kǃⁿq‸na kyuna′qa aₐ′qǃutsa′ne·k k.ɫo′‸ɫa." ɫaℇtxo′‸me·k.
qawunikℇ′t.se· ɫa·uɫpaɫnℇtℇ′t₁ne· ɫahaɫuk‸mℇ′se·. ɫao·knuqkup-
qǃaɫa′′mne·. n′u′pxₐne· pℇℇ′kǃaks sɫwa′se· nℇ′ɫse·ks paɫ sℇmℇtya-
xna′pse·. nℇt!ℇnmuqkupno·xun·qa′m·ℇk. nutsℇnqkupekℇ′m·ℇk.
qananuta′pse·. ta′xas qǃawatskℇ′nme·k. ta′xas sɫuk.ɫu′k‸ne·.
20 tsxa′n·e· skℇ′n·ku·ts, qake′₁ne·: "qa′ɫa kǃun·aqaɫo·qniya′xnu."
qakikℇ′ɫne·: "so′‸k‸ne·, paₐtǃ, qaqa′qna·n′ qo′‸ka·n′ na ka′min."
n′oqosaqǃmaxo′‸me·k. ta′xas wa′xe· nℇ′ɫse·k. n′u′pxₐne· ne₁s
kℇɫsaosa′qa·ps. nako′‸ne· nℇ′ɫse·k ne₁s aₐ′quɫ·u′qpko·ps. tsℇkǃkǃ-
o′‸ne·. nutsℇnqkupekℇ′me·k skℇ′n·ku·ts. ɫa·ts!ɲa′xe·. qawuɫℇ′₁t.se·
25 ɫa·psqǃawatskℇ′nme·k; ɫatsxa′ₐne·; qake′₁ne·: "ka· kℇnaqasaqa′ɫqa
nöpℇ′kǃa; husℇɫqǃo′k‸ne·." qakikℇ′ɫne·: "paₐtǃ, tsℇn qaqa′qₐna·n′
qo′‸ka·n′ na ka′min." tse₁ka′te·ts n′ℇ′nse· no′‸kwe·sis ta′xas
kuna′xe·ts n′o′qosaqǃmaxo′‸me·k. ta′xas wa′xe· nℇ′ɫs·e·k. nako′‸-
ne·ts tsℇkǃkǃo′‸ne· ne₁s no′‸kwe·′s. nℇt!ℇnmuqkupno·xun·qa′me·k
30 skℇ′n·ku·tsts nutsℇnqkupekℇ′me·k. qa·na′xe·ts qawuɫe·′t.se·
ɫa′psℇɫqǃawatskℇ′nme·k. ɫatsxa′n·e·: "pℇℇ′kǃak huɫa·′psℇɫqǃo′k‸ne·."
tsxanamℇ′s₁ne·, qakikℇ′ɫne·: "ɫʌ′n·a na qawa′kan′ na ka′min."
n′ℇ′nse· t!a′pℇswukna′na·s. n′oqo′‸saqǃmaxo′‸me·k. ɫaxa′xe·
nℇ′ɫse·k. naₐko′‸ne·. qawukǃo′‸ne·. ta′xas qataɫ′ℇskǃo′‸ne· ne₁s
35 t!a′pℇswukna′na·s. sℇɫqa′ₐɫo·qaɫnu′kǃune· nℇ′ɫse·k. qake′₁ne·

dead. | After Frog had cried, she took her bones. She laid them out | and put them together. She carried them to the water. Then she | threw them into the water. Frog went back to her tent. She went in ‖ and sat down. After a while, Chipmunk ran back into the tent | 45 the same way as she had been before. | She was glad. She jumped at her. She embraced her. She said to her: | "I am glad, grandmother, that we meet again." | That is the end. |

47. COYOTE AND BUFFALO [1]

Coyote went along. He found the head of a Buffalo Bull. He picked it up | and threw it away. Then he went on. He went along and | went about and came back the same way, there where he had gone before. He went along | and came back to the place where the head was, at the same place where the ‖ head of the Bull was. It 5 happened three times when he went along. Then he said to it: | "Why, I went here before, this way where you are lying, and you lie in the same place again." | He took a stone and smashed it. He took it and | scattered the pieces about. Then he started. He went and found a flat stone. | He threw his blanket over it. Then he lay down. While he was lying down, ‖ he cried. He said while crying: | 10

"Their mother Dog, [2] Q!uta′ptsek and Mis·qulo′ₐwom |
ha ha ho′ya; wes wis wis!" |

He heard noise of running. He arose. He looked around, | and there was nothing. "Oh, I thought I heard running; but it is nothing, ‖ because there are many passers-by who did it." He 15 lay down again. | After a little while he heard noise of running again. He raised | his head quickly. He saw a Bull approaching, | that ran after him. He jumped up quickly. | He started to run. He was pursued. He was out of breath and was tired. ‖ Then Coyote 20 spoke, and said: "Somebody shall help me." | He was told: "It is good, nephew, come to me." | He disappeared inside. Then the Bull arrived. He knew that (Coyote) | was in there. The Bull butted it. It was a stump. He split it in two. | Coyote ran away quickly. He started again. When he had gone a little ways, ‖ he was out of breath 25 again, and he spoke again, saying: "How far are you, | manitou? I am in danger." He was told: "Nephew, come to me, | come in." He saw it was a stone, and then | he disappeared in it. The Bull arrived. He butted it and | broke the stone in two. Coyote jumped up quickly ‖ and jumped away. He went along, and after a short distance | he 30 was out of breath again. Again he spoke: "I am already in danger." | Somebody spoke to him, and he was told: "Come, come to me." | That was a small bush. He disappeared inside. The Bull arrived | and butted it. He missed it. He could not hit ‖ the little bush with 35 his horns. The Bull could just not get it. Coyote said: | "Stop, stop

---

[1] For another version see p. 12.
[2] Dog is Coyote's wife; Q!uta′ptsek and Mis·qulo′ₐwom are his children.

skⁱ·n·kuᵗs: "ta′χas, ta′χas qa·qaskⁱ′nu·, hᴀntsᴅqataɫ′upɫa′p-
ne·." qake′ⱼne· nⁱ′ɫse·k: "so′ᵤkᵤne; ta′χas hutsqa·qaskⁿⁱ′sⁱne·."
qakiɫⁱ′ɫne· skⁱ·n·kuᵗs: "ta′χa ɫ′n·a·." ta′χas qanaɫ′aqa·t!oᵤχa′-
χe· skⁱ·n·kuᵗs. qake′ⱼne· skⁱ′n·kuᵗs: "hutsχaɫkuɫnakɫo′ᵤne·ts
40 huts!ᴅknoquknaɫa′ₐne·." qake′ⱼne· nⁱ′ɫse·k·: "so′ᵤkᵤne; huts!ᴅ-
knoquknaɫa′ₐne·. qa′psin koᵤtsᴅ′iknoqokna′la ?" qake′ⱼne·
skⁱ′n·kuᵗs: "kq!a·wo′ᵤqa·ɫ hutsɫⁱknoquknaɫa′ₐne·." qake′ⱼne·
nⁱ′ɫse·k: "at huqᵘa·ᴢknuqu′kᵤne· kq!awo′ᵤka·ɫ." qake′ⱼne·
skⁱ′n·kuᵗs: "ta′χa qa′psin at kᴀnsᴅᴢknoqo·′ko ?"—"aₐ′kmoq!o′-
45 ma·ɫ at husɫⁱknuqu′kᵤne·." qake′ⱼne· skⁱ′n·kuᵗs: "so′ᵤkᵤne·,
ta′χa hutsɫⁱknuquk ᵤnaɫa′ₐne·. naqa′ₐne· ka′min." ta′χas kuɫna-
k!o′ᵤne·. ta′χas nⁱᴢknuqu′kᵤne·. qake′ⱼne· skⁱ′n·kuᵗs: "na·sts at
tsqaqa′ₐne·, taχta′ neⱼs ktsyuna′qa aqɫsma′kⁿᴢk! saₐnⁱ′ɫwiyna′ₐ-
ta·m at ts!ᴢknuqu′kᵤne· at ktsɫa′soᵤks aₐ′kᴅɫwi·′ye·s." qake′ⱼne·
50 nⁱ′ɫse·k: "so′ᵤkᵤne·. hutsχaɫtsχan·atⁱ′sⁱne· ya·qaqa′ₐke· ka′min.
na· aₐ′kmaₐna·m o′k!ɫe·etna′m·u at koɫaqaha′k.ɫam·aɫa·k hu-
wakaɫtiɫⁱ′ne·. n′a′sne· katᴅɫna′mu. huɫahaya′χa katᴅɫna′m·u at
na·sts huɫaqaskam·a′ɫne·ts at qa·wa·ka˘a′ɫwa′χe· aqɫsma′knᴢk!ts
at hun′ʋpiɫⁱ′ɫne·." qake′ⱼne· skⁱ′n·kuᵗs: "ta′χas hᴀnts!ⁱ′ne·
55 ka′swu. huts!ɫats!ᴅnyaχnaɫa′ₐn·e· tᴅɫnamu′ne·s." tseⱼka′te· aₐko-
q!e·ᴢ′se·s swu′e·s skⁱ·n·kuᵗsts n′ume·tsᴀnq!ak.ɫe′ⱼse·. tsukᵘa′te·
aₐ′ktsama·ɫ′e·s ɫae·ta′χₐne· ta′χas ɫa·ᴢᴀnq!aqa′pse·. qakⁱ′ɫne·:
"ta′χas huɫts!ᴅnaχa′ₐɫa." ta′χas qa·nakⁱ′kⱼne· swʋ′tⱼmu. ta′χas
n′u′pχₐne· aₐ′kᴢk.ɫuna′me·s. qakⁱ′ɫne· skⁱ′n·kuᵗs swʋ′e·s·: "ta′χas
60 na hutsqaosaqa′ₐne·. ɫu′n·u·, ɫats!ᴅnya′χan′ tᴅɫnamu′ne·s."
ta′χas ɫats!ᴅnya′χₐne· tᴅɫnamu′e·s nⁱ′ɫse·k. ta′χas ɫatsukᵘa′te·.
ta′χas wanaqna′ɫne·. ɫaqa·oχa′χe· nⁱ′ɫse·k neⱼs ya·qaosaqa′ₐke·
skⁱ′n·kuᵗs. ta′χas nawu′kᵤne· skⁱ′n·kuᵗs. n′u′pχₐne· sɫ·awa′se·s
swʋ′e·s· ta′χas mⁱtya′χₐne· skⁱ·n·kuᵗs neⱼs aqɫsma′knᴢk!s.
65 n′u′pχa′ɫne· paɫ n′a′sⱼne· nⁱ′ɫse·k skⁱ·n·kuᵗs. n′oᵤneɫⁱ′ɫne·ts ta′χas
qa·qasknⁱ′ɫne·. ta′χas ts!ᴅnakⁱ′kⱼne· swʋ′tⱼmu. ta′χas χaₐtsa′n·e·,
ki·′as tⁱ′tqa·t!ts ki·′as paₐ′ɫkeⱼ. qaoχaɫ′ᴅtqa′ₐne·. tsχa′n·e·
nⁱ′ɫse·k; qakⁱ′ɫne· skⁱ·n·kuᵗs·: "na ki·′as katᴅɫna′mu tseⱼka′ten′,
ka· hᴀnqa′ɫwiy hᴀntstsukᵘa′te· tsχaɫⁱ′n·e· tᴅɫnamu′′ne·s."
70 ta′χas skⁱ·n·kuᵗs tseⱼka′te·. qaɫwi′yne·: "na ki·′ᴀn ktsaqu′n·a
naqants!ma′k!eⱼs ma′k!eⱼ. na ki·′ᴀn kwⁱ′ɫqa naqa′ₐɫsoᵤk. ta′χas
na huɫsᴅtso′ᵤkaɫ, na·ₐqa′ₐɫsoᵤk." qakⁱ′ɫne· nⁱ′ɫseks: "na hutsᴅ-
tsᵘkᵘa′te·." qakiɫa′′mne·: "ta′χas hutsyanqa·tsaɫa′ₐne·." tsχa-
maɫktsaɫa′′mne·, keⱼsoᵤk kiyu′kⱼyeⱼt. ta′χas yan·qa′ₐtse·. qa·na-
75 kⁱ′kⱼne· tᴅɫnamo′ᵤtⱼmu skⁱn·kuᵗs. n′u′pχₐne· suq!yuɫe·ⁱ′t.se·.
qakⁱ′ɫne· tᴅɫnamu′′e·s: "qoᵤ nak!amnaqaɫe·ⁱ′tke· qo· hᴀntska-
na′χe·. ka′min hutsχaɫ′uk!ena′χe·." ta′χas ts!ᴢna′χe· neⱼ ɫu′kpo.
ta′χas ts!ᴅnaɫ′o·k!ᵘina′χe· skⁱ·n·kuᵗs. ts!ᴅna′kⱼne·ts wa′sᴅaχa′χe·
neⱼs tsχaɫyaqana′ske· tᴅɫnamu′′e·s. ta′χas ɫaχa′χe·ts n′ᴢsakmu′-
80 n·e·. qawunekᴢt.se·ts ɫaχa′χe· neⱼ ɫu′kpo·. qaɫwi′yne· skⁱ·n·kuᵗs;

doing this to me! You can not kill me." | The Bull said: "Well, I'll let you go." | Coyote was told: "Now, come!" Then Coyote went near him. |

Coyote said: "I'll fill my pipe. ‖ We will smoke." The Bull said: 40 "It is well. Let us | smoke. What shall we smoke?" Coyote said: | "Let us smoke block tobacco." The Bull said: | "I don't smoke block tobacco." Coyote said: | "What do you smoke?"—"I smoke leaf tobacco." ‖ Coyote said: "It is well. | Let us smoke it. I have 45 some." Then he | filled his pipe. Then they smoked. Coyote said: "It will be this way | in later times, when there will be many people. When they are angry at one another, | they will smoke to make their hearts (feel) good."

The Bull said: ‖ "It is well. I'll tell you what happened to me. | 50 On this road, at the same place where my head lay, | my wife was taken away from me. I had two wives. When I went for my wives, | I came with them to this place. Then people came here, and | I was killed." Coyote said: "Now you will be ‖ my friend. 55 We shall get back your wives." Coyote looked | at the horns of his friend. The points were broken off. He took | his knife and sharpened them. Their points were sharpened again.

He said to him: | "Now let us go." Then the two friends went along. | They saw tents, and Coyote said to his friend: ‖ "I'll stay 60 here. Go on, go and get your wives back." | Then the Bull went to get back his wives. He took them back. | They made war on him. The Bull went back to where Coyote was staying. | Then Coyote arose. He saw his friend coming. | Then Coyote attacked the people. ‖ They saw there were two—the Bull and Coyote. They 65 were afraid of them, and | they left them. Then the friends went along. They were four— | two men and two women. They stopped there. The Bull spoke, | and said to Coyote: "Look at these my two wives! | Which one do you want to take? She shall be your wife." ‖ Coyote looked at her. He thought: "This younger one | 70 must have strong bones. The big one must be good. | I think I will take her. She must be good." He said to the Bull: "I | take this one." They said to each other: "We will part now." | They shook hands and said good-by. Then they parted. ‖

Coyote and his wife went off. He saw a mountain in front. | 75 He said to his wife: "That place looks like a valley. Go there. | I shall go roundabout." The Buffalo Cow went on. | Coyote went another way. He went quickly. He came back quickly | to the place where his wife was going. He arrived and sat down. ‖ After a 80 short time the Cow arrived. Coyote thought: | "I will shoot her.

"ta′χas huł′ɛ′łwa; ta′χas kutsχa′ł·e·k, kuhu·′′was." nei̭sts k.ła′-
χam nei̭ łu′kpo nasqasa′se·ts kmɛ′tχa· skɛ′n·ku·ts. ta′χas
n′ɛłwa′n·e· nei̭s ya̭aqakqa′pske· qawɔłeɛ′t.se· skɛkts!łanu′kse·.
ta′χas qaoχał′ɛsaknu′n·e· nei̭s a̭a′kɛkts!ła′ano̭uks. qa·nqa′me·kts

85 n′ɛła′n·e·. słiła′χa̭ne· tɛłnamu′′e·s nei̭s k.łɛ′łwa. qawunekɛ′t.se·.
n′uk!unłhutska′se· ka′a̭kens. yunaqa′pse·. n′uk!unł′ɛ′ki̭ne· nei̭s
k!ɛłwana′m·e·s. qałwi′yne· kts!o′ṷwuk skɛ′n·ku·ts; t!aptse·k-
pu′k!u̯ne·. n′upsłatwɛtsno·teχa′′mne·ts qa·tał·aluχu′se· a̭a′kɛkpu′-
k!u̯e·s. ta′χas n′ɛ′ki̭ne· nei̭ ka′a̭kei̭n nei̭s iya′mu′s. q!a′pχa̭ne·.

90 ta′χas łało′ṷse·. tsin saqno′ṷne· skɛ′n·ku·ts, nawo·′kṷne· słało-
χu′se· a̭a′kɛkpu′k!u̯e·s. qake′i̭ne· skɛ′n·ku·ts: "t!aptse·kpu′k!u̯so,
t!aptse·kpu′k!u̯so·!" qaoχa′χe·, tsɛn ma·′k!s n′ɛnqapta′kse·.
qałwi′yne·: "ta′χas huł′yaq!aχa′me·k." ta′χas n′ɛt!qaoχa-
kɛ′n·e· nei̭s ma̭ak!s. ta′χas sɛł′yaq!a′a̭ne·. qakełɛ′łne·: "pa̭at!,

95 at ma kuqa·′qanła′łtse·s ma̭ak!." qake′i̭ne·: "mɛ′ka̭ ma kqanɛ′-
ke·." tsei̭ka′te·ts n′ɛ′n·se· na′łme·t!s. qak.ła′pse·: "huts!ɛnł-
yaq!a′a̭ne·." qak.ła′pse·: "hɛntsχałhawɛtsqatkna′pi̭ne·." Ta′-
χas nawɛtsqatkɛ′n·e·. qak.ła′pse·: "ma̭ats tsmak!wɛtskɛ′n·e·;
hɛnłna′łmɛt!qatkɛ′na·p." ta′χas qakna′a̭ne·. qatsma·k!wɛtskɛ′n·e·.

100 tsuku̯a′te· na′łmɛt! a̭a′kuktsɛ′kei̭ns; qan·akɛ′n·e· nei̭s
a̭a′knu·′łma·ks, nei̭s k!ałmanu·′łma·ks. qakiłɛ′łne· skɛ′n·ku·ts:
"ye·′sɛnwuqo̭ukpɛ′tske·." at qasakinłɛ′si̭ne· a̭a·k!ałma′e·s; a̭a′ke· at
qake′i̭ne· skɛ′n·ku·ts: "huye·′sɛnwu′qo̭ukpɛ′tske·." no·tsɛnqku-
pɛkɛ′me·k na′łmɛt!. nałkɛ′n·e· a̭a′knu·′łma·ks. ta′χas mɛtya′χa̭ne·

105 skɛ′n·ku·ts, qaknu′te·. n′upsła′ti̭yił′ɛ′ki̭ne· na′łmɛt!, słało′ṷse·.
nei̭s qałamanɛnmɛ′te· nei̭s a̭a′ko·ktsɛ′kei̭ns. qakiłɛ′łne· skɛ′n·ku·ts:
"ɛn hɛnłɛn′o′ṷte·." ta′χas ts!ɛna′χe· na′łmɛt!. tsuku̯a′te· skɛ′n·-
ku·ts nei̭s a̭a′ko·ktsɛ′kei̭ns. n′ɛłta′χa̭ne·, pał kts!a′qa·ps. qa·kqa·′n-
wɛsqa′a̭ne· skɛ′n·ku·ts, tsin·ɛnqapta′kse· a̭a′q!a′n·a·ks. qał-

110 wi′yne·: "huł′ɛt!qaoχa′ke·nts kuts!aqtsa′kχo·." ta′χas n′ɛsak-
nu′n·e· kts!aqtsa′kχo· skɛ′n·ku·ts. qakiłɛ′łne·: "pa·t!, at ma ku-
qaqanła′łtse·s ma̭ak!." tsei̭ka′te· n′a′s·e· pa·′łkei̭s, n′ɛ′n·se·
ei̭′qo·łsts wa′ku·ks. qak.ła′pse·: "ta′χas huts!aqtsa′kχo·na-
ła′a̭ne·. nɛ′nko· ts!ɛ′na·nts, qo· hɛntstsuku̯a′te· qa′psi·n, hɛnts-

115 χałhału·′qki̭niłχnei̭mu′n·e·. hɛn·u′pχa na·qa′ski·łhanq!o·′ko·.
ta′χas hɛntsłats!ka′χe·." ta′χas ts!ɛna′χe· skɛ′n·ku·ts. n′a·′ka·n-
k!o′ṷne·; n′aqtsχo′ṷne· n′ɛtmase′i̭te·. qaosaqa′a̭ne· skɛ′n·ku·ts,
n′u′pχa̭ne·, taχ′as wɛɛnq!oko·′pse·. ta′χas łats′ɛna′χe·. ta′χas
k.ła·ła′χa·m. ło′ṷse· qa′psɛn. tsei̭ka′te· na′s a̭a′kits!ła′e·ns

120 swɛtsq!nu′se· wa′ko·ks, n′ao·′k!we·s nei̭s łuha·′wɛtsq!nu′se·
n′ao·′k!we·s nałχo′ṷse· t!na′mu′s n′ao·′k!we·s nałχo′ṷse.
hoq!ka̭ɛ′se·. ta′χas ło′ṷse· kɛ′ɛk nei̭s k.łɛ′łwa nei̭s iya′mu′s. ta′χa.

Then I will eat her. I am hungry." The | Cow arrived. As she
walked along, Coyote shot her. | He killed her. There she lay. A
little ways off there was a flat stone. | He sat down on the flat stone.
He sat there and ‖ began to cry. He cried for his wife whom he had   85
killed.

After a little while | many wolves arrived. They ate at once |
what he had killed. Coyote thought he would stand up, but he stuck
(to the stone). | He tried to get up, but he couldn't get off. | Then
the wolves ate the Cow. They ate it all. ‖ Nothing was left. Coyote   90
just got up. He arose. His backside came off from the stone. |
Coyote said: "Let me stick on, | let me stick on!"

He went there, and there were only bones. | He thought: "Well,
I will break the bones." He piled | the bones together, and he was
about to break them. He was told: "Nephew, ‖ I do not allow you   95
to break bones." He said: "That is so." | He looked, and there was
Badger. He was told: "I'll break the bones." | He was told: "You
shall hold my tail." | Then he held (Badger's) tail. He was told:
"Don't hold on too tightly, | you will badger my tail." He did so.
He did not hold the tail tightly. ‖ Badger Woman took the bladder   100
and put | the marrow into it. It was a big, round piece of marrow.
Coyote was told: | "I shall eat that much," and (Badger) passed her
hands close to her mouth. | Coyote also said: "I'll eat that much."
Then Badger | ran away quickly, carrying the marrow. Coyote
pursued her. ‖ He ran after her. Badger was eating all the time.   105
When she had finished, | she threw back the bladder. Coyote was
told: | "I suppose you want that." Badger went off. Coyote took |
his bladder. He licked it. It was greasy. |

Coyote was standing there. There were only the remains of broken
bones. ‖ He thought: "I will pile them together. I will pound them   110
to pieces." He | sat down. Coyote began to pound. He was told:
"Nephew, I won't | allow you to break bones." He saw two women.
They were | two birds.[1] He was told: "We will pound it. | Mean-
while go and get something that you may ‖ use for a spoon. When   115
you see that there is a fire, | come back." Coyote started. He took
a root out of the ground, | pounded it, and dried it. Coyote staid
there. | Then he saw a large fire. He went back, and | when he got
back, nothing was left. He looked up the tree, ‖ and there was one   120
of the birds. The other one was on another tree. | One carried the
grease; the other one, | the chopped bone. He had nothing to eat of
the game he had killed. Enough. |

---

[1] Species unknown.

48. THE ANIMALS AND THE SUN

Qaˑk.łuʹunam nʹɬwat!tkaʹaneˑ nasoʹukᵘeˑn. qakeʹᵢneˑ: "qaʹła's
tsxaʹłʹⱥns nataʹnⱥk!s?" taʹxas nakq!yⱥʹtᵢncˑ. k!oʹk!weˑ qakeˑ-
łʹłneˑ: "hⱥntsxałʹⱥˑncˑ." taʹxas tsxanatamnaʹmneˑ neᵢs k!oʹ-
k!weˑ ktsxaʹłinˑ nataʹnⱥk!s. taʹxas q!aʹpeˑ nułpałnetⱥtnaʹmneˑ

5 neᵢ ktsaqanⱥʹkeˑt. taʹxas ts!ⱥnaʹxeˑ neᵢ k!ɬwaʹt!teł ktsxaʹłⱥn
nataʹnⱥk!s. qałatⱥʹłneˑ qoʹkᵘiˑn. taʹxas ts!ⱥnˑaˑxeˑ. taʹxas
ktsⱥłmiʹyⱥt. kkanmiʹyⱥt nakiłwⱥtskiłⱥʹłneˑ ktsiʹwakmɛnuʹqkaˑ.
taʹxas yuwaˑkmnuqkaʹnˑeˑ qatałsoˑkᵘakaˑt.łⱥtⱥtᵢneʹᵢneˑ neᵢ
k!ⱥktⱥʹkmnuʹqka; nʹuʹpsłaˑtᵢyiˑłhamqoq!uʹkułʹaˑakat.łeˑtⱥtᵢneʹᵢ-

10 neˑ neᵢ kⱥyoʹʹkweᵢt; nʹupsłaˑtᵢyⱥlqaqaʹaneˑts kwałkwaˑʹyⱥt. ławaʹ-
xeˑ neᵢ nataʹnⱥk!. qakyaʹmneˑ: "siłsahaʹnˑeˑ naˑsts k!aqaʹqa
k!upsłaˑtᵢyiłhamqoq!uʹkułˑakat.łeˑtⱥʹtᵢneˑ." qakyaʹmneˑts qa.-
ⱥʹnˑeˑ. tseᵢkatⱥʹłneˑ, nʹoˑk!weʹᵢneˑ nʹɬwat!tⱥʹłneˑ: nʹⱥʹneˑ ⱥʹnła·k.
ktsⱥłmiʹyⱥt.s, taʹxas ts!ⱥnˑaˑxeˑ ⱥʹnła·k. kkanmiʹyⱥt yuwaˑkmɛ-

15 nuqkaʹnˑeˑ. taʹxas k!ⱥktⱥkmɛnuʹqkaˑ, namak!tsaʹakat.łeˑtⱥtᵢneʹᵢ-
neˑ na aʹmˑak. nʹupsłaˑtᵢyiłqaqaʹaneˑts kwałkwaʹyeˑt. taʹxas
ktsⱥłmiʹyⱥt.sts ławaʹxeˑ neᵢ nataʹnⱥk!. qakyaʹmneˑ tsxałqa.ⱥʹnˑeˑ
sⱥłsaʹhanłe.ⱥʹtᵢneˑ. kⱥt!qaoxaʹxaˑmts k.łahaʹkq!yeˑt. qakeʹᵢneˑ
skⱥʹnˑkuˑts: "hutsxałʹⱥʹnˑeˑ." qakyaʹmneˑ: "soʹukᵤneˑ." tsxałts!ⱥ-

20 nˑaʹxeˑ skⱥʹnˑkuˑts. taʹxas ts!ⱥnˑaˑxeˑ skⱥʹnˑkuˑts. ktsⱥłmiʹyⱥtts
q!uʹmneˑnaʹmneˑ. kkanmiʹyⱥtts yuwaˑkmɛnuqkaʹnˑeˑts kanuʹq-
kaˑ. nʹoˑk!ⱶⱥnłaʹtiłʹutᵢmeˑłⱥʹtᵢneˑ. ts!maˑk!eˑłsⱥłʹuʹtᵢmeˑłⱥʹtᵢneˑ.
taʹxas kiuʹkᵢyeˑt, aqłsmaʹkᵢnⱥk! nʹⱥtkⱥʹnˑeˑ keˑʹek. tsxaʹnˑeˑ neᵢ
nataʹnⱥk!; qakeʹᵢneˑ: "tsxałhaqaʹaneˑ kaˑkweʹsⱥnˑ." nułpałnⱥʹłneˑ

25 neᵢs k!aqaʹkeˑ ktsxałhaʹqaps kwⱥsⱥʹnˑeˑs. mⱥʹka nʹoniłoxa-
xaʹmnaˑm nⱥʹłeˑts at nʹuˑtmeˑłⱥʹtᵢneˑ. taʹxas at nʹɬaʹnˑeˑ łkaʹmˑu
neᵢs koʹuknaps nataʹnⱥk!s. at naqktsiyaʹmneˑ. qałwiʹynam
ktsxaˑʹłsoᵤkts paˑł qaqaʹnałʹutᵢmeʹᵢkᵤneˑ. taʹxas qaqałaˑtiłqa-
qaʹaneˑ yaˑqałaˑtiłʹonanuqkaʹkeˑ. łuqᵘałaˑtiłʹuʹtᵢmⱥłⱥʹtᵢneˑ neᵢ

30 kwałkwaʹyeˑt. ktsiłmiʹyeˑt qaˑnmⱥxuʹnenaʹmneˑ. tuʹxᵘa
nʹoⱶkwiłʹöpkwuʹmneˑ. ławaʹxeˑ skⱥʹnˑkuˑts. qakiłⱥʹłneˑ: "hⱥnts-
qa.ⱥʹnˑeˑ. hⱥnsahaʹnˑeˑ. ts!maˑk!eˑłsⱥłʹuʹtᵢmełe.ⱥʹtᵢneˑ nⱥʹnkoˑ."
qaˑnⱥt.łaʹaneˑ k!uʹk!we paʹłkeᵢ; nʹasqaʹłteˑ. qak.łaʹpseˑ: "hutsxałts!ⱥnaxałaʹaneˑ qoˑ yaˑkⱥʹɬtiyaʹmke nataʹnⱥk!." taʹxas ts!ⱥ-

35 nakⱥʹkᵢncˑ. k.łaʹxamts qakiłⱥʹłneˑ: "qaʹpseᵢn kⱥnseʹᵢłqaˑts?" qakeʹᵢneˑ: "huʹnułpałneˑtⱥtᵢnałaʹneˑ neᵢ ksakⱥłʹⱥʹtyam nataʹnⱥk!."
qakiłⱥʹłneˑ: "soʹukᵤneˑ. hⱥntsxałts!ⱥnˑaʹxeˑ." taʹxa nʹⱥʹnˑeˑ neᵢ
kwⱥʹlqa, taʹxⱥs ts!ⱥnaʹxeˑ. taʹxas q!uʹmneˑnaʹmneˑ. kkanmiʹyeˑt
taʹxas yuwaˑkmɛnuqkaʹnˑeˑ. nalaˑteˑʹqot!aʹmałⱥʹtᵢneˑ wⱥʹł-

40 naˑm. taʹxas k!ⱥktikmɛnuʹqkaˑ nʹupsłaˑtᵢyiłsoʹkᵘiłˑoˑxonatⱥtneʹᵢ-
neˑ. taʹxas kiuʹkᵢyit nʹutᵢmⱥt.łeⱥʹtᵢneˑ. nʹⱥtkᵢniʹyam nⱥʹłeˑts at
soᵤkᵘⱥłˑoˑʹxonaʹtⱥtneʹᵢneˑ. yaaⱥkaʹqktseᵢk at qaˑnˑmⱥłxoneʹᵢneˑ at

[Nos. 48–50. Told by Mission Joe and Felix Andrew]

48. The Animals and the Sun

There was a town. A chief gave his commands. He said: "Who | will be the Sun?" Then they began to talk about it. One of them was | told: "You shall be the Sun." After this one had been told | that he was to be the Sun, all heard about what ‖ was to be done. 5 Those who were told to be the Sun went. | The name (of this one) was Raven. Then he started. | It became dark. On the following morning they watched for him to come up. | He came up. It was not bright enough when | he came up. The day was always blackish. ‖ It was always like evening. The Sun came back. | They said: "This 10 way is bad. It is always | blackish." They said that he could not be it. | Another one was looked for. Chicken Hawk was sent. | It grew dark. Then Chicken Hawk started. On the following morning he went ‖ up. When he went up higher, the world looked yellow. | 15 It was always like that. He went down. | In the evening the Sun came back. They said: "You can not be it. | It looks like bad weather." [1] They assembled and talked it over again. Coyote said: | "I will be it." They said: "Well." Coyote was about ‖ to start. 20 Coyote started. At night | they slept. On the following morning Coyote went up. | When he went up, it began to be hot. It was fairly warm, and | then it was noon and the people cooked food. The Sun spoke, and | said: "Will there be any left for me?" It was heard ‖ what he said, and they left food for him. Even when they 25 went into | the shade, it was warm. The children began to cry, | for the Sun burned them. They went to the water, and they thought | it would be good, but the water was hot. It was the same | when the Sun went down. It became warmer and warmer until ‖ sunset. 30 When it was dark, they felt well. They had almost | been burned to death. Coyote came back. He was told: "You can not be it; | you are bad. You were too hot." |

There was one woman with two children. They said: "We will | go there where they are playing Sun." ‖ The two went. They ar- 35 rived there, and they were told: "Why do you come?" | They said: "We heard that they play Sun." | They were told: "It is good. You shall go." Then he, | the elder one, started. They slept. The next morning | he went up. In the morning it was coolish. ‖ He went high 40 up, and they always felt comfortable. | At noon it became warm, and when they were in the shade | it felt comfortable. They went swimming, and they felt well. | They felt cool. Then he came down. Then

---

[1] The narrator said that many others were tried, but he did not remember their names. See pp. 48, 116.

n'ɛtqo·t!ama'ɬne·. ta'ӽas k!unanu'qka·. ta'ӽas so'kᵘɹ·oӽo'natɛt-
ne'ᵢne· o·'k!ᵘqᵤna ksɹwaɬkwa'ye·t. ta'ӽas ktsɹmi'ye·t, ta'ӽas
45 ɬawa'ӽe· neᵢ nɛtsta'haɬ. q!a'pe· qaɬwiyna'mne· neᵢsts ktsӽa'ɬ'ɛn
    nata'n·eᵢk!. qakiɬɛ'ɬne· neᵢ nɛtsta'haɬ: "hɛntsӽaɬ'ɛ'n·e· nata'-
    n·eᵢk!." ktsɹmi'yɛt·sts ta'ӽas ɬats!ɛn·a'ӽe· o·'k!ᵘqᵤna ksɬa'matɛ'k-
    tseᵢɬ ktsӽa'ɬ'ɛn nata'neᵢk!s. neᵢ nao'k!ᵃe· nɛtsta'haɬ neᵢ ktsa-
    qu'n·a saosaqa'ₐne·. qakiɬɛ'ɬne·: "nɛ'nko hɛntsӽaɬts!ɛna'ӽe· na
50 ktsɹmi'yit. hɛntsӽaɬ'ɛ'n·e· ktsɹmetɹhnu'qka." ta'ӽas ts!ɛn·a'ӽe·.
    qawunekɛ'tᵢne· ktsɹmi'yeᵢt yuwakmɛnuqka'n·e· ktsɹmetɹhnu'q-
    ka· n'upsɬa'tᵢyilhu'k!ukyɛ'tᵢne· yɛ'sɛnwunmeyɛ'tke· tsɹme·yɛt-
    na'm·u. kkanmi'yɛt ɬawa'ӽe·. qakiɬɛ'ɬne·: "ta'tᵢne·s tsӽaɬ'-
    ɛ'n·e· yo·kwiyetna'm·us nata'n·eᵢk!s. nɛ'nko hɛntsӽaɬ'ɛ'n·e·
55 ktsɹme·tiɬhnu'qka·." na ki'a·s nata'n·eᵢk! n'asts n'ɛ'n·e·; n'ɛ'n·e·
    na ki'a·s nɛtsta'haɬ ta'ӽas q'a'pe· qaɬwiyna'mne· kse'ᵢɬ-
    soᵤkᵘts soᵤkᵘɹq!okna'mne·. ta'ӽas sɬoknɛ'ɬne·.

    Sa'hanɹwi'yne· skɛ'n·ku·ts. qaɬwi'yne·: "huɬo'piɬ neᵢ nata'-
    n·eᵢk!." ta'ӽas n'ɛt'wukᵘnɛ'ɬeᵢk; ta'ӽas a·'ke· n'aimaka'ₐne·.
60 ta'ӽas ts!ɛn·a'ӽe· tsɹme·yɛtna'mu's qo·s tsӽaɬya·qa'kaɬyuwa'k-
    mɛnu'qka·'ske·ts qaoӽa'ӽe·. qaosaqa'ₐne· kkanme'yit. ta'ӽas
    sukӽo'ᵤme·k neᵢs qaɬ'o'nɹqakqa'ₐne·. ta'ӽas na'wɛtsnuɬ-
    k!o'ᵤne·. ta'ӽas yu·wa'kmɛnuqka'n·e·. ta'ӽas suknuɬk!o'ᵤne·.
    ta'ӽas tsӽaɬmɛ'tӽₐne· qanaɬhaq!aku'pse· a'ₐk!e·s. ts'ɹq!an-
65 ku'pse·. n'ɹqanmɛ'te·. ta'ӽas naq!a'ɬɛkwaɛ'tᵢne·. no·sanoӽun-
    qa'ₐne·. qa·'mɛtɛnq!o·'kupӽu'se· nas yana'ha·ks neᵢs tsӽaɬya'ₐ-
    qana'mke·. ta'ӽas pa·ɬ kanɬu'kpqa·. ta'ӽas noɬu'qune·. ta'ӽas
    tsӽaɬ'hoᵤko'ᵤne·. n'u'pӽₐne· sɬqa'nama'namɛ'sᵢne·. qa·oӽaɬ'a·'qa-
    po·'ӽaɬ'ɛtӽo'ᵤme·k. wa·'mɛtɛnq!o·'kupӽu'se· ts!e·naɬ·u'qӽaɬha'-
70 q!a'ɬɛkwaɛ't.se·. o·'k!ᵘqᵤna ke'ᵢɬo·s tsa'ha·ɬs aₐ'kmana·'mists sɹ-
    ӽa·'tknu'kᵤne·. na aₐ'kik.ɬu'ᵤna·m n'upӽa'ɬne· neᵢ haq!aɬo·kwa'-
    et.[1] qakya'mne· qa'pseᵢɪ: "ksɬ'a'qaɬe·'e·t?" qakya'mne·: "lo'ᵤ-
    ne· skɛ'n·ku·ts, ɬɛntsӽaɬ'uɬa'n·e·." qake'ᵢne· skɛ'n·ku·ts: "ne·s
    tsӽaɬya·qa'naɬhaqa'ₐke· aq!sma'kneᵢk! na·sts at sqaqₐna'ₐne·
75 neᵢs tsӽaɬho'ᵤko· at tsӽaɬ'ɛtӽo'ᵤme·k qa·'s na·qana·man·a·'me·sts
    at tsӽaɬӽatknu'kᵤne·." ta'ӽa naₐ aₐ'kɛk.ɬu'nam qakya'mne·:
    "maₐts at qa'qₐnapmɛ'lkeᵢɬ neᵢs ya'qaqₐna'ₐke· skɛ'n·ku·ts;
    na·s tsӽaɬya·qa'naɬhaqa'ₐke· aq!sma'kneᵢk! maₐts at k.ɬɛn-
    q!o·ɛ'mu nata'n·eᵢk!s." qakya'mne·: "ta'ӽas hɛnsɬu'pӽₐne· at
80 hɛntsya·'qaqₐna'ₐke·." ta'ӽas soᵤkᵘɹq!okna'mne·ts ɬapa·'ts-
    qa'ₐtsa'mne·. ta'ӽas sɬqa·qa'sₐne·.

49. Coyote's Contests

    Qa·k.ɬuna'mne·ts kinelwi'ytik skɛ'n·ku·ts. qaɬwi'yne· paɬ
    ktsɬyuna'qwum neᵢts ya·qanakɹhaqwu'mke·. siɬkᵢniɬwiyteya'ₐte·
    neᵢs aₐ'kɛk.ɬuna'mɛs at ya'qaoӽaqaɬɛpnamɛ'ske·. qakɛ'ɬne· aɬ-

they felt comfortable, | because the Sun was setting. At night the ‖
youth came back, and all thought that he should be | the Sun. The 45
youth was told: "You shall be the Sun." | In the evening he came
back, because it was given to him | to be the Sun. The other youth,
the younger one, | staid there. He was told: "You shall go in ‖ the 50
evening; you shall be the Moon." Then he went off. | It had not been
dark long before the Moon went up. | It was always light throughout
the night. | On the following morning he came back. He was told:
"Your elder brother shall be | the Sun during the day. You shall be ‖
the Moon." These two became the heavenly orbs [Suns]. These | 55
two youths were thought to be good, | and they were glad. Then it
was decided. |

Coyote was angry. He thought: "I will kill the Sun." | Then he
made his bow, and he also had two arrows. ‖ Then he went in the 60
night to the place where the Sun was to come up. | He staid there.
On the following morning he took a good seat. | He lay on his stom-
ach. Then he aimed at the right place. | The Sun rose. He aimed
well | and was about to shoot. Then his arrow was burned. ‖ It burned 65
quickly, and he threw it away. Then everything was on fire. He
ran away. | There was fire on each side where he was going along. |
He ran and went into the water. | He was almost burned. He saw
a trail and | lay down on it. The fire arrived, and it turned back ‖
because there was no grass on the trail. | He was saved. The people 70
saw that the land was burning. | Some one said: "Why is this?"
They said: "Coyote is not here; | it must be he who has done it."
Coyote said: | "Later generations of people will do this. ‖ When there 75
is a fire, they will lie down on a trail. | Then they will be saved."
Then the people said: | "Don't do what Coyote has done. | Later
generations shall not | play Sun." Some one said: "Now you know
what ‖ to do." Then they were glad. They | scattered. That is 80
the end. |

49. COYOTE'S CONTESTS

There was a town. Coyote was thinking about (the future). He
thought | there would be many generations of people. He thought
of | the town where the people had been killed. He said to | his friends:

swʊ'eˑs: "hułts!maxa'ła hułts!małwats!na'ła." ts!ma'xe· n'ɛ'n·eˑ

5 naso'kᵘeˑn's skɛ'n·kuˑtsˑ, yama'kpaˑł, ma'ₐka, kiakqa'łoᵤk,
ɛ'nłaˑk, ła'toˑq! qoqu'skeˑ. wust�!ała'ₐneˑ neᵢ ta'xa kts!eˑ'nam.
łaxa'xeˑ sak.łunamɛ'sineˑ. qakiłɛ'łneˑ: "qa'psin kɛn'o'tkeᵢł?"
qake'ᵢneˑ: "hoᵤsdwats!nała'ₐneˑ." qakiłɛ'łne· tsxałsdwats!-
na'mneˑ kak!a'nwats!ti'yam. qakiłɛ'łnc· skɛ'n·kuˑts: "qa'ła

10 ktsxał'ɛsnɛ'łwaˑts!?" qake'ᵢne·, "tsxał'ɛ'n·eˑ ła'toˑq!." neᵢ
haₐk.ło'ᵤkᵘeˑ qake'ᵢneˑ: "kammna'ła tsxał'ɛ'n·eˑ sɛn'a." qakya'mneˑ: "ta'xa." ta'xas kxo'naˑm neᵢs wu'oˑs qoˑs qana'xeˑ
skɛ'n·kuˑts. qawa'kaˑł'u'pkaxona'kseˑ yaqso"meˑls. łuq!oxᵤ-
nɛ'łneˑ. qakɛ'łneˑ łatoq!na'nas: "husło·q!oxnɛ'łneˑ na yaq-

15 so"meˑł. neᵢ hɛnk!a'nwaₐts! hɛntsłaqawa·kawa'ts!neˑ hɛnts!-
qa·ka·ła·kawitsqo·'k!un·ka'kₐneˑ." ta'xas k!a'n·wats! neᵢ ki'as.
ta'xas neᵢ kyuna'qa aqłsma'kinɛk! nakdwitskɛ'łne· qa'łas ła-
yuwₐkmɛ'qoˑs ksɛ'ł'ips, ta'xas ktsxałtsłhu'qᵘa, sɛ'n·a n'ɛ'n·e·
kqa·hu'qᵘaˑł. at sł'aqaqa'pseˑ neᵢsts ła'xałwa'ts!xaˑłts at słqanał-

20 wa'ts!neˑ, sł'a'qaqa'pseˑ at kqaho'qᵘaˑł. ta'xas na'kdwɛtskełɛ'ł-
neˑ neᵢsts słwa·łkwayɛ't.seˑ. qakɛ'łneˑ skɛ'n·kuˑts łatoq!na'na's.
naₐ qa'skeᵢha·łuk.łe'et ta'xas tsxałtsł·a'yuwa·kme'wɛsu'qᵤne·
sɛ'n·a. ta'xas qoˑ hɛntsłaqanawa'ts!neˑ. ta'xas .to'xwa tsd-
wałkwayɛ't̠ineˑ qo's kdya'qanałk!anwa'tskeˑ sɛ'n·ats qakał'-

25 a·kałtsᵢmo'ᵤkᵤne·. ta'xas k!a'kałtsu'm·oˑkts qa'wuneˑkɛ't.seˑ
ła·awa·kmewisu'kᵤneˑ. ta'xas nałok.łeo't̠ineˑ so·kᵘiłq!o'kᵤna'm-
neˑ ko·qaka·"nam. ta'xas łats!ɛn·awa'ts!neˑ ła'tuq!na'na.
n'u'pxₐneˑ ktsdhoqᵘa'kaˑ. ta'xas k.łaaka'wats!.

Qake'ᵢneˑ neᵢ naso'ᵤkᵘeˑn skɛ'n·kuˑts: "ta'xas hutsłaₐts!maxa-
30 ła'ₐneˑ. paˑł kosłhoqᵘna'was." łaxa'xeˑ a"ke sa·k.łonamɛ'sineˑ.
qakiłɛ'łneˑ: "qa'psin kɛn'o'tkeᵢł?" qake'ᵢneˑ "husdwats!nała'ₐneˑ."
qakiłɛ'łneˑ: "qa'psin kałwa'ts!naˑm?" qake'ᵢneˑ: "qa'psin hɛn-
qałwe'ykeᵢł." qakiłɛ'łneˑ: "huts·dwats!nała'ₐneˑ kdnoqo'ykax-
na'mnaˑm." qakiłɛ'łneˑ: "qa'łaˑn· q!a·'kpakɛ'txoᵤł tsxałtshoqᵘa'ł-

35 neˑ." qakɛ'łneˑ skɛ'n·kuˑts ałaqa'łtˑeˑs: "qaˑ'ła ktsɛsnɛ'łwaˑts!?"
qake'ᵢneˑ ma'ₐka: "hutsxał'ɛ'n·eˑ." qakiłɛ'łneˑ: "maₐts, hɛnł-
q!akpakɛ'txoᵤł." qake'ᵢneˑ ktsxa'ł'eˑn n'ałsɛ'nteˑk. naqa'ₐneˑ
kqastsumqa'qa neᵢs kdnoqo'ykaxnamna'meˑs. qatałtsxa'n·eˑ
n'ɛ'nseˑ tsa'eˑs neᵢs ma'ₐka's. neᵢ ta'xa ha·k.ło'ᵤkᵘeˑ n'ɛ'n·eˑ

40 kqastsumqa'qa yu·wɛsq!a'naˑk. ta'xas k!ɛt!qaoxo'naˑm. ta'xas
yaₐkaxmɛtyaxna'mneˑ neᵢ ktsk.łaqna'naˑm. qanaqkupłałɛ'łneˑ
ma'ₐka. ts!ɛn'o'k!ᵘɛnłatił'ɛ'ktiˑkmɛtxo'ᵤlneˑ. n'o'k!ᵘɛnła'ₐt̠iyɛˑłts-
ha'qaɛydmo'xona·titmo'łneˑ. na'łq!anteᵢxa'łneˑ k.łaxa'nxoᵤł
łao·'niła·qxaqku'płałɛ'łneˑts ła·ts!ɛnmɛtxo'ᵤłne. qa'nqa'mik kia-

45 qka'łoᵤkts n'u'pxₐneˑ neᵢs tsa'eˑs. peɛ'k!aks paˑł tsł'ɛ'nseˑ up'na'-
moˑs. nuqo'kxamu'mek. ta'xas łaxanxo'ᵤneˑ neᵢs yu·wɛsq!a'naˑ-
ksts kqa·'naqkupła'łteˑ. ts!ɛnha'q!mak!ax·na'kseˑ neᵢsts kqa·na-
qkupła'łeᵢt. łaxanxo'ᵤneˑts k.łáqanaqkupła'łeᵢt. ta'xas qa'sd-

"Let us go and play with them!" They started. ‖ Coyote was their   5
chief. Woodpecker, Flicker, Hawk, | Chicken Hawk, Duck, and
Bluejay, seven of them, went. | They reached the town. They were
told: "What do you want?" | (Coyote) said: "We come to play."
He was told they would play | at diving. Coyote was told: "Who ‖
will play?" He said: "Duck shall be the one." The | people of the   10
town said: "Our (player) shall be Beaver." | Some one said:
"Ready!" Then they went to the shore. | Coyote went there. There
on shore was a canoe. | He pulled out the calking, and he said to the
little Duck: "I have taken the calking out of this canoe. ‖ When you   15
dive, come up here! You shall | stick your nose up through the hole."
Then the two dived, | and many people watched. Whoever | should
float dead on the water, he was to lose. Beaver | never lost. There-
fore he was selected when any one came to play with them. ‖ He   20
was never beaten. Then they were watched. | The sun was going
down. Coyote had said to the little Duck: | "When (you hear)
shouting, then Beaver comes up out of the water. | Then you may
come up, too." It was almost | sunset. Then at the place where
Beaver had dived ‖ bubbles came up; and not long after the bubbles   25
had come up, | he floated on top of the water. Then there was a
noise. They were glad | because he had won. Then the little Duck
dived back. | He knew that he would win. Then he came up. |

Chief Coyote said: "Now we will go on. ‖ We have won over you."   30
They came to another town, | and they were told: "What do you
want?" (Coyote) said: "We will play." | He was told: "What will
you play?" He said: "Whatever you | like." He was told: "We
will play boxing." | He was told: "Whoever is knocked down, he
will lose." ‖ Coyote said to his children: "Who will play?" | Flicker   35
said: "I'll be it." He was told: "No; you will be knocked down." |
He said he wanted to be the one. There was | an expert boxer. He
could not speak. | Flicker was the younger brother. ‖ The most expert   40
one in the town was Kneecap. Then they met. | They went against
each other, those who were to fight. Flicker was struck a hard blow, |
and at once he was thrown upward. He was always rolling about, |
and lost his senses. He was thrown back, | and he was struck again
from below. He was knocked back still farther. Hawk was sitting
there, ‖ and saw that his younger brother had almost been killed. | 45
Then he went out of his own body.[1] He went up to Kneecap | and
struck him hard. He gave him a hard knock | when he struck him.
He went up to him and struck him again. Then he | knocked a piece

---

[1] This was explained that his supernatural power went out of his own body to attack the enemy.

onmɛtxo′ᵤne·. ta′xas k!u′pxa ktsɬ′o′peɬ. ta′xas ɬahama′te·k-
50 tsɛ′ɬne· ma′ₐka. ta′xas ɬaqakxaɬ′ɛ′n·e·. ta′xas ɬao′kwaɬ-
aqana′mik ma′ₐka, peɛ′k!aks op′na′mus pa·ɬ ke′e·ns. ta′xas
a′′ke· sɬasa·′niɬhoqᵘaka′ₐne· skɛ′n·ku·ts.
     Qake′ᵢne· ta′xas: "hutsɬa·ts!ɛ′nax·aɬa′ₐne·." ta′xas kts!ɛ′na·m
ɬaxa′xe· saₐk.ɬunamɛ′sne. qakiɬɛ′ɬne·: "qa′psin kɛn′o′tke₁ɬ?"
55 qake′ᵢne· skɛ′n·ku·ts: "husɑwats!naɬa′ₐne·." qakiɬɛ′ɬne· tsxaɬsɑ-
wats!na′mne· k!ɛ′ke·ɬ. n′ɛtkɛnɬɛ′sᵢne· k!ɛ′k.ɬe·sts yunaqa′pse·.
qakiɬɛ′ɬne· skɛ′n·ku·ts aɬa·qaɬtɛ′tᵢmu: "qa·′ɬa ktsxaɬ′ɛsnɛ′ɬwa·ts!?"
qake′ᵢne· qoqu′ske·: "hutsxaɬ′ɛ′n·e." ta′xas tᵢnaqanxa′′mne· ne₁s
aₐ′kɛt.ɬana′me·′s. ta′xas n′ɛsaknu′n·e· qoqu′ske·. ta′xas naqaɬ-
60 pa′ɬne′ᵢne·   qo′s pɛ′k!a·ks qo′s ats!mɑq!aɬuk!puka′m′e·sts
lu′n·o′s. ta′xas n′ɛ′kneᵢts kaqaɬpa′ɬne·. pa·ɬ ksɬsokᵘa·ka′te· ne₁
k!ɛ′ke·ɬ. ɬe·etkeka′ɬhaqa′ɬpaɬne′ᵢne·ts k!o′kxats ɬɛtqawu′mne·.
ta′xas sɬhoqᵘaka′ₐne·. qake′ᵢne·: "ta′xas." ɬats!ɛnawɛsmaknɛ′ɬe·k.
     N′ok!ᵤᵐl′ɑkɑa′mne·. qake′ᵢne· skɛ′n·ku·ts: ktsqa′namna′ɬka
65 n′a·′qa·naɬhaqa·nak!aqɬa′ha·ɬs. qakiɬɛ′ɬne· skɛ′n·ku·ts: "hɛntsxaɬ′-
ok!ᵘe′ᵢne·, tax at hɛnqaɬtɛ′ɬeᵢkts hɛnske′ᵢne·." qake′ᵢne· ɬatoq!-
na′na: "hutsqanaxaɬa′ₐne· n′a·qa′naɬhaq!nukna′na." qakiɬɛ′ɬne·:
"hɛntsxaɬ′ok!ᵘe′ᵢne· tax at hɛnqaɬtɛ′ɬe·kts hɛnske′ᵢne·." qa-
ke′ᵢ ne· ma′ₐka ktsqanamna′ɬka n′a·′qanaɬhak!ak.ɬonukna′-
70 na′s. qakiɬɛ′ɬne·: "hɛntsxaɬ′ok!ᵘe′ᵢne· tax at hɛnqaɬtɛ′ɬe·kts
hɛnske′ᵢne·." qake′ᵢne· yama′kpa·ɬ ktsqa·′namna′ɬka n′a·′qa·na-
ɬhaq!a·′nqa·ts!ɬa′e·ns. qakiɬɛ′ɬne·: "hɛntsxaɬ′ok!ᵘe′ᵢne· pa·ɬ
at kɛnqa·ɬtɛ′ɬe·kts hɛnske′ᵢne·." qake′ᵢne· ki·aqka′t.ɬoᵤk ktsqa-
namna′ɬka n′a·′qa·naɬso·kᵘnusu′k!po·ns. ta′xas sɑ′ɛ′ɬkiɬ·a′mneᵢts,
75 sɑsa·nɑweynata′mnɛts sɑa·pa·tsqa·′′tse·. ta′xas sɑqaqa′sᵢne·.

50. THE WAR ON THE SKY

Qaₐk.ɬuna′mne·. naqa′pse· ɬuna′t!e₁s ha′nq!o. qaɬwe′yne·
ktsxaɬtso′ᵤkat. ta′xas tsak.ɬa′pse·. sa·niɬwe′ynɛts mɛ′txₐne· at
n′ak!ɬa′naqa′ₐne· a·k! sa′nak!ɬanakɛ′n·e· ne₁s kmɛtxa′m·u. ta′xas
ɬahosanᵤxunqa′ₐne·. qakɛ′ɬne papa′e·s: "so·q!ᵘne′ᵢto·." ta′xas n′u-
5 mɛtskɛnɬɛ′sne· aₐka′q!ne·′s. ta′xas wokqa′ɬne· ne₁ paɬke₁ ne₁ ki′e·p.
qaohu′ɬne· ne₁ a·k!. neyaxa′ɬne· wa′ta·k, n′ɛ′n·e· kq!ape·′ɬkqa·ts
nas a′m·a·ks. sɬqaɬwiynamɛ′sᵢne· ktsupxa·′ɬ′e·s ka·′s n′aqakeka-
nɛk!e·′ne· a·k!. ta′xas tɛnaxa′mne· ne₁s aₐkɛt.ɬana′me·s ya·qa-
kiɬkɛnɬɛ′ske· ne₁s a·k!s. n′o′ᵤne· n′ɛsɛ′nse· papa′e·s ne₁s a·k!s.
10 qae·ɬo′ᵤqaqna′ₐne· pa·ɬ ke′ɛns papa′e·sts sɑqata·′ɬtsxanatka′ₐxₐne·
n′oqo′′xaq!o·k.ɬoma′n·e· aₐ′ke′e·sts ne₁s qanaɬqaqna′ₐne·. qaɬwiy-
na′mne·. k.ɬsa′kqa a′m·a·kne₁s aₐkɑmi′yɛt.s.k.ɬsa′kq!nuk. ta′xas
qakya′mne· ktsxaɬts!ɛ′naɬ′anaxaka′ₐna·m. ta′xas k!o′k!ᵘe· n′ɛ′n·e·
kwu′ɬaq!makanɛ′ɬe·k. ta′xas wa·′ɪnɑtak!o′ᵤne·. n′upxaɬɛ′sᵢne·
15 ka·kq!meᵢɬmo·k!ona′ₐte·t. ta′xas ɬaa′k!ɬa·k kmɛ′txa·ts at
ɬaɛsk!o′ᵤne· ne₁s aₐq!anq!a′iks. ta′xas q!a·′pe· pa·ɬ kmɛ′txa·ɬts

off from him.   Then he knew that he could kill him, and he was given ‖
back to Flicker.   It was he again.[1]   Then | Flicker fought him down, 50
and that one was killed. | Thus Coyote won again in a bad manner. |

He said: "Now we will go."   They went, | and arrived at a town.
He was told: "What do you want?" ‖ Coyote said: "We will 55
play."   He was told | somebody would play eating.   Much food was
prepared. | Coyote and his children were told: "Who will play?" |
Bluejay said: "I'll be it."   Then they went into | the tent.   Blue-
jay sat down and ‖ began to talk of his great-great-grandfathers, who 60
lived long ago, and | those before them.   Then he ate and talked.
There was a great pile | of food.   He had not been talking very
long before he had eaten it all.   He was still hungry. | Then they
won.   (Coyote) said: "Enough!" They went along. |

At once they began to quarrel.   Coyote said ‖ he would take 65
them through swamps.   Coyote was told: "You | may go there
alone, for you like them, therefore you say so."   Little Duck said: |
"We will go through little lakes."   He was told: | "You may go
alone.   You like them, therefore you say so." | Flicker said he
would take them through young dry trees. ‖ He was told: "You 70
may go there alone.   You like them, therefore | you say so."
Woodpecker said he would take them through | thickly wooded
places.   He was told: "You may go there alone. | You like them,
therefore you say so."   Hawk said he would | take them through
places with scattered trees.   Thus they quarreled. ‖ They became 75
angry at one another and separated.   That is the end. |

50. THE WAR ON THE SKY[2]

There was a town.   There was Muskrat's brother's widow.   He
thought | he would marry her.   Then she refused him.   He was
angry and shot her. | The arrow was of a different kind.   He made
it in a different way, what he used for shooting her. | Then he ran
away.   He said to his grandmother: "——— (?)"[3]   Then ‖ his face 5
was torn up.   Then the dead woman was discovered. | The arrow
was not known.   They sent for Frog, who (was in the habit of going)
all | over the world.   They wanted to know where that | arrow came
from.   Then she (Frog) went into the house where | the arrow was
kept.   She herself knew that it was her grandson's arrow. ‖ She did 10
not know what to do, because it was her grandson, and she did not
want to tell on him. | She spat into her hands and nodded. | They
thought there must be a country in the sky, and that there must
be a lake. | Some one said they would go on the warpath.   One of
them | was able to shoot far.   He shot upward, and a noise was
heard ‖ as the point hit.   Then another one shot and | hit the notch 15
of the (first) arrow.   Then all of them shot, | but they did not reach

---

[1] That is to say, Hawk's power had entered Flicker, and now left him again.

[2] For another version see p. 87.

[3] My interpreters did not understand this sentence.   The word so·q!u·ne′ito· is derived from aa′ka′q!ne· ("face").

sɪnaˑɬaqaoqaxo'ₙmeˑk. qo'kᵘeˑn aₐˈkǃunkaˑˈkǃeˑs sɛlqaoxakɛ'nˑiˑts
ta'xas sɨtsmaˈkǃeˑɬˈoˑkᵘaxo'ₙmeˑk. ta'xas ktstsǃeˑnaxa'mists
qakeᵢne a'tsǃpoˑ: "hɛntsaˈwɛtskpayaˈtapkɛ'ɬneˑ. hutsǃai'mats-
20 sɬˈɛˈtkᵢnɛ'lɛk qoqa'pmoₙts hutsǃaimatswɛsɨɬnukteˈɬeˑk." n'upsaˈki-
ɬ'ɛtkᵢne'ɬekᵘ qoqa'pmoₙsts ktsǃɛnaxa'meˑ's. saˑnɛɬwi'yneˑ a'tsǃpo
kᵢma'teˑɬ. qunva'xₐneˑ neᵢs yaqanaɬwaˑqǃnonamɛ'skeˑts ɬaqǃa-
piɬ'umɛtskɛ'nˑeˑ. ɬaoˈkᵘiɬ'oˑkaxo'ₙseˑts saˑnɛɬwiynata'pseˑ pa'ɬkeᵢs
paɬ tsǃɛn kǃɛnqapta'keᵢs neᵢs aₐˈkɛkˑɬuna'meˑ's. ta'xas mɛte'xa'ɬneˑ
25 tsxaɬ'qǃakpaˈkɛtxo'ˑɬneˑ. qaˑkˑɬatnutɛ'ɬneˑ a'tsǃpotsta'xaskqǃawa-
tsɬ'nmeˑk. qonya'xₐneˑ aₐˈkɛnqǃaɬqa'eˑsts qasnɛnqa'meˑk. n'ɛnqapta'kseˑ ta'kǃaˑts. n'apakǃɛnɛ''nteˑ naˑs aₐˈkaˑ'mtǃeˑs qahaɬ'aka-
mɛnɬhaqa'peˑts ta'xas qanaɬ'antsoˑxa'xeˑ paɬ kˑɬaqaˑ'psɛɬxo'ₙne-
kuˈkˑɬoₙk. ta'xas kǃopɛnqanaxa''meˑsts qakiɬamnamɛ'sᵢneˑ: "naˑs
30 n'ɛ'nˑeˑ a'tsǃpo." qakeᵢne: "hoqᵘa.ɛ'nˑeˑ. hoqᵘa'kˑɬeˑk ksɛnˑakpa'-
meˑk kqaqunmetkpa'meˑk ka snaqanɛ'keˑts, naˑ kusɬ'aqaqa'ɬe-
kɛ'nmeˑk paɬ ta'kǃaˑts kskikɛɬmɛ'txa." ta'xas neᵢ kyuˑxa'xaˑm,
ta'xas tsǃɛna'xeˑ haˑnqǃo. ta'xas n'ɛtkɛ'nˑe kwɛ'ɬqǃnoks. ta'xas
n'ɛtɛt.ɬa'ₐteˑk paɬ at kyuna't.ɬa mɛˈkan o'kǃᵘeˑ ta'xas kqa'kyam
35 ksaˑkˑɬo'ₙnam. ta'xas kˑɬaxaxa'mis neᵢ.s aₐˈkikˑɬo'eˑs. ta'xas
wanaqna'ɬneˑ. n'omɛtskɛnɬɛ'sᵢneˑ aₐˈkɛt.ɬa'eˑs. neᵢsts kǃomɛtskɛ'nɬeᵢs
neᵢs hu'paksts n'upxa'ɬneˑ tɛ'tqaˑtǃ qaka'ˑɬakaxa'mneˑ kuɬwiya't!neˑ mɛtxa'kaˑts aₐˈkwumna'meˑ's. ta'xasts neᵢs yaˑqa'naɬ'-
omɛtskɛnɬɛ'skeˑ aₐˈkɛt.ɬa'eˑs neᵢsts n'oˑkǃɬaˈtiyɛɬqapeˑkɛ'meˑk.
40 n'omɛtskɛ'nɬeˑs aₐˈkɛt.ɬa'eˑsts at kuɬwiya't!neˑ. neᵢ tɛ'tqaˑtǃ
kmɛtxa'ka. ta'xas nakqǃeyɛ'tᵢneˑ. qakya'mneˑ ɬɛnɛ'nˑeˑ o'kǃ-
naˈmuɬatɛ'teˑk. ta'xas n'upxa'ɬneˑ paˈɬ n'ɛ'nɬatɛ'teˑk ˑhaˑnqǃo.
qakya'mneˑ: "ta'xas qaˑkaskɛ'nkeᵢɬ n'oˈknuqǃmeˑwumkǃoˑ-
nɛskɛ'ɬneˑ." ta'xas sɛlqaˑ'kaskᵢnɛ'ɬneˑ. ta'xas kˑɬaˑtsǃɛna'xam
45 ma yaqa'kaˑɬyoₙwaˑkaxa'mkeˑ. ɬaɬo'ₙneˑ paˑɬˑa'omɛtskᵢnɛ'ɬneˑ.
ta'xas sɛɬa'qaˈɬoqaˈɬnoˈkǃᵘɛ'nmeˑk nöpɛkǃanɛ''nteˑk. tsxa'nˑe
neᵢ kǃanaxa'kanaˈɬka. qakeᵢneˑ: "hutshaˑnˑiɬwukna'xnaɬa'ₐne
nu'mˑa aₐˈkǃakuxa'eˑs." ta'xas naˈniɬwoˑkᵘinxa'ɬneˑts n'upiɬ-
ɛ'ɬneˑ neᵢ nu'mˑa. ta'xas ɬoˑkᵘinkɛ'sᵢneˑ aₐˈkinqawa'eˑs. ta'xas
50 namatɛktsa'mneˑ qǃa'peˑ naqanqoˑ'wa ktsxa'ɬɛns aₐˈkɛnquˑ-
wa'eˑs. naqa'ₐne n'a'sneˑ swʋ'tᵢmu aₐˈkˑɬoₙm'. aₐˈke naqa'ₐne
swʋ'tᵢmu naˈɬaqɬɛ'lɛkts kiaqǃnoˈkᵘaₐt. n'a'sneˑ ˑneᵢ ke'soₙk
aₐˈkɛnqoˑ'wa neᵢ qawoxaknɛ'ɬneˑ. qakya'mneˑ: "maₐts hɛntsqa-
koˑkakɛnkɛ'ɬneˑ tsxaɬ'ɛ'nseˑ swʋ'tᵢmu." aₐˈkˑɬoₙm' swʋ'tᵢmu
55 qanqǃmaˑɬwanˑxoˑna'mneˑ qaɬwi'yneˑ kǃeˑɬɛ'kteˑɬ. ta'xas
kǃoˑˈkᵘɛɬhamatɛ'ktseˑɬ aₐˈkɛnqoˑ'wa's. ta'xas namatɛktsɛ'ɬneˑ neᵢs
swʋ'tᵢmu nasoˑkᵘinkɛ'steˑk. ta'xas kˑɬaqoˑnaxa'mneˑ neᵢ yaˑqa'-
kaɬyuˑwakaxa'mkeˑ. ta'xas kˑɬaˑonaqa'nˑoxu'nam. aₐˈkˑɬoₙm'
swʋ'tᵢmu namatɛ'ktseᵢɬ aₐˈkɛnqoˑ'waˑsts at qayaqa'hakɛ'nˑeˑ
60 paˑɬ kqa'ɬwiy ta'xta ktsa'qaps nɛnko'eˑs. ta'xas kˑɬa'ₐɬoₙsts
paˑɬ sɛɬkǃumnaˈqaɬaɬkɛ'nˑeˑ paˑɬ sɛɬo'ₙseˑ nɛnko'eˑs. ta'xas

down.   When Raven put his nose there, | then it reached the ground.
When they were going to start, | Wolverene said: "Wait for me.
It will take me two days ‖ to put away my things. It will take me 20
two days." He was still | putting away his things when they
started.   Then Wolverene became angry | because he was left.
When they had gone up, he took hold of (the arrows) and | tore them
down entirely.   They all dropped down. Then the women became
angry | at him because they were left alone in the town. They pur-
sued Wolverene, ‖ and he was about to be killed. They pursued 25
Wolverene, and he was out of breath. | He took up his sinews and
cut himself to pieces.   He changed himself | into a squirrel. He put
it under the belt which was | around his waist. Then he went back
somewhere, because he could do no more, | being tired. He went
around, and some one said: "Here ‖ is Wolverene." He said: "I am 30
not he; I am called | He-who-wants-to-act-differently-from-others-
and-who-does-not-care-for-whatever-may-be-done. | I am shooting
squirrels."

   Now, Muskrat, who had gone up, | started and made a large lake. |
He built tents for himself, many tents, although he was only one. ‖
There was a village. Then the people reached the village. They | 35
began to make war.   They tore up the tents. When the first one
was broken up, | a left-handed man was seen to come out. | They
shot (?) him in the stomach.   Then, when they tore up another |
tent, he came out again in the same clothing that he had worn
before. ‖ His tent was broken, and that left-handed man | was shot (?). 40
Then they began to speak, and some one said: "Maybe | he is always
the same one."   Then it came to be known that he was always the
same one; namely, Muskrat. | Some one said: "Stop shooting him—
shooting at his stomach." | Then they left him.

   Then they started back ‖ to the place where they had come from. 45
There was nothing. (The arrow chain) was broken down. | The
manitous did not know how to get down. | The war chief said: "We
will wait | at the drinking-place of Thunderbird." They waited for
the Thunderbird and | killed him. Then his feathers were taken off. ‖
Then they gave them to every one to be their feathers. | There were 50
two friends, the Bats; and there were | two friends, Golden Eagle and
Young Golden Eagle—two of them. Then the good | feathers were
laid aside. Some one said: "Don't touch | them, they are for the
friends."   The Bat friends ‖ nudged each other. They thought they 55
were meant.   Then | all the feathers were given out. Then the | two
chief friends were given feathers. They went back to | the place
where they had come up, and they began to fly down. When the
Bat | friends were given feathers, they passed them on. ‖ They thought 60
(the best ones) would be theirs. When (all the feathers) were gone, |
they knew they were mistaken. There was nothing for them.

łao·'nan·uxu'n·e· aₐ''k·ło·m'; sɛ't!e·s ne₁s qanułkɛ'n·e·. ta'χas
sɛlsqapɛn·quwa'ₐne·. yaqa'nła·lt ne₁s qa·l'ɑqa'nał'akunkɛ'n·e·
aₐ'kuqła'e·s. ta'χas sɛlsqapɛn·qowa'ₐne· at sɛłkᵤno·χo·mu'n·e·.
65 q!a'pe· kia'kχo· tsɛn łao·'naqanmɛ'te·k. q!u'me n'ɛ'ne· k!o·'-
k!ᵘil'aqtsχo'ᵤme·k. łaₐtkɛ'nełts at łaqa'tał'ɛtkɛnɛ'łne·. nöpɛ'k!a-
nɛ''nte·k q!a'pe· qunya'χₐne· łaₑ'tkɛnts pa·'mɛk at qa·sɛlqa-
oχakɛ'n·e· aₐ'kuła'k!e·sts at qałwi'yne· ktsła'so̧uksts at ła·qa·so'ᵤ-
kse·. naqa'pse· łunat!e'es q!u'me n'ɛ'nse· ya·qaoχał·a't₁yɑlqal-
70 we'yke· pa·'mik a'ₐ·ke· k.łqunya'χₐna·ps. ta'χas aₐ''ke·
qunyaχₐna'pse· ne₁s łunat!e'es qaoχaχa''mse·ts ta'χas ła·
q!a·'piłtsᴇmak!e'₁ne·. ne₁ yɛsaqapte'₁ke· k!anaχa'ka k.łaqa'-
łoqałnok!ᵘɛ'nme·k. qake'₁ne· ktsqa'piłno·k!ᵘɛ'n·mo· a'm·a·ks
k!anaχa'ka. ktsχałtsk'nam ne₁s ya·qaoχałao·naχonakɛ'ske·
75 aₐ'kɛłmi'yet·s. tsχał·ao·mok̆ᵘɑ'anaχa'ka. n'ɛ'n·e· ałtsa'ₐt₁mu
yama'kpa·ł. tá'χas k.łats̆k'na·mts k.łao·'na·m qo'sts łaya·qao-
χał·a'o·na·mke·. ta'χas łao·moka'χe·. ta'χas łake₁ka'mke·
ne₁s aₐ'qeya'mła·pshak.łeɛ'tske· qa'kɑ'u'pχₐne·ma·'łne· nöpɛ'k!a·s,
qak.ła'pse· "ɛn hɛntsłaya·qana'mke· hɛn·'u'pχa kia'kχo·. maₐts
80 hɛntsqunya'χₐne· hɛnła·'a·qaoχayɛksɛ'łe·k." ło'q̆ᵘałqakɛ'łne·:
"maₐts hɛntsqaoχa'yɛksɛ'łe·k n'a·'qakɑłhaq!anqots!!a'e·n'." ta'χas
sɛlyahał'antsakna'mne·. ta'χas kts̆k'na·m yama'kpa·ł ałtsa'ₐ-
t₁mu. qana'χɛtsqawa·'qa·l'upkaqa'iłuqu'se· to'ho·ls. qałwi'yne·
yama'kpa·ł ktsχał'u'pe·ł. qak.ła'pse· ma'ₐka·'s: "a· qanaqas-
85 nikɛ't₁ne·. kɛn'wɑ'atɑts χma kɛntsła·ɛ'sɪnqałnɛkɛtk₁na''te·t." ta'-
χasts l'ɛ'ne· ma'ₐka qa'ₐłɛn tsχałqunya'χats a·t a·nłaho·łqaiłu-
qu'se·ts at qawokᵘɛ'n·e·. qa'ₐłɛn ne₁s łaqal'u'pkałqaqa'pse·
wu'u·sts qa.u'pχₐne·ts pe.ɛ'k!aks pa·ł sl'o·'noq!wiyatqła'pse·
yawo'ᵤne·k!s. ta'χas ne₁sts n'ao·'k!we· kts̆k'na·m qa·na'χe·
90 qa'ₐłɛn łaχa'χe· ya·kɑłhaq!a·'nqots!łaɛ'nske·. sɛlwałkwayɛ'-
ts·e·ts kɛk₁yɛksɛ'łe·k. ta'χas kq!u·''mne· qahak.łe'₁tsne·ts
n'o·'k!ᵘɛnł'aqsa·'na·łɛnk!ałaq!nuχna'pse· ko̧ukuna'na·s. qałwi'yne·
χma hakamχune'₁ke· yama'kpa·ł naₐsts łɛn'ɑɛ'kte·ts qa.ɛn·tse'₁-
te·. ta'χas kq!u·''mne· pa·ł sɛłt!apts!e'₁se· ne₁s ko̧ukuna'na·s.
95 ta'χas słqa'qałqaqa'ₐne·. ta'χas pa·ł ksl'o·ʼk!ᵘɛ'l'ɛps ałtsa'e·s
yama'kpa·ł ksɑl'upła'pse·s yawo'ᵤne·k!s. n'ɛt₁numo·tstɛ'łne·
yama'kpa·ł. qake'₁ne·: "hułuq!ma·łk.łu·'nisna'ₐła aₐ'kuwuk.łe'-
et." ta'χas n'ana'χe·. ta'χas ko·'kᵘin ke'e·k. ta'χas k.łats̆k'kam
qo·'s aₐ'ko·'q!nu·ks. łaqawa'ₐka·ł yu·waqa'χe·. n'ɛsaknu'n·e·.
100 qaₐkił'u'pχₐne· nałmö'qtse·s. nałmö'qtse· n'ɛ'n·e· ne₁ kwɛ'łqa
tɛ'tqa·t!. ta'χas sa·'kiłhamatɛ'ktse· aₐ'kɛk.łeye·ɛ'se·s naₐs
a'm·a·ks. ne₁s qaha'χe· naₐs aₐ'k!ałe'et·s ne₁s k!u'pχa ·yama'k-
pa·ls ałtsa'ₐt₁mu's qakɛ'łne·: "a· ałkaha'tsa o·kᵘmɛtpɛsta'p-
ke₁ł." yama'kpa·ł sa·'hanłukpakta'pse· ne₁s hatsa''e·sts
105 sa·nɑwiyna'ₐte·ts tsukᵘa'te· aₐ'kte'₁mo·'s. χunmɛ'te·ts k!tu-
k.ła'ₐko·ps. tsukᵘa'te· aₐ'kɛ'łweys n'oqoχakɛ'n·e· ne₁s

Then | the Bats flew down, spreading out their blankets. | They used them for wings. The Flying Squirrel pulled out | his skin and used it for wings. He used it to fly with. || All the fish threw themselves 65 down. The Sucker was the | only one who was broken to pieces. All tried to restore him, but it could not be done. All the manitous | touched him; and when some one tried to fix him, he put | pieces of his own flesh on. They thought it would cure him, but he was not cured. | There was Sucker's brother's widow. He always wanted her to touch him. || Then she also went to him, and | his brother's 70 widow touched him. Then he | was well again.

Those warriors who were left behind | did not know how to get back. They said: "Being warriors, we shall finally reach the earth (?)." | They were about to start for the place where heaven and earth meet. || They were about to go to war. These were the brothers | Wood- 75 pecker. They started back to go down to the place | where they had come down. Then they reached the ground. When they came back, | at Nelson they met the manitous, | and were told: "When you go back, you will see a fish. Don't || touch it, wherever you may stay 80 over night." They were also told: | "Don't stay over night where there are thick trees." Then | they bewitched one another. Wood- pecker and his | brothers were going along; and while they were going along, they found a charr drifted ashore. | Woodpecker thought he would kill it. He said to Flicker: "Many things || have been done. 85 Have you a great name, and is it right that you make trouble? (?)" | Flicker was just about to touch the charr when it | went back into the water, and he did not touch it. It happened that the water was rolling in toward the shore, | and without his knowing it he was swallowed | by the Water Monster. Then the other one started and went along. || He came to a place where there were thick woods. 90 It was getting evening, | and he camped there over night. Then, while he was asleep, | a little toad went under his blanket. Wood- pecker thought | what he had been told did not mean anything, and he did not mind what was said to him. | Then he went to sleep. The little toad stuck on his body. || It was always like that. At one time 95 the younger brother | Woodpecker died. The Water Monster had killed him. A law had been made | for Woodpecker (?).

He said: "We will go around the mountains." | Then they went hunting. When the food was done, they started to come back | to the lake. They came up and sat down. || Then he saw Naḷmu'qtse.[1] 100 Naḷmu'qtse was a large | man. He was going about giving names | to the country. He followed this Kutenai River. He saw Woodpecker | and his brothers, and said to them: "O nephews! give me some food." | Woodpecker hated his uncle Naḷmu'qtse. || He was angry at 105 him, and took a whetstone, threw it into the fire until | it was red-hot. He took the heart of a Mountain Goat and put | the whetstone into

---

[1] See pp. 87 et seq.

aₐkteʼᵢmo·ʼs.　　 taʼχasts　　qakɛʼłne·　　kɬmaˑʼɫɴk!ało′ma·s.
taʼχas ts!ᴀnmɛʼte·.　n′uʼpχₐne·　nałmö′qtse·　neᵢs　ksɛlsa-
nɛlwiyna′ₐteˑł　n′ɛsqaq!ana`q!ne·ʼnɛ′łne·.　n′a·stsɛnło·χałhaq!ma-
110　nqaʼpse·.　qakeʼᵢne·:　"heʼhe　heʼhe　he·ʼ."　　qakeʼᵢne·:
"ksɛlsa·nɛlwiyna′tap ałkaʼtsa·, ksɛlyu·`k!kᵘa·kaʼta·p." k.łqaˑʼłʼat.-
łɛʼtᵢna·m knɛlwiʼynana′ke·.　taʼχas sɛlaoka′χe·　ɛs aₐko·ʼq!nu·ksts
n′uʼpχₐne· wɛʼtsweᵢts· tsɛʼtsqo·ms.　qakɛʼłne·　namatɛʼktse· keʼ-
eksts qakɛʼłne·:　"hᴀntsχałya`nału·q!nu`ku·kɛʼłne· hᴀntsqakeʼᵢne·
115　`mantsuk!ᶸna′łkił, mantsuk!ᶸna′łkił, mantsuk!ᶸna′łkił, man-
tsuk!ᶸna′łkił.′"　qakiłɛʼłne·:　"hᴀnqa·ełkᵢna′pke·ł hᴀntskɛʼłkułmoł-
kɛʼłne·."　taʼχasts qakeʼᵢne· neᵢ kianałuq!ᶸnoku′kwe·.　taʼχas
kts!ɛʼn·a·m naₐ qaoχałʼałtᵢna·wɛʼtsq!no·ks.　taʼχas at qaʼkɛlhaq-
wɛʼłne·ts at słqakɛʼłne·.　q!aʼpeᵢs kiaʼkχo·ʼs k.łʼuʼpa·ʼs aₐkɛt.-
120　łɛʼseˑs yamaʼkpaˑłs ktsχaʼłʼe·ks.　taʼχas k.łała′χaₐm taʼχas
q!aʼpe· kiaʼkχo· n′upaʼχe· qo·ᵤs aₐkɛt.łana′me·s.　qakiłɛʼłne·
yamaʼkpaˑł n′upsakmoχo′ᵤne· naso′ᵤkwe·n, taχta′ tsχałʼɛʼsnił-
toq!tsqak.łɛʼsᵢne·.　nawɛtskpayatɛʼłne·ts　waʼχe·　k!ɛʼk!o·mʼ.
taʼχas łaχaʼχe· namatɛktsɛʼłne· aₐko′ła·ʼs.　taʼχas k!ɛknu-
125　qo·ʼqo· paˑł yamaʼkpaˑł ałtsaʼₐtᵢmu q!aʼpe· keʼɛn tɛʼtqₐtˡs
n′o·k!ᶸita′mne·　paˑłkeᵢ　n′ɛʼnse·　ałnana′e·s　kaʼtska·ts.
taʼχasts kaʼtska·ts n′ɛʼsnɛlʼuʼpχₐne· k!ɛʼk!o·mʼs neᵢs k!e·k-
nuqo·ʼqus　pa·ł　pe·ʼk!a·ks　sɛlts!ᴀnne·q!ałˑe·kaku′pse·.
qakeʼᵢne·:　"kaˑʼas　kapapana′ła　k!aqa′qna."　neᵢs　qan-
130　mᴀq!ałʼɛ`kako′ᵤnets　naₐs　qaoχaq!ałɛkaqo′ᵤne·.　　taʼχas
sɛltsχa`natkaʼₐne·　neᵢs　ksaosaʼqa·ps　naₐs　aₐko·ʼq!no·ks.
taʼχasts sɛlhułtoq!tsqakeʼᵢne·.　taʼχas qakiłɛʼłne·.　taʼχas
huso′ᵤkᶸɛlq!o′ᵤkᵤne·:　"taʼχa łuʼn·u."　taʼχas łahołqkupɛlqakₐ-
naʼₐne·　kiaʼkχo·.　taʼχas ts!ᴀnałqanaʼʼnte· kiʼe·k.　at słaqa-
135　qaʼₐne·　kiaʼkχo·　naₐs　a·t　kia·`q!an·oʼho·s　n′ɛʼnse·　aₐko′-
ła·ks　neᵢs　kiʼe·k.　taʼχas　n′itaqna′me·ˡ　ktsχałʼoʼpił
yawo′ᵤne·k!s.　qakeʼᵢne·:　"taʼχas　hutsχałhułnu′qₐne·,
hutsχałʼɛts!kɛʼłne·."　taʼχas paˑł kaqa wuʼsa·q! n′o·k!ᶸił-
qałʼatɛʼłne·.　nułnu′qᵤne·ts.　qakeʼᵢne·:　"kaʼmin wuʼsaq!;
140　kaʼmin wuʼsaq!."　taʼχasts sɛlhałˑaχwaʼte·k n′uʼpskɛlqa`wił-
hułnu′qᵤne·.　at k!ɛktsno·ʼqo·.　taʼχas ła.upkaʼχe· ɛʼn·ta·sts
qaₐkiłqaʼₐtse·　yamaʼkpaˑł.　n′ɛʼsniłkᵢnu′qᵤne·　n′ɛtskɛʼłne·.
taʼχas k!uʼpχa·.　qałwiʼyne· ktsχałq!aʼkpakɛtqo·ʼke· aₐ`k-
łamʼɛʼse·s　ktsχałqaoχak.łɛʼkχa.　　wɛʼt!qkupqo·q!amˑakiʼne·ts
145　yu·`k!ka·ₐkaʼte·.　taʼχas neᵢs łu`qano·ʼtqo·kɛʼłne· neᵢs k.ło·ʼ-
qᶸak!ałe·ʼet.s　neᵢs　łałoka′χe·　ya·`kiłɛʼnske·.　ya`qona′ske·.
łaqaka′χe.　neᵢs yaknuso′ᵤkske.　qałwiʼyne· ktsχałqa`nałtsa-
qaʼna·m.　qunakᴀnχaʼłne·.　n′oʼła·n·e· yamaʼkpaˑł aₐ`ke·
łayu·`k!ka·ₐkaʼte·.　no·`k!ᶸłoqłaqłe·k!o·ʼłne·.　qakałtunwa`ₐkałha-
150　nuso′ᵤkᵤne·, słʼakaqaʼₐne· kqałʼat.łɛʼtna·m ya·knoso′ᵤkᶸe·.
łaₐtskaʼχe·ts　ɛs　yaₐkwuʼła·ks　aₐ`ke·　qa`oχałʼupaʼχe·.

it. Then he told him to open his mouth. | Then he threw it.
Nalmu'qtse knew that he was | angry with him. He nodded his head,
and (the whetstone) stood there just alongside of him. ‖ He said: 110
"He'he he'he he'!" He said: | "My brothers are angry with
me. I have escaped." | The name of that place was Little·
Heart.[1] Then he came down the lake and | saw a Water Bird[2] and
a Water Ousel. He spoke to them and gave them | food. He
said to them: "You will go along each side of the lake. You will
say, ‖ 'You are invited, you are invited, you are invited, | you are 115
invited, you are invited.'" They were told: "If you don't come
to me, your lake will be dried up." | Then those who went on each
side of the lake said so. | Wherever there is a bay here, there they
danced. | He said to them: "All the fish shall come ashore to the
tent of ‖ Woodpecker to eat (his food)." Then, when he came back, | 120
all the fish came ashore, there at the tent. Woodpecker | was told:
"The chief has not come back yet. He will | tell you something."
They waited for him, and the fish[3] arrived. | When he arrived, he
was given a pipe. Then he, ‖ Woodpecker, and his brothers, smoked. 125
They were all men. | Only one of them was a woman; namely, their
younger sister (a bird with yellow breast and gray feathers). | Then
the sister herself saw the fish smoking | and moving his eyebrows
while he was smoking. | He said: "Where is our grandson?" Then ‖
he moved his eyebrows in this direction. He moved them a little 130
ways. | Then he told them that (the grandson) was on this lake. |
He finished telling the news. Then he was told: "Now | I am glad.
Now go!" Then the fish went back into the water quickly. | Then
he had some food. ‖ The fish is like that. He is red on each side; | 135
that is the meat, the food (that he was given).

Now they made ready to kill | the Water Monster. Woodpecker said:
"I'll go into the water; | I'll search for him." Now they saw one person
named Long Legs. | He went into the water and said: "I am Long Legs, ‖
I am Long Legs." He was proud of himself. He had not gone | far 140
from the lake shore when he sank down. Next Woodpecker himself
went along the lake shore | and went into the water. He searched for
him. | Then he saw (the monster). He thought he would kick him dead
in the water. He intended to kick him | on the head, but the blow
glanced off from the head. ‖ He missed it. Then (the monster) was 145
chased this way along the | other big river. It came back this way by
way of Windermere. | It came back to Red Water. It thought it would
go along that river, | but it was stabbed by Woodpecker. The mon-
ster | escaped again. It was hit on the foot. There was some blood, ‖
and the water turned red. Therefore it is named Red Water. | It 150

[1] Name of a place east of Nelson, which was given its name by Nalmu'qtse owing to this incident.
[2] A small gray bird living on the lake shore.
[3] A small fish with large head and small tail.

qaʻoχaĺupaʻχe· aₐʻkiĺaʻłaquʼnoˑksts aqanaqoˑχuʼʼmne· yamaʻkpaˑł. namatɛʻktse· aₐˑkᵢyukᵘaʼeˑs nałmuχnaʼyiˑt tsu-
k!otiyaˑĺeˑs. qakɛʻlne·: "neᵢs hɛnʼuʼpχa łapskaˑĺaka'wats!ts

155 hɛntsqakɛʻlne·: ʻaˑ heʻiˑ.'ʼ" ma nʼoʼpsawɛtsaˑₐkɛʼnχa yamaʻkpaˑł
öpɟnaʻwe· yawoʼᵤnek!s. qakiłɛʻlne·: "naₐsts hɛntsqakɛʻlne·
tsχaˑłtsĺoʻnił/ˈsᵢneˑts hɛntsɟsoˑkqaʻoχakᵢnaʻχaneˑ." taʻχas
nʼoʻnaqoᵤq!ankɛʼmeˑk yamaʻkpaˑł sɟʻɛts!kɟqoˑkᵘɛʼneˑ. taʻχas
qakiłɛʻlne· nałmeχnaʼyet [1] łaₐpsaʻkχawaʼtsᵢne·. taχas na-

160 wɛtsnułkloʻᵤne·. qakeʻᵢne·: "aˑ, ma łaˑpsaₐwɛtsaˑkɛʼnχa
nałmuχnaʼyit uʼpiłnaʻwe· yawoʼᵤneˑk!s." maˑ kqaˑk.łaps
yamaʻkpaˑłs kts!ak!łanaʻke· siˑĺuʼpt!enmɛtɛˑłwiyχonaʼpse·
paˑł ksɟʻɛseka'teˑs. taʻχasts sɟyuˑk!kᵘaˑkaˑte·. taʻχasts
kᵤwuʼᵤkaˑt yawoʼᵤneˑk!s qak.łaʼpse·: "maˑ kułɛʼʼmˑqoˑł."

165 sɟpɛsnɛnmɛʼte· neᵢs ktsqunaʻₐkinχaʼmˑo. tsɟˑahoʼᵤsanuχun-
qaʼₐneˑ. taʻχas qakiłɛʼlne· nałmöʻqtse·: "łatsk/ʼnaˑnʼ
ɛn yɛsoʼᵤχaq!noʼᵤke·. hɛntsχałmaʼnuqk/ˈknatɛʼtᵢneˑ. maₐts kɛnˑła-
qayaʻₐqałqaʼₐtseˑ." nɛ/sts keʼᵢwaˑm yɛswaₐkaq!nuʼkske·
sɟqanaqlɛ/ˈkχₐneˑ ɛs aₐˑkwuk.łeʼets. sɟqasɟuˑnʼmɛtɛkɛʼneˑ.

170 taʻχas sɛʼłtsɛʼniłqoᵤqmɛχumuʼneˑ [2] aₐˑq!anaʻk!eˑs. taʻχas
yamaʻkpaˑł k.łaₐtskanuʼtqoˑł. taʻχas yunaqᵤwuʼmne· kanut-
quʼleˑł. skɛʼnˑkuˑts paˑł nɛʼneˑ· kałnukuʼpqa. kwaʼnχoˑ
nałkɛʼneˑ aₐˑkɛnuʼqłeʼs. taʻχas kwaʼnχoˑ tsχałtsłqaʻnaqkup-
łaˑʼłte· neᵢs qałtseᵢkataʼpseˑ. qak.łaʼpseˑ: "ma kułɛʼʼmˑqoˑł."

175 łaˑhoˑsaₐnχunqaʼₐneˑ naʼk!ᵢyu. taʻχasts qaʻsoᵤsaʻχeˑ. taʻχasts
nɛ/ˈsniłtsukᵘaʼte· neᵢs aₐˑknuʼqłeʼs. taʻχasts k.łaχaʼʼnχoˑ. neᵢs
qałtseᵢkataʼpseˑ. qakɛ/ʼlne·: "aˑ heʻi. keʼᵢło· tɛʼtqaˑt!; hoʼpaks
koɛʼsniłqanłaʼłeˑt yawoʼᵤneˑk!." aₐˑk.łamɛʼseˑs qaoχałaʼłteˑ.
taʻχas paˑł ksɟq!aqpakɛʼtχoˑ. taʻχas qaₐkɟʼoᵤmɛtsqaʼlne·.

180 taʻχas tsɛk!qaʼlne·. łaqakχałʼanaχaʼmne· maʼₐka aʼₐˑke łaʼtuq!
tɟnamoʼtᵢmuˑ. naₐs at paˑł kqaʻₐkɛsq!anˑmenuʼqło· łaʼtuq!ts
aʼₐˑke maʼₐka. taʻχasts sɟʼɛktoqoʼᵤmeˑk. taʻχasts nɛ/ʼsnił-
qakeʼᵢne· łaʼtuq!ts maʼₐka; paˑł łaʼtuq! tɟnamoʼᵤtᵢmo keʼen
k!oʻnoq!ᵘwiˑʼyatqułmuʼnˑaps yawoʼᵤneˑk!s yaqsoʼmɛˑĺeˑs. qakeʼᵢ-

185 ne· qoᵤsts haosaqaʼₐke· aₐˑkwumɛʼseʼs yawoʼᵤneˑk!s at ksɛn-
q!oᵤkoχaʼmeˑk yaqsoʼmɛˑĺeˑs at qaʻk.łaps: "maₐts k.łuˑ-
wɛʼłɛnq!oˑkoχaʼmeˑk. łoˑq!koˑps aqaɛʼseˑs. taʻχasts maʼₐka
sɟqasnanukχoʼlne· słɛʼneˑsqaʼpteˑk.

  Taʻχas nʼomɛtsqaʼlne· łuqᵘałɛʼsᵢne· aₐˑknokaʼk!eˑs. ts!ᵏᵢmɛt.-

190 kɛʼsᵢne·. na nałʼoˑnanmitoʼᵤke· na hanᵚmuʼk!ke· ɛsts nɛ/ʼnseˑ
aₐˑknokaʼk!eˑs. nʼaoˑk!ᵘists qoᵤs łałuqᵘanɛnˑmit.łɛʼsᵢne· qoᵤsts
yaₐkiłʼomitsqaʼłke·. taʻχasts słʼaqaˑĺat.łɛtitnaʼmne· yaₐkɛno-
kaˑʼke·. neᵢsts aₐˑkułaʻk!ɛsts taʻχas k!omɛtsqaʼłeˑs paˑtsnɛn-
mit.łɛʼsᵢne·. naₐsts iyɛʼsaˑts qaʻkiłhaqaʼₐke· aqłsmaʻkᵢnɛk!

came back to Long-Water Bay,[1] and | there it went ashore. It went ashore into a cave under water. There it went in. | Woodpecker gave his war bonnet and his | spear to Flicker, and said to him: "If you see it coming out of the water, ‖ say 'Ahei!'" Woodpecker was ready | to kill the Water Monster. He was told: "You must say this, 'Ahei!' | Then it will be afraid of you, and you will hit it in the right place." Then Woodpecker | stepped into the water. He waited for it. Then | he was told that Flicker was going there. He stood ‖ ready to spear the monster. He said: "Ah! Flicker is waiting to spear it. | He will kill the Water Monster." | Woodpecker had told him differently. He trembled for fear, for | the monster looked fierce. Then he missed it. When | the Water Monster saw him, it said to him, "I shall swallow you." ‖ Then Flicker let go the spear and ran away. |

Then Naᴌmu'qtse was told: "Start for | the end of the lake and shut up the water. Don't let it | go through." When he arrived at the end of the lake, | he kicked this mountain[2] and broke a piece off. ‖ Then he made the mud solid with his knees. | Then Woodpecker started in pursuit. Many were pursuing | the monster. Coyote was the fastest one. He caught up with it. | He carried his tomahawk pipe. He caught up with it, and was just about to strike it. | Then the Water Monster looked at him, and said, "I'll swallow you," ‖ and he ran away. Next Fox overtook him and | took the tomahawk pipe. When he caught up to it, | he looked at it, and said: "Ahei! there is no other man like me. I shall be the first | to strike the Water Monster." He hit its head, | killed it, and it was cut to pieces. ‖ Then it was cut open. Then Flicker and Duck | and his wife came out. Duck and | Flicker were white on each side. They washed themselves. Then | Duck and Flicker and Duck's wives, | those who had been swallowed by the Water Monster in their canoe, said ‖ that while they had been in the belly of the Water Monster | they had made a fire with their canoe. They had been told: "Don't | make a big fire; it might melt the fat (of the monster)." Then Flicker | was worn down to his present size. |

Then the ribs on one side of the monster were cut off. They were thrown away ‖ down the river. The one side of the ribs is now a cliff below. | Then the other side was thrown away, there | where it was being cut up. Therefore the cliff is named Standing Rib. | Then its body was cut up and was | scattered about where there are people. ‖

155

160

165

170

175

180

185

190

---

[1] South of Windermere. [2] Pointed out by the narrator.

195 ktsxaʼTⁿs keʼcᵏts aₐ`kuła´k!eˑs.  ta´xas  k.ła´łoᵤs  aₐ`ku-
ła´k!eˑsts q!akpayoˑtɛ´łneˑ naₐ aqłsmaʼkinck!. qoᵤsts yaₐ-
qaˋ`knuq!mɛ´łkeˑ saˋk!łqaskiki´łⁱtuʼkᵤneˑ. qakyaʼmneˑ ɛsts
ksuwɛ´suqs aₐ`koᵤk!ała´ₐk!eˑs. ta´xas ksɛłhonɛ´keⁱt qakiłam-
naʼmneˑ: "kaₐsts ktsxaʼTⁿs naₐ ha´kⁱłhaqaʼₐkeˑ aqłs-
200 maʼkinck! hoˑsłqaʼₐkiłʼoˋpiłnaˋla nʼɛ´sᵢneˑ amˑaʼk!eˑs." ta´xas
łatsokoˑknɛ´łneˑ waʼnˑmoˑ paˑł kpaₐtsɛnmuʼxoˑ. qak-
yaʼmneˑ: "naₐs tsxałʼɛ´nseˑ naₐ aqłsmaʼkᵢneˑk!. ta´xas
tsxałnʼɛ´nˑeˑ tsxałtsamnaʼneˑ na aqłsmaʼkᵢneˑk!. tsxał-
qayunaqaʼₐneˑ tsqaɛ´tełxoˋᵤmeˑk. ts!upsłaʼtɛyiłhaqaʼₐneˑ
205 mɛ´ka yunaʼqaps kwaˋnaqnaʼnapsts tsxałqatałʼoᵤktaʼpseˑ."
ta´xas sɛłhoknɛ´łneˑ. ta´xas słqaqaʼsᵢneˑ.

[No. 51. Told by Felix Andrew (recorded by Robert T. Aitken)]

51. THE GIANT

Qaₐk.łunaʼmneˑ kiʼas nɛtstaʼhał nʼɛnˑe tsaʼₐtᵢmoˑ. k!oˑkunmiʼ-
yɛt.sts nałʼanaʼxeˑ neᵢ tsaʼₐtᵢmo. qaˑkqaˑʼtseˑ neᵢ kwɛ´łqaˑ nʼuʼp-
xaneˑ kwɛ´łqłeˑʼsts, nʼɛłwaʼnˑeˑ łatskałoˑkałkɛ´nˑeˑ. ta´xas sɛłwał-
kwayɛ´t.seˑ, ta´xas nowaʼsᵢneˑ. qałweˑʼyne: "hułʼaq!amałʼɛłkoxaʼ-
5 mekts hutsxałˑuk!moxaʼmeˑk. hunheˑʼłⁱktskutsʼɛtwask!onɛ´łek."
ta´xas qasɛłxunmɛ´teˑ neᵢs kwɛ´łqłeˑʼsts kuʼkopsts nʼɛ´kᵢneˑ.
łɛtk!amxonełaxnɛ´seˑtsqałweˑʼyneˑ:"hułqasɛłˑoqaˑʼmek kułuk!mo-
xaˑʼmek." ta´xas qasɛłˑoˑqaʼmɛkts xunmɛ´teˑ. koˑʼkopsts ta´xas
nʼɛ´kᵢneˑ soˑkaxneʼᵢseˑ łaqasɛłˑoˑqᵘneˑts łaxunmɛ´tets łaɛ´kᵢneˑ.
10 nʼaimeyɛ´t.sits kq!apxaʼmɛk. ta´xas tsɛn ɛnqaptaʼkseˑ maʼk!eˑs.
ta´xas neᵢstsaʼcˑs k.łałaˑʼxasts, kkanmiʼyɛt.s qałweˑʼyseˑ:"hułts!ɛ-
nałɛ´tskɛł kaʼtaˑt." ts!ɛnaʼxeˑ. qaˑnaʼxeˑ neᵢs ma yaˋₐkɛłʼanaʼₐm-
keˑ. qaoxaʼxeˑ nułpałnitɛ´tᵢneˑ nałuk.łɛɛʼt.seˑ nʼɛtᵤwɛsqaʼₐneˑts
tsɛn k!apałteʼłcˑk. qahaq!yuˑminaʼseˑ qoˑsts paˑł qanak!aˋ-
15 pałtɛ´łeˑk. qaoxaʼxeˑts kᵢyuʼᵤxaˑm. qoˑnawɛtskɛ´kᵢneˑ sanɛnq!o-
kuʼpseˑ. qaoxaʼxeˑ nułpaˑʼłne paˑł nɛłkɛ´kseˑ neᵢs taˑʼt!eˑs paˑł
qakɛ´kseˑ: "heyâ´, ma kutsła´kɛł kaʼtsats kutsa.imɛtɛ´tᵢmo."
ta´xas qaoxaʼxeˑ k!uʼpxanaˋps mɛtyaxnaˑʼpseˑ qanłałtmonaˑʼpseˑ
aₐ`koˑqᵘt!eⅼɛ´seˑsts qanmɛtxomonaʼpseˑts nʼupłaˑʼpseˑ. qaₐ-
20 qwuʼmneˑts qakᵢyaʼmneˑ: "xma hɛ´nʼɛtskɛłkɛ´łne neᵢ tsaʼₐtᵢmu."
ts!ɛnaʼseˑ neᵢ kwɛ´łqa tɛłnamoˑʼeˑs nʼɛtsk.łaʼpseˑ. qaˑnaʼxeˑ neᵢ
paˑʼłkeᵢ. qanak!aˋpałtɛ´łeˑk nałukᵘłɛɛʼt.seˑ. qaoxaʼxeˑ qonawɛts-
kɛ´łneˑ sanaqₐanaˑʼkseˑ paˑł qakɛ´kseˑ: "heyâ´ ma kutsła´kiˑł kan-
xaʼłeⁱts kutsa.imɛtɛ´tᵢmo." nʼok!ᵘɛnłˑaaˑʼntsoxaʼxeˑ neᵢ paˑʼłkeᵢts
25 qakiłɛ´łne: "tapts!eʼᵢtɛnʼ ak!anoˋᵤkoˑ aₐ`qatwuʼmłatnɛ´smiˑł
tsxałqanłaˋʼłtᵢmunɛ´sᵢneˑ aₐ`koˑqᵘt!eˑʼeˑs. tsxałsłaˋʼłasqₐanapsɛ´sᵢneˑ
neᵢs noʼᵤkᵛeᵢs. tsxaˋʼłsłqataˑłtsɛnkɛnɛ´sᵢneˑ." ta´xas ktaʼptsleⁱt
noʼᵤkᵛeᵢs aₐ`qatwumłaʼₐt!eˑs. ta´xas k!q!aₐqat!oˑʼxam qanłałtaˑʼp-
seⁱts q!axoˑnaˑʼkseˑ aₐ`koqt!eⅼɛ´seˑs. paˑł kaˑʼłkɛn neᵢs aqaˑʼłt!eˑs

Its flesh was to be their food.   Then its body was gone entirely, | and 195
the people here had been forgotten, where | it was being carved.
There was no water there.   Some one said: "Is that | in the water
there its backbone?"   When it was all done, they talked | among
themselves.   "What shall belong to these ‖ people, because we killed 200
it on their own land?"   Then | they picked up the blood and scat-
tered it.   They | said: "This will belong to these people. | These peo-
ple will be few.   They will | not be many.   They will not increase,
but they will always remain; ‖ even if many make war against them, 205
they can not be exterminated." | Now it is finished.   The end. |

[No. 51. Told by Felix Andrew (recorded by Robert T. Aitken)]

51. The Giant[1]

There was a town.   One day | two men, brothers, went out hunting.
The two brothers were going along.   The elder one | saw a bighorn
sheep and shot it.   He carried it down.   Then toward | sunset he
became hungry.   He thought: "I'll make a fire ‖ and roast a piece of   5
meat.   When I have finished eating, I will hang up the meat and
dry it." | Then he threw a piece of the bighorn-sheep meat into the
fire.   When it was cooked, he ate it. | It was without taste.   He
thought: "I'll cut a piece of my own body and I'll roast it in the
fire." | Then he cut a piece off of himself and threw it into the fire.
When it was done, | he ate it.   It tasted good.   He cut off another
piece and threw it into the fire and ate it. ‖ After two days he had   10
eaten himself entirely.   Only his bones were left. | Then his younger
brother went home, and the following morning he thought: "I will
go and | look for my elder brother."   He started and went along to
the place where they had been hunting. | He arrived there and heard
a sound.   He stood still | and listened.   There was a hill.   He heard
the sound ‖ from that direction.   He arrived there and went up.. A   15
little ways off | there was a fire.   He went there, and he heard his
elder brother making that noise.   He was | saying: "Oh, I love my
brother, and it will take me two days to eat him!" | Then he arrived
there.   The elder brother saw him and ran after him. | He struck him
with his intestines, and threw him down with them and killed him. ‖
Those at home said they ought to look for the brothers. | The elder   20
one's wife started looking for them.   The woman | went along.   She
heard a sound somewhere.   She went there, and she saw him from a
little ways off | sitting down.   He was saying: "Oh, I love | my son!
It will take me two days to eat him."   The woman went along behind
a hill. ‖ Something told her: "Stick sharp stones on your clothing. | 25
He will strike you with his intestines, and the stones will cut them. |
Then he will not be able to catch you."   Then she stuck | stones on
her clothing.   She went nearer.   He struck her, | and his intestines

---
[1] See p. 272.

30 qawoqankɛ'nse·   neᵢs   no·łaqₐna'e·s.   łahe·tsi'nqkupe·kɛ'me·kts
mɛtyaxna·'pse·.   pał   ke'ɛns   ma·k!s   qata·łts!ɛna·'kse·.   łaqa·o·-
xa'xe·ts   qake'ᵢne·: "pał   q!a'pxₐne·   kanuł a'qₐna   tsa'e·s.   qał-
we·'yne·   a'ₐ'ke·   ktsxał'ɛ'txa   kanxałe'ᵢmił.   mats tsxa'xe·."   ta'xas
qakᵢya'mne·: "hułhoqᵘnaneya'ła."   qakᵢya'mne·: "qa'ła   ke'ɛn
35 kwiłɛ'łwey   tsxałqahaosaqa·'ₐne·ts   tsxał'upɛ'łne·   n'aqaske·'ł-
was."   qake'ᵢne·   skɛ'n·ku·ts: "hutsxał'ɛsi'niłqaha·o·saqa'ₐne·."
qakiłɛ'łne·: "ma·ₐts."   qake'ᵢne·   qaspɛ'ł'o·kᵘ: "hutsxał'ɛsi'niłqaha·-
osaqa'ₐne·."   qakiłɛ'łne·: "so'ᵤkᵘne·."   ta'xas   qaha·osaqa'ₐne·
qaspɛ'ł'u·kᵘts,   a'ₐ'ke·   tɛłnamo''ɛsts   xałe'e·s   neᵢ   tɛ'tqa·t!.   ta'xas
40 no'qᵘnane·ya'mne·.   qaosaqa'ₐne·   neᵢ   kqa'łsa.   qawunekɛ't.se·,
ta'xas   kts!ɛ'na·ɪn   qałspɛ'ł'okᵘ.   ta'xas   wa'xe·   neᵢ   tɛ'tqa·t!.   łało-
namɛ'sᵢne·.   n'asqapta'kse·   tɛłnamu''e·sts   xałe'e·s.   k!u'pxa   tɛłnamu''e·sts   qakɛ'łne·: "tskake'nin'   łka'm·u."   namatɛktsa'pse·,
ktsu'ᵤka·t.s   neᵢs   qa·ł'asqaoxaya'xₐne·ts   tsɛk!kɛ'n·e·.   qałwe·'yne·
45 ktsxa'ł'e·k.   qak.ła'pse·   tɛłnamu''e·s: "tskake'nen'   hutsxałts!i-
nał'iktuqo'ᵤne·.   saha'nse·   a'q!ołe'e·s."   namatɛ'ktse·   tɛłnamu''e·s.
tsukᵘa'te·   neᵢ   pa'łkeᵢ   ts!ɛnałxona·łkɛ'n·e·.   k!antso'xamts   n'ɛł-
qanmɛ'te·ts   n'ɛtsinqkupe·kɛ'm·e·k.   sɛłts!ɛnanxokᵘa'ₐne·.   k.ła·-
xan·xo·'ka·ts   qake'ᵢne·: "wa'xe·   neᵢs   yaqake·'ᵢkałhoqᵘnaneya-
50 mɛ'ske·.   n'upɛ'łne·   xałe'e·s."   ta'xas   qakiłɛ'łne·   qaspɛ'ł'oᵤkᵘ:
"ła·ts!ɛnamɛ'ł'en'ts   hɛntsxał'upɛ'łne·."   ta'xas   ła·ₐts!ɛna'xe·   qaspɛ'ł'oᵤkᵘ.   qaoxa'xe·   sɛɴʋmo'k!se·.   qanał'ɛtk!a'meknɛ'łe·k   qa'ₐłɛn
yɛ'sɛɴwosa·'q!ke·   qa'sɛɴwoᵤk!amɛ'se·.   ta'xas   qa·haosaqa'ₐne·.

Ta'xas   qahaosaqa'ₐne.   neᵢ   tɛ'tqa·t!.   łaqawa'ₐse·   tɛłnamu'e·s.
55 qałwe·'yne·: "hułts!ɛna'mi·łts   a'ₐ'ke·   kutsxał'u'pe·ł."   qaoxa'xe·
na's   ma   yaqana'ske·ts   ło'ᵤse·   n'uk!kɛkqa'pse·   neᵢs   xałe'e·sts
n'ɛ'kᵢne·.   ta'xas   ts!ɛna'xe·   neᵢs   yaqanaxamɛ'ske·.   qana'xe·
sɛɴʋmo'k!se·.   skɛkɛł'aq!asnamanamɛ'sᵢne·   ɛsts   qaosaqa'pse·
qaspɛ'ł'o·kᵘsts   qaoxa'xe·ts   qa·u'pxₐne·   neᵢs   ksa·'osa'qaps   qas-
60 pɛ'ł'o·kᵘs.   ta'xas   manq!ankɛ'me·k   neᵢs   ak!a'ₐme·s.   k!u'pxₐnaps
qaspɛ'ł'o·kᵘs   neᵢs   qał'ɛt!naqkupq!ałsa'q!se·ts   wat!mɛ'te·kna'-
pse·ts   xunaqo'ᵤne·.   ta'xas   n'ɛ'pᵢne·ts   ta'xas   ts!ɛna'xe·   qaspɛ'ł-
'o·ᵤkᵘ.   ta'xas.

[Nos. 52–77.   Told by Barnaby]

52.   NALMʋ'QTSE·[1]

IIo'ya's,   hutsxałqake'ᵢne·   yaqał'u'pke·   nalmʋ'qtse·   kapapa-
na'łɪ.

Qa·naqₐnu'kᵤne·   nalmʋ'qtse·.   ta'xas   tsxałqawunekɛ't.se·   ktsxa'ł'e·pnaₐsa'm·a·k's ktsxał·a'ło·.   qałwi'yne·: "ta'xas hułama'ₐt-
5 ke·ts   aₐ'kɛk.łiyi'e·s   na   a'm·a·k.   ktsxa·'łsɛłqaq!akpaya'ₐta·p ałka-
a·'qa·łt."   ta'xas   ts!ɛna'xe·.   ta'xas   namatɛ'ktse·   aₐ'kɛk.łiye·ɛ'-
se·s   naₐs   am·akɛ'se·s   ałaaqa'łt!e·s.   ta'xas   kq!a'piłhama'ₐtkits

---

[1] Several times the speaker used the form *Nalmʋqtsin*.

were torn. She carried her child. ‖ Her husband could not catch 30
her. She started to run, | and he pursued her. He was only bones.
He could not run fast. | She got back, and said: "My husband ate his
younger brother, | and he intended to bite my son. He is coming."
Then | they said: "We will move camp." Some one said: "Who has ‖
enough courage to stay and kill him when he comes?" | Coyote said: 35
"I myself shall stay." | He was told: "Don't." Crane said: "I my-
self shall | stay." He was told: "That is good." | Then Crane and the
wife and son of that man staid. ‖ They moved camp, but the three 40
staid there. It was not long before | Crane started. Then the man
arrived. There | was nobody left. Two only were there—his wife
and his son. When he saw | his wife, he said to her: "Give me the
child." She gave it to him. | When he took it, he took hold of it at
the two ends and tore it. ‖ He thought he would eat it. His wife 45
said to him: "Hand it to me. I shall | go and wash it. The dung
is bad." He gave it to his wife. | The woman took it and
carried it down to the water. Then she went behind. | She threw it
away. She began to run. She followed (the other people). When |
she reached them, she said: "He arrived at the place where we
moved camp. ‖ He has killed his boy." Then Crane was told: | "Go 50
back and kill him." Crane went back. | There was a steep bank. He
made a hole for himself. The hole was as long | as his legs. Then he
staid there. |

That man staid there. His wife did not come back. ‖ He 55
thought: "I'll go and kill her." He went | in the direction in
which she had gone. There was nothing there. Only his son was
lying there, | and he ate him. Then he started in the direction in
which she had gone. He went along | the steep bank. The trail
passed close to the bank, and | Crane staid there. He went there,
and did not know that Crane was staying there. ‖ He walked past 60
that hole. Crane saw him. | He stretched out his foot quickly and
kicked him over the bank, | and he fell into the water. Then he was
dead. Then Crane went off. | Enough. |

[Nos. 52–77. Told by Barnaby]

52. Naɫmu'qtse

Well, I am going to tell how our grandfather Naɫmu'qtse | died. |
Naɫmu'qtse was crawling about in the water. It was not (to be)
long before he was | to die in this world, which was to be without
him. He thought: "Now let me give ‖ names to this land, so that 5
my children may not forget me." | Then he started, and he gave
names | to the places of his children. He gave | names to this their

aₐ 'kik.łiye.ɛ'seˑs naₐs amˑaʼkˈleˑs; at qa.owuʼkᵤneˑ neᵢs keʼᵢkqaˑts
at nanuʼkᵤneˑ. tuʼxᵘa at qanałsoʼᵤkseˑ. neᵢs nɛ"nhaˑks neᵢsts qaʼ-
10 nam oˑʼkˈ!ᵘqᵤna at kaˑnuk sɛłʼaqaqaʼpseˑ neᵢs kˈałmanmiʼtuks.
kqaʼnaˑm mö̆ʼka nʼoʼᵤłoˑps at qananuʼkᵤneˑ. nʼuʼpxₐneˑ yamaʼkpaˑłs ałtsaʼₐtᵢmoˑs.   qoᵤs aₐˑkwok.łeʼet.s yuʼnoˑˑs qoᵤs qahaˑkˈła-
qomatɛʼtseˑ. yamaʼkpaˑł sakɛłsaˑniłwiʼyneˑ neᵢs haˑnqˈloˑˑs neᵢs
kuʼtskiˑks, taʼxas ktsˈkɛ'naˑm kˈłanaxaʼka neᵢs kqaˑnałwaʼhaˑm
15 kˈłanaxaʼka; taʼxas kˈlomɛʼtskin neᵢs aₐˑkₐmanaʼmes aʼts!poˑ.
kˈłupxaʼłeˑs pał sɛłhotskeʼᵢneˑ haʼnqˈloˑˑ. taʼxas kqałwiʼynam ktsła-
oˑkᵘaʼxam, pał nʼumɛtskɛʼnˑeˑ aʼts!po aₐˑkₐmanaʼmeˑs. łaqaˑtałʼu-
kaxaʼmneˑ. nʼɛtk!oʼᵤłneˑ nᵥʼmˑa. taʼxas kamaʼₐtił aₐˑkₑnqoʼwa
q!aʼpeˑ aq!oˑk.łuʼpqa. yamaʼkpaˑł ałtsaʼₐtᵢmu łoʼᵤseˑ nₑnkoʼeˑs.
20 taʼxas saˑnɛłwiʼyneˑ. neᵢs yaˑqaʼnaqaˑnuqkaʼskeˑ qanaʼxeˑ at
yaqaʼnałwat!ᴍᴇnuqkaʼskeˑ. łaqahałʼunaʼxeˑ. taʼxas łats!kaʼxeˑ
amˑaʼkˈleˑs. nʼuʼpxa aqłsmaʼkᵢnɛkˈls neᵢs łayaqₐkaʼmkeˑ at
nʼuʼkteˑ. qoᵤs qaₐkiˑłmɛʼtxₐneˑ kianuʼkxoˑˑs qawułe.ɛʼt.seˑ
aₐˑkuʼqˈlnuks. taʼxas keʼeˑk neᵢs kianuʼkxoˑˑs.
25   Nʼuʼpxₐneˑ neᵢs uʼmeˑˑs haqₐnuʼkskeˑ nałmᵥʼqtsins. pał
saʼkiłsanɛʼłwey yamaʼkpaˑł neᵢsts kˈluʼpxa neᵢs nułʼaʼqₐnaˑˑs.
saˑnɛkpaktaʼpseˑ. nʼuʼpxₐneˑ ksaˑkiłhamaₐʼtkiˑts aₐˑkik.łeyɛ'seˑs
naₐs aʼmˑaˑks. qałwiʼyneˑˑ: "hołʼuʼpił nʼɛʼnseˑ hatsaʼeˑs." qakɛʼłneˑ:
"kahaʼtsaˑ." nułpaʼłneˑ nałmᵥʼqtsin hatsaʼeˑs. qakeʼᵢneˑ:
30 "haʼi." qakiłɛʼłneˑ: "hutsxałheˑsɛʼsᵢneˑ. nʼɛₑnqaʼₐpskiłqahwasi-
kɛʼmeˑk kₑnsaˑkeˑłat.łeʼᵢteˑt." qakeʼᵢneˑ nałmᵥʼqtsin: "Háˑ,
hosoʼkᵘiłq!uʼkᵤneˑ." qakiłɛʼłneˑ: "malₑnk!ałɛʼman'."[1] yamaʼkpaˑł
xunakɛʼnˑeˑ noʼᵤkᵘeˑs nʼoqoxᵘakɛʼnˑeˑ aₐˑkɛʼłwiˑs kianuʼqxoˑˑs. neᵢs
kˈluʼtᵢmeˑˑs noʼᵤkweˑs. taʼxas nałmᵥʼqtsin malₑnk!ałmiaʼnˑeˑ.
35 taʼxas yamaʼkpaˑł ts!ₑnałʼonmɛʼteˑ neᵢs aˑkɛʼłwiˑs. pał kᴇnü̆p-
k!aqaʼqa yamaʼkpaˑł, aʼₐˑkeˑ qaqaʼₐneˑ nałmᵥʼqtsin. taʼxas
tuʼxᵘa ktsłaxmoʼxus nałmᵥʼqtseˑ. nʼuʼpxₐneˑ pał sɛłsaˑniłwiy-
nataʼpseˑ hatsaʼeˑs. naq!anˑaʼq!ₐnenɛʼłneˑ neᵢs aₐˑkɛʼłweˑys, neᵢs
łuwaʼxₐmoxuʼnˑeˑ neᵢ aₐˑkɛʼłwey. qakeʼᵢneˑ nałmᵥʼqtseˑ: "ę̆ˑ,
40 kinłqałʼat.łitɛʼtᵢnam kₑniłwiynanaʼkeˑ." mö̆ʼka ksɛłsaˑnɛłwiynaʼₐ-
tiˑł paʼₐmik sɛłʼat.łititmuʼnˑeˑ oˑʼkˈ!ᵘqᵤna kseʼᵢłkqaₐts ktsxałha-
maˑʼtkeˑts aʼₐˑkik.łiyeɛ'seˑs naₐs aʼmˑaˑks.
     Qakiłɛʼłneˑˑ: "maₐts hₑntsxałqaoxałq!uʼmneʼᵢneˑ na qaʼₐkiłhaq!-
aʼnquˑts!łaʼin." łuqᵘałqaˑkilkaʼₐneˑˑ: "maₐts hₑntsxałqunyₐxa-
45 kɛʼłneˑ toʼhoˑł naˑʼxqakqaʼyqokɛʼmeˑk toʼhoˑł." taʼxas ts!ₑnaqₐ-
nuʼkₐneˑ. taʼxas nʼɛʼnseˑ neᵢs tsᴇmaʼₐkk!unuq!ᵘwiyaʼₐtaps
yawoʼᵤnɛk!s maʼₐka.
     Qaˑnaʼxeˑ nałmö̆ʼqtseˑ. qałwiʼyneˑˑ: "hułaˑqˈ!małʼoʼᵤwoˑk
kułɛˑˑtˈ!eˑkaʼₐmeˑk." taʼxas nʼuwoʼkᵤneˑ. taʼxas tsᴇmaʼkˈ!aˑłeˑt!-
50 naotˈ!aˑłakaʼmeˑk. (pał koqᵘaʼkeˑ kwɛʼłqa nałmö̆ʼqtseˑ. neᵢsts
kˈloʼwok aₐˑkᵢyukwaʼeˑs woxomuʼnˑeˑ aₐˑkiłmiʼyit.s neᵢs

_____
[1] Or _malₑnk!ało'uman'_.

country.   He did not arise when he was going about, | but crawled on hands and feet.   It was almost the best way, ‖ for there is water 10 now where he crawled along.   Therefore the rivers have that width.[1] | He crawled along, even where there was much water.   He saw Woodpecker and | his brothers sitting in a row on the top of a mountain. |

Woodpecker was still angry at Muskrat, who | had lied at the time when the warriors started off, at the time when the warriors went up (to the sky), ‖ and when Wolverene tore their trail, | and they knew 15 that Muskrat had told a lie.   When they wished to come down again, | Wolverene had torn the trail, and they could not go down. | They shot the thunderbird, and they were given its feathers and | down. There were none for Woodpecker and his brothers. ‖ Then they got 20 angry.   They went to the place | where the sun goes down, and there they came down and returned | to their country.   When they saw the people, as they were going home, | they killed all.   Then they saw a mountain goat not far from | a lake, and they ate the goat. ‖

They saw below Naɫmu'qtse crawling along. | Woodpecker was still 25 angry; and when he saw the old man, | he hated him.   He knew that Naɫmu'qtse was still giving names | to the country.   Then he wished to kill his uncle.   He said to him: | "Uncle!"   Naɫmu'qtse heard his nephew.   He said: ‖ "Hai!"   He was told: "I'll give you 30 to eat.   Maybe you are hungry on account of your | going about and giving names to the land."   Naɫmu'qtse said: | "Oh, I am glad!" He was told: "Open your mouth."   Woodpecker | put a stone into the fire and put | the hot stone into the heart of the mountain goat. Then Naɫmu'qtse opened his mouth, ‖ and Woodpecker threw the 35 heart into it.   Woodpecker had manitou | power, and Naɫmu'qtse was the same way. | When Woodpecker reached him, Naɫmu'qtse knew that his nephew was evilly disposed | toward him.   He nodded to the heart, and it | fell down on one side.   Naɫmu'qtse said: "E, ‖ you will be named Little Heart."   Even though somebody was 40 angry with him, | he gave names to places, because he was walking about this world | in order to give names. |

(Woodpecker) was told: "Don't sleep where there is a | thick forest."   (Naɫmu'qtse) turned around, and said also: "Don't touch the ‖ charr while it is rolling in the water."   Then Naɫmu'qtse 45 crawled along in the water, | and there it was where Flicker was swallowed by the | Water Monster. |

Naɫmu'qtse went along.   He thought: "I'll stand up for a while. | I'll stretch myself."   He stood up and ‖ stretched his back.   (I said 50 Naɫmu'qtse was large.   When | he stood up, his war bonnet touched the sky.)   His | war bonnet fell down; and when his hat fell down, |

---

[1] That is, the rivers were formed on the trail which he made by crawling along.

aₐ‘kᵢyukwa′e·s.) qanaxu′n·e· neᵢs yaqanmoxu′ske· aₐ‘k!ayu-
kwa′e·s nɛnko′e·s aₐ″ke· neᵢs yaqanmoxu′ke·. qake′ₗne·: "kaₐs
na· qawaxₐmu′xo ka·k!ayu′kwa k.ĺqaĺ′at.letɛ′tnam wɛ′tsquwaṭ!."

55 ta′xas qanaxu′n·e, paĺ sĺu′pₐne· naso′ukᵘe·n naĺmȯ′qtse·.
neᵢsts na·moxu′kᵘe· ktsxa′ĺe·pts pa′ₐmc·k łao·k!ᵘc.ɛ′se·
k!at.łe′ᵢte·t.

Ta′xas hosꞁhułtsxamɛ′łne· ya′ₐqaĺu′pke· kaa·tsᵢmi· łq!a′łu-
k!ᵘpukamna′ła naĺmȯ′qtse·.

53. YA.UKᵁE′ᵢKA·M

Ho′yas, hutsxałtsxanemɛ′łne· yaqałaqa′ₐke· naso′ukᵘe·n ya.-
ukᵘe′ᵢka·m ktuna′xa neᵢs pɛ′k!a·ks.

(a) THE BIRTH OF YA.UKᵁE′ᵢKA·M

Qa·nɛt.ła′ₐne· wa′ta·k.· na̍qa′pse· tɛte′e·s qak.ła′kse· niłouqᵘat-
na′nas. at nałq!at!e′ᵢne· niłouqᵘatna′na. qakɛ′łne· wa′ta·k
5 tɛte′e·s: "at maₐts hɛntsxaĺ′e·ku′łne·[1] neᵢ a′ₐ‘k!a·q. ta′xta·
hɛnłatka′xa·m kaₐ‘kɛt.łana′ła at hɛnts!e·ku′łne·." naₐqsanmi′yɛt.s
at qaqna·pse· tɛte′e·s. k!ouk!unmi′yɛt.s ła·łq!at!e′ᵢne· nꞁouqᵘat-
na′na ława′xe· nok!unuq!ᵤma′ne· qałwi′yne·: "ho′yas, huĺe′ᵢko·ł
na aₐ″k!aq." n′e·ku′łne·. qakaĺ′akahe′ᵢse· tɛ′tqa·t!s n′ɛktsɛnuq-
10 kɛna′pse·. qałwi′yne· ktsxałtsɛ′ĺip. n′u′pxₐne· pa·ł n′ɛ′nse·
aₐ‘kɛt.łana′me·s neᵢs ya·qa·oxaĺ′ɛktsɛnuqkɛnɛ′łke. pa·ł sꞁ-
tsukᵘata′pse· tɛ′tqa·t!s. pał sꞁhałalitɛ′t ᵢne· neᵢ tɛ′tqa·t!.
qa′k.le·k aₐ‘kmɛnuqłu′nuk. qasaqa′ₐne·. ta′xas at n′ana′se·
neᵢs nułaqₐna″e·s. k.łuma′yit.s naqa′pse· aqa′łt!e·s. ta′xa
15 neᵢ łka′mu qaĺ′atɛ′łne· ya.ukᵘe′ᵢka·m. qaĺ′ata′pse· tɛtu′e·s
ma″e·s ya.ukᵘe′ᵢka·m′s. n′u′pxₐne· neᵢ tɛ′tqa·t! ktsxa′ĺe·ns
naso′ukᵘe·ns xałe′e·s słaqaqa′pse· kamaₐ‘tke·ts aₐ‘kɛk.łeyeɛ′se·s.

Ta′xa aₐ‘kmɛnuqłu′nuk naqa′pse· ta′t!e·s. saha′nse· ta′xa neᵢ
₊tɛ′tqa·t! at saniłwiynawe′ᵢne·. qaĺ′atɛ′łne· aₐ‘quxma′nuks. ta′xa
20 neᵢ tsa′ₐtᵢmu aₐ‘quxma′nuk nao′k!ᵘe· at sa·niłwiynawe ᵢne·,
nao′′k!ᵘe· neᵢ ktsaqu′na at· qasaniłwi′yne. tsɛmak!qa′pse·
aₐ‘kꞁwi′ye·s. ta′xas neᵢsts ka′qa ya.ukᵘe′ᵢka·m na·qt!oxa′-
nuk aₐ‘quxma′nuks at nałukułwita′kse·. ta′xas keᵢkqa·ts
ya.ukᵘe′ᵢka·m qak.ła′pse· ma″e·s: "atɛnsahankɛ′kq!aₐnxo′une·
25 xa′ₐne·s aₐ‘quxma′nuk. ta′xas pał kɛnsꞁwɛ′łqa ts!ɛnamɛ′łen′ neᵢs
sanɛt.ła′ₐne· papa″ne·s. qa′k.le·k wa′taks; at tsłakɛ′łne· q!a′pe·s
łka′m·u′s kwɛ′łqaps q!a′pe· aqłsma′knɛk! n′ɛ′nse· papa″e·sts
tɛte′e·s. n′ɛ′n·e· katɛ′te· wa′ta·k. neᵢsts hɛnłaxa′nme·ł n′u′pxₐneᵢs
tsxałqak.lɛ′sᵢne·.: 'kapa′pa, kułsꞁu′pxatsxałsłak.lɛ′sᵢne·' qo tax
30 hɛntsqa′ₐkiłk.lɛnq!u′le·k."

Ta′xas ya.ukᵘe′ᵢka·m ts!ɛna′xe· sanɛt.łanamɛ′sᵢne·. łaxa′xe·
tɛnawɛtskɛ′kᵢne·. n′u′pxₐne· tɛna′mu′s saosaqa′pse· sła·′tᵢyi-

---

[1] Pronounced continuously: maₐtsɛntsxałe·ku′łne·.

he also fell. He said when he fell: "The place where | my hat falls is to be called Ear." ‖ Then the chief fell and died. Naɫmu'qtse 55 fell and was nearly dead, and nevertheless | he named one more place. |

Now I have told you how Naɫmu'qtse, our great-great-grandfather generations back, died. |

53. YA.UK^UE'ₗKA·M

Well, I'll tell about Chief Ya.uk^ue'ₗka·m, | the Kutenai, long ago. |

(a) THE BIRTH OF YA.UK^UE'ₗKA·M

Frog was living in a tent. There was her granddaughter, named Young Doe. | Young Doe went picking berries. Frog said to ‖ her 5 granddaughter: "Don't go and drink at the water hole in the ice. | When you come into the house, drink here." For a few days | her granddaughter did so. One day Young Doe was picking berries again. | She came to be thirsty, and thought: "Let me drink | from the water hole." She drank. Then a man put out his hand ‖ to pull her 10 into the water. She thought she would die. She saw, however, there was | a tent where she had been taken into the water. | The man took her and married her. | The name of this man was White Stone. She staid there. | Then her husband went hunting. In the spring of the year she had a child. ‖ Then the child was called Ya.uk^ue'ₗka·m. His 15 father and | his mother called him Ya.uk^ue'ₗka·m. That man knew that his son would be | a chief, therefore he gave him this name. |

Then White Stone had an elder brother. That man was bad. | He was quick-tempered. He was named Gray Stone. Then among these ‖ brothers, Gray Stone, the one, was always angry; | the other, 20 the younger one, was not angry. He had a strong | mind. Then Ya.uk^ue'ₗka·m was like stones striking together (?). | Gray Stone made noise inside. Then when he went around, | Ya.uk^ue'ₗka·m was told by his mother: ‖ "Your father's brother, Gray Stone, does not 25 feel good when you are here. Now you are large, go to your | great-grandmother's tent. Her name is Frog. She loves all | children and all big people who are her grandsons | and her granddaughters. Frog is my grandmother. When you get there and she sees you, | she will say to you: 'My grandchild, let me see you and love you.' ‖ You 30 will always play there." |

Then Ya.uk^ue'ₗka·m started for the tent. He arrived and | looked in. He saw an old woman | sitting there in the rear with her back

ł·a‛n·taqanaqna′kse·. n′onɛ′łne·. pał ktsaqu′na sɛł′aimaktɛ′t¡ne·
ya.ukᵘe′¡ka·m. ta′χas tsχałsɛł′ɛtkɛ′n·e· qa′psins qᵤna·kₐna′χₐne·

35 q¡u′mne″nis ne¡s tɛłna′mu′s qa·nₐqa′me·k wa′ta·k, atqaq¡u′-
mne′¡ne·. n′uk¡ᵘnißhats!ₐłaqa′ₐne·. n′itχo′ᵤme·k. q¡u′mne′¡ne·.
ta′χas tɛnaχa′mne· ya.ukᵘe′¡ka·m. ta′χas k.łɛnq¡u′łe·k. n′u′p-
χₐne· ma qak.ła′pse· ma″e·s ne¡sts kqa′kχa·s. no′ᵤne· aₐ‛k.łɛtɛt!-
ɛ′se·s ma″e·s. ta′χas k.łɛnq¡o.imu′n·e·. kwałkᵤwa′yit.s łats!-
40 ɛna′χe· ma″e·s. k.łaχa′χam qak.ła′pse· ma″e·s: "qa′psin kɛ′nsi-
łats!ɛ′ka·″m ma kɛnsqaosa′qa· n′ɛ′n·e· papa″ne·s." qake′¡ne·
ya.ukᵘe′¡ka·m: "hun′onɛ′łne· n′ɛse¡kate′¡ne· ne¡ tɛłna′mu."
n′umats¡nata′pse· ałaknɛ′k!e·s. qak.ła′pse·: "taχta·″ hɛntsχałsła-
kɛ′łne·. q¡a′pe· łka′m·u atsłakɛ′łne·ɛs tɛłna′mu′s." qahak.łe′¡ts¡ne·
45 wa′ta·k nukᵤnuχa″mne·. n′u′pχₐne· k!aₐqałe′o·t.s ne¡s a′q¡a·′s
aₐ‛kɛt.ła′e·s. tse¡ka′te· pał n′ uła′se· łka′m·u′s. qake′¡ne·:
"ha·″ksa, katɛ′te·, kapa′pa, kłswa·″ka·m koa‛qałq¡u′mne′¡mił."
     Kanmi′yɛt.s a′′ₐ‛ke· łats!ɛna′χe· ya.ukᵘe′¡kam. ne¡sts k!u′pχa
kałikina′ₐtits łka′mu·′s wa′ta·k. "qa.u′pχₐne· qa′psins nɛ′n′ɛns
50 sɛł′aqake′¡ne· kapa′pa katɛ′te·." ta′χas n′ɛtkɛ′n·e· t!awuɛ′se·s
na′hek¡nanaɛ′se·s. pɛskɛ′n·e·. qałwi′yne·: "pał kosɛłq¡u′m-
ne″me·ł ne¡sts ktka′χa·′m. na′pit a′ₐ‛ke· hułaq¡u′mne″mił
tka′χa·m, ta′χas kuts!u′pχa qa′psin n′ɛ′n·e·." sɛł′aqaqa′pse·
k!asqana′qaps k!e·′tkin k.łɛnqo′¡mo·′s. qaosaqa′ₐne· wa′ta·k
55 nats!ałaqa′ₐne· n′ɛtχo′ᵤme·k q¡u′mne′¡ne·. a′ₐ‛ke· łao·ła′se·
ya.ukᵘe′¡ka·ms sɛł′a‛qał·aq¡u′mne′¡ne·. tɛnaχa′mne· ya.ukᵘe′¡-
ka·m. n′u′pχₐne· saₐkɛsqa′pse· t!awuna′na′s nahek¡na′na′s.
mit¡ya′χₐne· ne¡s t!awuna′na′s pał a′ₐ‛ke· n′ɛtkɛ′nse· tsa′ₐtsas.
ta′χas tsukᵘa′te· ne¡s t!awuna′na′s. n′anaχa″mne·. ta′χas mɛ′t-
60 χₐne· ne¡s tsa′ₐtsas. tuwo·′χa kwałkwa′yit.s q¡apnuq¡ᵘmok¡o′ᵤne·
ne¡s tsa′ₐtsas. łatnałkɛ′n·e·. łats!ɛna′χe· no‛kᵘnoχa″mne· wa′ta·k.
tse¡ka′te· ne¡s ma ke′¡tkɛn sła·tq¡a′nse· ne¡s nahek¡na′na′s. ne¡s
t!awuna′na′s skɛknoq!umɛ′se·. n′u′pχₐne· pał n′ɛ′nse· nɛtstahał-
na′na′s. qake′¡ne.: "ha·″ksa kapa·′pa kapa·″pa. k.łe′wa·m ku-
65 aqałwuł·e·e′tsme·ł." kanmi′yɛt.s qałwi′yne·: "mɛ′ka honats!a-
ła′ₐqa. maₐts kutsq¡u″mne·." ła.ɛtkɛ′n·e· tsa′ₐtsas. łapɛskɛ′n·e·.
n′ɛtχo′ᵤme·k. qałwi′yne·: "hołakqa′p′me·ł." qaoɛa′χe· yₐ.u-
kᵘe′¡ka·m. tɛnawɛtskɛ′łne·. pał sła·tkik.łe′¡tse· ne¡s tɛłna′mu′s.
qałwi′yne·: "pał ksi·łq¡u″mne·." ta′χas tɛnaχa″mne·. tsukᵘa′te·
70 ne¡s t!awuna′na′s aₐ″ke· ne¡s tsa′ₐtsas. ta′χas tsχałtsił′a-
nałkɛ′nse· tsχałk.łɛnq¡o′¡mo·′s: n′u′pχₐne· wa′ta·k. sukᵤno-
hu′s·e· aₐ‛kuq¡a·nt!ɛ′se·s ne¡s·łka′m·u′s so′ᵤkᵘse·. mit¡ya′χₐne·;
tsɛnkɛ′n·e·. qakɛ′łne·: "ha·″ksa, kapa·″pa, kapa·″pa." qa-
k.ła′pse·: "ta′χa·′s pɛskɛ′no·." ta′χas n′anaχa″mse·. ta′χ s
75 mɛ′tχₐne· tsa′ₐtsas ya.ukᵘe′¡ka·m. ta′χas wa′ta·k akɛł′se·s
n′ɛtkɛ′n·e· aₐ″ke· tsa′ₐtsas. ta′χas pał ksłu′pχₐnaps ya.u-
kᵘe′¡ka·m ne¡s tɛłna′mu′s. ta′χas qaosaqa′ₐne· pał ksak.-

toward the door. He was afraid. | Ya.uku̯e´ɩka·m was small, two
years old. Then he was going to throw something, to throw ‖ sleep 35
into the old woman. Frog was sitting there, and did not sleep. | She
became sleepy and lay down. She slept. | Then Ya.uku̯e´ɩka·m en-
tered. He began to play. | He knew, for his mother had told him,
how she was. He knew the belongings | of his mother. Then he
played with them in the evening and went ‖ back to his mother. When 40
he arrived, his mother said to him: "Why do you | come back? You
ought to stay with your grandmother." Ya.uku̯e´ɩka·m said: | "I was
afraid; that old woman looks terrible." | His parents laughed at him.
They said to him: "Later you will love her. | All children like that
old woman." Frog was asleep. ‖ She arose and saw that the inside 45
of her tent looked strange. | She looked, and she found out a child
had been there. She said: | "Oh, my grandchild, my grandchild has
arrived, and therefore I slept." |

In the morning Ya.uku̯e´ɩka·m started again, and Frog saw | the
evidence of a child having been there. "Nobody knows whether ‖ 50
it is my grandson or my granddaughter." Therefore she made a
bow and | a little basket. She put them down. She thought: "I
was asleep | when he came in. If I should go to sleep again, when |
he comes back I'll know what it is." That was the reason why | she
made the two kinds of toys. Frog was ‖ sleepy. She lay down and 55
slept. Again | Ya.uku̯e´ɩka·m came in. Therefore she went to sleep
again. | Ya.uku̯e´ɩka·m entered. He looked, and there was the little
bow and the little basket. | He ran for the little bow. She had also
made two figures of deer (of grass). | Then he took the little bow and
went out. He shot ‖ at the figure of the deer. When it was almost 60
evening, | the figure of the deer was torn to pieces. He carried it in
again and went back. Frog arose. | She looked at what she had
made, and the little basket was hanging there. | The little bow was
lying there. It was broken. Then she knew that her grand-
child was | a boy. She said: "O grandson, grandson! He must
have come while ‖ I was sound asleep." On the following morning 65
she thought: "Even if I do | feel sleepy, I'll not go to sleep."
She made a figure of a deer (of grass) and put it down. | She lay
down. She thought: "Let me lie down again." There was | Ya.-
uku̯e´ɩka·m. He looked in, and the old woman was asleep. | He
thought: "She is sleeping." Then he entered. He took ‖ the little 70
bow and the figure of the deer. Then he carried ǀ them out. He was
about to play with them. Frog saw him. His clothing was | bright
red. The child was good-looking. She ran for him | and took him.
She said to him: "O grandchild, grandchild!" | He said to her: "Let
me go!" Then Ya.uku̯e´ɩka·m went out and ‖ shot at the figure. 75
Frog had made an arrow | and the figure of a deer. Then | Ya.uku̯-
e´ɩka·m was seen by the old woman; and he staid there, on the pil-

ła·′′mχo′s ma′′e·s. ˙ta′χas wa′ta·k suk.łᵻk₁natᵻ′t₁ne· aₐ′kᴇmoχo-

χo.ᵻ′se·s papa′e·s. n′u′pχₐne· ne₁s ksuku′qła′ns. słaqaqa′psc·

80 ktsᴇma′k!iłsuk.łᵻk₁na′ₐte·t, aₐ′kᴇmoχoᵻ′se·s ya.uku̯e′₁ka·ms.

(b) YA.UKᵁE′₁KA·M OBTAINS ARROW WOOD

Ta′χas   wᵻłqa′ₐne· ya.uku̯e₁′ka·m: qałwi′yne·: "qa′psin

huł′e·′tke·n?" ne₁s pᵻ′k!a·ks ło′ᵤne· sq!u′m·o· na′s yᵻsłᵻ′tske·.

tsᴂn·ok!kᵻk.łe.ᵻ′t.se· yaki′łaqa˘a′ke·. o·′k!qᵤna kqawunᵻ′ki·t.s

ka′qa ya.uku̯e′₁ka·m słaqałqa.u′pχane· na′s a′m·a·ks. qake′₁ne·:

85 "hya· ła′qa a′k!ᵤwo·k huł′e·′tkᴂn ka′ak!."   ne₁s pᵻ′k!a·ks at n′ᵻ′-

n·e· a·k! sq!u′m·o· aₐ′k!ᵤwokᵘa′e·s, pał ke′₁ło′ᵤs sᵻł′a˘qa˘ke′₁ne·

ya.uku̯e′₁ka·m. qake′₁ne· wa′ta·k: "ha·′ksa, kapa·′′pa, kapa·′′pa,

iłqa′ha·ks qa·′kiłhaqa′ₐne· a′k!ᵤwo·k at qa′oχał′up₁na′m′ne·

naya′χał a′k!ᵤwo·k n′ᵼsᴂnkikiłwᵻtskᵻ′łne· k.ła′wła ne₁s a′k!ᵤwo·ks.

90 qa′ła łaχaya′χa at n′ᵻt!χₐna′pse· k.ła′wła′s." ta′χas ts!ᵼna′χe·

ya.uk·u̯e′₁ka·m. łaχa′χe· sawᵼsaqa′pse· n′a′se· qaspᵻ′ł′uks at

t!ało′ᵤkse· n′upχa′ka′s. ta′χas at n′u′pχₐne· k.ła′wła

kskaχa′m·e·s k!u′pχₐnaps qaspᵻ′ł′uks ya.uku̯e′₁ka·m qałwi′yse·

ktsχałt!a′łuks. qakᵻ′łne·: "a· maₐts tsχana′ₐtki·ł k.ła′wła. taχta·′

95 hułaqa′ham hᴂntstsχanatkᵻ′łne·." łaₐts!ᵼna′χe·. n′u′pχₐne· n′a′-

se· kianłᵻ′k!χo·′s, qałwi′yse· ktsχałt!a′łuᵤks. qakᵻ′łne·: "maₐts

tsχana′ₐtki·ł. taχta·′ hułaqa′ham he·′ntsχa·′natkᵻ′łne·." ła·ts!ᵼ-

na′χe·. n′u′pχₐne· n′a′se· sᵻ′n·a·′s. qałwi′yse· ktsχałt!a′łᵤuks

qakᵻ′łne·: "maₐts t!ało′ᵤkᵘe·ł."   ta′χas ya.uku̯e′₁ka·m n′u′pχₐne·

100 sq!u′m·o·′s sukᵘakate′₁se·. ta′χas tsukᵘa′te· a′k!ᵤwo·ks yu-

naqa′pse·. ta′χas q!a′pe·′s a′m·a·ks qawaχₐmᵻ′te·.   qake′₁ne·:

"taχta·′ pał ktsᵻyuna′q′wo·m na a′m·a·k χma ktsqa′qa tsᴂn

χma kts!u·′k!kᵻk.łe·′et.s am·a·′k!e·s sq!u′m·o·."   ta′χas q!a′pe·′s

a′m·a·ks at siłhaqa′ₐne· sq!u′m·o·. n′oła′n·e· ya.uku̯e′₁ka·m.

105   Ta′χas nałaχo′ᵤne· ne₁s a′k!ᵤwo·ᵤks. łats!ᵼna′χe·. łałaχa′χe·

sᵻ′n·a·′s. qakᵻ′łne·: "ta′χas tsχana′ₐtki·ł k.ła′wła." ta′χas t!ało′ᵤ-

kᵤne·. nułpa′łne· k.ła′wła sᵻ′n·a·′s, qake′₁ne·: "'yà, 'yà, qa′psin

ksᵻł·aqo·′łqałukułmi′yit?" qawuni·kᵻ′t.se· a′ₐke· t!ało′ᵤkᵤne.

kianłᵻ′k!χo·. a′ₐke· łaqake′₁ne· k.ła′wła qawunikᵻ′t.se· t!ało′ᵤ-

110 kᵤne· qaspᵻ′ł′uk a′ₐke· łaqake′₁ne· k.ła′wła. qakᵻ′łne· ałaqa′łt!e·s:

"anaχa′′mki·ł. k!aₐqanᵻ′ke·t?" n′anaχa′′mse· ałaqa′łt!e·s

n′u′pχa′s łało′ᵤse· sq!u′m·o·′s aₐ′kᵤwokᵘa.ᵻ′se·s. qak.ła′pse·:

"łało′ᵤne· sq!u′m·o·." sa·nilwi′yne· k.la′wła. nawasχo·′′mek.

tsukᵘa′te· aₐ′qa′tᵤwumła′t!e·s. n′ᵻ′nse· aₐ′qa′tᵤwumła′t!e·s

115 k.ła′wła′s aₐ′ku′qła·′s. qanaχa′′mne·. n′ᴂnqa′pte·k k.ła′wła′s.

n′anaχa′′mne· łatᵻk₁me·t₁ya′χₐne· ałaqa′łt!e·s. ła′ntaoχakᵻsink!-

ata′ksc·. qakᵻ′łne·: "koa·′qaka′te·?" qak.ła′pse·: "ni′n′ᵼse·ka·-

te·′ne·." ta′χas ła·′naχa′′mne· k.ła′wła. tse₁kat.łᵻ′k!ne·. n′u′p-

χₐne· n′ᵼsᴂnłᵻ′ksc· ya.uku̯e′₁ka·ms. nułpałnitᵻ′t₁ne· kuła′k.łe·′s nᴂts-

low of | his mother.   Frog made a good place | for her grandson to sit down on.   She knew that he had good clothing.   Therefore she made ‖ a really good place for Ya.uk^ue'ᵢka·m to sit down. | 80

(b) YA.UK^UE'ᵢKA·M OBTAINS ARROW WOOD

Now, Ya.uk^ue'ᵢka·m was growing up.   He thought: | "What shall I do?"   Long ago there were no service berries in this world. | There was just one place where there were some.   Because it was not long | since Ya.uk^ue'ᵢka·m was born, therefore he did not know this world. He said: ‖ "Hya! I wish there might be some arrow wood!   Then   85 I might make arrows."   Long ago | arrows were made of service-berry shoots.   There were none.   Therefore | Ya.uk^ue'ᵢka·m said so. Frog said: "O grandchild, grandchild! | far away there is arrow wood. | Those who go to get arrow wood die there.   Grizzly Bear watches the arrow wood. ‖ Whoever goes to get it, is bitten by   90 Grizzly Bear."   Then | Ya.uk^ue'ᵢka·m started.   He arrived where two Cranes | made a noise when they saw anybody.   Then Grizzly Bear knew | that somebody was coming.   When the Cranes saw Ya.uk^ue'ᵢka·m, they wanted | to make noise.   He said to them: "Oh, don't tell Grizzly Bear! ‖ When I pass again, then you may tell him."   95 He started again, and saw two | Marmots.   They intended to whistle. He said to them: "Don't | talk now!   Later on, when I pass again, you may talk." | He started again, and saw two Beavers.   They intended to make a noise. | He said to them: "Don't make a noise!" Then Ya.uk^ue'ᵢka·m saw ‖ plenty of service berries.   He took much 100 arrow wood. | He threw it all over the country.   He said: | "By and by there will be many people in this world.   It would not be right if service berries were | only in one place in the world."   Then there were | service berries in every country.   It was he, Ya.uk^ue'ᵢka·m, who did it. ‖

Then he put the arrow wood on his back.   He started back, and 105 came to | Beaver.   He said to him: "Now tell Grizzly Bear." Then (Beaver) made | a noise.   Grizzly Bear heard Beaver.   He said: "Yà, yà!—what does it mean? | I hear noise going back."   After a little while | the Marmots also made noise, and Grizzly Bear said so again.   After a little while ‖ the Cranes made a noise, and Grizzly 110 Bear spoke again.   He told his children: | "Go out (to see) what has been done!"   His children went out, and | they saw there were no more service-berry bushes.   They said: | "There are no more service-berry bushes."   Then Grizzly Bear became angry.   He sang. | He took his coat.   The coat of ‖ Grizzly Bear is a skin.   He put 115 it on and became a grizzly bear. | He went out and jumped near his children.   The two (children) jumped back. | He said to them: "How do I look?"   He was told: "You look terrible."   Then Grizzly Bear | went out.   He looked at the tracks, and he saw | that it was Ya.uk^ue'ᵢka·m.   He had heard that ‖ the youth had grown up and 120

120 ta′haƚs ktsxa′ƚⁱⁿs naso′ᵤkweˑns. ta′xas saˑniƚwiyna′ₐteˑ. ta′xas
    ts!ᴧna′xeˑ neᵢs ƚaya·ʻqana′skeˑ. ƚaxa′xeˑ sᴧ′nˑaˑ′s. qakᴧ′ⁱneˑ:
    "kaₐ kina·ʻqakᵢna′pkeˑƚ kᴧnsᴧlqa.upxa′keˑƚ nak.ƚqaha′xam?"
    qak.ƚa′pseˑ: "hoq!u′mnˑeˑʻnaƚa′ₐneˑ." ƚahats!ᴧna′xeˑ ƚaxa′xeˑ
    kiankᴧ′k!xoˑ′s. qakᴧ′ⁱneˑ: "kaₐ kᴧn′aˑʻqaqna′pkeˑƚ kᴧnsᴧlqa.up-
125 xa′keˑƚ nak.ƚqaha′xaˑm?" qak.ƚa′pseˑ: "hoq!u′mneˑnaƚa′ₐneˑ
    hosᴧlqa.u′pxₐnaƚa′ₐneˑ." ƚahats!ᴧna′xeˑ ƚaxa′xeˑ qaspᴧ′ⁱ′uks.
    qakᴧ′ⁱneˑ: "kaₐ kᴧn′aˑʻqana′pkeˑƚ kᴧnsᴧlqa.upxa′kiˑƚ naqƚqaha′-
    xa′m." qak.ƚa′pseˑ: "neᵢ ma kski·ƚwaƚ′niˑ′kit hoq!u′mneˑnaƚa′ₐneˑ
    hosᴧƚ′aˑʻqaƚqa.upxₐnaƚa′ₐneˑ." qakᴧ′ⁱneˑ: "taxta′ˑ. honuƚk′t!xa
130 ya.ukᵘe′ᵢkaˑⁿ hoƚa′waˑⁿ hutsxaƚ′upƚskᴧ′ⁱneˑ." sƚaˑ′tᵢyiƚ′aqₐneˑ-
    tsa′pseˑ neᵢs ᴧwat!na″eˑs. taxa neᵢ aƚswo̯′tᵢmu qaƚspᴧ′ⁱ′uk
    no′ʰᵤneˑ neᵢs ke′eˑns ya.ukᵘe′ᵢkaˑms sƚ′aqaƚ′oₒnᴧ′ⁱneˑ. ta′xas
    k.ƚa′wƚa ts!ᴧnanu′teˑ ya.ukᵘe′ᵢkaˑms. ta′xas n′u′pxₐneˑ ya.ukᵘe′ᵢ-
    kaˑⁿ k!u′pskaˑs k.ƚa′wƚas ktsxaƚ′u′pƚaps. n′ᴧtkᴧ′nˑeˑ nöpᴧ′k!aˑ′s.
135 qataƚ·axₐnxona′pseˑ. n′itkᴧ′nˑeˑ aₐʻqanq!ᵢyumᴧ′nˑas. ta′xas
    q!awats!ᴧ′nmeˑk k.ƚa′wƚa. qaƚwi′yneˑ ya.ukᵘe′ᵢkaˑm: "kaₐ
    huƚaˑʻaˑqaʻo̯xam ƚqaʻtaƚᴧ′t!xnap k.ƚa′wƚa?" qaƚwi′yneˑ: "hoƚa-
    ts!ᴧna′miˑƚ kaˑⁿa. ma ksaˑ′han ka′xa aₐʻquxma′nuk." ta′xas
    ƚaƚaxa′xeˑ ya.ukᵘe′ᵢkaˑⁿ ma″eˑs. qake′ᵢneˑ: "skanuta′pₐneˑ
140 k.ƚa′wƚa." aₐʻquxma′nuk qake′ᵢneˑ: "hê̄ː." n′owo′kᵤneˑ aₐʻqux-
    ma′nuk. nawasxo′ᵤmeˑk. n′ᴧtkᴧ′nˑeˑ nöpᴧ′k!aˑ′s. qake′ᵢneˑ: "huts-
    xaƚ′upᴧ′ⁱneˑ k.ƚa′wƚa." ta′xas n′ᴧnqa′pteˑk no′ᵤkᵘeˑs aₐʻquxma′-
    nuk. ta′xas tsukᵘa′teˑ t!ᴧna′mu′s q!apᴧts!aqa′meˑk. ƚaˑ′wᴧƚiƚ′iƚ-
    kuƚᴧ′sᵢneˑ. n′itxo′ᵤmeˑk neᵢs aq!a′saks aₐʻkᴧnq!u′kups. qawune-
145 kᴧ′t.seˑ ta′xas ƚaxa′xeˑ k.ƚa′wƚa. qake′ᵢneˑ, "oˑk!ᵘᴧnkᴧ′nkiˑƚ
    ƚaqƚanxo′ᵤnaˑƚ." qakᴧ′ⁱneˑ ya.ukᵘe′ᵢkaˑms: "qoqᵘawᴧ′sqan′
    aₐʻkuˑʻq!yuk!aƚaxwe′et." ta′xas wa′xeˑ k.ƚa′wƚa. n′u′pxₐneˑ
    ya.ukᵘe′ᵢkaˑms sawᴧsqa′pseˑ neᵢs aₐʻkuˑʻq!yuk!aƚaxweˑet.s.
    qake′ᵢneˑ k.ƚa′wƚa: "hàˑ, k.ƚseᵢƚhonmeƚa′k.ƚeˑ ya.ukᵘe′ᵢkaˑⁿ na-
150 so′ᵤkᵘeˑnts kutsxaƚ′o′piˑƚ." ta′xas aₐʻquxma′nuk n′owo′ᵤkᵤneˑ.
    ƚats neᵢs ƚuqᵘaƚitxo′ᵤmeˑk paƚ k!ᴧnqa′pteˑk no′ᵤkᵘeˑs. ta′xas
    sᴧƚ′u′tᵢmeku′meˑk. tsEmaˑ′k!ᴧƚ′u′tᵢmeˑ tsxaƚt!anoko′ᵤneˑ. ta′xas
    k.ƚᴧ′wƚa qake′ᵢneˑ: "hoya′suƚts!oˑpin′ƚaaˑtᴧqƚᴧxₐni′ˑyat ya.u-
    kᵘe′ᵢkaˑⁿ naso′ᵤkᵘeˑn." ta′xas mitᵢya′xₐneˑ. n′ᴧ′t!xₐneˑ. aₐʻqux-
155 ma′nuk neᵢs ƚoxaq!ana′q!ₐninᴧ′ⁱneˑ ya.ukᵘe′ᵢkaˑms neᵢs ƚoaˑ′q!-
    mawᴧsqa′ₐneˑ aₐʻkoˑʻq!yuk!aƚaxₐwe′eˑts ya.ukᵘe′ᵢka.m. ta′xas
    paˑƚ kts!opna′qƚiƚ k.ƚa′wƚa. n′ᴧ′t!xₐneˑ sq!ᴧmawᴧ′tsxₐneˑ aˑma′-
    ƚeˑt.s. maƚnaqƚᴧ′ⁱneˑ, paˑƚ n′ᴧ′nseˑ aˑmaˑ′ƚeˑts neᵢs kawᴧ′tsxa. tseᵢ-
    kaˑ′teˑ ya.ukᵘe′ᵢkaˑms neᵢs ƚonᴧ′k!q!yok!aƚaxwe′eˑt.s swᴧsqa′pseˑ.
160 qake′ᵢneˑ k.ƚa′wƚa: "hoˑyas, hoƚts!oˑ′pinƚaₐtᴧqƚᴧxₐni′ᵢyat ya.u-
    kᵘe′ᵢkaˑⁿ naso′ᵤkᵘeˑn." ta′xas aˑₐ′keˑ ƚaᴧ′t!xₐneˑ. aₐʻquxma′-
    nuk ƚatsᴧneᵢsƚoˑxᵘaq!anaq!ninᴧ′ⁱneˑ, ya.ukᵘe′ᵢkaˑms neᵢs ƚoaq!-
    mawᴧsqa′pseˑ. maƚnaqƚᴧ′ⁱneˑ k.ƚa′wƚa paƚ swᴧ′tsxₐneˑ aₐʻkuˑʻq! yo-
    k!aƚaxwe′eˑt.s. tseᵢkaˑ′teˑ ya.ukᵘe′ᵢkaˑms neᵢs sᴧʻoaq! mawᴧsqa′-

that he was to be a chief. Then he was angry at him. Then | he
started after the one who was going back. He came to the Beavers.
He said to them: | "What have you done to me? Why did you not
know that somebody passed by?" | He was told: "We were asleep."
He went on, and he came to | the Marmots. He said to them: "What
have you done to me? Why didn't you ‖ know that somebody passed 125
by?" He was told: "We were asleep, | therefore we did not know."
He went on, and he came to the Cranes. | He said to them: "What
have you done to me? Why did you not know that somebody
passed by?" | They said: "There was a snowstorm at that time, and
we were asleep. | Therefore we did not know." He said to them:
"After I have bitten ‖ Ya.ukᵘeʹᵢka·m, I'll come back and I'll kill you." 130
His servants were fooling him. | Then those friends the Cranes | knew
it was Ya.ukᵘeʹᵢka·m. Therefore they were afraid of him. Then |
Grizzly Bear pursued Ya.ukᵘeʹᵢka·m. Then Ya.ukᵘeʹᵢka·m knew
that Grizzly Bear | was coming to kill him. He called his manitou, ‖
and Bear could not catch up with him. He made a hill. Then Grizzly 135
Bear | became tired. Ya.ukᵘeʹᵢka·m thought: "Where | shall I go so
that Grizzly Bear can not bite me?" He thought: "I'll | go back to
my mother, but my uncle Gray Stone is bad." Then | Ya.ukᵘeʹᵢka·m
came to his mother. He said: "Grizzly Bear ‖ is pursuing me." 140
Then Gray Stone said: "Hé!" | Gray Stone arose. He sang. He
called his manitou, and he said: "I shall kill the Grizzly Bear."
Then Gray Stone became stone. | He took grease and rubbed himself
all over. | A large fire was made. He lay down near the fire. It
was not long ‖ before Grizzly Bear arrived. He said: "Open | the 145
door!" They said to Ya.ukᵘeʹᵢka·m: "Stand there by | the doorway."
Then Grizzly Bear arrived. He saw | Ya.ukᵘeʹᵢka·m standing there
by the doorway. | Grizzly Bear said: "Há! Chief Ya.ukᵘeʹᵢka·m is a
full-grown man. ‖ I shall kill him." Then Gray Stone arose and | lay 150
down the other way. He became stone. | He heated himself by the
fire. He became very hot, and was about to burst from the heat.
Then | Grizzly Bear said: "Well, I'll close my eyes. I will bite Chief |
Ya.ukᵘeʹᵢka·m." Then he attacked him. He bit him. ‖ Gray Stone 155
made signs to Ya.ukᵘeʹᵢka·m, who | (then) stood a little to the
other side of the doorway. | Grizzly Bear had his eyes shut when
he bit him, and he stood biting the post. | He opened his eyes
and had the post in his mouth. | He looked at Ya.ukᵘeʹᵢka·m. He
stood on the other side of the doorway. ‖ Grizzly Bear said: 160
"Well, I'll close my eyes and bite | Chief Ya.ukᵘeʹᵢka·m." Then
he bit again. Gray | Stone just made a sign to Ya.ukᵘeʹᵢka·m,
who | jumped to the other side. Grizzly Bear opened his eyes,
and he stood there biting the doorway. He looked | for Ya.u-
kᵘeʹᵢka·m, who was standing on the other side. ‖ Now Gray 165

165 pse·. ta′ɣasaₐ′quɣma′nuktsᴇma′k!ɖ′utᵢme′ᵢne·. qake′ᵢne· k.ła′wᵘ-
ła: "ta′ɣas hułakɛ′łwɛtskɛkɣₐne′ᵢya·t ya.ukᵘe′ᵢka·m naso′ᵤ-
kᵘe·n." ta′ɣas małᴇnk!ałma′ne· k.ła′wła. ta′ɣas aₐ′quɣma′nuk
t!anoko′ᵤne·. k.ła′wła aₐ′k!ałma′′e·s qanałtsᴇqan′mɛ′nɣoᵤqa′ₐ-
ne·. aₐ′quɣma′nuk. n′upsɖ′oqo′ᵤname·tɛ′łne·. aₐ′k!ałaɣɛkp!ɛ′-
170 se·s. łaqa′nał′anaɣa′′mne· aₐ′quɣma′nuk. k.ła′wła tuwu′nin-
muɣu′n·e·. aₐ′quɣma′nuk qo′s qana′qayqa′me·k. qake′ᵢne· ła-
ma·′tsɣmałataksa′pₐne·. ta′ɣas sɖ′opiłi′łne· k.ła′wła. ta′ɣa neᵢ
k.ła′wła pał k!ɛnqa′pte·k k.ła′wła′s. łaqa.ɛ′n·e· aqłsma′kᵢnɛk̓!s
qo′sts ktsɛ′ka·m aₐ′kɛt.ła′e·s. ta′ɣas pał k!ɛnqa′pte·k k.ła′wła′s.
175 ta′ɣas n′upsła′tᵢyiłɛ′n·e· k.ła′wła′s neᵢs k!u′płaps aₐ′quɣma′-
nuks. łaqa.ɛ′n·e· tɛ′tqa·t!s.

  Qo wɛsqa′ₐne· ya.ukᵘe′ᵢka·m. qałwi′yne·: "pał sɖqasts!oᵤmqa-
qa′ₐne· ka·ɣa aₐ′quɣma′nuk. k!u′pił k.ła′wła′s. łe′ᵢło aₐ′quɣma′-
nuk ɣma na·qan′u′płap k.ła′wła." qałwi′yne· ya·ukᵘe′ᵢka·m:
180 "ho′yas, hułtse′ᵢka·t kapa′pa wa′ta·k, kaₐs ɣma n′aqa′qana neᵢs
hu·l·aqaoɣa′mi·ł aₐ′kɛt.ła′e·s." qake′ᵢne·: "ho′yas łułama′ₐki·ł ɛn
k.ła′wła. hutsts!ɛnano·′kᵘitmɛ′łne· kapa′pa wa′ta·k, kaₐs ɣma a·-
qaha·te·na′łap." ta′ɣas łułama′ₐlne· k.ła′wła a′ₐke· aₐ′keᵢsi′ye·s.
ta′ɣas ts!ɛnanokᵘe′ᵢte· ya·ukᵘe′ᵢka·m. łatɛnaɣa′′mne· papa′′e·s.
185 qakɛ′łne·: "kapa′pa skanuta′pₐne· k.ła′wła." qake′ᵢne· wa′ta·k:
"ha·′ksa kapa·′pa, kapa·′pa. kaₐ ko·ł′aₐqₐkɛ′n·e·s koqo·qᵘahaq!-
a·′ł′e·n′. kqa′qₐna kɛ′nsił·aₐqa·wa·′ka·ɣa′′mktse·k. ɣma he·n·-
łaqao·ɣamɛ′łne· ałakᵢnɛ′k!ne·s. mɛ′ksan qasts!oᵤmqaqa′ₐne· ɣa′′-
ne·s aₐ′quɣma′nuk. ɣma n′upɛ′łne· k.ła′wła′s." n′uwo′kᵤne· wa′-
190 ta·k. nawaɣo′ᵤme·k. tsukᵘa′te· namɛ′t·a·s n′ɛtᵢnosła′q!tsa′ₐme·k.
tsukᵘa′te· aₐ′kɛnuq!ła·′nuk!ᵘɛ′n′es. qao·ɣₐkɛ′n·e· aₐ′k!ałaɣwitɛ′t!-
e·s. tsukᵘa′te· popo′′e·s. ta′ɣas nawɛtsᵢnułɣo′ᵤne· k.ła′wła′s. qa-
wuka′te· wa′ta·k neᵢs aₐ′ktsɛ′ka·′s kanukwe′ᵢtᵢmo′s ya.ukᵘe′ᵢ-
ka·ms qusɖqaqałtkaɣuna′kse·. ta′ɣas k!u′pɣa ya.ukᵘe′ᵢka·m
195 kułatɛ′qᵢnaps papa′′e·s. ta′ɣas n′a·ko·nkɛ′n·e· neᵢs aₐ′ktsɛ′ka·′s.
ta′ɣas k.ła′wła aₐ′k.ła′m′e·s n′o·niłkaɣu′n·e· qo′s łaq!anɣo′ᵤna·łs.
qaskałtkak!unka′kᵢne· k.ła′wła n′u′pɣₐne· wa′ta·k ta′ɣas ktka′-
ła·ms k.ła′wła·s neᵢs ya′qahakqa′pske· aₐ′kɛnu′q!łanok!ᵘɛ′n′e·s.
ta′ɣas tu′ɣᵘats q!a·piłtkano′ɣo·nła′′mse· k.ła′wła′s. qałwi′yne·
200 wa′ta·k: "ta′ɣas tu′ɣᵘa ł′a·pko·k!ᵤna·m′te·′ɣa kapapa′mi·ł."
ta′ɣas qanaqkupła′łte· aₐ′k.łamɛ′se·s k.ła′wła·s. ta′ɣas ksa·qɣa·-
łat!ɣo′ᵤme·k wa′ta·k, ya.ukᵘe′ᵢka·m n′akonqkupkɛ′n·e· ne′ᵢs
aₐ′ktsɛ′ka·′s. tɛkᵢmɛ′tɣₐno· aₐ′k.łamɛ′se·s k.ła′wła·s wa′ta·k
tsɛ′neᵢs qao·ɣaqkupła′łte· aₐ′kɛnu·q!łanuk!ᵘɛ′n′e·s. nan·u′qo.i·-
205 ɣo′ᵤne· aₐ′kɛnu·q!łanuk!ᵘɛ′n′e·s. n′u′pɣₐne· wa′ta·k pał sɖ-
k!umna′nta′pse· papa′′e·s. n′ɖa′n·e· pał ksɖ′ɖkiłɣa′mqana·-
na·′ksaps papa′′e·s sɖ′aqał′ɖa′n·e·.

Stone had become very hot. Grizzly Bear said: | "I'll watch and bite Chief Ya.ukᵘe′ᵢka·m." | Then Grizzly Bear opened his mouth, and Gray Stone | burst from the heat.[1] He flew into the mouth of Grizzly Bear. | Gray Stone went right through him, and came out ‖ at 170 his backside. Then Grizzly Bear fell back. | Gray Stone rolled himself about and said: | "I have soiled my flesh." Thus Grizzly Bear was killed. Then | Grizzly Bear was changed into a grizzly bear. He was not a person | when he started from the tent. Then he changed into a grizzly bear, ‖ and he remained a grizzly bear when Gray Stone 175 had killed him. | He was no longer a man. |

Chief Ya.ukᵘe′ᵢka·m stood there. He thought: "My uncle Gray Stone is skillful. | He killed the grizzly bear. If it had not been for Gray | Stone, Grizzly Bear would have killed me." Ya.ukᵘe′ᵢka·m thought: ‖ "Well, let me see my grandmother Frog. What may she 180 do | if I go back to her tent?" He said: "Well, cut off the head of | the grizzly bear. I'll drag it to my grandmother Frog. What | may she do for me?" Then the head of the grizzly bear and its paws | were cut off. Ya.ukᵘe′ᵢka·m dragged it along. He entered his grandmother's ‖ tent. He said to her: "Grandmother, Grizzly Bear is 185 pursuing me." Frog said: | "O grandson, grandson! what can I do for you? | What am I? Why do you come back to me? | You should go back to your parents. Your uncle | Gray Stone is very skillful. He ought to kill Grizzly Bear." Frog arose. ‖ She sang(?). She 190 took red paint and painted her legs. | She took a sharp flat stone and put it up by the doorway. | She took her hammer and stood ready to strike Grizzly Bear. Frog did not | see the rawhide strap with which Ya.ukᵘe′ᵢka·m was dragging the head. | (The head) was lying in the doorway. When Ya.ukᵘe′ᵢka·m ‖ saw his grandmother 195 ready (to strike), he pulled the strap. | Then the grizzly-bear head dropped down under the door. | Grizzly Bear put his nose into the tent. Then Frog saw | Grizzly Bear put in his head where the flat stone lay. | Almost the whole head of Grizzly Bear came in. Frog thought: ‖ "The head might jump at my grandson," | and she struck 200 the grizzly-bear head. | When Frog was striking it, Ya.ukᵘe′ᵢka·m pulled hard at | the strap and pulled the grizzly-bear head in. Just then Frog | struck it and hit her flat stone. She broke ‖ the flat stone. 205 Then Frog saw that her grandson | was fooling her.. She cried because | her grandson had done some damage. Therefore she cried. |

---

[1] Here the narrator indicated the flying about of the stone by clapping his hands.

(c) YA.UKᵁEʹₗKAᵀM OBTAINS FEATHERS

Taʹχas qaoˇsaqaʹₐne· ya.ukᵘeʹₗka·m. qakeʹₗne·: "łaʹqˑa aₐˈkₑn-
qoʹwa hułʹₑtkaχnₑʹlik." qakeʹₗne· waʹta·k: "nʹₑlqaˑłaqaʹₐne· aₐʹ-
210 kₑnqoˈʹwa neₗs sakq!ₐnuʹkᵤne· sakₑłhaqaʹₐne· kiaʹq!ła łuʹnˑqoʹ's,
at qaˈhałhaqaʹₐne· at qaˑupkaʹχe·. yakayaʹχa aₐˈkₑnqoˈʹwa's at
tsₑn tsuˇkuqkₑʹn·e· neₗs aₐˈq!aʹsoˑks, at qaˈhałaˈqaʹₐne· aₐˈkₑnqoˈʹwa nʹₑʹnse· k.łunqowaˈʹʹχo· kiaʹq!ła." taʹχas ya.ukᵘeʹₗka·m
ts!ₑnaʹχe·. k.łaʹχa·m nałkₑʹn·e· aₐˈkuʹk!ᵘpmaˑk!s. nʹuʹpχₐne·
215 pał tsᴇmak!kₑʹkse· papaʹe·s łoʹnˑqoʹs qaˈłaqaʹpse· kiaʹq!łaʹs.
taʹχa nʹₑʹne· qo kwₑʹłqa wuʹo neₗs yaqaoˇχaʹmke· ya.ukᵘeʹₗka·m
qoˑʹs aˈq!aʹsoˑks. qahanqaʹme·k. qaaˈłoˑqałnuʹk!ᵤne. kiaʹq!łaʹ·s.
nʹuʹpχₐne· naˑʹs aˈqaʹt!aks pał nʹuk!wiłsłaˑhatqaˈnwisquʹkse·,
mₑʹksaˑn qoʹs kiyunaʹqaps wₑlkaˈniłpałneχuʹse· k.łₑnq!uʹkse·.
220 nʹuʹpχₐne· neₗ k!oˑʹk!ᵘe kiaʹq!ła neₗs aₐˈq!aʹsq!nuks tₑʹtqaˑt!s
słaˑhatₑqaˈʹtse·. taʹχas nʹₑsakₗnuʹse·. sukᵤnusχuʹse· at qaˑuʹp-
χₐne· neₗs tₑʹtqaˑt!s. pał at k!upsłaˑtₗyiłˑaχayaʹχał aₐˈkₑnqoˈʹ-
wa. słʹaqaqaʹpse· kqaoˈhoˑ neₗ kiaʹq!ła neₗs tₑʹtqaˑt!s. qakeʹₗne·
ya.ukᵘeʹₗkaˑm, qakₑʹlne· neₗs k!oˑʹk!ᵘeʹ·s kiaʹqłaʹs: "haq!małʹ-
225 uʹpkaˑn'." qałwiʹyne· neₗ kiaʹq!ła: "ₑntsⁱupłaʹpₗne·." qatałʹ-
upaʹχe·. qakeʹₗne· ya.ukᵘeʹₗkaˑm: "maₐts onₑʹłoˑ. hutsχałqa.-
upłₑʹsₗne·. hutsχałʹₑtkₗnₑʹsₗne·. nₑntsχaˑłsoʹᵤkᵤne·." taʹχas nʹu-
paʹχe· neₗ kiaʹq!ła. nʹuʹpχₐne· tsₑnłaˑkateʹₗse· neₗs nₑtstaʹhałs.
qak.łaʹpse·: "hutsχałtsukᵘaʹte· aₐˈkₑnqowaʹʹne·s. hunałtsoʹᵤkwaˑt
230 hutsχałʹitₑnmakanₑʹsₗne·." taʹχas qałwiʹyne· neₗ kiaʹq!ła:
"pał ksₑlsukuʹqłaʹnt naₐ nₑtstaʹhał. naqaʹntsχałsukᵛₑnmakanₑʹ-
łaˑp.'' qakeʹₗne: "hoʹyas tsukᵘaʹteˑn'." taʹχas ya.ukᵘeʹₗkaˑm
łuʹʹnte· aₐˈkₑnqowaˑₑʹse·s neₗs kiaʹq!łaʹs. kułq!aʹpiłʹoʹᵤneˑt. taʹχas
tsukᵘaʹte· aₐˈkuk!pmaˑk!s ya.ukᵘeʹₗkaˑm. taʹχas t!aptsłaʹₐnte·
235 neₗs yaqakeʹₗkałukᵘₑʹnke· aₐˈkₑnqowaˑₑʹse·s. qakₑʹlne·: "taʹχa
łuʹnˑu łahułuʹqᵘeˑn'." taʹχas neₗ kiaʹq!ła łahułuʹqᵤne· qoˑʹs
aˑnłₑʹnqoʹs. qakₑʹlne·: "hoʹyas, neₗ qałwanwₑʹt!e·n'." taʹχas kiaʹ-
q!ła nit!naʹkₑswₑʹt!ₗne· neₗs qałwanwₑʹt!ₗne·. tsₑnłakateʹₗse aₐˈ-
kₑnqowaʹe·s. taʹχ qoˑ kₗyunaʹqa kiaʹq!ła nʹuʹpχₐne· qoʹs hanaʹ-
240 qₐnakₑʹske· tₑʹtqaˑt!s. qoʹs k!oˑˈk!ᵘiłʹₑlqawₑsqoʹkᵘes saˈqχałʹopaʹ-
qse·. nʹuʹpχₐne. k.łaqank.łaʹpseˑs qoʹs tₑʹtqaˑt!s k!uʹpaˑ's. taʹχas
k.łats!ₑʹkaˑs nas aˑnło'nₗqoʹs nʹuʹpχₐne· wanwₑʹt!se·. qₑʹn·a tsₑn-
łaˑkateʹₗse·. hàˑ, ne·sts k.łahoʹłoqs ya.ukᵘeʹₗkaˑm qakₑʹlne·: "łaqo-
namₑʹłeˑn' qo aₐˈkₑnₑk!namoˈʹne·s. tsχałʹupkaʹχe·. na·sts yaqaqaʹₐ-
245 ke· ku.ₑtkₑʹn·e·s q!aʹpe· hutsχałqałʹₑtkₑʹn·e·." taʹχas k.łałaʹχaˑm
aₐˈkₑnₑk!namuʹʹe·s mₑʹtsuˑk. taʹχa neₗ ko·łʹₑtkₑʹnaps ya.ukᵘeʹₗ-
kaˑms. qałʹatₑʹlne· mₑʹtsuˑk. k.łałaʹχaˑm qoʹs yaqaˈhałyunaqaʹpske· kiaʹq!łaʹs, nʹupχₐnaʹpse· yaqaˇqaʹpske· aₐˈkₑnqᵤwaʹʹe·s łaˑ-
łoʹᵤse· nʹak.łaˑnaʹqapqaʹpse· soʹᵤkse·. qakeʹₗne· mₑʹtsuˑk: "tseₗ-
250 kataʹpkiˑł kaₐ koaʹqaʹqa." qakiłₑʹlne·: "nₑntsₑʹnłakatₗmuʹn·e· ₑn
kqaₐkₑlhaʹqa aₐˈkwₑt!nₑʹsₗmiˑł." qak.łₑʹlne·: "hoʹyas neₗ qałwanwₑʹt!eˑn'." taʹχas mₑʹtsuk wankₑswₑʹt!ₗne·. nʹupχałₑʹsₗne· nʹₑseₗl-

(c) YA.UK^UE'_IKA·M OBTAINS FEATHERS

Then Ya.uk^ue'_ika·m staid there. He said: "If there were | feathers, I should feather my arrow." Frog said: "There are ‖ feathers 210 far off. There is a lake, and there are some ducks way out on the lake. | They stay there and do not come ashore. Those who go to get feathers | just pick them up along the shore. | The feathers are there. They come off from the ducks." Then Ya.uk^ue'_ika·m | started. When he arrived there, he carried ear ornaments. He discovered that his grandmother ‖ had spoken the truth. Way out on the lake 215 were some ducks. | It was a large (body of) water. Then Ya.uk^ue'_ika·m | went to the shore and sat down. He did not know how to get the ducks. | He saw one there swimming not far away; | but many ducks were making a noise with their mouths, playing. ‖ One Duck 220 saw the man | walking along the shore. Then (Ya·uk^ue'_ika·m) sat down. He was bright red. The Duck had never seen | a man. They always went to get feathers on shore. | Therefore the Duck did not know (what) a man (was). | Ya.uk^ue'_ika·m said to the one Duck: "Come ashore for a while." ‖ Duck thought: "He might kill me," and 225 did not come ashore. | Ya.uk^ue'_ika·m said: "Don't be afraid of me, I won't kill | you. I will make you (look) nice. You will be handsome." | Then Duck came ashore. It saw that the youth looked nice. | He said to Duck: "I'll take your feathers. When I have taken them, ‖ I'll pay 230 you for them." Then Duck thought: "This youth | is well dressed. Maybe he will reward me well." | He said: "Well, take them!" Then Ya.uk^ue'_ika·m | plucked out the feathers of the Duck. | He took them all off. Then Ya.uk^ue'_ika·m took the ear ornament and stuck it on ‖ where he had plucked off the feathers. He said: 235 "Now | go, swim away!" Then Duck swam away there, | far out to sea. (Ya.uk^ue'_ika·m) said (to Duck): "Well, move your wings!" Then | the Duck stretched out its wings and moved them. | Its feathers looked pretty. Then many ducks saw the man sitting there away off. ‖ That one floating about alone started to swim 240 ashore. | They knew that the man must have called it ashore. | When they saw it coming back, farther out to sea, they saw it spreading its wings. Oh, | they were pretty, ha! When (the Duck) began to swim back, Ya.uk^ue'_ika·m said to it: | "Go back there to your relatives! They shall come ashore. I'll make them all (look) in the same way ‖ in which I made you." Then, when (the 245 diver[1]) came back | to its relatives after it had been finished by Ya.uk^ue'_ika·m, | it was called Diver. When it arrived back where the many ducks were, | they saw how its feathers were. | It had pretty new ones. Diver said: ‖ "Look at me, how I am!" They said to 250 him: "You look pretty on account of the things that are on | your wings." He was told: "Go on, move your wings!" | Then Diver

---

[1] The duck had been transformed into a diver called *mitsuk*, smaller than a loon, with a long slender neck, white belly, and dark back.

so'ₐukse·. qake'ᵢne· mₑ'tsu·k: "qake'ᵢne· qo· nₑtsta'hał, kₑnł'-
upamₑ'łki·ł na·sts ya'xqał'itkᵢna'pke·, a'ₐ·ke tsxałqał'ₑtk-
255 nₑskₑ'łne·." ta'xas q!a'pe· kia'q!la n'upa'xe·. ta'xas ya.ukᵘe'ᵢ-
ka·m łokᵘₑ'n·e· a·ₐkₑnqowa.ₑ'se·s q!a'pe·s. qakₑ'łne·: "ta'xas
łahulqa'ₐtski·ł, kₑnła'k.łₑnq!o'yki·ł. na·s ·tsxałqaqa'ₐne. ts!up'-
na·'kot tsxał·awuqᵘa'ₐne· a·ₐkₑnqowanₑ'ski·ł. łuma'yit.s tsxał·a-
łuxu'n·e·. łaa'k!la·k at tsxał·aka'łak.łe'ᵢne·." ta'xas qakₑ'łne·
260 kia'q!la's: "ta'xas atinhołnoxokᵘₑ'łne·. suk.łₑ'tᵢne· neᵢ ₑ'nta.
q!a'pe· naqa'ₐne· a·ₐko'q!nuk na yₑsłₑₑ'tke· a'tₑntsq!apiłkqa-
tskₑ'łne·. taxta·' ts!upna'ko·t atₑntsławakₑ'łne· na·am·akᵢnₑ'ski·ł
mₑ'ksa·'n qo· ₑłqa'ha·k at n'ₑsqa·t!łe.ₑ'tᵢne·." ta'xas łahołqa·'
ₐtse· kia'q!la. sukᵘiłq!u'kₐne· ksukᵘił'itkᵢnₑ'ktsaps ya.ukᵘe'
265 ᵢka·ms. ta'xas tseᵢkata'mne· pał q!a'pe· so'ₐukse· a·ₐkₑnqowa''e·s
a·ₐku'k!pma·k!s. ta'xas ya.ukᵘe'ᵢka·m tsukᵘa'te· a·ₐkₑnqo'was,
łats!ₑna'xe·. ta'xas sₑł'ₑtkₑ'n·e· ya.ukᵘe'ᵢka·m na·s yₑsłe.ₑ't.ske· at
sₑłq!ape·łaqa'ₐne· kia'q!la a·ₐ'qsu'k!ᵘitna'mo's. neᵢs pₑ'k!a·ks kia'-
q!ła at qa.upka'xe· qo·s kwₑ'łqaps wu'o·s. łałaxa'xe· a·ₐ'kₑt.-
270 ła'e·s ya.ukᵘe'ᵢka·m.

(d) YA.UKᵁE'ᵢKA·M OBTAINS THE ARROW STRAIGHTENER

Qaosaqa'ₐne·. qake'ᵢne·: "ła'qa· koapₑswoₐuk!onₑ'łmo·." qake'-
ᵢne· wa'ta·k: "ło'ₐune· at qa·oxał'upna'mne· ya·keᵢł'aqa'ₐke·
a'pe·swok!onₑ'łmo·ł. n'isₑnkikₑłkₑ'n·e· kwₑ'łqłe·; at qaoxa'qał'-
opₑłka'ₐne· łaxa'yaxa'łe·s." ts!ₑna'xe· ya.ukᵘe'ᵢka·m. qałwi'yne·:
275 "hułts!ₑ'na·m, me'ᵢka n'u'płap kaha'tsa." n'ₑ'nse· ałₑtskₑ'ł'e·s
ma.ₑ'se·s ya.ukᵘe'ᵢka·ms kwₑ'łqłe·. łaxa'xe· san·ₑt.łanamₑ'sᵢne·.
tᵢnaxa''mne·. sanaqₐna'kse· nuł'a'qₐna's wuq!ła''mse·. ta'xa neᵢ
nuł'a'qₐna neᵢsts k!ₑseᵢłwu'q!ła'm sₑł'aqał'atₑ'łne· kwₑ'łqłe's.
qake'ᵢne· kwₑ'łqłe·: "qa'psin kₑ'n'oₐut?" qake'ᵢne· ya.ukᵘe'ᵢka·m:
280 "hun'o'ₐute· a'pₑswoₐuk!o'ₐuna·ł." qake'ᵢne· kwₑ'łqłe·: "ło'ₐune· nas
kakₑt.ła''mi·ł qo·s łe'ᵢnes a·ₐkₑnmₑ'tuks saq!a'n·e· hutsxał'ałqa'-
na'ntₑ'sᵢne·." ta'xas n'ałqana''nte·. neᵢsts kts!ₑ'ka·'m ya.ukᵘe'ᵢ-
ka·m papa''e·s tsxane·ta'pse· tsxałyaqakna'pske· neᵢs nuł'a'qₐna's tsxałyaqakₑ'n·ke·. ta'xas neᵢs k!ałqana''ntaps qak.ła'pse·:
285 "ta'xa łu'n·u. ₑn qa·'hałyu'ₐxᵘan' ₑs a·młu'n·us saq!a'n·e· hₑntsx-
ałtskałkₑ'n·e·." ta'xas n'u'pxₐne· ya.ukᵘe'ᵢka·m ta'xas kts!u'p-
łaps. yo·xa'xe· qo·s a·nqana'xe·. łayuxᵘa'xe·. tseᵢka'te· neᵢs
nuł'a'qₐna's pał sₑł·aho·łqu'łse· qo·s qayaqa'wo·'s. tsukᵘa'tse·
qa'psins. nₑłe·kxaqkₑ'nse·. wanuqkₑ'nse·. nawasxuna'kse·.
290 qakₑ·kse·:

"ał- qan- me·'-nit-ka'-na-we· he he- ha he he ha."

łaoqo·'xaqkₑ'nse·. ta'xas łats!ₑnaqu'łse·. ta'xas ya.ukᵘe'ᵢka·m
sukᵘₑł'u'pxₐne· yaqaqₐna'pske· neᵢs nuł'a'qₐna's. pał ksukᵘiłts-

moved his wings, and they saw that he looked nice. | Then Diver
said: "That youth said, 'You shall | go to the shore there. He will
make you look the same way as I am.'" || Then all the ducks 255
went ashore. Ya.uk^ue'₁ka·m | took off the feathers of all of them.
He said to them: "Now | swim out again and play. It will be this
way: | in the fall your feathers will be long again; in the spring they
will | come off, and others will grow." Then he said || to the ducks: 260
"You may fly to a nice place there back from the shore. There are |
lakes all over that place, and you shall visit all of them. | Then in
the fall come back here to this your country; | but there far away
it is very cold." Then the ducks swam away. | They were glad.
Ya.uk^ue'₁ka·m made them look nice. || Then they looked at one an- 265
other, and all the ear ornaments had become pretty feathers. | Then
Ya.uk^ue'₁ka·m took the feathers | and went back. Then Ya.uk^ue'₁ka·m
did this. There are | ducks all over the country in the summer time.
Long ago | the ducks did not come ashore out on the big sea. ||
Ya.uk^ue'₁ka·m went back to his tent. | 270

(d) YA.UK^UE'₁KA·M OBTAINS THE ARROW STRAIGHTENER

There he staid. He said: "I wish I had an arrow straightener!"
Frog said: | "There is none, but people die where there are | arrow
straighteners. Mountain-sheep Ram has them. He kills those | who
go to get them." Ya.uk^ue'₁ka·m started. He thought: || "Let me 275
start, even if my uncle should kill me." The Ram was | the brother
of Ya.uk^ue'₁ka·m's mother. He arrived there, and there was a tent. |
He entered. An old man with long hair was seated there. Now,
this | old man with long hair was called Bighorn. | Bighorn said:
"What do you want?" Ya.uk^ue'₁ka·m said: || "I want an arrow 280
straightener." Bighorn said: "There is none here | in my tent. It
is hanging on the other side of the river. I'll take you across in my
canoe." | Then he took him across. When Ya.uk^ue'₁ka·m was about
to come, | his grandmother had told him what the old man | would do
to him. When he had taken him across, Ya.uk^ue'₁ka·m was told: ||
"Now go on, climb up the mountain! Farther along it hangs. You | 285
shall bring it." Then Ya.uk^ue'₁ka·m knew that (Bighorn) intended
to kill him. | He went up and went on some distance. Then he
went up again. He looked at the | old man, who was going back in
his canoe. When he was in the middle of the water, he took | some-
thing, put it into the water, and shook it in the water, and sang, ||
saying: | 290

"I always take them across in my canoe, he he ha, he he ha!"[1] |

Then he put it back into the canoe and went back. Now, Ya.uk^ue'₁-
ka·m | knew very well what the old man had done. He had been·

---

[1] My interpreter could not translate the words of this song, but explained it in the way given here.

ẋana·''taps papa''e·s tsẋalya·qaqna'ₐke·. ta'ẋas kultse'ᵢkat neᵢs
295 nuł'a'qₐna's. neᵢs qana'ẋe· k!unanmⅇ'tuks. n'u'pẋₐne· sanₑt.-
łanamⅇ's̗ᵢne·. tₑnaẋa''mne·. ta'ẋas wa·miłnikⅇ't.se·. tsᴇma·k!ⅆ'-
ⅇsqat!łe.ⅇ't̗ᵢne·. qak.ła·pse· neᵢs kt̗ᵢna'ẋa'm: ''há·, qa'psins
ẋma ksiłaqaha'kqa ka'pₐt!?'' qak.ła·pse· aqsakaẋa·''mⅇ'łe·n'.
alkₑnu·k!ko·ẋa'maⅼ.   ta'ẋas   ya.ukᵘe'ᵢka·m   n'itẋo'ᵤme·k.
300 ta'ẋas n'o'ᵤyankᵢna'pse·. qao·saqa'ₐne·. qanła'łte· a'ₐ'kmaq!-
a'n'e·s. k.łayo''ẋam kwⅇ'łqłe·. n'ⅇtẋo'ᵤme·k yoᵤẋaqanmⅇ'te·
k!o·'ya·s. yoᵤẋaqanmitẋa'me·k. ta'ẋas sⅆqa.it!ko'ᵤne·   at
qa'kałqałⅇtkⅇ'n'e·. qa·hakqa'ₐne· neᵢ nuł'a'qₐna neᵢs qanła'łit
a·k'maq!a'n'e·s qo hanit.ła'ₐke·. qake'ᵢne· neᵢ nuł'a'qₐna: ''hoi,
305 skⅇ'kq!me·qo·ku'muqłⅇ'łko·.''   ya.ukᵘe'ᵢka·m   ku'n'me·ła·k.łe·
nₑtsta'hał· wunekⅇ't.se· a'ₐ'ke· k.łaqanła'łit aₐk'maq!a'n'e·s qo
hanit.ła'ₐke· a'ₐ'ke· łaqake'ᵢne· kwⅇ'łqłe· neᵢs ma sⅆya·qake'ᵢke·.
qake'ᵢne·: ''ta'ẋas maₐts ła.ⅇsqat!łe'e·t.'' ta'ẋa neᵢ nuł'a'qₐna
at sⅆⅇtkⅇ'n'e· nöpⅇ'k!as. qakiłⅇ'łne· ya.ukᵘe'ᵢka·m: ''ta'ẋa
310 łu'n·u. wa's·ⅆ·aqunamⅇ'łe·n'. neᵢ nuł'a'qₐna peⅇ'k!a·kstsẋał·a·-
ałqa·kaqu'łne· hₑnłaẋa'm·ił. n'upka'qo·ł maₐts tsupẋₐnⅇ's̗ᵢne·.
ta'ẋas yu'ᵤẋᵘa'm n'antso'ᵤẋᵘa'm·, ta'ẋas nⅇ'nko· hₑntsẋał·aoqo-
ẋaẋa''mne· yaqso''mił. ta'ẋas nₑntsłahołqu'łne· neᵢs yaₐqaqₐ-
na'ₐke· neᵢs kqa'łwi·y ktsẋał'u'płe·s. hₑntsẋałqakⅇ'n·e·. ta'ẋas
315 hₑnłaałqana'qo·ł hₑnłayo'ᵤẋwa'm. ta'ẋas hₑntsẋałyoᵤẋwaqa'n-
mitẋa'me·k k!o·'ya qa'psin. hₑntsa·wutsk!apałtⅇ'łe·k hₑn'u'pẋa
nakq!meqoᵤku'muqłⅇ'łko. a'ₐ'ke· łaha'q!me·qoᵤku'muqłⅇ'łko·.
ta'ẋas hₑntsẋałqake'ᵢne·: 'ta'ẋas maₐts ła.ⅇsqat!łe'et.'
ta'ẋas hₑntsẋał·aa·łqakaqu'łne· hₑntsẋałyoᵤẋa'ẋe·. tsẋałsak-
320 qa'ₐne·. tsẋał'ₑnqa'pte·k kwⅇ'łqłe·. ta'ẋas hₑntsẋałtsukᵘa'te·
a·'pe·swok!o·'naⅼ.'' ta'ẋas nułqakiłⅇ'łne· ya·ukᵘe'ᵢka·m. ta'ẋas
łats!ₑna'ẋe·. łaqao·ẋa'ẋe·. n'u'pẋₐne· neᵢs nuł'a'qₐna's qa:'łₑn
słu·'pkaqu'łse· qa.upẋₐna'pse·. ta'ẋas yoᵤẋa'se· neᵢs aₐ'kuq!yu'-
muk!s. ta'ẋas nₑnko'e·s ya.ukᵘe'ᵢka·m ła.oqoẋaẋa''mne· łahoł-
325 qu'łne·. sakⅆ'oqoha·kqa'pse· neₐs kwanu'qkins n'ⅇ'nse· a·'-
kułats̗ⅇ'se·s neᵢs at kwanu'qkₑns. ta'ẋas tsᵤkᵘa'te· ya.ukᵘe'ᵢ-
ka·m. tse̗ᵢka'te· neᵢ nuł'a'qₐna yaqso'mⅇ'ł'e·s pał peⅇ'k!a·ks
słⅇ'ahułqu'łse· ya.ukᵘe'ᵢka·ms. pał qatał'opⅇ'łne·. qakⅇ'łne·:
''ła.upkaqu'łe·n'.'' qatse̗ᵢkatⅇ'łne· neᵢ nuł'a'qₐna· yunaq!an-
330 ke'ᵢne·. ta'ẋas qayaqa'woᵤs qa'oẋałⅇt̗ᵤwitsqu'łne· ya.ukᵘe'ᵢ-
ka·m. tsukᵘa'te· aₐ'kułats̗ⅇ'se·s neᵢs nuł'a'qₐna's. qake'ᵢne·
neᵢ nuł'a'qₐna: ''maₐts qunya'ẋan' ⅇn hakqa'ₐkⅇ· ẋałe'ᵢne·.''
ta'ẋas kqunya'ẋa qake'ᵢne·: ''maₐts ẋunaqkⅇ'ne·n'.'' ta·'ẋas
kẋuna'qke·n. nawasẋo'ᵤmek ya.ukᵘe'ᵢka·m. qake'ᵢne·:

335   ''ałqanme·'nitka'nawe·, he he ha, he he ha!'' .

    Ta'ẋas n'ⅆu'n·e· neᵢ nuł'a'qₐna. ya.ukᵘe'ᵢka·m ła.upaqu'łne·.
łatₑnaẋa''mne· aₐ'kⅇt.ła.ⅇ'se·s. n'ⅇtẋo'ᵤme·k. yo·ẋa'qa·nmⅇtẋa'-

told | by his grandmother what he would do. Then, after he had
looked at the ‖ old man, he went down the river. He saw a tent | 295
standing there, and entered. Then there was a snowstorm. It was
very | cold. He was told to come in. "Ha! why | should my
nephew be lying here?" He was told: "Come in here | to your
brothers and sisters!" Then Ya.ukᵘeʼ₍ka·m lay down, ‖ and they 300
warmed him. He staid there and struck his testicles. | When
Bighorn went up again, he lay down and threw warm things on
him, | and he threw them on himself. Thus he was not cold. |
He always did so. The old man lay there while the tent owner
was striking | his testicles. The old man said: "Hoi, ‖ there is noise 305
of bursting eyes!" Ya.ukᵘeʼ₍ka·m was a full-grown | man. After
a long time the tent owner again struck his testicles, | and Big-
horn said again what he had said before. | Now he said: "Don't let
it be cold any more!" Then the old man | called his manitous.
Ya.ukᵘeʼ₍ka·m was told: ‖ "Go on; go there quickly! The old man 310
will soon be on this side of the water. | When you get there and he
comes ashore, don't let him see you. Then, | when he goes up, go
behind and get into | his canoe. Then go back in the canoe. Do the
same as he did | when he wanted to kill you. You shall do the same.
When ‖ you get across in the canoe, then go up and throw | warm 315
things on yourself. Then listen; and when you hear | again noise of
eyes bursting, | then say: 'Don't let it be cold any more.' | Then come
back in your canoe and go up. ‖ He will be lying there, and he will be- 320
come a mountain sheep. Then take | the arrow straightener." Thus
Ya.ukᵘeʼ₍ka·m had been told. Then | he started. He got there, and
he saw the old man just | coming back to this side in his canoe. (The
old man) did not see him. He went up the cliff | on the bank of the
river. Now Ya.ukᵘeʼ₍ka·m went aboard and went back. ‖ His penis 325
that he had moved in the water | and that he shook in the water was
lying in the canoe. Then Ya.ukᵘeʼ₍ka·m took it. | The old man
looked at his canoe, and Ya.ukᵘeʼ₍ka·m was already | on the water.
(The old man) had not been able to kill him. He said to him: | "Come
back to the shore!" (Ya.ukᵘeʼ₍ka·m) did not look at the old man, who
said this many times. ‖ When he was in the middle of the water, he 330
stopped there | and took the old man's penis. The old man said: |
"Don't touch the thing that lies there, son." | Then, when he touched
it, he said: "Don't put it into the water." When | he put it into the
water, Ya.ukᵘeʼ₍ka·m sang. He said:‖

"I always take them across in my canoe, he he ha, he he ha!" | 335
Then the old man cried. Ya.ukᵘeʼ₍ka·m went back ashore. |

me·k k!o·'yas qa'psins. qahakqa'ₐne·. ta'χas tsEma'k!il'ɛsqat!le·-
ɛ't.se·. nulpa'lne· n'asq!a'lilha'kq!me·qoᵤku'muql̷ɛku'pse· neᵢs
340 nul'a'qₐna's. qake'ᵢne· ya.ukᵘe'ᵢka·m: "ta'χas maₐts la.ɛsqat!-
le'e·t." ta'χas lao·kᵤnuχa"mne·. laalqanaqu'lne· ya.ukᵘe'ᵢka·m.
youχa'χe·. sakqa'pse· pal n'ɛnqapta'kse· kᵤwɛ'lqle·'s neᵢs nul'-
a'qₐna·'s. pɛtsχo'ᵤne· aₐ'kuqle.ɛ'se·s. ta'χas tsχal'ɛ'nse·
a'pɛswo·k!una'l'c·s. lats!ɛna'χe·. ta'χas a'ₐ'ke· sɛl'upɛ'lne· neᵢs
345 χma ktsχa'l'ɛns yaqao˘χa'qa·l'upᵢnamɛ'ske·. ta'χas lalaχa'χo·
papa"e·s. qao˘saqa'ₐne·.

(e) YA.UKᵁE'ᵢKA·M OBTAINS SINEW

Qake'ᵢne·: "la'qa· aₐ'kɛnq!a'lqa·, ta'χas χma ko·ɛtkaχₐnɛ'le·k."
qake'ᵢne· wa'ta·k: "ha·'ksa kapa·'pa, kapa·'pa; lo'ᵤne· aₐ'kɛn-
q!a'lqa·. ts!ɛnamɛ'le·n' neᵢ sanɛt.la'ₐne·; qa'k.le·k tɛ'tqa·t! ɛ'n-
350 tsu·k!s. sawɛsqa'pse· aₐ'kɛt.la'e·s. kaq!a'le·'s to'χᵘa tsχa·l'omɛts-
k!o'ᵤse· aₐ'kɛt.la'e·s. hɛntsχal'ɛlwamɛ'lne· hɛntsχaltsukᵘa'te·
aₐ'kɛnq!a'lqa·." ta'χas ts!ɛna'χe· ya.ukᵘe'ᵢka·m. laχa'χe·
aₐ'kɛt.la.ɛ'se·s ɛ'ntsuk!s aₐ'qo·la'ₐka·'s. tɛnaχa"mne·. qake'ᵢne·
ɛ'ntsuk!: "qa'psin kɛ'n'oᵤt?" n'u'pχₐne· ke'e·ns ya.ukᵘe'ᵢka·ms.
355 nulpalnitɛ't ᵢne· ka'qaps nɛtsta'hals kqaqla'ke·s ya.ukᵘe'ᵢka·ms,
ktsχa'le·ns naso'ᵤkᵘe·ns neᵢs tskqa·'k.laps ɛ'ntsuk!s: "qa'psin
kɛ'n'oᵤt?" nalatsukᵘɛ'kse·. qake'ᵢne· ya.ukᵘe'ᵢka·m: "husɛlwa'-
χe·." wɛlke'ᵢne· neᵢs ke'ᵢtsχa ya.ukᵘe'ᵢka·m. qake'ᵢne· ɛ'ntsuk!:
"maₐts wɛlki·kmɛ'le·n'. to'χᵘa tsχal'omɛtsk!o'ᵤne· ka·kit.-
360 lanala'e·s kaq!a'le·." qake'ᵢne· ya.ukᵘe'ᵢka·m: "ho'yasts
tskakɛ'ne·n' t!awu"ne·s." namatɛktsa'pse·. tseᵢka'te·, pal
saha'nse·. lawaq!wu'se· tsa.ɛ'se·s. qakɛ'lne· neᵢs k.lawa'q!wo·s:
"tskakɛ'ne·n' t!awu"ne·s." namatiktsa'pse·. tseᵢka'te·. to'χᵘa
pal so'ᵤkᵘse·. ta'χas la.anaχa"mne· ya.ukᵘe'ᵢka·m. mɛ'tχₐne·
365 neᵢs kaq!a'le·'s a'ₐ'ke· lamɛ'tχₐne·. ta'χas n'ɛlwa'n·e·. qakɛ'lne·:
"ta'χas tsukᵘa'tki·l aₐ'ku'la·k a'ₐ'ke· aₐ'ku'qla. hɛnts!alasqa
kɛ'lne· na aₐ'ku'qla. ka'mi·n tsɛn tsuk!ᵘe'ᵢne· aₐ'kɛnq!a'lqa·.
hutstsukᵘa'te·." ta'χas n'umɛtse'ᵢte· ɛ'ntsuk! altsa'ₐtᵢmo. ta'-
χas lats!ɛna'χe· ya.ukᵘe'ᵢka·m. k.lala'χa·m papa"e·s. qao˘sa-
370 qa'ₐne·. ta'χas n'ɛtkɛ'n·e· a'k!e·s. ta'χas q!a'pe·'s no·kᵘɛ'n·e·.

(f) YA.UKᵁE'ᵢKA·M OBTAINS FLINT

Qake'ᵢne·: "hol'u'pχa kaₐs naqa'ₐki·lha'qa a·qa'tsko·. hula-
ya'χa." qake'ᵢne· wa'ta·k: "ha·'ksa, kapa·'pa, kapa·'pa.
wule.ɛ't.se· ya ᵤkilaqa'ₐke· a·qa'tsko·. n'ɛ'n·e· tɛ'tqa·t!s neᵢ
a·qa'tsko·. pal ke'e·n no'ᵤkᵘe·ᵢs neᵢsts la·χa·m tɛ'tqa·t! qa'lwiy
375 ktsχaltso'ᵤkwa·t, neᵢs no'ᵤkᵘe·s at n'ɛnqa'pte·k tɛ'tqa·t!s.
ta'χas at qa'taltsukᵘatɛ'lne·." qalwi'yne· ya.ukᵘe'ᵢka·m: "hults!ɛna'me·l neᵢ no'ᵤkᵘe·." ta'χas ts!ɛna'χe·. laχa'χe· aₐ'kɛt.-

He entered the old man's tent and lay down. He threw | something warm on himself and lay there. Then it became very cold. | Twice he heard the bursting of eyes of the ‖ old man. Ya.uk^ue′_i- 340 ka·m said: "Don't let it be cold any more." | He arose. Ya.uk^ue′_i-ka·m went across. | He went up, and there he was lying. The old man had turned into a mountain sheep. | Ya.uk^ue′_ika·m chopped off its horn, which was to be | his arrow straightener. Then he started, and he also killed that ‖ which was to be killed by the people. Then 345 he went back to | his grandmother. He staid there. |

(e) YA.UK^UE′_iKA·M OBTAINS SINEW

He said: "If there were sinew, I should put feathers on my arrow." | Frog said: "O grandson, grandson! there is no sinew. | Go there. There is a tent. The name of the man is Mouse. ‖ His tent 350 stands there. Bull Moose almost breaks | his tent. You will kill him. You will take | the sinew." Then Ya.uk^ue′_ika·m started and came | to the tent of Mouse at A_aʻqoˑɫa′ka's.[1] He entered. Mouse said: | "What do you want?" He knew it was Ya.uk^ue′_ika·m. ‖ He had 355 heard that there was a youth named Ya.uk^ue′_ika·m | who was to be chief. When Mouse spoke to him, "What | do you want?" he whispered. Ya.uk^ue′_ika·m said: "I have come." | When Ya.uk^ue′_i-ka·m spoke, he spoke loud. Mouse said: | "Don't speak loud. Bull Moose might break our tent." ‖ Ya.uk^ue′_ika·m said: "Give me | your 360 bow." He gave it to him. He looked at it. | It was bad. (Mouse's) younger brother carried meat. He said to the one who brought the meat: | "Give me your bow." He gave it to him. He looked at it. It was almost | good. Then Ya.uk^ue′_ika·m went out. He shot ‖ the 365 Bull Moose, shot it again, and killed it. He said to them: | "Take the meat and the skin. You shall split | this skin. I shall take only one thing. I shall take the sinew." | Then Mouse and his brothers cut it up. | Ya.uk^ue′_ika·m went back, and arrived at his grandmother's (tent). ‖ He staid there. Then he made an arrow. 370 Then it was all finished. |

(f) YA.UK^UE′_iKA·M OBTAINS FLINT

He said: "If I knew where there is some flint, I should get it." | Frog said: "O grandson, grandson! | it is far away where the flint is. The flint is a man. | It is a stone. When a person arrives and intends ‖ to take it, then the stone becomes a man. | Then it can not be taken." 375 Ya.uk^ue′_ika·m thought: "I'll | go after that stone." Then he started,

---

[1] This is a small hill on the south side of St. Marys River, an isolated part of the lowest terrace in the valley of the Kootenay River. The hill is called A_aʻqoˑɫa′ka's.

łaꞏ′seꞏs. taꞏ′xas peꞏ′kǃaks nꞌⱭnqaptaꞌ′kseꞏ tⱭ′tqaꞏtǃs neᵢs
noꞌ₍ᵤ₎kᵘeꞏs, neᵢsts kǃuꞌpxₐnaps kꞏła′xaꞏm nꞌⱭnqaptaꞌ′kse. noꞌ₍ᵤ₎-
380 kᵘeᵢs. aꞌₐꞏkeꞏ neᵢs qaꞏwⱭtsᵢnuꞌkseꞏ at qaꞏkeᵢkaꞏkⱭnłⱭ′sᵢneꞏ.
ta′xas at sⱭłqanłałtmułⱭ′sᵢneꞏ. qaꞏ′ła nꞌⱭtⱭnmaꞏ′ka taꞏ′xas at
sⱭłtsukᵘaꞏ′teꞏ neᵢs noꞌ₍ᵤ₎kᵘeᵢs. taꞏ′xa neᵢ noꞌ₍ᵤ₎kᵘey at qakeᵢ-
kakⱭnⱭ′łneꞏ nⱭłkoꞌᵤtsǃap aₐ′ktsaꞏma·ł. at sⱭꞌaqaqaꞌₐneꞏ at
kǃⱭtⱭꞌnꞏmaꞏk neᵢsts nꞌitⱭnmaꞏkaꞏnⱭ′leᵢł aꞏqa′tskoꞏ at qatałꞌⱭn-
385 qaꞌ′pteꞏk noꞌ₍ᵤ₎kᵘeᵢs. qaꞏitⱭnmakanⱭ′łeꞏł at nꞌⱭnqaꞏ′pteꞏk tⱭꞌtqaꞏtǃs.
at qaꞏmaꞌₐteꞏ aₐ′kułaꞏ′kǃeꞏs. ta′xas yaꞏukᵘeꞏ′ᵢkaꞏm ktⱭnaꞏ′xaꞏm,
peꞏ′kǃaꞏks pał nꞌⱭnqaptaꞌ′kseꞏ tⱭꞌtqaꞏtǃs. qałwiꞌyne. aꞏqa′tskoꞏ:
"pał keꞏens nasoꞌ₍ᵤ₎kᵘeꞏns yaꞏukᵘeꞏ′ᵢkaꞏ′ms ktsxałwⱭⱭnmakanⱭꞌ-
łaps." qakeꞏ′ᵢne. aꞏqa′tskoꞏ: "qaꞏpsin kⱭꞌnꞌoᵤt?" qakeꞏ′ᵢne
390 yaꞏukᵘeꞏ′ᵢkaꞏm: "hunꞌoꞌᵤteꞏ aꞏqa′tskoꞏ." qakeꞏ′ᵢne aꞏqaꞏ′-
tskoꞏ.: "hⱭntsǃⱭtⱭnmakaꞌₐneꞏ, taꞏ′xas hutsⱭnqaꞏ′pteꞏk noꞌ₍ᵤ₎-
kᵘey, taꞏ′xas hⱭntstsukᵘataꞌ′pᵢneꞏ." qaꞏnqaꞏ′meꞏk yaꞏu-
kᵘeꞏ′ᵢkaꞏm. qałwiꞌyneꞏ: "hułꞌaꞏ′qₐneꞏts." taꞏ′xas łaꞏanaxaꞏ′-
mneꞏ. qaoꞏ′xaꞏ′xeꞏ tuwukxoꞌᵤnaꞏłs. qakⱭ′łneꞏ: "qakeꞏ′ᵢneꞏ
395 aꞏqa′tskoꞏ at kⱭnqₐtaꞌₐxoꞏ." qakeꞏ′ᵢne tuwukxoꞌᵤnaꞏł: "haꞏ-
slutskeꞏ′ᵢne aꞏqa′tskoꞏ, pał kutsmaꞏ′kǃeꞏ at wⱭłqałꞏunmⱭt-
xoꞌᵤneꞏ husaₐnłwiꞌynaₐt, kꞏłaqaꞏ′ke?" łaꞏanaxaꞏ′mneꞏ yaꞏu-
kᵘeꞏ′ᵢkaꞏm. łaqaoꞏ′xaꞏ′xeꞏ aꞏqa′tskoꞏs. qakⱭ′łneꞏ: "tuwukxoꞌᵤnał
słaꞏ′tᵢyilqakeꞏ′ᵢne. at kwⱭłqaꞏłꞏunmⱭtnukxoꞌᵤneꞏs." qakeꞏ′ᵢne
400 aꞏqa′tskoꞏ: "aꞏ:, slutskeꞏ′ᵢne tuwukxoꞌᵤnaꞏł. at qₐtaxonaꞏ′pᵢneꞏ
neᵢ huts!aqaꞏ′meꞏk at hutsᴇmakǃⱭ′ᵢneꞏ." łaꞏanaxaꞏ′mneꞏ
yaꞏukᵘeꞏ′ᵢkaꞏm. qaoꞏ′xaꞏ′xeꞏ tuwukxoꞌᵤnaꞏłs. qakⱭ′łneꞏ: "qakeꞏ′ᵢ-
neꞏ aꞏqa′tskoꞏ at kⱭnqₐtaꞌₐxoꞏ. kⱭnslutskⱭ′kᵢmiꞏł. neᵢs
ktsǃaqaꞏ′meꞏk, taꞏ′xas at ktsᴇmaꞏ′kǃeꞏ." qakeꞏ′ᵢne tuwu-
405 kxoꞌᵤnał: "qonamⱭ′łeꞏnꞌ kⱭnłqaꞏ′keꞏł kutskꞏłaqₐnaneꞏ′maꞏł." łaꞏ-
anaxaꞏ′mneꞏ yaꞏukᵘeꞏ′ᵢkaꞏm. qakⱭ′łneꞏ aꞏqa′tskoꞏs: "qakeꞏ′ᵢne
tuwukxoꞌᵤnaꞏꞏł, kⱭnkꞏłaqₐnaneꞏ′maꞏł." taꞏ′xas tsukᵘaꞏ′teꞏ aₐ′ktsa-
maꞏłꞌeꞏs tuwukxoꞌᵤnaꞏł, aₐ′keꞏ aꞏqa′tskoꞏ. qakeꞏ′ᵢneꞏ: "hoꞌyaꞏ
hułkꞏłaqₐnamnaꞏ′laꞏ." taꞏ′xas mitᵢyaxnaꞏ′mneꞏ qanłałtaꞏ′mneꞏ.
410 qⱭꞌnꞏa, aꞏqa′tskoꞏ łitiłxustⱭ′łeꞏk. wⱭłqaꞏłꞏuꞌnmⱭtnukxoꞌᵤłneꞏ.
taꞏ′xas yaꞏukᵘeꞏ′ᵢkaꞏm tsoꞏkokᵘⱭ′nꞏeꞏ aꞏqa′tskoꞏsts tuwukxoꞌᵤnaꞏłs. taꞏ′xas yunaqaꞏ′pseꞏ sakiłkꞏłaqₐnanaꞏ′mseꞏ. taꞏ′xas
tsukᵘaꞏ′teꞏ aꞏqa′tskoꞏsts tuwukxoꞌᵤnaꞏłs. paꞏtsⱭnmⱭ′teꞏ naꞏs
aꞏmaꞏks. qakeꞏ′ᵢneꞏ: "taꞏ′xas kꞏłqǃaꞏ′pełhaꞏ′qa aꞏqa′tskoꞏts
415 tuwukxoꞌᵤnaꞏł naꞏs aꞏmaꞏks. pał ktsxaꞏłwunⱭ′keꞏtꞏs ktsxał-
qahakⱭłhaꞏ′qa aqłsmaꞏ′kᵢnⱭkǃ naꞏs aꞏmaꞏks. at xma kts-
xałⱭsⱭłkⱭ′nꞏeꞏs nayaꞏ′xa aꞏqa′tskoꞏsts tuwukxoꞌᵤnaꞏłs." sakił-
kꞏłaqₐnaꞏ′mneꞏ swᵥꞌtᵢmo. qaꞏuꞌpxₐneꞏ peꞏ′kǃaꞏks słaꞏ′tᵢyiłpaꞏtsⱭn-
mⱭꞏ′tꞏseꞏ yaꞏukᵘeꞏ′ᵢkaꞏms. taꞏ′xas kułꞏeꞏ′tkin qaꞏ′psᵢns yaꞏukᵘeꞏ′ᵢ-
420 kaꞏm. qakⱭ′łneꞏ swᵥꞌtᵢmoꞏ′s: "taꞏ′xas qaqaskᵢnaꞏ′mkiꞏł.
ma kusⱭꞌaqₐnetsⱭ′skeꞏł. taꞏ′xas atⱭ′ntsxałꞏaqaⱭnkⱭ′łneꞏ aqłs-
maꞏ′kᵢnⱭkǃ neᵢs nayaxanⱭ′skeᵢł. taꞏ′xas husⱭꞌułⱭtkⱭ′nꞏeꞏ tsxałꞌ-

and arrived at | the house, and already the stone had become a man. |
When the stone saw him coming, it had changed its form, || and there 380
was another stone there where they get it from, | which is used to hit
(the flint).   Those who pay | can take the stone.   Then it is a stone |
from which they get arrow points and knives.   For this reason | they
pay for it; namely, that || the flint may not transform itself.   When 385
they do not pay, it turns into a man | who does not give his flesh.
When Ya.uk^ue′ᵢka·m entered, | the stone had already turned into a
man.   Flint thought: | "Ya.uk^ue′ᵢka·m is a chief; he will pay a great
deal." | Flint said: "What do you want?"   Ya.uk^ue′ᵢka·m said: || "I 390
want flint."   Flint said: | "You will pay for it.   Then I'll become a
stone. | Then you may take me."   Ya.uk^ue′ᵢka·m sat down. | He
thought: "I'll fool him."   Then he went out. | He went to Diorite,[1]
and said to him: "Flint says || you can not break him."   Diorite said: 395
"Oh, | Flint lies, I am strong.   I break him into big pieces | when I
get angry.   Why did he say so?"   Ya.uk^ue′ᵢka·m went out. | He
went back to Flint.   He said to him: "Diorite | always says he will
break you into big pieces."   Flint said: || "Oh, Diorite lies, he can not 400
break me. | When I grease my body, I am strong."   Ya.uk^ue′ᵢka·m
went out again | and came to Diorite.   He said to him: "Flint | says
you can not break him.   He says you are lying.   When he | greases
himself, then he is strong."   Diorite said: || "Go back and tell him 405
that I'll fight with him." | Ya.uk^ue′ᵢka·m went out again and said
to Flint: "Diorite says | you shall fight with him."   Then Diorite
took his knife, | and also Flint.   They said: "Well, | let us fight!"
They attacked each other and struck each other. || Oh, Flint lost. 410
Big pieces of stone were coming off from him. | Then Ya.uk^ue′ᵢka·m
took the flint and diorite. | He had much because they were fighting.
Then | he took the flint and diorite and scattered them over | this
world.   He said: "Let flint and || diorite occur all over this world. 415
For a long time people will be | here in this world.   It might be | diffi-
cult for them to get flint and diorite." | The friends were fighting.
They did not know that | Ya.uk^ue′ᵢka·m had scattered the stones.
When Ya.uk^ue′ᵢka·m finished doing this, || he told the friends: "Now 420
stop doing this to each other. | I cheated you.   You will not be | peo-
ple any more when they come to get you.   Now I have put an end

---

[1] Or some other tough stone.

ya·qaqa′ₐke· ne₁s u′s′me·ks.” ta′ӿas ɫapₑskₑna′mne· swʋ′t₁mo.
ta′ӿas ɫats!ₑnaɫӿo′ᵤne· a·qa′tsko·s ya.ukᵘo′₁ka·m. ta′ӿas
425 a·qa′tsko· q!apiɫaqa′ₐne. na′s a′m·a·ks.

(g) YA.UKᵁE′₁KA·M OBTAINS BOW WOOD

Ta′ӿas n′uk!qa·pɫo′ᵤse· tawu′′e·s. k!aɫa′ӿam ya.ukᵘe′₁ka·m
papa′′e·s. qake′₁ne·: “hol′u′pӿa kaₐs na· qa·kɫha′qa aₐ′k.ɫa′ₐkᵘo·.
hoᵤɫaya′ӿa.” qake′₁ne· wa′ta·k: “ha·′ksa kapa·′′pa, kapa·′′pa.
wuɫe.ₑ′t.se· ya·kɫhaqa′ₐke· aₐ′k.ɫa′ₐkᵘo· at qa·oӿaɫ′op₁na′mne·
430 naya′ӿa·ɫ.” ts!ₑna′ӿe· ya.ukᵘe′₁ka·m. wuɫe.ₑ′t.se· yaqana′mke·.
qana′ӿe·. nuɫpaɫnetₑ′t₁ne· nak.ɫe.ₑ′t.se·. qak.ɫa′pse· papa′′e·s·
ne₁sts qa′qa·ps ta′ӿas ktsӿaɫsɫa′ӿam. qa·na′ӿe·. nuɫpa′ɫne·
ta′k!a·ts· t!aɫo′ᵤkse·. taӿ ne₁ ta′k!a·ts at n′ₑt!ӿaka′ₐne·.
n′u′pӿₐne· ya.ukᵘe′₁ka·m ne₁s aₐ′kₑmana′m·e·s ne₁s qaɫya·nₑts!-
435 ɫa.ₑ′nse· yaₐkӿaɫa·′tqa·noӿu′nqa′pse·. n′ₑse·kate′₁se· at n′upɫ-
ka′ₐne· ne₁ aₐ′kₑts!ɫa′e·n. qataɫ′upₑ′ɫka ta′ӿas ta′k!a·ts at
n′ₑt!ӿaka′ₐne· ne₁s pₑ′k!a·ks yₑ′ske· k.ɫa′wɫa·′s aₜt qa′s₁ne·
ta′k!a·ts. at n′ₑse₁kate′₁ne·. tsukᵘa′te· tsuk!otiya′ɫ′e·s ya.u-
kᵘe′₁ka·m ne₁s qa·ɫ′ayanₑn·mo·ӿu′n·e· ne₁ aₐ′kₑts!ɫa′e·n qao˘ӿa-
440 q!aɫkₑ′n·e· tsuk!otiya′ɫ′e·s ya.ukᵘe′₁ka·m. ɫaqawane′₁se·. ta′ӿas
qayaqana′ӿe· ta′k!a·ts. ta′ӿas sa·nɫwi′yne·. qaɫwi′yne· ktsӿaɫ′-
ₑ′t!ӿa ya.ukᵘe′₁ka·ms. n′aₐko′ᵤɫne· ta′k!a·ts. n′upiɫₑ′ɫne· ne₁sts
ki′e·p ta′k!a·ts qakӿaq!ₐnu′n·e· tuq!tsqa′mna. na′s qa·nₑts!ɫa-
·ₑ′nse· qanaɫwa·haq!ₐnu′n·e·. qake′₁ne· ya.ukᵘe′₁ka·m: “a·ː,
445 ₑn taӿ kₑnɫe′e·n ta′k!a·ts. pa′ɫ ktsyu·na′qᵘo·m. taӿta·′ at
ӿma ke·ntsӿaɫₑt!ӿa′ka mₑ′ksa·′n k.ɫₑnq!oymu′n·e·s ɫka′m·u,
atₑnts!ₑ′t!ӿₐne· aₐ′ke′y′e·s.” ta′ӿas q!aӿo′ᵤne· ya.ukᵘe′₁ka·m
aₐ′k.ɫa·kᵘo′ᵤt!e·s. ta′ӿas pa·tsₐnmₑ′te·. qake′₁ne·: “ta′ӿas k.ɫq!a-
piɫha′qa ₑ′ts!na·t! na′s a′m·a·ks.” ta′ӿas sɫ′aqaqa′ₐne· kq!a-
450 piɫha′qa ₑ′ts!na·t!, at ke′e·ns aₐ′k.ɫa·kᵘo′ᵤt!e·s aq!sma′knₑk!.
ta′ӿas ɫats!ₑna′ӿe· ya.ukᵘe′₁ka·m.

(h) YA.UKᵁE′₁KA·M GOES TO THE END OF THE WORLD

Laɫaӿa′ӿe· papa′′e·s·. qakₑ′ɫne·: “kapa′pa, k!a′qa·s na
a′m·a·k?” qake′₁ne· wa′ta·k: “tsaqᵤna′ne· a′m·a·k.” qake′₁ne·
ya.ukᵘe′₁ka·m: “qa′psins a′m·a·ks at qake′₁ka·m nata′nₑk!?”
455 qake′₁ne· wa′ta·k: “wuɫe·ₑ′t.se·.” qake′₁ne· ya.ukᵘe′₁ka·m: “kaₐs
at k!a′qa·′oӿam nata′nₑk!.” qake′₁ne· wa′ta·k: “wuɫe·ₑ′t₁ne·
at yaqao˘ӿa′mke· nata′nₑk!.” qake′₁ne· ya.ukᵘe′₁ka·m: “huts-
ӿaɫ′u′pӿₐne· kaₐs at n′a·qake′₁ka·m nata′nₑk!. a′ₐke· hutsӿaɫ′-
u′pӿₐne· kaₐs at n′aqa′oӿa·′m nata′nₑk!. taӿta·′.”
460 Ta′ӿas husɫqaqaso′ᵤӿaɫ′upӿamₑ′ɫne· yaqaɫ′ₑtkₑ′n·ek naso′₁-
kᵘe·n ya.ukᵘe′₁ka·m ne₁ pₑk!a′k₁nₑk! aq!sma′k₁nₑk!.

to this as | it was going to be first." Then the friends let go of each
other. | Ya.ukᵘe'ᵢkaˑm carried the flint along, and now ‖ there is 425
flint everywhere in this world. |

(g) YA.UKᵁE'ᵢKAˑM OBTAINS BOW WOOD

Now, there was one thing that he did not have, a bow. When
Ya.ukᵘe'ᵢkaˑm came back | to his grandmother, he said: "Let me see
where there is bow wood. | I'll get it." Frog said: "O grandson,
grandson! | it is far away where bow wood is found, and those who try
to get it are killed." ‖ Ya.ukᵘe'ᵢkaˑm started. He went a long ways. | 430
He went along and heard a noise. His grandmother had told him |
that he would be near by when it would be like that. He went along
and heard | squirrels making a noise. That squirrel bit everybody. |
Ya.ukᵘe'ᵢkaˑm saw a tree standing on each side of the trail. ‖ They 435
struck each other continually. It looked terrible. The trees killed |
every one. If they could not kill him, the squirrels | bit him. Long
ago they were of the size of grizzly bears. | The squirrel was big and
looked terrible. Ya.ukᵘe'ᵢkaˑm took his spear, | and, when the trees
went apart, he ‖ put his spear across. Then they did not move any 440
more, and | he went through. Then the squirrels were angry and
tried | to bite Ya.ukᵘe'ᵢkaˑm, but the squirrel was stabbed and killed.
Then | the squirrel was dead, and from it crept a little animal, which |
climbed up the tree here. Ya.ukᵘe'ᵢkaˑm said: "Oh, ‖ you shall be 445
Squirrel. There shall be many of you. | You may continue to bite,
but you may bite only the hands of children | that play with you."
Then he chopped down | the bow wood and scattered it. He said: |
"Let cedar grow all over this world." Therefore ‖ cedar, that is 450
the bow wood of the people, grows everywhere. | Then Ya.ukᵘe'ᵢkaˑm
started back. |

(h) YA.UKᵁE'ᵢKAˑM GOES TO THE END OF THE WORLD

He came back to his grandmother, and he said to her: "Grand-
mother, how big is this | world?" Frog said: "The world is small."
Ya.ukᵘe'ᵢkaˑm said: | "From what place does the sun start?" ‖ Frog 455
said: "It is far." Ya.ukᵘe'ᵢkaˑm said: "Where | does the sun go
to?" Frog said: "It is far | where the sun goes to." Ya.ukᵘe'ᵢkaˑm
said: "I shall | look for the place where the sun starts from, and
later on I | shall look for the place where the sun goes." ‖

That is all I know about what Chief Ya.ukᵘe'ᵢkaˑm did | among the 460
people of ancient times. |

54. COYOTE AND YA.UKᵁE'ₗKA·M

(a) COYOTE AND THE FAT

Ts!ɛna'xe· skɛ'n·ku·ts n'as'ma'łne· ya.ukᵁe'ₗka·ms. qake'ₗne·
ya.ukᵁe'ₗka·m, qakɛ'łne· skɛ'n·ku·ts·: "saq!a'n·e· t!ɛna'm·u, at
n'o·kᵁ!qnałqasxa'łne· neₗ t!ɛna'mu." ta'xas łaxa'xe·. ta'xas
qa'sxₐne· ya.ukᵁe'ₗka·m. ta'xas ts!ɛna'xe·. łaxa'xe· skɛ'n·ku·ts

5 a'ₐ·ke· qasɛłu'xᵤne·. ta'xas a'ₐ·ke· ts!ɛna'xe·. ta'xas n'unuq!-
wiya'ₐte·. sukwaxane'ₗse· no·kᵁma·'nxa'me·k. qatsxana'ₐte·
ya.ukᵁe'ₗka·ms. łałoqałqa'ₐtse· skɛn·ku·ts. łalaxa'xe· neₗs t!ɛna'-
mu's yaₐqaq!a'nske·. ta'xas n'ɛ'kₗne·. nuqaxu'se· neₗs t!ɛna'm·u's.
yaqłei't.se· neₗs yaqaq!a'nske· neₗs t!ɛna'mu's neₗsts koqa'xo·

10 ts!ɛnaqayqa'ₐne·. ta'xas mitiya'xₐne· skɛ'n·ku·ts. qasɛłu'xᵤne·.
nanoq!wiya'ₐte·. n'u'pxₐne· pa·ł tsxałxunaku'se· neₗs t!ɛna'm·u's.
no·ᵤłu'se·. ta'xas łamitiya'xₐne· a'ₐ·ke· łaqasɛłu'xᵤne·. pɛ'sxₐne·
łamitiya'xₐne· a'ₐ·ke· łaqasɛłu'xᵤne; a'ₐ·ke· łapɛ'sxₐne·. ta'xas
xunaku'se·. ta'xas niktsinoku'se· neₗs t!ɛna'mu's. qawɛsqa'ₐne·

15 skɛ'n·ku·ts. qałwi'yne·: "ta'xas hułats!ɛ'na·m, ta'xas kułe'e·k neₗ
koqᵁasɛłu'xᵘa." ta'xas łats!ɛna'xe· skɛ'n·ku·ts. łaqaoxa'xe· neₗs
yaₐkɛłpɛsxa'ke· neₗs t!ɛna'mu's. łaqa.ɛ'nse· t!ɛna'mu's; n'ɛnqapta'k-
se· n'o'ᵤkᵁeys kamnu'qłu's. ta'xas qa·wɛsqa'ₐne· skɛ'n·ku·ts.
n'unuq!wɛtsta'pse· neₗs t!ɛna'mu's neₗs kxuna'qo's. qałwi'yne·:

20 "huł'itoᵤkwi'ke·n." ta'xas n'ɛtkɛ'n·e·. ta'xas kuno'ᵤko·ps, ta'xas
qunałqunok!o'ᵤne· neₗs yaqa·wɛso'qske· neₗs t!ɛna'mu's.

Qana'xe· ya.ukᵁe'ₗka·m łamanwɛtskɛ'kₗne· n'u'pxₐne· ło'ᵤse·
skɛ'n·ku·ts. qałwi'yne· ma kqaapɛ'se· skɛ'n·ku·ts. łats!ɛna'xe·
ya.ukᵁe'ₗka·m. łałaxa'xe· qo's yaqaq!a'nske· t!ɛna'mu's. ło'ᵤse·

25 neₗs t!ɛna'mu's. qawɛsqa'ₐne· pa·ł kiyaqłe'et.s. n'u'pxₐne· neₗs
pa·ł sɛłqanał'una·q!małɛ'kse· skɛ'n·ku·ts. a'ₐ·ke· neₗs t!ɛna'mu's
pa·ł sɛłqana·q!małɛkma'łse·. ta'xas ts!ɛnał'una'xe·. n'u'pxₐne·
qo's u'me·'s nanq!oku'pse·. n'u'pxₐne· skɛ'n·ku·ts qoᵤs pał
n'ɛ'nse·. qaoxał'una'xe·. n'u'pxₐne· pa·ł sɛłqa'oxałqunok!o'ᵤse·

30 neₗs yaqawɛsu'qske· t!ɛna'mu's. qa'sɛł'awak!muwɛsu'qse· neₗs
t!ɛna'mu's. skɛ'n·ku·ts qsakoxamu'n·e neₗs t!ɛna'mu's. k.ła'-
xa·m ya.ukᵁe'ₗka·m. qawukatka'ₐne· skɛ'n·ku·ts. n'u'pxₐne·
ya.ukᵁe'ₗka·m pa·ł sɛłk!umnaqałts!a'k̓ikta'kse· swᵘe's. qakɛ'łne·:
"qa'psins kɛn'u'pskeₗn?" naq!manaxwatɛ'łne· skɛ'n·ku·ts.

35 qake'ₗne·: "sukwa'xₐne·neła'pₐne·." qakiłɛ'łne·: "ma.uqak.łɛ's₁-
ne· at tse·n k!o·'kᵁ!qna·łqa'siłu'xwa·ł.¹" ta'xas tsukᵁa'te· ya.-
ukᵁe'ₗka·m a'ₐ·ki·ts. qa'oxałt!aptsakɛ'n·e· aₐ·ktsa'ma·łs. ta'xas
qunakna'xₐne· qo's t!ɛna'mu's. ta'xas n'umitse'ₗne· neₗ t!ɛna'-
m·u. ta'xas n'awak!moᵤsu'qᵤne·² neₗ t!ɛna'mu. ta'xas qakiłɛ'łne·

40 skɛ'n·ku·ts: "ta'xas ɛ'ke·n' q!a'pe·." ta'xas skɛ'n·ku·ts n'upka'nqu'łne· neₗs t!ɛna'mu's.

---

¹ I heard: K!owo·'k!qna·łqa'siłu'xwił.   ²Creston dialect: n'awakaqu'ne·.

54. COYOTE AND YA.UK^{u}E$'_i$KA·M

(a) COYOTE AND THE FAT [1]

Coyote went along with Ya.uk^{u}e$'_i$ka·m.   Ya.uk^{u}e$'_i$ka·m said, | he
said to Coyote: "Fat is hanging there. | They bite that fat once."
Then they got there. | Ya.uk^{u}e$'_i$ka·m bit off a piece.   Then he
started.   Coyote arrived ‖ and bit off once.   Then he went on.   Then   5
he swallowed. | It tasted good, and he wanted more.   He did not tell |
Ya.uk^{u}e$'_i$ka·m.   Coyote turned back.   He came back to where | the
fat was hanging.   Then he ate of it.   The fat fell down. | It was steep
where the fat was hanging.   When it fell, ‖ it began to roll.   Then Coy-   10
ote ran after it.   He bit a piece off | and swallowed it.   He saw that the
fat was about to roll into the water | where it was deep.   Then he ran
after it and bit off another piece.   He put it down with his mouth, |
ran after it, and bit off another piece, and he put it down with his
mouth.   Then | the fat fell into the water and sank.   Coyote re-
mained there. ‖ He thought he would go back and eat | what he had   15
bitten off.   Then Coyote started back.   He arrived | where he had put
down the fat with his mouth.   There was no fat.   It had become | a
white stone.   Then Coyote stood there. | He wanted to swallow
the fat which was in the water.   He thought: ‖ "Let me heat stones."   20
Then he did so.   When they were red-hot, | he took them with
sticks to where the fat was in the water. |

Ya.uk^{u}e$'_i$ka·m was going along.   He looked back, and he saw there
was no | Coyote.   He thought Coyote was not acting right.   Ya.u-
k^{u}e$'_i$ka·m went back. | He came to where the fat had been hanging.
There was no ‖ fat.   It was steep there.   He saw the | tracks of Coyote   25
going down, and also the fat | and the tracks going along with it.
Then he started down.   Way below he saw | a fire.   He saw Coyote,
who was there. | He went down.   He saw him carrying the stones
with sticks ‖ to the place where the fat was in the water.   A piece of   30
the fat came up to the top of the water. | Coyote took a mouthful of
the fat. | When Ya.uk^{u}e$'_i$ka·m arrived, Coyote did not see him.   Ya.u-
k^{u}e$'_i$ka·m saw | his friend suffering.   He said to him: | "Why did you
do that?"   Coyote was scared. ‖ He said it tasted good.   He was   35
told: "I told you | they take just one bite."   Then Ya.uk^{u}e$'_i$ka·m
took | a pole.   He fastened a knife to it.   He speared | the fat.   Then
the fat was broken up. | The fat came to the top of the water.   Then
Coyote was told: ‖ "Now eat all."   Then Coyote took | the fat ashore. | 40

---

[1] See p. 48.

(b) COYOTE AND THE GIANT

Ta′ҳas tsǃꞓna′ҳe· neᵢsts yaҳkana′mke·. qana′ҳe·. qake′ᵢne·
ya.ukᵘe′ᵢka·m, qakꞓ′ǁne· skꞓ′n·ku.ts: "sa⁀qǃa′ne· ǂka′m·u nankǃo·
ma′ǂne·. at n′iǂa′ne· neᵢ ǂka′m·u. at qa·tsꞓn·kǃapa·ǂteҳa′ǂne·.
45 ma′ₐtsꞓntstsꞓn·kǃapa·ǂtiya′ҳₐne·." ta′ҳas ǂaҳa′ҳe·. n′uǂpa′ǂne·
skꞓ′n·ku·ts neᵢs ǂka′m·u′s. seᵢǂ′ꞔa′se·. ta′ҳas k.ǂa′ҳam ya.ukᵘe′ᵢ·
ka·m qayaqana′ҳe·. qatseᵢka′te· neᵢs ǂka′m·u′s· ta′ҳas k.ǂa′ҳam
skꞓ′n·ku·ts a′ₐ·ke· qatseᵢka′te· neᵢs ǂka′m·u′s. qayaqana′ҳe·. qa·
wuǂꞓnqa′ₐtse· kǃumnanǂe·′kpayaҳwata′pse·[1] neᵢs ǂka′m·u′s. ǂaǂo′·
50 qᵘaǂqa′ₐtse· ǂaqaoҳa′ҳe· naqtu′qǃᵘatsqǃahe′ᵢne· aₐ′kaǂma.ꞓ′se·'s.
ta′ҳas tsutiǂa′pse· neᵢs aₐ′kꞓtsqahe′e·s neᵢs ǂkam·u′s. soᵤkikqǃa·
naҳna′pse·. ta′ҳas ǂaqa.iǂa′se· neᵢs ǂka′m·u′s. ta′ҳas tsǃꞓnanu·
qᵘeᵢҳuna′pse·. ta′ҳas n′u·pҳₐne· pa·ǂ tsҳaǂtsiǂ′unuqǃwiyata′pse·.
ta′ҳas n′akunǂa′tǃne· ǂaqa·taǂ′akaǂa′tǃne·.

55   Ta′ҳas n′u·pҳₐne· ya.ukᵘe′ᵢka·m ǂam·anwi·tskꞓ′kᵢne· ǂo′ᵤse·
skꞓ′n·ku·ts· swꞔ′e·s. pa·ǂ siǂaqa.iǂa′se· neᵢs ǂka′m·u′s. ǂaǂoqa·ǂ·
qa′ₐtse· ya.ukᵘe′ᵢka·m. ǂaǂaҳa′ҳe· neᵢs ǂka′m·u′s skꞓ′n·ku·ts. pa·ǂ
sꞔǂ′unuqǃwiyata′pse· neᵢs ǂka′m·u′s. tsukᵘa′te· ya.ukᵘe′ᵢka·m
aₐ′ktsa′m·a·ǂs n′a·komu′n·e· neᵢs ǂka′m·u′s aₐ′kǂamꞓ′ses.
60 ta′ҳas n′ꞓ′pᵢne· neᵢ ǂka′m·u. ya.ukᵘe′ᵢka·m tsukᵘa′te· skꞓ′n·
ku·ts· aₐ′k.ǂatǃꞓ′se·s ǂa·ǂitqǃuҳmaǂa·′tǃne· skꞓ′n·ku·ts. n′u·pҳₐne·
skꞓ′n·ku·ts pa·ǂ qaꞓ′nse· ǂka′m·u′s, pa·ǂ n′ꞓ′nse· e·′ka·′s.
ta′ҳas ǂatsǃꞓna′ҳe· swꞔ′tᵢmu·. nao·′kǃᵘe· ǂa·ǂꞓtqǃu′ҳmaǂa′tǃne·.

(c) COYOTE AND THE THUNDERBIRDS

Qa·na′ҳe· swꞔ′tᵢmu·. qakiǂꞓ′ǂne· skꞓ′n·ku·ts: "ne· hu·tsyaҳ·
65 qanaҳaǂa′ₐke· nꞓntsҳaǂhuǂpa′ǂne·   toᵤqǃᵘtsqa′mna.   ma′ₐ·
tsꞓntstsꞓnkǃapa·ǂtiya′ҳₐne·."   ta′ҳas   qa·na′ҳe·.   ta′ҳasts
nuǂpa′ǂne· neᵢs tuqǃᵘtsqa′mna′s. ta′ҳas tǃaǂo′ᵤkse·. ta′ҳas
qayaqana′ҳe· ya.ukᵘe′ᵢka·m, a′ₐ·ke· skꞓ′n·ku·ts qatsꞓnkǃapaǂ·
tiya′ҳₐne· neᵢs tuqǃᵘtsqa′mna·′s. ta′ҳas tǃaǂo′ᵤkse·. qake′ᵢne·
70 skꞓ′n·ku·ts: "a: kuǂse·qa·tsinkǃapaǂte′ᵢҳats ǂa:ko′ǂsak, ko′ǂsak,
ko′ǂsak." ta′ҳas neᵢs kǃaqa′·ke· skꞓ′n·ku·ts, ta′ҳas qa.u′pҳₐne·
peꞓ′kǃaks pa·ǂ ǂaqa′wumꞓkꞓ′n·e· swꞔ′tᵢmu. pa·ǂ sǂꞓktka′ҳe·.
ta′ҳas ǂaҳa′ҳe· qo′s toqǃᵘtsqa′mna·. ta′ҳas n′oqoҳa′ҳe· neᵢs
aₐ′kuqǃno·katǂꞓ′se·s. pa·ǂ n′ꞓ′nse· nꞔ′m·ananakꞓsta′ke·s. ҳa·ts′·
75 neǂ′oqoҳa′ҳe· swꞔ′tᵢmu skꞓ′n·ku·tsts ya.ukᵘe′ᵢka·m. ta′ҳas
qao⁀saqa′ₐne·. qakꞓ′ǂne· ya.ukᵘe′ᵢka·m neᵢs ǂka′m·u′s: "at
kǃaqa′·swo·k sǂa′wam a′ǂakꞓne·kǃne·ᵢskeǂ?" qak.ǂa′pse· nao·′kǃᵘe·:
"tu·′ҳᵘa at ·waǂkwayꞓ′t.se· ǂa′wam nao·′kǃwe·, at waǂkwa·
yꞓ′t.se· aₐ·′ke· ǂa′wam. n′ꞓseᵢkat.ǂꞓ′tetne′ᵢse· pa·ǂ ke′e·ns
80 aₐ′kwuk.ǂe·′et.s ǂawoqǃo·′ha·ks aₐ′knukҳuna′ke·s." qakꞓ′ǂne·
swꞔ′′e·s ya.ukᵘe′ᵢka·m: "hꞓntsҳaǂhuǂpaǂna′pᵢne·. hꞓnqa.·

[1] Felix Andrew: kǃumnanlu·′kpayaҳwata′psc·.

(b) COYOTE AND THE GIANT

Then they started to where they were going. They were going along. | Ya.uk^ue′ᵢkaˑm said, he said to Coyote: "A child is hanging in a cradle. | The child is crying. One does not listen to it. ‖ Don't 45 listen to it!" Then they arrived there. Coyote heard | the child crying. Then, when Ya.uk^ue′ᵢkaˑm arrived, | he went past. He did not look at the child. When | Coyote arrived, he also did not look at the child, and went past; | but he had not gone past far when he took pity on the child. ‖ He turned back and arrived there. He put his finger 50 into the child's mouth. | The child sucked his fingers and | found them nice. The child did not cry. Then his hand began to go into the mouth, | and he knew that the child was going to swallow him. | He pulled at his arm, but could not pull it out. ‖

Then Ya.uk^ue′ᵢkaˑm knew it. He looked back, and | his friend 55 Coyote was not there. The child was not crying. | Ya.uk^ue′ᵢkaˑm turned back, and he came to the child | which was swallowing Coyote. Ya.uk^ue′ᵢkaˑm took | his knife and stabbed the child's head with it. ‖ Then the child was dead. Ya.uk^ue′ᵢkaˑm took | Coyote's arm. 60 There was no flesh on Coyote's arm. Coyote saw | that it was no child, but a giant. | Then the friends went on. One of them had no flesh on his arm. |

(c) COYOTE AND THE THUNDERBIRDS

The friends were going along. Coyote was told: "The way where we ‖ are going along you will hear birds. Do | not listen to them." 65 Then they went along. Then | they heard the birds. They made a noise. | Ya.uk^ue′ᵢkaˑm went past, and also Coyote. He did not | listen to the birds that made a noise. ‖ Coyote said: "I am not listening to 70 you, but łāko′łsak, ko′łsak, | ko′łsak!" When Coyote said so, the friends, without knowing it, | were already raised from the ground. They were going up. | Then they arrived there where the birds were. They had gone into | their nest. These were two young thunderbirds. Both ‖ friends went in, Coyote and Ya.uk^ue′ᵢkaˑm. Then | they 75 staid there. Ya.uk^ue′ᵢkaˑm said to the children: | "Where is the sun when your parents come back?" One of them said: | "It is almost evening when the one comes back, and it is evening | when the other comes back. They look terrible." It was ‖ on rocks on 80 one side of the mountain, and Ya.uk^ue′ᵢkaˑm said | to his friend: "Listen to me! If you do not | listen to me, we shall die. You know |

ułpa′ɩnap, ta′ꭓas hutsꭓał′upnała′ₐne· pa·ł kɩn′u′pꭓa· pa·ł
ksɑ′ɛseka·ɩe·tɛ′t̡ne·. ła′wam nao·′k!ᵘe· tsꭓałqake′ɩne.: ʽha:
ku̅sukwɛ′łq!o·k. ta′ꭓas ksɑ′ɛtpötske·′me·k ałkaa·′qa·ɩt.′′′
85 n′u′pꭓₐnc· neɩs ke′ens naso·ᵤkᵘe·ns ya.ukᵘe′ɩka·ms sɑ′aqake′ɩne.
kso·ᵤkwi′łq!o·k k!u′pe·ɩs ałaqa′ɩt!e·s. ta′ꭓas wałoq!kᵘku·′t̡ne·.
t!ało′ᵤkᵤne· nꝟ′m·a. ta′ꭓas n′u′pꭓₐne· ławanuꭓu′n·c· nꝟ′m·a
qake′ɩne· nꝟ′m·a: ʽʽha: ku̅sokwɛ′łq!o·k. ta′ꭓas ksɑtsma·-
k!c·npötskɛ′nme·k ałkaa·′qałt.′′ (pałuqa·siłq!akpa′me·k. qaki-
90 łɛ′ɩne· skɛ′n·ku·ts: ʽʽneɩsts qa′ke· nꝟ′m·a[1] kso·ᵤkwɛ′łq!o·k.
tsꭓałqake′ɩne·: ′qa·ła at kuk.łokkakɛ′me·k, hutsꭓaɩ·o·qoka-
ꭓa′ktse·′′′ qakiłɛ′ɩne· skɛ′n·ku·ts: ʽʽneɩsts qak.ła′wa·s nꝟ′m·a
ʽhɛntsꭓało·wo′kᵤne·,′ hɛntsꭓałqake′ɩne·, ʽko·ᵤqᵘa·′sakɛ′me·k,
ko·ᵤqᵘa·sakɛ′me·k, at k!ɛ·′sne·ɩsakniya′we· ka′tsa o·′k!ᵘqᵤna
95 ksa·′ne·ɩk!one′ɩqa.′′′) ta′ꭓas ła.ɛsaknu′n·e· skɛ′n·ku·ts. qaki-
łɛ′ɩne· ya.ukᵘe′ɩka·m: ʽʽa: ɛnqaka·ɩ′it!nasa′q!e·n′. hutsꭓał′oqo-
kaꭓaktsɛ′s̡ne·.′′ ta′ꭓas n′ɛt!nasa′q!ₐne· ya.ukᵘe′ɩka·m. ta′ꭓas
qaoꭓak!ałma′ne· nꝟ′m·a. qa·psqa̅·qa·pse· łałɛt̡nułma′k̡ne·
ya.ukᵘe′ɩka·m. quna·kɛnꭓamu′n·e· tsu·ko·tiya′ɩ·e·s a·ₐkuk!p-
100 ła′ɩnkak!ɛ′se·s neɩs nꝟ′m·a′s. n′upɛ′ɩne· neɩs nꝟ′m·a′s. neɩs
a·ₐkoq!nokᵘatɛ′se·s n′umɛtsꭓo′ᵤse· yaqa·nał′unaꭓu′ske·. ta′ꭓas
qaosaqa′ₐne·. qakɛ′ɩne· neɩs łkam·ukᵘɛsta′ke·′s: ʽʽła′wa·m
tɛtunɛ′ske·ɩ qa′ke·: ′qa′psins ksɩ′umɛ′tse· kakɛt.łana′ła,′ hɛntsꭓał-
qakiłkɛ′ɩne·: ′ɛs qa′ka·ɩyuwaka′ke·′sqkatɛ′ɩe·k′′′ ɛn·a·ke·sɩn-
105 qame′ɩke· nöpɛ′k!a sɑ′umɛtsłoꭓonatɛ′t̡ne·. ta′ꭓas qawuni-
kɛ′t.se· ta′ꭓas a′ₐ·ke· ławałuꭓko·ku′t̡ne· a′ₐ·ke· łat!ało·′kᵘne·
nꝟ′m·a. ta′ꭓas a′ₐ·ke· ławanoꭓu′n·e· nꝟ′m·a neɩs ma ski·ɩya-
qake′ɩke· nao·′k!ᵘe· a′ₐ·ke· qake′ɩne·. qake′ɩne· nꝟ′m·a: ʽʽqa′ła at
ksakɛ′me·k, hutsꭓałwuqoqaꭓa′ktse·,′′ nuwu′kᵘne· skɛ′n·ku·ts neɩs
110 ma ski·ɩyaqake′ɩke·. a·ₐkɑ′aqake′ɩne·. naqᵤwɛ′ɩne·. qake′ɩne·:
ʽʽko·qwa·′sakɛ′m·e·k ko·qwa·sakɛ′m·e·k. k!ɛs′ne·ɩsakₐniya′we·
ka′tsa, o·′k!ᵘqᵤna ksa·niłk!one′qa.′′ ła.ɛsaknu′n·e· skɛ′n·ku·ts.
qake′ɩne· nꝟ′m·a: ʽʽɛnqa′ka·ɩ′it!ɩnasa′q!e·n′. hutsꭓałwu̅qo·qa-
ꭓaktsɛ′s̡ne·.′′ ta′ꭓas n′ɛt!ɩnasa′q!ₐne· ya.ukᵘe′ɩka·m neɩs
115 ma skɑɩyaqaka′pske· a·ₐ′′ke· łaqaqa′pse· a·ₐ′kɛinułma′k!e·s;
a·ₐ′′ke· łaquna·kɛna′ꭓₐne· a·ₐ′′ke· n′upɛ′ɩne·.

Qakɛ′ɩne· neɩs łkam·ukᵘɛsta′ke·s. ta′ꭓas ła.una·nuꭓuma·ɩnawa′sno·. qake′ɩne· nao·′k!ᵘe· neɩ łka′m·u. ta′ꭓas yuwa·′kaɩ′-
ɛsa′kₐnu·. ta′ꭓas ya.ukᵘe′ɩka·m yu·ꭓałɛsakₐnu′n·e· nao·′-
120 k!ᵘe·′s. qakɛ′ɩne· swꝟ′′e·s: ʽʽhɛntsꭓałałukᵘlitɛ′ɩe·k.′′ ta′ꭓas nuł-
nuꭓu′n·e· nꝟm·ana′na, neɩs qa·′natwa·nuꭓu′n·e·. ta′ꭓas nakɑ-
wutskɛ′k̡ne· skɛ′n·ku·ts. ta′ꭓas wɛ′ɩiłwa·nuꭓu′n·e·. ta′ꭓas na-
łuk.łiti′ɩe·k skɛ′n·ku·ts. ta′ꭓas łats!kaɩ′okᵘanuꭓu′n·e· łaqayaqa·-
hanuꭓu′n·e·. ta′ꭓas ła.u′nanuꭓu′n·e· qo·s a′m·a·ks. qakiłɛ′ɩne·
125 skɛ′n·ku·ts: ʽʽta′ꭓas a′ₐ·ke· nɛ′nko·. yu·wakaɩ′ɛsa′kₐnu skɛ′n-

they look terrible. When one of them arrives, he will say, | 'I am glad, now my children have something to eat.'" ‖ He knew that 85 Ya.uk^ue'ₗka·m was chief. | Therefore he said that he was glad that his children killed him (?).   Now it began to rain. | The Thunderbird made a noise. Then they saw the Thunderbird flying home. | Thunderbird said: "I am glad, now | I have something to eat for my children.". (I forgot something. ‖ Coyote was told that when the Thun- 90 derbird would say he was glad, | he would say, "Who is tired from walking? I shall take the marrow out of his leg." | Coyote was told: "When the Thunderbird says this to us, | get up and say, 'I don't get tired, | I don't get tired; my younger brother always gets tired because ‖ he is shaped badly.'") Then Coyote sat down again. | 95 Ya.uk^ue'ₗka·m was told: "Stretch your leg this way, I will pull out | the marrow with my mouth." Then Ya.uk^ue'ₗka·m stretched out his leg. Then | Thunderbird put his mouth there, and it was just as if Ya.uk^ue'ₗka·m had no more marrow. | Then (Ya.uk^ue'ₗka·m) threw his spear and stabbed ‖ the Thunderbird with it in the nape of the 100 neck. He killed the Thunderbird, who | broke his nest while he was falling down. Then | he was there. The two children were told: "When your father comes, | and if he says, 'Why is our nest broken?' | tell him: 'That happened when they came up.'" ‖ The two 105 manitous were sitting down in the place that was broken. It was not | long before it began to rain again, and the Thunderbird made a noise again. | Then the Thunderbird flew back; and this one | spoke in the same way as the other one had spoken. The Thunderbird said: "Who | is tired from walking? I shall pull out the marrow from his leg." Coyote arose ‖ and said this. He said the same as before. He 110 danced and said: | "I don't get tired from walking, I don't get tired from walking; my younger brother always gets tired | because he is badly shaped." Then Coyote sat down again. | Thunderbird said: "Stretch your leg this way, I will pull the marrow out of it." | Ya.-uk^ue'ₗka·m stretched out his leg ‖ the way he had done before, and 115 his marrow was as it had been before. | He threw his spear at him and killed him. |

Then he said to the two children: "Now fly down with us." | One of the children said: "Sit down on my back." | Then Ya.uk^ue'ₗka·m sat on the back of the one. ‖ His friend was told: "You shall make 120 a noise." Then | the young Thunderbird flew away. He flew upward. | Coyote was looking on. He flew way up. Then | Coyote shouted, and he began to come down. | He flew by. Then he flew down to the land. Coyote was told: ‖ "Now it is your turn. Sit on me, 125

ku·ts." yuxᵘal'ɛsakₐnu'n·e nao'k!ᵘe·'s. ta'xas a'ₐ'ke· wa·noxu'n·e·.
ta'xas a'ₐ'ke· ła·łukᵘlitɛ'łe·k. ta'xas a'ₐ'ke· ła·unanuxu'ne· na's
a'm·a·ks. sukᵘₐq!u'kᵘne· swʋ't¡mu skɛ'n·ku·ts. qakɛ'łne·: "ta'xas
at maₐts hɛntsłasa·nłwiyna'ₐte· aqłsma'k¡ne·k!. qa'la nutske·
130 qa·kɛ'k.łe·'s atɛn'tsaq!maxo'ᵤne·." ta'xas sɑtsxa·ma'łne· ya.u-
kᵘe'¡ka·m. ta'xas sɑ·ało'ᵤne· nʋ'm·a ne¡s aₐkamana'm·e·s at
ła·qao·pɑlka'ₐne· na's.   ta'xas tsɛn at t!ało·'kᵘne· nʋ'm·a

(d) THE ANIMALS MAKE THE SUN

Ta'xas la·ts!na'xe· swʋ't¡mu ne¡s ts!na'mke· swʋ't¡mu
skɛ'n·ku·ts nułpałne·tɛ't¡ne· tsxał'itk¡nɛ'łne· nata'nɛk!. ta'xas
135 sɑts!na'xe·. tsxał'ɛ'n·e· nata'ne·k!. na'qantsxa·łtsᵤkwa'te·ł
tsxa'ł'e·n nata'ne·k!. ta'xas sɑ'aqanakɛ'k¡ne· saki·łɛt!qaoxa-
xa''mne·. tsxał'ɛna'mne· nata'ne·k!. qała ne·n soᵤk tsxałtsu-
kᵘatɛ'łne·, tsxał'ɛ'n·e· nata'ne·k!. ta'xas łaxa'xe· ne¡s aₐki-
k.łuna'me·s. qakiłɛ'łne·: "kanmi'yit hɛntsxałts!na'xe·." n'iłik-
140 tɛ'łne· ya.ukᵘe'¡ka·m. ta'xas ktsiłmi'ye·t. wʋ'łna·ms ts!na'xe·
ya.ukᵘe'¡ka·m. ta'xas nawɛtskpayatɛ'łne·. ta'xas yuwa·'-
kme·nuqka'n·e·. nanoho's¡ne· nata'ne·k!. nuła'se· ya.ukᵘe'¡-
ka·m n'upsła't¡yił'ɛtnu'ste· aₐ'kuqła·'t!e·s. ta'xas n'upsła't¡yił'-
sukᵘnuhu's¡ne· aₐ'k.ło'ᵤk!wa. qa.ut¡mɑlɛ·'t¡ne·. so'ᵤkᵤne·. ne¡sts
145 k.ła'wa·m qakiłɛ'łne·: "nɛn so'ᵤkᵤne·; tsɛn·ok!ᵘe'¡ne· q!apiłso-
ᵤkᵘnuhu's¡ne· q!ape qa'pse·n nuła'n·e· ne¡ kenano'ho·s ya.u-
kᵘe'¡ka·m; at qa'tał'itkɛnɛ'łne· qa'psin o·'k!ᵘqᵤna q!apiłsoᵤkᵘ-
no'ho·s.

Qakiłɛ'łne· skɛ'n·ku·ts: "kanmi'yit ta'xas nɛ'nko." ta'xas
150 q!u'mne·na'mne·. wʋ'łna·ms ts!na'xe· skɛ'n·ku·ts. ta'xas yu-
wa·kme·nuqka'n·e·. ta'xas n'u·k!ᵘniłu't¡miłe.ɛ't¡ne·. ta'xas
kiyu'kᵘyi·t ta'xas tsma'k!e·ł'ut¡miłe.ɛ't¡ne·. n'ɛtkɛ'ne·ł nɛ'łe·, at
nupsła't¡yił'ut¡mił'e.ɛ't¡ne·. xunaqkɛ'ne·ł łka'm·u aₐ'kɛnmɛ'tu·ks
at no·ku·na'pse· ne¡s wu'o·s. q!apił'ut¡me'¡k¡ne·. me'ka ne¡
155 k!ɛsqa't!o·k qaqa'nał'ut¡me'¡k¡ne·. ta'xas n'upsat¡yiłtsxa'n·e·
ne¡ nata'ne·k!. ne¡sts k!u'pxa skɛ'n·ku·ts ta'xas k!e'¡ła·'s
łka'm·u·'s, qake'¡ne· k.łxonaqkɛ'nłe·s k!ɛsqa't!o·ks. a'ₐ'ke·n'u'pxa
n'ɛ'k.łe·s at qake'¡ne·: "hɛntsxałhɛsapkɛ'łne· tsxałaqa'ₐne·ka·
kwɛ'se·n'. hutsxał'ɛ'k¡ne· tsɛłme·'yit hułała'xa." ta'xas n'upsa·'-
160 tɛyɑłtsxanatka'ₐne· kaₐs n'a·qanɛ'ke¡ts ne¡ nata'ne·k!. ta'xas
naso'ᵤkᵘe·n sa·nłwi'yne·. qake'¡ne· skɛ'n·ku·ts qo· ksɑ'a'ynam
pa'łke¡; a'ₐ'ke· ne¡s ksɑtsɛnkɛ'na·m tɛ'tqa·t!ts pa'łke¡. ta'xas
kwa'łkᵤwa'yi·t, ne¡ tu'xwa ktsᵤwałkᵤwa'yit· n'upsła't¡yił'-
ut¡miłe.ɛ't¡ne·. tsɑłme·'yɛt.s ława'xe· skɛ'n·ku·ts. ta'xas quna'xe·
165 ne¡s ma ya·'kiłɛk.lɛ'ske·. ta'xas sɑquna'xe· ktsxa'ł'e·k kuwi-
sɛ'n'o·s, ma kqa'ke· ktsxała'qa·ps ku·sɛ'n'o·s.

Coyote." Coyote sat on the bird's back. | He sat on the back of the
other one, and he also flew up. | Then he shouted again, and he
flew back down to | the ground. The two friends, Coyote (and
Ya.uk^{u}e′ika·m) were glad. He said to the (Thunderbird): | "Don't be
angry with the people. ‖ You may scare whoever lies about you." 130
That was Ya.uk^{u}e′ika·m's prayer. | Then there were no more thunder-
birds. That is the reason | why they do not kill any one now. The
thunderbirds only make a noise. |

(d) THE ANIMALS MAKE THE SUN

The friends went along. The way the friends Coyote (and
Ya.uk^{u}e′ika·m) were going along | they heard that the sun was being
made. Then ‖ they started. He was to be the sun. Perhaps the 135
one who was to be taken | would be the sun. Therefore the two went
on together. | Some one was to be the sun. The one who was good
was to be taken. | He was to be the sun. Then they arrived at that
town. | They were told: "To-morrow you will start." ‖ They meant 140
Ya.uk^{u}e′ika·m. Then night came. Early in the morning Ya.uk^{u}e′i-
ka·m started. | They waited for him, and he went up. | The sun was
red. Because Ya.uk^{u}e′ika·m | always painted his clothing with
ochre, | therefore his shadow was bright red. It was not hot. It was
good. When‖he came back, he was told: "You are good. There is 145
only one thing, everything | is entirely red. Your red paint has done
it." | Ya.uk^{u}e′ika·m could not do it because he was | bright red. |

Then Coyote was told: "To-morrow you shall go." Then‖they 150
slept. Early in the morning Coyote started. Then | he went on.
At once it was hot. | At noon it was very hot. Shade was made, but |
it was always hot. The children were put into the water of the
river, | but the water burned them. The water was entirely hot.
Even ‖ cold water was hot. Then the Sun always talked. | When 155
Coyote saw a child crying, | he said: "Put it into cold water;" and
when he saw | the people eating, he said: "You will give me some-
thing to eat, something must be left for me. | I shall eat in the
evening when I return." Then the Sun‖told everything that was 160
being done. Then | the chief was angry. Coyote said: "Somebody
stole | a woman, also the man and the woman catch each other."
Then | it was evening; and when the sun had almost gone down, it
remained | always hot. At night Coyote came back. Then he went
to ‖ where they were eating. He went there to eat | what was left. 165
He said it should be left for him. |

(c) THE LYNX CHILDREN

A'ₐ'ke· łaχa'χe· k!o·'q!ᵘⁿnᴇnanak/ste·k. qanit.ła'ₐne· k!o·'q!ᵘne·
naqa'łt.se· t/namu''e·s n'asoqo'ᵤse·. ts!/na'χe· k!o·'q!ᵘne·
s/ts!/nal/ts!k/'łne·na'qpo·ks. tsχał'e·ʳko·łst/namu''e·stsχała'ko· łs
170 tsu'o·s. ta'χas łaχa'χe· yaki·łaqa'pske· sᵤwa'q!ₐmo·'s. ta'χas
n'its!k/'łne· k!o·'q!ᵘne·. k!o·ᵤkunmi'yet.s at n'ukᵘke·k/k/n·e·
at q!a'pχₐne·. ałaqa·hakey/ks/'łe·k. kanmi'yet.s at ła.its!k/'łne·,
a'ₐ'ke· at łao·k!ᵘkik/'łkin. ta'χas wune·k/'t.se· n'upsa't₁yił·o'ᵤse·,
at n'o·ᵤk!ᵘⁿnqa'nχₐne·. ta'χas w/qa'ₐne· nе₁ łkam·ukᵘ/'ste·k.
175 qak/'łne· ma'e·s: "qa'ła ke'e·n katituna'ła?" qak.ła'pse· ma'e·s:
"ne₁s qa·na'χe· titun/'ske₁ł." qak/'łne· ma'e·s: "qa'psiⁿs
ksł/'ts!ki·ł?" qak.ła'pse· ma'e·s: "s/ʾ·ts!k/'łne· sᵤwa'q!ₐmo·'s
n'/st/sk/'łne·. łaqawa'χe·." ne₁ łkam·ukᵘ/'ste·k nułpałni·t/'t₁ne·
ksaki·ł'/t!qaoχaχa'me·s ktsχał'ina'me·s nata'ne·k!s. qake'₁ne·
180 ne₁ łkam·ukᵘ/'ste·k ktsχałts!k/'na·m, ktsχa'ł'/n nata'ne·k!.
ta'χas ts!/na'χe·. qa·na'χe·. n'u'pχₐne· sakq!ₐnu'kse· sa·u˘-
sa˘qa'pse· nuł'a'qₐna·'s. n'u'pχₐne· sił'its!k/'łse· kia'kχo·s.
no'hᵤne· ke'e·ns titu'e·s. k!umnaqaqa'pse·. qak/'łne·:
"qa'psiⁿ k/'nsił'aqaosa'qa?" qake'₁ne· k!o·'q!ᵘne·. qak/'łne·:
185 "pe/'k!a·ks nᴇqa'ₐne· kaa·''qa·łt n'a'sne·, ta'χa husⱥtska'χe·,
husya'χₐne· na'qpo·kᵘ, tsχał'e·₁ko·ł kat/na'mu tsχa'ₐłtsuᵤt
kaa·''qałt. huqᵘa'tał'up/'łne·." qak.ła'pse· ne₁s n/tsta'ha·łs:
"hu'ya·'s a'ₐ'ke· łaqak/'łe·n'." qake'₁ne· k!o·'q!ᵘne·: "hutskuł-
mune'₁ki·ł." ta'χas n'u'pχₐne· ne₁ n/tsta'hałk/'ste·k notsu'kse·.
190 qake'₁ne· k!o·'q!ᵘne·: "ta'χas łakiłkułmune'₁ki·ł." ta'χas
ła.unakχu'n·e·. ta'χas n'u'pχₐne· ne₁ n/tsta'hałk/'ste₁k yunaqa'pse· sᵤwa'q!ₐmo·'s. ta'χas tsukᵘa'te· aₐ'k/nq!a'woks. ta'χas
q!akpa'kitne₁nχo'ᵤne· ne₁ sᵤwa'q!ₐmo. n'u'pχₐne· titu''e·s
słat/qkatk/'nse·. n'uk!łat/qkatk/'nse·. ta'χas n'umatsna'ₐte·.
195 tse₁ka'te· k!o·'q!ᵘne· sanmuχuna'kse· sᵤwa'q!ₐmo. qak.ła'pse·:
"ta'χas h/ntsχał'/tmase'₁te·." ta'χas no'hᵤne·. mitiya'χₐne·
sukᵘⱥq!o'ᵤkᵤne· k!u'pχa aₐ'qa'łt!e·s. qak.ła'pse· "hutsts!/naχa-
ła'ₐne· ne₁ ya'ₐkił'itiya'mke· nata'ne·k!. ta'χas n/'n·ko słats!-
/nam/'łne· t/namu''ne·s."

(d) THE ANIMALS MAKE THE SUN (CONTINUED)

200 Ta'χas ts!/na'χe· n/tstahałk/'ste·k. łaχa'χe· ne₁s aₐ'k/k.łu-
na'me·s. ta'χas qak.ła'pse· naso'ᵤkᵘe·n: "kanmi'yit h/ntsχałt-
ts!/na'χe·." nao·'k!ᵘe· ta'χas ktsiłmi'yit, w/'łna·ms ts!/na'χe·.
ta'χas yu·wakme·nuqka'n·e·. to'χᵘa n'/sqat.łe./'t₁ne·. ta'χas
tska·nuqka'n·e·. ta'χas to'χᵘa n'ut₁miłe./'t₁ne·. ta'χas
205 to'χᵘa kiyu'k₁yit. n'ut₁miłe./'t₁ne·. ta'χas kiyu'k₁yit. ta'χas
n'ut₁miłe./'t₁ne·. n'itk/n/'łne· n/'łe·. ta'χas łaqa·haq!akwu'm-

(e) THE LYNX CHILDREN

The two young Lynxes (Short Faces) arrived. There was the tent of Lynx. | His wife had two children, twins. Lynx started | to look for soup. His wife was to drink it in order to get ‖ milk. He 170 arrived where the salmon were. | Lynx looked for them. One day he got one. | He ate it all. He staid there another night. On the following day he looked again, | and he got one more. He was there a long time, but he kept nothing | because he ate it at once. Then the two children grew up. ‖ One of them said to his mother: "Who 175 is our father?" His mother said: | "Your father went that way." He said to his mother: "What | is he looking for?" His mother said: "He is looking for salmon for you, | but he did not come back." The two children listened, | and went together where somebody was to be the sun. ‖ The children said: "We will go, we shall be the sun." | 180 Then they started. They went. They saw a lake. | There was an old man. He was looking for fish. | They knew it was their father. He was poor. They said to him: | "What are you here for?" Lynx said, he said to them: ‖ "Long ago I had two children. Then I 185 started | to look for soup, which my wife was to drink to get milk | for my children. I can not kill them." He was told by the youths: | "Well, say that again." Lynx said: "I | raise the water with you." Then the two youths saw the water rising. ‖ Lynx said: "Let the 190 water go down with you." And | the water went down. Then the two youths saw | many salmon. They took sticks and | killed the salmon. They saw their father | going after them. He went after one to kill it, and they laughed at him. ‖ Lynx looked at the pile of 195 salmon. He was told: | "Now you try!" Then he knew it. He ran after them. | He was glad. He knew they were his children. He was told: "We are going | where they are playing sun. You | go back to your wife." ‖

(d) THE ANIMALS MAKE THE SUN (CONTINUED)

Then the two youths started, and they arrived at the town. | They 200 were told by the chief: "To-morrow you | will go." One night passed, and early he started. | Then he went up. It was almost cool. Then | he came up, and it was almost warm. When ‖ it was almost noon, it 205 was warm. Then at noon | it was warm. Shade was made. Then

ne·. naq!a′k_uwum at naqtsiya′mne· aɫaqahaq!ak_uwu′mne·.
n'upsat_iyɛɬ′ɛsqat!o′k_une· at qatsxa′n·e· nata′ne·k!. ta′xas
k!onanu′qk^ua. ta′xas to′x^ua ɫaqa.ut_imiɫe.ɛ′t_ine·. ta′xas kwaɫ-
210 kwa′ye·t. ta′xas ɫaqa.ut_imiɫe.ɛ′t_ine·. ta′xas wune·kɛ′t_ine·
kwat!me·nu′qka· wune·kɛ′t_ine. ta′xta· ta′xas ktsɛɬmi′yɛt,
ta′xas ɫawa′xe· ne_i nɛtsta′haɫ. qake′_ine· naso′_uk^ue·n: "sɛɫso′_u-
k_une· nata′ne·k!. ta′xas tsxaɫ′ɛ′n·e· nata′ne·k!s.'' qakiɫɛ′ɫne·
nao·′k!^ue·: "tsɛɫme′yɛt nɛ′n·ko· nɛnts!ɛna′xe·. ntsxaɫ′ɛ′n·e· tsɛ̨-
215 miyɛtna′mu.'' ta′xas ktsɛɫmi′yit. ta′xas ts!ɛna′xe· nao·′-
k!^ue· k!o·′q!^une·na′na. ta′xas yu·wakme·nuqka′n·e·. ta′xas
noq!ukyɛ′t_ine· sukwiɫo·k!ukyɛ′t_ine·; at to′x^ua n'ohu′ɫne· q!a′-
pe· qa′psin ne_i tsɛɫme·yɛtna′mu. to′x^ua wuɫe′it at wo·katɛ′ɫne·
qa′psin. ta′xas sɛɫso′_uk_une· tsɛɫme·yɛtna′mu nata′ne·k!. ta′xas
220 a′_ake· sɛɫtsuk^uatɛ′ɫne·. tsxa′ɫ'e·n nata′ne·k! tsɛɫme·yitna′mu.

Ta′xas kanmi′yɛt wʊ′hna·ms ts!ɛna′xe· skɛ′n·ku·ts. sɛɫsa-
nɛɫwiyna′_ate· nata′ne·k!s, o·′k!^uq_una kma′ta·ps naso′_uk^ue·ns.
ɫaxa′xe· qo·′s yaqa′ka·ɫyu·wakme·nuqk^ua′ske·. qawɛsaqa′_ane·
nawɛtsnuɫk!o′_une· nata′ne·k!s. ta′xas kiy_uwa·kmenu′qk^ua
225 n'upxana′pse· nata′ne·k!s ne_is ksɛɫsa·niɫwi′yna·t. ta′xas ɫuq^ua·ɫ-
sa·niɫwiynata′pse· naq!ako·ptse′_itse· a′k!e·'s n'u′pxane· paɫ
peɛ′k!a·ks sɛɫaq!aku′pse· a′k!e·'s. ta′xas neɫqa·nmɛ′te· a′k!e·'sts
t!awu''e·s. ta′xas nutsɛnqkupe·kɛ′me·k ne_is ya·qawaxmɛ′tke·
a′k!e·'sts t!awu''e·s. ta′xas naq!aɫikwa.ɛ′tse·. ta′xas nanuta′p-
230 se· ne_is a′_akɛnq!o′ko·ps. n'u′pxane· paɫ pɛ′k!a·ks sɛɫ'axa_anɛ-
xo·na′pse· a_a′kɛnq!o′ko·ps. n'u′pxane· sɛɫqa·hamanamɛ′s_ine·
qa'oxaɫ′ɛtq!ankɛkqa′_ane·. yu·haɫhaqaku′pse· sɛ′t!e·s. ta′xas
qa·taɫhoko′_une· qayaqanmɛte·nq!o·kupxu′se·. ta′xas at sɛɫa-
qaqa′_ane· at qa·taɫhaq!a′likwa′i·t a_a′k_ama′_anam. ta′xas
235 sɛɫ′ɛ′n·e· nata′ne·k!s k!o·′q!^une·nanakɛ′ste·k.

Husɛɫq!a'pqaɫq!a'nuxwa′te·

55. The People Try to Kill Ya.uk^ue′_ika·m

Ho′ya's a′_a'ke· hutsxaɫ·atsxamu′n·e· ya.uk^ue′_ika·m yaqaɫ'upi-
ɫɛ′ɫke·ts k.ɫa.itq!a·''nxa′m.

Qahak.ɫuna′mne· saosaqa′_ane· ya.uk^ue′_ika·m ne_is a_a′kɛk.ɫuna′-
me·s. n'ok!uniɫsa·haniɫwiynata′pse· aqɫsma′kinɛk!s. ta′xas n'ɛ′-
5 n·e· k_uwɛ′ɫqa nɛtsta′haɫ n'u′pxane· ktsxaɫ'upɛ′ɫe·ɫ. qaɫwi′yne·:
"ma'_atsuɫ'o′_uniɫ, ma'_atsuɫsa·niɫwi′ynat ka_akinɛk!na''mu, mɛ′ksa'n
ne_i yaksa′han qa′psin paɫ at ku'si·l'u′pe·ɫ.'' n'oniɫa′pse· aqɫs-
ma′kinɛk!s. qa.upxa′se· ka_as ɫaa·qakɛ′n·a·ps. ta′xas n'upɫa′p-
se·. xunmɛtqɫa′pse· a_a′kɛnmɛ′tuks. ta′xas aqɫsma′kinɛk! sukwɛɫ-
10 q!u′k_une· k!u'pi·ɫ ya.uk^ue′_ika·ms. ta′xas nuqona′me·k q!a′pe·.
qakiɫɛ′ɫne· qaspɛ′ɫ'uk: "hɛntsxaɫhanokwi''te· ^a_a'kuqɫu′pin. hɛnts-
xaɫt!ɛsɫe·kxok^ua′_ane·.'' ta′xas ts!ɛn'ɛɫu'nisna′mne·. n'ɛ′n·e·

they were not perspiring any more. | When they were perspiring, they swam in the water, and they stopped perspiring. | The water was always cool. The Sun did not talk. Then, | when he went down, it was not warm. Then ‖ he went down, and it was not hot. After 210 some time | he went down. Some time passed, and it became dark. | Then the youth came back. The chief said: | "The Sun is good. He shall be the Sun." The other one was told: | "You shall go at night." He was to be ‖ the Moon. Then it was dark. Then the 215 other | young Lynx started. He went up, and | the Moon shone brightly. Almost everything could be seen | by the Moon. They could almost recognize things at a distance. | Then the Moon was good, and ‖ he also was taken. He was to be the Moon. | 220

Early the next day Coyote started. | He was angry at the Sun, because the chief had rejected him. | He arrived at the place where the Sun rises. He staid there, | aiming at the Sun. Then, ‖ when he 225 saw the Sun coming up, he was angry. Then (the Sun) | was angry with him, and made his arrow burn. (Coyote) saw that | his arrow was burning. Then he threw away his arrow and his | bow. Then he ran, after he had thrown away | his bow and his arrow. Then the ground began to burn, and ‖ the fire pursued him. He saw that | the 230 fire had almost caught up with him. He saw there was a trail. | Then he lay down quickly, and his blanket was burned over, but | he could not burn, and the fire went by him. | Therefore the trails do not burn. ‖ Then the two young Lynxes were Sun and Moon. | 235

It is all finished. |

55. The People Try to Kill Ya.uk^ue'ˌkaˑm

Now I will talk more about Ya.uk^ue'ˌkaˑm, how he | was killed and came to life again. |

There was a village, and there was the tent of Ya.uk^ue'ˌkaˑm. | At one time the people became angry at him. He was now ‖ a full-grown   5 man, and he knew that he would be killed. He thought: | "Don't let me be afraid. Don't let me be angry at my people, only | at those bad things that I have killed." The people were afraid of him, | and did not know what to do with him. Then they killed him | and threw him into the river. The people were glad ‖ because they had killed   10 Ya.uk^ue'ˌkaˑm. Then they all broke camp. | Crane was told: "You shall drag a young tree. | You shall cover our tracks." Then they started. It was | winter time, and they made tracks on the snow.

wanu'yitna'mˑo neˑs aₐ'k!aɫukᵘⁱ'ɫ'eˑs. naqsanmi'yⁱt kuqnani'yam
qaoˇwⁱsu'qᵤneˑ   qo's   ya'wo's   ya.ukᵘe'ᵢkaˑm.   qa.u'pχₐneˑ
15 aqɫsma'kᵢnⁱk!neᵢs pⁱ'k!aˑks maeˑseˑs ya.ukᵘe'ᵢkaˑms ma kts!ⁱ'nas
ya'wo's wu'o's, ma kqahakiɫha'qaps ya.ukᵘe'ᵢkaˑms qo'sts ma
kqake'ᵢkaˑs wu'o's. sⁱⁿ'aqakⁱ'nˑeˑ kχunmⁱ'tqoˑɫ ya.ukᵘe'ᵢkaˑms.
ta'χas qawisu'qᵤneˑ ya.ukᵘe'ᵢkaˑm. ˑ ta'χas nⁱkᵢna'pseˑ kia'kχoˑ's
oˑ'k!ᵘqᵤna ke'eˑn up'na'moˑ's, sⁱⁿ'aqaqₐna'aneˑ neᵢ kia'kχoˑ keˑ-
20 eˑk aₐ'kuɫak!ⁱ'seˑs. n'u'pχₐneˑ ya.ukᵘe'ᵢkaˑm paɫ pⁱ'k!aˑks sɫaˑ-
tᵢyiɫ'ekₐna'pseˑ kia'kχo's aₐk.ɫⁱ'k!eˑs. qanaqɫⁱ'kχₐneˑ. qakⁱ'lneˑ:
"qa'psin kⁱnsⁱⁿ'ikᵢna'pkiˑɫ?" qak.ɫa'pseˑ neˑs kia'kχoˑ's: "huqa-
a'psiˑɫsaˑniɫwi'ynatawa'sₐneˑ. qa'psiˑn kⁱnsⁱⁿqana'qɫⁱkχₐna'was?
hosⁱⁿ'aeˑtkⁱnawa'sₐneˑ." ta'χas ɫa.upχa'meˑk ya.ukᵘe'ᵢkaˑm.
25 qak.ɫa'pseˑ neᵢs kia'kχoˑ's. "ta'χas ɫa.u'pan'. hⁱntsχaɫts!ⁱna'χeˑ.
neᵢ qanaχa'mneˑ. maₐts qaɫwi'yeˑn' kwunⁱ'keˑt kuqnani'yam.
nuɫa'nˑeˑ qaspⁱ'ɫ'uk nanukᵘe'ᵢteˑ aₐ'kuqɫu'pins. sⁱⁿt!ⁱsɫⁱkχo-
ka'ₐneˑ. qaɫwi'yneˑ kⁱntsqa.upχa'meˑɫ yaqanaɫu'nˑisnamⁱ'skeˑ."
ta'χas ya.ukᵘe'ᵢkaˑm ɫa.upa'χeˑ neᵢs ko'oˑs. ta'χas tseᵢka'teˑ.
30 n'u'pχₐneˑ yaqanak!aɫukiɫⁱ'skeˑ. ta'χas ts!ⁱna'χeˑ. naqanqaɫsan-
miˑ'yⁱt.s χaˑ'tsas k!u'pχa ko'oˑs. ta'χas n'u'pχₐneˑ qaˑqaₐ-
nⁱnq!oku'pseˑ neᵢs ko'oˑs. n'u'pχₐneˑ neᵢs wⁱ'ɫnaˑms kɫskⁱⁿqakχa-
ɫu'nˑisna'meˑs. ts!ⁱna'χeˑ qahaˇna'χeˑ. nuɫpa'hneˑ qaspⁱ'ɫ'uks
sᵤwasχuna'kseˑ. ɫaχa'nχo'ᵤneˑ. qakⁱ'lneˑ: "qa'psins kⁱnu'pskeᵢn
35 naₐ aₐ'kuqɫu'pin?" qake'ᵢneˑ qaspⁱ'ɫ'uk: "sⁱⁿ'aqsanmi'yⁱt.s
n'upili'hneˑ ya.ukᵘe'ᵢkaˑmˑ χunmitqulⁱ'ɫ'neˑ. sⁱⁿ'oniɫⁱ'lneˑˑ, na'pit
ɫa.eˑtq!a'n'χaˑm tsχaɫa''nχoɫunⁱ'stka; tsχaɫ'oˑkᵘⁱtka'ₐneˑ. husⁱⁿ-
qakiɫⁱ'lneˑ kuɫanoˑ'kᵘeᵢt na a'ₐ'kuqɫu'pin; na'pit ɫa.itq!aˑ'nₐχa'm
ya.ukᵘe'ᵢkaˑm tsχaɫqa.u'pχₐneˑ aₐ'kₐmana'meˑs." q!akpakit-
40 χo'ᵤneˑ qaspⁱ'ɫ'uks. ts!ⁱna'χeˑ ya.ukᵘe'ᵢkaˑm ɫaχaₐnχo'ᵤneˑ
tⁱⁿnamuⁱ'seˑs. a'ₐ'keˑ q!akpakitχo'ᵤneˑ. ts!ⁱna'χeˑˑ, n'u'pχₐneˑ
sⁱⁿnaχaˑmⁱ'sᵢneˑ. ɫaχa'nχo'ᵤneˑ. n'u'pχₐneˑ paɫ nⁱ'nse atsawa'-
ts!eˑs. sɫaˑ'hatᵢyiɫ'iɫa'seˑ, qakⁱ'kseˑ: "na'ₐs at ma qaˑniɫaɫa'pₐneˑ
kaatsa'wats! ya.ukᵘe'ᵢkaˑm; at ma o'niɫa'pseˑ aqɫsma'kᵢnⁱk!s.
45 na'sosanmeˑyⁱ'tskeˑ k!u'pɫaps, ta'χas kok!umnaqa'qa, koho'was.
k.ɫaqaoˑnⁱ'ɫaps aqɫsma'kᵢnⁱk!s. kanuɫ'a'qₐna k.ɫa'ɫo's tsa'eˑs."
naɫχo'ᵤseˑ aₐ'qaɫt!ⁱ'seˑs. ta'χa neᵢ ɫkₐmˑu qa'k.ɫeˑk neⁱ'ᵢts!uq!s.
ya.ukᵘe'ᵢkaˑm qunatsa'ₐχₐneˑ neᵢs ɫka'mˑu's. tseᵢkata'pseˑ,
nupχₐna'pseˑ. qakⁱ'lneˑ ma'eˑs neⁱ'ᵢts!uq!: "neᵢs nⁱ'nˑeˑ
50 ya.ukᵘe'ᵢkaˑm ka'χa." ta'χa ma'eˑs neⁱ'ᵢts!uq! ɫuqᵘaq!a'nkeˑ-
kⁱⁿwitskⁱ'kᵢneˑ. snⁱts!aⁱ'nseˑ. nantso'χa'χeˑ ya.ukᵘe'ᵢkaˑm.
neᵢs ktseᵢka'taˑps neᵢs atsawa'ts!eˑs, ɫo'ᵤneˑ. qaɫwi'yneˑ neᵢ
paˑ'ɫkeᵢ ksⁱⁿ'aqanⁱ'tsaps χaɫe'eˑs. qanɫa'ɫteˑ. qakⁱ'lneˑ: "aˑ:,
qa.u'pχa kaₐs n'aˑqaˑnikitnaɫa'peˑs k!upⁱ'ɫeˑs kaatsawa'ts!miɫ.
55 ksoᵤsaɫk!oˑmna'qaɫts!akⁱ'ktaksawa'seˑs aqɫsma'kᵢnⁱk!." ta'χas
ɫaeˑɫa'naχwa'teˑk neᵢs ke'at ya.ukᵘe'ᵢkaˑms, a'ₐ'keˑ ɫaqakⁱ'nˑeˑ
neᵢs ɫka'mˑu's ya.ukᵘe'ᵢkaˑm; a'ₐ'keˑ ɫaqaqna'ₐneˑ neᵢ paˑ'ɫkeᵢ

A few days after they had broken camp | in winter, Ya.uku e′ıka·m was down below. The people did not know ‖ that Ya.uku e′ıka·m's mother had gone | down into the water, and that Ya.uku e′ıka·m was born there | and had come from the water. Now, when they had thrown Ya.uku e′ıka·m | into the water in winter, then the fish ate him | because he was dead. Therefore the fish did so. ‖ They ate up his body. Ya.uku e′ıka·m knew at once that the fish | were eating of his feet, and he kicked them. He said: | "Why are you eating me?" The fish said to him: "We are | not angry at you. Why do you kick us? | We are restoring you." Then Ya.uku e′ıka·m knew himself.[1] ‖ The fishes said to him: "Go ashore! You shall go. | The people went in that direction. | Don't think that it is a long time since they broke camp. | Crane dragged a young tree along to cover their tracks. They thought you would not know which way they went." | Then Ya.uku e′ıka·m went ashore to the village site. He looked at it ‖ and saw which way they had gone. He started. After about | three or four days he saw a village site. He saw that there was | some fire left at the village site. He knew that they had started from there early in the morning. | He started and went along. He heard Crane | singing. He reached him, and said to him: "What are you doing ‖ with that young tree?" Crane said: "Several days ago | Ya.uku e′ıka·m was killed and was thrown into the water. We are afraid he may | come back to life, and he will go the way we are going and will kill everybody. | I have been told to drag along this young tree, so that, if he should come back to life, | he may not recognize the trail." Then (Ya.uku e′ıka·m) knocked ‖ Crane down. Ya.uku e′ıka·m went on, and reached | Crane's wife. Then he knocked her down. He started, and saw | somebody going along. He reached that person, and saw that it was his sister-in-law. | She went along crying. She said: "My brother-in-law Ya.uku e′ıka·m used to take me along this way. | The people were afraid of him, ‖ and the other day they killed him. Now I am poor. I am hungry, | for the people are not afraid of him. My husband's brother is no more." | She carried her child on her back. Her child's name was Duck.[2] | Ya.uku e′ıka·m poked the child with a stick. The child looked at him | and saw him; and Duck said to his mother: ‖ "Uncle Ya.uku e′ıka·m is here." Then the mother of Duck turned around and looked. | There was a tree, and Ya.uku e′ıka·m had gone behind it | when his sister-in-law looked at him. There was nothing there. The woman thought | her child had told a lie. She struck him. She said to him: "Oh, | don't you know how I feel because my brother-in-law has been killed? ‖ The people make us suffer." | She was crying while she was naming Ya.uku e′ıka·m; | and Ya.uku e′ıka·m

15

20

25

30

35

40

45

50

55

---

[1] Probably "came to his senses."   [2] Species unknown.

qanɫaʼɫteˑ xaɫeʼcˑs. qakeʼᵢncˑ ya.ukᵘeʼᵢkaˑm: "qaʼpsins kɛnʋʼps-
keˑn ɫkaʼmˑuⁱ hɛnt!aktsxoʼᵤncˑ." ɫoˑqᵘaʼq!ankikɛʼɫwitskɛʼkᵢncˑ

60 maʼeˑs nɛʼᵢts!uq! paɫ tsɛmak!kɛʼkscˑ xaɫeʼcˑs paɫ sɛɫwaʼse
ya.ukᵘeʼᵢkaˑms, paɫa.itq!anxaʼmscˑ. qakeʼᵢncˑ neᵢ paʼɫkeᵢ:
"hosoʼkᵘiɫq!uʼkᵤncˑ keʼʼnwaˑm. hok!umnaʼqaqwaɫaʼᵃncˑ. tsaʼₐneˑs nʼɛʼɫwa iyaʼmoˑʼs at tsukᵘaɫɛʼsᵢncˑ. kaʼmin tax na hunaʼmkeˑ
huɫaʼxeˑ hutsxaɫʼitkɛʼneˑ kaₐʼkɛʼt.ɫa, tsxaɫtsukᵘatɛʼɫneˑ ɫaaˑʼk!-

65 ɫaˑk aʼₐʼkeˑ atula.ɛt.ɫikᵢnatɛʼtᵢnˑcˑ, honuʼkweˑ aʼₐʼkeˑ at ɫatsu-
kᵘatɛʼɫncˑ. taʼxas tsiɫmiʼyɛt, taʼxas at ɫoʼᵤneˑ kaₐʼkɛʼt.ɫa. k.ɫaʼ-
waˑm k!aʼʼnam at yunaqaʼₐncˑ kaʼɫxoᵤɫ akuʼɫak tsʋʼpqa,
tsaʼₐneˑs at nʼoˑʼk!ᵘiɫ·oʼᵤscˑ, paɫ at nʼoᵤkᵘiɫtsukᵘaɫɛʼsᵢncˑ nʼɛʼɫwa
tsʋʼpqaˑʼs. taʼxas atoˑnowasₐnaɫaʼₐncˑ. tsɛɫmiʼyɛt.s nʼuʼxteˑk

70 nasoʼᵤkᵘeˑn at naqankɛʼɫneˑ ncʼᵢts!uq!s. at niktxonemuʼnˑeˑ
aₐʼk.ɫaʼmʼɛʼseˑs neʼᵢts!uq!s." qakeʼᵢncˑ ya.ukᵘeʼᵢkaˑm: "taʼxa
ɫuʼnˑu. ts!ɛnaʼkeˑiɫ hɛnɫaxaʼkeˑiɫ. hɛnʼeˑʼtkin aₐʼkɛt.ɫaʼʼneˑs
qaɫanqaʼɫwiy tsxaɫtsoʼᵤkᵘaˑt neᵢs kɛniɫk'natɛʼtmeˑɫ atɛntsqan-
ɫaʼɫteˑ. aʼₐʼkeˑ neʼᵢts!uq!s qaoˑʼxaɫʼɛtkɛʼnˑeˑ aₐʼqaʼtskoˑʼs aₐʼk.ɫa-

75 mʼɛʼseˑs." qakɛʼɫncˑ: "naqaʼnk.ɫeˑs nasoʼᵤkᵘeˑn, qaʼk.ɫeˑs
ktsɛktxoneʼʼmoˑ aₐʼk.ɫaʼmnɛʼsʼmiˑɫ, hɛntsxaɫqaʼoxaɫqaʼɫuqkaʼ-
ɫaʼmɛʼɫneˑ." taʼxas ts!naʼxeˑ maʼₐtᵢmoˑ neʼᵢts!uq!. ts!naʼxcˑ
ya.ukᵘeʼᵢkaˑm neᵢs yaqaʼnak!aɫukweˑɫɛʼsksˑ. nʼuʼpxₐneˑ tsaʼʼeˑs
qakɛʼɫncˑ: "kɛnʼɛʼɫwa iyaʼmoⁱ" qakeʼᵢncˑ: "pɛʼk!aˑks honʼiɫᵤ-

80 waʼnˑcˑ. tsukᵘatɛʼɫncˑ. aʼₐʼkeˑ hosɛɫaanaʼxcˑ at qaqaɫqaqaʼₐncˑ.
honʼɛʼɫᵤwa iyaʼmo at tsukᵘatɛʼɫncˑ. miʼka yunaʼqa at nʼoˑʼkuɫtsu-
kᵘatɛʼɫncˑ. taʼxas tsɛɫmiʼyɛt.s huɫaɫaʼxaˑm atoˑnowaʼsᵢneˑts aʼₐʼkeˑ
katɛɫnaʼmuts kaaʼₐʼqaɫt. hok!umnaqaqaʼₐncˑ." qakɛʼɫncˑ tsaʼʼeˑs
ya.ukᵘeʼᵢkaˑm: "taʼxa ɫuʼnˑu ɫa.eˑts!kɛʼɫeˑn' tsʋʼpqa. aʼₐʼkeˑ

85 hɛnɫaeʼɫᵤwa qaʼɫa qaʼɫwiy ktsxaɫtsoʼᵤkᵘat hɛntsxaɫmitiyaʼxₐncˑ.
hɛntsqanɫaʼɫteˑ. hɛntsqakɛʼɫncˑ: 'maₐts tsukᵘaʼteˑn', hɛnqaʼɫwiy
kɛntstsoʼᵤkᵘaˑt hutsmɛtxₐnɛʼsᵢncˑ.'" qakeʼᵢncˑ ya.ukᵘeʼᵢkaˑm:
"kaʼmin hutsxaɫqamɛʼtxₐneˑ tsʋʼpqa. taxtaˑʼ kanmeʼyɛt.s
hutsxaɫmɛʼtxₐncˑ." taʼxas ts!naʼxcˑ neᵢ tɛʼtqaˑt!. nʼupɛʼɫneˑ

90 tsʋʼpqaˑʼs, nutsaʼscˑ qaʼɫaˑs qaɫwiʼyscˑ ktsxaɫtsoʼᵤkᵘaˑts. mitᵢ-
yaʼxₐneˑ qanɫaɫtmuʼnˑeˑ aₐʼkɛnq!aʼwoˑks. qakɛʼɫncˑ: "naʼpit
hɛnqaʼɫwiy kɛntstsoʼᵤkᵘat na koɛʼɫᵤwa hutsʼupɛʼsᵢncˑ. ma
kɛnʼupɛʼɫkiˑɫ kaʼtaˑt. taʼxas hutsxaɫsaˑniɫwiynatɛskɛʼɫneˑ."
nʼoᵤniɫɛʼɫneˑ neᵢs k!aqaʼqₐna. k.ɫaʼxaˑm maʼₐtᵢmo neᵢʼts!uq!

95 taʼxas niɫikᵢnatɛʼtᵢneˑ tsxaɫyaqaʼʼnit.ɫaʼₐkeˑ. taʼxas kuɫʼeʼᵢtkiˑn,
taʼxas aʼₐʼkeˑ nʼɛtkɛʼnˑeˑ loᵤk!s. qaɫwiˑynamɛʼsᵢneˑ ktsxaɫtsu-
kᵘaʼt.ɫeˑs. mɛteᵢxakaʼₐncˑ. tuʼxᵘa qanɫaɫtᵢmumokᵘaʼₐncˑ aₐʼqu-
taʼɫʼeˑs. (neᵢs pɛʼk!aks aqɫsmaʼkᵢnɛk! at nʼɛʼnˑscˑ aqutaʼɫʼeˑs
noʼᵤkᵘeˑys popoʼeˑs; aₐʼq!aʼɫeˑs at nʼɛʼnscˑ ktsɛk!ɛts!ɫa.ɛnxoʼᵤmo.)

100 nʼoˑnck·ɛʼɫneˑ, at.skiɫqaqaqₐnaʼₐneˑts k!aqaʼqₐna. sɛɫaʼqaɫʼoˑniɫɛʼ-
ɫneˑ. toʼxᵘa ktsuwaɫkwaʼyit.s waʼscˑ nuɫaqₐnaʼʼeˑs. naq!awuʼscˑ.
nɛnkoʼeˑs sukˑɫeˑɛʼt.seˑ yaqaʼnɛt.ɫaʼₐkeˑ. yunaqaʼpscˑ aₐʼkoxneˑ-

did the same thing to the child; and the woman did the same again, she struck her child. Then Ya.uk‍ᵘe′ₗka·m said: "Why do you | do that to the child? You hurt him." The mother of Duck turned round quickly, ‖ and it was true what her son had said. Ya.uk‍ᵘe′ₗka·m 60 had arrived | and had come back to life. Then the woman said: | "I am glad that you arrived. We are poor. | When your brother kills game, they take it away from him. When I go along | and put up my tent, it is taken away from me; ‖ and when I go to another 65 place and make my tent and finish it, | it is taken away again. Then it is dark and I have no tent. | When the hunters come back and bring much deer meat, | your brother alone has not any, for they take away all | the deer he kills. Then in the evening we are hungry. When the chief defecates, ‖ they call Duck, and he must rub him | 70 with his head." Ya.uk‍ᵘe′ₗka·m said: "Now | go on! When you get there, make your tent, | and if any one wants to take the place that you have arranged, strike him; | and put flint on the head of Duck." ‖ He said to him: "When the chief calls you, and when he 75 tells you | to rub him with your head, then hit him with your head." | Then Duck and his mother started. Ya.uk‍ᵘe′ₗka·m started | and went along where the snow was trodden down. He saw his younger brother. | He said to him: "Don't you kill any game?" He said: "I have killed some, ‖ but it was taken away from me; and 80 I went hunting again, but it is like that always. | If I kill game, it is taken away from me. Even if it is much, it is all taken away from me. | Then in the evening, when I get home, I and my wife and child are hungry. | I am poor." Then Ya.uk‍ᵘe′ₗka·m said to his brother: | "Go on; look for deer! and ‖ if you kill it and some one tries 85 to take it away from you, go after him | and strike him, and say: 'Don't take it. If you try | to take it, I'll shoot you.'" Ya.uk‍ᵘe′ₗka·m said: | "I shall not shoot deer. Later on in the morning | I'll shoot some." Then the man started and killed ‖ a deer. Somebody went 90 up to him and intended to take it. He went after him | and struck him with a stick. He said to him: "If | you try to take what I kill, I'll kill you. | You have killed my elder brother; now I'll get angry with you." | Then they were afraid of what he had done. When Duck and his mother arrived, ‖ she cleaned a place for their 95 tent; and when she had finished, | she got firewood. Then they wanted to take it away from her, | but she went after them and struck them with her ax. | (In former times the people had for their axes | stone hammers and antler wedges, which they used for splitting trees.) ‖ The people were afraid, for she had not done before 100 as she did now; therefore they were afraid of her. | It was almost evening when her husband arrived. He carried meat. | She had a good place for their tent, and much wood. | Then at night the chief

yi′e·s. ta′χas ktsɛlmi′yɛt.s n′anaχa′′mne· naso′ᵤkᵘe·n n′u′χtc·k.
naqankɛ′łne· ne′ᵢts!uq!s. qakɛ′łne·: "ne:ts!uq!, pɛk!ako-
105 n′ɛt!ko′:ᵤne·." n′anaχa′′mne· ne′ᵢts!uq!, qao˘χal′qałuqkała′′mne·
aₐ′k!ała′χɛkpłɛ′se·s neᵢs naso′ᵤkᵘe·ns. qak.ła′pse·: "ma′qa·k,
ma′qa·k· n′upła′pₐne·. qa′psin łɛnsₐqła′n·e· aₐ′k.ła′mnɛ′s′mi·ł."
qatsɛnk!apałtɛ′łc·k ne′ᵢts!uq!. qa·waχₐmoχu′n·e· neᵢ naso′ᵤkᵘe·n.
pał sł′upła′psc· ne′ᵢts!uq!s. ta′χas sɛlqa′łsa˘ł′upɛłka′ₐne· χa′ₐtᵢmo
110 ne′ᵢts!uq!. ma k!upɛ′łi·ł qaspɛ′ł′uk tɛlnamo′′tᵢmo, a′ₐ′ke· k!upɛ′łi·ł
neᵢ naso′ᵤkᵘe·n. qao˘χaχa′mne·. tscᵢkatɛ′łne·. sao˘saqa′ₐne·
ya.ukᵘe′ᵢka·m. n′upχa′łne· pał′awa′χc·. tsχanatamna′mne·.
qakiya′mne·: "pał wa′χe· ya.ukᵘe′ᵢka·m, pał·aetq!anχa′′mne·
pał sł′aqaqₐna′ₐne· ne′ᵢts!uq! ała·kᵢnɛ′k!tᵢmo ksaha′nse·k." ta′χas
115 a:n′onełɛ′łne· ya.ukᵘe′ᵢka·m. ta′χas n′ɛ′ne· kwɛ′łqa naso′ᵤ-
kᵘe·ns neᵢs aₐ′kɛk.łuna′me·s.

Ta′χas husɛlq!apqałpałnɛmɛ′łne· yaqaqₐna′ₐke· neᵢs pɛ′k!a·ks
ya.ukᵘe′ᵢka·m.

56. COYOTE AND DOG

(a) COYOTE MISSES THE DEER

Qa′nɛt.ła′ₐne· skɛ′n·ku·ts, n′ɛ′nse· tɛlnamu′′e·s χa′ₐłtsin. n′ɛ′n·e·
wa·nuyɛtna′mu. χa′ₐłtsints a′ₐ′ke·[1] a·łaqa′łt!e·s qsama′łne· naya-
χaq!anu′kᵤne·. qa·nqułuk!pku′pse·. q!aχo′ᵤne·. neᵢs pɛ′k!a·ks
tsᵥ′pqa at nɛk!a′ₐkᵢne·. neᵢs kqła′χo· χa′ₐłtsin a·qułu′k!pkups
5 n′aqtsχuna′ktse· tsᵥ′pqa·, pał sank!a′ₐkᵢne· neᵢs k!aqtsχuna′ke·s
qakχałanaqu′mła·sχu′ne·. pał kwɛ′łko·s mitᵢya′χᵢne· χa′ₐłtsin
łaχa·nχo′ᵤne·. tsɛnqatkɛ′n·e· neᵢs tsᵥ′pqa·′s. qakɛ′łne· ałaqa′łt!e·s:
"łats!ɛnyaχa′ke·ł ała·kᵢne·′k!enɛ′ski·ł. tsχałmɛ′txₐne·." ła′ₐts!ɛn-
kɛsqku′pekɛ′me·k neᵢ łkam·ukᵘɛ′ste·k. nao·′k!ᵘe· qa′k.łe·k mɛs-
10 qoło·′′wum, nao·′k!ᵘe· qa′k.łe·k q!o·ta′ptse·k!. mɛsqoło·′′wum
n′ɛ′n·e· nɛtsta′ha·ł, q!o·ta′ptse·k! n′ɛ′n·e· na.u′te·. ła·łaχa′χe·
aₐ′kɛt.ła′e·s. qakɛ′łne· tɛtu′′e·s. qake′ᵢne·: "ka′ma kɛnts!na′me·ł
tsɛnkɛ′n·e· tsᵥ′pqa·′s." skɛ′n·ku·ts n′anmuqkupnu′χo·nka′me·k.
tsɛk!kɛ′n·e· aₐ′kuqłu′pe·ns, a′ₐ′ke· n′asɛlyaqe′ᵢte· mɛtsqo˘ko-
15 łɛ′łna·′s. łatᵢnaχa′′mne·. łoq!ᵘałkɛ′n·e· aₐ′ko·k!ᵘatsɛnko′′e·s.
qaoχa′χe·. yɛk!taχo′ᵤne· q!u′łᵤwa·s qaqsa˘qapta′kse· ki′e·k.
n′ɛ′kᵢne·. ta′χas n′itkɛ′n·e· t!awu′′e·s a′ₐ′ke· nai′maq!makaχnɛ′-
łe·k mɛtsqokołɛ′łna·′s. ta′χas ts!ɛna′χe·. łaχa′χe·. sawɛtsqatkɛ′n-
se· tɛlnamu′′e·s. nałikᵢnɛ′łe·k. pał kᵤwɛ′łko·′s neᵢs yaqa·′wɛts-
20 kɛ′nske· tɛlnamu′′e·s tsᵥ′pqa·′s. u′s′me·ks qa·′kiłt!ats!a′niłukᵘɛ′-
n·e·. qakɛ′łne·: "ta′χas pɛsła:′tɛkɛ′n·en′." ta′χas χa′ₐłtsin
pɛsła:tɛkɛ′n·e·. qanakɛtsłuχunɛ′łe·k tsᵥ′pqa·. mɛ′txₐne· skɛ′n·ku·ts.
qa′łe·n tsułuχo′ᵤse·. yuna·′kᵢnɛ′łne·. ta′χas naoko·qapka′ₐ-

went out. | He called Duck and said to him: "Duck, ‖ I am cold."   105
Duck went out and hit | the chief with his head. He said: "Stop, |
stop! It hurts me. Something must be on your head." | Duck did
not mind it. Then the chief fell down. | Duck had killed him.
Thus three were killed by Duck and his uncle ‖ — Crane and his wife   110
were killed, | and the chief was killed. They went there and looked,
and there was | Ya.uk*e′ika·m. They knew he had arrived. They
talked to one another, | and they said to one another: "Ya.uk*e′ika·m
has arrived. He has come back to life. | That is the reason why
Duck and his parents have done so, for they were angry." Then‖
they were more afraid of Ya.uk*e′ika·m. He was a great chief | in   115
the town. |

Now I have finished telling what | Ya.uk*e′ika·m did long ago. |

56. COYOTE AND DOG

(a) COYOTE MISSES THE DEER

Coyote lived in a tent. His wife was Dog. It was | winter
time. Dog and her children with her went out | for fuel. There was
a stump. She chopped it down. For a long time | a deer used to
have a hole there in the stump that Dog chopped down. ‖ The deer   5
was hit when it fell. There was its hole. It was broken. | The deer
jumped out quickly. There was snow on the ground, and Dog fol-
lowed the deer. | She caught up with it and caught it by the tail. She
said to her children: | "Go and get your parent. He shall shoot it." |
The two children started to run. One was named ‖ Misqoło′wum;   10
the other one was named Q!ota′ptsek!. Misqoło′wum | was a boy;
Q!ota′ptsek! was a girl. They arrived | at their tent and spoke to
their father. They said: "Mother says you should come | and take
the deer." Coyote ran out quickly. | He split a little tree[1] and he
broke in two a bush.[2] ‖ He went in again and pulled off quickly his   15
hair band. | He went there. He spilled rose hips, which were all the
food that they had. | He ate them. Then he made a bow, and he
quickly made two arrows | out of the bush.[2] Then he started. He
got there, and his wife stood there | holding the tail. He had snow-
shoes on his feet. There was much snow where ‖ his wife was hold-   20
ing the deer. First he tramped down the snow in front of her, and |
said to her: "Now let go!" Then Dog | let go of the deer. The
deer was running in the deep snow. Coyote shot. | Just then (the
deer) broke through the snow and fell. The arrow went over

---

[1] Species unknown.   [2] Species unknown; a bush with white berries that are not edible.

ne·. a′ₐ′ke· lamₑ′txₐne·. qa′łe·n yu·haqama·wₑsqa′pse· n′o·ne·łna·-
25 kᵢnₑ′łne·.   ta′xas   lałₑtka′ₐne·   skₑ′n·ku·ts.   ta′xas   tsʋ′pqa
ts!ₑna′xe·.   ta′xas   skₑ′n·ku·ts   sₒdyu·k!k^uaka′te·.   qa·qawₑsqa′ₐne·
xa′ₐltsin. nunuq!ᵘₑ′łe·k.   skₑ′n·ku·ts łuq!ᵘałkₑ′n·e· t!a′wumka″-
e·s.   qanaqku·płałtmu′n·e·   aₐ·k.ła·kwu′ᵤt!e·s   neᵢs   tsʋ′pqa·′s.
t!a′wumka″e·s   łae·tu·k!ᵘa·tsₑnk!une·mu′n·e·.   nutsₑnqkupekₑ′-
30 me·k   neᵢs   yaₐqana′ske·   tsʋ′pqaₐs.   pał   k.łałₑ′tᵤwoᵤt   qa′psins
a′qₐnₐ.

Qakₑ′łne·   xa′ₐltsins: "nₑ′ntsxa·ł′u′psᵢnama′łne·n′   łkam-
nₑ″nte·k."   qa′psin   tsxa′ł′o·ts   tₑłnamu″e·s   ałaqa′łt!e·s.   pał
ko′k.łoᵤk   xa′ₐltsints   aₐ·qa′łt!e·s.   n′ₑ′nse·   aₐ·quta′ł′e·s   nao″-
35 k!ᵘe·′s   n′ₑ′nse·   popo″e·s   sₒdq!axomu′n·e.   neᵢs   ło′ᵤk!ᵘs.   qa·qak-
qa′pse·.   łats!ₑna′xe·   aₐ·kₑt.ła′e·s.   k.łała′xa·m   tseᵢka′te·   ki′e·k
ła·ło′ᵤse·   q!u′łᵤwa·s.   qakₑ′łne·   ałaqa′łt!e·s: "qa′psins   ksiła′łukoᵤ-
kₑna′ła."   qak.ła′pse·:   "nuła′n·e·   ałka·kinₑk!na′ła."   ta′xas   nu-
quna′me·k.   nuwa′sᵢne·   pał   k!unuq!ᵤwu′łe·k.   kᵢᵧuk!ka′ₐka·t
40 tsʋ′pqa·′s   neᵢsts   a′ₐ·ke·   k!okxa′łe·′s   q!u′łᵤwa·s.   ta′xas   sₒd·itqa-
wumxo′ᵤme·k.

(b) COYOTE ROASTS SHREWS

Ta′xas   ts!ₑnałonₑ′sᵢne·.   nałxo′ᵤne·   aₐ′qułuma″e·s.   q!uta′p-
tse·k!   yuk^uₑkxo′ᵤłne·.   ta′xas   ts!ₑna′xe·   neᵢs   yaqa·na·q!małₑk-
ma′łske·   skₑ′n·ku·tsts   tsʋ′pqa·′s.   qa·na′xe·   skₑ′n·ku·ts.   ta′xas
45 n′anike′ᵢse.   aₐ·k!aqa′yt!e·s.   tseᵢka′te·.   n′u′pxₐne·   pał   yuna-
qa′pse·   tsₑnłana′na·′s,   pał   słaqaqa′pse·   k!anₑ′ke·′s   aₐ·k!aqa′y-
t!e·s.   tsᵤk^ua′te·   aₐ·kₑnq!a′wo·ks.   t!axo′ᵤne·   aₐ·k!aqa′yt!e·s.   pałts
yunaqa′pse·   neᵢs   łaqa·na·łikinₑ′łe·k,   a′ₐ·ke·   łayunaqa′pse·.   łat!a-
xo′ᵤne·.   ta′xas   wₑdkanmoxona′kse·   qa·nqu·łuk!pku′pse·.   sₑn-
50 mₑ′te·.   naqtsxoᵤna′kse·.   n′ₑ′łkᵢne·.   ta′xas   łuk!mo′ᵤne·.   qa·n
moxuna′kse·   a′ₐ·ke·   qao^uxa″nte·.   ta′xas   n′ₑ′kᵢne·.

Qa·nałonₑ′sᵢne·   xa′ₐltsin.   tᵢnoxa′xe·   skeᵢk!a″nqału′se·.   qake′ᵢ-
ne·   q!uta·′ptse·k!.   o·′k!ᵘqᵤna   kałxo′ᵤnaps   ma″e·s   sł′aqałsu·-
k^uił′u′pxₐne·.   qakₑ′łne·   ta′t!e·s: "qo·′s   nₑnq!okupxₐnₑ′kse·   tₑtu″-
55 e·s."   (O·,   pałutsik!małₑnkₑ′n·e·.   mₑ′ka   q!uta′ptse·k!   n′ₑ′sᵢnił′o-
mosa′xe·;   mₑsquło′ᵤwo·m   n′ₑ′sᵢniłhałxona′pse·   ma″e·s.)   qakₑ′ł-
ne·   tsu″e·s: "qo·′s   nₑnq!okupxₐnₑ′kse·   a′łka·kinₑk!nała″e·s."
qa·na′xe·   xa′ₐltsin   qałwi′yne·   neᵢ   łka′m·u   ke′e·ns   neᵢs   ka′no·ts
tₑtu″e·s   tsʋ′pqa·′s.   pał   kano′ho·s   neᵢs   aq!ułu′k!pkups   słaqake′ᵢ-
60 ne·.   qałwi′yne·   skumałe′e·ts.   ta′xas   n′aqat!o·xa′xe·.   ta′xas
suk^uₑdq!anke′ᵢne·   neᵢ   łkam·uk^nₑ′ste·k.   ta′xas   k!aqat!o·′xam   qa·
nawₑtskₑ′kᵢne·   xa′ₐltsin.   n′u′pxₐne·   pał   tsₑma·k!kₑ′kse·   ała-
qa′łt!e·s.   pał   nakumałe.ₑ′t.se·.   ta′xas   to′x^ua   łaxa′xe·.   suk^uił-
q!u′k̓ᵤne·   xa′ₐltsin   pał   ko·′wa·s.   ma   k.ła′ło·ᵤs   ki′e·k.   łaqatsxa′se·
65 ałaqa′łt!e·s.   k.ła′xam   łatseᵢka′te·   pał   n′u′pxₐne·   pał   qa.ₑ′nse·

it. Then he had one more arrow, | and he shot again. Just then (the deer) stood right on the snow, and the arrow went under it. ‖ Coyote had no more arrows. Then the deer | left, and it escaped 25 from Coyote. There stood | Dog. She was hungry. Coyote pulled off the bowstring. | He struck the deer with his bow stave. | He again used the bowstring as his hair band. Then the deer ran along. ‖ He was without a bow with which to do | anything. | 30

He said to Dog: "Take the children along." | What should his wife and his children go to get? | Dog and her children were tired· She had an ax ‖ and a hammer, with which she chopped the wood. | 35 It was left there. She went back to her house. When she came back, she looked for food, | and there were no more rose hips. She said to her children: "How does it happen that all our food is gone?" | She was told: "Our parent did it." Then | they moved camp. They were hungry because they had nothing to eat, the deer having been saved ‖ and the rose hips also having been eaten. Then 40 they had | nothing to eat. |

(b) COYOTE ROASTS SHREWS

They started, going away. She carried her parflèche. Q!ota'-ptsek! | was on top of it. Then Coyote started, and | went the way in which the deer tracks went. Coyote went along. Then ‖ his snow- 45 shoes were heavy. · He looked, and saw that there were many | shrews. Therefore his snowshoes were heavy. | He took a stick. He shook his snowshoes. There were a great many. | When he went on on his snowshoes, there were many more, and he shook them again. | There was a great pile. There was a stump. He threw it down, and ‖ it broke. He started a fire. Then he roasted the shrews. 50 There was a pile of them, | and he added more to them. Then he ate. |

Dog was going along. She walked through soft snow. | Q!ota'ptsek! said, because her mother carried her she could see well, | she said to her elder brother: "There our father is eating near a fire." ‖ (I 55 made a mistake. It was Q!ota'ptsek! who | was going along, and it was Misqoło'wum who was being carried by his mother.) He said | to his sister: "Our parent is eating by the fire." | Dog was going along. The child thought it was | the deer that his father pursued, for the stump looked red. Therefore he said so. ‖ He thought 60 the ground was bloody. They went near. | The two children talked, being happy. When they came near, | Dog looked that way. She saw that her children had told the truth. | The ground was bloody. Now they were almost there. | Dog was glad, for she was hungry· She had nothing to eat. | The children did not say any more. When 65 they arrived, she looked again, and she saw that it was not | meat

aₐ'ku'la·ks ne₍s ma kqa'łwi·y ksɛłkuma'ł·o·s, pał n'ɛ·nse· a·'q!u-
łu'k!pko·ps. n'e·t_uwɛsqa'ₐne·. tu'χ_uₐ nała'ₐne· o·'k!ᵘq_una ko'wa·s
słaqaqa'pse·. n'u'pχ_ane· pał ne₍s sɛnmuχona'kse· ka'łta·ts. tse₍-
kata'pse· skɛ'n·ku·ts. ta'χas at łats!ałama'ₐme·k skɛ'n·ku·ts.
70 qak.ła'pse·: "a: qa'psin kɛnsł'a'tstawɛ·'sqa pɛ'k!a·ks xma ha˘n-
pɛsχo'ₐne· łka'm·u kɛnłɛ'k_ama·ł ɛmałaqa'ₐke·. tsχał'ɛ·'nse· nɛn-
kuma'łne·s łkamnɛ·"nte·kts na ka'mi·n." tsukᵘa'te· ne₍s ka'łχo·
χa'ₐłtsin qo's qa'o˘χał'unmɛ'te·. tsukᵘa'te· ne₍s k!omowɛ·'sa·s,
ałaχo'ₐne·. qakɛ'łne·: "łao·kq!a'łe·łqasł'o·q!ᵘi·'yam ma koho·'-
75 was."

   Ta'χas ts!ɛna'χe· qaqa·kqa'pₐnaχwa'te·k. k!e·"ła mɛsquło'ₐ-
wo·m. ta'χas sɛłmatɛ'łne· tɛtu't₍mo mɛsquło'ₐwo·m. ts!ɛna'-
χe· ma'ₐt₍mo q!uta'ptse·k!. pał ki'e·n nɛtsta·hałna'na mɛsquło'ₐwo·m, sła˘qa˘qa'pse· kamatɛ'ktsi·ł skɛ'n·ku·ts χałe·'e·s.
80 q!ota'ptse·k! pał ki'e·n na·utena'na·s, sła˘qa˘qa'pse· ts_ukᵘa'-
ta·ps ma"e·s ta'χas qatał·aqa.e·ła'n·e· mɛsquło'ₐwo·m. n'u'p-
χ_ane· ksɛłma˘'ta·ps ma"e·s. ts_ukᵘa'te· χałe·'e·s skɛ'n·ku·ts.
qakɛ'łne·: "ta'χas maₐts łae·"'łan'. ne'₍na·m' naqa's₍na·m'
ma"ne·s nɛ·"nło·ₐs k!ałasχa'ma·ł tsχałatska'χe." pał ke'₍łoₐs
85 ki·'e·ksts k!aqa'ke·. qa'psins xma se·ł'ałasχa'ma·ts. ta'χas
n'ɛkma'łne· χałe·'e·s ne₍s ka'łta·ts. ta'χas ko_uł'ɛ'k₍ma·ł. nała-
χo'ₐne·. ts!ɛna'χe., qa·na'χe·.

(c) COYOTE AND THE BEAVERS

   Sakɛłaqa'pse· sɛ'n·a·'s. pɛsχo'ₐne· χa'łe·'e·s. qakɛ'łne·:
"hutsχałupkaₐnqu'łne·ts kuł'ɛk₍na·'ła." ta'χas n'umɛts-
90 kɛ'n·e· aₐ'kɛt.ła.ɛ'se·s ne₍s sɛ'n·a·'s a'ₐ'ke· aₐ'q!ankɛtsqa.-
ɛ'se·s. ta'χas łałɛtu'kse·. ta'χas n'umɛtskɛ'n·e· aₐ'qok!-
am'ɛ·se·s. n'upkaqkɛ'n·e· mo"q!ₐne·'s. a'ₐ'ke· ła.upkaqkɛ'-
n·e· mo"q!ₐne·'s. t!apts!aχa'ktse· χałe·'e·s. sukᵘatsk!ak!u'-
se·. n'u'pχ_ane· sɛ'n·a pał tsχałk!umna'nta'pse·. no'h_une·
95 pał n'ɛ·nse· skɛ'n·ku·ts. qakiła'mne·: "tsχał'o'_uktawa's₍ne·
hoł'u'ps₍yała'e·s." ta'χas sɛ'n·a n'upkaqkɛ'n·i·ł at nałnu-
ku'χ_une·. ta'χas sukᵘiłq!u'k_une· skɛ'n·ku·ts. ta'χas yunaqa'pse· k!upka'ₐnqo·ł sɛ'n·a·'s. ta'χas qa·qaskɛ'n·e·. ta'χas
n'ɛtskɛ'łne· ło·k!ᵘs. ta'χas n'ɛłqana'χe·. n'u'pχ_ane· sɛ'n·a
100 k!ɛłqa'na·s skɛ'n·ku·ts·. qakiła'mne·: "ta'χas huła'χuna-
χa'ła wu'o··." ta'χas q!a'pe sɛ'n·a łaχo·n·aqanmɛtqu'łe·k.
pał kqa'e·p ts_ɛn pał ksi·ł·aqa'qa·ps ne₍s wa"nmo·'s. mɛsquło'ₐwo·m aₐ'kok!ᵘa'tsk!ak!o·'we·s a'ₐ'ke· łaχunmitqu'kse·.
łaqanawa'ts!se· aₐ'qok!am'ɛ·se·s. nanukᵘe·ta'pse· mɛsqoło'ₐ-
105 wo·m. tsɛqa'nanukᵘita'pse·. sa'qχa·łya'n·qo·k!ame'₍se·. ła·-
asqanawa'ts!se·. naqankɛ'łne· tɛtu"e·s. nułpa'łne· χałe·'e·s
skɛ'n·ku·ts·. qakɛ'kse·: "kate·'tu, kate·'tu." łayik!ts!na'-
m·ok!am₍ni'łe·k." n'u'pχ_ane· skɛ'n·ku·ts ɛłqa'ha·ks qaₐkiła-

what she thought was bloody, but it was a stump. | She stopped and almost fainted from hunger.   It was so because she was hungry. | She saw that it was a pile of shrews. | Coyote looked at her.   Then Coyote rubbed [it on] his hair. ‖ She was told: "Why are you standing 70 about there?   You ought to have put down | the child.   Eat with them those that are spread out there.   They will be | for you and the children.   This will be mine."   Dog took what she carried | and threw it down.   She took it walking about. | She put it on her back. She said to him: "There is another disappointment.   I was‖ hungry." | 75

Then she started.   She left Misqoło'wum crying. | Then father and son, Misqoło'wum, were left behind. | Q!ota'ptsek! and his mother left him.   Misqoło'wum was a boy, | therefore he was given to Coyote. ‖ Q!ota'ptsek! was a girl, therefore | she was taken by her 80 mother.   Then Misqoło'wum could not help crying. | He knew that he was left by his mother.   Coyote took his son | and said to him "Don't cry!   As your mother is going along there, | if she does not find anything to eat, she will come back."   She had nothing ‖ to eat, 85 therefore he said so.   What should she have to eat?   Then | he and his son ate shrews.   They finished eating together.   He put the boy on his back | and started.   He went along. |

(c) COYOTE AND THE BEAVERS

There were some Beavers.   He put down his son.   He said to him: | "I'll take them out of the water, and we shall eat them."   Then he broke ‖ the dens of the Beavers and the beaver dams. | Then there 90 was no more water.   He broke open the dens | and took a young Beaver out of the water.   He took another | young Beaver out of the water.   He tied them on his child as ear ornaments. | Beaver saw him.   He was going to get the best of him.   He knew ‖ it was Coyote. 95 They said to one another: "He will kill us all. | Let us pretend to be dead."   When the Beavers were taken out of the water, they bled from the mouth. | Then Coyote was glad.   He had taken | many Beavers out of the water.   Then he stopped. | He looked for fuel. Then he went away.   The Beavers saw ‖ Coyote going away, and they 100 told one another: "Let us go back | into the water!"   Then all the Beavers went into the water.   All jumped back quickly into the water. | They were not dead.   It only looked like blood. | Misqoło'wum's ear ornaments also went into the water. | They dived into their holes.   They dragged Misqoło'wum in. ‖ They dragged him in. 105 There were two holes, one on each side, and one dived into each. | Then he called his father.   Coyote heard his son | saying: "Father, father!"   There was a turn | in the tunnel (into which they had gone). Coyote knew from far away that his | son was calling him.   He ran

qank.ła′pse· x̣ałe·′e·s. ła.utsinqkupek⁄′me·k. łaqao˘x̣a′x̣e·.
110 ło′ᵤse· x̣ałe·′e·s. nułpa′łne· ne₍s ya′wo′s qak.łⱶq!anło·u′kse·.
qao˘x̣a′x̣e· sł′a‵kak⁄′sᵤw⁄ts·a′q!ₐse·. nakunk⁄′n·e· ła·akak⁄′n·e.
q!akpakitk⁄sx̣o′ᵤne· ne₍s mo′q!ᵤne·′s. tse₍ka′te· ne₍s k₍yu-
na′qa·ps qa·qa·‵hake·łhakoma·′łe.⁄′t.se· pał sł′a‵sk⁄k⁄łk⁄′n·e.
mo·q!ᵤne·na′nak⁄sta′ke·s.

115   Ta′x̣as n⁄·to′kᵤwe·y₍k⁄′n·e·.   ta′x̣as nank!amu‵kupkin-
mu′n·e·. ta′x̣as ku′kups. ta′x̣as n′a‵qtsqₐne·s⁄′kse·. ts⁄n
aq!u′ta·łs s⁄łqao˘x̣ant⁄′ktse· x̣ałe′e·s., o·′k!ᵘqᵤna ktspo′q!ᵘ-
x̣ᵤne′s.   n⁄nko′e·s sk⁄′n·ku·ts ts⁄n aku′ła·ks tsx̣ałs⁄′-
⁄′k₍ne·. ta′x̣as n′⁄′k₍ne·. łatse₍ka′te· x̣ałe·′e·s. n′uno′qᵤwix̣ₐ-
120 na′pse· ts⁄n aq!u′ta·łs pał .ks⁄′ł′e·ks. qak⁄′łne· x̣ałe·′e·s:
"ho′yas łEm⁄′k!e·st." qao˘x̣ᵘa′nt⁄′ktse· ne₍s aku′ła·ks. łatsᵤ-
kᵘa′te·. n′⁄′k₍ne·. n′iła′x̣ₐne· x̣ałe·′e·s. ku′ł′i·k. ła·ts!⁄na‵-
łon⁄′s₍ne· sk⁄′n·ku·ts x̣ałe.⁄′t₍mu.

(d) DEATH OF COYOTE'S SON

Qa·na′x̣e·.   na· takx̣ax̣o′ᵤne· sk⁄′n·ku·ts. pa·′me·k w⁄l-
125 ninmox̣u′n·e· kts⁄nx̣o′ᵤme·k. tse₍ka′te· x̣ałe·′e·s. n′uma′tse·.
qałwi′yne·:‵ "a·:, kułsuk.likpa′kit ka·nx̣a′łe·. huła‵q!ₐma·ł-
ha·m⁄lu′qkᵘat⁄′łe·k." qa·kiłha·miłu′qkᵘat⁄′łe·k. ta′x̣as łaqa′-
w⁄łkikq!u′se· x̣ałe·′e·s. ts⁄n′a·‵witsł⁄lnukuna′se·. qałwi′yne·
ta′x̣as łaqao˘x̣a′x̣e·. qałwi′yne· ktsłaała′x̣o. qunya′x̣ₐne·
130 pał n′⁄′nse· up′na′m·o·′s, pał s⁄łhot!ₐn⁄‵nmitqa′pse·.
n′iła′n·e· qa·‵ₐkił′iła′n·e·. qake′₍ne·: "a·:, ·ta′x̣as qała ma·‵-
qa·ł·a′łoᵤsk k!utsx̣o′ᵤnaps ma qa‵łqa˘so˘kᵘ⁄′łq!o·k." ta′x̣as
tsx̣ak⁄lmat.lit⁄′łe·k, pał ks⁄′ł′e·ps x̣ałe·′e·s. qake′₍ne·: "a·:
na′s at k.łqa′qₐna aqłsma′k₍ne·k! n⁄′n′e·ps aₐ′kn⁄k!namo′′e·s
135 at tsx̣ałse: łqasa·no′x̣o′nx̣ona′pse· o·p′namo′′e·s." ko·łmat.lit⁄′-
·łe·k sk⁄′n·ku·ts, ta′x̣as ts!⁄na′x̣e·. ta′x̣as ts!⁄na′k₍ne·. łało′ᵤse·
kk!utsx̣o′ᵤnaps.

(e) COYOTE TRIES TO STEAL THE SUN

Qa·na′x̣e·. łax̣a′x̣e· sa·k.łunam⁄′s₍ne·. t⁄nax̣a·′′mne· qanit.-
łanam⁄′s₍ne·. n′⁄sakEnu′ne·. n′u′px̣ₐne· pa·′łke₍s sła·t₍yił-
140 a‵ntaqanaqₐna′kse·. n′u′px̣ₐne· łka′m·u′s sanaqna′kse· w⁄l-
wᵤ′mse·. qałwi′yne· sk⁄′n·ku·ts: "pał s⁄łso′ᵤkse· ma·′′e·s,
ks⁄łsa′han qo łka′m·u." qake′₍ne· ne₍ łka′m·u: "ka·′ma,
qałwi′yne· na nöp⁄′k!a: ‵kse′₍łsoᵤks ma·′′e·s, na łka′m·u
ks⁄łsa′han.′" qałwi′yne·: "a·: ks⁄łsa′han ne₍ łka′m·u. k!up-
145 x̣ałwi′ytap." qake′₍ne· ne₍ łka′m·u: "ka·′ma, qałwi′yne·
na nöp⁄′k!a: ‵a·: ks⁄łsa′han na łka′m·uts k!upx̣ałwi′ytap.′"
qałwi′yne· sk⁄′n·ku·ts: "a·: hutskiłpaq!ₐme·woma′ke·." qake′₍-
ne· ne₍ łka′m·u: "qałwi′yne· na nöp⁄′k!a: ‵a·: ks⁄łsa′han, huts-

quickly. He got there. ‖ His son had disappeared. He heard him 110
making noise in the water. | He went there. His legs stuck out.
He pulled at them, and took him out. | Then he knocked down the
young Beavers. He looked for | the many Beavers, but only the
bloody ground was left. | The two young Beavers were all he got. ‖

He made a hole in the ground. Then he made a fire and put the 115
meat into it. | When it was cooked, he took it out. | He put the
fat there for his son because it was soft. | He himself, Coyote, was
going to eat the meat. | Then they ate. He looked again at his
son, and he wished to eat ‖ what his son was eating, who was eating 120
fat. He said to his son: | "Let us change!" He put the meat there
and took back (the fat). | Then he ate. He made his son cry.
After they had eaten, | Coyote and his son moved camp. |

(d) DEATH OF COYOTE'S SON

He went along. Coyote slipped and fell. ‖ He slid down a long 125
distance until something stopped him. He looked at his son. He
laughed at him. | (Coyote) thought: "Let me make my son glad.
I'll | slide down on the snow for a little while." Then he slid
down. | His son did not laugh aloud. He just smiled. Then (Coyote)
thought | he would go back. He thought he would put him again
on his back. He touched him ‖ and he saw him. . He was frozen to 130
death. | He cried all the time. He said: "There is | nothing that
should prevent him from being glad (?)" Then | he threw his things
away because his son was dead. He said: "Ah! | This is what people
shall do when their relatives die. ‖ Then the dead will not be put 135
into bad condition." After | Coyote had thrown his things away, he
started. He went fast. There was nothing | to keep him back. |

(e) COYOTE TRIES TO STEAL THE SUN

He went along, and he came to a town. He entered a tent
there. | He sat down. He saw a woman sitting ‖ with her back toward 140
the fire. He saw a child sitting there | which had a big belly. Coyote
thought: "The mother is good, | but the child is bad." The child
said: "Mother, | this manitou thinks his mother is good, but her
child | is bad." He thought: "The child is bad; ‖ it knows my mind." 145
The child said: "Mother, | the manitou thinks this child is bad; it
knows my mind." | Coyote thought: "I'll burst his belly by kicking
him." | The child said: "The manitou thinks he is bad. | I will

kiłpaq!ₐme·woma'ke·.'"   qatsxa'n·e· ne₁ pa'łke₁. n'u·pxₐne·
150 skɛ'n·ku·ts· k!es₁nɛ't.ła·'s naso'ₐkᵘe·ns. łaa'ₐk!ła·k na ła·'a qa-
nɛt.łana'mne·, qawɛt.łana'mne·. tkaxa''mne· pa'łke₁ ne₁s yaqa`-
wɛsaqa'ₐke· skɛ'n·ku·ts. tse₁ka'te· skɛ'n·ku·ts n'ɛ'nse· tɛłnamu''-
e·s. qak.ła'pse·: "kaₐs kɛn·a·'qał·ati'ke·ł łka'm·u ksɛł'a·qała-
ti·'ke·. n'ɛ'n·e· papa'ne·s. kaₐs ke'e·n łka'm·u ma kinqsa'ma·ł."
155 skɛ'n·ku·ts qa·wa`xₐmit₁naxₐwa'te·k. n'ɛła'n·e·. qake'₁ne·: "nu-
t!a̤'nɛ·n·me·tqapₐmona'p₁ne·." qak.ła'pse· ne₁stɛłnamu''e·s: "na
a·qa't!a·k husɛnt.la'ₐne·. hułts!naxa'ła." ta'xas sɛłqaqa'pse·
ne₁s ma yaqakɛ'łke· xałe'e·s ne₁s ki·'e·ps: "ma kqa'ki·ł'e''na·m
ma''ne·s nɛ''nłoₐs k!ałasxa'ma·ł tsxał·ats!kax'e·." ta'xas sɛł·o'ₐse·
160 k!ałasxa'ma·ł xa'ₐłtsin sɛłałoqᵘałqa'ₐtse·. skɛ'n·ku·ts ta'xas ła-
tsₐkᵘa'te·. ta'xas t₁naxa''mne· xa'ₐłtsɛns aₐ'kɛt.łaɛ'se·s. ta'xas
n'ɛ'k₁ne. qak.ła'pse· tɛłnamu''e·s: "sakxa'xe· kała'qₐni·ł.
wałkₐwa'yi·t tsxał·awa'xe·. maₐts hɛntst₁naxa''mne·. ta'xta·
kanmi·'yit a'ₐke· łaqanɛ'ki·t. ta'xas hɛntst₁naxa''mne·.
165 tsɛłmi·'yet hɛnt₁na'xa·'m hɛntsqatse₁katɛ'łne·. at qaqa'ₐne· at
qaqana'ₐne· na naso'ₐkᵘe·n. n'ɛ'ne· nata·'nɛk!." ta'xas tsłimi'-
yit. ława'xe· kała'qₐni·ł. ta'xas q!a'pe· qaoˇxaxa''mne· ne₁s naso'ₐkᵘe·n aₐ'kɛt.ła'e·s. n'ɛt!qaoˇxałxo'ₐłne· tsₐ'pqa. ta'xas tsxana''mne·. ta'xas k.łanmu'ko·ł aₐ'ku'ła·k. ta'xas q!a'pe· tɛ'tqa·t!
170 quna'xe· ne₁s aₐ'kit.łana'me·'s. ta'xas nanmoku'łne·. łkamnɛ''nte·k q!a'pe· quna'xe·. n'ᴜpkawi'sɛłku'łne· ne₁s kanmuku'łe·'s.
ta'xas skɛ'n·ku·ts a'ₐke· quna'xe·. ta'xas sɛłma't·e· ke'₁tsxa·'s
tɛłnamu''e·s. ta'xas qsama'łne· łkamnɛ'nta'ke·s k!ᴜpka'łko·łs. qo's
a'pko·k!ᵘs qawaxₐmɛ'te· sɛ't!e·s. ta'xas k!ᴜpka·wɛsɛ'łko·ł tsu-
175 kᵘałɛ's₁ne· sɛ't!e·s. łaqawa'xₐmɛt.łɛ's₁ne· qo's aₐ'k!ała'xₐwu'e·t.s.
łat₁na'łkoₐł skɛ'n·ku·ts n'u·pxₐne· sɛtłɛ'se·s. łka'm·o's ne₁s
aₐ'k!ała'xₐwu'e·ts pa''me·k at qa'o·ˇxałyik!taku'łne·, a'ₐke· at
qa'o·ˇxał'upq!ₐmałɛkxo'ₐme·k. ta'xas ku'ko· aₐ'ku'ła·k, ta'xas
n'i·kɛ'łne·. ta'xas pał tsxało·k!ᵘiłqahisɛ'łne· skɛ'n·ku·ts· ne₁s
180 yaqa'hanqame'₁ke· at qanałhisa'mnamɛ's₁ne· at manq!ałe'₁ne· at
qakiłɛ'łne·: "hinqa.ɛstɛ'łne· ne₁stɛ'łne· ɛn łu'n·u." hanqame'ke·
łaa'k!ła·ks at n'atska·łkɛ'n·e·. at qakiłɛ'łne·: "hinqa.istɛ'łne·,
ne₁stɛ'łne· ɛn łka'm·u." ta'xas pał sł·ało'ₐse· aₐ'ku'ła·ks pał
sło·'k!ᵘiłqahisɛ'łne·. ta'xas łaanaxa'mna'mne·. yunaqaṅ-
185 qa'ₐne· kₐwisɛ'n·a·. skɛ'n·ku·ts nuk!ᵘiło'ₐse· kₐwɛsɛ'n'e·s o·'k!ᵘqₐ-
na·ts qahisɛ'łne·. ta'xas q!a'pe· ła·anaxa'mna'mne·. qake'₁ne·
skɛ'n·ku·ts: "ts!kakɛ'nki·ł ka'si·t! e·s ma kwɛ'ski·łqaoˇxa'ke·n."
qałwi'yne·a'pko·k!ᵘs ksa'kqa·ps sɛ't!e·s sł'aqake'₁ne·. qakiłɛ'łne·:
"is łu'n o·'s skikqa'ₐne·." tse₁ka'te· skɛ'n·ku·ts ne₁s aₐ'k!ałaxₐ-
190 wu'e·t.s skɛ·kqa'pse· sɛ't!e·s. skɛ·kq!ₐma'łse·, skɛ·kqoqᵘts!ała'₁se·.
łatsukᵘa'te·, ła·anaxa''mne·. łat₁naxa''mne· aₐ'kɛt.ła·ɛ'se·s tɛłnamu''e·s. qak.ła'pse·: "ki'n·e·k? kɛn·wɛ'łwo·m?" qake'₁ne· skɛ'n·
ku·ts: "a:waha·'. hoqᵘahisɛ'łne·, husɛłyanxu'n·e·." numats₁nata'p-

burst his belly by kicking him." The woman did not speak. Coyote knew ‖ that it was the tent of a chief. There was another | tent, 150 which was not large. A woman came in | where Coyote was. Coyote looked, and it was his wife. | She said to him: "Why did you say what the child said? | This is your grandson. Where is the child that went with you?" ‖ Coyote fell down crying. He said: | "He 155 froze to death." His wife said: | "My tent is near by. Let us start." Then it was | as he had told his dead son. He told him: "Your mother is going; | but if she has no one to share with her what she eats, she will turn back." Then Dog had no one ‖ to share with 160 her what she ate. Then she turned back. Then Coyote took her back. | He entered Dog's tent. Then | she ate. His wife said to him: "They have | started deer driving." In the evening they will come back. Don't go in. | In the morning they will do it again. Then you may go in. ‖ If you go in in the evening, they will not look at 165 you. | The chief always does that way. He is the Sun." | At night the deer drivers came back. Then all went to | the chief's tent. They piled up the deer. | Then they talked, and they boiled the meat. All the men ‖ went to the tent. Then (the meat) was being boiled. | 170 All the children went there, carrying water where the meat was being boiled. | Coyote always went there. He disobeyed his wife. | He went with the children who were bringing water. | There at the head of the tent he threw down his blanket. They brought in water. ‖ His blanket was taken and was thrown back to the door. | When 175 Coyote took water into the tent, he saw his blanket. The child | near the door always spilled water on it | and cleaned his feet on it. When the meat was done, | it was eaten, but nothing was given to Coyote. ‖ They were passing the food by the place 180 where he was sitting. He stretched his hand out, | but he was told: "It is not for you; it is for the next one." | Another one who was sitting there took it. He was told: " It is not for you; | it is for him, for that child." Then all the meat was gone, | and he did not receive anything to eat. Then all went out, and there was much ‖ food left over. Coyote had nothing left over, because | he 185 was not given anything. Then all went out. Coyote said: | "Give me my blanket; I put it there." | He thought that his blanket was lying at the head of the tent; therefore he said so. He was told: | "It lies over there." Coyote looked, and there was ‖ his blanket lying 190 at the door. It was dirty and wet. | Then he took it and went out. He went into the tent of his wife. | He was told: "Did you eat? Are you satiated?" Coyote said: | "Oh, no! I was not given anything.

se· tₐnamu′′e·s. qak.ła′pse·: "ma kinqa′qa·łqa′qa ne₁ pₑ′k!a·k,
195 at ma ke·n′upsła·t₁yiłmat ko·′ᵤtsxa. ma hoqaqlₑ′s₁ne·: ′maₐts
kintstna′xa.′ at qahisₑ′łne· tₑ′tqa·t! ne·nwam na′s aₐ′kik.łu-
na′me·′s. ta′xta· kanmi·′yit a′ₐ′ke· łaqanₑ′ke·. ta′xa· at t₁na-
xa′′mne·. ˙ ta′xas at na′łq!a·łhowu′mne·. swakałkinₑ′łne·
aₐ′ku′ła·k kutsxał′ₑ′k₁na′ła. huskiłhanmu′kᵤne·. is kikqa′ane·
200 ta′xas ₑ′ke·n′.′′ ta′xas skₑ′n·ku·ts tsxa′kił′ₑ′k₁ne·. ta′xas no-
wu′m′ne·. ta′xas q!u′mne′′ne·. wₑ′łna·ms naq!amałe′₁tsne·
skₑ′n·ku·ts. nułpałitₑ′t₁ne· aₐ′k.łuk.łe′et.s. qakiyamₑ′s₁ne: "hú,
hú, hú.′′ qake′₁ne· skₑ′n·ku·ts ne₁s kułpałnₑ′te·t k!aₐqakya′-
m·e·s, qake′₁ne·: "hú, hú, hú. kuł′ₑ′łwa k.łe′a·s wa′ma·t!
205 k.łakₑ′se·łnoho′sk!umk.łuwₑst!a′łama·łqałtₑ′łe·k k.ła′wła.′′ nuł-
pałnₑ′łne· skₑ′n·ku·ts· ne₁s k!a·′qa′ke·. n′ₑsłikpayaxₐwa′t₁ne·k-
tₑ′t₁ne·: "pa·ł k!anₑ′ke· ne₁s ke′as wa′ma·t! a′ₐ′ke· ne₁s kwist!a′ła
k.ła′wła. tsxałqa.ikₑ′t!ᵤwo· pał at qaha·′q!ₐwo·ktsamna′mne· qo
ta·′xa hak.łuna′mke·.′′ ta′xas ts!ₑna′mne·. aₐ′ke· skₑ′n·ku·ts
210 ts!ₑna′xe·. qanaxa′mne·. n′ₑsakₑmu′n′e· naso′ᵤkᵘe·n. ta′xas
ne₁s ya·qaha·nqame·′ke· naso′ᵤkᵘe·n. iłna·′hak qakₑ′₁kała′qₐ-
wu′mne·. łaxa′xe· skₑ′n·ku·ts. qayₐqana′xe· qo′s yₐqanaqₐ-
nakₑ′ske· naso′ᵤkᵘe·n u′s′me·ks. qa·′o·̆xał′ₑsakₑnu′n′e· qałwiy-
na′mne· ksₑłsana′qₐna skₑ′n·ku·ts. tsₑn ya·kqasts!ₑmqa′qa at
215 k!ₑ′s₁ni·ł′us′mo·ka·nqa′me·k. k!a·′qa′qₐna skₑ′n·ku·ts. ta′xas
q!a′pe· k.łaxa′xam. qake′₁ne· nata′nₑk!: "ta′xas łu′n·u ts!ₑna′-
ke·ł ne₁ wa·′kaq!yułeₑ′tke· ya·kₑnts!ₑłk!ₑku′kᵘi·ł hₑntsxał′ₑnkₑ′ł-
ne·.′′ n′iłiktₑ′łne· skₑ′n·ku·ts. o·′k!ᵘqᵤna ne₁s k!aqa′kₐna sₑł′aqa-
kiya′mne·. ta′xas n′owo′kᵤne· naso′ᵤkᵘe·n. ta′xas skₑ′n·ku·ts
220 a′ₐ′ke· n′owo′kᵤne·. ta′xas ts!ₑna′xe· naso′ᵤkᵘe·n. ta′xas
tsu′kᵤne·. nałkₑ′n′e· aₐ′kₑno·̆qᵘa′ₐkops. qao·̆xanq!o′kup-
q!o′ᵤne·. tse₁katₑ′łne· skₑ′n·ku·ts. ło′ᵤse· aₐ′kₑno·̆qᵘa′ₐko·ps.
k·a′łkₑn. qałwiyna′mne· tsxałqaqał′o·′k!ᵘe· nata′nₑk! ktsxał-
tsu′ko·. ta′xas skₑ′n·ku·ts qao·̆xakₑ′n′e· ma′ₐka·′s łₑ′n′e·s,
225 aₐ′kₑnqowa.ₑ′se·s ma′ₐka·′s. nutsinqkupekₑ′me·k. tse₁katₑ′łne·
ne₁s ya·qa·′naq!małe′₁ke· qanaq!ma·′k.łₑnq!oku′pse·. nuła′se·
ne₁s ma′ₐka·′s. ta′xas qakiłaq!maxoka′ₐne· skₑ′n·ku·ts. tse₁-
katₑ′łne· naso′ᵤkᵘe·n nata′nₑk!. taxta·′′ na′s qasna′xe·
peₑ′k!a·ks skₑ′n·ku·ts, qo·ᵤs nₑłqana′xe·. ta′xas ts!ₑnₑ′xe·
230 kała′qₐni·ł qanaxa′′mne·. n′upxa′łne· skₑ′n·ku·ts, pₑ′k!a·ks
ne₁s pał sₑł′awa′xe· pał słakamₑnqa′ₐtse· n′üpski·łqa.ₑłqana′xe·
ne₁ naso′ᵤkᵘe·n. skₑ′n·ku·ts łao·′k!qana′xe·. ta′xas mₑtxa′łne·
tsᵥ′pqa ne₁s yₐqa·′nałhanq!oku′pske· o′qo·ᵤks. qana′xe· skₑ′n·-
ku·ts. n′u′pxₐne· wa′ma·t!s n′a′s·e·. xa·′tsₑnł′ₑłwa′n′e·. qana′xe·
235 a′ₐ′ke· n′u′pxₐne· wₑst!a′łama′łqa·łtₑ′kse· k.ła′wła·s, a′ₐ′ke· n′u′-
kte·. ta′xas k.łats!ₑnaxa′mne·. n′u′pxₐne· skₑ′n·ku·ts at na′s
łaqoqᵘaha·′nłukpqa′pse· tₑ′tqa·t!s. at ło′ᵤse· qa′psi·ns. sanmo·ł-

I am starving." His wife laughed at him. | She said to him: "You are always like that. ‖ You always disobey me. I told you not | to go 195 in. A man who comes to this town is not given anything to eat. | At a later time, another day, when they do so again, then he may go in. | Then he is given enough to eat. Meat has been brought in | for us to eat. I have boiled it. It is there. ‖ Eat." Then Coyote began to 200 eat. Then | he was satiated and slept. Early Coyote awoke. | He heard a noise. People were saying: "Hu, hu, | hu!" Coyote said when he heard it (the same as) what they said. | He said: "Hu, hu, hu! let me kill two bucks ‖ and red (?) an old grizzly bear with seven young 205 ones." | They heard what Coyote was saying. It was frightful | what he said. "Two bucks and seven | grizzly bears are too heavy. Those will be nine. The people of that town don't carry meat for one another." | Then they started, and Coyote ‖ started, too. They were 210 going along. The chief sat down. Then | behind where the chief was sitting a row of men started. | Coyote got there. He went past the place where | the chief was sitting. Farther ahead he sat down. The people thought: | "Coyote is doing wrong. Only those who are skillful ‖ may sit at the head. Why does Coyote do so?" | Then they all ar- 215 rived. Sun said: "Go on | to the end of this mountain. Those who go quickly shall do it." | Coyote was meant. Because he had done so, therefore they said it. | Then the chief arose, and Coyote also ‖ arose. Then the chief started. | He started a fire. He carried pitch- 220 wood and he started a fire. | They looked at Coyote. He did not carry pitchwood. | They thought Sun would be the only one who would light a fire. | Then Coyote put flicker feathers on his moccasins. ‖ He ran. They looked at him; | and wherever he stepped, a fire started. | 225 The flicker did so. Then Coyote scared them. | Then they looked at Chief Sun. He had not gone far | before Coyote was way over there. Then the deer drivers started ‖ and went along. Coyote was seen 230 coming back already. | He went around in a circle. | The chief had not gone far when Coyote went the same way again. Then a deer was shot | where the fire was, in the circle of fire. Coyote went along, | and saw two bucks. He killed both of them. He went along, ‖ and he 235 saw seven grizzly bears—an old one and young ones. He killed them all | and started back. The men had nothing, and Coyote saw them |

kɛʼnʽeʽ neᵢs kǃɛʼɬwa. qaaʼɬuqᵘakɛʼnʽeʽ. qakɛʼɬneʽ: "a: ɬɛnɬoʼᵤneʽ kɛnʼɛʼɬwa x̣maʽnɬahaʼqǃwoktsaʼpᵢneʽ." qakiɬɛʼɬneʽ: "at qahaʼqǃₐ

240 woʽkktsamnaʼmneʽ." taʼx̣as ɬaɬunamɛʼsᵢneʽ. qaaʼɬuqᵘakɛʼnʽeʽ paɬ kqa.ikɛʼtǃᵤwoʽᵤs. nʼukǃuʼniɬʼakᵢmeʼʼnteʽ. qakɛʼɬneʽ neᵢs kǃakᵢmeʼʼneʽt: "a: tsx̣anataʼpkiɬ kaₐs koʼɬaʼqaʼkiʽn na koɛʼɬwa?" qak.ɬaʼpseʽ: "kɛnqaɬwiʼymeɬ keʼᵢɬoᵤs kǃɛʼɬwa? na k.ɬaqahaqaʼnqaʽts? at nɑkupx̣oʼᵤɬneʽ at tsɛqapqonaʼneʽ at ɬaaʽ-

245 pakǃeʽnkinɛʼɬneʽ aₐʼkaʽwutaʼmeʽs." taʼx̣as skɛʼnʽkuʽts nɑkup-x̣oʼᵤneʽ.[1] tsɛqapqonaʼseʽ. taʼx̣as ɬaapakǃneʼʼnteʽ neᵢs kuwɛstǃaʼ-laʼs k.ɬaʼwɬaʽʼsts neᵢs keʼaʽs waʼmaʽtǃs. ɬaʼutsɛnqkupekɛʼmeʽk. qaɬwiynamɛʼsᵢneʽ ktsx̣aɬhaʼɬkeʽks skɛʼnʽkuʽts paɬ ksiʽɬyunaʼqaʽps kǃɛʼɬwa. qanax̣aʼmneʽ. paɬ kaɬnokuʼpqa skɛʼnʽkuʽts nʼöpskiʽɬa-

250 qaɬax̣ax̣amʼɛʼsᵢneʽ k.ɬaqayaqaʼnaʽmomoʼkᵘa. k.ɬaɬaʼx̣aʽm ɬoʼᵤnteʽ k.ɬakaʼɬx̣oʽ.[2] qanaqɬɛʼkx̣aneʽ; tᵢnmitᵢkɛʼnʽeʽ neᵢs aₐʼkɛt.ɬanaʼmeʽs qǃaʼpeʽs ɬawɛɬqaʼpseʽ saʽmeʼᵢnmux̣uʼnaks neᵢs qa.ikɛʼtǃᵤwoʽs. taʼx̣as aʼₐʼkeʽ ɬahaqǃmax̣okaʼₐneʽ skɛʼnʽkuʽts.

Taʼx̣as tshmiʼyit ɬaeʽtǃqaoʽx̣ax̣aʼʼmneʽ nasoʼᵤkᵘeʽn aₐʼkɛt.-

255 ɬaʼeʽs. ɬaeʽkɛʼɬneʽ. skɛʼnʽkuʽts ɬaqatᵢnax̣aʼʼmneʽ at nuɬpaɬuɛʼɬneʽ skɛʼnʽkuʽts. paɬ k.ɬaʼloᵤ tɛʼtqaʽtǃ neᵢs aₐʼkik.ɬunaʼmeʼʼs; at qo-qᵘaʽkqaʽɬilqǃanɬoʼᵤkᵤneʽ skɛʼnʽkuʽts tɑnamuneʼntaʼkeʼs. sɬonɛʼɬneʽ waʼɬkᵤwaʽʼs ma kqoʼᵤnaʽm ma kqahɛʼsiʽɬ. ɬatᵢnax̣aʼʼmneʽ skɛʼnʽ-kuʽts tɑnamuʼʼeʽs. qak.ɬaʼpseʽ: "qaʼpsin kinsiɬqaoʼᵤnaʽm neᵢ

260 kǃɛtqaoʽx̣aɬɛʼkeʽɬ?" qakeʼineʽ: "a: waʼɬkᵤwaʽ ma kᵘqoʼᵤnaʽm ma koʼmatsqₐnaʽneʽyaʼₐtiʽɬ." tsǃɛnaʼx̣eʽ neᵢs yaʽqaʽhaʼqa-womɛʼskeʽ. tᵢnax̣aʼmneʽ, qaoʽsaqaʼₐneʽ. taʼx̣as kǃɛkinoqokuʼleʽs. taʼx̣as wunikɛʼtᵢneʽ ktsɬmiʼyit, taʼx̣as ɬaanaʼx̣aʼmnaʼmneʽ.

Nʼuʼpx̣aneʽ skɛʼnʽkuʽts neᵢs yaqahaʼnqameʼᵢkeʽ qaʼhaninʽqo-

265 maʼlseʽ aₐʼkuqɬatǃɛʼseʽs nawaspaʼɬeʽs. soʼᵤkᵘseʽ. qaɬwiʼyneʽ: "kutsx̣aɬʼaʼyniʽɬ." taʼx̣as qakeʼineʽ skɛʼnʽkuʽts: "a: kusɑʼaqaʼ-taʼɬʼanaʼx̣aʽʼm. kutsx̣aɬqahaʼk.ɬeʽts na aₐʼkɛt.ɬaʼʼnaʽm." taʼx̣as qǃuʼmneʼʼneʽ nataʼnɑkǃ. nʼupx̣aɬwiytaʼpseʽ nawaspaʼɬeʽ neᵢs kǃaqaʼɬwiy ktsx̣aɬʼaʼyniʽɬ. qatsx̣aʼnʽeʽ nataʼnɑkǃ. taʼx̣as wu-

270 nikɛʼtᵢneʽ ktsɬmiʼyit, nʼuʼpx̣aneʽ skɛʼnʽkuʽts qǃuʼʼmneʼs nawas-paʼɬeʽs. nuwoʼkᵤneʽ. tsᵤkᵘaʼteʽ neᵢs aₐʼkuqɬaʼntaʼmeʽs nʼaqsₐna-kɛʼnʽeʽ. ɬaanax̣aʼʼmneʽ. taʼx̣as tsǃɛnaʼx̣eʽ. qanaʼx̣eʽ. taʼx̣as qaɬ-wiʼyneʽ. taʼx̣as ksɑʼwɑleʼʼeʽts. nʼitx̣oʼᵤmeʽk, qǃuʼmneʼᵢneʽ paɬ kuʼk.ɬuʽk qahak.ɬeʼitsneʽ skɛʼnʽkuʽts. naqǃmaɬeʼᵢtsneʽ. nʼuʼpx̣ₐ-

275 neʽ aₐʼkɛʼkqǃyet.s. nʼukᵤnux̣aʼʼmneʽ, nʼuʼpx̣ₐnɛʽ paɬ nʼɛʼnseʽ neᵢs aₐʼkɛt.ɬaʼɛʼseʽs nataʼnɑkǃs. ma kwɑleʼʽeʽts yaqanaʼmkeʽ. kǃaʼqaʼ-qaʼps tsukᵘaʼteʽ neᵢs aₐʼkuqɬaʼntaʼmeʽs. qakeʼineʽ: "a: kǃeʽk-payaʼₐtaʽp na aₐʼkuqɬaʼʼntaʽm." ɬaqǃayakɛʼnʽeʽ. ɬaanax̣aʼʼmneʽ skɛʼnʽkuʽts. tsɑmeʽʼyit aₐʼʼkeʽ ɬatᵢnax̣aʼʼmneʽ. qahaqowuʼʼmneʽ.

280 taʼx̣as aₐʼʼkeʽ ɬaaʽnax̣aʼmnaʼmneʽ skɛʼnʽkuʽts. qakeʼineʽ: "aₐʼʼkeʽ

---

running by. | He had a pile of (game) what he killed. He did not know what to do with it. He said to them: "Evidently you have no game. | You ought to carry some meat home for me." He was told: "We do not ‖ carry meat for one another." Then there was 240 nobody left, and he did not know what to do with it, | with the nine animals. At once he called his manitous. He told those whom he had called: | "Tell me what to do with my game." | They said to him: "You think that they, those who went by, killed nothing. | They blow on it and it becomes small. ‖ Then they put it into their belts." 245 Then Coyote | blew on it, and (the game) became small. Then he put on | the seven bears and the two bucks. He ran back quickly. | They thought Coyote would not come home before night, because he had much game. | They went along, but Coyote was able to run fast. ‖ They were not home yet before he passed them. He got home. He 250 pulled off | what he carried on his belt. He kicked it into the tent, and | it was all big again, and the nine animals were piled up there. | Then Coyote scared them again. |

In the evening they assembled again in the chief's ‖ tent and ate 255 again. Coyote did not go in. They heard | Coyote. There were no other men in the town. | Somewhere Coyote made a noise where the women were. Coyote was afraid; | for when he had gone there the day before, he was not given anything to eat. Coyote entered | his wife's tent, and she said to him: "Why don't you go there ‖ where 260 they are assembled to eat?" He said: "Oh, yesterday I went there, | and they made fun of me." He went to the place where they were assembled. | He went in and staid there. Then they were smoking. | After a long time, in the evening, they went out again. |

Where he was sitting, Coyote saw a skin-drying ‖ frame (?) belong- 265 ing to his father-in-law. It was pretty. He thought: | "I'll steal it." Then Coyote said: "I can not go out; | I'll sleep here in this house." Then | the Sun was asleep. His father-in-law knew | what he was thinking about, that he was going to steal it. The Sun did not speak. Then, ‖ after a while, in the evening Coyote saw that his 270 father-in-law was asleep. | He arose and took the drying frame and put it under his blanket. | He went out again, started, and went along. | He thought he was far away, and he lay down and went to sleep. | Being tired, Coyote slept there. He woke up and heard‖ people talking. He arose, and he saw that it was | the tent of the 275 Sun. He had gone far, but this happened because he | had taken the drying frame. He said: "Ah! | I long for this drying frame." He hung it up. Then | Coyote went out. In the evening he came in again. They were assembled there. ‖ Then all went out again. 280

kutsłaqaha'k.łe·ts." n'itχo'ₙme·k. n'u'pχₐne· ta'χas kq!u''mne·'s
nata'nₑk!s. qawunekₑ't.se·. ktsłmi·''yit ta'χas łatsukᵘa'te· neᵢs
aₐ'kuqła'nta'me·s. n'anaχa''mne·. ts!ₑna'χe·. qałwi'yne·: "ta'χas
ₔqa'hak hułqa'na·m." ta'χas ts!ₑna'χe·. qa·na'χe· at nanłukp-
285 qa'ₐne·. ta'χas siłkanmeyₑ't.se· qałwi'yne·: "ta'χas ksₔwu-
ło·'ct.s." n'ₑtχo'ₙme·k. pał ko'k.łoₙk. ta'χas n'u'k!ₙniłq!akpa'ki-
tiłe'ᵢtsne·. qahak.łeₑ'ts₁ne·. na'q!noka'łna·χwatₑ'łne·. nu·kₙ-
nuχa''mne·, pał n'ₑ'nse· neᵢs ma yaₐ'qakχa'mke·. tsₙkᵘa'te· neᵢs
aₐ'kuqła'nta'me·s. qake'ᵢne·: "a: k!a·'qała'teᵢkₑ'n·a·p?" łaq!aya-
290 kₑ'n·e·. qak.ła'pse· nawaspa'ł'e·s nata'nₑk!s: "qa'psin kinsła-
tₑ'qₐna? kₑnqa'łwiy kₑntsχał'ana'χa·'m· n'ₑ'ne· ka·kₑ't.ła. na hₑnts!ₑ'na·m na a'qła ka·kₑ't.ła atₑnłaqa'haki·ł'itχo'ₙme·k·, hₑnqa'ł-
wiy ktsχa'ł'ₑn aₐ'kuqła''nt₁ne·'s, ta'χas tsₙkᵘa'te·n' kₑnłts!ₑ'-
na·n'. maₐts hₑntsχał'ₑtoₙsa‿qa'ₐne· tsₔme·'yit. yₑ'sₑnwun·me·-
295 yₑ'tke· tsₔme·yitna'mu. hₑnts!upsła't₁yiłqqa·'ₐtse·. kanmi·'yit
maₐts hₑnts!ₑtχo'ₙme·k. yₑ'sₑnwun·miyₑ'tke· yu·kᵘₑyₑtna'm·u.
maₐts hₑnts!ₑtoₙsa‿qa'ₐne· aₐ'ke· łatsiłmi·'yit; aₐ·'ke· hₑnts!ła-
kanmokₙnatₑ't₁ne· kanmi·'yit. qaha'łi·n kiyu'k₁yit, ta'χas
hₑnts!ₑsakₐnu'n·e·. hₑnqa'łwiy hₑnq!u''mne· so'ₙkₙne·. ta'χas
300 hₑntsₔ'anaχa''mne· ka·ki't.ła. ta'χas hutsłaqa'tsukᵘa'te·."
Ta'χas. husₔq!a'pqa·łq!a'nuχwa'te·.

57. COYOTE AND GRIZZLY BEAR

Qa.na'χe· skₑ'n·ku·ts. qaq!a‿yumena'se·. yuχa'χe·. n'u'pχₐne·
k.ła'wła·s sawₑtsqapχₐna'kse·. qałwi'yne· skₑ'n·ku·ts: "hułk.łₑn-
q!o'ymo·." qakₑ'łne·: "k.ławła, k!a·''ntsu." łaa'ntsuχaχa''mne·.
nułpa'łne· skₑ'n·ku·ts· sₔtsχa'se· k.ła'wła sₔ'ata'pse· sa·nił'a-
5 ta'pse·. qałwi'yne· k.ła'wła: "pał a'ₐ'ke· kₑntsχa·ł·aqa'ke·."
qaqana'wₑtskₑ'k₁ne· k.ła'wła. wunikₑt.se· łatseᵢka'te· skₑ'n·-
ku·ts k.ła'włas. qakₑ'łne·: "k.ła'wła kkoₙłwi·'yat!." ta'χas
n'u'pχₐne· k.ła'wła na's aₐ'kuq!yome'nas qa·kiłhaqank.ła'pse·
skₑ'n·ku·ts. ta'χas n'o·'ktse·k, nak.łatsu·łwitskₑ'łne· skₑ'n·ku·ts.
10 qawunikₑ't.se· skₑ'n·ku·ts łała·n'yunawitskₑ'łne· k.ła'wła·'s. qakₑ'łne·: "k.ła·'wła, ktsaqłiłna'na." skₑ'n·ku·ts łaa'ntsuχaχa''mne·.
ta'χas nutsₑnqkupekₑ'me·k k.ła'wła· mitiya'χₐne· skₑ'n·ku·ts.
qawunikₑ't.se· łała·n'yunawₑtskₑ'łne· ka·'s χₐma ts!a·qa'ki·ł
k.ła'wła·'s. qake'ᵢne· skₑ'n·ku·ts: "k.ła'wła —," qaq!ma·'łiłq!-
15 anło'ₙkₙne·. n'u'pχₐne· pₑ'k!a·ks pał sₔyuwa·kₑmi·tiyaχna'pse·.
k.ła'wła·'s skₑ'n·ku·ts. no:sa'no·χoₙnqa'ₐne· skₑ'n·ku·ts. mitiya'χₐnaps k.ła'wła·'s. qake'ᵢne· skₑ'n·ku·ts: "qa'χatsqano'χone-
kₑ'me·k qa'psin ktspułwina'ₐtam." ta'χas matka'ₐne· skₑ'n·ku·ts.
qana'χe· skₑn·ku·ts. łałoqᵘałqa'ₐtse· łałaχa'nχo'ₙne· k.ła'wła·'s.
20 qana'χe· k.ła'wła neᵢs aₐ'k.łₑkₑ's'e·s skₑ'n·ku·ts. nułpa'łne· na-
kₙwa'se·kna'kse· skₑ'n·ku·ts. pał sₔ'ałaχa·nχona'pse·. qałwi'y-

Coyote said: | "I'll sleep here again." He lay down. Then he knew that Sun was asleep. | It was not long before it was night. Then he took the | drying frame. He went out and started. He thought: | "Let me go far away." Then he started. He went along. || He ran. Then in the morning he thought | that he was far 285 away. He lay down. He was tired. Then at once he fell asleep. | He continued to sleep. Then he was awakened by the noise of talking. | He arose, and there he was where he had started from. He took the | drying frame. He said: "What is he trying to do with me?" and hung it up. || His father-in-law, Sun, said to him: "Why are you | 290 doing that? Do you want to go out of this my tent? | If you start here from the inside of my tent, when you lie down there, and if you | think this will be your clothing, then take it and go. | Don't stop at night. Keep on walking || a whole day and a whole night, until 295 morning. | Do not lie down the whole day and the whole night. | Don't stop anywhere until the next night. | Then walk through that night until the morning. Just at noon | you may sit down, if you think that you will sleep. Then it will be good. || You will be out of my 300 tent. Then I shall not take it back." |

Now I have told you all. |

57. COYOTE AND GRIZZLY BEAR

Coyote went along. There was a hill. He went up, and saw | Grizzly Bear eating there. Coyote thought: "I'll play with him." | He said to him: "Grizzly Bear, Short Tail!" | He hid behind (the hill). Grizzly Bear heard Coyote talking, calling him bad names. || Grizzly Bear thought: "You are sure to say that again." | Grizzly 5 Bear did not look. After a while Coyote looked again | at Grizzly Bear. He said to him: "Grizzly Bear, Left-handed One!" Then | Grizzly Bear knew that Coyote was on the hill calling him. | He pretended to eat again. He was looking without letting Coyote see it. || It 10 was not long before Coyote looked over the hill at Grizzly Bear. | He said to him: "Grizzly Bear, Small Eyes!" Coyote hid again. | Then Grizzly Bear ran. He pursued Coyote. | It was not long before he looked over the hill again to say something | to Grizzly Bear. Coyote said: "Grizzly Bear"—— He stopped quickly in his speech. || Coyote saw that Grizzly Bear was already coming right 15 up to him. | Then Coyote began to run away. | He was pursued by Grizzly Bear. Coyote said: "Things that want to catch each other | do not run fast together." Then Coyote left him behind. | Coyote was going along. He turned in a circle and got up to Grizzly Bear from behind. || Grizzly Bear was going along in the tracks of Coyote. 20 Coyote heard him | panting. He was getting near him. | He thought

ne· ktsχałtsɛ′nke· aₐᵏkᵤwiya′t!e·s. łoʻnaqu′młasχu′ne· skɛ′n·-
ku·ts neᵢs kuku′l′e·s. łuqᵘanɛ′n′me· teᵢχałitɛ′tᵢne· k.ła′wła.
qayaqana′χe· skɛ′n·ku·ts. qana′χe· k.ła′wła. a′ₐ·ke· łaqa·′qa-
25 na′ₐne· skɛ′n·ku·ts. qałwi′yne· k.ła′wła: "ta′χas kutstsɛ′nke·n
skɛ′n·ku·ts. kutsk′t!χa." łats! neᵢs łunɛk!łe′e·ts łunaqu′młas-
χu′n·e· skɛ′n·ku·ts k.ła′wła łats! neᵢs aₐʻkuya′t!e·′s łuqᵘanɛ′n·-
me·te′ᵢχałitɛ′tᵢne·. a′ₐ·ke· łaqa·wok·ᵘɛ′n·e·. qana′χe· k.ła′wła
qawułe.ɛ′t.se·. n′u′pχₐne· skɛ′n·ku·ts. s′na′se· pa·ł słuk.łu′ksɛ·.
30 łaxa′nχo′ᵤne·. ta′χas ya·kaqa·łwɛtske·kɛ′me·k skɛ′n·ku·tsts ła·-
wałuna′k!e·s. swɛtsnu′kse·. qałwi′yne· skɛ′n·ku·ts: "ta′χas
ktsχał′ɛ′t!χₐna·p k.ła′wła." qanał′akamɛnuta′pse· neᵢs aₐʻkwɛ′-
tsᵢno·ks. ta′χas tsχałtsɛnkᵢna′pse· k.ła′wła·s. ta′χas n′a·mił-
q!unaₐki′n·e· skɛ′n·ku·ts. qanaχu′n·e· skɛ′n·ku·ts· qakqa′ₐne·
35 wunikɛ′t.se·. qałwi′yne·: "qa′psins ksłqa.ɛ′t!χₐna·p k.ła′wła?"
na·łχunenała′pse· qap′sins aₐʻke′ᵢe·s. tseᵢka′te·. n′u′pχₐne· pał
słqana·ke·swɛtse′ᵢne· aₐʻkuqłe.ɛ′se·s nɛ′łse·ks. tseᵢka′te· k.ła′wła·s.
pa·ł na′s swɛsqa′pse·aₐʻk.łɛ′k!e·s. nu·kᵤnɛ′nmuqkupno·χunka′me·k.
mitiya′χₐne·. qakɛ′łne· neᵢs a·tiya·χqakɛ′kske· nɛ′łse·ks. qake′ᵢne·
40 skɛ′n·ku·ts: "fff."[1] ta′χas n′u′pχₐne· skɛ′n·ku·ts pa·lts oni-
ła′pse·. ta′χas mitiya′χₐne·. ta′χas k.ła′wła neᵢs ma skiłyaqaqₐ-
na′pske· skɛ′n·ku·ts. ta′χas a′ₐ·ke· qaqna′ₐne· ya·kaqa′łᵤwɛts-
kłaka′ₐme·k k.la′wła. sɛnmitu′kse·. nułu′qᵤne· n′akahe′ᵢne.
skɛn·ku·ts nao·′k!ᵘe·′s aₐʻku′qłe·s. n′asnałhołu′qske· k.ła′wła·s.
45 qanaqku′pła·łtᵢmu′n·e· maqku′pkpo·kχᵤmu′n·e· łats!naoʻ′k!ᵘe·′s,
a′ₐ·ke· n′akahe′ᵢne·, a′ₐ·ke· maqku′pkpo·kχᵤmu′n·e·. qaoχał′ał-
qana′kᵤne· k.ła′wła. n′ɛsakₐnu′n·e· skɛ′n·ku·ts. k!u′pa·q k.ła′wła
łaqana·ʻwitskɛ′kᵢne·. skɛ′n·ku·ts sła:tₐnaqₐna′kse·. qake′ᵢne·
skɛ′n·ku·ts: "k.ła′wła, ma kɛntsk·t!χₐna·p k.łukq!ᵘa·ʻłe·łqakya′me·s
50 k.ła′wła n′ɛ′tχₐne· skɛ′n·ku·ts·." k.ła′wła qatsχa′n·e· sɛl′-
onɛ′łᵢne·. tsɛmak!kɛ′kse· at qa·ʻit!χₐnapsɛ′sne· k.ła′wła·′s,
a′ₐ·ke· pał ksiłqsamunała′pse·s swuɛ′se·s nɛ′łse·ks. ta′χa·′s.

Husɛlq!a·′pka·łq!anuχwa′te·.

58. COYOTE AND FOX

Ho′yas, hutsχałhaqałq!anuχwa′te· swᵘ′tᵢmu skɛ′n·ku·tsts·
na′ₐk!ᵤyu yaqaqₐnaₐ′ke· neᵢs pɛ′k!a·ks.

(a) YOUNG COYOTE AND YOUNG FOX STEAL THE HOOP

Qa·nɛt.ła′ₐne· swᵘ′tᵢmo. naqa′łte· nɛtsta′hałs, aₐ′′ke· naqa′łte·
nɛtsta′hałs. skɛ′n·ku·ts tsɛłme·′yɛt.s at n′ananu′te·. qakɛ′łne·:
5 "ɛtskɛ′łe·n′ nöpɛ′k!a." ta′χas skɛ′n·ku·tsna′na tsɛłme′ᵢyɛt.s at
n′anaχa″mne·. at qaq!um′nenamɛ′sᵢne· łatka′χa·′m· ta′χas
n′u′pχa q!u″mne·′s swu″e·s na′ₐk!ᵤyu, ta′χas at qakɛ′łne·
χałe′e·s: "tsk·nał′ɛtskɛ′łe·n′ nöpɛ′k!a." ta′χas naₐk!ᵤyuna′na at

---
[1] Bilabial.

he would catch up with him on the right side. Then Coyote jumped
along his side. | Then he jumped around on the left side of
Grizzly Bear. | Coyote went past. Grizzly Bear was going along,
and ‖ Coyote did the same again. Grizzly Bear thought: "Now I'll   25
catch | Coyote. I'll bite him." Then Coyote jumped along on the
other side. | Then Grizzly Bear turned to the right side quickly | to
catch him, but again he could not catch him. Grizzly Bear went
along | a short distance, and saw Coyote. He was going along tired. ‖
He overtook him. Then Coyote was looking from one side to the   30
other. | His tongue was lolling. There was a big stone. Coyote
thought: "Now | Grizzly Bear will bite me." He chased him around
that stone. | Then Grizzly Bear was about to catch him, and | Coyote
was out of breath. Coyote fell down there. He lay there ‖ for a   35
time, and thought: "Why doesn't Grizzly Bear bite me?" | Then he
felt something on his hands. He looked at it, and saw | that he had
his hands in the horns of a buffalo bull. He looked at the Grizzly
Bear. | He was standing by his feet. (Coyote) stood up quickly | and
ran after him. He spoke to him in the way a bull bellows, and
Coyote said: ‖ "Fff!" Then Coyote knew that (Grizzly Bear) was   40
afraid of him. | He pursued him. The way Grizzly Bear had done,
that way | Coyote did to him. He also did the same. | Grizzly Bear
looked from side to side over his shoulders. There was a river. He
started to swim. Coyote put out | one of his hands with the horn
where Grizzly Bear was swimming ahead. ‖ He hit him with it. He   45
hit his backside, and he put out the other one | and with it also he
hit his backside. | Grizzly Bear swam across there. Coyote sat
down. When Grizzly Bear was across, | he looked back. Coyote
was sitting down. Coyote said: | "Grizzly Bear, you were going
to bite me. ‖ It should be once that that Grizzly Bear bit Coyote."   50
Grizzly Bear did not speak. He was afraid. | It is true, Coyote was
never bitten by Grizzly Bear, and | he was helped by his friend
Buffalo Bull. Enough. |

It is finished. |

58. Coyote and Fox

Well, I'll tell you about the friends, Coyote and | Fox—what they
did long ago. |

(a) Young Coyote and Young Fox steal the hoop

There were the friends. The one had a young son, and the other
one also had a young son. | Coyote sent out his son in the evening,
and said to him: ‖ "Look for manitou power." Then Young Coyote   5
went out at night. | The people were not yet asleep when he came
back into the tent. When | Fox knew that his friend was asleep,
he told | his son to go and look for manitou power. Then Young

n'anaẋa″mne˙. yɛsɛnwunmiyɛ't.ske˙ tsɛłmi˙yɛtna'm·o's. to'ẋᵘa

10 at kanmiyɛ't.se˙ łatka·ẋà·'m. ta'ẋas skɛ'n·ku·ts nokunu'ẋa at
tse̜ka'te˙ swu″e·s at sła·tke̜kɛsłɛ'̜itsma'łse˙ ẋałɛ.ɛ'se·s. ta'ẋas
wune·kɛ't.se· kqa'qₐna na'qsa·'s nata'nɛkls.

Qake'̜ne· skɛ'n·ku·ts: "ta'ẋas hun'u'pẋₐne· nakɛsqłɫẋuɳa'pse·
nöpɛ'k!a·'s kanẋa'łɛ·." ta'ẋas łaya'ẋa kk.łɛnq!oymu'łe·s. nułpał-

15 nitɛ't̜ne· ksakiłkɛ'nłe·'s ke'̜so·̜uks kk.łɛnq!oymu'łe·s. ta'ẋas sɛł·
aqakɛ'łne· swu″e·s na'ₐk!cyu's. ta'ẋa·s namatɛ'ktse· ẋałe·'e·s
skɛ'n·ku·ts nöpɛk!a'e·s, n'ɛ'nse· nöpɛk!a'e·s qasq!mamu'ẋo·'s
a̜ₐ″ke· hɛ'k!o·ks. na'ₐk!cyu namatɛ'ktse· ẋałe·'e·s k̜uɛłmu'ẋo·'s.

Ta'ẋas ts!ɛna'ẋe·. qa·na'ẋe·. naqsanmi·'yit.s kɛ'̜ikqa·ts ta'ẋas

20 łaẋa'ẋe· ne̜s a̜ₐ'kɛk.łuna'me·s. qahotsa'ẋe· n'ɛłqa'ₐkɛsu'̜usa°qa'ₐ-
ne·. ta'ẋas kanmi·'yit.ṣ k!unanu'qka·s, ta'ẋas nułpałne·tɛ't̜ne·
tsẋanamɛ'sɪne· a̜ₐ'kɛk.łuna'me·s. qakiyamɛ's̜ne·: "ta'ẋas k.łɛn·
q!o'yki·ł, ma ka'qa kɛnk.łɛnq!oymu'ke̜ł." ta'ẋas n'u'pẋₐne· ne̜s
a̜ₐ'kik.łuna'me·s n'anaẋa'mnamɛ's̜ne·. q!a'pe·'s tɛ'tqa·t!sts

25 pa'łke̜sts łka'm·u's. qao°ẋaẋamɛ's̜ne· qo̜us iłqa'ha·ks qaₐnɛt.ła-
namɛ's̜ne·. nakałkinłɛ's̜ne·. ta'ẋas n'oqoẋa·'łkɛnłɛ's̜ne· a̜ₐ'kɛk.łu-
na'me·'s. ta'ẋas naqts!ɛ'łukᵘaneyamɛ's̜ne·. n'u'pẋₐne·. ta'ẋas
ts!ɛnaqayt.łɛ's̜ne·. n'u'pẋₐne·. so̜ukɛ·'k.łetɛ'kse· ne̜s yaqa'naqay̜-
qa'pske·. ta'ẋas mɛte·'ẋałɛ's̜ne·. łaẋa'nẋo'̜ułe·s at qa·na·'qłɛkẋa-

30 łɛ's̜ne·. at so̜ukɛk.łitɛ'kse·. mɛte̜ẋa'łe·'s tsɛn ya·kkałn'uku'pqa·
nɛtsta·'hałni″nte·k. at n'ɛsniłaẋanẋo'̜une·. suk̜uiłnu·'k!̜uyok!aka-
te'̜se·. ta'ẋas k̜uwałkuwa'yi·ts qaₐqa'skɛnłɛ's̜ne·. łats!ɛna·'łkɛnłɛ'-
s̜ne· qo̜us k!ɫqa'nɛt.łana'me·'s. ta'ẋas ktsłmi·'yits n'̜opskiłqats-
ma·'k!i·łtsɛłme·yɛ't.se· qakc'̜ne· skɛ'n·ku·tsna·na: "ta'ẋas hułts!·

35 ɛnaẋa'ła kułtsukᵘata'ła." qak.ła'pse· swu″e·s: "maₐts pał k!up·
ski·łqaq!u'mne·'nam, huts!upẋₐna·łatɛ'łne·." qawunekɛ't.se· qa·
ke'̜ne· skɛ'n·ku·tsna·na: "ta'ẋas hułts!ɛnaẋa'ła kułtsukᵘata'ła."
a̜ₐ″ke· łaqak.ła'pse· swu″e·s: "huqᵘake'̜ne· maₐts kaₐs ksɛłq!u'″·
mne· aqłsma'k̜nɛk!." ta'ẋas qao°saqa'ₐne·. ta'ẋas k̜uwunɛ'ke·t.s

40 ta'ẋas n'u'pẋₐne· naₐk!cyuna'na ta'ẋas k.łalit.łuk.łe'e·t.s q!a'pe·'s
k.łq!u'mne·na'me·s. qakiłɛ'łne· skɛ'n·ku·tsna·na: "ta'ẋas hułts!ɛ·
naẋa'ła." n'upẋałɛ's̜ne· skɛ'n·ku·tsna'na pał skɛk.łe'̜itsne·. nu·
ła'se· ne̜s at k̜uwa·'sɛła·'wam n'ɛ'ts!ke·ł nöpɛ'k!a·'s. sɛł'aqaqa'pse·
k̜uwɛ'łe·ts. qakiłɛ'łne·: "maₐts q!u'″mne·n'. ta'ẋas hułqo·naẋa'-

45 ła." ta'ẋas q!a'pe· q!u'mne'″ne· aqłsma'k̜ne·k!. ta'ẋas ts!ɛn·
a'ẋe·. łaẋa'ẋe· qo̜us k!ɫqa'ₐnit.łana'mɛs. t̜naẋa'″mne·. n'u'pẋₐne·
mika ktsɛłmi·'yɛt.s qa.atsqa'pse· o·'k!ᵘq̜una ksu·'kᵘiłnu·'k!̜uyuk!a·
ka'te· ne̜ kk.łɛnq!o'ymuł. n'u'pẋₐne· ne̜s a·'k!a·łaẋwu'e·ts pał
słyakłe'̜itse· tɛłna'mukɛsta'ke·s. ẋa·tsɛni·łhakɛłkɛ'nse· po'po's

50 yake'ay tsẋałq!a·'kpa°ki·tẋumuna'pse· ne̜s po·po·'s tɛłna'mu's.
natsq!ₐna'ₐne·. qao°ẋa'ẋe· ne̜s yaqa·haq!a·'ha'nske·. tsukᵘa'te·
q!a'qₐne· a̜ₐ'kuqło·'kwats!ɛ'se·s. ta'ẋas nao·'k!ᵘe· nuk!ᵘe·n'·
wɛtskɛ'ne· łaq!anẋo'̜una·ł·s. ta'ẋas sɛłqawoẋo.ɛ'se· ne̜s a·'k!a·

Fox | went out. He staid out the whole night. ‖ When it was almost 10
morning, he came back into the tent. Then Coyote arose and |
looked at his friend. He was sleeping with his son. | They did so a
long time for several months. |

Then Coyote said: "I can tell by his eyes that my son has | mani-
tou power. Now let him go and get the toy." He had heard ‖ that 15
some one had a good toy. Therefore | he said so to his friend Fox.
Coyote had given to his son | his own manitou power, and his mani-
tou power was Moonlight-just-touching-the-Ground. | Fox gave his
to his son. (It was) Darkness-of-Night. |

Then they started. They went along. After they had gone along
for several days, ‖ they came to a town. They arrived there, and 20
they staid at a distance. | The following afternoon they heard | the
people talking. They said: "Now | play with your toy." Then they
saw | the people coming out—all the men, ‖ women, and children. 25
They all went there a little distance from their tents. | They brought
it out. Then they carried it into the camp. | Then they began to
shout. They saw how | they began to roll it about. They heard
(saw) that the thing they were rolling about had a nice sound. |
Then they went for it. They caught up with it and kicked it. ‖ It 30
made a good sound. They ran for it. Only youths who were very
fast could catch up with it. | It was pretty and bright. | Some time
in the evening they stopped. They took it back | to the farthest
tent. At night before it was very dark | Young Coyote said: "Now
let us go ‖ and let us take it!" His friend said to him: "No, | they 35
are not yet asleep, they will see us." It was not long before | Young
Coyote said: "Now let us go! Let us get it!" | The friend said
again: "I said no, the people are not asleep yet." | Then they staid
there. After some time ‖ Young Fox knew that it was quiet. All | 40
were asleep. Young Coyote was told: "Now let us go!" | Then it
was seen that Young Coyote was asleep. | This happened because
he returned early when he was looking for manitou power. There-
fore | he slept soundly. He was told: "Don't sleep! Let us go
there!" ‖ Then all the people were asleep. Then | they started. 45
They got there to the farthest tent. They entered; and they saw |
that, although it was dark, it was easily seen, because the toy
looked bright. | They saw two old people asleep in the doorway. |
Each held a hammer. ‖ They were to knock down with the hammer 50
whoever came to steal it. | They went in secretly. (The one) went to
the place where it was hanging, | took hold of it, and cut the string
with which it was hung up. The other one | held the door open.

łaxwi·'e·ts ne₍s tsł‿wu'xo·sts x̱ama n'ɛ·skik.letɛ'kse·. ta'x̱as
55 łaan·ax̱a''mne· qo‿us a·n'ɑqa'ha·ks. wu'q!max̱o'‿une· na'q!ma-
kik.letɛ'kse·. ne₍ tɑnamukᵘɛ'ste·k n'o·'kᵘinkɛ'sinmɛ'te·k ne₍s
kak.łe'e·ts. tse₍ka'te· ne₍s aₐ'k!a'ₐłmo·ks pał'o'‿use· ne₍ kk.łɛn-
q!oymo·ł. qał'atɛ'łne· aₐ'k!a'ₐłmo·k. qakiła''mne· tɑna'm·u:
"pał'o'‿une· aₐ'k!a'ₐłmok. pał n'ayna'mne·." ta'x̱as n'anakɛs-
60 x̱a''mne·. qake'₍ne·: "n'ayna'mne·, n'ayna'mne· aₐ'k!a'ₐł-
mo·k." wɑke'₍ne· ne₍s ke'₍tsx̱a. ta'x̱as ne₍ aₐ'kɛk.łu''na·m
qakiya'mne·: "yoqᵘake'₍ke· tɑnam·ukᵘɛ'ste·k." n'anax̱a'm-
na'mne·. qakiłɛ'łne·: "kaₐs k!a·qa·nałkɛ'n·e·ł." ne₍s qanank!o·-
nɛ'łne·. qake'₍ne·: "ne₍s qa·'ke·łhaq!make·k.letɛ'łe·k." ta'x̱as
65 wanaqna'łne· swʋ'tᵢmo·. qanax̱a'mne· n'u'px̱ał ne₍s na'mke·.
qak.ła'pse· swu''e·s skɛ'n·ku·tsna'na: "ma kamatɛ'ktse·'s
tɛtu''ne·s qa'psins. ɛtkɛ'ne·n'." ta'x̱as skɛ'n·ku·tsna'na naqte'₍te·
qasq!mamu'x̱o·s. n'ɛsqa·x̱ame·tɛ'łne·. qawunekɛ't.se·ts łakanmi-
yɛ't.se·. qak.ła'pse·: "a'ₐ·ke· ma kamatɛ'ktse·s łaa'k!ła·ks·."
70 a'ₐ·ke· łaₐaqte'₍te· n'ɛ'nse· hɛ'k!o·ks. qa.atsqa'ₐne· swʋ'tᵢmu.
ta'x̱as tsx̱ałtsɛnk₍nɛ'łne·. qak.ła'pse· swu''e·s skɛ'n·ku·tsna'na.
"ta'x̱as ts!kakɛ'ne·n' ɛn kina'łke·n." ta'x̱as ts‿ukᵘa'te· na'ₐk!ₑyu-
na'na ne₍s aₐ'k!a'ₐłmo·ks. ta'x̱as na'ₐk!ₑyuna'na naqte'₍te·
k‿uwɛlmu'x̱o·s. ta'x̱as n'ɛsqax̱ₐmetɛ'łne·. nułpałnɛ'łne·. qa.atski·k₍-
75 notx̱onɛ'łe·k. qakiya'mne·: "łun·ɛk!łe'et.s skɛk₍notx̱onɛ'łe·k."
qanax̱a'mne·. ta'x̱as łax̱a'nx̱o'‿ułne· skɛ'n·ku·tsna'na. tsɛnki·
nɛ'łne·. n'ɛsqax̱ₐmitɛ'łne· na'ₐk!ₑyuna'na. n'o·ła'se· ne₍s kta·
mu'x̱o·s. qakiłamna'mne·: "maₐts upɛ'łki·ł. tsx̱ał'i'n·e· kɛnk.-
ɛnq!oymo'kᵘi·ł." ta'x̱as łats!ɛna'x̱e· na'ₐk!ₑyuna'na. ła·hał-
80 kɛ'n·e· aₐ'ka'ₐłmo·ks. skɛ'n·ku·tsna'na ts‿ukᵘatɛ'łne·. n'ɛtuk!-
sa'ₐłne· skɛ'n·ku·tsna'na. ta'x̱as łaq!u'mne·na'mne·. łats!ɛna'x̱e·
na'ₐk!ₑyuna'na. qa·na'x̱e·. kanmiyɛ't.se· n'u'px̱ₐne· ma
ktsɛnkɛ'nłe·'s swu''e·s. ma kułpałnɛ'te·t ma kqakɛ'łamna'me·s
maₐts k.łupɛ'łe·s. ta'x̱as łaqa·na'x̱e· tsɑmiyɛ't.se·. to'x̱ᵘats
85 kanmi·yɛ't.se· ta'x̱as to'x̱ᵘats łałax̱a'x̱e· aₐ'kit.ła'e·s. ta'x̱as
łaqa'yte· ne₍s aₐ'ka'ₐłmo·ks. sukkᵘɛk.letɛ'kse·. ta'x̱as n'u'px̱ₐne·
ktsułpa'łnaps ałakinɛ'k!e·s. ta'x̱as nawasx̱o'‿ume·k. qake'₍ne·:

skɛ'n·ku·ts,   skɛ'n·ku.ts nu- pɛ· łe·'ł- ne· x̱a·ł e·'- ne·s.

skɛ'n·ku·ts qake'₍ne·: "hi'yá· kanx̱a'łe·" a'ₐ·ke. qake'₍ne·
90   na'ₐk!ₑyu, na'ₐk!ₑyu nupɑłe·'łne· x̱ałe·'ne·s.[1]

qake'₍ne. skɛ'n·ku·ts: "tse₍ka'te·n' ne₍s at ke·nqa·'k₍yukpu'k·
tse·'t x̱ałe·''ne·s. sɑ'upɛłɛ'łne·." a'ₐ·ke· łaqake'₍ne· na'ₐk!ₑyu-
na'na:
        skɛ'n·ku·ts, skɛ'n·ku·ts nupɛłe·'łne· x̱ałe·'ne·s.[1]

─────────────
[1] Tune as before.

Then it did not touch the doorway. | If it had touched it, it would have given a loud sound.   Then ‖ they went out.   There far off they 55 just touched it a little, | and it gave a slight sound.   The old couple at once got up quickly | when it sounded.   They looked for the hoop, but the toy had disappeared. | The toy was called "hoop."   The old woman said: | "The hoop is gone.   Some one stole it."   Then ‖ both of them went out, and said: "Some one has stolen the hoop, 60 some one has stolen the hoop!" | They shouted their words.   Then the people in the town | said to one another: "Listen to what the old couple are saying!"   They went out. | They were asked: "Which way has it been taken?"   It was pointed out to them. | They said: "There was a little sound of it in that direction."   Then ‖ the friends 65 were pursued.   The people went out.   They saw them going. | Then Young Coyote was told by his friend: "Your father gave you | something, use it."   Then Young Coyote untied | Moonlight-just-touching-the-Ground, and their tracks were lost.   It was not long before | it was daylight again.   He said: "He gave you something, too."   The other one ‖ then untied his moonlight.   The friends were not 70 visible. | When they were about to be caught, Young Coyote was told by his friend: | "Give me what you are carrying."   Then Young Fox took | the hoop.   Then Young Fox untied | Darkness-of-Night. Then he was lost (to his pursuers).   They heard only a rattling noise. ‖ They said to one another: "The other way is a rattling noise." | 75 They went that way and overtook Young Coyote. | He was caught. Young Fox was lost because he had the | Darkness-of-Night.   The people spoke to one another.   "Don't kill him!   He shall be your | toy."   Then Young Fox went back, carrying ‖ the hoop.   Young 80 Coyote was captured. | Young Coyote was tied up.   Then they slept again.   Young Fox started back | and went along.   In the morning he knew | that his friend had been taken.   He heard them talking together and saying | not to kill him.   Then he went along at night.   When it was almost ‖ morning, he almost arrived at his 85 tent.   Then | he began to roll the hoop.   It made a good sound. Then he knew | that his parents would hear it.   He sang, and said: |

"Coyote, Coyote, your child has been killed!" |

Coyote said: "Hiya', my son!"   Then he said:‖

"Fox, Fox, your child has been killed!" | 90

Coyote said: "See!   You didn't send your son to get manitou power, | and now he has been killed."   Young Fox said | again: |

"Coyote, Coyote, your child has been killed!" ‖

95 qake′ₑne· skᶓ′n·ku·ts: "hyá′·, kanxałna′na." qake′ₑne· na′ₐk!ₑyu:
    "qa′psin kₑnse′ₑłtsχa skᶓ′n·ku·ts? maₐts he′ₑtsχan′. ta′xta· ła-
    wa′xa·′m hutsχa·ł′upχₐnała′ₐne· qa′ła n′ᶓ′snił′upᶓ′ł·e·s χałe·′e·s."
    ta′xas skᶓ′n·ku·ts łaqatsχa′ne·. tsₑnanqa′me·k. ta′xas nułpa′łne·
    swᵥ′tₑmo· skᶓ′n·ku·ts aₐ·kik.lite·yeᶓ′se·s aₐ·k!a′ₐłmo·ks. sukᵤnikᶓ′-
100 te·nała′pse·. a′ₐ·ke· to′xᵤa at łae·ła′n·e· nułpałnᶓ′te·t kqakiya′m-
    ne·s k!upᶓ′ł·e·s χałe·′e·s. ta′xas aqa′t!a·ks łaqaskakik.łe·tᶓ′łe·k
    aₐ·k!a′ₐłmo·k. qakiłᶓ′łne· skᶓ′n·ku·ts: "ok!ᵘₑnkᶓ′ne·n′ laq!an·
    xo′ᵤnał." ta′xas skᶓ′n·ku·ts nowu′kᵤne·. n′uk!ᵘe·nkᶓ′n·e·,
    łaₑsakₑnu′n·e·. ta′xas waqa′yne· aₐ·k!a′ₐłmo·k. tkaqa′yne·
105 ne·s aₐ·kᶓt.łana′me·s. qawa·kaqa′yne·. sła:tkikqa′ₐne· na′ₐk!ₑyu.
    qawanxa′′mne· ne·s kułpałnᶓ′te·t kawasχomeya′me·s. qaoχa-
    qa′yse· yaqakqa′ₐke· na′ₐk!ₑyu ne·s aₐ·k!a′ₐłmo·ks. to′xᵘa
    qanaχu′se· qakχaqa′yse· skᶓ′n·ku·ts yaqa·hanqame′ₑke·.
    qa′o˘χałqanaχu′se· ne·s aₐ·k!a′ₐłmo·ks. ta′xas sᶓłtsχanata′pse·
110 k!ᶓs′nᶓ′ł·e·ps χałe·′e·s skᶓ′n·ku·ts. qa·waχamitnaχwa′te·k k!e·′′la.
    qake′ₑne·: "hiyá′· kanxałna′na, kanxałna′na." ta′xas ława′xe·
    na′ₐk!ₑyuna′na. łatkaχa′′mne·. qake′ₑne·: "hoqᵘa.u′pχₐne· ka·n′-
    aqanᶓ′ke·t mᶓ′ksa·n honułpałnetᶓ′tₑne· ne·s ktsₑnkᶓ′n·e·ł.
    k!u′pχa·ł ta′xas ku˘sᶓᶓsqₐχamᶓ′te·ł qakᶓłamna′mne·: 'maₐts
115 upᶓ′łki·ł, pał kₑnsᶓᶓsqₐχamᶓ′tki·ł kₑnk.łₑnq!o′ymo′ᵤkᵘi·ł tsχał′-
    ₑnqa′pte·k kₑnk.łₑnq!oymo′ᵤkᵘi·ł.′ ta′xas kuł·atskᶓ′ka·m."
        Ta′xas qa·nᶓt.ła′ₐne· swᵥ′tₑmo· skᶓ′n·ku·ts at ła′ₐpsiłqake′ₑne·
    skᶓ′n·ku·ts: "ta′xas hułts!ᶓnał′anaχakana′ła." naqa′sₑnwunᶓ′-
    ke·ts qak.ła′pse· swu′′e·s: "ta′xa·s hułts!ᶓna·ł′anaχakana′ła.
120 ta′xas łₑnłaqao·kᵘiₑqa′ₐne· aqłsma′kₑnᶓk!." ta′xas ts!ₑnakᶓ′kₑne·
    swᵥ′tₑmo·. nuk!qape′ₑne· na′ₐk!ₑyuna′na pał ka′qa·ps kk.łₑn-
    q!o′ymo· qao·k.łikpa′me·k. ta′xas łaχa′xe· swᵥ′tₑmo· aₐ·kᶓk.łu-
    na′me·s. qawitsa′xe· qaₐkᶓsu·wᶓsa˘qa′ₐne·. k!unanu′qkwa·s
    nułpałnetᶓ′tₑn·e·. tsχanamᶓ′sₑne· qoᵤs aₐ·kik.łuna′me·s. qakiya-
125 mᶓ′sₑne.: "ta′xas anaχa′′mki·ł kᶓnlik.linq!o′yke·ł." qawunᶓ-
    kᶓ′t.se·, ta′xas n′akaχa′mnamᶓ′sₑne·. q!a′pe·′s ne·s at
    yaqanekᶓ′tske· ne·s aₐ·k!a′ₐłmo·ks tsχałk.łₑnq!oymu′łe·′s qanikᶓ′-
    tse·. ta′xas ᶓna·′haks n′akaχa′mnałᶓ′sₑne· χałe·′e·s. nałqo-
    ma′tiłᶓ′sₑne·. n′u′pχₐne· na′q!apq!li·sa′kse· ma wuq!ła′′mse·,
130 k!a′qa˘qa′pqaps. ta′xas qa·naqkupłi·kχałᶓ′sₑne·. nutsₑnqkupekₑ-
    na′kse·, ta′xas miteχałᶓ′sₑne·. łaχa′nxo′ᵤłe·s at qanaqłᶓ·kχa-
    łᶓ′sₑne·. ta′xas skᶓ′n·ku·ts k!umna′nłᶓkpakta′pse·. qake′ₑne.:
    "ta′xas hułqonaχa′ła, kuł·atsukᵘata′ła." qake′ₑne· na′ₐk!ₑyu:
    "ma′qa·k. hutsχał′ᶓtkᶓ′n·e·." naq!a·naq!neᶓ′ₑne· na′ₐk!ₑyu.
135 ta′xas skᶓ′n·ku·tsna′na n′o·k!ᵤniłhałnokupqa′ₐne·. łaqa′łaχa′n-
    xo′ᵤłne·. łats!ₑnaq!anaq!neᶓ′ₑne· na′ₐk!ₑyu. łats!ₑna′xe· skₑn-
    ku·tsna′na. łaqa′łaχa′nxo′ᵤłne·. łało·′qᵘałqa′ₐtse·. ta′xas na′ₐk!ₑ-
    yu ts!e·q!a·naq!neᶓ′ₑne·. ta′xas skᶓ′n·ku·tsna′na nutsqa·nkaqu-
    pe·kᶓ′me·k. ta′xas q!a′pe· n′umats!na′mne· k.łaqałaχa′ₐnxoᵤł

Coyote said: "Hiya', my little son!" Fox said: | "Why did you 95
talk, Coyote? Don't talk! Later on, | when he arrives, we shall know
whose child has been killed." | Then Coyote said no more. He was
just sitting there. Then | Coyote and his friend heard the noise of the
hoop. ‖ They felt glad, but they also almost cried when they heard 100
some one saying | that his child had been killed. Then there was
noise of | the hoop. Coyote was told to open the door. | Then Coyote
arose and opened it. | He sat down, and the hoop came rolling in.
It rolled ‖ into the tent. It came along rolling. Fox was lying 105
down. | He did not move. Then they heard some one singing. | The
hoop rolled to where Fox was lying. It almost | fell down, but went
rolling on to where Coyote was sitting down. | There the hoop fell
down. Then they told him ‖ that Coyote's son was dead. He fell 110
down crying, | and said: "Hiya', my little son, my little son!"
Then Young Fox arrived. | He entered the tent, and he said: "I do
not know what has happened, | but I heard that he was taken. | He
was seen when they lost sight of me. They said among themselves:
'Don't ‖ kill him! Since you have lost sight of your toy, he shall | 115
become your toy.' Then I went back." |

Then Coyote and his friends lived in the tent. Coyote often said: |
"Let us make war on them!" After some time | his friends said to
him: "Now let us make war on them! ‖ Probably the people are no 120
longer uneasy." Then the two friends started. | Young Fox was left
alone. Because he had the toy, | he was not lonesome. Then the
friends reached the town. | They did not go near. The two stopped. |
When the sun was going down, they heard talking there in the town. ‖
It was said: "Now go out to play!" It was not | long before they 125
came out. Everything that | used to be done with the hoop when
they were going to play with it was done now. | Then his son was
taken out. They were all around him. | They saw that his hair was
all cut. ‖ He used to have long hair, but now he was changed. Then 130
they kicked him hard. | He started to run, and they pursued him.
When they caught up with him, he was kicked again. | Then Coyote
pitied him. He said: | "Let us go nearer! Let us take him back!"
Fox said: | "Wait, I'll do something!" He made a sign with his
head. ‖ Then all of a sudden Young Coyote ran fast. They could not 135
overtake him. | Fox again made a sign with his head, and Young
Coyote started again. | They could not catch up with him. He made
a turn. | Fox made a quick sign with his head. Then Young Coyote
ran their way. | Then all laughed because they could not overtake ‖

140 skɛ'nˑkuˑtsna'na. me'ka yaka'ɬnoku'pqa ɬaqaɬaxa·'nxo'ᵤne,
slaˇqaqa'ₐneˑ k!omats!nata'mnam. qawaka'xeˑ skɛ'nˑkuˑtsna'na;
ta'xas tsᴇma'k!iɬ·aqamɛte·xa'ɬne· ne¡s yaqa·'kɛsosaqa'pske·
aɬakinɛ'k!e·'s. ɬaɬaxa'xe·. nowokᵘɛ'ste·k swʋ'tᵢmo· na'ak!ₑyu.
n'upxa'ɬne· paɬ sɛ·lats?kua'te·xaɬe·'e·s. qakiɬamna'mne·: "ta'-
145 xas maₐts tse¡ka'tke·ɬ swʋ'tᵢmo· skɛ'nˑkuˑts. at saˇha'ne·. xɪɦa
ts!upɬawa'sᵢne." ta'xas ɬats?kna'xe· swʋ'tᵢmo·. Hiyá·', q!a'pe·
n'iɬana'mne·. k.la·'ɬok.lɛnq!o'ymo·ɬ ne¡ aₐ'kɛk.ɬu·''na·m. ta'xas
ɬaqa·na'xe· skɛ'nˑkuˑts swʋ'tᵢmo·. ɬaɬaxa'x'e·. ta'xas soᵤkᵘiɬ-
q!o'kᵤne·.

(b) COYOTE GAMBLES WITH SALMON

150   Qa·nɛt.ɬa'ₐne· swʋ'tᵢmo·. ta'xas naqa'pse· kk.lɛnq!o'ymo.
nulpaɦne·tɛ'tᵢne· qaye¡k!ɛna'mo¹ qa'qaₐps aₐ'k!a'ₐlmo·ks
swʋ'tᵢmo's skɛ'nˑkuˑtsts na'ak!ₑyu's. ts!ɛna'xe·. ts!ɛnaɬuwa'ts!-
xne·. qaɬwi'yne· ktsxaɬho·'qᵘa ne¡s aₐ'k!a'ₐlmo·ks. sukᵘaₐkɛ'nˑe·
qaye¡k!ɛna'mo, sɬaqaqana'ₐne· kts!ɛnaɬuwa·ts!xa. pɛ'k!a·ks
155 n'upxaɬ·'sᵢne· sukᵘaₐkɛ'nˑe· skɛ'nˑkuˑts at qawuɬaxa''mne·.
ta'xas sɛ·ltspo·ɬwiynatɛ'ɬne·, mɛ'ksa·'n na'ak!ₑyu at qa·haɬwa'-
ts!ne·. qaɬwiynamɛ'sᵢne· ksaₐna'ₐki·n. ta'xas ɬaxa'xe· qaye¡k!ɛ-
na'mo. naqu'ɬne· nɛtsta·'haɬnɛ''nte·k, nok!ᵘe'¡se· aɬ'aɬɛtskɛ'l'e·s·
qsama'ɬne. k.la'xa·m qakɛ'ɬne· swʋ'tᵢmo·'s skɛ'nˑkuˑts: "ho'ya's
160 huɬa'ɬᵤwats!na'ɬa." qake'¡ne· skɛ'nˑkuˑts: "qa'psin kutsaɬwats!-
na'ɬa?" qakiɬɛ'ɬne·: "kaɬq!a'ha·ɬt." qake'¡ne· skɛ'nˑkuˑts:
"so'ᵤkᵤne·. hutsaɬwats!naɬa'ₐne·." ta'xas n'anaɬ'ɛtku'ɬne·.
ta'xas naɬᵤwats!na'mne·. qake'¡ne· na'ak!ₑyu: "maₐts ɬha'ɬᵤwats! xaɬe·''ne·s. kanxa'le· hɛnts!ɛsni·lkᵢne·ma'ɬne·." ta'xas naɬ-
165 wats!na'mne·. qawunikɛ'tᵢne· nuqᵘa'ɬne· skɛ'nˑkuˑts. a'ₐ'ke·
ɬa·ha'ɬᵤwats!na'mne· a'ₐ'ke· ɬahoqᵘa'ɬne· skɛ'nˑkuˑts. ta'xas
q!a'pe·ɬuqᵘa'ɬne· xa'ₐtᵢmo na'ak!ₑyuna'na. pɛ·'k!a·ks nuqᵘa'ɬne·
aₐₐk!a'ₐlmo·kᵘa'e·s. paɬ ne¡sts k!o·'tᵢmo·ɬ. ta'xas qa·nqa'me·k
skɛ'nˑkuˑts. qakɛ'ɬne· na'ak!ₑyuna'nas: "ts!ɛnamɛ'le·n' tɛtu''ne·s,
170 hɛntsxaɬqakɛ'ɬne· k.ɬamatɛ'ktsap kmaɬu'q!ᵘɬi·ɬs." ts!ɛna'xe·
na'ak!ₑyuna'na. qakɛ'ɬne· tɛtu''e·s: "qake'¡ne· ka'xa
kɛnɬama'ₐtke·ts kmaɬu'q!ᵘɬi·ɬs." qaɬwi'yne· na'ak!ₑyu: "qa'psins
k!ɛ'ɬke·t? ksɛlqaha·matɛ'ktsa·p qa'psins k!aqa'ke·." qakɛ'ɬne·
xaɬe·'e·s: "ts!ɛnamɛ'le·n', kɛnɬqa'ke·ɬ qa'psins n'ɛ'ɬke·t."
175 ɬats!ɛna'xe·. qakiɬɛ'ɬne· skɛ'nˑkuˑts: "qake'¡ne· katɛ'tu qa.u'pxa
qa'psins hɛn'itkɛ'tᵢmi·ɬ." qake'¡ne· skɛ'nˑkuˑts: "a: xma
ɬqsa·nmu'ki·ɬqa.u'pxa? ts!ɛnamɛ'le·n' kɛnɬqa'ki·ɬ, maₐts
kɬtsɬakɛ'ɬktsa·p." ɬats!ɛna'xe· ne¡ ɬka'mˑu ɬaquna'xe· tɛtu''e·s.
qakɛ'ɬne·: "qake'¡ne· maₐts kenɬtsɬakɛ'ɬki·ts kinɬama'ₐtki·ts.
180 mi'ka hɛnwiɬɛ'ɬwiyna'ₐtme¡ɬ. ktsxa·ɬstɛ'le·k." n'u'pxaₐne· na'ₐ-

---
¹ Story name of salmon; modern name swaʹqǃmo.

Young Coyote. Even the fastest runners could not catch up 140
with him. | Therefore they laughed about it. Young Coyote came
along. | They could not catch up with him at all. Then he came
to | where the parents were. Fox and his friend arose. | Then it
was known that he had taken back his son. They told one another:‖
"Don't look at Coyote and his friend! They are bad. | They might 145
kill us." Then the friends started back. Hiya! they all | cried,
because they had no toy in that town. | Coyote and his friend went
on. They arrived at home, and | they were glad. ‖

(b) COYOTE GAMBLES WITH SALMON

Then the friends lived in their tent. They had the toy. | The Salmon 150
heard that the friends | Coyote and Fox had the hoop. He started
to gamble with them. | He thought he would win the hoop. Salmon
was a good | gambler, therefore they started to gamble. Long ago ‖ it 155
was known that Coyote was a good gambler, but he did not keep it
up. | Therefore they tried their luck with him; but Fox never gam-
bled. | They thought he was a bad gambler. Then Salmon arrived, |
traveling by canoe. They were young men, and one (woman) their
sister | went with them. When they arrived, (Salmon) said to Coyote
and his friend: "Let us ‖ play!" Coyote said: "What shall we play?" | 160
He was told: "The hiding game (lehal)." Coyote said: | "Well, let
us gamble!" Then they made a fire outside, | and they began to
gamble. Coyote said: "Don't | let him gamble! Your son and my
son shall be partners." Then ‖ they played. It was not long before 165
Coyote lost the game; and | he played again, and Coyote lost. Then |
he lost everything. Young Fox and his uncle had lost | the hoop.
That is what they wanted to get. Coyote sat down, | and said to
Young Fox: "Go to your father ‖ and tell him to give me the thing 170
striped crosswise." Young Fox went. | He said to his father: "Uncle |
says you shall give him the thing striped crosswise." Fox thought:
"What | does he mean? He did not give me anything. Why should
he say that?" He said | to his son: "Go to him and ask him what
he means." ‖ He went back, and Coyote was told: "My father says he 175
doesn't know | what you mean." Coyote said: "Oh, how should |
he not know it? Go to him and tell him not | to keep it from me
because he likes it." The child went back and came to his father. | He
said to him: "He says you should not keep it back because you like it,
but give it to him, ‖ even if you should like it very much. He wants 180
to bet with it." Then Fox knew (what it was). | Then he gave it to

k!ₑyu pɛ'k!aˑks ma kamatɛ'ktsaps t!a'nqoˑts· aₐ'kɛnuq!ᵘma'ₐ-
na's. "kɫtsχaɫ'ɛ'ɫkiˑts." nakakɛ'nˑe· neᵢs t!a'nqoˑts· aₐ'kɛnuq!ᵘma·'na'·s. namatɛ'ktse·. qakɛ'lne·: "χma haˑk!aˑmχoneˑ'ᵢke·
na·s tsɫɛnts!iɫɛ'kte·." ɫats!ɛnaɫkɛ'nˑe·. namatɛktsɛ'lne· skɛ'nˑkuˑts.
185 qakiɫɛ'lne·: "qake'ᵢne· katɛ'tu naₐsts hɛnˑaqan'ɛɫkɛ'tᵢmiˑɫ."
qake'ᵢne· skɛ'nˑkuˑts: "kaₐ χma ku.ɛ'ɫkeˑt." qake'ᵢne·
na'ₐk!ₑyu: "maₐtsɛntsaˋq!maɫ·aha'ɫwats!kɛ'lne·. huts!ts!ɛna'χe·."
qakiɫɛ'lne· skɛ'nˑkuˑts: "qake'ᵢne· katɛ'tu kɛntsa'wɛtskpa'ya't
ktsχaɫts!ɛ'ka." ta'χas n'ɛ'tiɫmoˑmaɫqana'meˑk na'ₐk!ₑyu.
190 qawunekɛ't.se· skɛ'nˑkuˑts na'qaˑnke'ᵢne·. qake'ᵢne·: "a: hɛnˑ-
k!utsta'pne·. pɛ'k!aˑk χma huɫa'qᵘa'meˑk." qaoˑχa'χe· na'ₐ-
k!ₑyu. qakɛ'lne· skɛ'nˑkuˑtsna'na's: "huts!asnaɫa'ₐne·." ta'-
χas quna'χe·. ta'χas naɫᵤwa'ts!ne·. nanɛɫkɛ'nˑe·. nawasχo'ᵤ-
meˑk. qaɫq!anɛ'lne·.
195   "hun'aˑ'qaˇna·meˇnɛˋleˑlts k.lqa'eˑnwu'nˑe·."

Ɫaaˑ'k!laˑks a'ₐ'ke· nawasχo'ᵤmeˑk. qaɫq!anɛ'lne.:

          "huno'qⁿaˋlts k.l'u'pᵢnaˑm."

Qawunekɛ't.se· nuˇqᵘaka'ₐne·. ɫaeˑtetɛ'leˑk qayeᵢk!ɛna'mo.
a'ₐ'ke· ɫaˑɫᵤwaˑts!ne·, a'ₐ'ke· ɫaoqᵘaka'ₐne·. n'ɛ'sniɫhanɛɫkɛnma'ɫne·
200 skɛ'nˑkuˑtsna'na's, mɛ'ksaˑ'n na'ₐk!ₑyuna'na skɛ'nˑkuˑts n'ɛ'sɛ-
nɫhoqᵘa'ɫne·. ta'χas q!aˋpiɫhoqᵘa'ɫne· qayeᵢk!ɛna'mo. qake'ᵢne·
qayeᵢk!ɛna'mo: "χma keˑnqawakate'ᵢkiˑɫ aɫkaaˋleˑtskiɫna'ɫa."
qake'ᵢne· na'ₐk!ₑyu: "so'ᵤkᵤne·; paɫ kɛ'nsiɫqake'ᵢkiˑɫ." ta'χas
stɛ'leˑk, a'ₐ'ke· ɫa.uqᵘa'ɫne· qayeᵢk!ɛna'mo. ta'χas ɫaɫitstɛ'leˑk.
205 ɫats!ɛna'χe· n'ɛɫa'nˑe· oˑ'k!ᵘqᵤna ku'qʷaˑɫ nana''e·s. qake'ᵢne·
na'ₐk!ₑyu: "χaɫe''neˑs tsχaɫ'ɛ'nse· tɛɫnamu''eˑs, kanχa'leˑ paɫ
k!u'pskiɫtsaˇqu'nˑa." ta'χas skɛ'nˑkuˑts naqa'pse· papa''eˑs.
naɫaɫitɛ't.se· χaɫe·''eˑs.

(c) SALMON WOMAN TRIES TO DROWN COYOTE

Qaˑnˑɛt.ɫa'ₐne· swɛ'tᵢmoˑ. ta'χas naqa'lte· skɛ'nˑkuˑtsna'na.
210 n'oˑ'k!ᵘniˑɫiɫa'nˑe· neᵢ paˑ'ɫkeᵢ. paɫ ka'qaˑps yaqso'mɛ'ɫ'e·s.
oˑ'k!ᵘqᵤna koˑqᵘa'ka na'ₐk!ₑyu sɛɫa·'qaˇqa'pse· qa'qaˑps
yaqso·''miˑls. n'ok!ᵘiniˑɫ'eˑtaqₐna'meˑk neᵢ paˑ'ɫkeᵢ. n'u'pχₐne·
skɛ'nˑkuˑts paɫ tsχa'ɫsiɫ·ats!ɛna'se·ˑ neᵢs papa''e·s, a'ₐ'ke·
n'itaqₐna'meˑk skɛ'nˑkuˑts tsχaɫqsama'ɫne· χaɫe·''e·s neᵢs
215 ktsts!ɛ'na·s. qaɫwi'yne· na'ₐk!ₑyu: "ma ksaₐnɫc'et neᵢ
aₐ'kɛnmɛ'tuk. huɫqsa'maˑɫ. χma ktsχa'ɫ'eˑp χaɫe'tᵢmo
skɛ'nˑkuˑts." ta'χas a'ₐ'ke· n'itaqₐna'meˑk na'ₐk!ₑyu. ta'χas
ɫaoˑqoχaχa''mne· neᵢ. paˑ'ɫkeᵢ yaqso·''miˑls. qakeɫɛ'lne·:
"ma'qaˑk, huts!oqoˑχaχa··''mnɛ·." ta'χas n'ɛɫa'nˑe· neᵢ paˑ'ɫkeᵢ.
220 qakɛ'lne· χaɫe·''e·s na'ₐk!ₑyu: "hɛntsqa'oˇsaˇqa'ₐne·. hutsχaɫ-
qsama'ɫne·. χma tsχaɫ'upeɫ'lne· χaɫe'ᵢtᵢmu skɛ'nˑkuˑts." ta'χas
n'oqoˑχaχa''mne· na'ₐk!ₑyu. ta'χas ts!ɛnaqu'ɫne·. n'us'mokaˑˑnˑ-

him. | "He must mean the partridge tail." Then he took out the partridge | tail and gave it to him. He said to him: "I think he meant just this. | He must have meant it." (The boy) took it back and gave it to Coyote. ‖ He was told: "My father says you must 185 have meant this." | Coyote said: "What else should I mean?" | Fox said: "Don't gamble for a while. I shall go." | Coyote was told: "My father said you should wait for him. | He is coming." Then Fox got ready. ‖ It was not long before Coyote shouted, saying: "You | 190 let me wait. I ought to have back already what I have lost." Fox arrived there, | and said to Young Coyote: "Let us be partners!" Then | he went there, and they gambled. He moved his hands in the game and sang. | He sang thus: ‖

"Whenever I am pointed out, the gambling bone will disappear." | 195

And he sang also another song. He sang thus: |

"If I lose, they'll die." |

It was not long before he began to win. Salmon bet again. | They gambled, and Fox won another game. Young Coyote was his partner. ‖ While Young Fox and Coyote themselves had lost, | now Sal- 200 mon lost everything. Salmon said: | "You ought to stake against our sister." | Fox said: "It is well, since you say so." | They staked, and Salmon lost again. They had nothing else to stake. ‖ He started 205 home, and cried because he had lost his younger sister. | Fox said: "She shall be your son's wife. My son | is still too young." Then Coyote had a daughter-in-law. | She married his son. |

(c) SALMON WOMAN TRIES TO DROWN COYOTE

The friends lived together. Then Young Coyote had a child. ‖ At 210 once the woman began to cry. She had a canoe. | Because Fox had won, therefore they had | a canoe. The woman got ready at once. Coyote saw | that his daughter-in-law was going home. Then | Coyote also got ready to accompany his son where ‖ he was going. Fox 215 thought: "There are bad places in that | river. Let me go along. Coyote and his son might die." | Then Fox also got ready. | The woman went aboard the canoe. She was told: | "Wait; I'll get aboard." Then the woman cried. ‖ Fox said to his son: "You stay 220 here; I'll go along. | Coyote and his son might be killed." Then | Fox went aboard, and the canoe started. | The woman was seated in the

qaʼmeˑk neᵢ paˑʼlkeᵢ. qaːnaquʼlneˑ. sanłaxapqłeʼᵢse. łaxaquʼlneˑ. qakeʼᵢneˑ skɛʼnˑkuˑts: "maqaʼₐk upaquʼleˑnʼ hutsxałʼɛntanał-
225 xoʼᵤneˑ łkaʼmˑu." qaqałwiʼyneˑ neᵢ paˑʼlkeᵢ. nʼiłaʼnˑeˑ. taʼxas
łaxaquʼlneˑ neᵢs aₐˑkaxaʼpqłeˑʼs. nʼuʼpxₐneˑ naʼₐk!ₑyu ksɛlsaˑnɛl-
wiynaʼₐtaps neᵢs paˑʼlkeᵢs. naqaʼpseˑ aₐˑkuktsɛʼkeˑns naʼₐk!ₑyu.
qakɛʼlneˑ neᵢs xałeʼᵢtᵢmoˑʼs skɛʼnˑkuˑtsˑ: "qanaxaʼʼmkeˑł na aˑ-
kuktsɛʼkiˑn." taʼxas qanaxaʼʼmneˑ xałeʼᵢtᵢmo skɛʼnˑkuˑtsts
230 naʼₐk!ₑyu. maʼnwitskaxₐnɛʼleˑk koˑʼs naʼₐk!ₑyu. taʼxas watła-
quʼnˑeˑ yaqsoʼʼmiˑl. nʼiktsɛnoquʼnˑeˑ. qałwiʼyneˑ neᵢ paˑʼlkeᵢ
taʼxas ktsᵎuʼpił. neᵢ aₐˑkuktsɛʼkiˑn yoˑkuquʼnˑeˑ. aːnk!onanmɛʼ-
tuks łaʼwaˑkaquʼnˑeˑ yaqsoʼʼmiˑl. manwɛtskɛʼkᵢne. neᵢ paˑʼlkeᵢ
słaˑtkeˑk!aqoˑmatɛʼtse pał qaˑuʼpseˑ.

235   Łaːts!ɛnaquʼlneˑ. qaˑwułeʼɛʼt.se aʼₐˑke łaˑʼpsanłaxapqłeʼᵢseˑ.
aːnɛʼseˑkałetɛtneʼᵢse. qakeʼᵢne skɛʼnˑkuˑts: "maˑʼqaˑk, hutsxał-
ɛntaʼnałxoʼᵤne kapaʼpa." qaˑtsekataʼpse neᵢs paˑʼlkeᵢs. taʼxas
łaxaquʼlneˑ. aʼₐˑke łaːɛtkɛʼnˑeˑ naʼₐk!ₑyu neᵢs aₐˑkuktsɛʼkeˑns.
łaoˑqoxaxaˑʼʼmneˑ xałeʼᵢtᵢmo skɛʼnˑkuˑtsts naʼₐk!ₑyu. łamaːʼn-
240 wɛtskaxnɛʼleˑk koˑʼs, aʼₐˑke łaɛktsɛnuquʼse yaqsoʼmɛʼłeˑs.
aːnk!onanmɛʼtuks łaaˑwaˑkkɛmɛnxoˑnuʼqᵤneˑ yaqsoʼʼmił. łaakaˑ-
qanxaʼʼmneˑ naʼₐk!ₑyuts skɛʼnˑkuˑts xałeʼɛtᵢmo. tseᵢkataʼpse
neᵢs paˑʼlkeˑs. słaˑtkeˑk!aqoˑmatɛʼtᵢneˑ, aʼₐˑke pałaqaˑupłaʼpseˑ.

(d) SALMON WOMAN TRIES TO KILL COYOTE IN HER TENT

Taʼxas słałaxaʼxeˑ aₐˑkɛt.łaʼeˑs neᵢ paˑʼlkeᵢ. qałwiˑʼyneˑ: "taʼxas
245 kaałɛʼtskeˑł ktsxałʼɛsnił'oˑʼkᵘiˑt." qaˑq!aˑnmoqts!ɛnuʼkseˑ, qaʼoˇ-
xałʼupaquʼlneˑ. łaˑeˑłeˑkxaxaˑʼʼmneˑ heᵢ paˑʼlkeᵢ. qanak.łɛʼkxₐneˑ
neᵢs yaqsoʼʼmiˑls. qałwiʼyneˑ ktsxałyɛʼk!tałqoku'mˑoˑ. nʼasqaʼnał-
hotsinqaʼₐtseˑ sahanłeɛʼt.se. qaaˑłoqaqₐnaʼₐneˑ ałswʊʼtᵢmoˑ pał
ksahanłeʼɛt.s. naʼₐk!ₑyu qaoˇxaqaˑnmeˑtxoʼᵤneˑ yaʼq!eᵢts. taʼxas
250 qanaʼxeˑ ałswʊʼtᵢmo. youˇxaʼxeˑ. sɛnt.łanamɛʼsᵢneˑ. k.łatᵢnaʼxaˑʼm
neᵢ paˑʼlkeᵢ qakeʼᵢneˑ: "husiłwamˑaʼlneˑ kɛnłˑokᵘɛʼtkiˑł." nʼeˑłɛʼkte
taˑʼt!eˑs. taʼxas ktinaʼxaˑm neᵢ ałswʊʼtᵢmo neᵢs qaₐkqaʼpseˑ
nɛtstaˑʼhaˑłs, nuwuʼkseˑ nʼanaxaʼʼmseˑ. nuwuʼkseˑ nʼaʼsˑeˑ tɛlnaʼ-
moˑʼs tsᵤkᵘaʼt.se aʼtsuˑʼs nʼanaxaʼʼmseˑ. wunekɛʼt.seˑ łatkaˑ-
255 kɛsxaʼʼmseˑ nałkɛʼnseˑ nʼɛt!qaʼpseˑ aₐq!ułɛʼseˑs xaʼₐltsins.
xonałyeˇk!tałɛʼsᵢneˑ. taʼxas q!aˑpeˑłʼɛ́nk!omatiyamɛʼsᵢneˑ. nʼit-
xoniyamɛʼsᵢneˑ. taʼxas naq!akoʼᵤneˑ neᵢs aₐˑq!uˑłeˑs xaʼₐltsin.
taʼxas sahanoquʼnˑeˑ. aₐˑkiłaqakɛʼnˑeˑ neᵢs aₐˑkuktsɛʼkeˑns
naʼₐk!ₑyu. wunekɛʼt.seˑ, taʼxas łaqasaˑhanoquʼseˑ. łaoˇk!ᵘinki-
260 nɛʼlneˑ seʼit!. tseᵢkatɛʼlneˑ naʼₐk!ₑyu. słaˑtkeˑk!aqoˑmatɛʼtᵢneˑ. pał
aʼₐˑkeˑ sɛlaqaˑtałʼoktɛʼlneˑ.

     Taʼxas tsɛlmiyɛʼt.seˑ. qak.łaʼpse neᵢs nułʼaʼqₐnaʼːs: "łoʼᵤneˑ
qayeᵢk!ɛnaʼmo. tsɛlmiʼyet hɛntsałnuˑʼqᵘakɛʼlneˑ. hɛnts!eˑkɛʼlneˑ."
taʼxas tsɛlmiˑyɛʼtᵢneˑ. taʼxas ts!ɛnaʼxeˑ naʼₐk!ₑyu, tsxałhaquʼlne.

bow. They traveled along. There was a cascade. They came to it. | Coyote said: "Wait; paddle ashore! I'll carry the child alongshore." || The woman did not want to do it. She cried. | Then they 225 arrived at the cascade. Fox knew | that the woman was angry with them. Fox had a bladder. | He told Coyote and his son: "Go into this | bladder." Then Coyote, his son, and Fox went in. || Fox had his 230 pipe in the hole of the bladder. Then | the canoe upset and sank. The woman thought | they were dead, but the bladder floated. Farther down the river | the canoe came up again. The woman looked back, | and there they were sitting together. They were not dead. ||

She turned back. Not far away there was another cascade, | a still 235 more terrible one. Coyote said: "Wait; I'll | carry my grandchild along the shore." The woman did not look at him. Then | they arrived there, and Fox worked again at his bladder. | Coyote, Fox, and the boy went in again. || He held the pipe at the edge of the 240 hole. Then their canoe went down again. | A little farther down the river the canoe emerged again. | Coyote, Fox, and the child came out. The woman looked at them, | and they all sat down together, and again she had not killed them. |

(d) SALMON WOMAN TRIES TO KILL COYOTE IN HER TENT

Then the woman got back to her tent. She thought: || "My brother 245 shall kill all of them." There was a smooth precipice there. | They went ashore. The woman landed, and kicked | the canoe. She thought she would upset it. | Then they climbed up a bad place. The friends did not know what to do | when they came to the bad place, but Fox had thrown tobacco on it. Then || they went on, and the friends 250 reached the top. There was a tent. When the woman entered, | she said: "I bring them all; kill them all." She meant (spoke to) | her elder brother. When the friends arrived there, a young man was lying down. | He arose and went out. Two old women also arose. | Each took a dish and they went out. After some time || the two 255 came back again, carrying (the buckets) filled with dog manure. | They threw it into the fire. Then all the people covered their heads and | lay down. The dog manure was burning, | and there was bad smoke in the house. Fox did the same thing with the bladder. | After some time there was no smoke. They took off || their blankets 260 and they looked at Fox. They were all sitting there together, | and again they had been unable to kill them. |

Then at night they were told by an old man: "There is no | salmon. At night you shall carry torches. Then you shall eat." | In the even-

265 skⲉ'n·ku·tsna'na. tsχaⱡ'aₐko'ₐne· n'o·k!ᵘe'ᵢne· nⲉtsta'haⱡna'na.
tsχaⱡhaⱡnu'qₐne· skⲉ'n·ku·ts· tsχaⱡqawu˘sa˘qa'ₐne·. qakiⱡⲉ'ⱡne·
skⲉ'n·ku·ts: "maₐts hⲉntsq!u'mne'ᵢne· hⲉnts!upsa't·ᵢyiⱡtse·ᵢka'te·
aₐ'kⲉnq!o'ko·. hⲉnq!u''mne· tsχaⱡ'upⱡⲉ's·ᵢne·." ta'χasts!ⲉnaqu'ⱡne·
na'ₐk!ⲉyu n'ⲉ'n·e· ka'qo·ⱡ. skⲉ'n·ku·tsna'na tsχaⱡ'ⲉ'n·e· k!a'ₐko·
270 qayeᵢk!ⲉna'mo·'s. neᵢ nⲉtsta'haⱡna'na tsχaⱡ'ⲉ'n·e· kawⲉtsnu'qᵘa-
ku'pk!o·. ta'χas skⲉ'n·ku·ts qao˘sa˘qa'ₐne·. ta'χas wune·kⲉ't.se·
at ⱡaa·na·'wⲉtskⲉ'kᵢne· skⲉ'n·ku·ts. qakiⱡⲉ'ⱡne· skⲉ'n·ku·ts:
"hⲉn'u'pχa ⱡaqawⲉⱡₐnq!u'ko·, ta'χas hⲉntsⱡaa·naχa''mne·. ta̅'χas
hu'tsiⱡ'upⲉⱡamnaⱡa'ₐne·;tsχatsiⱡ'aqₐqa'ₐne· neᵢ aₐ'kⲉnq!u'ko·." qa-
275 wunekⲉ't.se· ⱡaa·na'wⲉtskⲉ'kᵢne·. n'u'pχₐne·, ta'χas ⱡaqawⲉⱡₐnq!u-
ko'pse· qoₐs yaqso''mi·ⱡs. ta'χas n'u'pχₐne·. ta'χas k.ⱡ'upⲉ'ⱡam-
na'me·s. qoₐs aₐ'k!a·'ⱡaχwe'ets ya·wⲉsqa'pse· tⲉⱡna'mo·'s nawⲉts'-
nuⱡχomuna'pse· po'po·'s. ⱡa·qa'nam tsχaⱡyaqχa·'ⱡaⱡta'pse·.
neᵢsts k!u'pχa ktsₑqapqu'na·'s aₐ'k!aⱡmokuwa'ets qoₐs yaqso''-
280 mi·ⱡs, qaⱡwi'yne· ta'χas ktsⱡaa·na'χam. qawunekⲉ't.se· ⱡatⲉkₐmuq-
kupᵢno·'χunaqna'kse· neᵢs nⲉtsta'haⱡna'na·'s. qakⲉ'kse·: "n'ⲉⱡa-
wa's·ᵢne· nö'pⲉ'k!a." ta'χas skⲉ'n·ku·ts qaⱡwi'yne·: "qaⲉ'n·e·
huⱡtsqa'e·p, paⱡ ksⲉⱡ'ⲉse·ka'te· qo po'po·. mⲉ'ka ke'e·n tⲉⱡna'mo·
qo kᵘawⲉ'tske·n, mⲉ'ksa paⱡ ke'e·n no'ₐkᵘey qo po'po·. ktsχaⱡ'o˘-
285 piⱡmu'na·'p." ta'χas ⱡaqao˘χaqu'mⱡasχu'n·e· skⲉ'n·ku·ts. qaⱡwi'y-
ne·: "huⱡ'a'qₐne·ts." k!o·''pχₐna·ps neᵢs tⲉⱡna'mo·'s ta'χas
ktsχaⱡtsⲉⱡ·aana'χa·'m. ta'χas neᵢ tⲉⱡnamukᵘⲉ'ste·k yu·waka'ⱡat!-
χunia'ₐte· χa'tsⲉnⱡ'asqₐwa·'χₐme·tⲉnsaq!χu'neya'ₐte· skⲉ'n·ku·ts
ktsχaⱡq!akpakⲉ'txo·. tₐ'χas ⱡaⱡa·'χaqu'mⱡasχu'n·e· skⲉ'n·ku·ts.
290 n'itqkupq!a'nwⲉsqa'ₐne·. ta'χas tⲉⱡnamukᵘⲉ'ste·k qaⱡwi'yne·
ta'χas ktsχaⱡsⲉⱡ·aqayaqa'wa'ₐqumⱡa'ₐsχo·'s, ta'χas qana'qkup-
ⱡa'ⱡte·, paⱡ skⲉ'n·ku·ts k!itqkupq!anwⲉ'sqa. ta'χas neᵢ tⲉⱡnamukᵘⲉ'ste·k ya·'haⱡqanaqku'pⱡaⱡta'mne·. qaha·'ⱡe·n aₐ'k.ⱡa'm'e·s
qao˘χaⱡχuna'mne·. χa'tsⲉniⱡq!akpakitχona'mne·. ta'χas ⱡats!-
295 na'χe· skⲉ'n·ku·ts. qoₐs yaqa'haⱡ·a.upaqⱡamⲉ'ske· ⱡaqao˘χa'χe·.
ⱡaχa'χe·. ta'χas na'ₐk!ⲉyuts skⲉ'n·ku·tsna'na ⱡa·upaqu'ⱡne·. qa'ₐ-
ⱡe·n sⲉⱡqa'kiⱡa'mnamⲉ's·ᵢne·: "qaⲉ'nse· ⱡqa'q!akpakitχo'ₐna·ps tⲉⱡna'mu's skⲉ'n·ku·ts, sⲉⱡ'aqaⱡ·aqawa'χe· naₐs ⲉ'nta·'s." sⲉⱡtsχa'n·e·
skⲉ'n·ku·ts, qake·ᵢne·: "a: husⲉⱡ·awa'χe·, qa·upⱡa'pᵢne· tⲉⱡnamu-
300 kᵘⲉ'ste·k. huⱡuqᵘa·ⱡk!umna''nte·." ta'χas n'una'tsᵢne· wⲉⱡke'ᵢ-
ne·. at qakq!u'n·e· skⲉ'n·ku·ts: "χo:χo:χo:" n'u'pχₐne· na'ₐk!ⲉyu
k.ⱡ'u'pe·ⱡs tⲉⱡna'mu·'s, k!u'pske·ks k!u'm·a·ts. qakⲉ'ⱡne·: "ta'χas
woa˘sa'qₐnan' ⱡa˘oqo˘'wakaχa'm'e·n'. to'χᵘa ⱡe·'wam kwa'nₐ-
qnana'wa·'s."

(e) FOX KILLS SALMON

305 Neᵢsts wa'ⱡkᵤwa·s· ke·'ᵢwam na'ₐk!ⲉyu neᵢsts ktᵢna'χa·'m
aₐ'kⲉt.ⱡana'me·s, ma k!u'pχa nⲉtsta'haⱡs ma k!aka'χa·''ms. ta'χas
neᵢ nⲉtsta'ha·ⱡ χuna'χe· neᵢs aₐ'kⲉnmⲉ'tuks. ta'χas n'itkⲉ'n-

ing they started.   Fox was to paddle, ‖ Young Coyote was to spear 265
(the fish), and the boy was to carry the torch. | Coyote was to remain (in
the tent).   Coyote was told: | "Don't sleep.   Look at the | fire.   If
you should fall asleep, they will kill you."   Then they paddled away. |
Fox paddled.   Young Coyote was the one to spear ‖ the salmon, and 270
the boy was to hold the torch. | Coyote remained (in the tent) for
some time. | Coyote looked out.   Coyote was told: | "If you should
see a small fire, then come out.   Then | we are about to kill one an-
other.   For that reason the fire will be thus." ‖ It was not long before 275
he looked out again.   Then he saw that the fire | in the canoe was
small.   Then he knew that they were about to kill | one another.
There on each side of the doorway stood an old person. | They were
holding a hammer each, ready to strike with it | if any one should
want to go there.   Then they would strike from each side.   When
he saw the light in the canoe getting smaller, ‖ he intended to go out. 280
It was not long before | the boy came running in, and said: | "The
manitous have killed us!"   Coyote thought: | "I shall certainly die.
That hammer is terrible.   Although only an old woman | is holding
it, nevertheless the hammer is made of stone, and she will ‖ kill me 285
with it."   Coyote jumped there.   He thought: | "I'll fool them!"
When that old woman saw that he | was about to go out, then the
old people lifted their hammers | to hit him.   They both stood with
legs apart, ready to strike Coyote. | They were about to knock him
down.   Then Coyote jumped there. ‖ He stopped quickly.   The 290
old people thought | he would jump through between them, and
they struck; | but since Coyote stopped quickly, the old people |
struck each other right on their heads.   They | hit each other and
killed each other.   Then ‖ Coyote started to go to the place where they 295
had landed.   He went there | and got there.   Then Fox and Young
Coyote paddled ashore. | They were just telling each other: "Certainly
the old woman has knocked down | Coyote, therefore he has not come
to the shore." | Then Coyote talked, and said: "I am here.   The
old people have not killed me. ‖ I have made trouble for them."   Then 300
he laughed aloud. | He laughed thus: "So, so, so!"   Fox knew now |
that he had killed the old people, and that he laughed for this reason.
He said to him: | "Hurry up!   Come aboard!   Those who | make war
on us are coming." ‖

(e) FOX KILLS SALMON

Then Fox saw a youth coming out—the same one | whom he had seen 305
the day before when he arrived and entered the tent. | The youth
went down to the river.   Then | he transformed himself into a salmon.

meˑk, nʾɛnqaʾpteˑk   qayeˑkǃna'moˑ's.   tsχałsaˑniłwiynaʾateˑ
swʊʾtᵢmoˑs na'akǃₑyu's. qałwiʾyneˑ ktsχałuʾpił ma kqaʾkeˑł-
310 kǃumna''ntaps neᵢs k.łaʾχałwaʾtsǃχa. (pał husłaʾtᵢyiłtsɛkǃma'-
łɑnkɛʾn'eˑ. mɛʾka skɛʾnˑkuˑtsna'na nʾɛʾsᵢneˑłhaquʾlneˑ; na'akǃₑyu
nʾɛʾsᵢneˑłaₐkoʾuneˑ qayeˑkǃɛna'moˑs.) ta'χas neᵢs kułqoˑł. qana-
quʾlneˑ. nʾuˑpχaneˑ qayeᵢkǃɛna'moˑs. noˑʾhune neˑ na'akǃₑyu keˑeˑns
neᵢs waʾłkᵤwa''s ma kǃakaʾχaˑ'ms nɛtsta'hałs. nʾuˑpχaneˑ
315 k.łeˑnqaptaʾkeˑs qayeᵢkǃɛna'moˑsˑ. tsχałaʾₐkoˑ at neᵢs łuqᵘₐ-
qǃaˑłkɛʾn'eˑ neᵢ nɛtsta'hałna'na aₐʾkɛnqǃuˑkoˑps. saˑqana'ₐneˑ
maₐts k.łsukqaˑoˑχałaʾₐkoˑs na'akǃₑyuˑ's. pał keˑeˑns taʾtǃeˑs
neᵢs   ktsχałaₐkoˑ'łeˑs.   nʾuˑpχaneˑ na'akǃₑyu   yaˑʾqaqʾna'-
pskeˑ neᵢs nɛtsta'hałna'nas. qałwiʾyneˑ: "hułaʾqaneᵢts."
320 neᵢs łukᵘiˑkaʾseˑ neᵢs kiaʾkχoˑ's neᵢs łuˑʾqᵘankǃonɛʾlneˑ.
qakɛʾlneˑ neᵢs nɛtsta'hałs neᵢs nʾɛʾn'eˑ kaˑmkeˑ qayeᵢkǃɛna'-
moˑ. sɛłaqₐnɛʾtseˑ neᵢs yaqakaʾskeˑ. qanaqǃałkɛʾn'eˑ aₐʾkɛnqǃuˑkoˑps neᵢ nɛtsta'hał. ta'χas suk.łaₐkoʾuneˑ na'akǃₑyu.
kǃuˑpχa neᵢ nɛtsta'hał pał słaˑqanetsaʾpseˑ na'akǃₑyu's
325 qakɛʾlneˑ: "maₐts qaˑoˑχałaʾₐkoˑn' aₐʾkᵤwuˑ'm'eˑs. qaˑ-
oˑχałaʾₐkoᵤn' aₐʾqaʾtǃeˑs." aʾₐˑkeˑ neᵢ nɛtsta·hał sɛłqałwiʾyneˑ
ktsχałuʾpił na'akǃₑyu's. neᵢsts qaˑoˑχałaʾₐkoˑ aₐʾqatɛʾseˑs
na'akǃₑyu. ta'χas χma yɛkǃtaʾseˑ yaqsoʾmɛʾłeˑs. neᵢs kqaʾk.łaps:
"maₐts aₐʾkᵤwumʾɛ'seˑs." qatsɛʾnkǃapałtiyaʾχₐneˑ qaoˑʾχałaₐₐkoʾu-
330 neˑ aₐʾkᵤwumʾɛʾseˑs. nʾuˑʾkǃuᵘniˑłuˑkᵘǃqₐnuχonuʾqᵘneˑ qayeᵢkǃɛna'-
mo. nʾuˑpχaneˑ neᵢ nɛtsta'hał pał sɛłupɛʾsᵢneˑ taʾtǃeˑs. ta'χas
qaoˑʾχaqǃankɛʾmeˑk neᵢs oˑkǃuᵘeʾhaks yaqsoʾ'miłs. yɛkǃtałqo-
kᵘɛʾn'eˑ. ta'χas nʾɛnqaʾpteˑk qayeᵢkǃɛna'moˑs neᵢ nɛtsta'hałna'na.
ta'χas łatsǃɛʾnałʾupaʾχeˑ aₐʾkɛt.łaʾeˑs k.łałaʾχaˑ'm. ta'χas sɛłaqₐ-
335 keʾᵢneˑ: "nʾupławaʾsₐneˑ," qałwiʾyneˑ mɛʾksa ta'χas ktsupɛʾłeˑ's
neᵢs kǃukǃqaʾpeˑ's. aʾₐˑkeˑ nʾaˑsiłupłaʾpseˑ, ta'χas qałsaˑkiłkina'-
pseˑ. ta'χas na'akǃₑyu swʊʾtᵢmo łatsǃɛnaquʾlneˑ neᵢs kǃuʾpił nɛtsta'haˑłs. naqaʾpseˑ aₐʾkoˑkǃuᵘatskǃak.ło.ɛʾseˑs. łołama'ₐneˑ nʾoqo-
χakɛʾn'eˑ yaqsoʾ'mɛʾłeˑs. aʾₐˑkeˑ wuˑqǃłaˑ''mseˑ. (at qaqana'ₐneˑ
340 neᵢs pɛʾkǃaˑks aqłsmaʾkᵢnɛkǃ. waˑ'naqₐna'nam qaʾła nʾuˑpił
nasoʾᵤkᵘeˑns at łułamaʾneˑ at łatsǃɛnałkɛʾn'eˑ· amʾaˑkǃeˑs.)
ta'χas sɛłkanmiyɛʾt.seˑ qakiłɛʾlneˑ χaleʾᵢtᵢmo skɛʾnˑkuˑts: "maₐts
hɛntsłamaʾnᵤwɛtskiˑkɛʾlneˑ." qaˑnaquʾlneˑ. ta'χas yuwaˑ'kmɛ-
nuqkaʾseˑ, ta'χas yuˑnaqaʾₐneˑ neᵢ aqłsmaʾkᵢnɛkǃ neᵢ haₐk.łoᵤ-
345 kᵘeˑ. ta'χas wanaqₐna'n'eˑ na'akǃₑyu's. qałwiʾyneˑ skɛʾnˑkuˑts:
"mɛʾka pɛʾkǃaˑk hunaʾqanła.łqanaʾqułnaʾₐła." łamaʾ'nᵤwɛts-
kɛʾkᵢneˑ. qakeʾᵢneˑ: "sukᵘakateʾᵢneˑ kᵤwaˑ'naqₐnana'waˑs."
qak.łaʾpseˑ na'akǃₑyu's: "qaʾpsin at kɛnsɛłqatsoʾᵤkᵘat koʾᵤtsχa
ma huqᵘak.łɛʾsᵢneˑ: 'maₐts kɛnłaʾqanawɛʾtskeˑk.'" ta'χas
350 nʾɛtwɛtsquʾlneˑ swʊʾtᵢmo skɛʾnˑkuˑts. mɛʾka kǃałsɛʾnteˑk kaʾqoł
qataławanχa''mseˑ yaqsoʾmɛʾłeˑs. ta'χas łaχaʾseˑ kᵤwanaq-
qna'naps. tsukᵘaʾteˑ neᵢs aₐʾk.łamʾɛʾseˑs neᵢs nɛtsta'hałs.

He was going to attack | Fox and his friends. He thought he would kill them, because he had been beaten ‖ when he had gone to play 310 with them. (I have been all the time making a mistake. | It was Young Coyote who paddled, and Fox | who speared the salmon.) Then they paddled along. | They saw a salmon. Fox knew it was | the youth who had come out the day before. He knew ‖ that he had 315 turned into a salmon. When Fox was ready to throw his spear, | the boy put the torch to the other side. He did this so | that Fox should not hit the salmon, | for the one to be speared was his elder brother. Fox knew what | the boy was doing. He thought: "I'll fool him!" ‖ The fish was coming along on one side, but he pointed 320 the other way. | He said to the youth: "Salmon is coming there." | He fooled him in regard to the side whence it was coming. | The youth turned the torch, and Fox speared him. | When the youth saw that Fox had fooled him, ‖ he said to him: "Don't hit it in the belly; | 325 hit its tail!" The youth thought | the salmon would kill Fox if he should hit its tail, | because then he would upset the canoe. When Fox was told: | "Don't hit its belly," he would not listen, but he hit it ‖ in the belly. The salmon at once turned sideways. | The boy 330 saw that his brother was killed. Then | he stepped on one side of the canoe, fell into the water, | and became a salmon. | Then he went back to his tent and arrived there. Then ‖ he said: "They have killed us." 335 He thought the one remaining might also be killed, | as two had been killed. Then three had been killed.[1] | Then Fox and his friends went on paddling. | The youth who had been killed wore ear ornaments. They cut off his head | and put it into the canoe. He also had a long braid. ‖ (In olden times the people used to do this. When they 340 made war and some one killed | a chief, they cut off his head and took it back to their country.) | Then in the morning Coyote and his son were told: "Don't | look back!" They paddled on. At sunrise | many people from a large camp ‖ came to make war on Fox. Coyote 345 thought: | "They are already paddling after us." He looked back | and said: "A great many are making war on us." | Fox told him: "Why don't you obey me and do | what I tell you? Don't look back!" Then ‖ Coyote and his friends stopped. No matter how hard 350 they tried, | they could not move their canoe. Then the warriors arrived. | (Fox) took the head of the youth. | He lifted it up and

---

[1] The two old people and the Salmon.

n'ɛktkakɛ'nˑeˑ qakɛ'łneˑ: "aˑ naˑ kɛn'oˑ'tki·ł?" pɛsuqkɛ'nˑeˑ.
n'iktseˑnuqu'seˑ. łahaqu'łneˑ. n'uˑk!ᵘniłˑawa'nxa''mseˑ yaqso'-
355 mɛ'ł'es. pał słxatkɛnu'kᵤneˑ. neᵢ kᵢyuˑna'qa ta'xas qa'oˑxał'-
ɛ'tᵤwitsqu'łneˑ neᵢs yaˑqa'nałɛktsenoqu'skeˑ aₐ'k.łamˑɛ'seˑs
nɛtsta'hałs. ta'xas na'ₐk!ₑyu sɛˀats!ɛna'xeˑ łaqatseᵢkatɛ'łneˑ.

(f) TURTLE RESCUES THE SALMON HEAD

Qakeˑ'ᵢneᵢ neᵢ yaqaˀsɛnqa'łtkeˑ neᵢs nɛtsta'hałs: "qa'ła
łatso'ᵤkᵘaˑt naₐs aₐ'k.łamˑɛ'seˑs kanxałeˑ''mi·ł. maˑ koˑoˑk!qa'p-
360 qa·łt na.u'teˑ. tsxałsałeˑtɛ'tᵢneˑ." ta'xas q!a'peˑ aqłsma'kinɛk!
n'anᵤwa'ts!neˑ. pał k!o'ᵤło qatakᵢnɛ'łneˑ. ta'xas qa·'łɛn
kiyu'kᵢyit qakeˑ'ᵢneˑ ka'xax—n'uk!ᵘe'ᵢneˑ nɛtsta'haˑł qał'a-
tɛ'łneˑ ka'xaxs—: "hutsxałk!anᵤwa'ts!neˑ. qak.ła'pᵤneˑ ka'xax
neᵢ tuq!tsqa'mna ka'xax, at kuˑtsqaqₐna'pmił, pał kᵢnupxa'-
365 kił ka'xax at kqasts!u'mqa'qa k!a'nᵤwats!. hutsxał'akoˑ-
kᵘɛnmɛ'łneˑ, keˑ'ᵢtsxa ka'xax." ta'xas neᵢ nɛtsta'hał qakeˑ'ᵢneˑ:
"hutsxałk!anᵤwa'ts!neˑ. ta'xas hɛntsła.upa'qułkɛ'łneˑ aₐ'kɛt.ła-
nɛ'ski·ł. kanmi'yɛt, qa·'łɛn kiyu'kᵢyit ta'xas hutsłaaˀwaₐka-
wa'ts!neˑ. ta'xas heᵢnˑtsłaqo'kwaqo·łkɛ'łneˑ." ta'xas łats!ɛnaxa''-
370 mneˑ. kanmi'yit qa·'łin kiyu'kᵢyit qakiya'mneˑ: "ta'xas maˑ
ktsxał·aaˀwaₐka'wa·ts! ka'xax. ta'xas łaqunamɛ'łkił." ta'xas
q!a'peˑ łaholqła'mneˑ. naˀwɛtskpayatɛ'łneˑ. qa·'łin kiyu'kᵢyit
łaaˀwaₐkawa'ts!neˑ. łahałkɛ'nˑeˑ aₐ'k.łamˑɛ'seˑs neᵢs nɛtsta'hałs.
ta'xas tsᵤkᵘa'teˑ neᵢs na.u'teˑs. naqsanmeˑ'yɛt.s ke'eˑns
375 tɛłnamu''eˑs. naqan'okunmi'yɛt.s aˑ·'s at qatsxa'seˑ. ta'xas
at tsɛnˑmałatikɛ'nˑeˑ k.łe'ᵢtsxaˑs at qat!aq!tała'pseˑ. ta'xas
q!utse'ᵢteˑ. n'uma'tseˑ pał n'uktukᵘe'ᵢseˑ aₐk!ałmaɛ'seˑs.
łama'teˑ.

Ta'xas husɛłq!apqałq!anuxwa'teˑ qayeᵢk!ɛna'mo.

59. COYOTE AND THE DUCKS

Ho'ya's, hutsxałhaqałq!anuxᵘa'teˑ skɛ'nˑkuˑts xałe'ᵢtᵢmo neᵢs
pɛ'k!aˑks yaₐqałetkɛ'nkeˑ kia'q!łaˑ's.
Qahana'xeˑ skɛ'nˑkuˑts. nałxo'ᵤneˑ xałe'eˑ's. xuna'xeˑ. skɛkq!ₐ-
nu'kseˑ. qak.łayi'ɛ'tᵢneˑ yaₐqaˀwɛsiłqo'ᵤk!awa'ts!eˑkina'xanam-
5 na'mkeˑ. n'uˑpxₐneˑ skɛ'nˑkuˑts qo'ᵤs łuˑnˑqo's yunaqa'pseˑ
kia'q!łaˑ's. nonuˀq!ᵤwitsta'pseˑ. qaaˑłoˑqałnu'k!ᵤneˑ. qałwiˑ'yneˑ:
"hoˑ'yas huł'a'qₐneˑts kia'q!ła." qakɛ'łneˑ xałe'eˑ's: "ho'yas,
eᵢ'ˑ'la·n'. qało'ᵤkᵘin': ˀa·łskáˑ'tˑles katɛtó:'.'" ta'xas neᵢ łka'nˑu
qakeˑ'ᵢneˑ neᵢs yaqak.ła'pskeˑ tɛtu''eˑs. ta'xas skɛ'nˑkuˑts a'ₐ'keˑ
10 n'eᵢ'ła'nˑeˑ. qało'ᵤkᵤneˑ: "a·łˑka'skat, a·łˑka'skat." ta'xas
n'uk!ᵘe'ᵢneˑ kia'q!ła qo'ᵤs a·nɛłqa'haˑks qawɛsqu'łeˑk. qakɛ'łneˑ
ałaqa'łt!e·s: "ma'qaˑk tsɛnk!apa·łteᵢxa'ki·ł qo'ᵤs n'ɛ'nˑeˑ nöpɛ'k!a
yo'qᵘakeˑ'ᵢkeˑ." ta'xas neᵢ kᵢyuna'qa kia'q!ła tsɛnk!apałtɛ'łe·k
pał słła'seˑ qo'ᵤs nöpɛ'k!aˑ's. qakiła''mneˑ: "ts!ɛ'nałˀupamɛ'łki·ł,

said to them: "Is this what you want?"   He put it into the water. |
It sank.   Again they paddled, and their canoe moved right away. ‖
They were saved.   Then the crowd stopped | on the water when the   355
head of the youth sank. | Fox went on.   They did not look back
again. |

(f) TURTLE RESCUES THE SALMON HEAD

Then the one who was the father of the youth said: "Who | will
get this head of my son?   I have one more child, ‖ a daughter.   He   360
shall marry her."   Then all the people | dived.   They went into the
water, but could not get it.   Just at | noon Turtle—a young man
called | Turtle—said: "I'll dive.   Turtle, | the animal, said to me | I
should do it, because you know ‖ Turtle is an expert diver.   I'll try." | 365
Thus said Turtle.   Then that youth said: | "I'll dive.   You shall
paddle back to the shore to your tents. | To-morrow, just at noon, I'll
come out of the water; | then paddle back here."   Then they went
back. ‖ On the following day, just at noon, they said to one another: | 370
"Turtle was to come up at this time.   Go back to him."   Then | they
all paddled back and waited for him.   Just at noon | he emerged,
carrying the head of the youth. | Then he took the girl.   For several
days she was ‖ his wife.   For one or two days she did not talk.   Then | 375
he teased her to make her talk, but she wouldn't talk with him.
Then | he tickled her, and she laughed.   Her mouth had a bad smell. |
He left her. |

Now, I have told you about the Salmon. |

59. COYOTE AND THE DUCKS[1]

Well, I'll tell you about Coyote and his children |—what they did,
a long time ago, to the Ducks. |

Coyote was going along, carrying his son.   He went down to a
lake. | It is named Where-they-fight-with-Broken-Pieces-of-Wood-
in-the-Lake. ‖ Coyote knew that far away there were many | Ducks.   5
He was hungry for them, but had no way of getting at them.   He
thought: | "I'll fool the Ducks."   He said to his son: "Go on; |
shout, 'O my father's brothers-in-law!'"   Then the child | said what
his father had told him.   Then Coyote also ‖ cried.   He shouted: "O   10
my brothers-in-law! O my brothers-in-law!"   Then | one Duck was
swimming farther away on the water.   He said | to his children:
"Wait; listen [to] what the manitous | are saying!"   There were
many Ducks.   They listened | to what the manitous were crying.

---

15 hʌntsxaꞁ·a‘k.ꞁiꞁkɛ′ꞁne· qa′psins.”   ta′xas n’ok!ᵘe′ᵢne· tsꞁɛ′naꞁ’u-
pa′xe·. qakɛ′ꞁne·: “qa′psin kʌnske′ᵢke‘ꞁ?” qake′ᵢne· skɛ′n·ku·ts:
“ha: hʌnsɛly ɛlna’nstawa′sᵢne· k!aqa′ₐꞁsoᵤk ke·nk.ꞁʌnq!o′ykeꞁ.
koa‘qa·ꞁqa‘taꞁhoꞁqatsa′ꞁa.” ꞁatsꞁɛna′xe· neᵢ kia′q!ꞁa·. qake′ᵢne·:
“paꞁo‘siꞁyɛlna’nstaꞁa′ₐne· kok.ꞁʌnq!oyaꞁa′e·s.” qake′ᵢne· neᵢ

20 k!u‘k!ᵘe·: “ꞁu′n·o·s upamɛ′ꞁkiꞁ. hʌntsxaꞁtsukᵘatkɛ′ꞁne·. kʌnꞁ-
k.ꞁʌnq!oyma′tkiꞁ.” ta′xas n’upa′xe· kia′q!ꞁa. n′ɛtkɛ′n·e· xaꞁɛ′ᵢtᵢ-
mo’s skɛ′n·ku·ts ktsxaꞁqa.ɛktsᵢnu′qos mɛ′ksa·’n qa·hamatɛ′ktse·
aₐ‘kʌnqowa.ɛ′se·s. qakiꞁɛ′ꞁne· skɛ′n·ku·ts xaꞁɛ′ᵢtᵢmo: “ta′xas
huꞁqsana′ꞁa.” ta′xas qsama′ꞁne· kia′q!ꞁa·’s skɛ′n·ku·ts xaꞁɛ′ᵢtᵢ-

25 mo. ta′xask.ꞁunq!oyma′ꞁne· kia′q!ꞁa·’s. naₐkiꞁk.ꞁʌnq!u′ꞁik kia′q!ꞁa
at nuꞁqan·oxu′n·e· neᵢs· k.ꞁoha′kq!ₐnuᵤks n’aꞁoᵤxaqa′n·uxu′n·e·.
skɛ′n·ku·ts at ꞁa.upa′xe· at n’ɛntana′xe·. xo’na·m at nuꞁu′qᵤne·,
at ꞁaho·′ꞁqa′n·uxu′n·e· kia′q!ꞁa. at ꞁa′tsᵢne·’s ꞁaꞁo′ᵤxaqa′n·u-
xu′n·e·. tse·n·o‘k!ᵤniꞁ′ɛtnu‘mo·tstɛ′ꞁne· skɛ′n·ku·ts. qakɛ′ꞁne·:

30 “saha′n·e· at kʌnhuꞁqa′n·oxo′kᵘiꞁ. ta′xas at maₐts ꞁaqa˘qa˘-
na′pkiꞁ. ata′qkiꞁ paꞁ k!oho‘psiꞁqayaₐqa′ₐꞁha·k. at neᵢ qa‘ꞁ’a-
aꞁ·qaꞁaqa′pkiꞁ, at q!a′pe· hʌn·tsawats!kɛ′ꞁne·.” ta′xas qaki-
ꞁa′mne· kia′q!ꞁa: “paꞁ sɛlso′ᵤkᵘse· qoᵤs yaₐqake′ᵢke· nöpɛ′k!a.
huꞁqa′qₐnawaꞁa′e’s.” ta′xas kia′q!ꞁa at qaqₐna′ₐne·. neᵢs tsɛl-

35 mi·′yɛt.s at ꞁa.upa′xe· skɛ′n·ku·ts. at qusqaₐkᵢyiksɛ′ꞁe·k ɛ′nta·s.
ta′xas n′ɛtkɛ′n·e· skɛ′n·ku·ts a′ₐkɛts n’aꞁqanamxonɛ′ꞁne· neᵢs
aₐ‘kʌnuxo′ᵤnuks. ta′xas kia′q!ꞁa qaha′wats!. at qaqoᵤqakɛ′n·e·
u’s′me·ks. at q!a′pe·’s n′ɛtuk!sa′ₐne·. a′ₐke· ꞁaqaha′wats!s
qaqakɛ′n·e·. ɛlna′haks ꞁaqaha′wats!s at ꞁa.ɛ′tuk!sa′ₐne·. qakɛ′ꞁne·

40 kia′q!ꞁa·’s: “ta′xa neᵢ hʌnts!ɛnawa′ts!kiꞁ at ts!upᴇna·qꞁɛ′ꞁkiꞁ.
maₐts ata‘kiꞁwi·tske′ᵢkiꞁ.” ta′xas sɛl′ɛlkɛlwi’yne· skɛ′n·ku·ts.
xma ktsxaꞁwo′ᵤkats aₐ‘kak!o′’e·s kia′q!ꞁa·’s. ta′xas naqsan-
mi·′yɛt.s kqa′ke·ᵢn, ta′xas yunaqa′pse· ke’e·k skɛ′n·ku·ts.
tse·n n’u′pxₐne· kia′q!ꞁa paꞁ ꞁaqaso‘kᵘaₐkatɛ′ᵢne·. qakiꞁa′mne·:

45 “paꞁu’sɛltsa‘mnaqapta‘teyaꞁa′ₐne·.” qake′ᵢne· k!o·′k!ᵘe· kia′q!ꞁa:
“neᵢ qakaꞁo′ᵤme· yaₐqaₐnit.ꞁa′ₐke· skɛ′n·ku·ts at ts!anɛ′mse·
k!a‘ꞁikwa.ɛ′tᵢne·. ho′yas, ts!ɛnamɛ′tkiꞁ, kʌnꞁtseᵢkatmɛ′ꞁkiꞁ aₐ‘-
kɛt.ꞁa′’e·s.” ta′xas n’uk!ᵘe′ᵢne· kia′q!ꞁa qaꞁ’atɛ′ꞁne· mɛ′tsoᵤk
ts!ɛnawa′ts!ne·. k.ꞁa′xa·’m aₐ‘kɛt.ꞁa.ɛ′se·s. n’upa′xe·. n’u′pxₐne·

50 yunaqa′pse· k!ɛtma′se·’ts kia′q!ꞁa·’s. n’u′pxₐne· paꞁ n’ɛ′nse·
skɛ′n·ku·ts·. ꞁatsꞁɛna′xe·. k.ꞁaꞁa′xam qake′ᵢne·: “paꞁ n’ɛ′n·e·
skɛ′n·ku·ts paꞁ sɛlo‘ktawa′sᵢne·.” ta′xas n’ɛla′n·e· kia′q!ꞁa.
qakiꞁa′mne· kia′q!ꞁa: “kanmi·′yɛt.s a′ₐke· ꞁaqaqₐna′was.
hʌntsxaꞁhakɛlwɛ′tski‘ᵢkɛ′ꞁne·. neᵢ hʌnts!ɛnawa′ts!kiꞁ hʌntstse′ᵢ-

55 katkɛ′ꞁne· qa′psin naₐqantsxa′ₐꞁo neᵢs aₐ‘kʌnoxo′ᵤnuks.” ta′xas
kanmi·′yɛt.s ts!ɛnaꞁᵤwa′ts!te·k kia′q!ꞁa neᵢs k.ꞁua′kq!nuks.¹
neᵢ u’s′me·k q!a′pe· nakɛlwɛtskɛ′kᵢne·. qawiꞁe.ɛ′t.se· n’u′pxₐne·

_____

¹ Barnaby: k.ꞁuha′kq!nuks.

Some one said: "Go ashore ‖ and ask him something." Then one of 15
them went ashore. | He said to him: "Why do you say that?"
Coyote said: | "We wanted you. You are playing nicely. | We are
not able to go on the water." The Duck started, and said: | "They
are wishing for us. They want to have our way of playing." Then ‖
one of them said: "Go ashore. Take them | and play with them." 20
Then the Ducks went ashore. They made it so that | Coyote and his
son should not sink, but they did not give them | their feathers.
Coyote and his son were told: "Now | let us go together!" Then
they went out together—Coyote, his son, and the Ducks. ‖ Then they 25
played with the Ducks. While they were at play, all the Ducks | flew
along to another lake. They flew there. | Coyote went ashore over-
land. When he came to the water, he swam, | but the Ducks flew
again to the other lake. | All at once Coyote laid down a rule. He 30
said to them: ‖ "It is bad for you to fly away. Don't do it any
more. | Swim there through the middle of the water. | Arrange your-
selves in a line right across, and all of you dive together." Then | the
Ducks said to one another: "It is good, what the manitou says. | Let
us do it!" Then the Ducks did so. ‖ At night Coyote went ashore. 35
He stepped on shore. | Then Coyote made something to stretch
across | the brook. Then the Ducks came diving along, and did not do
anything. | The first one he tied, the next one that came diving
along | he let go, and the last one that dived coming along he tied
again. He said ‖ to the Ducks: "When you start diving, close your 40
eyes. | Don't look!" Coyote was clever. | (He thought) they might
see his trap. They | did so for several days. Then Coyote had much
food. | The Ducks just knew that they ceased to be many. They
said among themselves: ‖ "We are getting few in number." One Duck 45
said: | "The wind is blowing from the place where Coyote's tent is. |
It gives a smell of burnt fat. Now go and look into his | tent." One
Duck was called Great Diver.[1] | He dived and came to Coyote's
tent. He went ashore, and saw ‖ many dried ducks. Then he 50
knew that it was | Coyote. He went back: and when he came
back, he said: "It is | Coyote. He is killing all of us." Then the
Ducks cried. | The Ducks said among themselves: "He will do the
same to us to-morrow. | Look out when you dive! You will see ‖
whether there is anything in the stream." Then | on the following 55
day the Ducks started diving to another lake. | The first ones all
looked, and it was not long before they saw | something right across

---

[1] Mot-head (?).

sal'ałqaqo‘na‘kse· qa'psins. łałuqawa'ts!ne·. qake'ine· sk‹'n‑
ku·ts: "a: hᵻna‘łᵤwiyktse;k‹'łne·[1] ma.ots!o‚ukt‹sk‹'łne·." ta'xas
60 łaqa‘qa‘qna‚ane· kia'q!ła. ta'xas at łaho'łnoxu'n·e·.

　　Qa‚anit.ła'ane·[2] k!o·'q!ᵤne·. n'anaxa''mne· ne;s qakałom‹'se·.
n'aqłu'k!ᵤne· ts!an‹'mse· k!a'likwa.‹'tse·. ts!ᵻn·mek!u'n·e·.
łaxa'xe· ne;s a‚a'ku'q!ᵘnoᵤks. n'u'px‚ane· pał sn‹łaxna'kse· sk‹'n‑
ku·ts. qona‚akₐina'x‚anc· q!u'mne·''nis. xa'ts;niłq!u'mne'₍ine·
65 x‚ałe'₍itᵢmo sk‹'n·ku·ts. tsukᵘa'te· ne;s kia'q!ła·'s k!o·'q!ᵤne·.
qonya'x‚ane· a‚aqat!‹'se·s sk‹'n·ku·ts. nakunk‹'n·e·. wo‘qapqa't.se·
a'‚a'ke· x‚ałe.‹'se·s. qak‹'n·e·. tsukᵘa'te· a‚akaq!‚ane.‹'se·s. nakun‑
k‹'n·e·. wo‘qapq!‚ane'₍ise·. łats!ᵻna'xe·. naq!amałe'₍itse· x‚ałe'e·s
sk‹'n·ku·ts. tse;kata'pse· sak.łe'₍itsne·. n'upx‚ana'pse·. wo‘qap‑
70 q!nc'₍ine·, wo‘qapqa't₍ine·. ta'xas n'umats;nata'pse· x‚ałe''e·s
ne;s k!łaqaqa'pka. naq!nuka'łnaxwata'pse· tse;ka'te· x‚ałe''e·s.
n'u'px‚ane· k!a‚aqa‘qa'pqaps ne;s ya‚aqa‘qa'‚ake·. a'‚a'ke· qa‘qa'p‑
se·. tse;ka'te· ne;s kia'q!ła·'s. łało'‚use· ke'e·k. qahao‘sa‘qa‚ane·.
qak‹'łne· x‚ałe''e·s: "ne; hu·tsqana'xe·." ts!ᵻna'xe· sk‹'n·ku·ts.
75 n'u'px‚ane· san‹t.łanam‹'s;ne·. n'u'px‚ane·. n'‹snit.ła‚ase· k·łoq!ᵘ‑
ne·'s. n'u'px‚ane· pał n'‹s;nił'ayn‹ła'pse· ki'e·k. q!u''mne·tse'₍ite·.
łatsukᵘa'te· ne;s kia'q!ła·'s. qonya'x‚ane· a‚aqat!‹'se·s tsa‑
qanak‹'ne·. a'‚a'ke· qak‹'ne· x‚ałe·‹'se·s. tsᵻn qas‹łakaqa'p‚uwᵻts‑
qatnana'se·. qonya'x‚ane· a‚akaq!ne.‹'se·s ne;s qałyaptsak‹'ne·.
80 k!o‚uqa'pq!nenana'se·. łats!ᵻna'xe·. naq!amałe'₍its;ne· x‚ałe'₍i‑
tᵢmo k!o·'q!ᵤna, n'u'px‚ane· ya‚aqaqapqa'‚ake· łało'‚use· ki'e·k.
ta'xas słaqaqa'‚ane· sk‹'n·ku·ts kᵤwok!u'nka·k kᵤwo'qa·t.
n'uła'se· k!o·'q!ᵤne·'s. sa‘qa‘qa'‚ane k!o·'q!ᵤne· kk!o·qu'na·'s
a‚a'k!unka'k!e·s kk!oqu'na·'s a‚aqa't!e·s. n'uła'se· sk‹'n·ku·ts.
85 　　Ta'xas hus‹łq!apqałq!anuxwa'te· sk‹'n·ku·ts yaqał'‹tk‹'nke·
kia'q!ła·'s **ne**;s p‹'k!a·ks.

60.. Coyote Kills Panther and Liberates the Salmon

Ho'yas, hutsqałq!anuxwa·'te· swa' k!u'pła·ps sk‹'n·ku·ts·.

(a) coyote kills panther

Qa·n‹t.ła'ane· sk‹'n·ku·ts sałet‹'t;ne· xa'‚ałtsins. ts‹łmi·'y‹t.s
qake'ine· xa'‚ałtsin: "kanmi·'yit.s xma hᵻnts!na'mełk‹'łne· ała‑
tsa·n‹'ski·ł ne; san‹t.ła'ane·. qa'k.łe·k swa's. at qahuwa's;ne·
5 m‹'ksa·'n at n'u'p;yit!e'₍ine·." kanmi·'yit.s no·kunoxa''mne·‑
sk‹'n·ku·ts. qake'ine·: "ts!kak‹'ne· ka·ku'qła·nt." ta'xas xa'‑
‚ałtsin namat‹'ktse· n'‹tuqła·'nt‹'k.łe·k sk‹'n·ku·ts. ta'xas ts!ᵻ‑
na'xe·. łaxa'xe· san‹t.ła'e·s swa's. t;naxa''mne·. ha: yunaqa'pse·
a‚a'ku'ła·ks. t‹łnamo.‹'se·s sła·t‹nts!łko'se·. ała·qałt!‹'se·s ła·ł‹'‑
10 tkins a·'qu'qt!e·s, swa's ła·t;niłkaxan‹'kse·. qatse;kata'pse·.

[1] Barnaby: hᵻn·a‘łᵤwiᵢktseyek‹'łne·.
[2] Barnaby: qahan‹t.ła''ne·.

the water. They dived and went back. Coyote said: | "Oh, you
have a (good) mind! I was going to kill you all." ‖ The Ducks did 60
not do it any more, but flew again. |

There was the tent of Lynx. He went out. The wind was
blowing this way, | and he smelled the burning fat. He started, fol-
lowing the smell, | and arrived at the lake. He saw that Coyote had
much to eat. | Then he made him sleep; and both slept, ‖—Coyote and 65
his son. Lynx took the Ducks. | He took Coyote by his tail and
pulled it. Then he had a long tail; | and he also took his son. He
took his face and pulled it | so that he had a long face. Then he
started back. Coyote's son woke up, | and he saw (his father) sleep-
ing. He saw that he had a long face ‖ and a long tail. Then the 70
son laughed at him | because he was that way. He woke him up.
He looked at his son, | and he saw that he was different from what he
had been; | and he looked at the Ducks, and there was no food.
They staid there. | He said to his son: "I'll go that way." Coyote
started ‖ and saw a tent. He knew it was the tent of Lynx. | He 75
knew that he had stolen the food. He made him sleep, | and he took
back the Ducks. He took hold of his tail | and pushed it in, and he
did the same to his son. Just a little piece of the tail remained
sticking out. | He took his face and pushed it in, ‖ and he had a short 80
face. Then he went back. Lynx and his son awoke. | They saw
how they were, and that there was no food. | Therefore Coyote has a
long nose and a long tail. | Lynx did it. And therefore Lynx | has
a short nose and a short tail. Coyote did it. ‖

Now I have told you about Coyote, what he did to | the ducks 85
long ago. |

60. Coyote Kills Panther and Liberates the Salmon

Well, I'll tell you a story how Panther was killed by Coyote. |

(a) COYOTE KILLS PANTHER

Coyote had a tent. He was married to Dog. In the evening |
Dog said: "To-morrow you shall go to your uncle. | His tent is
there. His name is Panther. He is not hungry, but ‖ he is very 5
stingy." On the following morning Coyote arose. | He said: "Give
me my clothes." Dog gave | Coyote his clothing. Then he started,
and arrived | where the tent of Panther was. He entered. Oh,
there was much meat. | His wife was scraping fat off a skin. His
children were cleaning guts. ‖ Panther was putting feathers on his 10
arrows. They did not look at him. He sat down, and | thought:

qaːnqa′meˑk. qałwi′yneˑ: "ɬnqawoˑˑkata′pneˑ." łaˑanaxa″mne.
łaqaˑo˘xałkɛkqǃowasxoneyikɛ′meˑk. łatᵢnaxa″mneˑ. pał sɛɬqa-
tseᵢkata′pseˑ. qaˑ″nqa′meˑk. nanuqǃuwɛˑłeˑk. pał koˑ′was. neᵢs
kǃu′pxa aₐˑku′łaˑks tsɛma′kǃiłuwa′sₐneˑ. łaaˑnaxa″mneˑ. sɛɬa-
15 tsǃɛna′xeˑ ɬtqawumxo′ᵤmeˑk. kǃała′xaˑm aₐˑkɛt.ła′eˑs.

Tsɛɬmiˑ′yɛt.s qake′ineˑ: "kanmiˑ′yit hutsuqnaˑneyała′ₐneˑ.
naqa′ₐneˑ kakᵤwɛ′seˑ. hoqᵘatsǃkałxo′ᵤneˑ." qałwiˑ′yneˑ xa′ₐɬtsin:
"ma n′upᵢyitǃe′ᵢneˑ kǃaqa′qₐna." kanmiˑ′yɛt nuqᵤna′meˑk.
kǃaxało″neˑs qakɛ′łneˑ skɛ′nˑkuˑts tɛɬnamu″eˑs: "aː wa′siłqun-
20 yaxamɛ′lin′ aₐˑku′łaˑks. ɬn′ɛ′kᵢneˑ." ta′xas xa′ₐɬtsin tsǃɛna′xeˑ
qoᵤs aₐˑkɛt.łana′meˑs. tᵢnaxa″mneˑ, qatseᵢkatɛ′łneˑ. qaˑ″nqa′-
meˑkˑ, qake′ineˑ.: "husiyaxamɛ′łneˑ kᵤwɛsɛ′n′eˑs skɛ′nˑkuˑtsˑ."
qatseᵢkatɛ′łneˑ. kwune′ᵢkeˑts ła.aˑnaxa″mneˑ. nonoqǃwɛ′łeˑk,
pał koˑ′was neᵢsts kǃu′pxa aₐˑku′łaˑks kǃumnaqaqa′ₐneˑ.
25 łałaxa′xeˑ. qake′ineˑ: "hoqᵘaˑmateˑktsɛ′łneˑ."

Qake′ineˑ skɛ′nˑkuˑts: "pa′mek kɛnłamatɛ′ktseˑł. ɛs aₐˑkǃa-
łaxawu′eˑts ma ksaˑqǃaˑnqakiłhoł′itkinɛ′łneˑ." łaqaoˑxa′xeˑ
xa′ₐɬtsin. tᵢnaxa″mneˑ a′ₐˑkeˑ łaqaˑtseˑkatɛ′łneˑ. waˑhaˑwɛts-
kɛ′kᵢneˑ. n′up′xₐneˑ naₐs pał sqǃa′nseˑ. pał nułu′ksałɛ′sᵢneˑ.
30 qake′ineˑ: "nasts ke′eˑns?" ta′xas tsukᵘa′teˑ. łuqᵘawɛts-
kɛ′kᵢneˑ swa′. nu′pxₐneˑ peɛ′kǃaks pał tsxaˑłtsił′oˑkᵘakɛ′nseˑ.
naₐs qaˑkqa′pseˑ no′ᵤkᵘeys. tsᵤkᵘa′teˑ. pał kᵤwaha′łaˑtǃ
xa′ₐɬtsin qanaqkupłałtᵢmu′łneˑ neᵢs no′ᵤkᵘeys. qaˑ′łɛn tsuo″eˑs
qaoˑxaqkupiłxo′ᵤłneˑ. qake′ineˑ swa′: "aː ksaˑn̂łaˑtᵢyaˑkaˑteˑ
35 hułɛn′ɛ′steˑ. ałkaqa′łtᵢmiˑł at koˑsił′anakɛ′tsᵢmiˑł." łaaˑn-
muqkupnoxo′niłkikwakɛ′meˑk xa′ₐɬtsin.

Kǃała′xaˑ′m kułpa′łeˑn skɛ′nˑkuˑts tɛɬnamu″eˑs. nałɛnqǃo′yłoˑ-
kᵘa′ₐmeˑk. n′anmuqkupnu′xoqa′meˑk. tsɛkqłopnaˑxnaktse′ᵢteˑ.
n′ɛtkɛ′neˑ tǃawu′eˑs; a′ₐˑkeˑ xałe″eˑs n′ɛtkɛ′neˑ tǃawuna-
40 naɛ′seˑs; tɛɬnamu″eˑs n′ɛtkɛ′neˑ popoɛ′seˑs; a′ₐˑkeˑ swɛ′n′eˑs
n′ɛtkɛ′neˑ poponanaɛ′seˑs. qakɛ′łneˑ: "ta′xas hułtsǃɛnaxa-
ła′eˑs. hutsxał′uteˑma′łneˑ kaˑntɛtqa′tǃmaˑł; nɛ′nko hɛntsxał′-
uteˑma′łneˑ pa′łkeᵢma′łneˑ′s; nɛ′nko hɛntsxał′uteˑma′łneˑ
nɛtstaˑhałnaˑnama′łneˑ′s; nɛ′nko hɛntsxał′uteˑma′łneˑ naˑuˑteˑ-
45 naˑnama′łneˑ′s." ta′xas tsǃɛna′xeˑ. qaoˑxa′xeˑ. qakɛ′łneˑ tɛɬ-
namu″eˑs: "hɛntsxało˘kǃᵘeˑłaːtikiniktsa′pₐneˑ łaqǃanxo″naˑł."
ta′xas xa′ₐɬtsin oˑkǃᵘɛnkenɛ′ktseˑ nułaqₐna′eˑs. tɛnaqǃaxo′ᵤxᵤneˑ
swa′s; a′ₐˑkeˑ łatᵢnaqǃaxo′ᵤxᵤneˑ. ta′xas tɛnnitᵢya′xₐneˑ swa′s
skɛ′nˑkuˑts. tsɛnkɛ′neˑ. qaˑwɛtski′neˑ. ta′xas n′u′pxₐneˑ pał
50 sɛł′ɛ′pseˑ. pɛskɛ′neˑ. tseᵢka′teˑ. qaˑha′łeˑn pał sɛł′wakᵢni-
łɛ′sᵢneˑ tɛɬnamu″eˑs popoɛ′seˑs. tsxałsɛɬqanłałtᵢmułɛ′sᵢneˑ. mitᵢ-
ya′xₐneˑ ławakᵢnɛ′łneˑ neᵢs pa′łkeᵢs. ławakᵢnɛ′łneˑ qanaqkup-
ła′łteˑ. qǃakpaˑ′kitxo′ᵤneˑ. tseᵢka′teˑ. qaˑha′łeˑn pał tsxałsɛɬmiˑ′t-
xamułɛ′sᵢneˑ tǃawuɛ′seˑs xałe″eˑs. wakᵢnɛ′łneˑ neᵢs łka′mˑu.
55 mɛ′txₐneˑ a′ₐˑkeˑ n′upɛ′łneˑ. tseᵢka′teˑ swɛ′n′eˑs. n′u′pxₐneˑ

"Maybe they did not see me." He went out again. He went back coughing. | He went in again. They did not look at him, | and he sat down. They did not give him anything to eat, and he was hungry when he saw the meat. | He was very hungry. He went out and went home without anything to eat. ‖ He arrived at his tent. | 15

In the evening he said: "To-morrow we will move. | My food is there. I did not bring it." Dog thought: | "He was stingy, therefore he did so." On the following morning they moved their camp. | When they got there, Coyote said to his wife: "Oh, go quickly ‖ and   20 get meat, that you may eat!" Dog left | for that tent. She entered, but they did not look at her. She sat down. | She said: "I came for the food that you gave to Coyote." | They did not look at her. After a long time she went out. She did not get anything to eat. | She was hungry when she saw the meat. She was poor. She went back ‖ and said: "They didn't give me anything." | 25

Coyote said: "Try again. It may be given to you. It is | hanging ready made by the doorway." Dog went there again. | She entered, and they did not look at her. She looked up. | She saw it hanging here. It was all tied up. ‖ She said: "Is this it?" Then   30 she took it. | Panther looked around, and saw that she was taking it down. | A stone was lying there. He took it; and when Dog put her arm up, | he struck her with the stone. He struck her hard right on the breast. | Panther said: "Oh, you bad-looking one! ‖ This is   35 not for you. I am hunting for my children." | Then Dog ran out quickly, howling. |

When she came back, Coyote heard his wife. He uttered his war cry | and ran out quickly. He split a young tree | to make a bow, and made a small bow for his son. ‖ He made a hammer for his wife,   40 and for his daughter | a small hammer. He said to them: "Let us go now! | I'll go against my fellow man;—you go against | your fellow woman.—You shall go against | your boy companion,—and you shall go against your girl ‖ companion." Then they started. They reached   45 there, and he said | to his wife: "Open the door for me." | Then Dog opened the door for her husband, and he shot into the tent of | Panther. He shot in again. Then Coyote attacked Panther. | He took him and held him. When he knew that ‖ he was dead, he put him down.   50 He looked, and just then (the female Panther) was taking | the hammer from his wife. She was about to strike her with it. | Then he attacked her and took it from that woman. He took it from her and | struck her down. He looked, and just then his son was about to shoot | with his bow. (The Panther boy) took it from him. ‖ (Coy-   55 ote) shot him and killed him. He looked at his daughter, and saw |

qa'ₐleˑn paɫ tsχa'ɫsⱥɫqanɫaɫtᵢmuɫⱬ's̩neˑ poʹponana.ⱬ'seˑs. mitᵢ-
yaʹχₐneˑ q!akpakitχoʹᵤneˑ neᵢs na.uteˑnaʹnas. taʹχas naoʹkteˑ.

    Qakⱬ'ɫneˑ: "taʹχas kⱬnɫaʹqlakⱬʹnˑkiˑɫ. maₐts umⱬtskⱬʹnˑkiˑɫ."
taʹχas nʹⱬtkⱬʹneˑ. q!apⱥɫuqɫaʹₐteˑ. taʹχas qanaχaʹʹmneˑ ts!ⱬna-
60 wⱬsʹnokᵘeᵢteˑ qoᵤs qaₐnk!aɫuˑk!oʹpokaʹmseˑ. taʹχas tᵢnaɫu-
nⱬʹs̩neˑ neᵢs aₐˑkⱬt.ɫa.ⱬ'seˑs swaʹs skⱬʹnˑkuˑts. taʹχas nʹⱬtkaχanⱬʹ-
ɫeˑk. tⱬnamuʹʹeˑs sɫaːtⱬnts!ⱬtk!oʹᵤseˑ; aɫaqaʹɫt!eˑs sɫaːtⱬɫⱬʹtkⱬns
aₐˑquʹqt!eˑs.

(b) COYOTE PRETENDS TO BE PANTHER

    Taʹχas tsⱬɫmiʹyⱬt.s nʹuʹpχₐneˑ χaʹₐltsin at yaqₐnaʹpskeˑ
65 swaʹs. taʹχas tsχanaʹₐteˑ skⱬʹnˑkuˑts. taʹχas qaqₐnaʹₐne-
neᵢs at yaqaqₐnaʹpskeˑ swaʹs. nowoʹᵤkᵤneˑ q!aʹpeˑ. taʹχas
naqankⱬᵢneˑ. naqankⱬʹɫneˑ iyaʹmˑoʹs. qakeʹᵢneˑ: "o: kumᴇ-
noˑʹktsaʹykiˑɫ." nʹoˑʹk!ᵤniɫhuɫpaɫnitⱬʹtᵢneˑ neᵢs aₐˑkᵤwok.ɫeʹeˑts
nak.ɫe.ⱬʹtseˑ ˑχunanoqokupkⱬʹnˑeˑ. tkaʹχams iyaʹmˑo; neᵢs
70 uʹsʹmeˑks mⱬtχₐneˑ. taʹχas tsχaʹkiˑɫtkaχaʹʹmseˑ. ⱬnaʹhaⱡks
aʹₐkeˑ ɫamⱬʹtχₐneˑ. taʹχas sⱬɫaɫoʹᵤseˑ. q!uʹmneᵢneˑ. kan-
miʹyit nʹanaχaʹʹmneˑ. skeˑⱬsqaʹpseˑ nⱬʹlyaˑps. nomⱬtseʹᵢteˑ.
taʹχas nʹitkaχanⱬʹɫeˑk skⱬʹnˑkuˑts. χaʹₐltsin ɫots!ⱬtk!oʹᵤneˑ;
aɫaqaʹɫt!eˑs nʹⱬtkⱬnseˑ aₐˑquʹqt!eˑs. tsⱬɫmiˑʹyⱬt.s aʹₐkeˑ
75 ɫaqaqₐnaʹₐneˑ. qakeʹᵢneˑ skⱬʹnˑkuˑts: "aː, ksakqaˑnq!aⱡeˑɫ-
nⱬʹkeˑt." taʹχas ɫahaˑʹqankⱬʹɫneˑ iyaʹmˑoʹs. taʹχas ktkaʹ-
χaʹms mⱬtχₐneˑ. taʹχas tsχakiɫmⱬʹtχₐneˑ; q!aʹpeʹs mⱬtχₐneˑ,
mⱬtχₐneˑ, mⱬtχₐneˑ. neᵢs yisaʹskeˑ aʹₐk!eˑs qaʹɫeˑn ɫaɫoʹᵤseˑ,
aʹₐkeˑ k.ɫaʹɫoᵤs neᵢs iyaʹmˑoʹs. q!uʹmneʹᵢneˑ. kanmiˑʹyⱬt.s
80 nʹanaχaʹʹmneˑ. nʹaskikqaʹpseˑ, neᵢs ma ksukᵘakaʹteˑs ɫoʹᵤseˑ.

    Tsⱬɫmiˑʹyⱬt nuɫpaɫnitⱬʹɫneˑ aₐˑk.ɫuk.ɫeˑʹit.s neᵢs aₐˑkᵤwok.ɫeˑʹets.
nⱬɫkⱬʹkseˑ neᵢs ma kmⱬʹtχa sⱬɫukaχaˑʹnmetⱬʹt.seˑ. taʹχas
ktsⱬɫmiˑʹyⱬt.s qak.ɫaʹmneˑ iyaʹmˑoˑ: "ⱬnqa.ⱬʹnˑeˑ swaʹ. sⱬɫʹaqakᵢna-
waʹs̩neˑ. ts!ⱬnaʹkiˑɫ. hⱬntstseᵢkatkⱬʹɫneˑ qaʹɫa keʹeˑn." ts!ⱬnaʹχeˑ
85 kanuʹq!ɫaqɫenaʹna. k.ɫaʹχaˑm neᵢs qanaʹχeˑ yaqanawiˑtso-
mⱬʹskeˑ. nʹaqɫuʹk!ᵤneˑ nʹuʹktok.ɫe.ⱬʹt.seˑ. qaoˇχaʹχeˑ. nʹuʹpχₐneˑ
sanmoχunaʹkseˑ swaʹs aɫaqaɫtⱬʹtᵢmoʹs. qaoˇχaʹχeˑ aₐˑkⱬt.ɫa.ⱬʹseˑs.
tⱬnawⱬtskⱬʹkᵢneˑ. nʹuʹpχₐneˑ paɫ nʹⱬʹnseˑ skⱬʹnˑkuˑts. taʹχas ɫats!ⱬnaʹχeˑ ɫaqawuʹliˑɫqanaʹχeˑ t!anukqɫoʹᵤkᵘneˑ. qakeʹᵢneˑ skⱬʹnˑ-
90 kuˑts: "hóy, qaʹpsins k!uʹpski iyaʹmˑu." aːnuwunikⱬʹt.seˑ
aːnʹiɫqaˑʹhaks aʹₐkeˑ ɫatɫaʹnukqɫoʹᵤkᵤneˑ. aʹₐkeˑ ɫaqakeʹᵢneˑ
skⱬʹnˑkuˑts: "hóy, k!oˑʹkᵤnaˑk iyaʹmˑu." taʹχas ɫaɫaχaʹχeˑ
kaʹnuq!ɫaqɫenaʹna. aʹₐkeˑ nʹⱬk!namuʹʹeˑs qakⱬʹɫneˑ: "paɫ
ɫaqa.ⱬʹnˑeˑ swaʹ, paɫ nʹⱬʹnˑeˑ skⱬʹnˑkuˑts. huwuʹkqᵤneˑ swaʹ aɫa-
95 qaɫtⱬʹtᵢmuˑ saˑnmoχoʹᵤmeˑk. paɫ nʹoʹᵤktⱬʹneˑ."

    Qakeʹᵢneˑ q!aʹpeˑ iyaʹmˑu: "hulsaˑniɫwⱬynataʹla skⱬʹnˑkuˑts."
q!aʹpeˑ qakeʹᵢneˑ: "hoʹya." taʹχas ɫaowoˑʹkᵤneˑ skⱬʹnˑkuˑts

that she was about to be struck with her little hammer. | (Coyote) attacked that girl and knocked her down. He had killed them all. |

He said to them: "Now pull their skins off. Don't tear them." | They did so. They skinned them entirely. Then they put them outside. ‖ They dragged them to an old fallen stump, and | Coyote 60 moved into Panther's tent. Then he put feathers on his arrows. | His wife scraped the fat off the skin, and his children cleaned | the guts. |

(b) COYOTE PRETENDS TO BE PANTHER

Then it was evening. Dog knew what Panther used to do, ‖ and 65 she told Coyote about it. Then they did | what Panther used to do. He arose, and called all of them. | He called the Game. He said: "Oh, | come down quickly!" At once they heard noise coming down from the mountains. | They put pitchwood on the fire, and the Game came in. ‖ The first one he shot. They began to come in, and the 70 last one | he also shot. Then there was no more. They slept. | The following morning they went out, and there were two sheep lying there. He skinned them. | Then Coyote put feathers on his arrow. Dog cleaned | the fat off the skin, and the children cleaned the guts. When it was dark, Coyote ‖ did the same. He said: "Oh, it's no use 75 to try to do what you ought to do!" | Again he called the Game. Then, | when it came in, he shot. He kept on shooting all. | He shot, he shot, he shot, until his arrows were spent | and there was no more game. Then he slept. On the following morning ‖ he went out. 80 There were only two of them. The big number (which he had shot) were not there. |

In the evening he heard a sound on the mountains. | Those whom he had shot were making a noise. It was the noise of their suffering. | Then in the evening the Game Animals said to one another: "That is not Panther. Why does he do that to us? | Go and look and see who it is." Little Flathorn started. ‖ When he arrived, he 85 went where the wind was blowing. | He smelled a stench. He went there, and saw | Panther and his children piled up. He came to his tent, | looked in, and saw that Coyote was there. Then | he started back. He was not far away when he began to snort. Coyote said: ‖ "Oh, what does the Game say?" After a little while, | when he was 90 farther away, he snorted again; and Coyote said again: | "Oh, the Game found something!" Then Little Flathorn got back | and told his relatives: | "That is not Panther; it is Coyote. I found Panther ‖ 95 and his children piled up there, all killed." |

Then all the Game Animals said: "Let us make war on Coyote!" | All said: "Well." Then Coyote and his children arose. | He called

ała·qałtɛ'tᵢmu. ta'χas łaha·qankɛ'łne· iya'm·u·'s. ta'χas
nułpałnetɛ't ᵢne· aₐ'kik.łe'et.s neᵢs n'a'ₐta·'s aₐ'k ᵤwok.łe·'et.s.
100 qałwi'yne· skɛ'n·ku·ts: "ktsχałsɛts!ka·ł'o'kᵘas iya'm·u·'s."
n'ok!uniłwat!no'k!ᵤne·. q!a'pe· iya'm·u q!a'piłwat!no'k!ᵘin-
χa'łne· skɛ'n·ku·ts. ta'χas n'u'pχₐne· skɛ'n·ku·ts pał sɛlsa·nił-
wiynata'pse· iya'm·u·'s. ta'χas n'o'k!ᵤnɛ'ɛtɛEmu'ma·łqana'-
me·k neᵢs at yaqaqana'ₐke· wanaqₐna'me·k. nutsqanq!łała'ₐ-
105 kinχa'me·k. n'apa'k!e·nłoᵤk!onemu'ne· ma'ₐka·'s aₐ'kɛnuq!-
ma'ₐna's. ta'χa·s na·łat.łɛnq!oyło·ka'me·k. ta'χas naqa'nkikqa'me·k. ta'χa·s q!a'pe·ł'ᵕmi'tsit.łaχumu'łne· no'ᵤkᵘeys. ta'-
χas q!akpakitχo'ᵤłne· q!uta'ptse·k!. ta'χas qałsaqa'pte·k mɛsqoło'ᵤwum ała·kinɛ'k!tᵢmo. qa'kqanq!ła'ła·nk!a'te·k. taχas a'ₐ'ke·
110 q!akpakitχo'ᵤłne· mɛsqoło'ᵤwum. ta'χas n'asqa'pte·k tɛlnamo'ᵤ-
tᵢmo skɛ'n·ku·ts. qa'ₐkɛsqank!a'te·k. ta'χas a'ₐ'ke· q!akpakit-
χo'ᵤłne· χa'ₐltsin. n'uk!qape'ᵢne· skɛ'n·ku·ts. qakqa·nkeᵢkqa'-
me·k. ta'χa·s łało'ᵤne· no'ᵤkᵘey neᵢs n'a'ₐta·'s a'ₐ'kuk.łe·'e't.s.
ta'χas łaqawa·t!e·no'ᵤk!ᵤne· iya'm·u. ta'χas at łatsukokᵘɛ'n·e·,
115 at wune·ke·'t.se· ławu'kᵘqa no'ᵤkᵘeys. ta'χas łało'ᵤne·. qa·-
wɛsqa'ₐne· skɛ'n·ku·ts. ta'χas sɛlqata·'nuk!nɛ'łne·.

Qoᵤs łaqana'χe· kanuq!łaqle·na'na. qa·kqa'pse· aₐ'kɛnuqła'ₐ-
nuks tsaqona'se· ts!ɛnał'unałałtᵢmu'n·e· skɛ'n·ku·ts. qake'ᵢne·:
"ho'ya, hakɛłwɛtskɛ'tki·ł skɛ'n·ku·ts." qa·wɛsqa'ₐne· skɛ'n·-
120 ku·ts. nułpa'łne· nałuk.łee·'tse·. qake'ᵢne·: "hóy." pał kpaqtse·
na'na neᵢ no'ᵤkᵘey nała·t.łoᵤk.litɛ'łe·k n'iłkɛ'kse· neᵢs qałmaq!-
ała''mne· skɛ'n·ku·ts. sqa'nq!a·łk!apałtᵢya'χₐne· neᵢs kałuk.-
litɛ'ke·s. maqku'pła·'mχomo'łne·. q!akpakitχo'ᵤłne· skɛ'n·ku·ts.
sa·ka'χmoχu'n·e. aₐ'kᵢnɛnmoχo''e·s qake'ᵢne·: "kuł'inqa'pte·k
125 aₐ'kɛnu·q!ᵕła·k!a'ₐko·." qakaχₐmoχu'ne· aₐ'kɛnu·q!ᵕła·k!a'ₐko·.
sɛnmɛtu'kse· qa·'oχałχunaku'n·e· neᵢ aₐ'kɛnu·q!ᵕłak!a'ₐko·.

(c) COYOTE STEALS THE SALMON

Ts!ɛnaqu'ne·. qa·naqu'ne·. sa·k.łunamɛ'sᵢne·. sɛnkɛtsqa'pse·.
qao·χałtsinoqo'ᵤme·k. at yaqa'o·χałqsa·k!ołɛ'ske·. qawɛsaqa'ₐne·
na·utekɛ'ste·k. ts!ɛnyaχha·k!o'ᵤne·. n'u'pχₐne· neᵢs łoᵤk!ᵤs so'ᵤ-
130 kse·. qake'ᵢne·: "ho'ya·'s hułtsu'ᵤkᵘa·t. ktsχa·ł'e·n' kaa'tsu."
ts!ɛnałkɛ'n·e·. ta'χas n'o·qo·χakɛ'n·e· kia'kχo·'s neᵢs atsu''we·s.[1]
qao·ka'χₐne·. tsɛlmi·'yɛt q!ayakɛ'n·e·, ktsiłm·i'yɛt ta'χas n'ɛ'kᵢne·
skɛ'n·ku·ts neᵢs kia'kχo·'s. n'aqsanaχa''mne· neᵢs na·u'te·s. kanmi''yɛt.s n'u'pχₐne· neᵢs atsu''we·s n'aqsa·kɛłkɛ'n·e· nao·'k!ᵘe·.
135 qak.ła'pse· ała'e·s: "qe·'na·, nɛlɛn'o·kᵘa'χₐne· ka·kᵤwɛsen·a'ła."
ta'χas la·u'pkaqkᵢnɛ'łne· ya'qa. łae·kɛ'łne·. tsɛlmi·'yɛt.s a'ₐ'ke·
łaq!a·yakɛ'n·e· kᵤwɛse'n'e·s. kq!u''mne· skɛ'n·ku·ts a'ₐ'ke·
łaɛ'kᵢne· neᵢs kia'kχo·'s k!oqoha'kqa·ps. k!o·'kχa n'aqsa-

again for Game.   Then | noise was heard high up on the mountains.‖
Coyote thought the Game would begin to come down, | but all at once 100
all the Game Animals threw down stones.   They all threw stones at |
Coyote.   Then Coyote knew that | the Game Animals were making
war on him.   At once he got ready. | He did as he always does when
going to war.   He put stripes on himself ‖ and pinned tail feathers 105
of the red flicker on himself. | Then he gave a war cry and jumped
sideways. | His whole tent was torn up by the stones. | His son
Q!uta′ptsek! was knocked down.   Then three, Misqoło′wum | and her
parents, were left over.   They were jumping back and forth.   Then ‖
Misqoło′wum was knocked down.   Now two were left, Coyote and 110
his wife. | They two jumped back and forth.   Then Dog also was
knocked down, | and Coyote alone was left over.   He was jumping
back and forth. | Then there were no more stones up on the moun-
tain, | and the Game Animals did not roll down any more.   They
picked up some more, ‖ and after some time they found stones.   Then 115
there were no more.   Coyote was standing there. | They could not
kill him. |

   Little Flathorn went that way.   There a small sharp flat stone
was lying. | He hit Coyote with it.   He said: | "Well, look out,
Coyote!"   Coyote was standing there. ‖ He heard a noise.   He said: 120
"Hey!"   It was a | thin stone which made the noise.   Then he put
his | head sideways quickly.   He was listening for the noise. | He was
hit hard on the head and was knocked down. | He began to fall, and
as he was falling he said: "I'll turn into ‖ a piece of wood."   Then 125
a piece of wood fell from his body, and he fell | into the river in the
form of a plank. |

(c) Coyote Steals the Salmon

   He drifted down.   He drifted along.   He came to a town.   There
was a fish trap. | He stopped where they went to dip water.   There
were | two girls, who went to get water.   They saw a good piece of
wood, ‖ and one said: "Well, let me take it to use it for my dish!" | 130
She carried it and put fish into her dish.   She did not eat all. | In
the evening she put it up.   At night | Coyote ate the fish.   He went
under the girl's blanket. | On the following morning the one looked
for the dish, and it was with her. ‖ Her friend said to her: "Oh, 135
you must have eaten all that was left over!" | They took the fish
trap ashore and ate again.   At night they again | put up the food
that was left.   When they were asleep, Coyote | ate again the fish
that was in the dish; and when he had eaten all, | he went under the

naxa″mne· ne¡s nao·′k!ᵘe·s na.u′te·′s. wɛ′łna·ms k!okᵤnu′x̣ᵘa·′m
140 łatsnao·′k!ᵘe· na.u′te·′s. naqsakɛłk¡na′pse· ne¡ aₐ′kinu′qła·k!a′ₐ-
ko·. qakiła′mne· ne¡ na.u′te·: "qináₐ niłin′okᵘa′x̣ane· ka·kᵤ-
wɛse·na′ła." qake′¡ne·: "atoqᵘa·′e·k¡nała′ₐne·. at k!aqa′qa?"
qałwi′yne· skɛ′n·kuⁱts: "a: qake′¡ki·ł, 'kɛnłqa′e·n skɛ′n·kuⁱts,'
kɛnłx̣unmitqła′pki·ł." qake′¡ne· ne¡ na.u′te·: "a: kɛnłqa′e·n
145 skɛ′n·ku·ts." łax̣unmitqu′łne·. łats!ɛnaqu′n·e· skɛ′n·ku·ts.
qa·naqu′ne·.

(d) COYOTE LIBERATES SALMON

N'u′px̣ₐne· n'a′se· na.u′te·′s sakɛłhałq!at!e′¡se· n'upa′x̣e·
skɛ′n·ku·ts. n′ɛtkɛ′nme·k łka′m·u·′s qoᵤs qana′x̣e·. at łǎ′qa·̔-
nax̣u′n·e· pał ktsǎqu′na ne¡ łka′m·u. nupx̣ana′pse· ne¡s
150 na.u′te·′s. qake′¡ne· ne¡ na.u′te·: "qoᵤs n′ɛ′n·e· łka′m·u pał
sɛłso′ᵤkune·. hułmiti̔yax̣na′ła qa′lam·a·tka tsx̣ałsqa′łte·."
ta′x̣as mit¡ya′x̣ane· ne¡ ała′t¡mu. nao·′k!ᵘe· qa·k.łe·k p!e·q!s;
nao·′k!ᵘe· qa·k.łe·k wu′tswi·ts. pe·q! ho′paks n′ɛsnił·ax̣a·x̣e·.
tsᵤkᵘa′te· ne¡s łka′m·u·′s. qake′¡ne·: "hutsx̣ał·asx̣omu′neya-
155 ła′ₐne·." ta′x̣as łats!ɛnałkɛ′n·e· ne¡s łka′m·u·′s. su·kᵘiłq!u′-
kune· ka′qa·ps aₐ·qa′łt!e·s ke·′e·ns nɛtsta̔hałna′na·s. kts!ɛ·
tak.łe′¡kin wɛ′łqaps at kts!a′ₐna·s. ta′x̣as k.łała′x̣a·′m, ta′x̣as
qawɛsaqa′ₐne·. kanmi·′yɛt.s qa·łq!at!e′¡ne·. kanmi·′yɛt.s a′ₐ·ke.
łaqa·łq!at!e′¡ne·. sɛłk!utsx̣o·na′pse· ne¡s aₐ·qa′łt!es, pał k!a-
160 nɛ′ke·′s· sɛłqatałhałx̣o′ᵤne· a′ₐ·ke· pał k!upskiłqa′e·ns x̣ma
ł'u·k!qa′pe·′s. ta′x̣as słaqaqa′pse· k.łaqa·ta·łhałq!a′t!e·. n′u′p-
x̣ₐne· skɛ′n·ku·ts yaqaqₐna′pske· nao·′k!ᵘe·′s at łan·taqa-
he′yse· at q!akpa·kitx̣o′ᵤse· sᵤwa′q!ₐmo·′s. at n′ɛk¡nała′pse·
wałkᵤwa′yi·ts. łats!ɛnao·′k!ᵘe·′s at ła·ntaqahe′yse· at q!akpakit-
165 x̣o′ᵤse·. tunwaka′kins at n′ɛ′nse· aₐ·kɛnq!u′tsa·ks. at n′ɛk¡-
nała′pse·. so′ᵤkse· ne¡sts k!aqa′qa·ps. ta′x̣a·s yuna·nmiyɛ′t.se·
k.łaqa·hałq!a′t!e· ne¡ na.u′te·kɛ′ste·k, o·′k!ᵘqᵤna ke·′e·ns aₐ·qa′ł-
t!e·s. ne¡s tsɛłmi·′yɛt.s nao·′k!ᵘe· at n′a′skik.łe¡tsma′łne·, łatsɛł-
mi·′yɛt.s łats!ɛnao·′k!ᵘe· at n′askik.łe¡tsma′łne·. qakiła′mne·:
170 "ta′x̣as sɛłtsa̔mnaqapta′te·k aₐ·kuq!łe′e·t kuek¡na′ła. ho′ya·′s
hułtse¡kata′ła na łka′m·u x̣ma n′a·̔qa·′nhoq!u′tsko· ne¡s hoła̔-
q!at.łakᵤwała′e·s." nao·′k!ᵘe· qoᵤs qa′ox̣anq!okupko′ᵤne·. qa-
kɛ′łne· ne¡s łka′m·u·′s: "ho′ya·s hoq!u′tsko·n·." ne¡ łka′m·u
tsᵤkᵘa′te· aₐ·kɛnq!a′wo·ks; nuq!u′tskune·. qake′¡ne· ne¡ na.u-
175 te·kɛ′ste·k: "pa·ł siłqa·ts!o·′mqaqa′ₐne·. ta′x̣as łqaosa′qa
kuła′łq!at!nała′e·s." ta′x̣as ts!ɛna′x̣e· ła·hałq!at!e′¡ne·. tse¡ka′te·
skɛ′n·ku·ts qoᵤs ła·″nta·′s. n'u′px̣ₐne· pał skɛkq!nu′kse· pał
słit!qa′pse· sᵤwa′q!ₐmo·′s. qaǒx̣a′x̣e· nao·′k!ᵘe·′s. tse¡ka′te·
qoᵤs ła·″nta·′s. n'u′px̣ₐne· pał sɛkt!qa′pse· aₐ·kɛnq!u′tsaks. ta′x̣as
180 qałwi′yne·: "hułe′ay!" ta′x̣as n′ɛtk!a·mok!o′ᵤne·. qa·ǒx̣a·
k!amok!o′ᵤne· ne¡s aₐ·kɛnmɛ′tuks. kᵤwałkᵤwa·′yɛt.s ława′se·

blanket of the other girl.   Early the other ‖ girl arose.   The plank 140
was with her. | Then the girls said to each other: "Oh, you must
have eaten all the food that was left!" | They said: "We did not eat
it.   How does it happen?" | Coyote thought: "Oh, say: 'May you not
be Coyote?' | Throw (the dish) into the water!"   Then the girls said:
"Oh, may you not be ‖ Coyote?" and they threw it into the water. 145
Coyote swam on and | drifted along. |

(d) COYOTE LIBERATES SALMON

He saw two girls picking berries.   Coyote went ashore | and trans-
formed himself into a baby.   He went there. | A small child fell
from his body, and a girl saw him. ‖ The girl said: "There is a child. | 150
It is nice.   Let us run for it, and the one who gets there first shall
have it for her child!" | Then the friends ran for it.   One was
named Night Hawk, | the other was named Snipe.[1]   Night Hawk
reached there first | and took the child.   She said: "We will both
own it." ‖ Then she carried the child back.   She was glad | to have 155
the child.   She was going to raise the boy; | and when he was big, he
was to hunt.   Then they got home and | staid there.   In the morning |
she did not pick berries, and also the following day | she did not pick
berries.   She was prevented by her child. ‖ It was heavy.   She 160
could not carry him on her back, and | he could not stay alone.
Therefore she could not pick berries. | Coyote saw what the one was
doing.   She put her hands behind | the tent and knocked down
salmon.   Then she ate with him. | In the evening the other one put
her hand back behind the tent.   She knocked at it, ‖ and she took out 165
a fawn.   He ate with her. | That was a nice way.   For many days
the two girls | did not go to pick berries on account of that child. |
When it was dark, he staid with the one; | and when it was dark
again, he staid with the other one.   (The girls) said to each other: ‖
"There are not many berries left for us to eat.   Let us | see whether 170
the boy can put out a fire if our home should be on fire." | The one
then started a fire, and said | to the child: "Now put out the fire."
The child | took a stick and put out the fire.   Then the two girls said: ‖
"He is clever.   He may stay here. | Let us go and pick berries." 175
Then they started to pick berries.   Coyote looked | there at the back
of the tent, and he saw a lake | there which was filled with salmon.
He went to the other side and looked | behind the tent, and he saw
that it was full of fawns.   Then ‖ he thought: "Let me steal them." | 180
He dug a ditch along toward the river.   In the evening | his mother

---

[1] The species is uncertain.   It was described as a bird smaller than a snipe, whose call is " Hust!"

ma'e·s. suku̇ilq!u'kse· kqaha·'q!at.la'ᵃko·. naqsanmi·'yɛt.s at
qaqᵃna'ᵃne·. ta'xas skɛ'n·ku·ts qaya'qak!amok!o'ᵤne· tsɑ̱mi·'-
yɛt.s. qałwi'yne· skɛ'n·ku·ts. "ta'xas kanmi·'yɛt.s kutsxa'ł'ay."
185 tsɑ̱mi·yɛt.s. kkanmi'yɛt.s łats!e·nałq!at!e'ᵢne·. ta'xas łaqa'-
pitsqałwi'yne· pał ta'xas kqasts!u'mqa·qaps xałe'e·'s. skɛ'n·-
ku·ts no·yɛ't!te· sᵤwa'q!amo·'sts aₐ'kɛnq!u'tsa·ks. ta'xa·s tu-
no·xa'xe· neᵢs k!a'łma·nmɛ'tuks sᵤwa'q!amo. n'o·'k!ᵘiłq!a'k-
pakitxo'ᵤne· aₐ'kɛnq!u'tsa·ks. ta'xas naq!akuptse'ᵢte· neᵢs
190 aₐ'kɛt.łana'me·s. neᵢs aₐ'kɛnq!u'tsa·ks xunmɛ'te·. ta'xas
ts!na'xe·. qaₐkiłhałq!at!e'ᵢne·. ała'tᵢmo·. nao·'k!ᵘe· łaqana·-
witskɛ'kᵢne·. n'u'pxₐne· aₐ'kɛnq!u'kups aₐ'kɛt.ła'e·s. qake'ᵢne·:
"a: ma ko·ᵤpxa'mił to'xᵘa ktsxałqała'łke·n's łka'm·u·'s.
tseᵢka'te·n' yo·qᵘałe.ɛ'tke· kakɛt.łana'ła naq!ako'ᵤne·." ta'xas
195 łats!na'xe·. łałaxa'xe·. n'u'pxₐne· łało'ᵤse· aₐ'kɛt.ła'e·s q!ap-
ku'pse·. qo·ᵤs qayaqa'wo·'s swɛsku'pse· xałe·''e·s mak!ɛ'se·s.
pał noku'pse·. qa.u'pxₐne· neᵢs ke'e·ns aₐ'kɛnq!u'tsa·ks
mak!ɛ'se·s. ta'xas n'ɑ̱a'n·e·. nao·'k!ᵘe· qao·xa'xe· neᵢs ke'e·k.
tseᵢka'te· ła·ło'ᵤse· aₐ'kɛnq!u'tsa·ks. nao·'k!ᵘe· qao·xa'xe·.
200 tseᵢka'te· a'ₐke· ła·ało'ᵤse· sᵤwa'q!amo·'s k!aₐqałe'e·t.s pał
sɑ̱qakxanmitu'kse· qao·xanmitu'kse· neᵢs k!ałmanmɛ'tuks.
tseᵢka'te·. n'u'pxₐne· qo·ᵤs słuyɛt!ɛ't.se· skɛ'n·ku·ts neᵢs ke'e·k
pał sɑ̱'ay'nła'pse·. qakiła'mne·: "pał n'ɛ'n·e· skɛ'n·ku·ts neᵢ
łka'm·u qo·ᵤs n'ɛ'n·e· pał sɑ̱'aynława'sᵢne·." ta'xas miti-
205 ya'xₐne·. nao·'k!ᵘe· qananłukpqa'ₐne· naqaps łka'm·u·'s. nao·'-
k!ᵘe· qananłukpqa'ₐne·, a'ₐke· naqa'pse· łka'm·u·'s. qa.u'pxₐne·
neᵢs at ma k!askik.łe'ᵢtsmał pał sɑ̱haqa'ł·ta·'ła'pse·. qakɛ'łne·
skɛ'n·ku·ts·. qake'ᵢne·: "hóy, pa·'me·k łae·sawa'sₐno. naqa'ₐne·
łka'm·u." skɛ'n·ku·ts n'anuxo·'nłatᵢmo'me·k. tsamna'se· łału-
210 qałqa·'ₐtse·. neᵢs yɛsa'ske·. qakɛ'łne·: "hayó:, hó." ta'xas
q!a'pe·'s no·yɛ't!e·t. ta'xas n'iła'n·e· neᵢ ała'tᵢmo. k!aynɛ'łaps
skɛ'n·ku·ts ke'e·k.

(e) COYOTE MEETS THE FISHERMAN WOLVERENE

Ta'xas qa·na'xe· skɛ'n·ku·ts. n'u'pxₐne· sa·nkɛtsqa·pse·.
qakɛ'łne· sᵤwa'q!amo·'s "ma'qa·k, hutsxał'u'pxₐne· na aqłsma'-
215 kinɛk!." ta'xas sᵤwa'q!amo qahaqa'ₐne·. qao·xa'xe· skɛ'n·ku·ts
qakiłhaqawi'łse·. łaxaxe·. n'upxₐna'pse· neᵢs na.u'tɛnɛ'nta'ke·s.
łaxa'xe·. n'upxₐna'pse·. nok!ᵘe'ᵢne· nɛtsta·'hałna'na qak.ła'pse·
ałtsu''e·s: "lu'n·u·'s ła tsɛ'na·'n titu''e·s. ɛsxałqakɛ'łne· ke''wa·s
nö·pɛ'k!a·s." łats!na'xe·. k.łała'xa·'m. qakɛ'łne· titu''e·s:
220 "wa'xe· nö·pɛ'k!a. qake'ᵢne· ałka'tsu kułatska'mi·ł." qake'ᵢne·
a'ts!pu: "ka·'s k!aqa·'qa?" qakɛ'ᵢneᵢ neᵢ nɛtstahałna'na: "słama'ł-
ne· aₐ'q!u'na·qs, n'apa'k!inłuk!unɛmu'ne· ma'ₐka·'s aₐ'kinuq!u-
ma'ₐna·'s. nutsqanq!lalakɛ'nme·k." qake'ᵢne· a'ts!pu: "n'i'n·e·
skɛ'n·ku·ts. at qa.apɛse'ᵢne·. maₐts tse·ka'tke.ᵢł." łats!na'xe· neᵢ

arrived. She was glad, for the tent was not burned. It happened thus several days. | Then Coyote had completed the ditch. At night | Coyote thought: "To-morrow I shall steal them." ‖ It was night. 185 On the following day they went again to pick berries. | They were not afraid now, because their child was clever. | Then Coyote began to drive the salmon and the fawns. | The salmon reached the large river. At once he knocked down | the fawn. Then he burned ‖ the 190 tent. He threw the fawn into the fire. Then | he started. The friends had gone to pick berries. One of them | looked back and saw their tent on fire. She said: | "Oh, I almost knew what would happen to the child! | Look how our tent looks! It is burning." Then ‖ they 195 went back. When they arrived there, they saw that their tent was gone. | It was all burned, and there in the middle the child's bones | were burning. He was burned. They did not know that they were the fawn's | bones. They cried. The one went to get food. | She looked, and there were no more fawns. The other one went there, ‖ and she also saw that there were no more salmon, | and she saw the 200 water running down in a stream to the wide river. | She looked, and she saw that Coyote was driving their food | which he had stolen from them. Then they said to each other: "Oh, that child was Coyote, | he who robbed us!" Then ‖ they pursued him. The one ran along, 205 and gave birth to a child. | The other one was running along, and also gave birth to a child. They did not know | that he had slept with two. They said to Coyote, | they said: "Coyote, oh, leave us something to eat for this child! There are | children." Coyote shook his blanket, and a few turned back. ‖ He said to the others, "Hayo ho!" 210 Then | he drove all of them. Then the friends cried because | Coyote had stolen their food. |

(e) COYOTE MEETS THE FISHERMAN WOLVERENE

Then Coyote went along. He saw people fishing. | He said to the Salmon: "Wait until I see the people!" ‖ Then the Salmon stopped. 215 Coyote went there, | and arrived where they were dancing. Some girls saw him; | and when he arrived, a boy was told by | his elder sisters: "Go to your father and tell him that | a manitou has arrived." The boy went back. When he came there, he said to his father: ‖ "A manitou has arrived. My elder sister told me to come." 220 Wolverene said: | "How does he look?" The boy said: | "He has a white blanket, and tail feathers of the flicker are pinned to it. | He is striped." Wolverene said: "That is | Coyote. He is not straight.

225 nɛtsta'haɫna'na. ɫaɫa'x̣a·'m. qakɛ'ɫne· aɫtsu''e·s: "qakɛ'kse·
katitu'miɫ ke'e·ns skɛ'n·ku·ts. maₐts k.ɫtse'ₖka·t at kqaapɛ'se·'s." ta'x̣as ɫahaqᵤwɛ'ɫne·. ɫats!ɛna'x̣e· skɛ'n·ku·ts. qakɛ'ɫne sᵤwa'q!ₐmo·'s: "ta'x̣a·s ts!ɛna'ki·ɫ. tsak.ɫᵤwa'sₐne·
a'ts!pu." neᵢ ta'x̣a hak.ɫuna'mke· qa'k.ɫe·k naso'ᵤkᵘe·n ats!pu.

(f) COYOTE MEETS THE FISHERMAN SPARROW.

230   Qaᵢna'x̣e· skɛ'n·ku·ts. ɫax̣a'x̣e· saᵢk.ɫunamɛ's ᵢne·. neᵢ ta'x̣a
hak.ɫuna'mke· qa'k.ɫe·k naso'ᵤkᵘe·n mɛts!qa'qa·s. qakɛ'ɫne·
sᵤwa'q!ₐmo·'s: "ma'qa·k hutsqonamɛ'ɫne· na aqɫsma'kᵢnɛk!"
qaoᵛx̣a'x̣e· skɛ'n·ku·ts. n'u'px̣ₐne· sakiɫaqᵤwɛ'ɫse· na·utenɛ'n-
ta'ke·s. k!u'px̣ₐna·ps no·k!ᵘe''se· nɛtstahaɫna'nas. qakiɫɛ's ᵢne·:
235 "ɫats!ɛ'na·'m tɛtu''e·s tsx̣aɫqakɛ'ɫne· ke''wa·s nŭpɛ'k!a·s."
ɫats!ɛna'x̣e·   neᵢ   nɛtsta'haɫna'na.   k.ɫaɫa'x̣a·'m   tɛtu''e·s
qakɛ'ɫne·: "wa'x̣e· aqɫsma'kᵢnɛk!." qak.ɫa'pse· tɛtu''e·s: "ka·'s
k!a·qa'qa·?" qakɛ'ɫne·: "sɫama'ɫne· a'q!o·'ᵤna·qs setsa'ₐne·
ma'ₐka·'s. nutsqa'nq!ɫa'ɫakɛ'nme·k." qakeɛ'ᵢne· mɛts!qa'qa·'s:
240 "ɫu'n·u·'s ɫats!ɛnamɛ'ɫne· aɫtsu''ne·s. tsx̣aɫtsᵤkᵘa'te·. n'ɛ'nse·
skɛ'n·ku·ts. ka·'as n'aɫkɛlkɛ'n·e· k!ɛ'k.ɫe·'s·." ta'x̣as ɫats!ɛna'x̣e·.
ɫaɫa'x̣a·'m qakɛ'ɫne· aɫtsu'we·'s: "paɫ n'ɛ'nse· skɛ'n·ku·ts;
qakɛ'kse· su''e·s k.ɫtsu·'kᵘat. ka·'a·s atkkɛ'ɫke·ns k!ɛ'kɫe·'s."
ta'x̣as tsᵤkᵘa'te· aₐ'keyɛ'se·s skɛ'n·ku·ts· neᵢ na·u'tenɛ'nte·k.
245 yawɛtsɫat!kɛ'n·e·.   ta'x̣as   naqᵤwiɫma'ɫne·.   neᵢ.sts   ka'qᵤwiɫ
qaɫq!anɛ'ɫne·: "paɫ n'ɛ'n·e· skɛ'n·ku·ts; huɫsalɛ'te·tna·ɫa." ta'x̣as
kuɫa'qᵤwe·ɫ. ta'x̣as ɫats!ɛna'x̣e·. ɫaqaoᵛx̣aɫx̣una'x̣e· skɛ'n·ku·ts.
qakɛ'ɫne· sᵤwa'q!ₐmo·'s: "hoqᵘa'tsakɛ'ɫnaɫatɛ'ɫne·."

(g) COYOTE LEADS THE SALMON INTO THE FISH TRAP

Ta'x̣as qaoᵛsaqa'ₐne·. tsɛlmi·'yɛt.s na'wasx̣o'ᵤme·k skɛ'n·ku·ts.
250 qakeɛ'ᵢne·: "x̣ma ɫqsaᵢnma·kᵢnɛ'ke·t; x̣ma ɫqsaᵢnma·kᵢnɛ'ke·t;
kqa'kᵢyam ksanoᵛkts ᵢyɛnkɛ'tsqa x̣ma ktsqa'qx̣aɫx̣atkᵢnu'-
kᵤnam." ta'x̣as kqu''mne· skɛ'n·ku·ts. wɛ'ɫna·ms qakɛ'ɫne· sᵤwa'-
q!ₐmo·s:'"hɛntsx̣aɫ'o·k!ᵘiɫo·'qox̣akɛ'ɫne· neᵢ aₐ'kɛ'tsqa." wɛ'ɫna·ms
qakɛ'ɫne· tɛlnamu''e·s: "qakɛ'ɫe·n' su''ne·s k.ɫqo'ᵤna·m aₐ'kɛts-
255 qa'e·s." qakɛ'ɫne· neᵢ pa'ɫkeᵢ su''e·s. qakiya'mne·: "kɛnɫx̣u'na·'m
aₐ'kɛtsqa''ne·s." ts!ɛna'x̣e· mɛts!qa'qa·s. x̣una'x̣e·. n'u'px̣ₐne· n'o·-
k!ᵘe''se· sᵤwa'q!ₐmo·'s sawɛsqa'pse·. ta'x̣as ɫa·upa'x̣e·. tsx̣a'n·e·.
qakeɛ'ᵢne·: "upkaqk!o'ᵤke·ɫ sᵤwa'q!ₐmo. n'o·k!ᵤwɛsqa'ₐne· aₐ'kɛ'ts-
qa·ps." ta'x̣as n'aₐko'ᵤɫne·. ta'x̣as n'ɛt!qa·oᵛx̣aɫ'ɛkɛ'ɫne··. tsɛl-
260 mi·'yɛt.s a'ₐ'ke· ɫaha·'wasx̣o'ᵤme·k skɛ'n·ku·ts. qakɛ'ɫne· sᵤwa'-
q!ₐmo·s. "tsɛlmi·'yɛt hɛntsx̣aɫ'a·sɛlo·qox̣akɛ'ɫne· aₐ'kɛ'tsqa." wɛ'ɫ-
na·m's qakɛ'ɫne· tɛlnamu''e·s: "qakɛ'ɫe·n' su''ne·s k.ɫx̣u'na·'m
aₐ'kɛtsqa''e·s." qaoᵛx̣a'x̣e· mɛts!qa'qa·'s. n'u'px̣ₐne· n'aswɛsqa'pse·
sᵤwa'q!ₐmo·'s. ɫa·upa'x̣e·. tsx̣a'n·e·. qakoɛ'ᵢne·: "aₐ'ko'ᵤke·ɫ
265 sᵤwa'q!ₐmo. n'a·swɛsqa'ₐne·. ta'x̣as x̣o·'nax̣a''mne·. n'ako'ᵤɫne·.

Don't look at him." The boy went back. ‖ When he came back, he 225
said to his sisters: "Father said, 'That is | Coyote. Don't look at
him. | He is not straight.'" They continued to dance, and Coyote
started on. | He said to the Salmon: "Go ahead! Wolverene does
not want us." | The chief of that town was named Wolverene. ‖

(ƒ) COYOTE MEETS THE FISHERMAN SPARROW

Coyote went along. He came to a town. | The chief of that town 230
was named Sparrow. He said to | the Salmon: "Wait! I'll go to
the people." | Coyote went there, and he saw the girls dancing. |
When they saw him, they said to a boy: ‖ "Go to father and tell him 235
that a manitou has arrived." | The boy started; and when he ar-
rived at his father's, | he said to him: "A person has arrived." His
father said to him: "How | does he look?" He said to him: "His
blanket is white, and he has tail feathers | of the flicker pinned to it.
He is striped." Then Sparrow said: ‖ "Go back to your sisters and 240
tell them to take him. It is | Coyote. Sometimes he carries food."
Then the boy went back. | When he arrived, he said to his sisters:
"That is Coyote. | Your father says you should take him. Some-
times he carries food." | Then the girls took Coyote's hand. ‖ They 245
took him by the arms and danced with him; and while they danced, |
they sang, "This is Coyote; we will marry him." After | they had
danced, they went there. Coyote went back to the river, | and said
to the Salmon: "They want us here." |

(g) COYOTE LEADS THE SALMON INTO THE FISH TRAP

Then they staid there. In the evening Coyote sang. ‖ He said: 250
"It would look strange (?). | Although they have a trap, they are
starving. They ought to be saved (?)." | Then Coyote slept. Early
he said to the Salmon: | "One of you shall go into the trap." Early |
he said to his wife, 'Tell your father to go to his trap.'" ‖ The
woman said so to her father. She said: "Go to the water, | to 255
your trap." Sparrow started and went down, and he saw one | sal-
mon in it. Then he went ashore and spoke, | and said: "Take the
salmon ashore. There is one in the trap." | Then it was speared.
They assembled and ate it. ‖ In the evening Coyote sang again, he 260
said to the Salmon: | "In the evening two of you shall go into the
trap." | In the morning he said to his wife, 'Tell your father to go
down | to his trap.'" Sparrow went there, and he saw the salmon in
the trap. | He went ashore, spoke, and said: "Go and spear ‖ the 265
salmon in the trap." Then they went to the water. The two were

n'upkakɛsiłkinɛ'łne·. a'ₐ'ke· ła.ɛt!qao˘xaɬ'ikɛ'łne·. tsɑmi'yɛt a'ₐ'ke·
łaha·'wasxo'ₐme·k skɛ'n·ku·ts. qakɛ'łne· sₐwa'q!ₐmo'·s: "tsɑmi·'-
yɛts hɛntsxałqałsało·qohakɛ'łne· aₐ'kɛ'tsqa." ta'xas q!u'mne'ₐne·
skɛ'n·ku·ts. wɛ'łna·ms qakɛ'łne· tɑnamu"e·s: "qakɛ'łe·n' su"ne·s

270 k.łxu'na·'m aₐ'kɛtsqa'e·s." qao˘xa'xe· mɛts!qa'qa·s. n'u'pxₐne·
qałsa'se· sₐwa'q!ₐmo'·s. ła.upa'xe·. tsxa'n·e·. qake'ₐne·:
"aₐko'ₐke·ł sₐwa'q!ₐmo qałsa'n·e· aₐ'kɛ'tsqa·ps." xunaxa"'mne·,
n'aₐko'ₐłne·. a'ₐ'ke· ła.it!qa`o˘xaɬ'ikɛ'łne·. ta'xas to'xᵘa· no-
wumna'mne· o·'k!ᵘqₐna kqa'łsa sₐwa'q!ₐmo·. tsɑmi·'yɛt xu-

275 na'xe· skɛ'n·ku·ts. qakɛ'łne· sₐwa'q!ₐmo·'s: "ta'xas hɛntsxaɬ'-
ɛt!qapkɛ'łne·. aₐ'kɛ'tsqa." wɛ'łna·ms qakɛ'łne· tɑnamu"e·s:
"qakɛ'łe·n' su"ne·s k.łₐwa'siłxu'na·m' aₐ'kɛtsqa'e·s." wɛ'łna·ms
xuna'xe· mɛts!qa'qa·s. n'u'pxₐne· n'ɛt!qa'pse· sₐwa'q!ₐmo'·s neₐs
yɛsłe.ɛ'tske·. ła.upa'xe·, tsxa'n·e·. qake'ₐne·: "nɛtsta`hahɛ"nte·k,

280 tsukᵘa'te·n' kɛn'aₐko"'mo· sₐwa'q!ₐmo·. kɛnłupkanu'qk!o·
sₐwa'q!ₐmo·. to'xᵘa· tsxaɬ'omɛtsłu˘xo·natɛ'tₐne· aₐ'kɛ'tsqa·ps.
sukᵘakate'ₐne·." ta'xas xunaxa'mne·. n'upxa'łne· tu'xᵘa·
tsxaɬ'omɛtsłu˘xo·natɛ'tₐne· sₐwa'q!ₐmo·. ta'xas n'aₐko'ₐłne·
q!a'pe· tɛ'tqa·t!. pa'łkeₐnɛ"nte·k n'upkawɛ'siłxo'ₐne·. ta'xas

285 n'itk!a'nekɛ'łne·. ta'xas sukᵘakate'ₐne· k!ɛtₐmase'ₐtił. qao˘sa-
qa'ₐne· skɛ'n·ku·ts. pɛ'k!a·ks naqa'nqo'ₐqᵘa·ɬ'a'sqa·łt.

Qake'ₐne·: "ta'xas hutsłaqo·ₐqana'xe·." ta'xas sɑ·amatka'ₐne·.
ta'xas ktsłama'tka skɛ'n·ku·ts ma'niłyaqkɛ'nme·k.[1] qakɛ'łne·
sₐwa'q!ₐmo·'s: "ma·ts at naₐ hintsqanakɛ'łne·. naₐ k.łuqᵘan·-

290 mɛ'tuk atɛnsqanakɛ'łne·."

Ta'xas husɑq!apqałq!a'nuxwa'te·.

61. ORIGIN OF THE SEASONS

Ho'yas, hutsxałhaqałpałne'ₐne· neₐ pɛ'k!a·k yaqałɛɛ'tke· na
a'm·a·k. qa·hakiłaqₐwu'mne· neₐ pɛ'k!a·k at wuku'tₐne· wanu·-
yɛtna'mots aqsu·'k!witna'm·o.

Qa·hak.łuna'mne·. n'ɛ'n·e· wanu·yitna'm·o. n'ok!ᵘe'ₐne· tɛ't-
5 qa·t! qak.łe·k skɛ'n·ku·ts. tɛnaxa"'mne· tɑna'mu's namatiktsa'-
pse· ke·'e·ks. ta'xa neₐ tɑna'm·u qa'k.łe·k ta'k!a·ts. qake'ₐne·
ta'k!a·ts: "ta'xa·s si·ɬ·ało'ₐne· ko'e·k. pał k!u'pski·łwunɛ'ke·t
ktsxaɬ·uma'yit. kaₐ kuts!aqa'qₐna ła'łoₐ ko'e·k." qake'ₐne·
skɛ'n·ku·ts: "ho'yas, e"łan'. ta'xas tkaxa"mna·m hɛn·qakɛ'łe·ł:
10 'qa'psin kɛnsiɬ'e'ₐ'ła?' atɛntsqatsxa'n·e·. łało'ₐna·m hɛn·o·'kułqa-
kɛ'łe·ł ta'xas ɑna'hak hutsxałqak.łɛ'sₐne·: 'kɛn'u'pske· k!a'qa·ł-
wunɛ'ke·t ktsxaɬ·uma'yit ksi·ɬ·a'ło· kɛ'n·e·k. hɛntsxałqake'ₐne·:
'hé'i.'" ta'xas skɛ'n·ku·ts łaanaxa"'mne·.

Ta'xas ta'k!a·ts qałwi'yne· pał siłso'ₐkse· nas yaqake'ₐke·.
15 ta'xas n'i'ła'n·e·. wɑke'ₐne· k!e'ₐła. neₐ aₐ'kɛk.łu"nam qaki-

---
[1] This is the portage between Columbia Lakes and the Kutenai River.

speared | and were taken up. Then they assembled and ate them.
In the evening | Coyote sang again. He said to the Salmon: | "In
the evening three of you shall go into the trap." Then Coyote
slept. | In the morning he said to his wife: "Tell your father ‖ to go   270
down to his trap." Sparrow went there, and saw | three salmon. He
went ashore, spoke, and said: | "Spear the three salmon in the
trap." They went down | and speared them. Then they assembled
and ate them. Then they had almost | enough to eat, because there
were three salmon. In the evening ‖ Coyote went down and said to   275
the Salmon: "Now | fill up the fish trap. In the morning he said to his
wife, | 'Tell your father to go down early to his trap.'" In the morn-
ing | Sparrow went down. He saw that the fish trap was full at | that
place. Then he went ashore, spoke, and said: "Boys, ‖ take your   280
spears and spear and throw | ashore the salmon. They are almost
breaking the trap. | There are plenty of them." Then they went
down. It was seen that the salmon almost | broke it. Then all the
men speared them, | and the women carried them ashore. Then ‖ they   285
were cut. Then they were plenty, and they were dried. | Coyote
staid there. He already had two children. |

He said: "Now I'll go to some other place." Then he left his
wife. | When Coyote was about to leave, he put himself across the
water. He said to the | Salmon: "Don't go this way. You shall
go ‖ the other way." [1] | 290

Now I have told the whole story. |

61. Origin of the Seasons

Well, I will tell you a story of what happened long ago in this |
world. They were staying at a certain place a long time ago, | and
summers and winters were long. |

There was a town. It was winter time. A man ‖ named Coyote   5
went into the tent of an old woman, who gave him | food. The old
woman was named Squirrel. Squirrel said: | "There is no more
food, and it is a long time | before spring will come. What shall I do?
There is no more food." Coyote said: | "Well, cry. Then if the
people come in and ask you, ‖ 'Why do you cry?' don't answer.   10
When they have all spoken to you, | I shall say to you, 'Do you say |
that your food will be gone long before spring comes?' Then you will
say, | 'Yes!'" Then Coyote went out. |

Squirrel thought that what he had said was good. ‖ Then she   15
cried. She cried aloud. The people in the town said: | "What is

---

[1] This is the portage between Columbia Lakes and Kootenay River.

ya′mne·: "qa′psins k!u′pske· tɛna′mu?" qunaxamɛ′sįne·.
n′ak.lilɛ′hne·, at qatsxa′n·e· tsɛn oᵤk!ᵘe′įse· k!e′įla wɛlke′įne·.
ta′xas q!a′pe·'s n′ak.lilɛ′lne·. qatsxa′n·e· tɛna′mu. quna′xe·
skɛ′n·ku·ts. qakɛ′lne· neįs tɛna′mu's: "kɛn′u′pske· k!a′qałwu′-
20 ko·t ksɛ·a′ło· kɛ′n′e·k?" łaqa.iła′n·e· neį tɛna′mu. qake′įne·:
"hê′." qakiya′mne·: "ka𝒶s kuła·′qakįna′łats k.łuma′yit."

A′𝒶ke· łaa′k!la·k sa𝒶k.łuna′mne· qoᵤsts qa′ha˘kiłkįnɛ′lne·
a𝒶′kiłk!aku′ko·t. ta′xa·s n′ɛt!womła′a·s nata′nɛk!, ta′xas qo
aqlsma′kįnɛk! at naqte′įte· łuma′yitna′mo's, aqsuk!ᵘitna′mo·'s,
25 ts!upna′ku·tna′mo·'s. ta′xas at łɛ·tuk!sa′𝒶ne· wanu′yitna′mo's.
sɛ·′aqakiya′mne·: "ka𝒶s ts!a·′qakɛn·i·ł." qakiya′mne·: "hułts!ɛ·-
nałayna′ła."

Ta′xas ts!ɛnaxa′mne·. ta′xas neį haq!a·n·ukkᵘa′ke·. sɛ·′ɛn·mi-
sa′n·e· nata′nɛk! kᵤwanu′yit, tsxał′a·ɛ′nme·sa′n·e· nata′nɛk!ktsxa-
30 ł′uma′yit. łaxaxa′mne· neį a𝒶′kɛk.łu′′na·m. qakiya′mne·: "qa′ła
ya·k!a′tsq𝒶na, tsxał′ɛ′sįniłqana′xe·." n′ok!ᵘe′įne· nɛtsta′ha·ł.
n′upxa′lne· ke′e·n k!a′tsq𝒶na. qakiłɛ′lne·: "ɛ′snił′a′yen′." ta′xas
ts!ɛna′xe·. to′xᵘa ktsxała′xam neįs a𝒶′kit.łana′me's, n′ɛtkɛ′n·e·
nöpɛ′k!a·s. ta′xa·s kuł′e′tke·n tsxanałta′pse· nöpɛ′k!a·s tsxałya-
35 qaq𝒶na′ke· tįna′xa′m qoᵤs yaqahaq!a′nske·. tsukᵘa′te· ɛ′łwa·s.
tɛnaxa′′mne· neįs a𝒶′kit.łana′me·s. ta′xa neį k.łaxa′xam qa-
kiya′mne·: "ya·kᵤwułɛ′le·k tsxał′ɛ′sįniłtsukᵘa′te· neįs n′a·kałk-
ɛ′nłe·s. tsxał′ɛlqanmɛ′te·. ya𝒶ktsɛma′k!qa𝒶 qoᵤs tsxałqa𝒶sa˘qa′𝒶-
ne· qoᵤs haq!a′nuqlɛɛ′tske· tsxałqawaxamɛt.lɛ′sįne·. natska′łke·n
40 tsxał′u·k!ᵘñił′o′mɛtskɛ′n·e·."

N′ok!ᵘe′įne· tɛ′tqa·t! tsɛmak!qa′𝒶ne· n′ɛ′nse· nöpɛk!a′e·s
k.ła′wła's. qakiłɛ′lne·: "nɛ′nko· hɛnts!ɛ′sįnił′omɛtskɛ′n·e·." ta′xas
neį nɛtsta′ha·ł ktina′xa′m. n′u′pxₐne· sawɛsaqa′pse· tɛna′mu·'s.
qak.ła′pse·: "ta′xas sɛ·′ɛ′n·e· qayaqa′wokᵘanu′ye·t." qakɛ′lne·:
45 "ka𝒶s ke′e·n łuma′yɛtįna′mu." qak.ła′pse·: "neįs q!a′n·e·."
qakɛ′lne·: "ka𝒶s ke′e·n aqsuk!ᵘitna′mu?" a′𝒶ke· tsxaneta′pse·.
nawɛtskɛ′n·e· neįs ɛ′łwa·s. qao˘xawɛtse′įne· a𝒶′kɛnq!o′kups. qał-
wi′yse· neįs tɛna′mu's ksɛ·′u′tįmiyaku′mek pał k!ɛ′sqat!le′et.s.
qa·upxa′se· neįs ksɛ·′ut įmɛ′nko· neįs ɛ′łwa·s. wune·kɛ′t.se· ta′xas
50 tsɛma′k!ił·oqᵘɛnku′pse·. mitįya′xₐne· neįs tɛna′mu·'s, t!ap!ts!-
e′įte· a𝒶′k!lałma.ɛ′se·s. ta′xa·s mitįya′xₐne· neįs kqa′kiks ke′e·ns
łumayitna′mu's. łukᵘ′ɛ′n·e·, n′anałkɛ′n·e·. ta′xas neį tɛna′mu n′a·n-
muqkupnuxunqa′me·k. qałwi′yne· ktsxa·′łtsxa. qa′tałtsxa′ne·.
pał kt!a′pts!e· a𝒶′k!lałma′e·s. Tse·n·upxałɛ′sįne· pał qoᵤs n′ɛ′n·e·
55 tɛna′m·u at wanła′t!ne· at ne·'s qa′nank!unɛ′lne·. mɛte·xa′lne·.
k.łaxaxa′me·s qao˘xank!unɛ′lne· a𝒶′kɛt.ła′e·s neįs qanank!unɛ′l-
ne·, tɛnawɛtskɛknam·ɛ′sįne· ło′ᵤse· neįs łumayɛtna′mo·'s. tseįka-
tɛ′lne·, n′upxa′lne· pał qoᵤs n′ɛ′n·e· aqlsma′kįnɛk! nałkɛ′n·e·.
wanaq𝒶na′lne·. qałwiyna′mne· ktsxał′o·′kti·ł neį ki′ay. ta′xas
60 to′xᵘa tsxał·axa′nxo′ᵤlne· pał qoᵤs n′ɛ′n·e· łaa′k!la·k nuq!ɛyu′n-

the old woman saying?" They went there, and questioned her. She did not speak. She was just crying aloud. | Then all had questioned her, but the old woman did not speak. Coyote went there. | He said to the old woman: "Do you say ‖ that you will have no more 20 food for a long time?" Then the old woman cried no more. She said: | "Yes!" The people said: "What shall we do to make spring come?" |

There was another town, and there they kept | the seasons. After twelve months had passed, these | people would untie the springtime and the summer time and ‖ the fall of the year. Then they would tie 25 up again the winter. | Therefore they said: "What shall we do with them?" They said among themselves: | "Let us go and steal it!" |

Then they started. Now, those up in the sky counted that the winter would last six | months, and that six months more would pass ‖ before spring came. They arrived at that town, and said: "Who- 30 ever | can walk secretly shall go there." There was a boy. | It was known that he could walk secretly. He was told: "You shall steal it." Then | he started. He almost came to the tent. He worked | his manitou power. After he had done so, his manitou spoke to him, and told him ‖ what he was to do when he entered, and where it was 35 hanging. He took some gum. | He entered the tent; and when he arrived, they said: | "Whoever can throw farthest shall take it, after it has been thrown out. | Then he shall throw it away; and the one who is strongest shall stay on | the prairie on the hillside. It will be thrown there; and when he catches it, ‖ he shall tear it at once." | 40

There was one very strong man. His manitou was | Grizzly Bear. He was told: "You shall tear it." Then | the youth went in. He saw an old woman standing there. | She said to him: "It is midwinter." Then he said to her: ‖ "Where is the springtime?" He was 45 told: "It is hanging there." | He said to her: "Where is the summer?" and she told him. | He was holding the gum. He held it in his hand close to the fire. | The old woman thought that he was warming his hands, for it was cold. | She did not know that he was heating the gum. After some time ‖ it melted. Then he attacked the 50 old woman and stuck | (the gum) on her mouth. Then he went to get the thing in which she had said | the springtime was kept. He pulled it off and carried it out. Then the old woman | ran out quickly. She intended to speak, but could not speak. | (The gum) was stuck on her mouth. It was just seen that ‖ the old woman was moving her 55 arms, pointing in a certain direction. They went that way. | When they got there, she pointed to her tent. She pointed that way. | They looked in, and the springtime was gone. They looked for it, | and it was known that the people were carrying it away. | Then they made war on them. They wanted to kill all those who had stolen it. When ‖ they were about to overtake them, another one | 60

kɛ'n·e· neᵢs kałkɛ'nłe·s.   ta'xas n'ɛ'n·e· neᵢ kwułɛ'łe·k pał ta'xas
tu'xᵘaktsxała'xa·skwanaqna'naps. tsǃɛnmɛ'te· qoᵤsaqǃa'nuk,łe.ɛ'-
tske·.   sła·twɛsqa'ₐne· neᵢ ktsɛma'kǃqa.   n'ɛtkɛ'n·e· nöpɛkǃa'e·s.
n'ɛnqa'pte·k k.ła'wła·'s. natskałkɛ'n·e·.   pał ktsɛma'kǃqa tsɛma-
65 kǃe·''se· neᵢs kǃoqoha'kqaps n'umɛtskɛ'n·e. nałumɛ'se·.   qa'tałye-
ku'ne· kqawunɛ'kit k.łałɛ't.łu.   ta'xas sɛł·umayɛ'tᵢne·.   ta'xas at
sɛł'aqaqa'ₐne· kǃɛnmɛ'sa nata'nɛkǃ łuma'yit a'ₐ'ke· at kǃɛn·mɛ'sa
nata'nɛkǃ wanu'yit. nuła'n·e· neᵢ tɛlna'mu. k.ła'lo·s ke'e·k.

Ta'xas husłqǃapqałqǃanuxᵤwa'te· neᵢ pɛ'kǃak yaqałe.ɛ'tke· na·
70 a'm·ak.[1]

62. COYOTE JUGGLES WITH HIS EYES

Ho'yas, hutsxałtsxamɛ'łne· yaqaqa'pske· kǃe·'tkin skɛ'n·ku·ts
aₐ'kaqłilna'me·s neᵢs pɛ'kǃa·ks.

Qa·na'xe· skɛ'n·ku·ts.   n'u'pxₐne· tɛ'tqa·tǃs qoᵤs qaha'n·-
łukpqa'pse·.   n'itwɛsqa'pse·.   qaŏxa'xe· skɛ'n·ku·ts.   n'u'pxₐne·
5 neᵢs tɛ'tqa·tǃs nutsɛnqkupikna'kse·.   ła·ɛtwɛsqa'pse·.   n'u'pxₐne·
pał neᵢ's qanałwaₐhakɛłwɛtskɛ'kse·.   łahatsǃɛna'se·.[2] ta'xas łaxa'-
xe·. qa.upxₐna'pse·.   n'u'pxₐne· ła.ɛtwɛsqa'pse·. pał sɛł'akakɛ'nse·
aₐ'kaqłɛł'ɛ'se·s.   pał sɛłɛktikmɛ't.se· neᵢs yaqanmoxu'ske· aₐ'ka-
qłɛłɛ'se·s qanmuqkup'noxonakna'kse·. n'ɛtwɛsqa'pse· neᵢs qa-
10 nałwa·kɛłwɛtskɛ'kse·.   łaqawaₐkał'ukaxu'se· aₐ'kaqłiłɛ'se·s. ła-
haqłɛ'łse·.

Qałwi'yne· skɛ'n·ku·ts: "hòya'sułtsukᵘa'tmeł aₐ'kaqłɛ'łe·s.''
ta'xas łunikqaŏxa'xe·.   qawoᵤkata'pse· a'ₐ'ke· ła.ɛtᵤwɛsqa'p-
se·.   n'akakɛ'nse·.   n'iktikmɛ't.se·.   nutsɛnqkupikna'kse· a·''ke·
15 skɛ'n·ku·ts mitᵢya'xₐne·.   n'atskałkɛ'n·e· neᵢs aₐ'ka·qłiłna'me·s.
ta'xa neᵢ tɛ'tqatǃ qanałwa·wɛtsła''mne·.   łaqaŏ'kaxu'se·
aₐ'kaqłɛ'łe·s.   pał sił·ałɛtqłɛ'łne·.   tsǃɛna'xe·.   ta'xa neᵢ k.łałɛ'tqłił
qał'atɛ'łne· nu'ktsnaqǃa''nkam.   łałitqłɛ'łne· ˋnuktsnaqǃa''nkam.
tsǃɛna'xe·. qoᵤs u's'me·ks qaŏxa'xe· skɛ'n·ku·ts n'ɛtwɛsqa'ₐne·.
20 qaka'wɛtsɛtsqǃahe'yne· qa·''hₐłin' aₐ'kaxapakǃɛ'se·s.   qaŏxats-
qǃahe'yne·.   tu'xᵘa qanaxu'ne· nuktsnaqǃa''nkam.   ła·hatsǃɛna'xe·
a'ₐ'ke· łaqaqₐna'ₐne· skɛ'n·ku·ts, a'ₐ'ke· tu'xᵘa ła'qǃakpakit-
kǃo'ᵤne· aₐ'ka'xapakǃɛ'se·s.   qałwi'yne· nuktsnaqǃa·''nkam ''pał
sɛłqapsqaqa'ₐne· naqa'ₐne· nuła'n·e·.   napit a·''ke· łaqa'qa,
25 mɛ'ka n'ɛ'se· maₐts ku'tsxałɛ'ntseᵢt ku'tsxałqanaqǃa'łey.'' a·''ke·
łaqaₐhaqǃana'ₐne·[3] skɛ'n·ku·ts mɛ'ka kǃɛ'se·s nuktsnaqǃa''nkam
nas qana'qkupqǃałe'yne·. n'u'pxₐne· tɛ'tqa·tǃs nałkᵢne'ᵢse·
tsɛnkɛ'n·e·. kǃu'pxa skɛ'n·ku·ts ksɛłtsɛnkɛ'neł qake'ᵢne·: ''a:
maₐts qoᵤqakɛ'nu. hutsxał·ama'tiktsɛ's ᵢne· aₐ'kaqłɛ'łne·s.'' qa-
30 tsɛnkǃa'pałtɛ'łe·k nu'ktsnaqǃa''nkam. tsɛnkᵢnɛ'łne· skɛ'n·ku·ts.

[1] The youth who stole the spring was LYNX (kǃo'uqune·).
[2] Pierre: łaₐtsǃɛna'se·.
[3] Pierre: łaqaₐqǃana'ane·.

took hold of what they were carrying. It was he who could throw
farthest. When the pursuers were almost | about to overtake them,
he threw it. There on the prairie on the hill | the strong one was
standing. He worked his manitou power | and turned into a Grizzly
Bear. He caught it because he was strong. ‖ The thing that con- 65
tained it was strong. He tore it. | There was wind. It was not.
long before there was no more snow, and it was spring. | Therefore
spring has six months, and there are six | months winter. The old.
woman did it when there was no food. |

Now I have told you how ‖ the world was long ago.[1] | 70

62. COYOTE JUGGLES WITH HIS EYES

Well, I'll tell you what Coyote did with | eyes long ago. | Coyote
went along. He saw a man | running along and stopping. Coyote
went there. He saw ‖ the man running along and stopping again. 5
He saw | that he was looking up. He went on and arrived there. |
The man did not see him. He saw that he stopped again and that
he was taking out | his eyes to throw them up. | Then he ran to the
place where the eyes were going. The man stopped ‖ and looked up. 10
His eyes came back down, and | he had his eyes again. |

Coyote thought: "Well, I'll take his eyes." | Then he went be-
hind him. (The man) did not see him. He stopped again. | He
took them out and threw them up. He started to run. ‖ Coyote also 15
ran after them and caught the eyes. | Then the man looked up, but his
eyes did not come down again. | He was without eyes. He went on.
The one without eyes was named Snipe. | Now Snipe had no eyes. |
He went on. Coyote went ahead there and started. ‖ He stretched 20
out his fingers and just put them into Snipe's orbits. | Snipe almost
fell down. Then he went on, | and Coyote did the same again, and
he almost put his fingers again | into his orbits. Snipe thought:
"It is just as though | somebody was doing this. If it should happen
again, ‖ even if it hurts, I shall not mind it. I shall just stretch my 25
hands out." | Coyote did so again. Even though it hurt him, | Snipe
just stretched out his hands. He felt that there was a man, | and he
took hold of him. When Coyote knew that he was caught, he said:
"Oh, | don't do anything to me! I will give you your eyes." ‖ Snipe 30
would not listen. Coyote was caught. | His eyes were taken out, and

---

[1] The young man who stole the bag containing the spring was Lynx.

nakaqɬiłkₙnɛ́ɬneˑ. t!apts!akɛ́nˑeˑ nuktsnaq!a⁰nkam neᵢs aₐ́kaqłдˀɛˑseˑs skɛ́nˑkuˑts. ta´χas ławoᵤkat.litɛ́tᵢneˑ. nˀuˊpχₐneˑ sᵤwɛˑtskɛ́nˑseˑ aₐ́kaqłɛˑˀłˑeˑs. wakₙnɛ́ɬneˑ nutsₙnqkupekɛ́meˑk nuk tsnaq!a⁰nkam. łałitqłɛ́ɬneˑ skɛ́nˑkuˑts. łats!ₙna´χeˑ nuktsna-

35 q!a⁰nkam aₐ́kik.łuna´meˑs. k.łała´χaˑm qakeˊᵢneˑ huwałkₙnmɛ́ɬ- neˑ aₐ́kaqłɛˑˀłˑeˑs skɛ́nˑkuˑts. qahaᵛna´χeˑ skɛ́nˑkuˑts. ta´χas k!umnaqaqaˊₐneˑ. nˀuˊpχₐneˑ k.łats!ła´eˑns. qałwiˊyneˑ at ma keˊᵢsoᵤks ɛˑˀłˑwaˑs qakqankikeˊᵢneˑ. nˀuˊpχₐneˑ pał sq!a´nˑseˑ ɛˑˀłˑwaˑs. łukᵘɛ́nˑeˑ nˀoqoᵤχakɛ́nˑeˑ. woᵤkat.łeˑtɛ́tᵢneˑ. nɛ́tskɛ́ɬneˑ

40 łaa´k!łaks. ta´χas keˊᵢsoᵤks. tsukᵘa´teˑ. t!aptsłakɛ́nˑeˑ. łahaqłɛ́ɬneˑ skɛ́nˑkuˑts. ts!ₙna´χeˑ. nˀuˊpχₐneˑ yaₐqakeᵢka´skeˑ nuktsnaq!a⁰nkam. qahana´χeˑ. pał k!utᵢmełeˊit.s, łuqᵘɛ́nˑkuˊpseˑ neᵢs ɛˑˀłˑwas. nˀunaχuˊseˑ. łałɛtqłɛ́ɬneˑ skɛ́nˑkuˑts. qaˑhana´χeˑ. ta´χas łak!umnaqaqaˊₐneˑ. nˀuˊpχₐneˑ naknuχonuˊkseˑ. qałwiˊyneˑ at

45 ma keˊᵢsoᵤk aₐ́qoᵤq!łɛ́ᵗᵇp. qanaqaˑnkikeˊᵢneˑ. nˀupχałkₙneˊᵢteˑ t!aptsłakɛ́nˑeˑ. łahaqłɛ́ɬneˑ skɛ́nˑkuˑts. ts!ₙna´χeˑ qahana´χeˑ. pał at ktspuˊq!ⁿeˑ neˑ aₐ̍qoˑq!ᵘłɛ́ᵗᵇp. paq!ₐmeˊᵢseˑ łaa´psiła´litqłɛ́ɬneˑ skɛ́nˑkuˑts. qaˑna´χeˑ. nułpa´ɬneˑ łka´mˑuˑs sqankɛ́kseˑ. qakɛ́kseˑˑ: "tsúˊàː." aₐ́keˑ naqaᵤnkiyamɛ́ₛineˑ. "qa´psin?"

50 qakeˊᵢneˑ neᵢ łka´mˑuˑ. "naₐs skɛˀkiłˊwдk!ałaχapa´kseˑ." qałwiˊyneˑ skɛ́nˑkuˑts: "k.łaˊqa ławiˊˑyaˑɬ." qanaqankikeˊyneˑ. nˀuˊpχₐneˑ pał naqa´pseˑ ławiˊˑyałs. łukᵘɛ́nˑeˑ neˊˑs kwɛ́łqaps. nˀoqoᵤχakɛ́nˑeˑ aₐ́kaqłɛˑˀłˑeˑs. łahaqłɛ́ɬneˑ skɛ́nˑkuˑts. łaₐpsaqłɛ́ɬneˑ ławiˊˑyałs. qałwiˊyneˑ: "ta´χaˑs kuˊsдˑaha´qliɬ." qaoᵛχa´χeˑ

55 neᵢs łka´mˑuˑs neᵢs ma kaqa´nkiˑłs tsuɛ́seˑs. qałwiˊyneˑ neˑˊ łka´- mˑu keˊeˑns tsuˊˑweˑs. qatseᵢka´teˑ. ta´χas k.ła´χam skɛ́nˑkuˑts tsₙnkɛ́nˑeˑ neᵢs łka´mˑuˑs. łukᵘɛ́nˑeˑˑ aₐ̍kaqłдˀɛˑseˑs. ta´χaˑs łahaqa´pseˑ aₐ́kaqłɛˑˀłˑeˑs. qoᵤs qaoᵛχa´χeˑˑ qaₐkiłyunaqa´pseˑ ławiˊˑ- yałs. qakeˊᵢneˑ: "tsúˊàːˑ. naˑs skiˀkiłwдk!ała´χaˑpa´kseˑˑ." ta´-

60 χas nˀ́ₛaknuˊneˑ. ta´χas qaoᵛχa´χeˑ neᵢ naˑuˊteˑ. nˀₛqaˑna- kₐna´kseˑ tsiya´ˑeˑs. ta´χas nałq!atłeˊᵢneˑ. nˀowoˊkᵤneˑ skɛ́nˑkuˑts. qaoᵛχa´χeˑ. tsₙnˑkɛ́neˑ neˑˊs naˑuˊteˑs. nakakɛ́neˑ aₐ́kaqłдˀɛˑseˑs.

     Ts!ₙna´χeˑ. łaχa´χeˑ aₐ́kдk.łuna´meˑs. qoᵤs aₙnˑiłqa´haks qa´nɛˊt.ła´s tдna´muˑs. tₙnaχa⁰mneˑ. ta´χas nˀɛ́kᵢneˑ. qakɛ́ɬneˑˑ:

65 "ka at k!aₐqanɛ́kit na haₐk.łuna´mkeˑ?" qak.ła´pseˑ qakiłwał- kₙnłɛ́ₛineˑ skɛ́nˑkuˑts aₐ́kaqłɛˑˀłˑeˑs saˀkдk.łukmułɛ́ₛineˑ. aₙn- wunɛ́kit.s tsχałwa´χeˑ ałkatɛ́teˑ. tsχałts!ₙnałχuna´pᵢneˑ. qa- kɛ́ɬneˑˑ: "at kinawasχoˊᵤmeˑk?" qakeˊᵢneˑ neᵢ tдna´mu. "pał kuˊsiłhułˑaˀk.łeˑ; tsₙnyaₐkeˊᵢsoᵤk tɛˊtqaˑt!ts pa´łkeᵢ at nˀɛˊsᵢ-

70 nˀiłhaqₐwɛ́ɬneˑ." q!akpakitχoˊᵤneˑ neᵢs tдna´muˑs. łuqła´ₐteˑ. nˀдqanmɛ́teˑ neˑˊs aₐ́kułak!ɛ́seˑs. aₐ́kuqłaɛ́seˑs qanaχa⁰mneˑ. nˀₛaknuˊneˑ. qawunekɛ́t.seˑ taˑˊχas wa´seˑ neᵢs tɛteɛ́seˑs. nˀa´sₐneˑ neᵢ naˑuˊteˑ. keˊwam qakɛ́ɬneˑˑ: "katɛ́teˑ ta´χas husyaχnawa´ₛineˑ. ta´χasts łaha´qᵤwдna´mneˑ. hutsts!ₙnałχu-

75 nawa´ₛineˑ." ta´χas nałaχoˊɬneˑ skɛ́nˑkuˑts. ts!ₙnałχoˊᵤineˑ.

Snipe put on | Coyote's eyes. Then he could see again. He knew
(Coyote) | had taken his eyes from him. Then Snipe ran away, | and
Coyote had no eyes. Snipe went back ‖ to his town. When he ar-   35
rived, he said: "I brought | here Coyote's eyes." Coyote went
along. | He was poor. He knew there were trees. He thought | the
gum would be good. He felt for it, and noticed gum hanging down. |
He took it off and put it in. He could see with it. He looked for ‖
another one. Then it was good. He took it and stuck it on. | Then   40
Coyote had his eyes back. He started. He saw the place from which
Snipe | had come. He went along. It was hot, and the gum melted. |
It fell down, and Coyote was again without eyes. He went along.
Then | he was poor again. He knew there was a creek there. He
thought: ‖ "The foam will be good." He felt for it. He found it   4
and | stuck it on, and Coyote had eyes again. He started and went
along. | The foam was soft. It burst, and Coyote was again with-
out eyes. | He went along and heard a child speaking. | He said:
"Sister!" He also heard some one calling. "What is it?" ‖ said   5
that child. "Here is a big berry patch." | Coyote thought: "There
must be huckleberries." He felt for them with his hands. | He
knew there were huckleberries. He picked off a big one | and put it
in his eyes. Then Coyote had eyes again. He had huckleberries
for his eyes. | He thought: "Now I have eyes again." He went to
where ‖ the child was calling for his sister. The child thought | that   5
his sister was coming. He did not look. When Coyote arrived, | he
took hold of the child, took out his eyes, and so | he had eyes again.
Then he went there where there were many huckleberries. | He said:
"Sister, here is a big berry patch." Then he ‖ sat down. The girl   6
went there where | her younger brother was sitting. She picked ber-
ries. Coyote arose and | went there. He took hold of the girl and
took out her eyes. |

Then he started and came to the town. There at one end | was
the tent of an old woman. He entered and ate. He said to her: ‖
"What are they doing in this town?" He was told: | "Coyote's eyes   6
were brought here. They are using them to obtain good luck. |
After a little while my granddaughters will come. They will carry
me." | He said to her: "Do you sing?" The old woman said: | "I
am old. Only young men and women dance." ‖ Then he killed the   7
old woman, took off her skin, | and threw away her body. He went
into her skin | and sat down. After a short time her granddaughters, |
two girls, came. When they arrived, they said: "Grandmother, | we
came to get you. They are dancing again. We will take you over
there." ‖ Then they took Coyote on the back. He was carried   7

k.łaxa′łxoᵤł qakɛ′łneˑ neᵢs na.u′teˑs: "hutsxałhawasxo′ᵤmeˑk,
a′ₐˑkeˑ hutsxałhaqᵤwɛ′łneˑ."

Ta′xas k.ła′xaˑm qakeʹᵢneˑ neᵢ na.u′tekɛ′steˑk; qakeʹᵢneˑ:
"tɛ′łnaˑ a′ₐˑke ktsa′qᵤwiˑł." qakeʹᵢneˑ nuktsnaq!aˑ′′nkam:
80 "so′ᵤkseˑ a′ₐˑke tsxałhaqᵤwɛ′łneˑ tɛłna′mu." ta′xas naqᵤwił-
na′mne. ta′xas skɛ′nˑkuts n′u′pxₐneˑ yaₐqaneˑkɛ′tskeˑ. qaki-
łɛ′łneˑ tɛłna′mu: "ta′xas nɛ′nkoˑ hawasxo′ᵤna′m." ta′xa neᵢ
haˑkiłhaqᵤwɛˑłna′mkeˑ at qakiya′mneˑ.:

"aː ksak.łukmoˑ′łeˑs skɛ′nˑkuˑts skɛ′nˑkuˑts aₐˑkaqlɛ′łˑe·s."

85 Ta′xas tɛ′łnaˑ nawasxo′ᵤmeˑk neᵢs yaₐqakiyamɛ′skeˑ. a′ₐˑke
qakeʹᵢneˑ. pał kqa′eˑn tɛłna′mu, pał ke′eˑn skɛ′nˑkuts. łɛtk!aˑ′ł-
mukᵘa.ɛ′tᵢneˑ neᵢ yaₐkiłhaqᵤwiłna′mkeˑ. qakiłɛ′łneˑ neᵢ na.u′te-
kɛ′steˑk: "owokɛ′nkiˑł tɛłna′mu, kɛ′nłhanułkɛ′nkiˑł, pał k!um-
naqa′qa." ta′xas neᵢ na.u′tekɛ′steˑk n′owokɛ′nˑeˑ tɛteʹ′es. ta′xas
90 naqᵤwiłna′mne. n′alsɛntᵢya′mneˑ, oˑ′k!ᵘqᵤna tɛłna′mu k!ɛsᵢniłha-
wasxo′ᵤmeˑk. sukᵘiłq!ukna′mneˑ. ta′xas woˑnikɛ′tᵢneˑ ka′qᵤwɛ′ł-
nam. ta′xas qakeʹᵢneˑ neᵢ tɛłna′mu: "k.łpɛskɛ′nˑiˑł yaₐkawas-
xo′ᵤmeˑk." at nałkɛ′nˑeˑ neᵢs aₐkɛqłɛ′ɛ′seˑs skɛ′nˑkuˑts. ta′xas
skɛ′nˑkuˑts nałkɛ′nˑeˑ neᵢs aₐˑkɛqłɛ′łˑe·s. qaₐkiłhaˑ′qᵤwɛłna′mneˑ.
95 ta′xas n′upxałɛ′sᵢneˑ neᵢ tɛłna′mu łaqaaˑ′psiłpałnɛxu′neˑ. ta′xas
słq!awa′ts′neᵢnaxwa′teˑk. ta′xas to′xᵘa tsłaqawɛ′łpałnɛ′łneˑ.
ta′xaˑs łaxa′liˑłq!anło′ᵤkᵤneˑ aₐˑk!aˑłaxweʹ′ets. ta′xas łałɛtke′ᵢ-
neˑ. n′ɛtᵤwɛsqᵤwu′mneˑ. łaqahaˑ′qᵤwiłna′mneˑ. qakiya′mneˑ.
"tsukomɛ′łkiˑł, tseᵢka′tkiˑł tɛłna′mu. łɛnsɛ′łupekɛ′meˑk." tsu-
100 ku′łneˑ. tseᵢkatɛ′łneˑ neᵢ tɛłna′mu. n′upxa′łneˑ sakqa′pseˑ
aₐˑkuqła′eˑs neᵢ tɛłna′mu. ło′ᵤneˑ tsɛn aₐˑkuqła′eˑs n′ɛnqap-
taˑ′kseˑ. nułpałnɛ′łneˑ skɛ′nˑkuˑts qo′ᵤs aˑn′ɛłqa′haˑks. sɛł′u-
maˑ′tsᵢneˑ. qakiya′mneˑ: "pał n′ɛ′nˑeˑ skɛ′nˑkuˑts, pał qa.ɛ′nˑeˑ
neᵢ tɛłna′mu ka′qᵤwił. pał n′upɛ′łneˑ skɛ′nˑkuˑts, pał tsɛn
105 n′ɛ′nˑseˑ aₐˑkuqłaɛ′seˑs."

Ta′xas husɛł′q!aˑ′pqałq!aˑnuxwa′teˑ skɛ′nˑkuˑts yaqałʹɛtkɛ′nkeˑ
aₐˑkɛqłɛ′łˑe·s.

63. COYOTE AND DEER

Hutsxałhaqałq!anuxwa′teˑ skɛ′nˑkuˑts neᵢs yaqałɛtkɛ′nkeˑ
tsu′pqaˑ′s.

Qaˑhak.łuna′mneˑ. neᵢs pɛ′k!aˑks tsu′pqa at n′ɛtˑ!xaka′ₐneˑ.
at qa.upsła′tᵢyił′anaxa′mneˑ. tsɛn ya·kqasts!umqa′qa tɛ′tqaˑ′t!
5 at n′ɛsᵢnił′ana′xeˑ. yaₐk.łitaka′teˑ at n′ɛt!xₐna′pseˑ tsu′pqa′s.
ta′xa ne·′ hak.łuna′mkeˑ oˑ′k!ᵘqᵤna ksa′han tsu′pqa nowasᵢna′-
mneˑ. qałwi′yneˑ skɛ′nˑkuˑts: "hułts!ɛnał′a′ₐnaˑnᵢ." qakiłɛ′łneˑ:
"maₐts aˑ′naˑn′ ł′ɛ′t!xₐneˑs tsu′pqa." qakeʹᵢneˑ skɛ′nˑkuˑts: "aˑ′
hutsxałʹɛtkɛ′n·eˑ nöpɛ′k!a. tsxałqa.et!xₐna′pᵢneˑ tsu′pqa." ta′xas
10 ts!ɛna′xeˑ skɛ′nˑkuˑts. qo′ᵤs qana′xeˑ n′itkɛ′nˑeˑ nöpɛ′k!as.

along. | While he was being carried there, he said to the girls:
"I will sing, | I will dance." |

When the two girls arrived, they said: | "The old woman also
wants to dance." Snipe said: ‖ "Well, she also shall dance." Then   80
they danced. | Coyote knew what was done. | The old woman[1] was
told: "Now you sing!" Then, | while the dancing was going on,
they sang— |

"Try to get good luck out of Coyote's, Coyote's eyes!" ‖

The old woman sang that which was said. She also | said so. She   85
was not an old woman; she was Coyote. There was no | light where
they were dancing. The two girls were told: | "Let the old woman
stand up. Lead her. She is poor." | Then the two girls made their
grandmother stand up. ‖ They danced. They tried hard, because   90
the old woman was singing. | They were glad. They danced for a
long time. | Then the old woman said: "Let go what you sing about." |
They carried the eyes of Coyote. Then Coyote carried | his eyes.
They were dancing about. ‖ Then it was noticed that (the voice) of   95
the old woman was going down. | She was almost out of breath.
Almost they could hear her no more. | Then she was heard singing
by the doorway. Then she was not heard any more. | They stopped,
and did not dance any more. They said: | "Bring a light! Look for
the old woman! She may have died of fatigue." ‖ Light was made,   100
and they looked for the old woman. Then they saw the skin lying
there. | The old woman was gone. | Only her skin remained. They
heard Coyote some distance away. He laughed, | and they said: "It
was Coyote, it was not the old woman, | who danced. Coyote killed
her. It was only ‖ her skin." | 105

Now I have told you what Coyote did to | his eyes. |

63. COYOTE AND DEER

I'll tell you how Coyote made the | Deer. |

There was a town. Long ago the Deer used to bite the people. |
They never went out hunting. Only the men who were skillful ‖ went   5
hunting. Those who were unskillful were bitten by the Deer. | There
was that town. They were hungry because the Deer was bad. |
Coyote thought: "Let me go hunting!" He was told: | "Don't go
hunting! The Deer might bite you." Coyote said: "Oh, | I'll work
my manitou power. The Deer shall not bite me." ‖ Coyote started.   10

---

[1] That is, Coyote.

qake′ɪne· nöpɛ′k!a·: "tsxana″'tu kaₐs kuts!aqa′ke·n tsu′pqa. ho-
qałwi′yne· hutsxał′itkɛ′n·e·. ta′xta· neᵢ yuna′qa aqɪsma′kᵢnɛk!
naₐs a′m·a·ks kaₐs at kts!aqa′qₐna. pał ktsx̣a′t′e·ns ke′e·k at
xma ktsxał′upsła′tᵢyił′u′płₐps." qak.la′pse· nöpɛk!a′e·s: "so′ᵤ-
15 kᵘne·. hutsxałqak.lɛ′sᵢne·. ta′x̣a łu′n·u. ts!ɛ′na·n′ mitᵢya′x̣ₐ-
ne·s tsu′pqa. hɛntsxałtsɛnkɛ′n·e· hɛntsxał·ukᵘinmɛ′łne· aₐ′q!o-
na′n′e·s. hɛnts!ɛtkinmɛ′łne· aₐ′kuła′k!e·s tsxałso′ᵤkse·; a′ₐ′ke·
hɛnts!ɛtkɛnmɛ′łne· a·qa′t!e·s." ta′xas ts!ɛna′x̣e· skɛ′n·ku·ts. qoᵤs
qa·na′x̣e· at n′a·′q!o·k! tsu′pqa. ta′x̣as at mɛte·′x̣aka′ₐne·. qa·ha-
20 kq!anqłupɛ′nse· neᵢs yaₐqa′kałomɛ′ske· neᵢs łuna′x̣e· skɛ′n·ku·ts.
n′u′px̣ₐne· neᵢs a′q!a·s nak.łuxonatɛ′tse· tsu′pqa·′s n′u′px̣ₐne·
ksɛłmɛtᵢya′x̣ₐnaps. pɛskɛ′n·e· t!awu″e·s. ta′x̣as n′u′px̣ₐne· tun-
waka′se· tsu′pqa·′s mitᵢya′x̣ₐne·; tsɛnkɛ′n·e·. qaoᵛx̣aya′x̣ₐne·
aₐ′k!ałma.ɛ′se·s. łukᵘɛ′n·e· aₐ′q!onan′ɛ′se·s. ta′x̣as nawɛtskɛ′n·e·.
25 q!apiłso·kᵘɛ′n·e· aₐ′kułak!ɛ′se·s. tsukᵘa′te· tsa′ha·ɫs, so′ᵤkse· neᵢs
tsa′ha·ɫs. t!apts!akɛ′n·e·. kuł′e·′tki·n łapɛskɛ′n·e·. qakɛ′łne·:
"ho′ya·′s t!anukqło′ᵤkᵘe·n′ na ke·nłqa′na·n′." ta′x̣as tsu′pqa
t!anukqło·ᵤkᵘɛ′n·e· neᵢs qana′x̣e·. neᵢs qałyuwa·kaq!ałqa′tᵢne·.
tsɛnłakate′ᵢne· tsu′pqa. pał ke′so·ᵤks aₐ′kuła′k!e·s, ke′ᵢso·ᵤks
30 aₐ′qa·′t!e·s. qakɛ′łne· skɛ′n·ku·ts tsu′pqa·′s: "ta′x̣as hosɛłułɛtkᵢ-
nɛ′sᵢne· tseᵢka′ta·m′ hɛnyuqᵘa·ɫtsɛnłakate′ᵢke·. ta′x̣as at maₐts
hɛntsła.ɛ′t!x̣ₐne· aqɪsma′kᵢnɛk!. ta′x̣as atɛnts!oᵤnɛ′łne· hɛn′u′px̣a
atɛntsxałt!anukqło′ᵤkune·; atɛntsxałhosanu·x̣on·qa′ₐne·. tsɛn
ya·kqasts!umqa′qa at tsisᵢniłupłɛ′sᵢne·. ya·k.łitaka′te·. at tsxał-
35 qa.upłɛ′sᵢne·. taxta·′ yuna′qa aqɪsma′kᵢnɛk! pał ktsyuna′qaps
k!u′płₐps a′ₐ′ke· at xma kɛnts!u′pe·ł." ta′x̣as sɛłhołɛtkɛ′n·e·
skɛ′n·ku·ts ke′ᵢso·ᵤks qa′psins.

Łahats!ɛna′x̣e· skɛ′n·ku·ts, n′u′px̣ₐne· tsu′pqa·′s. n′ɛłwa′ne·.
a′ₐ′ke· łats!ɛna′x̣e·. a′ₐ′ke· ła′e·łwa′n·e· łaa′k!łaks. ta′x̣as
40 łahats!ɛna′x̣e· ła.aimax̣o′ᵤne· tsu′pqa·′s. łałax̣a′x̣e· aₐ′kɛk.-
łuna′me·s qoᵤs a·nɛłqa′haks qahaqa′pse· łkamnɛ′nta′ke·s.
tse·n tseᵢkata′pse·. si·łaq!max̣omu′n·e· neᵢs k.ła.aima′x̣o· tsu′p-
qa·′s, o·′k!ᵐqᵤna at k!upɛ′łka·s. qakɛ′łne· neᵢs łkamnɛ′nta′ke·s:
"qa′psin tsɛn kɛ′nsiłtseᵢkata′pkeᵢł; awu′tkeᵢł. at tsxałqake′ᵢne·
45 łkamnɛ′nte·k taxta·′ yuna′qa aqɪsma′kᵢnɛk! n′u′px̣a łkamn-
ɛ′nte·k ławaq!ₐwu·na′me·s at tsxał′awu′te· ta′x̣a neᵢ aₐ′kɛk.-
łu″nam. at tsxał′upx̣a′łne· k.łapska·q!ₐwu·na′me·s k!u′pske·
łkamnɛ′nte·k." qa.u′px̣ₐne· neᵢ łkamnɛ′nte·k kaₐs ł′aqa′ke·.
qak.la′pse· skɛ′n·ku·ts. qake′ᵢkeł: "hó· hó· wú." ta′x̣as łkamn-
50 ɛ′nte·k q!a′pe· qake′ᵢne· neᵢs kułpa′łmił łkamnɛ′nte·k neᵢsts
k!łaqa′ke·. qakiya′mne·: "qa′psin sk!u′pske· łkamnɛ′nte·k."
n′anax̣a′mna′mne·. qakiya′mne·: "tseᵢka′tkeᵢł skɛ′n·ku·ts
sɛł′awaq!ₐwu′n·e·. ła.aimax̣o′ᵤne· tsu′pqa·′s." tseᵢkatɛ′łne·
skɛ′n·ku·ts pał sɛł′awaq!ₐwu′n·e·. qake′ᵢne· skɛ′n·ku·ts: "ta′x̣a·s

Then he worked his manitou power. | He said to the manitou power:
"Tell me, what shall I do to that Deer? | I want to change it.   Later
on there will be many people | in this world.   What will they do for
their food? | It might always kill them."   His manitou said: "It is
good. ‖ I will tell you.   Go on! and if the Deer runs after you, | take 15
it and pull out its teeth | and make it so that its meat shall be good,
and | make a tail for it."   Then Coyote started. | He went, and the
Deer smelled him.   Then the Deer pursued him.' ‖ There was a bunch 20
of little trees in the direction from which the wind came.   Coyote
went around this way. | He saw a thicket.   Deer made noise, and he
noticed | that it would go for him.   He put down his bow.   Then he
saw | the Deer coming out.   Coyote ran after it and took it.   He took
it | by the mouth and pulled out its teeth.   Then he held it, ‖ and he 25
made its body good.   He took grass, nice | grass, and stuck it on.
After he had changed it, he let it go, and said to it: | "Go on, snort!
Go this way!"   Then Deer | snorted and went along.   It put up its
tail quickly. | The Deer was nice.   Its body was nice.   Its tail was
nice. ‖ Coyote said to the Deer: "Now I have finished with you. | 30
Look at yourself!   Look how nice you are!   Now don't | bite people!
You shall be afraid of them.   When you see them, | you shall snort.
You shall run away. | Only skillful people shall kill you.   Unskillful
ones ‖ shall not kill you.   Later on, when there are many people and 35
when there will be enough | to kill animals, you may be killed." |
Then Coyote finished making things good. |

Coyote started on, and he saw a Deer and killed it. | He went on
and killed another one.   Then ‖ he went back.   He carried two Deer. 40
He reached the town. | A little ways from the town, children | were
playing.   They just looked at him, and he scared them with the two
Deer he was carrying, | because they used to kill people.   He said to
the children: | "Why are you looking at me?   Shout for joy! ‖ That 45
is what children will say.   Later on, when there are many people and
when children see | somebody carrying meat, they will shout for joy.
Then it will be known in the town | that somebody is bringing meat.
Therefore the children shall shout." | The children did not know how
to do it. | Coyote said to them: "Say 'Hohowu!'"   Then ‖ the chil- 50
dren all said so.   When they heard what the children were saying,
they all said: | "Why do your children say that?" | They came out
and said: "Look at Coyote! | He is carrying two Deer."   Coyote
was looked at. | He was carrying meat. Coyote said: "Now ‖ go out 55

55 ana′keᵢɫ. hun′itkɛ′nˑeˑ tsu′pqaˑ tsχaɫ′aqa.ɛt!χₐniskɛ′ɬneˑ n′oˑ-
kweʼᵢqapqa′ₐneˑ tsu′pqa.''

Taʼχas husⱺq!aʼpqaɫq!anuχwa′teˑ skɛ′nˑkuˑts neᵢs pɛ′k!aˑks
yaqaɫʼitkɛ′nˑkeˑ tsu′pqaˑ′ʂ.

64. COYOTE AND TREE CHIEF

Hoʼya′s hutsqaʼɬanuχwa′teˑ k!aˑk!ɬanˑaq!oʼχᵤmaɬeˑ′et.

(a) COYOTE BECOMES TREE CHIEF'S FRIEND

Qaoˇsaˇqa′ₐneˑ skɛ′nˑkuˑts. nuɫpaɫnetɛ′tᵢneˑ ka′qaˑps nⱺsta′-
haˑɫs ka′qaps nⱺsta′haˑɫs ksaoˇsa′qaˑps. qaɫwi′yɬneˑ: "huɫts!-
ⱺna′miˑɫ. ktsχa′ɫʼeˑn kaˑ′swu neᵢ nⱺsta′haɫ paɫ kqa′kyam
5 kqasts!oʼmqa′qa.'' taʼχa neᵢ nⱺsta′haɫ qaɫʼatɛ′ɬne k!aˑk!ɬa-
nˑaq!oʼχᵤmaɬeˑ′et. ts!ⱺna′χeˑ skɛ′nˑkuˑts. qoᵤs qana′χeˑ. n′ɛtkɛ′ne
kᵤwɛʼɫqᵤwaʼt!eˑʼs. nʼu′pste skɛ′nˑkuˑts yuˑhanqa′moˑk. paɫ k.ɫⱺt-
q!uχma′saq! tsukᵘa′teˑ aʼɫaˑs. qanakɛ′nˑeˑ aₐˑksa′q!eˑs. taʼχas
wɛɫkɛ′sqɬeˑk!aʼɬneˑ. qaₐnmɛtu′kseˑ yaqaₐnet.ɫaʼₐkeˑ k!aˑk!ɬanˑa-
10 q!oʼχᵤmaɬeˑ′et. ɬeʼᵢneˑs qoᵤs qaʼqaɫχona′pseˑ kwɛʼɫqᵤwat!s
skɛ′nˑkuˑts. k!uʼpχa maʼeˑs k!aˑk!ɬanˑaq!oʼχᵤmaɬeˑ′et, qakeʼᵢneˑ
neᵢ tⱺna′mu: "aː kseʼᵢɫsoᵤk qo haʼmkeˑ ɬeʼins swu′eˑs
kanχaʼɬeˑ.'' nuɫpaɫnitɛ′tᵢneˑ qoᵤs ktsχana′meˑs skɛ′nˑkuˑts.
qayaqana′χeˑ. maʼteˑ neᵢs χaɫtsɛ′nʼeˑs kᵤwɛʼɫqᵤwat!s. ɫaχa′χeˑ
15 neᵢs tⱺna′muˑʼs. tⱺnaχa′′ɪnneˑ. qakɛ′ɬneˑ: "kaₐ kɛ′nskiɫʼaₐqa′ke
qoᵤ kuˇqᵘaʼham ɬeʼᵢneˑ.'' nʼu′pχₐneˑ neᵢ tⱺna′mu neᵢs paɫ
nʼɛ′nseˑ neᵢs nⱺsta′haɫs. ma kskⱺlyⱺna′ₐntstaps. qakɛ′ɬneˑ
skɛ′nˑkuˑtsˑ: "aː ma koqᵘa′keˑ ɬeʼeˑns swu′eˑs kanχaʼɬeˑ.''
qaoʼᵤneˑ neᵢs keʼeˑns skɛ′nˑkuˑtsˑ. taʼχas slaˇqaˇqa′pseˑ
20 ktsoʼᵤkᵘat ktsχaʼɫʼeˑns swuɛ′seˑs χaɫeˑ′′eˑs. nʼu′pχₐneˑ neᵢs
χaɫeˑ′′eˑs ktsχaʼɫʼeˑns nasoʼᵤkweˑns. qaoˇsaˇqa′ₐneˑ skɛ′nˑkuˑts
aₐˑkɛt.ɫa.ɛ′seˑs swu′eˑs.

(b) COYOTE TRIES TO KILL TREE CHIEF

Naqsanmi′yɛt.s qakɛ′ɬneˑ swu′eˑs: "huɫts!ⱺnaχa′ɫa aₐˑkɛk.ɫoʼᵤ-
naˑm.'' nʼu′pχₐneˑ paɫ tsmak!kiyamɛ′sᵢneˑ paɫ tsχaɫʼitkɛ′nseˑ
25 qaʼpsins neᵢs nⱺsta′haˑɫsˑ nuɫpaɫnetɛ′tᵢneˑ qoᵤs aₐˑkɛk.ɫuna′meˑs
neᵢs kqaoˇwⱺsa′qa qaki′kseˑ nasoʼᵤkweˑns ktsχaɫhamaˑ′tkɛts
swinʼɛ′seˑs neᵢs nⱺsta′haɫs. taʼχas sⱺlaqaqa′pseˑ kqaʼɬwiy ksχaɫʼ-
eˑ′tkⱺn swu′eˑs ktsχaɫʼu′piɫts ktsχaɫʼɛ′sᵢniɫtsuʼᵤkᵘat neᵢs nasoʼᵤ-
kᵘeˑns swɛnʼɛ′seˑs. taʼχas ts!ⱺna′χeˑ neᵢs aₐˑkmana′meˑsˌ taʼχa
30 neᵢ nⱺsta′haɫ at qa.ⱺlqana′χeˑ aₐˑkɛt.ɫaɛ′seˑs ma′eˑs. at qaₐqona-
′χeˑ yaₐˑkiɫwⱺlk.ɫunamɛ′skeˑ. skɛ′nˑkuˑts taʼχas keʼeˑns swu′eˑs,
taʼχas nʼⱺlqanama′ɬneˑ. nʼu′pχₐneˑ skɛ′nˑkuˑts ksank!aʼₐmeˑs. keʼ-
eˑns aₐˑkinuʼkweᵢt!ɛ′seˑs kaʼₐkeˑnˑs. qaɫwi′yɬneˑ skɛ′nˑkuˑts: "neᵢs
kuˑ′tsχaɫqaʼₐkiɫʼu′piɫ kaˑ′swu.'' taʼχas ɫaχa′χeˑ. taʼχas yuna′qaɫpaɫ-

hunting. I will change the Deer, and it will not bite you; | but the Deer is wild." |

Now I have told what Coyote did long ago | to the Deer. |

64. COYOTE AND TREE CHIEF[1]

Well, I will tell you about Tree Chief. |

(a) COYOTE BECOMES TREE CHIEF'S FRIEND

There was Coyote. He heard about a youth. | There was a youth. He thought: "I'll go, | and the youth shall be my friend, because it is said ‖ that he is clever." The name of this youth was Tree Chief. | 5 Coyote started. He went along. He met | a mule. Coyote took him and rode him. Because his legs were lean, | he took moss and stuffed his legs. Then | he had big calves. Tree Chief's tent was on a river. ‖ Coyote came riding along on the mule | opposite (the tent). When 10 Tree Chief's mother saw him, the old woman said: | "Oh, I wish the passer-by would be my son's friend!" | Coyote heard her talking. | He went past. He left his mule and came ‖ to the old woman. He 15 entered, and said to her: "What did you say | when I passed there on the other side?" The old woman saw that | he was a youth. She was pleased with him. She said | to Coyote: "I said this: 'I wish you would be my son's friend.'" | She did not know that it was Coyote. Therefore ‖ she took him to be her son's friend. She 20 knew that | her son was to be a chief. There was Coyote | in his friend's tent. |

(b) COYOTE TRIES TO KILL TREE CHIEF

After several days he said to his friend: "Let us go to the town!" | He knew that it was true that ‖ the youth was going to do something. 25 He had heard there in the town | while he was there [he was told] that the chief would give | his daughter to that youth. Therefore he thought | he would make him his friend. He wanted to kill him and take the | chief's daughter for himself. They went along a trail. ‖ The youth did not want to leave his mother's tent. He would never 30 go | to the big town. When Coyote had become his friend, | he took him along. Coyote saw a pit. It was | a trap of Wolf. Coyote thought: "Here | I shall kill my friend." Then they arrived there.

---

[1] Literally, "different kind of tree."

35 nʹ<ne· skʹnˑkuˑts. at qoᵤqᵘanaqaˈlenk!onʹⁱlneˑ. taˑχas saqₐnaʹ'-
neˑ maₐts k.ltseᵢkat.leʹᵢteˑts nasts yaqaoˇχaqaˈnq!ankinakʹⁱskeˑ.
taˑχas toʹχᵘa tsχaⁱˑaχaʹχeˑ neᵢs aₐ·k!aʹₐmes. taˑχa neᵢ aₐ·k!aʹₐmeˑ
natsleⁱʹtᵢneˑ oˑʹkᵘ!qᵤna keˈen aₐ·kaʹk!o. qaʹnam ˑqaʹpsin, at
qaoˇχaⁱaₐqapwaχₐmoχuʹnˑeˑ q!aʹpeˑ qaʹpsin, tsuʹpqa, k.ⁱaʹwⁱa;
40 q!aʹpeˑ qaʹpsin at qaoˇχaⁱʹʹpᵢneˑ neᵢs aₐ·k!aʹₐmeˑs.   qaoˇχakʹⁱk-
neˑ swᵥʹtᵢmo. taˑχas ⁱaχaʹχeˑ neᵢs ⁱaqaˈnank!onʹⁱlneˑ skʹnˑkuˑts
wuqkupχoʹᵤneˑ swᵥʹeˑs.   naₐqapwaₐχamʹtχoʹᵤneˑ neᵢs aₐk!aʹₐ-
meˑs. tseᵢkaʹteˑ skʹnˑkuˑts. qakeʹᵢneˑ: "hyáˑ kaʹswo. hutsχaⁱˑa-
qaʹⁱoᵤqaⁱnuk!nʹⁱsᵢneˑ paⁱ ksⁱwit!k!aʹₐmeˑ." tsʹnskeʹᵢneˑ paⁱ ksⁱⁱ-
45 qoquʹnteˑk. qakʹⁱlneˑ: "yuwaₐkaqanˑmʹⁱteˑn' aₐ·kuqⁱaʹ'ⁿtneˑs.
taˑχas hutsⁱayuwaₐkaknʹⁱsᵢneˑ." paˑ'meˑk skʹnˑkuˑts nakun-
kʹⁱneˑ swᵥʹeˑs. ⁱaqaˈtaⁱyuwaₐkakenˑmuʹnˑe aₐqaʹt!eˑs. sʹt!eˑs
nʹⁱnseˑ aₐqaʹt!eˑs. taˑχas sⁱʹaqakʹⁱlneˑ ksⁱʹaqataʹₐkeˑn. sⁱuˑts-
keʹᵢneˑ. qa.akunχaʹ'mneˑ. taˑχas k!ak!ⁱanˑaq!oχᵤmaⁱeˑʹet yuwaₐ-
50 kmʹⁱteˑ aₐ·kᵢyukwaʹeˑs. q!aʹpeˑs qaʹpsins yuwaˈₐkmʹⁱteˑ. taˑχas
ⁱaⁱʹtqⁱaʹ'ⁿte. qakeʹᵢneˑ skʹnˑkuˑts: "aₐˑke yuwaₐkaqaˈnˑmit-
q!uˑ'kˑⁱo'mak!oʹᵤnam." taˑχas ⁱaⁱʹtq!uk.ⁱumaʹneˑ k!aˑ'k!ⁱanˑaq!oˑ-
χᵤmaⁱeˑʹet. neᵢs aₐˑq!uk.ⁱumaʹeˑs at nʹⁱnqaptaʹkseˑ. k!uʹ''mtsaks.
aₐ·k.ⁱaʹmˑeˑs at qaₐwʹtsq!anuʹseˑ kiaq!akuʹtats neᵢsts nʹiⁱqaʹⁿ-
55 mitq!uk.ⁱumak!oʹᵤmek paⁱ at k!ⁱnqaptaʹkeˑs k!uʹ''mtsaks, neᵢsts
kiak!akuʹtats at nʹⁱʹkseˑ neᵢs k!uʹ''mtsaks. taˑχas kq!aʹpiⁱtsoʹᵤ-
kᵘat skʹnˑkuˑts qaʹpsins. taˑχas ts!ⁿaʹχeˑ. naʹₐteˑ qaʹsnaⁱ's
naqaʹpseˑ aₐˑkʹnuqⁱeʹᵢt!eˑs; nayuˇkwaʹₐneˑ. naʹₐte kiak!akuʹ-
tats. q!apⁱʹhaqoka'mseˑ aₐ·kuqⁱaʹ'ⁿt!eˑs.

60   ⁱaχaʹχeˑ neᵢs aₐ·kʹk.ⁱunaʹmeˑs. tunoχaʹχeˑ aₐˑkinuqⁱeʹets
naqts!ⁱdukᵘaʹₐmeˑk. qakᵢyaʹmneˑ: "hoʹyas waʹχeˑ k!aˑ'k!ⁱanˑaq!oˑ-
χᵤmaⁱeˑʹet." tseᵢkatʹⁱlneˑ qoᵤ kaʹmkeˑ. qawakaʹχeˑ. waʹχeˑ aₐˑ-
kʹk.ⁱunaʹmeˑs. qakiⁱʹⁱlne: "qoᵤs sⁿt.ⁱaʹₐneˑ nasoʹukᵘeˑn." qaⁱ-
wiʹynamʹⁱsᵢneˑ taˑχas ksⁱqoʹᵤkam neᵢs k!aqaʹkeˑks nasoʹᵤkᵘeˑns.
65 ktsχaⁱ'saⁱʹtit swⁿʹⁱseˑs. tᵢnaχaʹ'mneˑ. peⁱʹk!aˑks nuⁱsoᵤkᵢnⁱʹsᵢneˑ
aₐˑkmoχoʹeˑs, oˑʹkᵘ!qᵤna keˈen nasoʹᵤkᵘeˑns. tⁱnamuʹ'eˑs nasoʹᵤkᵘeˑn suˇkᵘⁱq!uʹkseˑ neᵢs keˑ''wam. qa.uʹpχₐneˑ neᵢ na.uʹteˑ neᵢs
keˈeˑns skʹnˑkuˑts. pʹⁱk!aˑks qakiⁱqaoˇsaˇqaʹpseˑ naₐs aₐˑkik.-
ⁱunaʹmeˑs. neᵢs k.ⁱaqoʹᵤkᵘaʹ's. ⁱaqa.oʹᵤneˑ nʹⁱnseˑ nuⁱaqₐnaʹ'eˑs.
70 sukᵘⁱq!uʹkᵤneˑ. nʹⁱsaknuʹnˑeˑ skʹnˑkuˑts. naʹₐteˑ kiak!akuʹtats.
nʹiⁱqanmitq!uk.ⁱumak!oʹᵤmeˑk. at nʹunanuχuʹseˑ neᵢs kiak!a-
kuʹtats at nʹⁱʹkseˑ neᵢs k!uʹ''mtsaks. at ⁱaqaoˇχanuχuʹseˑ
aₐˑk.ⁱaʹ''mˑeˑs.   taˑχas   k!uʹpχₐnⁱaʹps aⁱʹatsawaʹts!eˑs neᵢs
k!aqaʹqaˑps aₐq!uk.ⁱumaʹ'eˑs. at·tsᵤkᵘaʹt.seˑ at ⁱaqa.ʹⁱkseˑ neᵢs
75 tuq!tsqamnaʹeˑs. qawunekʹⁱt.seˑ yanχuʹseˑ neᵢs kiak!akuʹtats.
taˑχas skʹnˑkuˑts yanχuʹseˑ kiaq!akuʹtⁿts, aʹₐke ⁱaⁱitq!uˑ'k.ⁱu-
maʹneˑ. taˑχas sⁱk!uʹ'mnaqaⁱalkʹⁱneˑ neᵢ nasoʹᵤkᵘeˑn. taˑχa neᵢ
nasoʹᵤkᵘeˑn qaⁱ'atʹⁱlneˑ kiaq!ₐnoʹkwaₐt.

Coyote was talking all the time. ‖ He pointed at everything, so that 35
his friend should | not look at the place where he was to step. | Then
they had almost arrived at the pit. The pit was | hardly visible
because it was a trap. If anything goes along there, | it falls into it;
everything—deer, grizzly bear, ‖ everything—dies there in the pit. 40
The friends went there. | They arrived; and while Coyote was point-
ing at different things, | he pushed his friend. He threw him into
the pit. | Coyote looked, and said: "Hya, friend! I shall have no |
way of getting you out, for the pit is deep." He just said so on
purpose. ‖ He said to him: "Throw up your clothing, | then I'll get 45
you up." Coyote pulled | his friend slightly. He could not get him
up with his tail. His blanket | was his tail. Therefore he told him
that he could not do any more, | but he was telling him a lie.
He did not pull. Then Tree Chief ‖ threw up his war bonnet. 50
He threw up everything. | Then he was without clothing. Coyote
said: "Spit up your spittle." | Then Tree Chief had no more spittle. |
It became sea shells. | A sparrow hawk was sitting on his head.
When ‖ he spat, his spittle changed into shells, and | the sparrow 55
hawk ate them. When | Coyote had taken everything, he left. He
had | a shield. He had a tomahawk. He had a war bonnet.
He had the sparrow hawk. | His clothing was fringed. ‖

He arrived at the town. He came out on a prairie, | and shouted. 60
The people said: "Oh, Tree Chief has arrived!" | He was coming
along. He came nearer, and arrived at | the town. He was told:
"There is the tent of the chief!" They thought | that he was coming
to marry the chief's ‖ daughter, according to what the chief had said. 65
He entered, and the place was ready prepared for him, | because he
was a chief. His wife | was glad when he came. The girl did not
know | that he was Coyote. He had staid at this town already. |
When he came back, she did not know that he was (not) her hus-
band. ‖ She was glad. Coyote sat down. He had the sparrow hawk. | 70
When he spat, the sparrow hawk would fly down | to eat the shells.
Then it flew back | to his head. When his sisters-in-law knew that |
his spittle was thus, they took it, and ‖ the bird would not eat any 75
more. It was not long before the sparrow hawk was starving. | Then
Coyote let the sparrow hawk starve, and he had no saliva. | Now,
the chief had made a mistake. | The name of the chief was Golden
Eagle. |

(c) WOLF RESCUES TREE CHIEF

Qao῎sa῎qa′ₐne· ne₍ nuł′a′qₐna qa′k.łik ka′ₐke·ns. qasts!o′m-
80 qaqa′ₐne· k!ana′ktse·k sł′aqał′atₑ′łne· ka′ₐke·ns. kanmi·′yₑt.s
ts!ₑna′x̣e· aₐ′kₑnok₍we′₍t!e·s ka′ₐke·n. łax̣a′x̣e· n′umₑtsłe·ₑ′t.se·.
qałwi′yne· ktsx̣ałha′qa   qa′psin   ła′nyonawₑtskₑ′k₍ne· ne₍s
aₐk!a′ₐme·s. n′u′px̣ₐne· sanaqₐna′kse· łka′m·u·′s tsa῎qona′se·.
qakₑ′łne·: "a: matsꞮₑtₑtx̣ₐna′pₐne·." qałwiyk₍na′pse· ne₍s
85 łka′m·u·′s: "mₐₐts u′pło·. łats!ₑnamₑ′łe· tₑłnamo′₍ne·s. hₑnts-
x̣ałts!kakikma′łne·." łats!ₑna′x̣e· ka′ₐke·n. łałax̣a′x̣e· aₐ′kₑt.-
ła′e·s. qakₑ′łne· tₑłnamu″e·s: "hults!ₑnax̣ała″e·s. sao῎sa῎qa′ₐne·
łka′m·u· kaₐ′kₑn·ok῍e′₍t₍mił. hutsx̣ał′akak₍nała′ₐne·." ta′x̣as
ts!ₑnakₑ′k₍ne· tₑłnamo′₍t₍mo. k.ła′x̣am tse₍ka′te· ne₍ tₑłna′m·u
90 ne₍s łka′m·u·′s. qałwi′yne· pał sₑłqa′psqakₑsqłₑ′łne· k!a῎k!łan·a-
q!o῎x̣₍małe·′et. qałwi′yne· ne₍ łka′m·u: "hałwa′ts!ke₍ł qa′ła
ho′paks n′ₑsₑnłtsuk῍a′taₐp tsx̣ałₑ′n·e· kapa′pa."   ta′x̣as
qake′₍ne· ne₍ tₑłna′mu·s: "huła′łwats!na′ła. qo₍ qa′o῎x̣a′n
kₑnłts!ka῎kitsmₑ′ke·n′. ka′min ne₍ hutsqao῎x̣a′x̣e· a′ₐ′ke huts-
95 x̣ałtskakₑ′tsmek₍′n·e·. qała ho′pa·ks n′ₑsnł·ax̣a῎kitsmₑ′ke·n
tsx̣ałtsuk῍a′te·. na′pit ho′pa·k hₑn′ₑ′s₍niłtso′₍k῍at hₑntsx̣ał′-
upₑ′łne·. na′pit hun′ₑ′s₍niłwa῎sił·ax̣a῎kitsmₑ′ke·n tsx̣ałₑ′n·e·
kapa′pa." qake′₍ne· ka′ₐke·n: "ho′ya." qałwi′yne· ka′ₐke·n:
"pał kₑłsa′han na łka′m·u. kutsx̣ałq!akpakₑ′tx̣o·."   ta′x̣as
100 nalwa′ts!ne· tₑłna′muts nuł′a′qₐna. ts!ₑnakₑtsmekₑ′n·e·. x̣i′n·a
ne₍ tₑ′tqa·t! pał tsx̣ałts!ₑna′k₍ne·. ħe₍ tₑłna′mu qats!e·kₑtsme·
kₑ′n·e·. naq!a′naq!ₐne′ne·. ta′x̣as qa′kx̣ałwasaqₐna″ne· ne₍ tₑłna′-
mu. ne₍ nuł′a′qₐna ła′qawasa῎qₐna″ne·. qaha′łe·n′ qayaₐqa′na-
q!ałe′yne· ne₍ tₑłna′mu ne₍s aₐk!a′ₐme·s. sₑłkₑne′₍se· ne₍s łka′mu·′s
105 nakunkₑ′n·e·. n′e·łqa῎kakₑ′n·e·. ne₍ nuł′a′qₐna ta′x̣as a′ₐ′ke
qayaₐqanaq!ałe′yne·; ło′₍se· ne₍s łka′m·u·′s. qake′₍ne·: "ya:
hoyu῎k!k῍aₐka′te·." ta′x̣as łaana῎kₑsx̣a″mne·. tse₍ka′te· ne₍s
łka′m·u·′s tₑłna′mu. qałwi′yne·: "pₑ′k!aks maon′u′px̣ₐne· k!a῎k!-
łan·aq!o῎x̣₍małe·′et nas tsₑmak!qa῎kₑsqłₑ′łne· ne₍s ke′e·n łka′-
110 mu·′s." ta′x̣as łats!ₑna′x̣e· aₐ′kₑt.ła′e·s ka′ₐke·n. łaso₍k῍ₑ′n·e·
aₐ′kₑn·ukwe′₍t!e·s. k.łałax̣a′łkin ne₍s łka′m·u·′s ne₍ tₑłna′m·u
ta′x̣as n′ₑktuqo′₍ne·. suk῍ₑłq!u′k₍ne· ka′qaps papa′e·s.

(d) TREE CHIEF PROVIDES FOOD FOR HIS GRANDPARENTS

Ta′x̣as to′₍x῍a wₑłqa″ne· ne₍ łka′m·u. qakₑ′łne· papa″e·s:
"kapa′pa, ke′₍ło· aₐ′kₑnq!a′łqa?" qak.ła′pse·: "a: kapa′pa,
115 ło′₍ne· ne₍ n′uła′qₐna." qakₑ′łne· ne₍s łka′m·u·′s: "kaₐs
x̣ma k!aₐqa῎ke₍ka′ke·n?" n′ₑtskₑ′łne· ne₍ tₑłna′m·u wu῎kq₍ne·
tsaqona′se·. namatₑ′ktse· papa″e·s. n′itkₑ′n·e· t!aqu′mo′s ne₍
łka′m·u. nanawₑtsk!o′₍ne·, łatkakₑ′n·e·. q!apx̣o′₍se· wₑ′suk!ᵘs.
łu″nte· a′ₐ′ke ła·ana῎wₑtsk!o′₍ne·. łatkakₑ′n·e·. a′ₐ′ke łaq!ap-

(c) WOLF RESCUES TREE CHIEF

An old man named Wolf lived there.   He was an expert ‖ hunter.   80
Therefore he was named Wolf.   In the morning Wolf | started for his
trap.   He got there, and it was broken. | He thought that there must
be something in his trap. | He looked down into the pit and saw a small
child sitting there. | He said to him: "You soiled this place for me."
The child caused him to think: ‖ "Don't kill me.   Go back to your   85
wife, | then come back with her."   Wolf started back, and arrived at
his tent. | He said to his wife: "Let us go!   There is | a child in my
trap.   We will take him out."   Then | the couple went.   They arrived,
and the old woman looked ‖ for the child.   She thought his eyes looked   90
like those of Tree Chief. | The child thought: "Bet who | will get me
first.   He shall be my grandparent."   Then | the old woman said:
"Let us bet!   Go over there | and start to dig, and I'll go here and ‖
I will also begin to dig.   Whoever first gets down to him | shall take   95
him.   If you take him first, you may kill him. | If I get him first,
he shall be | my grandson."   Wolf said: "Well."   Wolf thought: |
"The child is bad; I will kill him."   Then ‖ the old woman and her   100
husband raced digging.   Oh, | the man was digging fast!   The woman
was not digging fast. | She nodded her head.   Then the old woman
began to dig fast, | and her husband was not fast.   The old woman
just went through | to the pit.   She felt of the child ‖ and pulled him   105
out.   She pulled him away.   Then the old man also | pushed his hand
through, but there was no child.   He said: "Ya, | I missed it."   Then
both went out.   The old woman looked | at the child.   She thought:
"Long ago I saw Tree Chief. | His eyes were like those of this ‖ child."   110
Then Wolf went back to his tent.   He fitted up | his trap.   When
the old woman brought back the child, | she washed him.   She was
glad to have a grandson. |

(d) TREE CHIEF PROVIDES FOOD FOR HIS GRANDPARENTS

Then the child was almost grown up.   He said to his grandmother: |
"Grandmother, is there no sinew?"   She said to him: "O grand-
son! ‖ there is none here."   The old man said to the child: "Where | 115
should he get it from?"   The old woman looked for it and found | a
small piece.   She gave it to her grandchild, and the child made a
netted ring. | He held it outside on the point of a stick.   He brought
it in, and it was loaded with birds.[1] | He took them off and held it

---

[1] A bird smaller than a robin, yellow at the tips of the feathers, with a single feather on top of its head.

120 ҳo'ᵤseˑ wɛˈsuk!ⁿs. qakɛˈɬneˑ papa''eˑs: "kapa'pa". qanawɛts-
kɛˈkᵢneˑ neᵢ tɛɬna'mˑu. sɛnˑmoҳuna'kseˑ tuq!tsqa'mnaˑ's. qak.-
la'pseˑ "ɛtkɛˈnˑeˑn' kuɬ'ikᵢna'ɬa." sukᵘiɬq!uˈkᵤneˑ neᵢ tɛɬna'mˑu.
  Kanmeˑ'yit.s qakɛˈɬneˑ papa''eˑs: "keˈᵢɬo aₐˈk!a'ₐq!yu
qayaₐqa'ɬaˑm?" qakeˈᵢneˑ neᵢ tɛɬna'mˑu: "ɬo'ᵤneˑ." qakeˈᵢneˑ neᵢ
125 nuɬ'a'qₐna: "tɛɬna'mˑu kɛnsᵤwaka'wisiɬkɛˈnkeˑts ҳma ksiɬa'-
qaps." n'ɛtskɛˈɬneˑ neᵢ tɛɬna'mˑu. n'u'pҳₐneˑ sawɛtsqa'pseˑ. qakɛˈɬneˑ: "naₐs n'ɛˈnˑeˑ tsaqᵤna'neˑ." qakeˈᵢneˑ neᵢ ɬka'mˑu: "pa·-
meˑktskakɛˈneˑn'." n'itkɛˈnˑeˑ t!aqo'moˑ's neᵢ ɬka'mˑu. n'anaɬ-
kɛˈnˑeˑ. nuk!ᵘi'nkɛˈnˑeˑ ɬaq!anˑҳo'ᵤnaɬs qo's aˑnɛɬqa'haˑks qaoˑ-
130 ҳa'ҳeˑ. qakɛˈɬneˑ papa''eˑs: "hɛnts!ɛˈɬink!oma'tek." ts!ɛnaqa'yteˑ
neᵢs t!aqo'moˑ's qoᵤs aₐˈk!aɬaҳwe'et.s. qakɛˈɬneˑ neᵢs t!aqo'-
moˑ's: "paˑ'meˑk hɛnts!ɛˈɬuqɬaҳo'ᵤneˑ neᵢ nuɬ'a'qₐna. at qatsɬak.-
la'pₐneˑ." qaoˑҳaq!a'yneˑ neᵢ t!aqo'mo. qakeˈᵢneˑ neᵢ nɛtsta'-
haɬna'na: "yu'wa, yu'wa, yu'wa, kapa'pa. tsҳaɬ'aₐkonɛˈsᵢneˑ
135 iya'mo." naɬokᵤmɛˈseˑ. qa.okᵤnoҳa''mneˑ neᵢ tɛɬna'mˑuts neᵢ
nuɬ'a'qₐna. n'ok!ᵘinq!aɬkɛˈnˑeˑ sɛˈt!eˑs. n'u'pҳₐneˑ iya'mˑo's paɬ
sɛɬtka'qumɬasҳu'seˑ aₐˈkɛt.ɬa'eˑs. ta'ҳas toˈxⁿa ts!aₐkuna'pseˑ.
neᵢ nɛtsta'haɬna'na qunaₐkᵢna'ҳₐneˑ. n'upɛˈɬneˑ. ɬaqaoˑҳa'ҳeˑ.
qakɛˈɬneˑ: "kapa'pa. ta'ҳas omɛtse'ᵢtkeˑɬ." n'ukᵤnoҳa''mneˑ
140 neᵢ tɛɬna'mˑu. n'u'pҳₐneˑ sakqa'pseˑ qayaₐqa'ɬaˑms. sukᵘiɬ-
q!uˈkᵤneˑ. ta'ҳas n'omitse'ᵢteˑ. qakɛˈɬneˑ papa''eˑs: "maₐts
yɛˈk!tan' aₐˈkᵤwumˑa'ɬq!oɬ ɬa'ntaoҳakɛˈneˑn', a'ₐkeˑ aₐˈku'-
qɬa'm." n'oqoᵤҳakɛˈnˑeˑ ya't!aps. qakɛˈɬneˑ: "kapa'pa, a'ₐkeˑ
ɬa'ntaoҳakɛˈneˑn'." ta'ҳas tɛɬna'mˑu n'ɛtk!anɛˈɬneˑ. n'itma-
145 se'ᵢteˑ. tsɛɬmi'yɛt.s q!o'mnɛˈᵢneˑ. wɛˈɬnaˑms n'ukᵤnuҳa''mneˑ neᵢ
nɛtsta'haɬna'na. qakɛˈɬneˑ: "kapa'pa, hutsҳaɬ'ɛˈkᵢneˑ kɛɬku'ɬka."
qakeˈᵢneˑ neᵢ tɛɬna'mˑu: "ɬo'ᵤneˑ kiɬku'ɬka." qakeˈᵢneˑ neᵢ
ɬka'mˑu: "ma kɛnɬa'ntaaҳa'keˑn. tseᵢka'teˑn'." qaoˑҳa'ҳeˑ neᵢ
tɛɬna'mˑu. tseᵢka'teˑ neᵢs aₐˈkᵤwumˑa'ɬq!oɬs. n'ɛnqapta'kseˑ kiɬ-
150 ku'ɬka's. qasɛɬuk!o'ᵤktseˑ papa''eˑs a'ₐkeˑ neᵢ nuɬ'a'qₐna.
a'ₐkeˑ n'ɛˈkᵢneˑ kiɬku'ɬka's. kanmiˑ'yit qakeˈᵢneˑ neᵢ nɛtsta'-
haɬna'na: "kapa'pa, keˈᵢɬo aₐˈk!a'ₐq!ᵢyu ɬu'kpoˑ." qakeˈᵢneˑ:
"ɬo'ᵤneˑ." qakeˈᵢneˑ neᵢ nuɬ'a'qₐna: "ma ka'qaps. ɬka'mˑu hama-
tɛˈktseˑn'." n'ɛtskɛˈɬneˑ. wu'kqₐneˑ. qakɛˈɬneˑ papa''eˑs: "naₐs
155 n'ɛˈnˑeˑ tsaˑqᵤna'neˑ." qakɛˈɬneˑ papa''eˑs: "paˑ'meˑk tskakɛˈ-
nˑen'." namatɛktsa'pseˑ. n'ɛtkɛˈnˑeˑ aˑnwɛɬqa'pseˑ t!aqo'moˑ's neᵢs
ma qa'kiɬyaₐqakɛˈnˑkeˑ, a'ₐˈkeˑ ɬaqakɛˈnˑeˑ neᵢs wa'ɬkᵤwas k!o'pi
qayaₐqa'ɬaˑms n'ɛˈnseˑ sɛˈt!eˑs. neᵢ nɛtsta'haɬna'na neᵢstsoᵤsaₐn-
miyɛˈt.skeˑ k!o'piɬ ɬu'kpoˑ's n'ɛtkɛˈnˑeˑ sɛˈt!ɛˈseˑs papa''eˑs.
160   Neᵢs yaₐqaₐnit.ɬaₐ'keˑ ɬeˈᵢneˑs aₐˈkɛnmɛˈtuks qaₐk.ɬunamɛˈsᵢne
neᵢsts qa.oˑҳaɬtsukᵘatka'ₐneˑ skɛˈnˑkuˑts neᵢ nɛtsta'haɬ qakɛˈɬneˑ
papa''eˑs: "kapa'pa; hamatɛˈktsu kiɬku'ɬka. hutsts!ɛnyaҳaₐ-
k!o'ᵤneˑ." namatiktsa'pseˑ papa''eˑs kiɬku'ɬkaˑps. peɛˈk!aks
n'u'pҳₐneˑ neᵢ nɛtsta'haɬna'na neᵢs aₐˈkɛnmɛˈtuks tsҳaɬ'u'pҳₐneˑ

out again.   He took it in, and again ‖ it was loaded with birds.   He 120
said to his grandmother: "Grandmother!" | The old woman looked,
and there was a pile of birds. | She was told: "Prepare them.   Let
us eat."   The old woman was glad. |

In the morning he said to his grandmother: "Is there no leg skin |
of a yearling buffalo calf?"   The old woman said: "There isn't
any."   The old man said: ‖ "Old woman, do you bring it, that there 125
may be some!" | The old woman looked for it.   She saw some.   She
said to him: | "Here it is.   It is a little piece."   The child said: |
"Give it, anyhow."   The child made the netted ring.   He took it
out. | He opened the door a little farther.   He went there. ‖ He said 130
to his grandmother: "Cover your head with your blanket."   Then
he began to roll | the netted ring to the door.   He said to the ring: |
"Surprise them a little; the old man does not like me." | Then the
netted ring rolled along there.   The boy said: | "Go away, go away,
go away, grandmother!   The game will hook you." ‖ There was noise 135
of running, but the old woman and the | old man would not get up.
When he threw back his blanket, he saw the game | jumping into the
tent.   It was about to hook them.   Then the | boy threw his lance
and killed it.   He went there. | He said to her: "Grandmother, cut
it up."   The old woman arose, ‖ and saw a yearling.   She was glad. | 140
Then she skinned it.   He said to his grandmother: "Don't | spill the
guts.   Put them behind in the tent, and also the hair." | She put the
coagulated blood inside.   He said to her: "Grandmother, put it also
behind in the tent." | Then the old woman cut it up and dried the
meat. ‖ In the evening they slept.   Early next morning the boy 145
arose, | and he said: "Grandmother, I'll eat pemmican." | The old
woman said: "There is no pemmican."   The | child said: "You put
it away.   Look!"   The old woman went there. | She looked at the
guts.   They had become pemmican. ‖ His grandmother took a piece, 150
and also the old man, | and they all ate pemmican.   In the morning
the boy said: | "Grandmother, is there no edge piece of the skin of a
buffalo cow?"   She said: | "There is none."   The old man said:
"There is some; give it to the child." | She looked and found it.
She said to her grandson: "There is a ‖ small piece."   He said to his 155
grandmother: "Anyway, give it to me." | She gave it to him.   He
made a larger netted ring, | the same as before, and he made it in the
same way as the day before, when he killed | the yearling.   That was
his blanket.   On the same day the boy | killed a cow and made a
blanket for his grandmother. ‖

Across the river from where the tent was there was the town | 160
where Coyote was married.   The youth said to | his grandmother:
"Grandmother, give me pemmican; I'll draw water." | His grand-
mother gave him pemmican. | The youth knew already that at the

165 naso'ₐkᵘeˑnssuwɛnˑ'ˑseˑs. taˈxassɑtsₐkᵘaˈteˑ kɑkuˈɬkaˈs. ts!ɛnaˈ-
     xeˑ. xonaˈxeˑ. nˈuˈpxₐneˑ naˑuˈteˑs. namatiktseˑ. qakɛˈɬneˑ:
     "ɬats!ɛnɑɬkɛˈnˑeˑnˈ. hɛntsxaɬ'eˑkɛˈɬneˑ. maₐts tsxaɬˈuˈpxₐneˑ neᵢ
     tɛˈtqaˑt!. qaˈk.leˑs maˈˈneˑs 'qaˈɬa k!ɛˈseˑn naₐs kiɬkuˈɬkaˈsˑ' hɛn-
     tsxaɬqakɛˈɬneˑ: ˈnɛˈsᵢneˑɬamatiktsaˈpᵢneˑ xunyaxak!onaˈweˑˈˈˈ
170 taˈxas ɬats!ɛnaˈxeˑ neᵢ naˑuˈteˑ. nɛˈnseˑ suwɛˈnˈeˑs kiaq!ₐnuˈ-
     kᵘat nasoˈₐkᵘeˑn. aˈₐˈkeˑ neᵢ nɛtstaˈhaɬ ɬats!ɛnaˈxeˑ.

     Kanmiˈyɛt.s qakɛˈɬneˑ papaˈˈeˑs: "keˈᵢɬoˑ aₐk!aˈₐq!ᵢyu
     nɛˈɬseˑk?" qakɛˈᵢneˑ neᵢ tɑnaˈmˑu: "ɬoˈₐneˑ." qakeˈᵢneˑ. neᵢ
     nuɬaˈqₐna: "makaˈqaˑps. hamatɛˈktseˑnˈ ɬkaˈmˑu." wuˈkqₐneˑ:
175 namatɛˈktseˑ. qakɛˈɬneˑ: "naₐs nɛˈnˈeˑ tsaqₐnaˈneˑ." qakeˈᵢneˑ:
     "meˑˈka ktsₐquˈna hamatɛˈktsu." nɛˈtkɛn t!aqoˈmoˈs wɑqaˈpseˑ.
     at sɑˈitkɛˈnˑeˑ nöpɛˈk!aˑˈs at sɑˈaqaqaˈpseˑ miˈka tsₐquˈnas neᵢs
     ak!aˈₐq!ᵢyuˈs at kₐwɛˈɬqaˑps t!aqoˈmoˈs. neᵢs at yaₐxqakɛˈnˈkeˑ
     neᵢs qayaₐqaˈlaˑ'ms qaˈₐɬin at ɬaqaˈɬatikɛˈnˑeˑ nˈupɛˈɬneˑ nɛˈɬseˑks.
180 taˈxas aₐˈˈkeˑ naqaˈpseˑ sɛˈt!eˑs neᵢ nuɬaˈqₐna. qayaₐqaˈwaₐ-
     q!anq!ɛˈɬseˑ. neᵢs nˈoqoₐxaˈkeˑn yaˈt!aps aₐˈkuˈqɬaˈs. nupaˈkeˑn.
     kanmiˈˈyet.s ɬatuˈnwaₐ kaˈkeˑn at nɛnqaptaˈkseˑ k!ɛtq!anxoˈₐɬis;
     at qayaₐqawaₐq!anq!ɛˈɬseˑ sɛˈt!eˑs. taˈxas nˈoₐkuɬhaɬamaˈɬneˑ
     aɬpapaˈtᵢmo. taˈxas yunaqaˈpseˑ kiɬkuˈɬkaˈs, yunaqaˈpseˑ aₐˈquɬo-
185 maˈˈeˑs.

     Qakɛˈɬneˑ papaˈˈeˑs: "hamatɛˈktsuˑ kiɬkuˈɬka. hutsts!ɛnyaˈ-
     xak!oˈₐneˑ. hutsxaɬpɛˈtsekɛˈmeˈk." qak.laˈpseˑ papaˈˈeˑs: "atɛnsɑˈ-
     waˈsɑq!aˈpxₐneˑ." qakɛˈɬneˑ: "atunamatɛˈktseˑ xunyaxaₐk!oˈ-
     naˈweˑ." taˈxas ts!ɛnyaxaₐk!oˈₐneˑ. kxuˈnaˑm aˈₐˈkeˑ ɬaxokwaˈ-
190 seˑ neᵢs naˑuˈteˑs. namatɛˈktseˑ. qakɛˈɬneˑ.: "hɛntsxaɬ'eˑkɛˈɬneˑ.
     qaˈk.leˑs maˈˈneˑs: 'qaˈɬa at k!ɛsniɬamatɛˈktseˑsˈ' hɛntsxaɬ-
     qakɛˈɬneˑ: ˈat nˈɛsniɬamatiktsaˈpᵢneˑ xunyaxaₐk!onaˈweˑ.ˈˈˈ qakɛˈ-
     neˑ "maₐts atɛntsxaɬhɛsˈkɛˈɬneˑ neᵢ tɛˈtqaˑt! neᵢs nuɬaqˈnaˈˈeˑs
     tsuˈˈneˑs."

(e) TREE CHIEF VISITS THE TOWN OF GOLDEN EAGLE

195   Neᵢ aₐˈkik.luˈˈnaˈm taˈxas tsEmaˈk!eˈɬowask.lunaˈmneˑ. ɬoˈₐ-
     neˑ iyaˈmˑu ɬuˈkpoˑ. sɑˈɛt.ɬatsuˈteˑ k!aˈk!ɬanaq!oˈxₐmaɬeˑˈet.
     sɑsaₐniɬweynaˈₐteˑ skɛˈnˈkuˑts. sɑˈaqaqaˈpseˑ. k!ɛt.ɬaˈₐtsuˑt
     ɬuˈkpoˈs. qakɛˈɬneˑ neᵢs naˑuˈteˑs: "kanmiˈˈyit hɛntsxaɬsoₐkᵘɛˈ-
     nˈeˑ kaɬaˈxa. hutsɬaxaˈxeˑ aₐˈkɛt.ɬanɛˈskiˈɬ." ɬats!ɛnaˈxeˑ neᵢ
200 naˑuˈteˑ. k.ɬatᵢnaˈxaˈm aₐˈkit.ɬaˈeˑs namatɛˈktseˑ maˈˈeˑs neᵢs
     kiɬkuˈɬkaˈs. taˈxas nɛˈˈkseˑ; aₐˈˈkeˑ nɛˈkseˑ suˈˈeˑs. aₐˈˈkeˑ
     namatɛˈktseˑ neᵢs tsuˈweˑs, neᵢs skɛˈnˈkuˑts tɑnamuˈˈeˑs, neᵢsts
     kskɛˈk.leᵢts skɛˈnˈkuˑts. nukᵘnaˈkₐne, nˈupinqanawitskɛˈɬneˑ
     tiɬnamuˈˈeˑs. qakɛˈɬneˑ: "qapsqaqaˈₐneˑ nɛnsɑˈɛˈkᵢneˑ qaˈpsin."
205 qatseᵢtakaˈpseˑ tɑnamuˈˈeˑs. qak.laˈpseˑ maˈˈeˑs: "qaˈɬa k!ɛˈsin
     naₐs kiɬkuˈɬkaˈs?" qakɛˈɬneˑ: "nɛˈsᵢniɬhamatiktsaˈpᵢneˑ xun-
     yaxaₐk!onaˈweˑ." kiaq!ₐnuˈkwaˑt nasoˈₐkᵘeˑn qaɬwiˈyneˑ:
     "taˈxas hoɬˈuˈpxa qaˈɬa k!ɛˈsin naₐs koɛˈkᵢmiɬ." nˈaˑnaxaˈˈmneˑ

river he was going to see ‖ the chief's daughter. He took the pemmi- 165
can, started, | and went to the river. He saw the girl and gave it to
her. He said to her: | "Take it back home and eat it. Don't let
that man see it. | If your mother asks who owns this pemmican, say
to her, | 'The one who draws water all the time gave it to me.'" ‖
Then the girl started back. She was the daughter of the | chief 170
Golden Eagle. The youth also went back. |

In the morning he said to his grandmother: "Is there no leg part
of the skin | of a bull?" The old woman said: "There is none."
The old man said: | "There is some; give it to the child." She
found it ‖ and gave it to him. She said to him: "Here! It is small." 175
He said: | "Even though it is small, give it to me." He made a large
netted ring. | He worked his manitou power; and although the edge
of the skin was small, | it became a large netted ring. He did the
same way | as he had done with the yearling. Just as he had done
that, he killed the bull. ‖ Then the old man also had a blanket. 180
There was a painting in the center of it. | When she had put the
coagulated blood in the skin and put it away, | and when she
brought it out the next day, it was tanned, | and there was a paint-
ing in the center of the blanket. Then the grandparents and the
grandson all had blankets. | They had much pemmican and many ‖
parflèches. | 185

He said to his grandmother: "Give me pemmican. I'll draw
water. | I'll eat it on my way." | She said to her grandson: "You
eat it too quickly." He said to her: "I give it to the water carrier." |
Then he went to draw water. When he came to the water, ‖ the girl 190
also came. He gave it to her. He said to her: "Eat it. | If your
mother asks you who gave it to you, then | say to her, 'That one
gave it to me himself who goes to the river to draw water.'" He
said to her: | "Don't give any of it to the man, your | elder sister's
husband." ‖

(e) TREE CHIEF VISITS THE TOWN OF GOLDEN EAGLE

The people in that town were very hungry. There were no | buffa- 195
loes. Tree Chief had hidden them. | He was angry at Coyote.
Therefore he had hidden the buffaloes. | He said to the girl: "To-
morrow prepare | my seat; I'll go to your tent." The girl went
back. ‖ When she entered the tent, she gave the pemmican to her 200
mother. | Then she ate. Her father also ate, and | she gave some to
her elder sister, Coyote's wife, while | Coyote lay asleep. He felt
uneasy. He looked sideways | at his wife. He said to her: "It looks
as though you were eating something." ‖ His wife did not look at 205
him. Her mother said: "Who owns | this pemmican?" She said
to her: "The one who always draws water gave it to me." | Chief
Golden Eagle thought: | "Now I'll see who owns what I eat."

kiaq!ₐnu′kwaˑ′t. łukᵘɛ′nˑeˑ aₐ′q!uˑk.łupqaˑ″eˑs. n′ɛktikmɛ′teˑ.

210 qaₐnɛts!łaɛ′nseˑ qawaχₐmɛ′teˑ. n′ɛnqapta′kseˑ kiaq!ₐnu′kᵘaˑ′t.s.
neᵢs at qakał′itkɛ′nˑeˑ kiaq!ₐnu′kᵘaˑ′t.s; sł′aqaqa′pseˑ kqa′k.łik
kiaq!ₐnu′kᵘaˑ′ts. tsχa′nˑeˑ. qake′ᵢneˑ: "naₐs swɛtsq!ₐnu′neˑ
kiaq!ₐnu′kᵘaˑ′t. mɛtχa′keł q!a′peˑ łka′mˑuts nɛtsta′haˑłts
kwɛ′łqa tɛ′tqaˑt!ts kułˑaˑ′k.łeˑ tɛ′tqaˑt!. qa′ła n′ɛ′tk!oˑ tsχał′ɛ′nseˑ

215 tɛłnamuˑ″eˑs kaswɛ′nmiˑł. ma k!ok!qa′peˑ″s." ta′χas q!a′peˑ tsu-
kᵤatɛ′łneˑ t!a′wu. n′anaχa′mnaˑ′mneˑ neᵢ aₐ′kik.łoˑᵤnaˑm pał
kᵤwɛłk.łoˑᵤnaˑm. yunaqᵤwu′mneˑ łka′mˑuts nɛtsta′hałts
tɛ′tqaˑt!ts kułˑaˑ′k.łeˑ, q!a′peˑ mɛtχa′łneˑ. qake′ᵢneˑ kiaq!ₐnu′-
kᵘaˑ′t. "at tsχał′oˑk!q!ₐnq!aχuˑχwa′łneˑ." ta′χas mɛtχa′łneˑ.

220 skɛ′nˑkuˑts n′oˑk!ᵘᵢłmɛ′txₐneˑ, mɛ′txₐneˑ, mɛ′txₐneˑ. ta′χas
numatsnatɛ′łneˑ skɛ′nˑkuˑts. ta′χas q!a′peˑ mɛtχa′łneˑ. łoˑᵤneˑ
k!ɛ′sk!oˑ. n′u′pχₐneˑ k!aˑk!łanaq!oˑχᵤmałeˑ′et ksakiłmitχa′łeˑ′s
kiaq!ₐno′kᵘaˑ′t.s. qatsχanatɛ′łneˑ pał ktsaqu′na. qałwiyna′mneˑ
kqaˑ′nkqa′kₐna. tsɛnˑöpk!a′qał′u′pχₐneˑ neᵢs k!aqanɛ′kets.

225 n′ɛtkɛ′nˑeˑ t!awunana′eˑs aₐ′k!nana′eˑs. ts!ɛna′χeˑ. qaoˑχa′χeˑ.
łaχa′χeˑ neᵢs aₐ′kɛk.łuna′meˑ′s, pał q!a′peˑ k.łałaha′qᵤwom.
n′upχa′łneˑ qoᵤs qaka′χeˑ łka′mˑu słₐtqaˑ′nˑmitaₐk!onɛ′łeˑk
qoᵤs yɛsałha′qᵤwomɛ′skeˑ qoᵤsts qake′ᵢkaq!aχo′ᵤχᵤneˑ. tsa-
mna′neˑ k!u′pχa neᵢs łka′muˑ′s. skɛ′nˑkuˑts n′u′k!ᵘᵢłsłahaˑ′t‍ᵢ-

230 yilmɛ′txₐneˑ. mɛ′txₐneˑ. qahaˑ′łɛn łamɛ′txₐneˑ skɛ′nˑkuˑts neᵢsts
kɛnmɛ′txa′s łka′mˑu′s n′upχaₐłˑ′sᵢneˑ neᵢ łka′mˑu n′ɛsk!oˑᵤneˑ
neᵢs kiaq!ₐnu′kᵘaˑ′ts. skeᵢkmitk!oˑᵤneˑ. n′u′pχₐneˑ skɛ′nˑkuˑts
skeᵢkmu′χos. mɛtya′χₐneˑ. k!oka′χus n′uq!ᵢyunkɛ′nˑeˑ n′u′pχₐ-
neˑ neᵢs kqa′eˑns a′k!eˑs. n′aˑkaq!ałkɛ′nˑeˑ a′k!eˑs, łoˑqᵘałqaₐna-

235 q!ałkɛ′nˑeˑ. łahotsɛnqkupekɛ′meˑk. łahałk!oˑᵤneˑ. qake′ᵢneˑ.:
"nawa′spaˑł, nawa′spaˑł." wɛłke′ᵢneˑ. qakɛ′łneˑ nawaspa′łˑeˑs:
"hon′itk!oˑᵤneˑ kiaq!ₐnu′kᵘaˑ′t." n′uk!ᵘe′ᵢneˑ tɛ′tqaˑt! qakɛ′łneˑ:
"skɛnˑkoˑ′ᵤts, at qoᵤqᵘaₐkiłso′ᵤkᵘeˑn′ naₐqanɛ′keˑt kaₐs ksɛ′łˑeˑn
tseᵢka′teˑn′; n′ɛ′nˑeˑ ktskɛ′q!ła ɛn kɛna′łk!oˑ qoᵤs sɛłk!oˑᵤneˑ

240 łka′mˑu ma ksɛłɛ′tk!oˑ." tseᵢka′teˑ skɛ′nˑkuˑts neᵢs kaˑ′łk!oˑ, pał
n′ɛ′nseˑ ktskɛ′q!ła′s. ta′χas numatsɛna′mneˑ neᵢs k!aqa′qₐna
skɛ′nˑkuˑts. qałwi′yneˑ. aₐ′kˑeˑ ktsł′atsu′ᵤkᵘaˑt kiaq!ₐnu′kᵘaˑ′ts
swɛnɛ′seˑs, pał kk!omna′ₐneˑt kiaq!ₐnu′kᵘaˑ′t.s kqa′łwiy
χma kχaˑ′tsniłsakɛ′tet swɛnɛ′seˑs. ta′χas łatᵢnaχa′mnaˑ′mneˑ

245 aₐ′kɛt.łaˑ″naˑm. qakiya′mneˑ: "pał sɛłtsaqᵤna′neˑ neᵢ łka′mˑu
ktsχałha′qaps tɛłnamuˑ″eˑs." mɛ′ksan kiaq!ₐnu′kᵘaˑ′t qałwi′y-
neˑ: "mɛ′ka ktsaqu′na neᵢ łka′mˑu kutstso′ᵤkᵘat. ktsχa′łˑins
nuł′aqₐna′eˑs ka′swiˑn."

    Taˑ′χas tsɛmiˑ′yit q!o′mneˑna′mneˑ k.łała′χaˑm k!aˑk!łana-

250 q!oˑχᵤmałeˑ′et papaˑ″eˑs łaₐłkɛ′neˑ kiaq!ₐnu′kᵘaˑ′t.s. qak.łaˑ′p-
seˑ papaˑ″eˑs: "qa′ła k!ɛ′sᵢnił′ɛ′tk!o?" qake′ᵢneˑ: "ka′min."
qak.łaˑ′pseˑ: "qapsins kɛnsɛł′itk!oˑ′ᵤmo?" qakɛ′łneˑ: "naₐs n′ɛ′nˑeˑ
kat!a′wu." pał ktsaqu′naˑ′s neᵢs t!awuˑ″eˑs. qałwi′yneˑ ˑneᵢ

Golden Eagle went out, | took a feather of his body, and threw it up. ‖
There was a tree. Where he threw it, (the feather) became an 210
eagle. | He always used to make eagles, and therefore his name was |
Golden Eagle. He spoke, and said: "Here on the tree | a golden
eagle is sitting. Let all the children, youths, | big men, and old men,
shoot at it! Whoever kills it shall ‖ marry my daughter, the one who 215
remains." Then they all | took their bows. The people of that town
went out. | It was a big town. There were many boys, youths, | men,
and old men, and all shot at it. Golden Eagle said: | "Every one
shall have one shot." Then they all shot. ‖ Coyote shot once. He 220
shot, shot. Then | they laughed at him. They all shot, but no one |
hit it. Tree Chief knew that they were shooting | at the golden
eagle. He was not told about it because he was small. They
thought | he would not be able to do it. He just discovered through
his manitou power what was happening. ‖ He made a small bow and 225
a small arrow. He started. He went there. | He arrived, and all
the people were outside. | They saw the boy coming, shooting away
while he was coming along. | Then just from the edge where they
were he shot. | Only a few saw the boy. Coyote was still shooting, ‖
shooting. Coyote just shot again. When | the child shot, they knew 230
that he had hit | the golden eagle. It fell down. Coyote saw it fall
down. | He ran after it. When it reached the ground, he took
hold of it. He | saw that it was not his arrow. Then he took out his
arrow and exchanged it (for Tree Chief's arrow). ‖ He began to run. 235
He had (the bird) on his arrow. He said: | "Father-in-law, father-in-
law!" He shouted. He said to his father-in-law: | "I killed the
golden eagle." One man said to Coyote: | "Try to be sensible. What-
ever may have happened, this is not it. | Look at it! It is a prairie
chicken you are carrying. There, that ‖ boy has it on his arrow. 240
He shot it." Coyote looked at what he was carrying. | It was a
prairie chicken. Then they all laughed at what Coyote had done. |
He thought he would take Eagle's other | daughter, because he had
fooled Golden Eagle before. He thought he | ought to marry both
his daughters. Then all went into ‖ the tent. They said: "The 245
boy | is too small to have a wife." But Golden Eagle thought: |
"Even if the boy is small, I'll take him to be | the husband of my
daughter." |

At night, when the people slept, Tree Chief's ‖ grandmother came. 250
She carried the golden eagle. | His grandmother said to him: "Who
killed it?" He said: "I did." | She said to him: "What did you kill
it with?" He said to her: "With | my bow here." His bow was

255 tɛlna'm·u: "ta'χas naqan tsłama'tap kapa'pa pał kqa'e·n
k.lɛ'tk!am kiaq!anu'kᵘa·'t naso'ᵤkᵘe·n.   qa.ɛ'nsiłqao''ła·."
   Kwałkwa'yɛts ts!ɛnyaχaₐk!o'ᵤne. ła.u'pχane· ne¡s na.u'te·'s.
qakɛ'łne·: "kanmi·'yit kiyu'k¡yit hutsłaχa'χe·." n'u'pχane·
ne¡ na.u'te· ne¡s k!ɛ'tk!o·'s kiaq!anu'kᵘa·'t.s ne¡sts
260 ke'e·ns ne¡s at kɛ'saps kɛlku'łka·'s. ta'χas łats!ɛna'χe·. kan-
mi·'yit.s qakɛ'łne· papa''e·s: "ta'χas hutsχał·ama'tɛskɛ'łne·.
wa'łkᵤwa ne¡ kᵤwa'łke·n kiaq!anu'kᵘa·'t n'ɛ'n·e· kohoqᵘa'ka
nałwats!na'mne·. hunoqᵘaqa''ne· pa'łke¡ hutsχałts!ɛna'χe·."
qake'¡ne· ne¡ tɛlna'm·u: "qa'ła sᵤwɛ'n'e·s?" qake'¡ne· ne¡
265 nɛtsta'hałna'na. "kiaq!anu'kᵘa·'t swɛ'n'e·s." qake'¡ne· ne¡
tɛlna'm·u: "łqa'e·n naso'ᵤkᵘe·n χma hoqᵘaha'matɛ's¡ne·."
n'iła'n·e· ne¡ tɛlna'm·u qak.ła'pse· papa''e·s: "maₐts
e''ła·n'. hutsχałqamatɛ's¡ne·." qake'¡ne· ne¡ tɛlna'm·u: "kɛn·-
tsχała'łχo· aₐ'ku'ła·k?" qake'¡ne· ne¡ nɛtsta'hałna'na: "kan-
270 mi·'yit tsχałyu·naqa''ne· aₐ'ku'ła·k ne¡ aₐ'kik.łu''na·m.
hutsχał'ɛtkɛ'n·e·." qake'¡ne· ne¡ tɛlna'm·u: "so'ᵤkᵤne·. tɛlnamu''ne·s tsχałtskaya'χₐne· aₐ'ku'ła·ks. tsχał'ɛ'kine· kiaq!a-
nu'kᵘa·'t."
   Tsɛlmi·'yit.s taχas ts!ɛna'χe· ne¡ nɛtsta'hałna'na. n'an-
275 tsuχa'χe·. ta'χas ła.ɛtkɛ'nme·k ne¡s ma yaₐqaqa'ₐke· ne¡s
qa·wɛsa'qa ma'e·s. łaqaqa''ne· naqoka''mse· aₐ'koqła''nt!e·s.
naqa'pse· qasna'ł'e·s a'ₐ'ke· łahaqa'pse· aₐ'kinuqłe'¡t!e·s.
naqa'pse· poponana'e·s. łahaqa'pse· aₐ'k¡yukᵘa'e·s; łahaqa'pse·
ak.ła'm'e·s kiak!aku'ta·'t.s a'ₐ'ke· ła.ɛ'nse· aₐ'q!uk.huma'e·s
280 k!u''mtsaks. ta'χas q!a'pe·'s łahaqa'pse· ne¡s ma yaₐqaqa'pske· aₐ'k.łɛtɛ't!e·s, ne¡s kqao·sa'qa ma'e·s. ta'χas ts!ɛna'χe·
aₐ'kik.łuna'me·s; aₐ'ke· ła.ɛ'n·e· kᵘwɛ'łqa nɛtsta'hałs. kt¡na'-
χa'm aₐ'kɛnuqłe·'et.s naqts!ɛlu·kᵘa'ₐmik. nułpałnɛ'łne· qoᵤs
aₐ'kik.łuna'me·s. qakiya'mne·: "ho'ya·'s sɛlwa'χe· k!a'k!ła-
285 naq!o·χᵤmałe·'et." tse¡katɛ'łne·. n'upχa'łne· ska'χe·. ta'χas
n'anaχa'mna'mne·. qawaqa'χe·. qakiłɛ'łne·: "qoᵤs sn'ɛt.-
ła'ₐne· naso'ᵤkᵘe·n." qa.oho'łne· ne¡s wa'łkᵤwa·'s ma
k!ɛ'tk!o· kiaq!anu'kᵘa·'t.s. mɛ'ksan ne¡ na.u'te· a'ₐ'ke·
kiaq!anu'kᵘa·'t n'u'pχane·   ne¡sts ke·'ɛns ne¡s wa'ł-
290 kᵤwa's ma k!ɛ'tk!o·'s kiaq!anu'kᵘa·'t.s. ta'χas ne¡ na.u'te·
t!aχo'ᵤne· łaχa.ɛ'se·s suk.łɛk¡natɛ'tine· tsχałyaₐqa·na'qanakɛ'ske·
nuł'aqₐna''e·s. ta'χas qona'χe·. tɛnaχa''mne·. pɛ'k!aks
nułɛkna.ɛ'tse· aₐ'kɛnoχo'e·s. ta'χas n'ɛsak¡nu'ne·. pɛ'k!aks
ne¡ na.u'te· n'ɛtkɛ'n·e· tsχałyaₐqaₐwɛtsq!anu'ske· kiaq!a-
295 ku'ta·'t.s. sanqa'me·k skɛ'n·kᵤ·ts. ta'χas n'a'sₐne· ki'haₐt
kiaq!aku'ta·'t.s sᵤwɛ't¡mo. at wunekɛ't.se· n'ɛlqanmɛt-
q!ok.łɛmak!o'ᵤmik, at n'ɛlqapta'kse· k!u''mtsaks, at
t!alo'ᵤkᵤne· kiaq!aku'ta·'t. at n'unanoχu'ne·. at n'ɛ'k¡ne·
ne¡s k!u''mtsaks. ta'χas skɛ'n·kᵤ·ts sa·niłwi'yne·. nałnu'kp¡ne·.

small. ‖ The old woman thought: "Now my grandson may leave me, | 255
because Eagle Chief was not without high rank. | Maybe he did not
do it." |

In the evening he went to get water, and again he saw the girl. |
He said to her: "To-morrow at noon I shall come." The girl knew |
that he had shot the golden eagle. ‖ It was he who had given her 260
pemmican. Then she started again. | On the following day he said
to his grandmother: "I shall give you | the golden eagle that I brought
yesterday. This is what I won | by playing. I won a woman. I
shall go there." | The old woman said: "Whose daughter is she?"
The youth said: ‖ "She is Golden Eagle's daughter." The old woman 265
said: | "If he were not chief, I should not give you up." | The old
woman cried. Her grandson said to her: "Don't | cry! I shall not
leave you." The old woman said: | "Do you want to carry meat
along?" The boy said: ‖ "To-morrow there will be much meat in 270
that town. | I shall make it." The old woman said: "It is well. |
Your wife will come for meat. The eagle will eat | it." |

In the evening the boy started. ‖ He went behind the tents. He 275
made himself look the way he used to be | when he was with his
mother. His clothing was fringed. | He had a shield and he had a
tomahawk. | He had a little hammer and he had a war bonnet, and |
on his head was a sparrow hawk. His saliva was ‖ shells. He had 280
everything that he used to have | when he was with his mother. He
started | for the town, and he was a large youth. | When he came
out of the prairie, he shouted, and the people in the town heard it. |
They said: "Well, Tree Chief arrives." ‖ They looked at him, and 285
they saw him coming. Then | they went out. He arrived. He was
told: "There is the | chief's tent." On the day before, | when he shot
the eagle, he was not recognized. Only the girl and | Golden Eagle
knew that he was the one who had ‖ shot the golden eagle on the pre- 290
vious day. Then the girl | shook his bed. She prepared the seat |
where her husband was to sit. Then he went there. He entered. |
His place was prepared. He sat down. | The girl had prepared the
place for Sparrow Hawk to sit down. ‖ Coyote was sitting there.
Then there were two | friends who had each a sparrow hawk. After
some time he spat, | and his saliva turned into shells. | The Sparrow 295
Hawk screeched, flew down, and ate | the shells. Then Coyote was
angry. He was ashamed. ‖

(f) TREE CHIEF PROVIDES FOOD FOR THE PEOPLE

300　Tsɛɫmi·′yits kq!o·′′mne· n′u′pxₐne· k!a‛k!ɫanaq!o‛xᵤmaɫe·′et
nowas′namɛ′sᵢne· neᵢs aₐ‛kik.ɫuna′me·s. wɛ′ɫna·ms qakɛ′ɫne·
tɛɫnamu′′e·s: "hɛntsxaɫqakɛ′ɫne· su·′′ne·s, tsxaɫtseᵢka′te· aₐ‛ku-
q!ɫiɫme′e·s." ta′xas ts!ɛna′xe·. wɛ′ɫna·ms qakɛ′ɫne· su′′e·s neᵢ
pa′ɫkeᵢ: "qakᵢya′mne· kɛntstse′ᵢkat aₐ‛kuq!ɫiɫme′′nis." ta′xas
305　kiaq!ₐnu′kᵘa·′t tseᵢka′te· a′ₐ‛kuq!ɫɛɫme′e·s. n′u′pxₐne· yuna-
ɫ·′kse· ɫu′kpo·s. n′anaxa′′mne· kiɫpa′ɫnekɛ′me·k. qake′ᵢne·
nɛtsta‛hahɛ·′′nte·k: "ɫatsᴇma·k!kɛ′ne·n′ aₐ‛kuqɫa′ɫaₐk." ta′xas
ɫatsᴇmak!kᵢnɛ′ɫne· aₐ‛kuqɫa′ɫaₐk. qa:na′xe· k!a‛k!ɫanaq!oxᵤma-
ɫe·′et. skɛkts!ɫa‛nuqɫe.ɛ′t.se·. tsxa‛kɛɫ′itqana′ₐqₐne· aₐ‛q!uɫ′ɛ′se·s
310　ɫu′kpo·s. yunaqa′pse· k!itqana′qa. ta′xas kuɫ′itqana′′qa. ta′-
xas naɫuk.ɫɛtᵢya′xₐne·. qakɛ′ɫne·: "hú′hú′huˇyá·′." ta′xas
neᵢs aₐ‛q!u′ɫ′e·s ɫu′kpo· q!a′pe· n′uwo′kᵤne· n′ɛnqa′pte·k ɫu′kpo·.
ta′xas nanuxu′nqa′′ne·. ta′xas ts!ɛna′xe·. qa:′ɫɛn kiyu′kᵢyi·t.s
ta′xas ɫaxa′xe· aₐ‛kuqɫa′ɫaₐks. n′upxa′ɫne·‛ ska′xe· yunaqa′ₐne·
315　ɫu′kpo·. qakiɫamna′mne·: "ska′xe· ɫu′kpo· soᵤkɛ′nki·ɫ. maₐts
ɫsa′′nqa." ta′xas wa′xe· ɫu′kpo·. ta′xas qasa′nqa′′ne·. q!a′pe·
wat!qa′me·k. sanmoxo′ᵤme·k ɫu′kpo·. yunaqa·′′ne· n′ɛt!qa′ₐne·
neᵢs aₐ‛kuqɫa′ɫa·ks. ta′xas q!a′pe· aqɫsma′kᵢnɛk! tsukᵘa′te·.
qakᵢya′mne·: "q!a′pe· tsukwa′tki·ɫ, hɛntsqaqa‛naɫtsukwatkɛ′ɫne·
320　aₐ‛ku′qɫa." ta′xas tsukᵘatɛ′ɫne· q!a′pe· qoᵤs yu′n·o·′s aₐ‛kuq!-
yumɛ′n·a·′s. ɫaqawaₐqaɫyuwaₐka′xe· k!a‛k!ɫanaq!o‛xᵤmaɫe·′et.
n′ɛsakᵢnu′ne·. ta′xas q!a′pe· tsukᵘatɛ′ɫne·. kiaq!ₐnu′kᵘa·′t
naso′ᵤkᵘe·n tsᵤkᵘa′te· sɛ′kse· ɫu′kpo·′s. n′u′pxₐne· nawaspa′ɫ′e·s
qaokᵘa′se·. qoᵤs sɫatᵢnaqₐna′kse·. ta′xas q!a′pe·′s tsukᵘat.ɫɛs′ᵢne·
325　ke′ᵢsɛks ɫu′kpo·s. qakɛ′ɫne· swɛ′n′e·s: "paɫ ku′k.ɫo·k k!a‛k!ɫa-
naq!o‛xᵤmaɫe·′et, sɛɫqaoˇkwa′xe· naₐs. n′ɛ′ne· ke′ᵢse·k ɫu′kpo·.
tsᵤkᵘa′te·n′. a′ₐ‛ke· sukqᵤwa′ate·. tsxaɫ′ɛ′n·e sɛ′t!ne·s." neᵢs
tsk.ɫa′wam k!a‛k!ɫanaq!o‛xᵤmaɫe·′e·t, ɛna′haks wa′xe· ɫu′kpo·
n′uk!we·′′ne·, nuɫ·ak.ɫe′ᵢne·, tuna′kₐne· q!apq!uɫqa′′ne·. a′ₐ‛ke·
330　wat!kaxo′ne· qoᵤs na′ₐtaₐs. qawaₐkaɫts!ɛnxo′ᵤme·k at qa.ikɛ′ɫne·
qoᵤ kqa′qa paɫ ksɫhuɫ·a′k.ɫe·. sɛɫ′a‛qaɫqatseᵢkatɛ′ɫne·. n′u′pxₐne·
k!a‛k!ɫanaq!o‛xᵤmaɫe·′et neᵢs k!aqa′keᵢks nawaspa′ɫ′e·s ktso′ᵤ-
kᵘats k!u′k!e·′s ke′ᵢsiks ɫu′kpo·′s. ta′xas ɫa.una′xe·. qaoˇxa′xe·
neᵢs ktu′ᵤna·ks ɫu′kpo·′s q!apq!u′ɫqaps. wat!kᵢmɛ′te·‛ qawa-
335　ka′xe· tɛɫnamu′′e·s. qakɛ′ɫne·: "qa′psins kɛnsɛɫtso′ᵤkᵘat na
ɫu′kpo· paɫ kiyuna′qa aqɫsma′kᵢnɛk! xma tsukᵘa′te· qoᵤ kᵤwa′t!-
kᵢme·t. huɫqonaxa′ɫa, hutsxaɫ′umitse′ᵢte·." ta′xas qona′xe·
n′umitse′ᵢte·. ta′xas numatsɛnata′pse· skɛ′n·ku·ts, k!o‛k!iɫ-
q!apq!u′ɫqaps ksɛɫ′umɛ′tse·t. ta′xas tsxa′ne· skɛ′n·ku·ts.
340　qakɛ′ɫne·: "qa′psins kɛn′u′pske·n? at qa.ikɛ′ɫne· ɛn kqa′qa.
ma′te·n′ neᵢs skikqa′pse· ɫu′kpos ma ksɛɫtso′ᵤkᵘat kiaq!ₐnu′-
kᵘa·′tsɛ′kse·,a′ₐ‛ke·sukqᵤwa′ₐte·. tsxaɫsɫama′ɫne· tɛɫnamu′′ne·s."

(ƒ) TREE CHIEF PROVIDES FOOD FOR THE PEOPLE

At night, when Tree Chief slept, he knew | that the people in the 300
town were starving.　In the morning he said | to his wife: "Tell your
father to look at the fortune-telling place." | Then she started.　In the
morning the woman said to her father: | "He says you shall look at
your fortune-telling place."　Then || Golden Eagle looked at his fortune- 305
telling place.　He saw many | tracks of buffalo cows.　He went out
and shouted.　Then | the youths said: "Make the buffalo fence
strong."　Then | the buffalo fence was made strong.　Tree Chief went
along. | There was a large prairie.　He began to pile up the manure
of || buffaloes, much of the same kind.　After he had piled it up, | he 310
shouted at it.　He said to it: "Hu, hu, hu, ya!"　Then | all the buffalo
dung arose and became buffalo cows. | Then he rounded them up.
Then he started.　Just as soon as he arrived | at the buffalo fence, he
saw many buffaloes coming. || The people told one another: "The buffa- 315
loes are coming.　Be careful!　Don't | let them disperse!"　The buffaloes
arrived.　They did not disperse, and they all | went over the precipice.
They were piled up.　Many buffaloes filled up | the buffalo drive.
Then all the people took them. | They said: "Take everything.
Take even || the skin."　Then they were all taken up the hillside. | 320
Tree Chief came up the hill. | He sat down, and all were taken.
Chief Golden Eagle | had taken the fat of the buffaloes.　He saw his
son-in-law, | who did not go down.　He remained sitting on top.　Then
all the || fat buffaloes had been taken.　(The chief) said to his daughter: 325
"Tree Chief is tired. | Therefore he did not come down.　Here is
a fat cow. | Take it.　It also has good hair.　That shall be your
blanket." | When Tree Chief came back, one buffalo cow came along
behind the others. | It was old, thin, and full of sores.　It also ||
slid down from above.　It stopped up there.　It was so old that 330
it was not good to be eaten, | therefore it was not looked at.　Tree
Chief knew | what his father-in-law had said when he took | one fat cow.
Then he went down.　He went to | the lean buffalo, the sore one.
He let it slide down. || His wife came, and he said to her: "Why did 335
you take that | buffalo?　There are many people.　They ought to take
what slides down. | Let us go and skin it!"　She went and | skinned
it.　Then Coyote laughed | at them because they skinned one sore one.
Coyote spoke, || and said to him: "Why do you do that?　That kind 340
is not eaten. | Leave this cow lying there.　Eagle has taken | a fat
one with good hair on it for a blanket for your wife." | They did not

qatse¡katɛ́ɬne· skɛ́n·ku·ts.   ne¡sts k!aqa′ke·. qaɬwi′yne· kiaq!ₐ-
nu′kᵘa·′t paɬ ksɛ́ɗqa′ɬwiyts, ksa·̆′qₐna qatsχa′ne· mɛ́ksa·′n
345 skɛ́n·ku·ts nomats¡natka′′ne·. ta′χas n′umɛtse′¡te· k!a`k!-
ɬanaq!o`χᵤmaɬe·′et.

    Namatɛ́ktse· a′k!e·s tɛ́namu′′e·s k!a`k!ɬanaq!o`χᵤmaɬe·′et.
qakɛ́ɬne·: "at maₐts wuχo′ᵤmun′ χa′ₐɬtsin a′ₐ′ke·ɬka′m·u." ta′χas
n′umitse′¡te·. tse¡ka′te· naso′ᵤkᵘe·n qa′ɬas nɛ́n′e·ns u′s′me·ks
350 ke′¡siks k!omɛ́tse¡ts q!a′pe·′s sɛ́kse·. qao·̆χa′χe· nawaspa′ɬ′e·s.
ma ksɛ́umɛ́tse¡ts kuɬ·a`k.le·′s. tse¡ka′te· paɬ nɛ́′nse u′s′me·ks
ke′¡se·ks ɬu′kpo·s.

    N′u′pχₐne· skɛ́n·ku·ts ne¡s kama′ₐtkits tɛ́namuɛ́′se·s aₐk!ɛ́′se·s
swu′e·s. a′ₐ`ke· namatɛ́ktse· tɛ́namu′′e·s a′k!e·s. qakɛ́ɬne·:
355 "hawɛtskɛ́n·e·n′. maₐts at wuχo′ᵤmo·n′ qa′psin." qa·wɛsqa′pse·
tɛ́namu′′e·s k!a`k!ɬanaq!o`χᵤmaɬe·′et. q!akpa′me·k ne¡ pa′ɬki¡
ne¡s ma·. k!aqa′k.ɬaps nuɬaqₐna′′e·s. paɬ ko′wa·s χa′ₐɬtsin ne¡s
k!u′pχa aₐku′ɬa·ks. ta′χas n′aɬtsɛ́n·te·k ke′e·k wa′′nmo·′s.
qa.u′pχₐne· ne¡ pa′ɬke¡ paɬ sɛ́ɬwuχomu′n·e ne¡s kawɛ́tske·n′ aₐk!s.
360 qanaχu′se· paɬ sɛ́ɬ′u′pse·. qakɛ́ɬne· tɛ́namu′′e·s k!a`k!ɬana-
q!o`χᵤmaɬe·′et: "ma hoqak.ɬɛ́′s¡ne· maₐts kɛ́nɬwu′χo·. ne¡s ɬaqal-
wuχo′ᵤmon′ ɛs aₐk!s." ɬawuχomu′n·e· ne¡ pa′ɬke¡ ne¡s χa′ₐɬ-
tsins aₐk!s ɬa.ɛ́tq!a′nχa′′mse·.

    N′u′pχₐne· skɛ́n·ku·ts ne¡s k!aqanɛ́ke·ts. naₐs qaha′se·
365 χa′ₐɬtsins qanaqkupɬa′ɬte·. q!akpakitχo′ᵤne·. qakɛ́ɬne· tɛ́na-
mu′′e·s: "qa′psins kɛnu′pske·n? maoqak.ɬɛ́′s¡ne· maₐts kinɬwu-
χo′ᵤmo ɛs kaa′ₐk!mi·ɬ. ne¡s ɬaqaɬwuχo′ᵤmon′." ne¡ pa′ɬke¡ ne¡s
ɬaqaɬwuχomu′n·e·. sɬaha`tk̈ikqa′pse·. ɬaₐqa.itq!a′′nχa′′mse·.

    Qakɛ́ɬne· tɛ́namu′′e·s k!a`k!ɬanaq!o`χᵤmaɬe·′et: "qonamɛ́ɬe·n′
370 ne¡s kɛnɬqaɬwuχo′′mo ɛs kaa′ₐk!mi·ɬ qoᵤ χa′ₐɬtsin. qa′ɬa n′ɛsɛnɬ-
ɛntsɬakɛ́ɬne·." qao·̆χa′χe· ne¡ pa′ɬke¡ ne¡s qaɬwoχomu′n·e· ne¡s
ak!s χa′ₐɬtsins. ɬa.itq!a′nχa′′mse·. ta′χas skɛ́n·ku·ts n′umats¡-
natɛ́ɬne· ne¡s k¡yunaqχowu′me·s.

    Ta′χas kuɬ′umɛ́tse¡t k!a`k!ɬan·aq!o`χᵤmaɬe·′et qakɛ́ɬne·:
375 "ta′χas qoᵤ nawɛsiɬkɛ́′nen′ aₐku′ɬak kaₐkɛt.ɬanaɬa′e·s." paɬ
k!ɛsɛ́ku′ma·ɬs qa.aɬoᵤqakɛ́n·e· ne¡ pa′ɬke¡. qakɛ́ɬne· tɛ́namu′′e·s
k!a`k!ɬan·aq!o`χᵤmaɬe·′e·t: "oqoᵤnaɬχo′ᵤmon′ · sɛ́t!nɛ́′smi·ɬ."
ta′χas ne¡ pa′ɬki¡ noqoᵤna·wɛsq!owomu′n·e sɛ́′t!e·s. qaɬwi′yne·
ne¡ pa′ɬke¡ ktsχaɬyɛ́′k!ta aₐkᵤwum·aɬq!ols. qak.ɬa′pse·: "maₐts
380 yɛ́′k!ta. qaqa`naɬts!ɛnaɬχo′ᵤmo·n′ ɛs a′ₐ`kᵤwuᵤms." ta′χas ne¡
pa′ɬke¡ ts!ɛnaɬχo′ᵤne· ne¡s a′ₐ`kᵤwuᵤms qa.yɛ́k!ta′ane·
aₐ′q!uɬ′ɛ́′se·s.

    Ta′χas tsɛ́dmi·′yɛt·s paɬ k!ɛsku′ma·ɬs sɛ́t!e·s. ne¡ pa′ɬke¡ qaɬ-
wi′yne· ktsχaɬɛ́ktɛ́′qo·sɛ́t!e·s. qak.ɬa′pse· nuɬ·aqₐna′′e·s: "maₐts
385 ɛktɛ̈′qo·n′. qaqa`naɬ′upakɛ́′ne·n′; a′ₐ`ke· ne¡ a′ₐ`kᵤwum ne¡
qa′qaps aₐ′q!uɬ′e·s a′ₐ`ke· upakɛ́′nen′; a′ₐ`ke· ne¡ aₐ`ku′qɬa

look at Coyote, (and did not listen to) what he said. Golden Eagle
thought: | "He wants it, therefore he did not speak." But ‖ Coyote 345
laughed at them. Then Tree Chief | skinned it. |

Tree Chief gave his arrow to his wife. | He said to her: "Don't
touch it! Don't touch the dogs and children with it!" Then | he
skinned it. The chief looked (to see) who had most ‖ fat when they 350
scraped off all the fat. He went to his son-in-law. | He was skinning
the old cow. Then he saw that it was | the fattest buffalo. |

Coyote saw that his friend had given his arrow | to his wife, and he
also gave his arrow to his wife. He said to her: ‖ "Keep it. Don't 355
let it touch anything." | The wife of Tree Chief stood there. The
woman forgot | what she had been told by her husband. When her
hungry dog | saw the meat, it tried to eat the blood. | The woman did
not know that she touched it with the arrow that she was holding; ‖
(but when she did so, the dog) fell down and died. Tree Chief said 360
to his wife: | "I told you not to touch it. | Touch it again with your
arrow." The woman touched the dog | with the arrow, and it came
to life again. |

Coyote saw what had happened. He passed by ‖ a dog, struck it, 365
and killed it. He told his wife: | "Why did you do that? I told you
not to touch it | with the arrow. Touch it again with it." The
woman | touched it again, but it still lay there. It did not come to
life again. |

Tree Chief said to his wife: "Go there and ‖ touch the dog with my 370
arrow! Whoever owns a dog likes it." | The woman went there and
touched | the dog with the arrow. It came to life again. Then
Coyote was laughed | at by the crowd. |

Tree Chief said to his wife after she had skinned (the buffalo): ‖
"Carry the meat there into our tent!" | It was bloody, and the woman 375
did not know what to do. Tree Chief said to his wife: | "Carry it in
your blanket!" | The woman carried it in her blanket. The woman
thought | she would spill the guts. He said to her: "Don't ‖ spill 380
them! Carry them in with the stomach." Then | the woman car-
ried the stomach, and did not spill | the guts. |

Night came. Her blanket was bloody. Then the woman thought |
she would wash her blanket. Her husband said to her: "Don't ‖ wash 385
it! Just put it aside; and also the stomach | and the guts, put them

oqo_uxakɛ'ne·n'; ya't!ap a'_a'ke· kɛnl'upa'ke·n." ta'xas qaq_a-
na"ne· ne_i pa'lke_i ne_is ya·qak.la'pske· nulaq_ana"e·s.

Skɛ'n·ku·ts k!u'pxa ne_is k!aqa'q_anaps s_uwu'e·sts ats_awa'ts!e·s
390 a'_a'ke· qakɛ'lne· tɛlnamu"e·s łqa'q_anaps noqo_una'wɛsq!o_u-
womu'se· sɛt!ɛ'se·s. ta'xas tsɛlmi·'yɛt.s ne_is yaqaq_ana'pske.
tɛlnamu't_imo·'s k!a'k!łan·aq!o'x_umałe·'et.s a'_a'ke· qała'taˇqnap-
ma'łne· tɛlnamu"e·s.

Kanmi·'yɛt.s wɛ'łna·ms k!ok_unu'x^ua'm tɛlnamu't_imo k!a'k!ła-
395 n·aq!o'x_umałe·'et. ta'xas n'ɛ'k_ine·. qakɛ'lne· tɛlnamu"e·s:
"ka_as ke'en kɛlku'łka hutsxal'ɛ'k_ine·." qak.la'pse·: "tux^ua ła'q·a
kɛlku'łka?" numa'ts_ine·. qakɛ'lne·: "ts'ma_an·quk^uałxo'_une· ɛs
kɛkqa"ne·." qak.la'pse· tɛlnamu"e·s: "tux^ua łe'e·n' kɛlku'łka
ma n'ɛ'n·se· a_a'q!u'l'e·s." qakɛ'lne·: "tunwakakɛ'n·e·n'. kɛnłtse'_i-
400 kat." ta'xas ne_i pa'łke_i tunwaka'qkatkɛ'n·e· pał k!anɛ'ke_is.
tse_ika'te· pa·ł n'ɛnqapta'kse· kɛlku'łkas. łaqa.ɛ'n·se· a_a'q!ul'ɛ'se·s
łu'kpo·s. ta'xas n'ikɛ'lne·. qakɛ'lne·: "tunwakakɛ'ne·n' sɛt!ne·s."
qak.la'pse·: "tux^ua ła'q·a ksa'kqa; ma n'ok!^ue'_ine· ma q!apku-
ma'łne·." qakɛ'lne·: "tu·nwakakɛ'n·e·n'. kɛnłtse'_ika·t." ts_uk^ua'te·
405 ne_i pa'łke_i ne_is ma k!ɛsɛku'ma·ls sɛt!e·s. łaqaqo_uqaqa'pse·
n'ɛnqapta'kse· wu'p_inɛk!s. sukuq!łɛ'lse·. qakɛ'lne· tɛlnamu"e·s:
"a'_a'ke· ne_i ma kin'upa'ke·n tse_ika'te·n'." tse_ika'te· ne_i
pa'łke_i ne_is a_a'ku'qła's ma k!upa'ke·n. n'ɛnqapta'kse·
k!ɛtq!anxo'_ułes. qaya_aqa'wa_aq!anq!łɛ'łse·. ne_is ma kq!apq!u'ł-
410 qaps ma ksa_anqo'_uwa·ts, o'k!^uq_una ma ksɛlhuł·a'k.łe's ne_is
łu'kpo·s, q!a'piłso'_ukse· a_a'q_uwat!ɛ'se·s.

Ta'xas skɛ'n·ku·ts kułatkɛ'ki·lwɛ'tskeł swu"e·s yaqaqa-
na'pske·. ta'xas a'_a'ke q_aq_ana'_ane·. łitiłqaqa'pse·. xasɛnmi-
tu'qse· sɛt!ɛ'se·s tɛlnamu"e·s, ne_is a_a'ku'qła·'s ma k!upa'ke·n
415 qa_aqała'til'ɛ'n·se· a_a'ku'qła·'s; ne_is a'_a'k_uwums ma k!upa'ke·n
qaoqała'til'ɛ'nse· a_a'q!ul'ɛ'se·s łu'kpo·s. ne_iła'se· tɛlnamu"e·s
ne_is k!a'qałk!umna'_anet. qakɛ'lne· ne_is ats_uwa'ts!e·s k!a'k!ła-
n·aq!o'x_umałe·'et: "ma_ats łae'_iła·n' la.upa"nte·n'." ta'xas ne_i
pa'łke_i skɛ'n·ku·ts tɛlnamu"e·s ła.upa"nt.se· ne_is qa'qałsɛt!ɛ'-
420 se·s ma kxasɛnmɛ'tuqs; ne_is a_a'ku'qła's ne_is a_a'kwum·a'łq!oł·s.
mɛ'ksa'n kiaq!_anu'k^ua·'t qa·'łɛn ya·qaqa'pske· k!a'k!łan·a-
q!o'x_umałe·'ets k!e·'tkɛns, a'_a'ke· qal'ɛ'tk_inɛktsa'pse· suk'ni-
kit'nała'pse· k!u'pxa nawaspa'l'e·s yaqaqa'pske· k!e·'tkɛns.
mɛ'ksa'n nao·'k!^ue·'s nawaspa'l'e·s nałnu'kp_itsta'pse· ne_is
425 k!a'qał·ałnukpqa_aka'te·na'la_aps.

Ta'xas ne_is kwunɛ'kit.s qakɛ'lne· ats_uwa'ts!e·s k!a'k!łana-
q!o'x_umałe·'et: "ta'xas łatse_ika'te·n' ne_i kɛn'upa'ke·n. kɛnl'ɛ'k_i-
ma·ł łkam'nɛ"nte·k kɛlku'łka's." tse_ika'te· ne_i pa'łke_i. pał n'ɛnqapta'kse· kɛlku'łka's ne_is skɛ'n·ku·ts ma kqatal'e'_itkin. a'_a'ke·
430 ne_is ki'a·s sɛt!e·s, a'_a'ke· tse_ika'te· a'_a'ke· xa'ts_iniłso'_ukse·. ta'-
xas sɛlhoł'ɛtkɛ'n·e· ke·'so_uks qa'psins k!a'k!łan·aq!o'x_umałe·'et.

aside too, also the skin; | put the coagulated blood into it and put it aside." Then | the woman did as her husband told her. |

Coyote saw what his friend and his sister-in-law were doing, ‖ and he told his wife to do the same. She carried it | in her blanket. When evening came, Coyote's wife did the same | as Tree Chief's wife was | doing. |

Early in the morning Tree Chief and his wife arose. ‖ Then they ate. He said to his wife: | "Where is the pemmican? I'll eat." She said to him: "Is there any | pemmican?" He laughed, and said to her: "You brought it in. | There it is." His wife said to him: "Is that pemmican? | Those were guts." He said to her: "Bring it out and look at it." ‖ Then the woman pulled it out slowly. It was heavy. | She looked at it, and it had turned into pemmican. There were no more | buffalo guts. Then it was eaten. He said to her: "Pull out your blanket." | She said to him: "Is there one? There was one, but it was all bloody." | He said to her: "Pull it out and look at it." The woman took ‖ the bloody blanket. It was no more that way. | It had become a new one with beautiful stripes. He said to his wife: | "Look also at the other things we put aside." The woman looked | at the skin which she had put aside. It had become | a tanned skin with a painting in the middle, although it had been full of sores ‖ with bad hair, for it had been an old | buffalo cow. Its fur was very good. |

After Coyote had watched what his friend was doing, | he did the same, but nothing happened. | His wife's blanket remained stiff, and the skin that she had put aside ‖ remained rawhide, and the stomach which she had put aside | remained as before. It was buffalo dung. His wife cried, | because he had given her trouble. Tree Chief said to his sister-in-law: | "Don't cry! Put them back again." Then the| woman, the wife of Coyote, put back again her ‖ own blanket, the rawhide, and the guts, | but Golden Eagle did just the same as Tree Chief. | He did the same to him. He was glad | when he saw what his son-in-law had done, | but his other son-in-law made him ashamed. ‖ He was ashamed on account of what he had done. |

After a while, Tree Chief told his sister-in-law: | "Look again at the things you have put aside. Eat | pemmican with the children." The woman looked at it, and it had turned | into pemmican. Coyote had not been able to do it. And there ‖ were also two blankets. She looked at them, and both were good. Then | Tree Chief finished his good work. |

390
395
400
405
410
415
420
425
430

Tsɛłmi·'yit.s qakɛ'łne· tɛłnamu''e·s skɛ'n·ku·ts: "a: hɛntsqakɛ'łne· su''ne·s tsχałtseᵢka'te· aₐku'q!łiłme'e·s." ts!ɛna'χe·
skɛ'n·ku·ts. ta'χas tsχałsɛłskɛn·ku·'tstik. wɛ'łna·ms tseᵢka'te·
435 aₐ'kuq!łiłme'e·s kiaq!ₐnu'kuₐ'·t. łɛt.łi'kse· qa'psins. łatᵢna-.
χa''mne·. qana'χe· skɛ'n·ku·ts. skikiłhaqa'pse· aₐq!uł'ɛ'se·s.
tsχa'kił'ɛtqana''qₐne·. kuł'itqana'ₐqa ta'χas nałuk.łitᵢya'χₐne·
łu'kpo·s. qawanaχa''mse· neᵢs aₐq!uł'ɛ'se·s łu'kpo·s. qak.ła'țᵢ-
yił'ɛ̦ᵤwa't!te·, pałsɛłqatał'ɛ'nse· łu'kpo's. łahutsinqkupekɛ'me·k.
440 ła qana'χe·. łałaχa'χe·aₐ'kɛk.łuna'me·s. łayuχa'χe· aₐ'koq!yu-
mɛ'n·as. qake'ᵢne·: "kqa'sɛłsa''nqa iya'mu." Wɛłke'ᵢne· neᵢs
ke'ᵢtsχa. qake'ᵢne·: "wu'ptseᵢł ła'psa'ke·soᵤsa'qapnałka''ne·."
nłɛ'kte· k!a'k!łan· aq!o'χᵤmałe·'ct.s neᵢsts k!ₐqa'ke·. (neᵢ k!ₐqa'k-
ya·m wu'ptsoł at qakya'mne· qawunɛ'ke·t.s ktsᵤkuₐ'tka.)
445 ta'χas ła.una'χe· aₐ'kɛk.łuna'mes neᵢs k!a·'qa'ke· skɛ'n·ku·ts.
ta'χas n'umatsnatɛ'łne· pał wa'łkᵤwas kᵢyuna'qa łu'kpo k!upɛ'-
łeᵢł. słaqaqa''ne· kqawanχa''mnam. n'ɛtkɛnɛ'łᵢne· aₐ'ku'ła·kts
a'ₐ'ke· aₐ'ku'qła·. ta'χas skɛ'n·ku·ts łatᵢnaχa''mne· aₐ'kɛt.ła''e·s.
słₐa·'tkikqa'ₐne· k!a'k!łana·q!o'χᵤmałe·'et. a'ₐ'ke· łaqaₐke'ᵢne·
450 skɛ'n·ku·ts neᵢs ma yaqake'ᵢke·. qoᵤs kqaₐke'ᵢłtsχa aₐ'kuq!yu-
mɛ'n·a's n'ukᵤnuχa''mse· k!a'k!łan·aq!o'χᵤmałe·'et qak.ła'pse·:
"kaₐ kɛn'aqa'ke·? a'ₐ'ke· łaqa'ke·n'. kɛnłɛtke·kq!a'naqana'meᵢk
neᵢ ma kɛna'ₐqapwa'χ'mitχo'ᵤnap aₐ'kinokwe·'t!e·s ka'ₐke·n?"
ta'χas tsukuₐ'te· aₐ'kuk!paχma'kups k!a'k!łan·aq!o'χᵤmałe·'et,
455 łqa'łwiy ktsχał'u'peł skɛ'n·ku·ts·ts χma n'upɛ'łne· słaqaqa'pse·
ksɛłtso'ᵤkuat aₐ'kuk!paχma' kups. ta'χas qanłałtɛ'łne· skɛ'n·ku·ts.
ła.a'naqa'yiłχo'ᵤłne·. qakiłɛ'łne·: "ta'χas hutsχał·aqa.upχₐna'mna·
ła'ₐne·. hɛnqa'łwiy kɛntsχa'łʹip hɛntsχał·aqukuₐ'χe· na ka'min."

Ta'χas husłq!a'pqałq!anuχwa'te· k!a'k!łan·aq!o'χᵤmałe·'et.
460 to'χuₐ n'ɛ'n·e· kᵤwɛ'łqa qa'psins neᵢsts łqa'k.łaqₐnane'ᵢmał
skɛ'n·ku·ts kaₐsts χma n'aqa'qa.

(g) THE END OF THE WORLD

Ho'ya's, ta'χas hutsχałq!apqałq!anuχuₐ'te· k!a'k!łan·aq!o'χᵤ-
małe·'et naso'ᵤkuₑ·n kk.łaqₐnane·''mał skɛ'n·ku·ts.

Ta'χas neᵢsts kk.łaqₐna'na·m skɛ'n·ku·ts swᵥ'țᵢmo· ts!ɛn·a-
465 qayiłχo'ᵤłne· skɛ'n·ku·ts, neᵢs yaₐqa'n·aqa'n·uqka'ske· qa-
naqayiłχo'ᵤłne· skɛ'n·ku·ts. pał koquₐ'o·pχₐna'ła kaₐ n'ɛ'n'e·ns
at yaqa'o·χał·aona'mke· nata'nɛk! qa'o·χałqa·qaskᵢnɛ'łne·
skɛ'n·ku·ts. qakiłɛ'łne·: "na ta'χa qao·sa'qa·. maₐtsɛntsłak-
qa'ₐtse· q!a'pe· a'm·a·k. taχta·' o'ne·k kiyu'kᵢyit ta'χas
470 hutsła·upχₐnɛ'șine·. ka'min neᵢ hutsłaqana'χe· qo's at yaqa'qa·łyuwaka'mke· nata'nɛk!. qo· hutsqaₐnqa'mik. ta'χas
nɛ'ntsχa naso'ᵤkuₑ·n ktsχał·a'ło· na a'm·a·k, ta'χas hutsłao-
wo'kᵤne·. hutsłatska'χe·. nɛ'nko· skɛ'n·ku·ts a'ₐ'ke· hɛntsła-

At night Coyote said to his wife: "Oh, | tell your father to look at his fortune-telling place." Coyote started. | Now, Coyote was going to play. Early in the morning ‖ Golden Eagle looked at his fortune- 435 telling place. There were no tracks. He came in again. | Coyote went along. There was some manure. | He piled it up; and after piling it up, he yelled | at the buffaloes; but the buffalo manure did not move. He tried to drive the buffaloes, | but he could not move them. He ran back. ‖ He went along, and came to the town. 440 He went up a hill, | and he said: "The buffaloes have dispersed." He shouted | his words. He said: "The bridegroom is staying with his wife!" | He meant Tree Chief by these words. (They | used to call bridegrooms those who had not been married long.) ‖ Then the people 445 of the town went down when Coyote had said this. | They laughed at him, because the day before many buffaloes had been killed; | but now they did not move. The people prepared the meat | and the skins. Then Coyote entered his tent, | and Tree Chief lay there. Coyote said also ‖ what Tree Chief had said before, when he spoke on 450 the hill. | Tree Chief arose. He said to Coyote: | "What did you say? Say it again. Don't you know what you did | when you pushed me into the trap of Wolf?" | Then Tree Chief took a firebrand. ‖ He 455 wanted to kill Coyote. He might have killed him. Therefore | he took up the firebrand. Then Coyote was struck. | He was struck while he was running out. He was told: "We shall never meet again. | If you want to die, come back to me." |

That is the end of the story of Tree Chief. ‖ He would have been 460 the greatest one | if he had not fought with Coyote. |

(g) THE END OF THE WORLD

Now I'll finish the story of Tree | Chief's fight with Coyote. |

When Coyote and his friend fought, ‖ Coyote was beaten away west- 465 ward. | Coyote was being beaten. Although we do not know | the place where the sun goes down, there Coyote was left. | He was told: "You shall stay here. Don't | go about any more through the whole world. Later on, at the end of the world, ‖ I'll see you again. I shall 470 go back that way | where the sun rises. There I shall stay. When | the chief says that this world shall be no more, then I'll | arise. I'll

owo′kᵤne·. a′ₐke· hₐntsɫats!na′xe· qₐyaₐqa′wo a′m·a·k huts-
475 xaɫqa′ₐkil′upxₐnamnaɫa′ₐne·, hutsxaɫtsxamaɫktsaɫam·naɫa′ₐne·.”
Ta′xas hutsₑmak!ɫsₐq!a′piɫtsxamɛ′ɫne· yaxqaɫ′ₐtkɛ′nke·
swᵥ′tᵢmo k!ak!ɫa′n·aq!o′xᵤmaɫe·′etts skɛ′n·kᵤ·ts neᵢs pɛ′k!a·ks
a′ₐ‘ke· neᵢs taxta·′′ tsxaɫya‘qa·′qna′ₐke· o′nₐks kiyu′kᵢyit.s.

65. RAVEN

Ho′ya·′s hutsqaɫq!anuxwa′te· qu′kᵘe·n.

(a) THE ORIGIN OF DEATH

Qa·k.ɫuna′mne·. tsxa′ne· naso′ᵤkᵘe·n, qake′ᵢne·: “at tsxa-
ɫa·sq!a‘liɫupna′mne·.” q!a′pe· qaɫwiyna′mne· neᵢs yaqake′ᵢke·
naso′ᵤkᵘe·n. qu′kᵘe·n qaqaɫwi′yne, o′k!ᵘqᵤna at ke′e·k aₐ-
5 ka′q!e·ɫs, paɫ ke′en naso′ᵤkᵘe·ns tsukᵤat.ɫɛ′sᵢne· ke·′tsxa.
Naqsanmi·′′yit tsxa′ne· naso′ᵤkᵘe·n. qake′ᵢne·: “huɫ′ipiɫna-
ɫa′e·s aɫaqa′lt!e·s qu′kᵘe·n.” qakiya′mne·: “mɛtxa′ki·ɫ tsa·′tsa,
a′ₐ‘ke· na.utenɛ′′nte·k ɛtkupkɛ′nki·ɫ. hₐntsxaɫa·qatsk!o′mi·ɫ-
kɛ′ɫne· xaɫe′e·s qu′kᵘe·n; a′ₐ‘ke· hₐntsxaɫyu·witsxomₐkɛ′ɫne·
10 sᵤwu′n′e·s.” ta′xas mɛtxa′ɫne· tsa·′tsa. naqatsk!uɫɛ′sᵢne· xa-
ɫe′e·s qu′kᵘen; neᵢ kanₐts!ɫaɛ′nxo· na.uten ɛ′′nte·k neᵢs tsxaɫ-
yaqa′nmoxu′ske·‘aₐkₐts!ɫa′e·ns qawaxmɛt.ɫɛ′sᵢne· swu′n′e·s qu′-
kᵘe·n. tsxana′mne·. qakiya′mne·: “na·qatsk!uɫɛ′sᵢne. xaɫe′e·s
qu′kᵘe·n.” a′ₐ‘ke· ɫatsxana′mne·. qakiya′mne·: “yuwitsxu′se·
15 swu′n′e·s qu′kᵘe·n.” qake′ᵢne· qu′kᵘe·n: “ta′xas at′a·sq!a‘liɫ-
up′na′me·s.” qak.ɫɛ′ɫne·: “paɫ kɛ′n′e·n naso′ᵤkᵘe·n. pɛ′k!a·k
ma ke·′ntsxa.”

(b) WHY THE ANT HAS A THIN WAIST

Ta‘xa neᵢ ha·kiɫhakq!ayɛ′tke·, ta′xas ts!ₐxu′na at tsₑmak!-
ka·′mtɛ′ɫe·k, sa‾qₐna′ₐne· k.ɫɛte·tɫa·mna′me·s. tu′xᵘa n′aɫasxa′-
20 m·e·k. n′o·ktsqapxomna′ne·.

(c) RAVEN HIDES THE GAME

Ta′xas qatakɛ′n′e· qu′kᵘe·n paɫ qa‾qa′l′a·′sqa·lt. ta′xas
saₐnɫwi′yne· qu′kᵘe·n. n′e·ɫatsu′n′e·. q!ape·l′ɛatsu′te· iya′m·u′s
ɫu′kpo·s, kamqoq!u′ko·ls iya′m·u′s. ta′xas n′ɛskaxₐmetɛ′ɫne·
qu′kᵘents a′ₐ‘ke· i′ya′m·u. q!a′pe·ɫkqaₐtsa·′′mne· paɫ sₐ′ɛskaxₐ-
25 metɛ′ɫne·. qa.upxa′ɫne· kaₐs naqa′nam qu′kᵘe·n. n′upxaɫɛ′sᵢ-
ne· k!o·′ɫa. ta′xas wune·kɛ′tᵢne· nowasna′mne·. wune·kɛ′tᵢne·;
ta′xas q!a′pe· tunakᵢna′mne·.
Qaɫwi′yne· qu′kᵘe·n: “hults!ɛ′na·m aₐkik.ɫu′′nam na·qanha′qa
kiya′nxo·.” ta′xas ts!na′xe·. n′ₐtkɛ′nme·k qu′kᵘe·ns. nuhu-
30 xu′n′e·. ɫaxanoxu′n′e· aₐkɛ·k.ɫuna′mo·s. na′ₐta·s qa·nuxu′n′e·.

come back.   You, Coyote, will also | arise, and you shall come back.
In the middle of the world || we shall meet.   Then we shall shake 475
hands." |

This is the very last of the story of what | the friends Tree Chief
and Coyote did | long ago, and what they will do at the end of the
world. |

65. RAVEN

Well, I'll tell you about Raven. |

(a) THE ORIGIN OF DEATH

There was a town.   The chief spoke, and said: | "Everybody shall
die twice."   Everybody wished for what the chief said; | but Raven
did not want it because he eats || eyes.   Since he was chief, his word   5
was taken. |

After some days the chief spoke, and said: "Let us kill | Raven's
children!"   They said: "Shoot at a grass figure, | and the girls shall
get fuel.   Then you shall shoot | Raven's son, and you shall chop a
tree down and make it fall on || his daughter."   Now they shot at the   10
grass figure, and Raven's son was shot. | The girls chopped down a
tree; and when the tree was about | to fall, Raven's daughter was
thrown under it. | They talked, and said: "Raven's son has been
shot," | and they said: "A tree fell || on Raven's daughter."   Raven   15
said: "Now they shall die twice." | He was told: "You are a chief,
and already | you have spoken." |

(b) WHY THE ANT HAS A THIN WAIST

Then, when they were talking, Ant tightened his belt | in order to
bury the dead.   He almost || cut himself in two, and was small after   20
that. |

(c) RAVEN HIDES THE GAME

Then Raven could not succeed.   He had had two children.   Then |
Raven was angry.   He hid himself and hid all | the buffaloes.   (Both)
were lost, | Raven and the game.   All went on, but he was lost. || It   25
was not known where Raven had gone.   It was known | that he had
done it.   For a long time they were hungry.   After a long time |
they all became thin. |

Raven thought: "Let me go to the town to see if | they are starv-
ing."   Then he started.   He transformed himself into a raven.
He flew || away and flew back to the town.   He flew about above   30

n'u'pxₐne· ǩtq!a·nǩe.ǫ't.se·. n'u'pxₐne· k.ło·wasna'me·s. łatsǩna-
noxu'n·e·.

Qakiya'mne·: "kaₐs kuł'a·qakᵢna'ła qu'kᵘe·n kułtsᵢnkᵢna'łᶏ?"
qakiya'mne·: "kanmi·'yit maₐtsᵢnts!a·naxakᵢ'łne·.   sᵢ'n·a
35 tsxalqaqało·k!ᵘe'ᵢne· k!ana'xa pał k!ᶅkᵢ'łwiy. tsxał'u'pxₐne·
kaₐs tsxał'a·qa'qₐna." ta'xas kanmi·'yit qawanxa·'mna'm-
ne·. n'anaxa·''mne·. qoᵤs a·n'iłqa'haks qao·xa'xe· n'itxo'ᵤ-
me·k, neᵢs qałṭowukqa'ₐne· pał ko·'wa·s. łałᶅtqawu'mne· qaps-
qakqa'ₐne· op'na'mo·s.

40   Qawᶅsa·qa'ₐne· qu'kᵘe·n. qałwi'yne·: "a'ₐ·ke· hułats!e·'nam
aₐ·kᶅk.łu''na·m." a'ₐ·ke· łae·tkᶅ'nme·k qu'kᵘe·ns. nułnuxu'n·e·.
łaxa·noxu'n·e· aₐ·kik.łuna'me·s. n'u'pxₐne· sᶅ'n·a·'s qoᵤs
a·n'iłqa'haks sakqa'pse·. qałwi'yne·: "há·, ma k!ᶅkᶅ'łwiy
sᶅ'n·a. qa.u'pxa kaₐs naqa'ₐkiła'qaps łu'kpo·s." pał k!ᶅnqa'pte·k
45 qu'kᵘe·ns, słaqa·qa'pse· qałwi'yne·: "hułe'e·k aₐ·kaqłe·'ł'e·s
sᶅ'n·a." ta'xas n'unanuxu'n·e. yuwaxamᶅᵗnka'me·k a'ₐ·kᵤ-
wum'ᶅ'se·s sᶅ'n·a·'s. pał kqa'łwiy ksᶅ'ł'e·ps. qa.onᶅ'łne·. tsᶅnk-
ina'pse· sᶅ'n·a·'s. qake'ᵢne· sᶅ'n·a: "hutsᶅnkᶅ'n·e· qu'kᵘe·n."
       Ta'xas q!a'pe· n'anaxana'mne·. mitiyaxa'łne· qu'kᵘe·n.
50 tu'xᵘa at xatkᶅ'n·e· sᶅ'n·a pał ko·'wa·s qatsᴇmak!qa'ₐne·.
qu'kᵘe·n pał ke'ᵢse·k tsᴇmak!qa'ₐne·. ta'xas łaxaxa'mne·.
ta'xas tsinkinᶅ'łne· qu'kᵘe·n. ts!inałkinᶅ'łne· naso'ᵤkᵘe·ns
aₐ·kit.ła.ᶅ'se·s. ta'xas q!a'pe· qonaxa'mne·. tuk!xo'ᵤłne·
aₐ·kit.ła''na·m. pał kᵤwᶅtk.ło'ᵤ'na·m q!ape·łq!u'ntkałhaqᵤwu'm-
55 ne·. skᶅ'n·ku·ts wa·q!ₐnu'n·e· aₐ·k!a''nqo·'s. ta'xas qa'nał-
ᶅᵗnakᶅ'łwᶅtskᶅ'kᵢne· skᶅ'n·ku·ts. ta'xas tsxana'mne·. qaki-
ᶅ'łne· qu'kᵘe·n: "ta'xas tsxanatawa's'nu kaₐs kᶅn'aqa'ke·n
iya'm·u. nowas'na'mne·. kᶅn'it.ła'ₐtso·t. k!umnaqaqa'ₐne·
łka'm·u." qatsxa'n·e· qu'kᵘe·n. yᶅk!ta'kse· aₐ·kaqłᶅ'ł'e·s. sᶅ'i-
60 ła'n·e· ktsxa'ł'e·p. tsxałqa.u'pełᶅ'łne· pał ke'en naso'ᵤkᵘe·n,
pał ke'en aₐ·kik.łu''na·m. n'ᶅ'nse· a·na'e·s aₐ·ka'qłe·łs łu'k-
po·s. ta'xas łukᶅnłᶅ'sᵢne· a·na'e·s. n'ikłᶅ'sᵢne·. qakiłᶅ'łne·:
"wasa'qₐna·n' he'ᵢtsxan." qatsxa'n·e· qu'kᵘe·n. wa·wᶅtskᶅ'kᵢ-
ne·. n'u'pxₐne· skᶅ'n·ku·ts pał n'ᶅ'nse· qoᵤs aₐ·k!a·''nqo·s.
65 n'u'pxₐne· ma kqawᶅkᶅ'łwiys skᶅ'n·ku·ts. qałwi'yne·: "ta'xas
pał hutsxatkᵢnu'kᵤne·." qake'ᵢne· qu'kᵘe·n: "kaₐ kuł'a·'qaqa'ła·'m." wᶅke'ᵢne·. n'u'pxₐne· skᶅ'n·ku·ts nank!ata'kse·.
qałwi'yne·: "ta'xa·s pałutsqa.ᶅ'pᵢne·." qakiłᶅ'łne·: "wasa'-
qₐna·n' he'ᵢtsxan." a·n'ᶅ'siłpałne·xu'n·e·. qake'ᵢne·: "kaₐ
70 kuł'a·'qaqa'la·'m." łahułnuxu'n·e· skᶅ'n·ku·ts. łao·k!onᶅn'-
me·'nxoᵤnqa'ₐne· qu'kᵘe·n. łaananuxu'n·e·. yuk!kᵘaka·
tᶅ'łne·. skᶅn·ku·ts ta'xas n'ᶅkiłᶅ'łne·.

       Qała'k'ne·s qa·nałwa·nuxu'n·e· qu'kᵘe·n. ta'xas łaqawoᵤ-
katᶅ'łne·. a·n'a·n naqts!ᶅqłᶅ'łne·. qake'ᵢne·: "qò· qò· qò·."
75 sa·niłwi'yne· skᶅ'n·ku·ts. tsᵤkᵘa'te· a·m·a·ks qawaxamᶅ'te·

the town. | He saw that there was nothing moving. He knew that they must be hungry. | Away he flew. |

They said: "What shall we do with Raven that we may catch him?" | They said: "Don't go out to-morrow. Beaver ‖ shall be the 35 only one to go out, for he is wise. He will know | what to do." Then the next day they did not move. | He went out. He went some distance, lay down, | and lay on his back hungry. His stomach was empty, and he lay there | just like dead. ‖

Raven staid there. He thought again: "I'll go back to | the 40 town." He transformed himself into a raven. He flew away | and flew to the town. He saw Beaver lying | a little ways off. He thought: "Oh, Beaver is wise, | but he doesn't know where the buffaloes are." Since he had become ‖ a raven, he thought: "Let me eat 45 Beaver's eyes." | He flew down. He sat down on Beaver's belly. | Because he thought he was dead, he was not afraid. | Beaver took him. Then Beaver said: "I caught Raven." |

All ran out to get Raven. ‖ He almost got away from Beaver, 50 because Beaver was hungry and weak. | Raven was fat and strong. Then the people arrived. | Raven was caught and taken to the chief's | tent. They all went in. The tent was ballasted. | It was a big tent, and they were all around it. ‖ Coyote climbed up to the top 55 of the tent. | Coyote was looking in through the smoke hole. Then they spoke. | They said to Raven: "Now, tell us, what did you do with | the game? The poor children are hungry. You have hidden it." | Raven did not speak. He wept. ‖ He cried, because he was to 60 die. They were not to kill him, because he was a chief, | because it was a town. He wore around his neck the eyes of buffaloes. | They took off his neckwear and ate it. They told him: | "Quick, speak!" Raven did not speak. He looked up, | and saw Coyote there in the smoke hole. ‖ He knew that Coyote was a coward. He thought: 65 "Now | I'll be saved." Raven said: "Which way | shall I put my head?" He shouted. He saw Coyote, who was scared. | He thought: "Now I shall not die." They said to him: "Quick, | speak!" He shouted louder, and said: "Which way ‖ shall I put my head?" Then 70 Coyote flew up, and | Raven jumped out. He flew out. | He was saved. Coyote was scolded. |

Raven flew straight up, and was lost to sight. | Magpie had clear eyes. He said: "Qo, qo, qo!" ‖ Coyote became angry. He took dirt and threw 75

aₐ'kaqłił'ᶻ'seˑs. qats!upɛnaqłᶻ'łneˑ a'n'aˑn. snakⱦwᶻtskᶻ'kᵢneˑ.
ta'χas yik!ta'kseˑ aₐ'kaqłᶻ'l'eˑs pal k!ᶻ'tqaˑps a'mˑaˑks sⱦ'aqaqa'pseˑ. qake'ᵢneˑ: "neᵢs łału'qᵘanoχu'n'eˑ."

    Ta'χas tsⱦmi·'yⱬt nakq!eyᶻ'tᵢneˑ. qakiya'mneˑ: "qa'ła· ktsxał-
80 ts!ᶻ'naˑm neᵢs łayaqananoχu'skeˑ?" qakiya'mneˑ qaqanu'k.łoˑ
    a'ₐ'keˑ tiłna'ₐkoˑ. kanmi·'yit ts!ᶻna'χeˑ nᶻi nⱬtsta'hałkᶻ'steˑk.
    qaˑna'χeˑ. sⱦqawa·'kannitu'kseˑ qakałtunwaˑkawitsomᶻ'seˑ.
    na'qtseˑk!a'sⱦaka'kₐneˑ. ta'χas ts!ᶻnałtsₐqana'χeˑ. qaˑna'χeˑ.
    n'u'pχₐneˑ sant.ła'namᶻ'sᵢneˑ. n'ᶻsnit.ła'ᶻseˑ tⱦnamukᶻsta'keˑs.
85 łaχa'χeˑ. qa.u'pχₐneˑ kaₐs at naqa'qₐnaps. n'u'pχₐneˑ yunaˑ-
    kᶻ'kseˑ łu'kpoˑ. qakiła'mneˑ: "kaₐs kuł'aˑqakina'łⱬ?" qake'ᵢ-
    neˑ: "hułⱬtkᶻna'ła nöpᶻ'k!a." naoˑ'k!ᵘeˑ n'ᶻnqa'pteˑk qaqa-
    nu'k.łoˑ's, naoˑ'k!ᵘeˑ n'ᶻnqa'pteˑk no'kⁿeys. qaoˑsa'qaₐneˑ
    tⱦna'mˑu naoˑ'k!ᵘeˑₐ ts!ᶻnyaχak!o'ᵤneˑ. χuna'χeˑ a'ₐk!aₐqs.
90 n'u'pχₐneˑ tsₐqu'naˑ's χa'ₐłtsins saoˑsa'qa'pseˑ qoᵤs a'ₐk!aₐqs.
    saˑnⱬkpakta'pseˑ. χunaqkᶻ'n'eˑ neᵢs a'ₐk!aₐqs. ta'χas net!ko'ᵤ-
    neˑ neᵢ tsⱬt!na'na. łatskᶻna'χeˑ neᵢ tⱦna'mˑu. naoˑ'k!ᵘeˑ tⱦna'-
    mˑu a'ₐ'keˑ ts!ᶻnyaχak!o'ᵤneˑ. n'u'pχₐneˑ tsⱬt!na'nas; qoᵤs
    a'ₐk!aₐqs saoˑsa'qa'pseˑ. tu'χ"a tsχałhut!nᶻ'nmitqa'pseˑ. k!u-
95 mna'nłⱥkpakta'pseˑ. tunaknana'seˑ. tsuk"a'teˑ, ts!ᶻnałkᶻ'n'eˑ.
    k.łatᵢna'χaˑm qak.ła'pseˑ neᵢs tⱦnamumaⱦ'eˑs: "qa'psins kⱬn'-
    u'pskeᵢn?" qakᶻ'łneˑ: "k!umnaqaqa'ₐneˑ at tsχałᶻ'kᵢneˑ maˑk!s.
    ta'χas q!a'peⱬn'oˑ'kⁿᵢnoktsiyamᶻ'sᵢneˑ, sⱦtska'χeˑ na tsⱬt!na'-
    na." naoˑ'k!ᵘeˑ tⱦna'mˑuts!ᶻnya'χₐneˑ a'ₐqanuˑks tsχał'a'qtsχo·
100 waˑ'tskₐnaˑ's. qana'χeˑ. skᶻkqa'pseˑ soᵤ'kseˑ a'qₐnuˑks. ts!ᶻnał-
    kᶻ'n'eˑ. qa.u'pχₐneˑ ma kskiłχunmᶻ'tquł neᵢs nⱬtsta'hałs, naoˑ'-
    k!ᵘeˑs n'ᶻ'nseˑ neᵢs a'qₐnuˑks. tᶻnałkᶻ'n'eˑ. ta'χas sⱦ'ⱬtkᶻ'n'eˑ
    nöpᶻ'k!as neᵢ nⱬtsta'hałkᶻ'steˑk. ta'χas qaoˑsa'qaₐneˑ aₐ'kⱬ-
    t.ła.ᶻ'seˑs tⱦna'mˑu's a'ₐqła's. qaoˑsa'qaₐneˑ naqsanmi·'yⱬt.s,
105 ta'χas n'ᶻ'kᵢneˑ neᵢ nⱬtsta'hałkᶻ'steˑk. at qa.u'pχₐneˑ neᵢ tⱦna'-
    mukᶻ'steˑk at n'askik.le'ᵢtseˑ neᵢs tsⱦmi·'yⱬt.s. kanmi·'yⱬt.s at
    łaᶻ'n'seˑ naoˑ'k!ᵘeˑs χa'ₐłtsins, naoˑ'k!ᵘeˑs at łaᶻ'n'seˑ no'kⁿeys.
    ta'χas n'u'pχₐneˑ neᵢ nⱬtsta'hałkᶻ'steˑk at yaqaqna'pskeˑ at
    ława'seˑ łu'kpoˑs neᵢs aₐ'kⱬt.ła.ᶻ'seˑs neᵢs tsⱦmeˑyⱬtna'mu's.
110 naoˑ'k!ᵘeˑ's qoᵤs qaq!a'nseˑ aₐ'koˑktsᶻ'keˑns aₐ'k!a'łaχweˑ'ets,
    naoˑ'k!ᵘeˑ's qoᵤs qaq!a'nseˑ aₐ'kiłq!a'łukps. ta'χas k.ła'waˑs
    łu'kpoˑs ta'χas at wankᶻ'n'seˑ naoˑ'k!ᵘeˑ's aₐ'koˑktsᶻ'keˑns, naoˑ'-
    k!ᵘeˑ's at wankᶻ'n'seˑ aₐ'kiłq!a'łukps.

    Tsⱦmiyᶻ't.seˑ qak.ła'mneˑ: "ta'χaˑs hułaᵢts!ᶻnaχa'ła aₐ'kik.łuˑ'-
115 naˑm ma kowa'snaˑm. hułⱬtsuk"ata'ła łu'kpoˑ." ta'χas
    ts!ᶻna'χeˑ. n'u'pχₐneˑ pal su'k"akate'ᵢseˑ łu'kpoˑs. naoˑ'k!ᵘeˑ
    neᵢ nⱬtsta'hał paq!ₐmeˑk!o'ᵤneˑ neᵢs aₙkok"tsᶻ'keˑns. naoˑ'k!ᵘeˑ
    tsuk"a'teˑ neᵢs aₐ'kiłq!a'łukps. ta'χas ts!ᶻna'χeˑ naoˑ'k!ᵘeˑ.
    ta'χas ła.ᶻ'n'eˑ u's'meˑks. naoˑ'k!ᵘeˑ ts!ᶻna'χeˑ. qoᵤs tsₐqa'haks
120 yᶻsoᵤχa'łhaqa'pskeˑ łu'kpoˑs. ta'χas wankᶻ'n'eˑ aₐ'kiłq!a'łukps.

it | into his eyes. Magpie did not shut his eyes. He was looking up. | Then his eyes began to water. They were filled with dirt. Therefore | they are this way. He said: "Raven flew back this way." |

Then at night they held a council. They said: "Who will || go the 80 way he flew back?" Then they said: "Jack Rabbit | and Hare." On the following day the two youths started. | They went along. There was a river there. The wind blew toward them, | and they took his scent. Then they started, going up the river. | They saw a tent. It was the tent of two old women. || They arrived there. 85 They did not know what it was. They saw many | tracks of buffaloes. They said to each other: "What shall we do?" | One said: "We will work our supernatural powers." One turned into a jack rabbit.[1] | The other became a stone. They staid there. | One of the old women went to draw water. She went to a water hole in the ice. || There she saw a little dog near the water hole. | She did 90 not like it, and pushed it into the water hole. Then | the young dog was cold. The old woman went back. The other old woman | also went to draw water. She saw the pup there at the | water hole. It was almost frozen to death. || She pitied it. It was thin. She took 95 it and started carrying it. | She went in, and said to her companion: "Why did you | do that?" She said to her: "It is poor; it will eat bones. | They must all be starved. Therefore this pup came here." | The other old woman went to get an anvil stone to pound || dried 100 meat. She went along, and there was a good stone. | She started to carry it. She did not know that she had thrown into the water the one young man, | and that the other one was a stone. She carried it in. Then | the two youths worked their manitou powers. They staid there | in the tent of the old women. They staid there several days. || Then the two youths ate. The old women did not 105 know it. | The two slept together during the night. On the following morning | the one was again a dog, and the other was a stone. | The two youths saw what happened | when the buffaloes came to that tent every night. || There was a bladder hanging by the door, | and 110 there was a bunch of claws hanging there. When | the buffaloes came back, they shook the bladder | and the claws. |

At night they said to each other: "Let us start back to the town || where they are hungry! Let us take back the buffaloes!" Then | they 115 started. They saw a great number of buffaloes. One | of the youths burst the bladder with a stick; the other | took the bunch of claws. Then the one started. That one was | first. Then the other one started. There at the source of the river, || where the buffaloes were, 120

---

[1] Evidently an error, for later on he is a pup.

ta′ẋas nawasẋo′ume·k. qake′ine·: "qwa:, qwa:, qaqanu′k.ɫu;
qwa:, qwa:, qaqanu′k.ɫu ts!ka′m·a′ɫe· iya′m·u."

N′u′pẋₐne· tɬnamukᵘɛ′ste·k paɫ sɬ·aqayaqaha′se· iya′m·u′s.
qakiɫa′mne·: "a: paɫ sɬ·aqayaqa·′ẋe· iya′m·u·." nao·′k!ᵘe· wan-

125 kɛ′n·e· aₐ′kuqtsɛ′k·ens. ɫɛtkɛk.ɫe·tɛ′kse· paɫ kpa′q!ame·k!o′uɫe·s.
nao·′k!ᵘe· mitᵢya′ẋₐne· aₐ′kiɫq!a′ɫukps. ɫo′use·. tseᵢka·te· neᵢs
tsɛt!na′nas. qaɫwi′yne· ktsɬwa′t!e·t ktsẋaɫ·ama·′nme·te·′ẋa·s.
ɫo′use·. n′u′pẋₐne· nawasẋona′kse·. paɫ n′iɫkɛ′kse·. qake′ine·:
"qa′psin kinsɬtso′uk·ᵘat neᵢ tsɛt!na′na? n′uɫa′n·e· sɬ·ayniɫa-

130 wa′sᵢne· iya′m·u′s. ma hun·o·′kɛsqɫɛ′t!ne· qaqanu′k.ɫo·. ma
husɬẋunaqkɛ′n·e·. kɛntka′ɫke·n."

Ta′ẋas tɬnamukᵘɛ′ste·k tsᵤkᵘa′te· popo′e·s. qao̯ẋa′ẋe· neᵢs
aₐ′k!aɫoko·ɛ′se·s iya′m·u′s. yaoẋaɫ′etuwɛsqa′ₐne·.   ta′ẋas
nawɛtsᵢnuɫẋo′une·. qaɫwi′yne· ktsẋaɫq!akpakɛ′tẋo· qaqanu′k.-

135 ɫo·′s.

N′uk!uɫmatɛ′ɫne· kaq!u′ɫqa. ta′ẋas ɫaɫaẋa′ẋe· neᵢ nɛtsta′haɫ
n′u′pẋₐne· neᵢs tɬnamukᵘista′ke·s paɫ qoᵤs n′ɛ′nse· nawɛts-
nuɫẋona′pse·. mitᵢya′ẋₐne· neᵢs kaq!u′ɫqa·ps. n′ɛtkɛ′nme·k qaqa-
nu′k.ɫo·′s. tsɛna′ẋₐne· aₐ′kuɫatsɛ′se·s. qayaqa′wo′s aₐ′ksaq!ɛ′-

140 se·s qa·wisnuẋo′nẋu′ne·. qanaqkupɫa′lte· neᵢ tɬna′m·u. n′i-
tɛnme·tnu′qɫasaq!ẋo′une·. nao·′k!ᵘe· tɬna′m·u a′ₐ′ke· qanɫa′lte·
nao·′k!ᵘe·saq!ɛ′se·s; a′ₐ′ke· n′itɛ′nme·tnu′qɫasaq!ẋo′une·. ta′-
ẋas neᵢs aₐ′kɛt.ɫa′e·s q!a′pe′s aₐ′quɫo·ma′′e·s ts!ɛnaqayqa′pse·.
o′k!ᵘqᵤna·ts ho·q!ᵘka′e·s ts!ɛnaqayqa′pse· nao·′k!ᵘe· mitᵢya′ẋₐ-

145 ne· t!ɛnamo′′e·s. tsɛnkɛ′n·e· qoᵤs qana′kₐnuqẋuna′pse·. nao·′-
k!ᵘe· mitᵢya′ẋₐne· neᵢs qa·′qayqa′pse· ho·q!ᵘka′e·s. tsɛnkɛ′n·e·
qoᵤs qanakₐnuqẋuna′pse·. ta′ẋas ẋa′tsɛnɫẋa′tke·n. qoᵤs qao̯·
ẋakɛsɛnmɛtnaẋowa′tik k!e′iɫa·.

Ta′ẋas hu·sɬq!apqaɫq!anuẋwa′te· qu′kᵘe·n ki·′ay iya′m·u′s.

66. The Deluge

Ho′ya′s, hutsqaɫq!anuẋwa′te· ɛ′nɫa·k yawo′une·k! neᵢs k!u-
pɛ′ɫam.

Qa·nɛt.ɫa′ₐne· ɛ′nɫa·k n′ɛ′n·se· tɬnamu′′e·s kia′wa·ts; at n′a-
na′ẋe· ɛ′nɫa·k; kia′wa·ts at naɫq!at!e′ine· ɫawi·′ya·ɫs. naqsan-

5 mi·′yit.s qaₐq!anu′kse· at yaqa′o̯ẋaɫq!at!e′ike· kia′wa·ts. ta′-
ẋas tsẋaɫ·ats!ɛna′ẋe· naq!ako′une·, a′ₐ′ke· tsẋaɫ′iku′ɫne·.
qao̯ẋaɫẋuna′ẋe· neᵢs aₐku′q!ɴuks kia′wa·ts. ta′ẋas
n′iku′ɫne·, ta′ẋas a′ₐ′ke· na′qtse·k. qa.kiɫa′qktse·k ta′-
ẋas ɫa.upka′ẋe·. n′u′pẋₐne· neᵢs wu′os n′o·k!ᵘni·ɫhotsu′kse·.

10 tseᵢka·te· paɫ qoᵤs n′ɛ′nse· kaɫ′upka′ske· qapsins n′upka′se·.
n′u′pẋₐne· paɫ n′ɛ′n·se· yawo′unɛk!s. ta′ẋas n′upka′se·. qak.-
ɫa′pse·: "hun′otɛ′sᵢne·. hutsẋaɫtsukᵘatɛ′sᵢne·." paɫ ktsɫa′kiɫ

there he shook the claws | and sang, saying: "Qwa, qwa, Jack Rabbit! | Qwa, qwa, Jack Rabbit! Bring the game!" |

The two old women saw the game going by. | They said to each other: "The game is passing along." The one shook ‖ the bladder. 125 It made no noise. It had burst. | The other one went to get the claws. They were not there. She looked for | the dog. She thought she would send it in pursuit to get them back. | It was not there. Then she knew that he was singing, and that he was the one. She said: | "Why did you take that little dog? He has done it. He has stolen ‖ our game. I knew by his eyes that he was Jack Rabbit. | 130 Therefore I put him into the water, and you brought him in." |

Then the two old women took hammers, and they went | to the trail of the game in the snow. They stood on each side, ready to strike with their hammers. | They thought they would strike Jack ‖ Rabbit. | 135

One scabby bull was left behind. The youth came back, | and saw the two women ready to strike him. | Then he ran after the scabby bull. He transformed himself into a | jack rabbit. He held on with his teeth to the bull's testicles, and was ‖ hanging down between his 140 legs. One of the old women struck it | and flattened out one leg (of the scabby bull). The other old woman struck him | on the other leg and made it flat. Then | all the parflèches in the tent began to roll out; and | because the fat and marrow began to roll, the other old woman ran after it. ‖ She caught it, and it dragged her along. | 145 The other one ran after it, and the fat and marrow were rolling this way. She took it, | and it dragged her along. They could not hold it. | They fell down crying. |

Now I have told how Raven stole the game. |

66. THE DELUGE[1]

Well, I'll tell how Chicken Hawk | killed the Water Monster. {

There was the tent of Chicken Hawk and his wife Grouse. | Chicken Hawk went hunting, and Grouse picked huckleberries. ‖ For 5 several days Grouse picked berries near a lake. | Then she would start again. She perspired and wanted to drink. | Grouse went to the water of that lake. Then | she drank and she swam. After swimming, | she went to the shore again. Then she noticed that the water was rising. ‖ She looked at it, and there it was where something came 10 ashore. | She saw that it was the Water Monster. He came ashore, and | said to her: "I want you; I'll take you!" She loved | Chicken

---
[1] See p. 40.

ɛ'nła·ks; ne₁sts k!aqa'k.łaps yawo'ᵤnik!s n'o·nɛ'łne· pał at k!u-
pɛ'łka·'s.   ta'χas qałwi'yne·, qak.ła'pse· "hutsχał'ɛ'k₁ne· ła-
15 wi·'yał."   ta'χas namatɛ'ktse·.   ta'χas pał ktsɛłwałkwa'yɛt.s
ta'χas ktsłats!ɛ'na·m pał ktsła'kił nułaqₐna''e·s ɛ'nła·ks.   łało'ᵤ-
se· ławi·'ya·ls ktsχa'l'e·ks ɛ'nła·ks.   mɛ'ka ksɛłwałkwa'yit.s ła-
hałq!at!e'₁ne·. sa·hankɛ'n·e·. ta'χas łats!ₓna'χe· aₐ'kɛt.ła'e·s. k.ła-
ła'χam tsɛma'k!iłtsɛłmeyɛ't.se.   k.łała'χam pe·ɛ'k!a·ks łaₐpsaₐ-
20 osaqa'pse· ɛ'nłaₐks. namatɛ'ktse·. n'o·nɛ'łne·. qakɛ'łne·: "hoqᵘasoᵤ-
kᵘɛ'n·e· na ławi'₁yał. husa·'haniłχone'₁nc·. huqᵘa·hałq!at!e'₁ne·.
honupsłatqa'nkikqa'ₐne· yɛsɛnwunme·yɛ'tke·."   ne₁sts k.łats!ɛ'-
nam kia'wa·ts n'u'pχₐne· ne₁s tuq!tsqa'mna·s kia'wa·ts, n'ɛ'n·se·
nöpɛk!a'e·s. sɛł'aqa'k.łe·k kia'wa·ts. q!akpakitχo'ᵤne·. .tsu-
25 kᵘa'te·, qa'sɛłtsukwa'te·.   ne₁s ktsiłmi·'yit.s n'aqtuq!ᵤwakɛ'n·e·.
qake'₁ne·: "n'ise'₁ne· kaa'k.ła·m'. hutsχałqa.ɛ'k₁ne·."   ta'χas
n'itχo'ᵤme·k. nałokaχanmitɛ't₁ne·.   at qawunekɛ't.se·, at
łao·kᵤnuχa''mne·. at ława'łne·. at n'ɛ'n·se· aₐ'kma'k!tsuks
ne₁s kᵤwa'łna·'t. n'ɛ'n·se· ne₁s ma k!aqtuk!wa'kin tuq!ts-
30 qa'mna·s. qaₐpsiłsa·niłχone'₁ne· o·'k!ᵘqᵤna ksɛł'o·'nił nułaqₐna.''e·s, sɛł'aqaqa'pse· k!a'qₐne·ts.

  Kanmi·'ye·t.s łaana'χe· ɛ'nłaₐk. qake'₁ne· kia'wa·ts: "mɛ'ka
koqᵘaₐpsɛłχo'ᵤne· hutsłats!e·'nałq!at!e'₁ne· ma ksa·'hankɛ'n'e·k
ławi·'yał ne₁s wa'łkᵤwa·s." ta'χas ts!ₓna'χe· kia'wa·ts, a'ₐ·ke·
35 łaqa.ł'ɛtkɛnma'łne· yawo'ᵤnik!s. a'ₐ·ke· łaqaₐqa'pse· kałq!at!e'₁-
ke·ts ɛ'nłaₐks. k.łaχa'χam aₐ'kɛt.ła'e·s ta'χas a·nɛse.ɛł'ukᵘa'χa·n-
mɛtɛ't₁ne· kia'wa·ts. kanmi·'yɛt.s wɛ'łna·ms qake'₁ne· kia'wa·ts:
"pa'me·k hutsχał·a·hałq!at!e'₁ne· mɛ'ka kusa·niłχo'ᵤne·. to'χᵘa
hułe'e·p pał kɛntsłaqa'e·k qa'psin aₐ'koq!łe·'et hunałq!a't!e·.''
40 a'ₐ·ke· łats!ₓna'χe· kia'wa·ts.

  Ta'χas nuko·'yiłχone'₁ne· ɛ'nła·k. qałwi'yne·: "pał sɛłqapsqa˘-
qa'pse· qaₐpse·'łsa·niłχone'₁ne· katɛłna'mu. ho'ya·s hułts!ɛ'na·m
qoᵤs at yaqa'o·˘χałq!at!e'₁ke·." ta'χas ts!ₓna'χe· ɛ'nłaₐk. łaχa'χe·
sao˘sa·˘qa'pse· tɛłnamu''e·s sła·t₁yiłhawasχona'kse·. qałwi'yne·.
45 n'u'pχₐne· pał qasa·niłχone'₁se·. qao˘sa·˘qa'ₐne·. ta'χas tu'χᵘa
wałkᵤwayɛ't.se·. ts!ₓna'χe· kia'wa·ts qoᵤs aₐ'ku'q!nuks.
qake'₁ne·: "ho'ya·s hułts!ₓna'łpe·'st kanuł'a'qₐna yawo'ᵤnik!."
tse₁ka'te· ɛ'nłaₐk qoᵤs yaqao˘χa'ske· nawasχona'kse· tɛłnamu''e·s. kχo'na·s n'u'pχₐne· qoᵤs wu'o·s qawaₐkał'upka'se·
50 yawo'ᵤnik!s. qao˘χa'χe· kia'wa·t nałkɛ'n·e· ławi·'yał·s. ta'χas
k!u'pka·m yawo'ᵤnik!. małɛnk!ałma'n·e· n'aqtu'q!waqₐχa'ktse·
ne₁s ławi·'yał·s. ta'χas n'ɛsak₁nu'n·e· kia'wa·ts ne₁s qawa'ₐqa-
łupkaqo'ᵤme·k yawo'ᵤnik!. ta'χas at wɛłke'₁ne· kia'wa·ts
k!o'ma·ts wɛłka·'niłpa·'łne·χoma'łne· yawo'ᵤnik!s. ta'χas
55 to'χᵘa ktswałkᵤwa'yit.s ta'χas ła·'hułqa'ₐtse· yawo'ᵤnik!.
ta'χas łats!ka'χe· kia'wa·ts. nawasχo'ᵤne·. qake'₁ne·: "ta'χas

Hawk when the Water Monster spoke to her. She was afraid that
he would | kill her. Then she thought thus, she was told: "I'll eat ‖
huckleberries." Then she gave them to him. In the evening | she 15
started back. She loved her husband, Chicken Hawk. | There were
no huckleberries which Chicken Hawk was to eat. Even though she
had picked until the evening, | she had done badly. Then she went
back to her tent, | and arrived when it was very dark. When she
arrived, Chicken Hawk ‖ was already there. She gave it to him. She 20
was afraid. She said to him: "I did not | get many huckleberries. I
felt ill. I did not pick berries. | I have been lying down all day."
When Grouse was going back, | she saw the bird grouse, who was | her
manitou. Therefore she was called Grouse. She knocked it down. ‖
She took it, and at night she took a piece of it into her mouth. | She 25
said: "I have a headache; I will not eat." | She lay down. She
groaned. After a little while | she got up again. She vomited.
She vomited yellow water. | That was the bird that she had swal-
lowed. ‖ She was not sick at all. She did so because she was afraid 30
of | her husband, whom she deceived. |

In the morning Chicken Hawk went out hunting. Grouse said:
"Even | though I am not feeling well, I'll go to pick berries. | Yester-
day I did badly picking huckleberries." Grouse left, and ‖ she did the 35
same with the Water Monster. She did also the same, and | picked
berries for Chicken Hawk. When she arrived at the house, she
groaned still more. | Early the next day Grouse said: | "Although I
am sick, I'll go and pick berries. | If I should happen to die, you
would not eat any more of the fruit that I pick." ‖ Then Grouse 40
started again. |

Chicken Hawk felt uneasy. He thought: "Maybe | my wife is not
sick. I'll go there | where she is picking berries." Chicken Hawk
started. He came to | the place where his wife was. She was sing-
ing. He thought ‖ he knew that she was not sick. He stood there. 45
When it was almost | evening, Grouse started for the lake. | She said:
"I'll give something to eat to my husband the Water Monster." |
Chicken Hawk looked on, (and saw) his wife going and singing. | She
went to the shore. He saw the Water Monster coming out of the
water. ‖ Grouse went there. She carried the huckleberries. | When 50
the Water Monster came ashore, he opened his mouth, and she emp-
tied | the huckleberries into his mouth. Then Grouse sat down. | The
Water Monster was coming ashore. Then Grouse shouted, | and she
and the Water Monster laughed and made noise. ‖ When it was almost 55
evening, the Water Monster went back into the water. | Then Grouse
started for home. She sang. She said: | "It is getting evening,

ksɗwałkᵤwa′yi·t   me·ʻka   husa·nkɛ′nmił   kuwałq!at!e′ᵢke·ts
ławi·′yałs kanuł′a′qₐna ɛ′nła·k.''

Ta′ꭓas saₐnɗwi′yne· ɛ′nła·k. łats!ɛna′ꭓe·. qałwi′yne· ɛ′nła·k:
60 "kutsꭓał′u′pi·ł   yawo′ᵤnik!   pał   at   ksa′ha·n·,   pał   at   k!upɛ′łka.
ksɗqa′łwiy ktsꭓał′u′pła·p ksɗaqa′ke·n katɗnamo′′mi·ł.'' ta′ꭓas
łats!ɛna′ꭓe·. łałaꭓa′ꭓe· aₐ′kɛt.ła′e·s. wo·q!ᵘmaₐne·kɛ′t.se· ktsɗ-
mi·′yɛt.s nułpa′łne· tɗnamu′′e·s neᵢs aₐ′kmana′me·s. nałukᵘa-
ꭓa'nmetɛ′tse·. n′u′pꭓane· ma· kqaₐpsiłsa·haniłꭓo′ᵤne·s. łatkₐꭓa′-
65 mne· kia′wa·ts. na′łukᵘatsła′′mne·. namatɛ′ktse· nułaqₐna′′e·s
ławi·′yałs. qakɛ′łne·: "ta′ꭓas a·nutsɛmak!iłsa·nɗꭓone′ᵢne·.
a′ₐ'ke łasaha′n·e· ɛn ławi·′yał.'' qa.ɛ′kᵢne· ɛ′nła·k neᵢs ławi·′yałs.
łaqao˘ꭓakɛ′n·e·. qakɛ′łne· tɗnamu′′e·s: "hutsꭓałqa.ɛ′kᵢne· at
saha′n·e· aₐ′qoᵤłaqpika′e·sts aₐ′q!utsk!a′ła·kna′na. hɛnqa′łwiy
70 kułe′·e·k iktu′qo·n′. ta′ꭓta huts!ɛ′kᵢne·.'' n′ɛtꭓo′ᵤme·k kia′-
wa·ts. qake′ᵢne·: "hutsꭓałqa.ɛktuqo′ᵤne·. hutsɛma·k!iłqaₐpsił-
ꭓone′ᵢne·.   hutsakqa′ₐne·.''   ta′ꭓas   kq!u′′mne·   wɛ′łna·ms
qake′ᵢne· kia′wa·ts: "a′ₐ'ke hutsłaha·łq!at!e′ᵢne·. yunaqa′ₐne·
ławi·′yał sɗa′qałyɗna′ntsta′pₐne·.''

75 Qake′ᵢne. ɛ′nła·k: "at sukᵘa′qₐna·n′.'' ta′ꭓas łaqatsꭓa′ne·
łaa′k!ła·ks ɛ′nła·k. ta′ꭓas sɗtsꭓanatɛ′łne· kia′wa·ts ktsꭓa′l′e·p
aₐ′'ke yawo′ᵤnik!s. ta′ꭓas ts!ɛna′ꭓe· kia′wa·ts. tsukᵘa′te· ɛ′nła·k
a′k!e·s n′a′se·. n′ɛtkɛ′n·e· nüpɛ′k!a·s neᵢs a′k!e·s. pał kqasts!-
o′mqa′qa yawo′ᵤnik! sɗ′aqaqa′pse· ɛ′nła·k k!e′ᵢtke·n nüpɛ′k!a·s
80 neᵢs a′k!e·s, ktsꭓałmitꭓa′m′o yawo′ᵤnik!s. ta′ꭓas ts!ɛna′ꭓe·.
k.ła′ꭓam qao˘sa˘qa′ₐne· nułpa′łne· kia′wa·ts sła·ₐtᵢyiławasꭓo-
na′kse·. ta′ꭓas qao˘ꭓa′se·. ta′ꭓas a′ₐ'ke n′upka′se· yawo′ᵤ-
nik!s. ta′ꭓas n′upꭓana′mse·. łaꭓa′ꭓe· qawoᵤkₐta′pse· k.ła′-
ꭓa·′m. pe.ɛ′k!a·ks nuł′ɛ′kᵢne· yawo′ᵤnik! neᵢs ławi·′yałs kałq!a′-
85 t!e·ᵢs kia′wa·ts. łaꭓa′ꭓe· ɛ′nła·k. qakɛ′łne·: "a:swo·.'' tseᵢkata′p-
se· yawo′ᵤnik!s pał pe.ɛ′k!a·ks sɗmɛ′tꭓₐne·. qake′ᵢne· yawo′ᵤ-
nik!: "hoyasułu′′mqo·ł.'' ɛ′n·ła·k qa.oniła′pse·. ta′ꭓas mɛtꭓa′łne·
yawo′ᵤnik!. ta′ꭓas łahułqa′ₐtse· neᵢs wu′o·s. kia′wa·ts mitᵢya′-
ꭓane· ɛ′nła·ks. qakɛ′łne·: "kanuł′a′qna ɛ′nłaₐk. ma kutsł′ak.-
90 łe·s.'' qake′ᵢne· ɛ′nła·k: "hɛntsꭓałqak!u·mna'nłikpayaꭓwuta′-
pₐne·. nɛnk!umna′nta′pₐne·.'' mitꭓa′łne· kia′wa·ts. n′upi-
łɛ′łne· neᵢsts yaqa'hakqa′ₐke kia′wa·ts qakꭓanoꭓu′n·e· toq!ts-
qa′mna. qake′ᵢne· ɛ′nła·k: "ta′ꭓas hɛntsꭓałɛ′n·e· kia′wa·ts.
atɛntsꭓał′ɛkɛ′łne·.''

95 Ta′ꭓas łats!ɛna′ꭓe· ɛ′nła·k. yawo′ᵤnik! neᵢs k.ła.ɛktsɛ′nqa·ts
wu′o·s qoᵤs qayaqa′wo·s aₐ′ko·'q!nuks qa′o˘ꭓał′itꭓo′ᵤme·k
pał k!ɛskᵤwu′m·a·′ł. natstkiłqa.ü′pᵢne·. ta′ꭓas n′e·ku′łne· neᵢsts
yɛsq!nu′kske·. n′oᵤkoku′ꭓₐne· na· aₐ′qanmɛ′tu·k aₐ′qan·oꭓu′-
nukna′na aₐ′qana·q!nukna′na. q!apeł′ałe·tu′kᵤne·. n′aqsanmi′ᵢ-
100 yit ta′ꭓas n′ɛtskiłɛ′łne· wu′o pał sɗq!a′pi·łhoma·słɛ.ɛ′tᵢne·. ta′ꭓas
to′ꭓᵘa tsꭓało·kᵘᵢnukᵤna′mne·. n′oła′n·e· ko·k!ᵤnuq!łuma′nam

and I have done badly picking | huckleberries for my husband Chicken Hawk." |

Then Chicken Hawk was angry. He went back. Chicken Hawk thought: ‖ "I'll kill the Water Monster. He is bad. He kills people. | He wants to kill me doing this to my wife." Then | he went back. He arrived at home. After a while, | when it was dark, he heard his wife groaning on the trail. | He knew that she was not sick. Grouse came in. ‖ Her head was tied up. She gave huckleberries to her husband, | and said to him: "I was still more sick, | and the berries are bad." Chicken Hawk did not eat the huckleberries. | He put them back, and said to his wife: "I'll not eat them. | The leaves and twigs are bad. If you want ‖ me to eat them, wash them. Then I'll eat them." Grouse lay down. | She said: "I will not wash them. I am very ill. | I will lie down." Then, after she had slept, in the morning | Grouse said: "I'll pick berries again. There are many | huckleberries. I like to do it." ‖

Chicken Hawk said: "Take care!" Chicken Hawk did not say | anything else. Then it was said that Grouse | and the Water Monster should die. Grouse started. Chicken Hawk took | his two arrows, and he worked his manitou power over his arrows. | The Water Monster is skillful. Therefore Chicken Hawk worked his manitou power ‖ over his arrow, to shoot the Water Monster with it. Then he started. | When he arrived where she was, he heard Grouse singing along. | Then he went there. The Water Monster also came ashore. | Then they met on shore. He arrived there. They did not see him | when he came there. The Water Monster had already eaten the huckleberries ‖ which Grouse had picked. Chicken Hawk arrived. He said to him: "O friend!" | The Water Monster looked at him, and at once he shot at him. The Water Monster said: | "I'll swallow him." Chicken Hawk was not afraid of him. The Water Monster was hit. | Then he went towards the water. Grouse went to | Chicken Hawk, and said to him: "My husband Chicken Hawk, I love you." ‖ Chicken Hawk said: "I will not take pity on you. | You brought me into trouble." Grouse was shot and | was killed. There where Grouse lay a bird flew up. | Chicken Hawk said: "You shall be grouse. | You shall be eaten." ‖

Then Chicken Hawk started. When the Water Monster sank down | in the water in the middle of the lake, he lay down, | for he was wounded in the belly. After a while he died. He drank | the whole lake. He drank all the rivers and all | the creeks and little lakes. There was no more water. ‖ For several days the people looked for water, but everything was dry. | They were about to die; it happened

60
65
70
75
80
85
90
95
100

ɛ'nla·k pał k!o'ʊła. qake'ɪne·: "hutsχał'akʊkᵘɛ'n·e· wu'o, na'-
pe·t hoqᵘasts!u'mqa'qa, hutsχał·ae·ko·łnała'ₐne·. mɛ'ksa'n no-
kuyakate'ɪne· yawo'ʊnik!. a:nts!ak.ła'nałsa·nɑłwiynata'pₐne·."

105 nawasχo'ʊme·k ɛ'nla·k. ta'χas ts!ɪnaχa'mne· qoʊs yaqa'hakqa'ₐke· yawo'ʊnik!. tsukᵘa'te· ɛ'nla·k a'k!e's łaakakɛ'ne· neɪs
aₐ'k.łuktsum·o.ɛ'n'e·s   yawo'ʊnik!.   qakał'akanoχunu'kʊne·.
ta'χas n'e·kułɛ'łne·. pał sɑχa'tkɪnukʊna'mne·. ta'χas łats!ɪnał'-
upaχa''mne· aₐ'kik.łu·''na·m.

110 N'upχa'łne· pɛ'k!a·k pał sɑhotsu'kʊne·. a:n'u'pału'nisna'mne·.
łaχaq!asu'kʊne·. a:n'upału'nisna'mne·. a'ₐ'ke· łała'χaq!asu'kʊ-
ne·. ta'χas nutsɪnqatsa'mne· aₐ'kʊwuk.łe·'et. ta'χas notsu'kʊne·,
notsu'kʊne·, notsu'kʊne·. ta'χas youₓaχa'm'ne· aₐ'kʊwuk.łe·'et.
n'upsna·łhotsu'kʊne·. ta'χas tsχałqawunekɛ'tɪne·   ktsχał·a'ło
115 a'm·a·k. o·k!ᵘwina'm·o ɛ'nla·k nawasχo'ʊme·k. ɛ'nla·k n'ɛ'n·se·
nöpɛk!a'e·s neɪs tuq!tsqa'mna·'s ɛ'nła·ks sɑ'aqał'atɛ'łne· ɛ'nła·ks.
n'akakɛ'n·e· aₐ'kɪnuq!ma'ₐna·s neɪs tuq!tsqa'mna''s ɛ'nła·ks.
n'eyakɛ'n·e·. qakɛ'łne· aqɪsma'kɪnɛk!s: "hakɑłwitskɛ'łki·ł naₐ
a'ₐ'kɪnuq!ma'ₐna. na'peɪt n'asqa·'łsama'q!łeɪłnoʊke·łqaya'qa'-
120 qa'q!a'soʊk, ta'χas tsχałało'ʊne· na a'm·a·k. hutsχałałonała'ₐne·.
ts!oʊktawa'sₐne· yawo'ʊnik!. na'peɪt hoqᵘasts!o'mqa'qa tsχał·-
a'unakχo'ʊne·; hutsχatkɪnuknała'ₐne·." ta'χas nakiłwitskiłɛ'łne·
neɪs k!eya'ke·n ɛ'nla·k aₐ'kɛnuq!ma''na·s. ta'χas nawasχo'ʊme·k
ɛ'nla·k. ta'χas n'ok!ᵘiłqayaqa'qaq!aso'ʊkʊne· neɪs aₐ'kuq!łɛ'łe·s
125 a'ₐke· qayaqaqaq!aso'ʊkʊne· kqayaqa'wuha'q!łił. nawasχo'ʊmek
ɛ'nla·k. a'ₐ'ke· łaχaq!asu'kʊne· neɪ k!oʊkoqa'pq!łił. n'upχa'łne·
tsɪnukχo'ʊme·k. qakiłɛ'łne·· ɛ'nla·k tsɪnukχo'ʊme·k. qake'ɪne·:
"hakiłwitskɛ'łki·ł." nawasχo'ʊme.k ɛ'nla·k. qakiłɛ'łne·: "ła·una-
kχu'n·e·." qake'ɪne·: "ta'χas hosɑqa'tał'u'pnała'ₐne·." nawas-
130 χo'ʊme·k. ta'χas łats!ɪnał'unakχu'ne·. ta'χas łats!ɪnał'unało'-
nɪsna'mne·. ta'χas ła·unaχa'mne· aₐ'kuk!płe·'et. ta'χas wu'o
łałaχaq!ₐsu'kʊne· neɪ ma yisaq!aso'ʊkʊe·. soʊkᵘiłq!ukʊna'mne·.

Ta'χas husɑłq!a'pqałq!anuχwa'te· ɛ'nla·k yawo'ʊnik yaqał'ɛtkɛ'nke· neɪs pɛ'k!a·ks.

67. WOLF

Ho'ya's, hutsχałtsχa'ne· yaqał'ɛtkɛ'nke· ka'ₐke·n neɪs pɛ'-
k!a·ks.

Qa·hak.łuna'mne·. qak.łik tɛ'tqat! ka'ₐke·ns. salitɛ'tɪne· łaa'-
k!łaks aₐ'kik.łuna'me·s pa'łkeɪs qak.ła'kse· nɑlo'ʊqats. n'e·'tkɪns
5 ła'n'e·s tɑłnamu''e·s at saha'nse·. n'e·'tkɪns łan'ɛ'se·s tat!ɛ'se·s
at so'ʊkse·. sa·niłwi'yne· ka'ₐke·n. łama'te· tɑłnamu''e·s. łats!ɪ-
na'χe· neɪs aₐ'kik.łu'e·s. k.łała'χam qake'ɪne·: "hułts!ɪna'χała'e·s
aₐ'kɪk.łu'e·s katɑłna·m·u. hutsχałwanaqₐnanała'ₐne·." ta'χas
ts!ɪna'χe·. k.ła'χam n'upχa'se· ska·'t!e·s. neɪs ska·'t!e·s nöpk!a˘'-
10 qa'qa'pse·, sa˘'qa˘'qa'pse· k!u'pχa''s neɪs ksa·haniłwi'ynaₐt.

on account of thirst. | Chicken Hawk did it. He said: "I'll try to get back the water. | If I am clever, we shall drink again, but | it is dangerous. The Water Monster may make war on me in another way." || Chicken Hawk sang, then he went along to the place where | the 105 Water Monster lay. Chicken Hawk pulled his arrow | out of the wound of the Water Monster. Then the water came flowing out, and | the people drank. They were all saved. Then | the people of the town went back to the shore. ||

Now, it was seen that the water was rising. They went farther 110 away from the shore. | The water reached up there. They went still farther away from the shore, and again the water reached there. | They climbed the mountains. The water rose, | rose, rose. They went to the top of a mountain. | It was still rising, and it seemed that in a little time all the land would be gone. || Then Chicken Hawk 115 sang in the same way. The chicken hawk was | his manitou; that is, the bird chicken hawk. Therefore he was called Chicken Hawk. | He opened his sacred bundle (which contained) the tail of the bird chicken hawk. | He placed it upright, and said to the people: "Watch this | tail. If the water passes the three stripes of the tail, || then the world will come to an end. We shall all be drowned. | The 120 Water Monster will kill us all. If I am clever, | the water will go down, and we shall be saved." Then they watched | the tail that Chicken Hawk had put up. Chicken Hawk sang. | Then the water reached the first stripe. || The water also passed the second stripe. 125 Chicken Hawk was singing, | and the water also reached the third stripe. Then it was seen | that the water ceased to rise. They said to Chicken Hawk that it had ceased to rise. He said: | "Watch it!" Chicken Hawk was singing. He was told: | "The water is going down again." Then he said: "Now we shall not die." He sang. || Then the water went down. Then they all went down. | They came 130 down to the foot of the mountain. Then the water | reached back to its own place, and everybody was glad. |

Now I have told you what Chicken Hawk and the Water Monster | did in olden times. |

67. WOLF

Well, now I will tell you what Wolf did | long ago. |

There was a town, and a man was named Wolf. He was married | to a woman in another camp. Her name was Doe. || When his wife 5 made moccasins for him, they were bad. When she made moccasins for her elder brothers, | they were good. Wolf was angry. He left his wife. | He went back to his town. When he arrived, he said: "Let us start for | my wife's town. Let us fight them!" Then | they started. When they arrived, his brother-in-law knew it. He had manitou || power. Therefore he knew that they were angry at him. | 10

nawasxo'ᵤmik kianq!alᴇna'na. qakᴇ'lnᴇ. tᴇlnamu''e·s: ''pᴇ'-
k!a·ks tsxalsa·nilwi'ynatawa's̲ₐne· ka'ₐke·n. n'ᴇtk!amе'ᵢnᴇ.
qanaxa'ntsᴇ'ᵢte· tᴇlnamu''e·s a'ₐke· xalе'·e·s. ta'xas laxa'xe·
neᵢ kᵢyuna'qa kᵤwanaqₐna'mik neᵢs aₐ'kmoxo''e·s kianq!al-
15 na'na. o·'k!ᵘqᵤna ksᴅ'e·tkᴇn nöpᴇ'k!a·s n'ᴇtkᴇ'nmi·k tsu'pqa·'s.
n'ᴇnqa'pte·k neᵢs yaqak.lе'ᵢkе·. n'iktka'xe· qoᵤs qa·witsq!ayu-
lе.ᴇ't.sе·. qao·xal'yuxa'xe· qan'yu'n·o·'s. ta'xas ka'ₐke·n k!o·
kᴇ'tka. n'ᴇtskᴇ'lnᴇ ska't!e·s neᵢs ya·qa·nmu'xo·nakᴇ'skе· neᵢs
k!okᵘᴇ'le·s. n'u'pxₐnе· pal·o'ᵤse· ska't!e·s. n'u'pxₐnе· ma kᵢnö'p-
20 k!aqa'qaps. qalwi'ynе·: ''ku'tsxalqatanu'k!ᵘe·n.'' qao·xa'xe·
aₐ'kmoxo.ᴇ'se·s. nawasxo'ᵤme·k, n'ᴇnqap'te·k ka'ₐke·ns. woᵤ
ka·tе·. o'k!ᵘqᵤna ksᴅ'e·'tke·n nöpᴇ'k!a·s sl'aqaqa'psе· kᵤwo'ᵤ
ka·t aₐ'k.lik!ᴇ'se·s ska't!e·s. neᵢs yaqanalᴇ'kskе· qanawiskᴇ'kᵢnе·.
woᵤka·tе· qoᵤs qa·witsq!ayulе.ᴇ't.sе· qoᵤs qanyu'n·o's sᴅlqaka·o·
25 wᴇsqa'psе· ska't!e·s. n'ᴇktka'xe· ka'ₐke·n. n'u'pxₐnе· neᵢ k!ᴇn
qa'ptek kianq!alna'nas ksᴅts!ᴇ'n·as ka'ₐke·ns. nᴇnko'e·s n'ᴇkt
ka'xe·. qa'ₐlin'iktka'xe· laxa'sе· ka'ₐke·ns neᵢs la'witsq!ayu-
lе.ᴇ't.sе·. qao·xal'una'xe·ts layoᵤxa'xe· qanyu'n·o·s neᵢsts k!u'-
n·a·m ka'ₐke·n qoᵤs ma yaqa·'wisqa'pskе· ska't!e·s. sawᴇslᴇ'ksе·.
30 tseᵢka'tе· qoᵤs lе'ᵢne·s hawᴇtsq!ayulе.ᴇ't.skе· qoᵤs qanyu'n·o·'s
sᵤwᴇsqa'psе·. a'ₐ·kе· la.iktka'xe· ka'ₐkᴇn. n'u'pxₐnе· kianq!al-
na'na ksᴅts!ᴇ'na·s ka'ₐke·ns. ts!ᴇnal'una'xe· aₐ'kᴇnmᴇ'tuks. qal
wi'ynе·: ''hults!ᴇna'm·il kapa'pa k!ᴇ'k!oᵤm'.'' k!ᴇ'k!oᵤm' sanᴇt.
la'ₐnе· qoᵤs lе'ᵢne· aₐ'kᴇnmᴇ'tu·ks. ta'xas ka'ₐke·n k.laxal
35 wulikᵢna'ₐte·t qoᵤs ma yaₐqa·'ₐwᴇsqa'pskе· ska't!e·s. lo'ᵤsе·. sᴅl
qanal'unaq!malᴇ'ksе·. mᴇtᵢya'xanе·. qalwi'ynе· ka'ₐke·n: ''ma
ksa'han k!ᴇ'k!oᵤm. qa.ᴇnsᴅltsxalhamatᴇ'ktsa·p. na'pe·t huqᵘ
alaxa·''nxo· tᵢna'xa'm¹ papa''e·s, ta'xas kutsᴅyuk!ka'ₐka·t.''
ts!ᴇnaxе·. k.la'xam kianq!alna'na ktᵢna'xa'm² laₐtᴇnqa'mik
40 k!ᴇ'k!oᵤm' qak.la'psе· papa''e·s: ''a· qoᵤqalеtᴇ'l·o. sᵢnuta'
pane· ka'ₐke·n.'' qatseᵢkatka'ₐne· k!ᴇ'k!oᵤm. a'ₐ·ke· laqake'ᵢne.
kianq!alna'na. qatse'ᵢkata'psе· k!ᴇ'k!oᵤms. neᵢsts n'ᴇkᵢno·
qu'ko· k!ᴇ'k!oᵤm at qake'ᵢne·: ''saₐk, sa'k sak sa'k sak.'' a'ₐ·ke·
laqake'ᵢne·: ''wa·saqₐnapmᴇ'le·n'. aₐqa't!a·ks ma qaska'xe·
45 ka'ₐke·n.'' qake'ᵢne· k!ᴇ'k!oᵤm: ''ksa·nla'luk.lе'ᵢte·t; ma ke'e·n
ska't'ne·s, ma kintslakilе'ᵢmal. qa'psins ksᴅsa·nᴅwiyna'ₐte·s.''
qake'ᵢne· kianq!alna'na: ''wasa'qₐnan'. toxᵘa tsxalwa'xe· ka'ₐ
ke·n. tsxal'ᴇt!xna'pₐnе·.'' qake'ᵢne· k!ᴇ'k!oᵤm: ''ke'e·n ka'ₐ
ke·ns?'' qake'ᵢne. kianq!alna'na: ''hê, n'ᴇnqa'pte·k ka'ₐke·ns.''
50 qake'ᵢne· k!ᴇ'k!oᵤm: ''nᴇ'nko· kᴇn'ᴇtkᴇ'nme·k iya'm·u tsu'pqa?''
qake'ᵢne· kianq!alna'na: ''hê, ta'xta na· la'a husᴅlaᴇtkᴇ'nme·k
tᴇ'tqa·t!. ta'xas husᴅltkaxa''nnе·.'' qake'ᵢne· k!ᴇ'k!oᵤm: ''ᴇn
qa'o·xal'ᴇtxo'ᵤna·m'.'' n'ᴇtxo'ᵤme·k kianq!alna'na. qumya'-

The two-year-old Buck sang. He said to his wife: | "The Wolves
are mad at us." He dug a hole, | and let his wife and his son go in.
Then | the many warriors arrived where the young Buck was sitting. ‖
Because he was working his manitou power, he had become a deer, | 15
and he became what his name was. He went up a mountain. | He
went up there to the top. Wolf | killed all the people. He looked
for his brother-in-law. Where those who had been killed were piled
up, | he did not see his brother-in-law. He knew that he had manitou
power. ‖ He thought: "I shall not be able to kill him." He went | 20
to his seat and sang. Then he became a wolf. | He looked; and
because he was working his manitou power, he saw | the tracks of his
brother-in-law. Then he went that way. | He looked, and saw him
on top of a mountain. ‖ His brother-in-law was standing there, facing 25
this way. Wolf went up. Then the one | who had become a young
buck saw him. Wolf started to go up to him. | He just began to go up;
and when Wolf arrived, there was another high mountain. | He went
down, and went up toward the top. | When Wolf was going down, at
the place where his brother-in-law had been standing, there were his
tracks. ‖ He saw another high mountain on the other side, and he 30
was standing on top. | Again Wolf went up. The Buck saw | the
Wolf starting, and went down to a river. | He thought: "I'll go to my
father's mother, Fish."[1] Fish's | tent was on the other side of the
river. When Wolf stepped ‖ down to the place where his brother-in- 35
law had been standing, he was not there. | He saw his tracks going
down. He followed them. Wolf thought: | "Fish is bad. Maybe
he will not give him to me. If I | do not catch him, and if he enters
his grandfather's tent, I shall not be able to get him." | He started.
When the Buck arrived and went in, Fish was sitting inside. ‖ Fish 40
was told by his grandson: "Put me somewhere. | Wolf is pursuing
me." Fish did not look at him. Buck spoke again. | Fish did not
look at him. | He said while he was smoking: "Sak, sak, sak, sak, sak!" |
(Buck) said again: "Hurry up! The Wolf is close by. He is coming
along." ‖ Fish said: "What you say is bad. He is | your brother-in- 45
law. You loved each other. Why is he angry at you?" | Buck said:
"Hurry up! Wolf has almost arrived. | He'll bite me." Fish said:
"Is he a wolf?" | Buck said: "Yes, he has become a wolf." ‖ Fish 50
said: "Can you transform yourself into a deer?" | Buck said: "He is
just outside. I became | a man again when I came in." Fish
said: | "Lie down there!" The Buck lay down. | Fish touched his

---

[1] Species unknown; a small fish with large head and small tail.

x̣ane·, k!ɛ'k!oᵤm aₐ'q!atkɛ'n'e·s; n'ɛ'n·se· aₐ'q!atkɛ'n'e·s tsu'p-
55 qa's. yuwax̣ametɛ'ktse· kianq!ałna'na's. qakɛ'łne.: "maₐts
wanx̣aₐmɛ'łe·n'." qałwi'yne· kianq!ałna'na: "koqᵘałwi'ymi·ł
ktsqoqᵘakɛ'n·ap, kusɛłtkax̣a''mi·ł." pał tsɛn k!o·'k!ᵘcᵢs pa'l'ya's
kiwa'x̣ame·t k!ɛ'k!oᵤm. pał kᵤwɛ'łqa kianq!ałna'na. tunwaka-
kɛswi·ts·a'q!ₐne·. ta'x̣as n'u'px̣ane· tᵢkax̣a''mse· ka'ₐke·ns.
60   Qałwi'yne· kianq!ałna'na tax̣as kts!u'k!ᵘnił'u'px̣ₐnaps ka'ₐ-
ke·ns. qapɛs'noła'akatqłɛ't!ᵢne·. qatsɛᵢkata'pse·. a'ₐ'ke· ka'ₐ-
ke·n ła.ɛtkɛ'nme·k tɛ'tqa·t!s. neᵢsts ktsx̣ałtᵢna'x̣a·'m aₐ'kɛt.ła.-
ɛ'se·s k!ɛ'k!oᵤm's. qakɛ'łne·: "kɛnqa.u'px̣a kianq!ałna'na?"
qatsɛᵢkata'pse· neᵢs ma skiłyaqakɛ'nskeᵢ kiaq!ałna'nas, a'ₐ'ke·
65 qaˇkina'pse·. natstawitsnu'te·. tax̣ta·'ts keᵢ'tsx̣a k!ɛ'k!oᵤm.
qakɛ'łne·: "ksa·nłałuk.łe·ᵢte·t ma ke'e·n ska't'ne·s; ma kintsła'-
kełˑe·ᵢma·ł. qa'psins kinsɛłsa·'niłwi'ynaₐt?" qakeᵢne· k!ɛ'k!oᵤm:
"k!ɛtkɛ'nme·k iya'm·u's kianq!ałna'na?" qakeᵢne· ka'ₐke·n:
"hê, n'ɛnqa'pte·k." qakeᵢne· k!ɛ'k!oᵤm: "qa'psins tsma·'qsi·łt-
70 ka'x̣a·'m kaₐkɛt.ła''mi·ł. pał ke'e·n tsu'pqa's, at tkax̣a''mne·
ka.ₐkɛt.ła''mi·ł neᵢs ke'e·n tɛ'tqa·t!s. anax̣a'mɛ'łe·n'. kɛn x̣unmɛt-
qu'łeᵢk̇. at qaqₐna''ne· iya'm·u." łaanax̣a''mne· ka'ₐke·n. n'ɛtkɛ'-
n·e· tsa'ₐtsa·s k!ɛ'k!oᵤm. wasaˇqana'ₐne·. aₐ'k!anqu't!e·s qanał'-
anmɛ'te·. n'ɛnqapta'kse· tsu'pqa's neᵢs tsa'ₐtsa·s qoᵤs łe'ᵢne·'s
75 qawɛtsᵢnu'qse·. neᵢs k.łaana'x̣am ka'ₐke·n, n'u'px̣ane· qoᵤs
łe'ᵢne·'s pał sᵤwɛtsᵢnu'qse· neᵢs kianq!ałna'nas. łatᵢnax̣a''mne·
ka'ₐke·n. qakɛ'łne· k!ɛ'k!oᵤms: "hamatɛ'ktsu yaqso''mił. hun'-
u'px̣ane· tsu'pqa qoᵤs łe'ᵢne·'s." qakeᵢne· k!ɛ'k!oᵤm: "pał kɛnqa'ke· kɛn'ɛnqa'pte·k ka'ₐke·n; a'ₐ'ke· kianq!ałna'na k!ɛnqa'p-
80 te·k tsu'pqa's. tax̣ta·' ka'ₐke·n mɛte'ᵢx̣a tsu'pqa's x̣unmɛtqu'-
kᵘe·'s aₐ'kɛnmɛ'tu·ks, a'ₐ'ke· ka'ₐke·n at tsx̣ałałqana'qₐne·."
qakeᵢne· ka'ₐke·n: "ha: pał qaqa'ₐne·." łaanax̣a''mne· ka'ₐke·n.
n'ɛtkɛ'nme·k. ka'ₐke·ns n'ɛnqa'pte·k. ta'x̣as n'ałqana'qₐne·. sɛl'a-
qanɛtsa'pse· k!ɛ'k!oᵤms pał kqa'e·ns tsu'pqa·'s qoᵤ sawɛtsnu'q-
85 ske·, pał ke'e·ns tsa'hałs k!e·'tkɛns tsu'pqa's. qa.ɛ'n·e· tsu'pqa
qawɛtsnu'qkᵘe·, n'ɛ'n·e· tsa'hał. neᵢsts k.łaana'x̣ams ka'ₐkens;
kianq!ałna'na łao·'kᵤnux̣a''mne·. qakɛ'łne· k!ɛ'k!oᵤms: "ałqana'ntap'mɛ'łe·n'. hutsx̣al'upɛ'łne·. pał k!o·'kᵘit ka'ₐkɛnɛk!na-
mo'ᵤmił." ta'x̣as k!ɛ'k!oᵤm n'owo'ᵤkᵤne·. tsukᵘa'te· sɛ't!e·s.
90 nałakɛ'n·e·. tsukᵘa'te· aka''mt!e·s. tsukᵘa'te· a·k!ₐyukᵘa'e·s. tsukᵘa'te· pał'ya''e·s. qakeᵢne· kianq!ałna'na: "wasa'qₐna·n',
pɛ'k!aks tsx̣ał'ałqana'qₐne·." qakeᵢne· k!ɛ'k!oᵤm: "kaà: tax̣ta·'
na's n'ɛ'n·e·." ta'x̣as n'anax̣a''mne·. x̣un·aqkɛ'n·e· yaqso'mɛ'l'e·s.
qawasaˇqna'ₐne·. ta·'x̣as tu'x̣ᵘa tsx̣al'ałqana'qₐne· ka'ₐke·n.
95 ta'x̣as n'oqoᵤx̣ax̣a''mne· k!ɛ'k!oᵤm a'ₐ'ke· kianq!ałna'na. tsukᵘa'te· kse'ᵢe·s k!ɛ'k!oᵤm. x̣unaqkɛ'n·e· nakun·kɛ'n·e·. tu'x̣ᵘa
ła'x̣a·'nx̣o'ᵤne· ka'ₐke·ns neᵢs łoᵤx̣ᵘakɛ'n·e· kse'ᵢe·s. naqu'łne·.
ta'x̣as łax̣a·'nx̣o'ᵤne· ka'ₐke·ns. ta'x̣as kianq!ałna'na tsx̣ałmɛ't-

mittens, which were mittens of deer (skin). ‖ He threw them on Buck, 55
and said: "Don't | move!" Buck thought: "I thought he | would
do something for me, therefore I came in." There was just one
mitten | which Fish threw on him. Buck was big, | and his legs
stuck out. Then he saw Wolf come in. ‖

Buck thought he would be seen by Wolf, | and did not turn 60
his eyes from those of Wolf, who did not see him. Now Wolf |
retransformed himself into a man. When he was about to enter the
tent | of Fish, he said to him: "Didn't you see Buck?" | He did
not look at him. He did the same as he had done with Buck. ‖ He did 65
the same. (Wolf) was coaxing him. After a while Fish spoke, | and
said to him: "Your talk is bad. He is your brother-in-law. |
You loved each other. Why are you angry at him?" Fish said: |
"Did Buck transform himself into game?" Wolf said: | "Yes, he
transformed himself." Fish said: "Why should he ‖ come into my 70
tent if he is a deer? If he should come | into my tent, he would
become a man. Go out. Maybe | he went into the water. Game
does that." Then Wolf went out. | Fish made a figure of grass.
He hurriedly threw it out of the smoke hole. | The figure became
a deer, which stood there on the other side of the water. ‖ When 75
Wolf went out, he saw | Buck standing in the water on the other side.
Wolf went in again, | and said to Fish: "Give me a canoe. I | see
a deer on the other side." Fish said: "You | said you became a
Wolf, and Buck became ‖ a deer. Later on, when a wolf runs after a 80
deer and it goes into the water | of a river, then a wolf also will swim
across." | Wolf said: "Is that so?" Wolf went out. |

He transformed himself into a wolf. He became one. Then he
swam across. | Fish had told a lie. It was not a deer standing in
the water; ‖ it was grass that he had made into a deer. It was not 85
a deer | that was standing in the water; it was grass. When Wolf
had gone out again, | Buck arose, and said to Fish: | "Take me
across, so that I may kill him, for he killed all my relatives." |
Then Fish arose, took his blanket, ‖ and put it on him. He took his 90
belt and took his hat. He took | his mittens. Buck said: "Hurry
up! | He is about to swim across." Fish said: "He is still here." |
Then he went out and launched his canoe. | He did not hurry. The
Wolf had almost gotten across. ‖ Then Fish and Buck went aboard. | 95
Fish took his paddle, put it into the water, and pushed with it. He
almost | caught up with Wolf. Then he put the paddle in on the
other side. He paddled, | and caught up with Wolf. Then Buck

x̣ane· ka′ₐke·ns. qawukata′pse· neᵢs qałᵤwoxo′ᵤne· yaqso′-
100 m′l′e·s naq!mak/k.łe·t/kse·. ka′ₐke·n nułpa′łne· yaqso″mils.
tse̜ka′te· ne̜s ma swₑts̜nu′qse· kianq!ałna′nas: p′k!a·ks pał
tsx̣ałs/łm/tx̣ana′pse·. qak/′łne·: "a: ska′tᵤwa· ma kutsła′k.łe·s
maₐts ŭ′pło·." qake′̜ne· kianq!ałna′na: "h/n·tsqak!u′mnan-
łŭkpayax̣wuta′pₐne·. h/n·″o·″kt·e· kaₐk̜n/k!na″mu." ta′x̣as mit-
105 x̣a′łne· ka′ₐke·n. n′upił/′łne·. qake′̜ne· k!/′k!oᵤm: "ta′x̣as łats!/-
nam/′łe·n′ t/łnamu″ne·s. x̣ałe″ne·s k!ułmnaqaqa′ₐne·."

    Ta′x̣as husłq!apke′̜ne· yaqanik/′tke· ne̜ p/′k!ak.

68. SKUNK

    Ho′ya′s, hutsx̣ałhaqałpałne′̜ne· yaₐqaqa′pske· k!c·tke·n tsa′ₐ-
timo x̣a′x̣a·sts wu′qt!e· ne̜s p/′k!a·ks.
    Qa·hanit.ła′ₐne· tsa′ₐtimo x̣a′x̣a·s n′/′n·se· tsa′e·s wu′qt!e·s.
a′ₐ·ke· qanit.ła′ₐne· wa′ta·k n′a′se· alt/te″e·s, n′/′n·se na′młat!sts
5 q!u′tsa·ts.
    Nuwa′s̜ne· q!u′tsa·ts aₐ′ku′ła·ks. qake′̜ne·: "hao′m·
hao′m·." qak.ła′pse· t/te″e·s: "ha·′ksa kate·′te, kate·′te,
qa′psin k̜n′u′pske·?" qake′̜ne· q!u′tsa·ts: "hunuwa′s̜ne·."
qak.ła′pse· t/te″e·s: "tsukᵘa′te·n′ qa′psin k̜ns/łho′·was."
10 qake′̜ne· q!u′tsa·ts: "aₐ′ku′łak husłowa′s̜ne·." qak.ła′pse·
t/te″e·s: "tsukᵘa′te·n′ aₐ′k̜nx̣amulu′ła·k k̜nłe′·e·k." qatsu-
kᵘa′te· q!u′tsa·ts. qak.ła′pse·: "k̜nsiłho′·was na qa′tsuk?"
qak/′łne·: "hé̜." qak.ła′pse· t/te″e·s wa′ta·ks: "ts!̜n′am/′łki·ł
wu′qt!e. tsx̣ał/′n·e· nuła′qₐnan/′ski·ł. maₐts/ntsx̣ałtse̜katk/′łne·
15 x̣a′x̣a·s. at saha′n·e. ts/ntsx̣ałok!ᵘe′̜ne· wu′qt!e· nułaqₐnan/′s-
ki·ł. at qahowa′s̜ne· wu′qt!e·. qasts!u′mqaqa′ₐne· k!a″na·m."
    Ta′x̣as ts!̜na′x̣e· nana′ₐtimo na′młat!ts q!u′tsa·ts. qak.ła′pse·
t/te″e·s: "h̜n·łax̣a′ki·ł /łqa′hak h̜ntsqao̮·s/′qapk/′łne·. tax̣ta·′
wałkᵤwa′yit.s h̜n′upx̣am/′łki·ł ła′wa·′m wu′qt!e·. ta′x̣as
20 h̜n·tsu′tsamiłk/′łne·." k.ła′x̣a·m nana′ₐtimu a·n′/łqa′haks
qaha̮·o̮·saqa′ₐne·. n′u′px̣ₐne· x̣a′x̣a·s pe̜/′k!a·ks kaₐqat!o′ᵤ-
x̣ᵘa·s na.u′te·k̜sta′ke·s pał k̜nŭpk!aqa′qa. słaqaqa′pse·
k!u′px̣ₐ qaho̮·saqa′ₐne·. sła′ₐt̜yił′aqtsakx̣o′ᵤne·. n′/tk/′n·e·
nŭp/′k!a·s. tsukᵘa′te· s/t!/′se·s tsa′e·s. n′ałak/′n·e·. n′anax̣a′mne·
25 ne̜s nŭp/k!a′e·s ta′x̣as naqtsakx̣o′ᵤse·. qake′̜ne· q!u′tsa·ts:
"ta′x̣as hołhutsax̣a′′ła qoᵤs n′/′n·e· wu′qt!e·. pał saho̮·-
saqa′ₐne·." qak.ła′pse· tsu″we·s: "qa/′n·e· wu′qt!e qoᵤ
k!aka′x̣a·′m. n′/′n·e· x̣a′x̣a·s." qake′̜ne· q!u′tsa·ts: "qoᵤsts
k!aka′x̣a·′m wu′qt!e·. sła·t̜yiłkikk.łux̣onat/′t̜ne· x̣a′x̣a·s qoᵤs
30 a′qła·′s." qak.ła′pse· tsu″e·s: "qao·ła′n·e· x̣a′x̣a·s̜ qoᵤ
kᵘa′k.ło·x̣una′ₐte·t. n′uła′se· nŭp/k!a′e·s x̣a′x̣a·s." wune·k/′t.se·,
ta′x̣as n′als/nte·k q!u′tsa·ts. qak.ła′pse· tsu″e·s: "ta′x̣a łu′n·o
hoł·qunax̣a′′ła. maₐts/ntsqo·′qᵘałwi′yne· qa′e·n wu′qt!e· pał

was about to shoot | Wolf, who did not see him. He touched his canoe, ‖ and it made a little noise. Wolf heard the canoe. | He looked 100 at it, and Buck was standing in the water, | about to shoot him. Wolf said to him: "O brother-in-law! I love you. | Don't kill me!" Buck said: | "I shall not take pity on you, for you have killed all my relatives." ‖ The Wolf was shot and killed. Fish said: | "Go 105 back to your wife. Your son is poor." |

Now I have told all that happened in olden times. |

68. SKUNK

Well, I'll tell you what happened, what the brothers | Skunk and Fisher did long ago. |

Skunk and his brother lived in a tent. Fisher was his younger brother. | There also was the tent of Frog and her granddaughters, Chipmunk and ‖ Big Chipmunk. | 5

Chipmunk was hungry for meat, and said: "Haom, | haom!" Her grandmother said to her: "O granddaughter, granddaughter! | what do you mean?" Chipmunk said: "I am hungry." | Her grandmother said to her: "Take whatever you hunger for." ‖ Chipmunk said: 10 "I am hungry for meat." | Her grandmother said to her: "Take a little piece of dried meat. Eat it." | Chipmunk did not take it. She was told: "Do you want fresh meat?" | She replied: "Yes." Then her grandmother, Frog, said to her: "Go to | Fisher. He shall be your husband. Don't look at ‖ Skunk. He is bad. Only Fisher 15 shall be your husband. | Fisher never is hungry. He is a skillful hunter." |

Then the sisters Chipmunk and Big Chipmunk started. | Their grandmother said to them: "When you get there, stay at a distance. After a while, | in the evening you will see Fisher coming back. Then ‖ you may go near." When the sisters arrived (at the tent), | they 20 staid at a little distance. Skunk knew already | that the two girls were coming. He had manitou power; therefore | he knew that they were there. He was always pounding bones. He worked | his manitou power. He took his younger brother's blanket, put it on, and went out, ‖ and his manitou pounded bones. Chipmunk said: | 25 "Let us go near! There is Fisher. | He is at home." She was told by her elder sister: "That is not Fisher | who came out, it is Skunk." Chipmunk said: | "Where Fisher came out, there is always the noise of Skunk pounding (bones) ‖ inside." She was told by her elder sister: 30 "It is not Skunk who | makes the noise. Skunk's manitou does it." After a while | Chipmunk insisted. Then her elder sister said: "Well, | let us go, but do not feel badly about it if it is not Fisher. |

kɛ'nsɛɬ'alsɛ'nteˑk. ma kqa'keˑ katɛtena'ɬa taxtaˑ'' waɬk̥uwa'yiˑt.s

35 kutsqunaxaɬa'e·s ɬa'wa·s wu'qt!e·s.''

Ta'xas ts!ɛna'xe·. k.ɬa'xa'm t̥naxa''mne· n'u'pxₐne·
nok!ᵘo'yse· xa'xa·s. ɬunamɛ's̥ne·. namatɛktsa'pse· aₐku'ɬa·ks
xa'xa·s. ta'xas n'ɛ'k̥ne·. qak.ɬa'pse·: ''ɬe'n'o·tiktsɛskɛ'ɬne·
kamɛ'nmiɬ tɛte·nɛ'skiˑl.'' n'ɛt.lɛk̥natɛ't̥ne· xa'xa·s qoᵤs ɬa''nta·s.

40 qakɛ'ɬne·: ''na qahosaqa'pkiˑɬ.'' ta'xas neᵢ nana'ₐt̥mo ɬa'n-
taoˑxa'xe·. qakɛsusa'qa'ₐne·. ta'xas xa'xa·s sla·'t̥yiˑɬ'a'qts-
xo'ᵤne· wa'tsk̥na's.

Ta'xas ɬawa'xe· wu'qt!e·. qakɛ'ɬne· ta't!e·s: ''ts!ɛnyaxa'ₐ-
k!o'ᵤn'. hutseᵢku'ɬne·.'' qawaxametɛ'ktse· aₐ'kuqɛ'ᵢt!e·s.

45 wuɬɛɛ't.se· wuo'e·s wu'qt!e·. qaɬwi'yne· xa'xa·s qa.ɛ'n·se·
ɬtsxaɬqatso'ᵤkᵘaˑt naₐs na.u'te·'s wu'qt!e·. ta'xas k!o·'wo·k,
tsukᵘa'te· wa'tsk̥na's xa'xa·s. ɬa'ntawaxametɛ'ktse· neᵢs
nana'ₐt̥mo·'s. qake'ᵢne· xa'xa·s: ''a'ɬasᴇsᴇs, a'ɬasᴇsᴇs.''
ta'xas tu'xᵘa kts!ana'xa'm qake'ᵢne·: ''maₐts wa'nkɛskɛskɛs.''

50 ta'xas kts!ɛ'na'm xa'xa·s qaɬwi'yne·: ''paɬ ksɛlwuɬe·'et.s
wuo'e·s wu'qt!e·. huɬqa'oˑxam kawu'o·.'' ta'xas ɬaxa'xe·.
qsaₐk!o'ᵤne· ɬa'hutsɛnqku'pekɛ'm·ek xa'xa·s. qaɬwi'yne·: ''huɬ-
wasɛɬ'alaxa'miˑɬ. qaɛnsɛltsqatso'ᵤkᵘaˑt neᵢs na.utekɛsta'ke·s.''
ɬalaxa'xe·. namatɛ'ktse· tsa''e·s neᵢs wu'o·s. tsukᵘa'te·

55 wu'qt!e·. n'u'pxₐne· paɬ n'ɛ'nse· wuo.ɛ'se·s xa'xa·s. qoᵤs ɬa'qawaxₐmɛ'te·. qakiɬɛ'ɬne· xa'xa·s: ''kaₐs ksɛɬ'e'n kawu'o·.
n'ɛ'n·e· wuo'ne·s.'' namatiktsɛ'ɬne· ɬaa'k!laks aₐ'ku'qɬe·'s.
qakiɬɛ'ɬne·: ''ts!ɛnyaxa'ₐk!o·n' kawu'o·.'' ts!ɛna'xe· xa'xa·s.
qsaₐk!o'ᵤne·. ɬaska'xe·. ta'xas ɬatts!ɛna'k̥ne· yɛk!taqaɬku-

60 kᵘɛ'n·e·. na ta'xa· sakiɬhaqa'naq!nu'k̥ne· neᵢs nuɬa'se· neᵢs
kuyɛ'k!taqaɬku'kᵘe· xa'xa·s. ta'xas k.ɬaɬa'xa·'m. namatɛ'ktse·
tsa''e·s wu'o·s.

Kuɬ'e·'ᵢkul wu'qt!e· qakiɬɛ'ɬne· xa'xa·s: ''ts!ɛnyaxa'q!ᵤwin'.''
neᵢsts ksak̥mu'xo· wu'qt!e· n'u'pxₐne· k.ɬa'xa·s na.u'tekɛsta'-

65 ke·s. k!o'ᵤtaps, xa'xa·s pɛ'k!a·ks ktso'ᵤkᵘaˑt.s. ta'xas sɛɬsa'-
handwiyna'ₐte· ta't!e·s. tsukᵘa'te· aₐ'qu'qt!e·s wu'qt!e·.
n'itnu'ste· neᵢs aₐ'qu'qt!e·s iya'm·u's. ta'xas neᵢ aqu'qt!e·
at qaɬ'atɛ'ɬne· wɛlma'pes. neᵢsts kqakɛ'ɬiɬ xa'xa·s k.ɬts!ɛnyaxa'-
q!ᵘo·. namatiktsɛ'ɬne· neᵢs k!ɛtnu'sɬe·'s aₐ'qu'qt!e·s. qakiɬɛ'ɬne·:

70 ''hɛntsxaɬts!ɛna'k̥ne· paɬ ksɛlwaɬk̥wa'yiˑt.'' ta'xas qaɬwi'yne·
xa'xa·s ta'xas qa.ɛ'n·siɬtsqatso'ᵤkᵘaˑt wu'qt!e· naₐs na.u'tekɛsta'ke·s. aₐ'ke· ɬatsukᵘa'te· wa'tsk̥na's. qanaɬ·a''nta·wa·xₘ-
mɛ'te·. qakɛ'ɬne·: ''a'ɬasᴇsᴇs, a'ɬasᴇsᴇs. maₐts wa'nkɛskɛskɛs.''
ta'xas ts!ɛna'xe· xa'xa·s. k.ɬa'xam neᵢs yaₐqaₐhaˇkqa'pske·[1]

75 aₐ'ku'ɬa·k. ta'xas n'ɛ'tuqɬuk!samu'n·e· neᵢs aₐ'kts!ɛ'ka·s.[2]
qa.u'pxₐne· neᵢs ke'e·ns aₐ'qu'qt!e·s. qaɬwi'yne· ke'e·ns
aₐ'kts!ɛ'ka·s. paɬ k!ɛtnu'sɬe·s. ta'xas n'alaxo'ᵤne·. k.ɬao'ᵤwo·k

---

[1] Pierre: yaₐqaₐkqa'pskeˑ.   [2] Pierre: aₐ'kts!ɛ'ka·'s.

You urge me very much. Our grandmother said after a while, in the evening, ‖ when Fisher comes home, then we should go there." | 35

Then they started. When they arrived, they entered, and saw | Skunk alone, nobody else. Skunk gave them meat. | Then they ate. He said: | "Your grandmother wants me to marry you." Skunk prepared a place in the rear of the tent. ‖ He said to them: "Stay 40 here." Then the sisters | went to the rear of the tent and staid there. Skunk was | pounding dried meat all the time. |

Then Fisher came home. He said to his elder brother: "Go | and get some water. I want to drink." He threw his drinking horn to him. ‖ Fisher's water was far away. Skunk thought: | "Fisher might take 45 the girls." Then he arose. | Skunk took dried meat and threw it backward to | the sisters. Skunk said: "Divide-de-de-de it." | When he was almost going out, he said: "Don't move-ve-ve-ve!" ‖ Then 50 Skunk started. He thought: | "Fisher's water is far away. I shall go to my water." Then he arrived there | and dipped it up. Skunk started to run. He thought: "I | want to get back quickly. He might take those girls." | He came back and gave the water to his younger brother. Fisher took it, ‖ and knew that it was Skunk's 55 water. Therefore he threw it back. | Skunk was told: "This is not my water, | it is your water." He was given another horn, | and was told: "Draw some of my water." Skunk started. | He just dipped up the water and came back. He came back quickly, ‖ and 60 spilled it while running. Now there remain many little lakes, the result of | what Skunk spilled while walking. Then he came home and gave | the water to his brother. |

After Fisher had drunk, he said to Skunk: "Go and get my game." | Fisher had known while he was away that the two girls had arrived, ‖ and that they wanted him, and that Skunk had already taken them. 65 Therefore | he was angry at his elder brother. Fisher took entrails. | He painted the entrails of the game red. These entrails | are called "rectum." Then Skunk was told to bring in | the meat. He was given the painted entrails. He was told: ‖ "Go quickly, because the 70 sun is getting low." Then Skunk thought | that Fisher might take those two girls. | Again he took dried meat and threw it backward. | He said: "Divide-de-de-de it. Don't move-ve-ve-ve!" | Then Skunk started. When he came to the place where the meat was, ‖ he 75 tied it with that line. | He did not know that it was entrails. He

q!aqa′pse· ne₁s a₋ᵃkts!ɛ′ka·s. qake′₁ne· ҳa′ҳa·s: ‶hyà·.
ko·q!ᵤa‵kakɛ′nmo ka′tsa.″ ta′ҳas n′e·sqa‵t.łe.ɛ′t₁ne·.

80   Ta′ҳas ne₁s kts!ɛ′nam ҳa′ҳa·s. qake′₁ne· wu′qt!e·: ‶ta′ҳas
tu′nᵤwaka′ki·ł. qa′psin kɛnsɛłwa‵se·łhutska′ki·ł. taҳta·′ kuła′-
wam ta′ҳta ҳma hɛnhutskakɛ′łne·. ta′ҳas e′₁ke·ł a₋ᵃku′ła·k.
hɛnuł′e′₁ke·ł hutsu‵qₐnaniyała″ne·.″ ta′ҳas n′ɛ′k₁ne· nana′₋ₐ-
t₁mo a₋ᵃku′ła·ks.

85   Ku′ťe·k qakiłɛ′łne·: ‶ta′ҳas ho·łuqna‵neya′ła. saha′ne·
ҳa′ҳa·s. nöpk!aqaqa′₋ₐne·. tsҳaľo·ktawa′s₋ₐne·.″ qake′₁ne· wu′q-
t!e·: ‶ɛs ła″nta·s q!a‵piłhaqa′pse· hoq!ka′e·s. q!a′pe·′s ·aka‵-
kin·mɛ′łki·ł.″ ta′ҳas ne₁ nana′₋ₐt₁mo naka″nte· ne₁s huq!ka.-
ɛ′se·s ҳa′ҳa·s.

90   Qake′₁ne·: ‶ka₋ₐ ko′ľa‵qanaҳa′ła noᵤlitɛ′t₁ne· ka₋ₐkit.ła′₋ₐmil
ҳa′ҳa·s.″ qake′₁ne· q!u′tsa·ts: ‶hułts!ɛnaҳa′ła ka₋ₐkɛ′t.ła.″
ta′ҳas ts!ɛna′ҳe·. t₁naҳa″mne·. qa‵tałtɛnaҳa″mne· wu′qt!e·
pał tsa‵łe.ɛt₁nana′se·. qake′₁ne· na′młat!: ‶hułts!ɛnaҳa′ła ka₋ₐ-
kɛ′t.ła.″ k.ła′ҳam kt₁na′ҳa·′m, a′₋ₐ′ke· qa‵tałt₁naҳa″mne· wu′q-

95 t!e·. qake′₁ne· wu′qt!e·: ‶ta′ҳa·s hułts!ɛnaҳa′ła ka₋ₐkɛ′t.ła,
mɛ′ksa′n noᵤłetɛ′t₁ne· ҳa′ҳa·s ka₋ₐkɛt.ła″mił.″ ts!ɛna′ҳe· n′itkɛ′-
n·e· nöpɛ′k!a·s wu′qt!e·. qa₋ₐkɛ′snɛts!ła.ɛ′nse·. n′ɛtkɛ′nme·k.
n′ɛnqa′pte·k ne₁s tsɛma‵k!i·łwu′qt!e·s. n′ɛtkɛ′n·e· nao·′k!ᵘe·s
tɛłnamu″e·s. n′ɛnqapta′kse· ne₁s tsɛma‵k!iłna′młat!s. a′₋ₐ′ke·

100 n′ɛtkɛ′n·e· nao·′k!ᵘe·s tɛłnamu″e·s. n′ɛnqapta′kse· ne₁s tsɛ-
ma‵k!iłq!u′tsa·ts. ta′ҳas waq!₋ₐnu′n·e· ne₁s a₋ᵃkɛts!ła′e·ns.
      Qahosaqa′₋ₐne·. ta′ҳas ҳa′ҳa·s ne₁s kwa₋ₐ′miłnɛ′ke·ts, nu-
ła′n·e· wu′qt!e·, sɛľa‵qaľɛsqat!łe.ɛ′t.se·, qałwi′yne· ktsҳałhot!-
nɛmmitqa′ptse₁t ta′t!e·s. ta′ҳas ҳa′ҳa·s n′ɛt!ko′ᵤne·. at łaq!-

105 a₋ₐkqa′pse· ne₁s a₋ᵃkts!e·ka′e·s. qa.u′pҳane· ne₁s ke′e·ns wɛł-
ma′pis. qałwi′yne·: ‶ta′ҳas hułe′₁ma·t na₋ₐ a₋ᵃ‵ku′ła·k.″ pał
ta′ҳas ksɛtsɛłmi·′yɛt.s ta′ҳas ma′te·. łats!ɛna′ҳe·. k.łała′ҳam
n′u′pҳₐne· pał nuqᵤna′ne·yamɛ′s₁ne·. łtɛnq!oku′pse·. ta′ҳas
n′ɛła′ne·. qałwi′yne·: ‶kułtsҳa′ľe·p pał ksiľɛ′sqat!łe′et.″

110 qake′₁ne· ҳa′ҳa·s: ‶ka′yap! naso·′ᵤkᵘe·n, naso·′ᵤkᵘe·n.″ tse₁-
ka′te· hoq!ka′e·s. łało·′ᵤse·. q!a′pe₁s.ło·′ᵤse·. n′u′pҳₐne· n′o-
k!ᵘɛ′se· sawɛtsqa′pse· hoq!ka′e·s. ts₋ₐqanaҳa″mne·. sukwił-
q!u′kᵤne·. qałwi′yne·: ‶ta′ҳas kusɛłҳa′tk₁no·kᵘ.″ qawɛsa-
qa′₋ₐne· ne₁s ktsɛłme·′yɛt.s. wɛłna·ms nułpałnɛ′łne· sɛłtsҳa′ne·.

115 qakiłɛ′łne· ne₁ nana′₋ₐt₁mo na′młat!: ‶kɛn′o·′ᵤkuľakakɛnmɛ′łki·ł
hoq!ka′e·s?″ qake′₁ne· na′młat!: ‶ma kuo·ᵤkᵘi·ľaka‵kɛ′n·mi·ł.″
qake′₁ne· q!u′tsa·ts: ‶ma kou·k!ᵘi·ľqaakakɛ′nmi·ł.″ qake′₁ne·
wu′qt!e·: ‶ta′ҳas tsҳaľo·ᵤktawa′s₁ne· ҳa′ҳa·s. saha′ne·.
n′ɛ′nse· nöpɛk!a′e·s ne₁s hoq!ka′e·s. ta′ҳas sɛłqa‵taľɛ′p₁ne·.

120 ta′ҳas tsҳałsa₋ₐnɛłwiynatawa′s₁ne·.″
      Łaakaҳa″mne· ҳa′ҳa·s. nawasҳo·′ᵤme·k. n′ɛtkɛ′n·e· nöpɛ′k!a·s.
n′ɛnqa′pte·k ne₁s tsɛma‵k!iłҳa′ҳa·s. ne₁s pɛ′k!a·ks wɛłqa′₋ₐne·

thought it was | a line. It was painted red. He put it on his back.
When he arose, | the tump line broke. Then Skunk said: "Oh, | I
broke my brother's tump line!" Then it became cold.‖

When Skunk started, Fisher said: "Now | come out! Why did you   80
come here early? Later on, | when I came back, then you ought to
have come. Now eat meat! | After you have eaten, we will move
away." Then the sisters ate | meat. ‖

When they had eaten, they were told: "Now let us move! Skunk   85
is bad. | He has manitou power. He will kill us all." Fisher said: |
"There in the corner of the tent are all his rotten bones. Take
them all out." | Then the sisters took out Skunk's | bones. |

Fisher said: "Where shall we go? Skunk knows the place where   90
my tent is." | Chipmunk said: "Let us go to my tent!" | Then
they started. They entered; but Fisher could not | go in, for it was
too small. Then Big Chipmunk said: "Let us go | to my tent!"
When they arrived, they went in, but Fisher could not go ‖ in. Fisher   95
said: "Then let us go to my tent, | although Skunk knows the place
of my tent!" | Then Fisher worked his manitou power, and two trees
stood there. He transformed himself, | and became a real fisher. He
transformed one | of his wives, and she became a real big chipmunk;‖
and he transformed his other wife, and she became | a real chipmunk.   100
Then they climbed one of the trees. |

They staid there. Then Skunk, when there was a wind storm, |
which Fisher had made, and therefore it was cold, thought his | elder
brother would cause him to freeze to death. Then Skunk was cold.‖
He left his tump line at the door. He did not know that it was   105
entrails. | He thought: "I'll leave this meat." | Then, when it was
dark, he left it. He went on. When he came back, | he knew that
they had moved camp. There was no fire. Then | he cried. He
thought: "I'll die, because it is cold." ‖ Skunk said: (?) "Chief,   110
chief!"[1] | He looked for his rotten bones. They were all gone.
Then he saw | that there was one rotten bone in a hole. He went in.
He was glad. | He thought: "Now I am saved." | He staid there
that night. Early in the morning he was heard talking. ‖ Then the   115
sisters were asked: "Big Chipmunk, did you take out all | his rotten
bones?" Big Chipmunk said: "I took them all." | Chipmunk said:
"There is one bone that I did not take." Then Fisher said: | "Then
Skunk will kill us all. He is bad. | That rotten bone is his manitou.
Now he can not die. ‖ He will make war on us." | 120

Skunk came out. He sang. He worked his manitou power. | Then
he became a real skunk. Long ago the skunk was large. | He killed

---

[1] My interpreter could not translate this sentence.

xa′xa·s. at n′upɛ′łne· q!a′pe·'s qa′psins, mɛ′ka tsema′k!e·s.
ne₁sts k!ɛnqa′pte·k tsema′k!iłxa′xas·. nawasxo′ᵤme·k. qake′₁-
125 ne·: "a·q!ono′ᵤko· no′ᵤkᵘey, a·q!ono′ᵤko· no·′kᵘe·; aₐ′ki·łq!a-
n·otsa′ko· maₐ′k!." kuławasxo′ᵤme·k. qake′₁ne·: "pa·′me·k
k.łaqoᵤka·łuqłe·′et ne₁s łunik!łe′et.s." łuqᵘa′q!o·łu′kpₐne·. ła·łi-
tɛts!ła.ɛ′nse·. ne₁s łunik!łe′et.s łuqᵘa′q!o·łu′kpₐne·, a′ₐ′ke·
ła·łɛtɛts!ła.ɛ′nse·. n′asqa′pₐnɛts!ła.ɛ′nse·, nao·′k!ᵘe·'s qao˘xaq!o·-
130 łu′kpₐne·. n′akaqku′piłqaqₐna′pse·. ałtɛłnamo′ᵤt₁mo·s wu′qt!e·s
ne₁s k.łohanɛts!ła′e·ns qahoxaqa′n·muqłu′k!ᵘatsq!a′nse·.[1] ła′ts₁-
ne₁s łoᵤxa′q!olu′kpₐne·. ła′ts₁ne₁s łaluᵤqwaqkupi′łqaqₐna″ne·
ałtɛłnamo′ᵤt₁mo· wu′qt!e·. qahakiłatsu′kpₐne·[2] xa′xaˑs. nuk.łu′-
kᵤne· q!u′tsa·ts. n′ukᵘaxu′n·e·. qao˘xa′xe· xa′xaˑs ne₁s q!u′-
135 tsa·ts qanaqa′n·q!o·łu′kpₐne· aₐ′k!ałma.ɛ′se·s q!u′tsa·ts. nutka·′-
wumaku′pse·. ta′xaˑs lamɛ′txane· ne₁s tɛłnamo′ᵤt₁mo·s wuqt!e·s.
a′ₐ′ke· n′ukᵘaxu′n·e· namłat!. ne₁s ma skiłyaₐqakɛ′nke· q!u′-
tsa·ts. a′ₐke· qakɛ′n·e·. ta′xas n′uk!ᵘqape′₁ne· wu′qt!e·.
wune·kɛ′t.se· k!a·tsukpu′xₐnaps xa′xaˑs. ta′xas ḳu′k.łuk
140 wu′qt!e· a′ₐ′ke· n′ukᵘaxu′n·e· n′oᵤktɛ′łne· ałtɛłnamo′ᵤt₁mo·
wu′qt!e·.

Qao˘xa′xe· xa′xaˑs. tsukᵘa′te· ne₁s nana′ₐt₁mo·′s, ła.ɛtkɛ′n·e·.
ła.ɛtq!a′nxa″mse·. ta′xas n′ɛ′n·se· tɛłnamu″e·s.

Qake′₁ne· xa′xaˑs: "ta′xaˑs kaₐ ko·łaₐqanaxa′ła? saha′n·e·
145 wu′qt!e·. ła.ɛtq!a″nxaˑm′ tsxał′oᵤktawa′s₁ne·." qake′₁ne·
na′młat!: "hułts!ɛnaxa′ła kaₐkɛ′t.ła." ne₁sts k!oᵤkᵘɛ′tka xa′xaˑs
ta′xas ła.ɛtkɛ′nme·k tɛ′tqa·t!s. a′ₐ′ke· ła.ɛtkɛ′n·e· pa·′lke₁s ne₁s
nana′ₐt₁mo·′s. łaqa.ɛ′nse· ne₁s tsema′k!ɛłna′młat!sts q!u′tsats.
ta′xas ts!ɛna′xe· aₐkɛt.ła″e·s na′młat!. tɛnaxa″mne·. tsałe′itna-
150 na′se·. qake′₁ne· xa′xaˑs: "łaa′kaxa′m′e·n′." łaakaxa″mne·
na′młat!. ta′xas xa′xaˑs n′atsu′kpₐne·. ta′xas n′umɛtskɛ′n·e·
no′ᵤkᵘeys. ta′xas wdɛɛ′t.se·.[3] tɛnaxa″mne·. ta′xas ktsɛłmi·′yɛt.s
n′ɛtxo′ᵤme·k. qayaₐqawahakqa′ₐne·[4] xa′xaˑs, yanaxuna′kse·
ałtɛłnamu″e·s. ta′xas wune·kɛ′t.se·. ktsɛłmi·′yɛt.s qaq!u′mne′₁-
155 se· ałtɛłnamu″e·s. qakɛ′łne·: "ta′xas hułq!u′mne·na′ła.
hunuk.łu′kᵤne·." qatsɛn·k!apałtiyaxna′pse· at q!utseta′pse·.
sk₁na′pse· maₐts k.łq!u″mne·. ta′xas tsema′k!iłhats!ałaqa″ne·
xa′xaˑs. qakɛ′łne·: "ta′xaˑs, taxta·′ atutsła·k.łɛnq!oyała″ne·;"
at łaq!utse₁ta′pse·. ta′xas q!u′mne′₁ne· xa′xaˑs; mɛ′ka kq!u-
160 tse′₁tił qa·tał·a·haq!małe′₁tsin. n′u′pxₐne· ne₁ nanaₐt₁mo
ta′xas ksɛłtsema′k!iłq!akpakɛ′t.le₁ts xa′xaˑs. qakiła′mne·:
"ta′xas hoł·ats!ɛnaxała′e·s wu′qt!e·. ta′xas łaowo′kᵤne·. tsukᵘ-
atɛ′łne· xa′xaˑs. pał ke′e·n aₐ′kᵤwuk.łe·′et ne₁s yaₐqahank!an-
me′₁ke·,[5] ne₁s łoqᵘak₁nɛ′łne· xa′xaˑs. n′ɛ′nse· aₐ′k ła′m·e·s ne₁s

[1] Pierre: qao˘xaqa·n·muqłu·k!ᵘatsq!a·nse·.
[2] Pierre: qaₐkiłatsu′kpnac·.
[3] wdɛɛ′tsc· FAR.
[4] Pierre: qayaₐqawaₐkqa′·nc·.
[5] Pierre: yaₐqaₐnk!anme′ike·.

everything, even strong animals. | When he became a real skunk, he sang, ‖ and said: "Burnt rocks, burnt rocks, remains of a burnt | bone!" 125 He finished singing. He said: | "There is a faint sound on the other side." Then he sent out his fluid, | and the tree was no longer standing there. Then he sent his fluid to the other side, and | the tree was no longer standing there. There were two trees left. He sent his fluid to one of them. ‖ Fisher and his wives came out quickly | and jumped 130 across to the other tree. | He sent his fluid to the other side, and | they jumped again to the other tree, Fisher and his wives. Skunk sent out his fluid. | Then Chipmunk was tired and fell down. Skunk went to Chipmunk ‖ and sent his fluid into her mouth. | Then her 135 belly swelled up. Then he shot with his fluid at Fisher's (other) wife, | and Big Chipmunk also fell down; and as he had done to Chipmunk, | he did to her also. Then only Fisher remained. | After some time Skunk shot his fluid again. Then Fisher became tired ‖ and 140 also fell down. He killed Fisher's wives and | Fisher. |

Skunk staid there. He took the sisters, and he restored them to life. | Then they became his wives. |

Skunk said: "Where shall we go now? Fisher is bad. ‖ If he should 145 come to life, he will kill us all." Big Chipmunk said: | "Let us go to my tent!" When Skunk had killed them all, | he became a man again, and the sisters became women. | They were no more a real big chipmunk and a chipmunk. | Then Big Chipmunk started for her tent. They entered. ‖ It was too small. Skunk said: "Come out!" Big Chip- 150 munk came out. | Then Skunk shot his fluid, and the stone broke. | Then it was a large place. They entered. At night | they lay down. Skunk lay in the middle, | and his wives were on each side. After some time, when it was dark, ‖ his wives did not sleep. He said to 155 them: "Let us sleep! | I am tired." They did not listen to him, but they tickled him. | They did this so that he should not go to sleep. Then Skunk became very sleepy. | He said to them: "It's enough. Let us play later on." | They tickled him again. Then Skunk slept; and even though they tickled him, ‖ he did not wake up. The sisters 160 saw | that Skunk was really dead asleep; and they said to each other: | "Now let us go to Fisher!" They arose. | They took Skunk. The hole was on a mountain, | and they turned Skunk the other way. His

165 aₐ‘k!a‘łaxwi′e·ts, neᵢs yaₐkił′nske· aₐ‘kₐwuk.łe·′et.s n′ɛ′n·se·
aₐ‘ksa′q!e·s. ta′xas łaanaxa″ɪmne· neᵢ nana′ₐtᵢmo. nawasxo′ᵤ-
me·k. n′ɛtkɛ′n·e· nöpɛ′k!a·s neᵢs ma yɛsk!ame′ᵢke· na′mła·t!.
qasqapłe.ɛ′t.se· xa′xa·s. q!a‘piłtsɛnxuna′pse· no′kᵘeys. ta′xas
łats!ɛna′xe· na′młat! nana′ₐtᵢmo yaₐqaₐkqa′pske· wu′qt!e·s.

170   K.łała′xam łaetkɛ′n·e· ła.ɛtq!a″nxa′ɪms, ta′xas k.łao′ᵤwuk
wu′qt!e· n′u′pxₐne· ałtɛnamu″e·s. qakɛ′łne·: "kaₐs ke′e·n
xa′xa·s." qak.ła′pse·: "qoᵤ sawɛtsqa′ₐne· aₐ‘kₐwuk.łe·′et.s."
qakɛ′łne·: "ta′xas hułts!ɛnáxa′ła ɛłqa′ha·k a′m·a·k. at
saha′n·e· xa′xa·s; mɛ′ka neᵢs ktsɛma′k!e·s no′kᵘeys kɛn′-
175 ɛtkɛnmɛ′łki·ł tsxał′umɛtskɛ′n·e·. tsxał·aakaxa″mne·." ta′xas
ts!ɛna′xe· ałtɛłnamo′ᵤtᵢmo wu′qt!e·. ma′te· am·a′k!e·s.

       Qahak.łe′ᵢtsᵢne· xa′xa·s. naq!małe′ᵢtsᵢne·. n′u′pxₐne· pał
sɛłsaxuna′pse· tɛłnamu″e·s. qake′ᵢne·: "a·nłu′n·u qa‘ha-
xone′ᵢki·ł, hɛntsaxu′napkɛ′łne·." qawanxa′ₐmse·. a′ₐ‘ke· łaqa-
180 kɛ′łne·: "a·nłu′n·u qa‘haxune′ᵢki·ł." neᵢs qałwanxo′ᵤne·,
n′u′pxₐne· tsɛmak!e′ᵢse·. ta′xas wanxa″mne·. pał q!a‘pił-
hawɛtsxuna′pse·. pał sᵤwɛtsqa′ₐne· no′ᵤkᵘeys, pał q!a‘pił-
q!u′ntkaxuna′kse· neᵢs yɛ′ske·. yana′ha·ksts nas yu′n·u-
nɛk!xo′e·s. pał sɛł·aqa′tałwanxa″mne·. ta′xas n′iła′ne·,
185 qałwi′yne·: "ta′xas kułtsɛ′ł′e·p." n′u′pxₐne· mɛ′ka at ma
k!umɛ′tskin no′ᵤkᵘeys. ta′xas n′atsu′kpₐne·. qaₐkił′atsu′k-
pₐne· n′atsu′kpₐne·, n′atsu′kpₐne·. wune·kɛ′t.se· k!a′ₐtsukp,
ta′xas ławansa′q!ₐne·. qahakił′atsu′kpₐne·, ta′xas łaq!a‘-
piłwanxa″mne·. na′tstkił′atsu′kpₐne· ta′xas wɛłe.ɛ′t.se·. pał
190 sɛłqa′tał·a.u′pxₐne· kiyu′kᵢyit.s. qałwi′yne·: "neᵢ hułinłŭ-
qᵘa‘xo′ᵤme·k." neᵢs łuqᵘaxa′mne·. ta′xas łaatsu′kpₐne·.
wunɛkɛ′t.se· n′u′pxₐne· tsaₐk!aₐłmi′yitnana′se·. pał sɛł·a-
tsu′nok!o′ᵤne·. qake′ᵢne·: "hà: ma qa‘psqawe·′sɛłno′hos."[1]
ta′xas a′ₐ‘ke· łaatsu′kpₐne·. ta′xas a·n′ałmak!anu′kse·. ta′xas
195 nuk.łu′kᵤne· k!a′ₐtsukp. qałwi′yne.: "ho′ya′s hułtse′ᵢka·t
naqa‘sᵢmak!a′ₐnu·k." n′akakɛ′n·e· aₐq!ułu′kp!e·s. qao̯xakɛ′n·e·
a′ₐk.ła′ₐkᵤwu′ᵤt!e·s neᵢs aₐ‘q!ułu′kp!e·s n′anak!o′ᵤne·.

       Qahana′xe· qu′kᵘe·n. n′u′pxₐne· yaₐqakₐna′pske· xa′xa·s
qoᵤs qawɛsqa′ₐne· ła′a·s. neᵢsts k!ana′k!o· aₐ‘q!ułu′kp!e·s
200 xa′xas. naₐs aₐ‘kaq!ne′e·s qu′kᵘen naₐs qahak!o′ᵤse·[2]
qatseᵢka′te·. kwunɛ′ke·t.s łatᵢnak!o′ᵤne· xa′xa·s aₐ‘q!ułu′k-
p!e·s. naku′m·seke′ᵢte·. qake′ᵢne·: "k.łɛtɛ′m·sɛkqłɛ′lxo qu′kᵘe·n
k.łqa′qoqᵘa′kam at k!u′k!ᵘił. qao‘k!qaxo′ᵤme·k." pał kqa-
tse′ᵢka·t.s n′upxa′se· neᵢsts ktsxał·a′kum·sɛ′keᵢt. sɛł·a′qał-
205 qatseᵢka′te·. łaan·ak!o′ᵤne·. qake′ᵢne· xa′xa·s, nawasxo′ᵤ-
me·k. qake′ᵢne.:

       "Ha′p ho·he′ha; ha′p ho·he′ha; ha′p ho·he′ha."

---
[1] Pierre more quickly: qa‘psqawɛsłno′hos.
[2] Pierre: qaₐk!o′usẽ·.

head was ‖ toward the door, and his legs lay toward the mountains. | 165
Then the sisters went out again. They sang. | They worked their
manitou power, and the size of Big Chipmunk's hole | was almost the
size of Skunk. The stones squeezed him all over. Then | Big Chip-
munk and her sister went back to where Fisher lay. ‖

When they got there, they restored him to life; and when Fisher 170
arose, | he saw his wives. He said to them: "Where is | Skunk?"
They said to him: "He is in a hole in the mountain." | He said to
them: "Let us go to a far-away country. | Skunk is bad. No matter
how strong the stones ‖ you made, he will break them, he will come out 175
again." Then | Fisher and his wives started and left the country. |

Skunk was asleep. He woke up, and knew | that his wives hurt him.
He said: "Move away a little! | You hurt me!" They did not move;
and ‖ he said again: "Move away a little!" He pushed them, | and 180
he noticed that (what he touched) was hard. Then he moved, | and
everything was tight on his body. He was in a hole in the rock. It
was all | around him on each side of his body and on top of his body. |
He could not move. Then he cried. ‖ He thought: "I must die." He 185
knew that he even | used to break rocks. Then he sent out his fluid.
He went on sending out his fluid, | sending out his fluid, sending out
his fluid. After he had sent out his fluid for some time, | he could
move a leg. He went on sending out his fluid, and | he could move
all around. For a long time he sent out his fluid, and then the space
was large. ‖ He could not see the daylight. He thought: "Let me | lie 190
the other way," and he turned the other way. Then he sent out his
fluid again. | After some time he saw a little hole. The rocks opened. |
He said: "Oh, it looks like a star!" | He sent his fluid again. Then
the hole was larger. Now ‖ he was tired sending out his fluid. He 195
thought: "Now let me see | how large the hole is." He took out his
musk bag and put it on the end of | his bow. He stuck it out. |

Raven was going along at this time. He saw what Skunk was
doing. | He stood there outside; and when Skunk put out his musk
bag ‖ here in front of Raven, he passed it in front of him. | He did not 200
look at it. After some time Skunk took his musk bag in again. | He
smelled of it, and said: "It might smell like the eye of Raven. |
Maybe he is coming this way. He is one who is always going about."
(Raven) had not looked at it, | because he knew that (Skunk) would
smell of it. Therefore ‖ he had not looked at it. (Skunk) put it out 205
again. Skunk sang, | and said: |

"Hap ho he ha! hap ho he ha! hap ho he ha!" |

N'ɛtkɛ'nmeˑk qu'kʷens. n'ɛnqa'pteˑk neᵢs tsɛma'k!iɫqu'kʷins.
nuq!ᵢyu'k!o'ᵤneˑ neᵢs aₐ'q!ulukp!ɛ'se's ẋa'ẋaˑs. nulnuẋu'n'eˑ
210 paɫ k!ɛnqa'pteˑk neᵢs tsɛma'k!iɫqu'kʷins, sɗ'aqaɫhuɫnuẋu'n'eˑ.
n'u'pẋₐneˑ ẋa'ẋaˑs neᵢs aₐ'kikqapẋuneyiɛ'se's qu'kʷins. qake'ᵢneˑ:
"Yàˑ." ɫatkaq!aɫkɛ'n'eˑ aₐ'k.lak_uwo'_utle's. ɫo'_use aₐq!oɫu'kp!-
e's. ta'ẋas n'iɫa'n'eˑ. qake'ᵢneˑ: "ka'yap! naso:'kʷeˑn, ka'yap!
naso:'kʷeˑn, naso:'kʷeˑn." paɫ ke'eˑns ktsɛmak!qa'pᵢmo neᵢsts
215 ktsukʷa't.le's siɫ'a'qaɫwɛlke'ᵢneˑ k!e'ᵢɫa. qake'ᵢneˑ: "hɛn'-
upsɫa'tᵢyiɫmaˑn'ɫo_uk!a'paɫnuẋ'watɛ'ɫik. tseˑn k!a'paɫtɛ'ɫam' kaₐ
kts!aₐqa'naɫu'kʷiɫmiˑ'yit." ta'ẋas tsɛn k!a'paɫtɛ'ɫik ẋa'ẋaˑs.
n'u'pẋₐneˑ qa'ɫakna'sqa'naɫwaₐkikqa'pẋuna'kseˑ qu'kʷins. ɫaₐps-
keᵢkaɫ'okʷa'kikqapẋuna'kseˑ. ta'ẋas q!a'kqapẋuna'kseˑ. qa-
220 ke'ᵢneˑ: "qo_u ɫu'nˑu at ma kuqaˇha'ₐɫkqaₐts naₐ ɫa:'n'a
qa'oˇẋaɫ'a.u'n'aɫu'kʷɛlmiˑ'yit." qahakqa''neˑ ẋa'ẋaˑs. tsukʷa'te
aₐ'ktsₐma'ɫ'eˑs. ɫu'q_uneˑ aₐ'ksa'q!eˑs. n'anakɛ'n'eˑ. paɫ k!u'kts-
ɫe.ɛtna'nas. tsẋaɫ'aqa'taɫ'anaẋa''mneˑ. sɗ'aqaqₐana''neˑ k.ɫu'qʷa
aₐ'ksa'q!eˑs. k!ana'keˑn. a'ₐkeˑ ɫu'q_uneˑ nao'ˑk!ʷe's. a'ₐkeˑ
225 n'anakɛ'n'eˑ. ɫu'q_uneˑ aₐ'k.la't!eˑs. a'ₐkeˑ n'anakɛ'n'eˑ. neᵢs
k!uk!qa'pe'ˑs aₐ'k.la't!eˑs. ɫu'q_uneˑ. n'anaqayqa'pseˑ. ta'ẋas
ɫalo.u'seˑ aₐ'q!onakiɫma'k!eˑs. nawasẋo'_umeˑk. qake'ᵢneˑ:

　　　"Huɫ'a:'naqa'yuk!aˇ'ɫaˑkka''meˑk;
　　　huɫ'a:'naqa'yuk!aˇ'ɫaˑkka'meˑk."

230　　Ta'ẋas saˑkẋaqayqa'pseˑ aₐ'ko_uk!aɫa'ₐk!eˑs. ta'ẋas ɫa.a-
naqayqa'pseˑ. qao'ˇẋaqayqa'mˑeˑk nao'ˑk!ʷe's aₐ'k.la't!e's
tsukʷa'teˑ nao'ˑk!ʷe's ɫat!apts!akɛ'n'eˑ. tsukʷa'teˑ aₐ'ksa'q!e's
a'ₐkeˑ ɫaẋa'tsᵢniɫt!apts!akɛ'n'eˑ. ta'ẋas ɫao·wo'ˑk_uneˑ ẋa'ẋaˑs.
ta'ẋas ẋa'ẋaˑs qawɛsqa'ₐneˑ. saha'n'seˑ. k.ɫa'ɫo's aₐ'quqt!e'e's.
235 qao'ˇẋa'ẋeˑ. tsukʷa'teˑ aₐ'ku'laˑɫs. qanakɛ'n'eˑ. to'_uẋʷa so'_ukʷseˑ.

　　　Ts!ɛna'ẋeˑ neᵢs ma yaₐqana'nuẋu'skeˑ qu'kʷins. neᵢs ɫawat!-
ɛ'naks. qana'ẋeˑ. wat!a'ẋeˑ. ts!ɛnaɫhuɫqa'ₐtseˑ aₐ'kɛnuqɫe'eˑt.s.
wuɫe.ɛ't.seˑ. ta'ẋas ɫaẋa'ẋeˑ aₐ'kik.luna'meˑs. neᵢsts k.ɫa'ẋam
qu'kʷin ɫa.ɛtkɛ'nmeˑk tɛ'tqaˑt!s qu'kʷin. ta'ẋas qake'ᵢneˑ:
240 "husɗwaɫkinmɛ'ɫneˑ aₐ'q!oɫu'kp!e's ẋa'ẋaˑs." ta'ẋas q!a'pe·
sukʷiɫq!ukna'mneˑ. qakiya'mneˑ: "ta'ẋas ẋa'ẋaˑs at tsẋaɫ'a-
qa.upɛ'ɫneˑ q!a'pe'ˑs qa'psins. k.ɫa'ɫo_us aₐ'q!oɫu'kp!e's." ta'ẋas
at k.ɫɛnq!oymoɫɛ's_ineˑ. ta'ẋas wuneˑkɛ't.seˑ kk.ɛnq!o'ymoˑɫ,
ta'ẋas ɫaẋa'ẋeˑ ẋa'ẋaˑs. n'upẋa'ɫneˑ k.ɫa'ẋam tɛ'tqaˑt! qakiɫɛ'ɫ-
245 neˑ: "qa'ɫa kɛ'n'eˑn?" qake'ᵢne ẋa'ẋaˑs: "neᵢ ɫu'nˑqo aₐ'ki-
nuqɫe·'et hoqʷaqa'ẋeˑ. hoqʷa'k.le·k k.ɫu'nˑqo·ke'ᵢkaqts!ɗa-
mˑa·ɫwuẋonɛ'ɫikhɛnma'wo." qakiɫɛ'ɫneˑ: "qo_us sn'ɛt.ɫa'ne·
naso'_ukʷe·n qa'k.leᵢk qu'kʷins. n'ɛ'n'eˑ ta'ẋta· ke''wam naₐs
aₐ'kik.luna'meˑs, naɫkɛ'n'eˑ ẋa'ẋaˑs aₐ'q!ulukp!ɛ'se's. a'ₐkeˑ
250 n'ɛ'n'eˑ naso'_ukʷe·n qa'k.leˑk k.ɫa'wɫa. n'a's_ineˑ naso'_ukʷe·n
na aₐ'kik.ɫu''nam." quna'ẋeˑ ẋa'ẋaˑs aₐ'kɛt.laɛ'se's qu'kʷins.

Raven transformed himself into a raven. He became a real raven. |
He took hold of Skunk's musk bag with his bill. Then he flew away, ‖
because he had become a real raven, therefore he could fly. | Skunk 210
noticed the flapping of the wings of Raven, and said: | "Oh!" He
pulled in his bow quickly. His musk bag was gone. | Then he cried,
and said: "(?) . . . chief, | chief!" for his power ‖ had been taken 215
away from him; therefore he cried. He said (to himself): | "You
always make too much noise about your ears. Now, listen whether |
the sky will make noise!" Then Skunk listened. | He noticed that
Raven went right up. | Then it came down making a noise. Then
the noise stopped. ‖ He said: "There, farther along, I walk about. 220
Here, on this side, | went down the noise from the sky." Skunk was
lying there. He took | his knife and cut off his leg. He pushed it
out. | Because the hole was small, he could not get out. Therefore
he did so. He cut off | his leg. He pushed it out. He also cut off
the other one and ‖ pushed it out. He cut off his arm and put it out, 225
too. | Now there was one arm left. He cut it off, and it rolled out.
Then | all his limbs were gone. He sang, and said: |

"Let my back roll out, |
Let my back roll out." ‖

Then his back rolled out. Then he rolled out. | He rolled himself 230
on his one arm. He took | the other one and stuck it on. He took
his leg, and he | stuck on both of them. Then Skunk arose.
Then | Skunk stood up. He was bad. He had no entrails. ‖ Then he 235
went and took leaves and put them in. Then he was almost good. |

He started to the place where Raven had flown, there across
the mountains.[1] | He went along. He went across the mountains,
and he went along the prairie. | Far away he came to a town.
When Raven had arrived, | he had transformed himself into a man.
Then he said: ‖ "I have brought with me Skunk's musk bag." Then 240
they were all | glad. They said: "Now Skunk will | no longer kill
everything. He has no musk bag." Then | they played with it. They
played with it for a long time. | Then Skunk came. A man was
seen coming along. He was told: ‖ "Who are you?" Skunk said: 245
"I come from that prairie | over there. I am named | Coming-from-
the-Prairie-far-away-with-Head-washed-with-White-Clay-carrying-
my-Bow-Sideways." He was told: "Over there is the tent | of the
chief. His name is Raven. He just came | to this town and brought
Skunk's musk bag. Now, ‖ there is also a chief named Grizzly 250
Bear." There were two chiefs | in this town. Skunk went to Raven's

---

[1] Through Crow's Nest Pass.

ne₁s k.łaxa′łke·n qu′kᵘin a₋′q!ułukp!ɛ′se·s xa′xa·s n′ɛtkɛ′n·e·,
n′ɛnqapta′kse· tsɛt!na′nas. ne₁sts kt₁na′xa′m xa′xa·s na₋s
a₋·ka′łaxwu′c·ts qa₋nłuk!ᵘa′tse· tsɛt!na′nas. mit₁yaxna′pse·.
255 sukᵘiłq!u′kse·. qake′₁ne·: "k!a₋qakɛ′n·ap tsoᵤt?" sɛł′ouna′pse·
ts·ił′aqakɛna′pse·. mɛ′ksa′n qu′kᵘin qao′ᵤne· qałas nɛ′n·c·ns.
ta′xas n′ɛsaknu′n·e· xa′xa·s. namatɛkts·ɛ′łne· ke′e·k. ta′xas
n′ɛ′k₁ne·. saha′n·se· ne₁s ke′e·k pał k.ła′łoᵤs qa′psins
oqonɛ′k!c·s. qawɛl′ił′ɛ′k₁ne·. k.łaqa′e·k. saha′n·se· oqonɛ′k!e·s,
260 o·′k!ᵘqᵤna k!oqo′ᵤsałxasɛnmɛ′tko. qakiłɛ′łne·. qake′₁ne· k.ła′wła:
"kɛnłts!ɛna′mi·ł." n′owo′kᵤne·. łaanaxa′′mne· xa′xa·s ne₁s
ya₋qa′kxał′owo′ᵤkᵘe· qahakqa′pse· a₋′ku′ła·ks. qake′₁ne· łka′-
m·u: "wa′nasksks·ɛ′kqa a₋′ku′ła·k." qake′₁ne· qu′kᵘin: "ma₋ts
ɛ′ke·n′. n′ɛ′n·e· kxa′tkxa·ł. at qa·ɛ′k₁ne· łka′m·u. huts!ɛ′s₁-
265 nił′ɛ′k₁ne·." t₁naxa′′mne· xa′xa·s a₋′kɛt.ła·ɛ′se·s k.ła′wła′s a′₋·ke·
namatɛkts·ɛ′h̓e· ke′e·k. a′₋·ke· qawɛl′ił′ɛ′k₁ne·. kqa₋qa′ske·n
łaanaxa′′mne·, a′₋·ke· qahaˇkqa′pse·¹ a₋′ku′ła·ks ne₁s ya₋qa′-
kxał′owo′ᵤkᵘe·. a′₋·ke· n′ɛs₁nił′ɛk₁ne· k.ła′wła. n′ɛ′nse· ne₁s ke′e·k
xa′xa·s ne₁s at k!ɛ′k.łe·s o·k!ᵘqᵤna k.ła′łoᵤs a₋′kᵤwu′m′e·s. ne₁s
270 nɛ′n′e·k at sɛł·aqaˇya′₋qanmuxo′se·.

    Ta′xas tu′xᵘa tsxałwałkwayɛ′t.se· n′anaxa′′mne· qu′kᵘin.
qake′₁ne·: "ta′xa·′s akaxa′′mki·ł kɛnła′k.łɛnq!o′ykі·ł, ma ka′qa
kɛ′nk.łɛnq!oymu′kᵘi·ł." ta′xas q!a′pe· n′anaxa′mna′mne·. ta′xas
n′anałkinɛ′łne· ne₁ tsɛt!na′na. qoᵤs a·n′ɛlqa′haks pɛskɛnɛ′łne·.
275 ta′xas qanaqłɛkxa′łne·. nutsɛnqku′pe·kɛ′mek.· mit₁yaxa′łne·.
łaxa·′′nxoᵤł at qanaqłɛkxa′łne·. ta′xas xa′xa·s k!umna′nłuk-
pakitmu′łne· a₋′q!ułu′kp!e·s. ne₁sts k!u′pxₐnaps to′xᵘa nit₁ł
yaxna′pse· łaqu′łqaq!ana′q!nenɛ′łne·. qałwi′yne· xa′xa·s. "pa′-
ko·xasɛnmɛ′tko·, xma ktsxał′o′płap. ta′xta: kanmi·′yit.s kutsła-
280 tso′ᵤkᵘa·t." tsɛłmi·′yɛt.s qa·′qaskɛnɛ′łne· kk.łɛnq!o′ya·m. ta′xas
xa′xa·s xuna′xe· a₋′kɛnmɛ′tuks. xunakuxu′′mne·.· ntɛk.łu′mqu′ł-
ne·. kanmi·′yit.s q!apenma′tswɛsk.ło′mqu′łek. k!o·nanu′qkwas
ta′xas k.łak.łɛnq!o′yam. qałwi′yne·: "ta′xas kutsłatso′ᵤkᵘa·t
ka′q!o′łukp." qa:kiłk.łɛnq!oya′mne·. ta′xas xa′xa·s qoᵤs
285 a·n′ɛlqa′haks qa′oˇxał′ɛsaknu′ne·. ta′xas qałwi′yne·: "qa·ɛ′n-
sɛłtsqa.u′pła·p." na₋s łaqahanut.łɛ′s₁ne·. qoᵤs wɛ′łił′ɛlqana′se·.
łału′qᵘałqa·′′tse·. łats!ka′se·. ta′xas n′aq!ana′q!ₐnenɛ′łne· łahuts-
qa·′nkaqkupɛkina′kse·. qawaka′se·. łaqałaxa′′nxołɛ′s₁ne·. ta′xas
xa′xa·s qana′we·tsɛnk!a′ₐk₁ne·. łaqaoˇxa′se· a₋′q!ołu′kp!e·s.
290 łɛtsaqanaxa′′mse· qanmitxuna′pse·. ła.owo′kᵤne· xa′xa·s. qaki-
łamna′mne·: "ta·xas ma₋ts tsₑ₁katemo′kᵘi·ł xa′xa·s pał n′ɛ′ne·
sɛł·atsukᵘa′te· a₋′q!ołu′kp!e·s." łało′ᵤne· kk.łɛnq!o′ymuł.
    Ta′xas husɛlhułtsxamu′ne· ya₋qaˇqna′ₐke· tsa′ₐt₁mo xa′xa·s.

---

tent. | Raven brought out the musk bag. He worked over it, | and it became a pup. Skunk did not go in. | The pup was tied up at the doorway. It went to him || and was glad. He said: "What did they 255 do to me, Tso·t?" It knew him; | therefore it did so. But Raven did not know that it was he. | Then Skunk sat down. He was given food. Then | he ate. The food was bad, for there was nothing | in him. He did not eat much. He did not eat more, because his insides were bad, || because he was dry inside. He was told by Grizzly 260 Bear: | "You should go on." He arose. Skunk went out, and where | he stood up, there was meat. A child said: | "There lies some meat." Raven said: "Don't | eat it. He dropped it from his mouth. Children must not eat it. I'll || eat it myself." Skunk 265 entered Grizzly Bear's tent and | was given food. Here again he could not eat much. When he stopped, | he went out; and there was meat again where he stood up, | and Grizzly·Bear himself ate it. It was what Skunk had eaten. | Because he had no belly, when he ate, || it went right through him. | 270

Then, when it was about evening, Raven went out. | He said: "Come out and play! | You have a toy." Then they all went out. Then | they brought out the pup. A little distance away they put it down.|| Then they kicked it. It ran, and they ran after it. | When they 275 caught up with it, they kicked it. Then Skunk had pity | on his musk bag. When it saw him, it almost | ran up to him. Then he nodded his head the other way. Skunk thought: | "I am thirsty. It might hurt me. Later on, to-morrow, || I'll take it back." At 280 night they·stopped playing. Then | skunk went to the river. He jumped in and soaked himself. | In the morning and all day he soaked himself. When the sun was going down, | they played again. He thought: "I'll take back | my musk bag." They went on playing. Then Skunk || sat down a little ways off. He thought: | "It 285 might hurt me." They chased it toward him, and it went there. | Then it turned back and came back. Then he nodded his head to it, | and it came running this way. It came, and they could not catch up with it. Then | Skunk turned himself toward it, and his musk bag went to him. || It got into·him again and threw him down. 290 Skunk got up. | They said to one another: "Don't look at him, for it is Skunk. | He himself took back his musk bag." Their toy was gone. |

Now I have told what Skunk and his brother did. |

69. Frog and Antelope

Ho′ya′ṣ hutsxałhaqałpałne′ₑne· ne₁s pɛ′k!a·ks yaₐqałhoqᵘa′ke.
nɛ′ɫtuk!ᵘpts wa′tak.

Qaₐhak.łuna′mne·. qał′at.lititna′mne· ts!oᵤts!u′q!ᵘa. n′ɛ′n·e·
naso′ₙkⁿe·ns nɛ′ɫtuk!ᵘp: nɛlnukupqa′ₐne· nɛ′ɫtuk!ᵘp. mɛ′ka yaₐ-
5 kałnuku′pqa at nuqᵘna′pse· nɛ′ɫtuk!ᵘps. ta′xas q!a′pe· nuqᵘa′łne·
nöpɛ′k!a. qaₐk.ło′ᵤne· wa′ta·knɛ′′nte·k. ta′xa n̓aso′ₙkⁿe·n
wa′ta·k qałwi′yne·: "ho′ya′ṣ huł′a′yne·ł nɛ′ɫtuk!ᵘp." qakɛ′łne·
aₐ′kik.łu′′e·s: "hołałwats!małna′ła   nɛ′ɫtuk!ᵘp." qak.ła′pse·:
"kaₐs kuł′a·qak₁na′ła nɛ′ɫtuk!ᵘp? pał kałnuku′pqa." qakɛ′łne·:
10 "hułts!naxała′e·s q!a′pe· hutsxałhałwats!małnała′ₐne·." ta′xas
qakɛ′łne· aₐ′kɛk.łu′e·s tsxałyaₐqaqna′pske·. qake′₁ne· q!a′pe·
wa′ta·k: "ho′ya·′s pał sɛlso′ₙkᵤne· kɛnkɛnłwi′yte·k." qake′₁ne·
ne₁ naso′ₙkⁿe·n: "hutsts!na′xe·, huts!uk!ᵘe′₁ne·. taxta′′ na′pit
qa′łwiy kanmi·′yit.s ta′xas hutsqunaxała′′ne·." qake′′ne·
15 wa′tak: "so′ₙkᵤne·." ta′xas ts!na′xe·. k.ła′xam nɛ′ɫtuk!ᵘps
qakɛ′łne· nɛ′ɫtuk!ᵘp wa′taks: "qa′psin kɛusɛlqo′ₙkam kaₐkɛ′t.ła?"
qake′₁ne· wa′ta·k: "hosɛlqokᵘa′xe· hɛn·a′qantsqaouɛ′łap kutsa′ł-
wats!na′ła." n′uma′ts₁ne· nɛltuk!ᵘp. qałwi′yne·: "tsɛ′namts
yaₐkkałnuku′pqa kuse′₁łmat. k!aqa′ke· wa′ta·k." qakiłɛ′łne·
20 wa′tak: "tsɛn·a′pe·t hɛnqa′łwiy k.łe′e·n kaₐ′k.łe′₁te·t aₐ′k.litɛ′-
t₁ne·s. tsɛn tsɛmatiktsa′p′ne·." qake′₁ne· wa′ta·k: "ha· hosu-
kᵘiłq!u′kᵤne· kutstso′ₙkᵘat aₐ′k.litɛ′t₁ne·s." ta′xas n′omats₁na-
tɛ′łne· pał kqa′e·n ke·′ma·t nɛ′ɫtuk!ᵘps k!aqa′ke·. qake′₁ne·
wa′ta·k: "kanmi·′yit qa′ₐlin[1] kiyu′k₁yit hutsxałwa′xe· huts-
25 qsama′łne· kaₐkɛ′k.łu·." ta′xas łats!na′xe· wa′ta·k. k.łała′xa·m
qakɛ′łne· aₐ′kɛk.łu′e·s: "ta′xas huts!aynihała′ₐne· nɛ′ɫtuk!ᵘp
ała′ₐqałtɛ′t₁mo." kanmi·′yit.s ts!na′xe· wa′tak. q!a′pe· yunaₐ-
qa′ₐne· pa′łke₁ kqsa′mał ne₁s tɛ′tqa·t!s wa′taks. ta·′xas tu′xᵘa
ktsła′xam aₐ′kɛk.łu′se·s. qake′₁ne· wa′ta·k ne₁ naso′ₙkⁿe·n.
30 "su′kᵘiłqaakaxana′mne·. ta′xas ts!na′ki·ł hɛnts!ɛ′txone₁kɛ′łne·
ne₁ at yaₐqanaxa′mke·. qa′ₐlin atɛnyɛsɛnwonɛn·mitk!one₁kɛ′łk₁e·
hɛn·tsqa′sin′wun·iłkikɛ′łamkɛ′łne·." ta′xas quna′xe· wataknɛ′′-
nte·k qoᵤs at yaₐqa′kxa·xamɛ′ske·. ta′xas n′ɛtxo′ᵤme·k q!a′pe·.
ne₁s at yaₐqa′naxamɛ′ske· łaxanoqoyɛqa′ₐne· qoᵤs at yaₐqa′o˘-
35 xałakamɛnqaₐtsamɛ′ske· ta′xas kuł′e′₁tke·n. ta′xas ne₁ yɛsa′k·e·
quna′xe· aₐ′kik.łuna′mis. qakiya′mne·: "ta′xas wa·′taknɛ′′nte·k
sɛłwa′xe·, ma ktsałwats!nała′ₐwas." ta′xas n′anaxa′mna′mne·
q!a′pe·. ta′xas qɯnaxa′′mne· at yaₐqakxaxa′′mke·. ta′xas
n′itɛtiya′mne·[2] suk.litɛ′t₁ne· wa′tak. q!a′pe·′s na k!aqo·′x′ma-
40 qa′pse· aₐ′k.lɛtɛ′t!e·s. ta′xas n′itɛtałɛ′łne·. wɛłtiya′mne· pał
kqałwi′yna·m ktsxałhu′qᵘa·ł wa′tak. nɛnko′′e·s pał k!u′pxa
ktsxałhoqᵘa′ka, qakiya′mne·. ta′xas nɛ′ɫtuk!ᵘp n′itwɛsqa′ₐne·.

---

[1] Barnaby: qaha′łin.   [2] Pierre: n′it·ɛya′mne·.

69. FROG AND ANTELOPE[1]

Well, I'll tell you how, long ago, | Frog won over Antelope. |
There was a town. It was named Fish Hawk Nest.[2] | Antelope
was chief. Antelope runs fast. Even ‖ the best runners were beaten 5
by Antelope. He was a manitou, and won over everybody. | There
was a town of Frogs. Then Chief | Frog thought: "I'll cheat Ante-
lope." He said to | his tribe: "Let us play with Antelope!" They
said to him: | "What shall we do with Antelope? He runs fast."
He said to them: ‖ "We shall go, all of us. We shall play with him." 10
Then | he told his people what to do. All the Frogs said: | "Well,
your thoughts are good." That chief said: | "I'll go alone. Later
on, if | he agrees, to-morrow we shall go." The Frog said: ‖ "It is 15
well." Then he started. When he arrived at Antelope's (tent), |
Antelope said to Frog: "Why do you come to my tent?" | Frog said:
"I come here to see if you are not afraid to run a race with me." |
Antelope laughed. He thought: | "Even if he runs fast, I can easily
do (leave behind) what Frog says." Frog was told: ‖ "If you agree, 20
my property shall be your property. | You may give it to me."
Frog said: "Go; | I am glad. I'll take your property." Then they
laughed at him | because he could not do (leave) what Antelope said.
Frog said: | "To-morrow just at noon I'll come, ‖ accompanied by my 25
tribe." Then Frog started. When he came home, | he said to his
tribe: "Now we will cheat Antelope | and his children." On the fol-
lowing morning the Frogs started, all of them. | There were many.
The women went along with the men Frogs. When they almost | came
to the town, the chief Frog said: ‖ "Before any one comes out, go and 30
lie down | on the trail they go. Just at that distance jump! | You
shall be that far apart." Then the Frogs went | to the starting
place, and all of them lay down | on the way they were to run. ‖
They lay down up to the point where the track turned. When this 35
was all done, others went | to the town. They said: "The Frogs |
have come to play with us." Then all of them went out. | They went
to the starting place. Then | the Frogs bet their property. All
their clothing was blue. ‖ Then they bet with them. They staked 40
much, | because they thought the Frogs would be beaten. They
thought | they themselves would win. Thus they spoke among them-

---

[1] See p. 42.   [2] A place in Tobacco Plains.

n'umatsna'ₐteˑ ɛneˑnɛ'k!eˑs. sakqa'ₐneˑ wa'tak. ta'ẋas tseᵢka'tcˑ
nɛ'ltuk!ᵘps. qakiya'mneˑ: "ta'ẋa łu'nˑu." ta'ẋas wa'tak
45 peɛ'k!aks n'ɛktɛkmɛnẋo'nqa'ₐneˑ. ta'ẋas nɛ'ltuk!ᵘp n'uma'tsᵢneˑ.
suk.likpakta'pseˑ ɛnenɛ'k!eˑs. qats!na'kᵢneˑ, neᵢsts k.łaˑ
ẋamɛnẋoˑ'nₐqa wa'tak, n'ɛtẋo'ᵤmeˑk łaa'k!łak wa'tak. n'ɛk-
tɛkmɛnẋoᵤnqa'ₐneˑ. ta'ẋas q!a'peˑ qaqₐna'ₐneˑ wa'tak. ta'ẋas
nɛ'ltuk!ᵘp qats!na'kᵢneˑ. qawułeɛ't.seˑ, ta'ẋas mata'pseˑ.
50 ta'ẋas aːnts!na'kᵢneˑ nɛ'ltuk!ᵘp. ta'ẋas tsᴇmaˈk!iłmata'pseˑ.
ta'ẋas ts!na'kᵢneˑ. mɛ'ka kts!ɛ'naˑk nɛ'ltuk!ᵘp, ta'ẋas wa'tak
u's'meˑks n'ɛ'nˑeˑ. ta'ẋas k.łaˑ'ẋam tsẋałya'ₐkiłakamᵢnqa'ₐtskeˑ.
neᵢsts wułɛkᵢna'ₐteˑt wa'tak at neᵢs łału'qᵘał'itẋo'ᵤmeˑk. ta'ẋas
k.łałuqᵘa'tqaˑts nɛ'ltuk!ᵘp. ta'ẋas peɛ'k!aˑks wa'tak wɛłˑdˑaˑdˑ-
55 qana'ẋeˑ. ta'ẋas tsᴇmaˈk!ił'ałɛ'nˑteˑk nɛ'ltuk!ᵘp. n'u'pẋₐˑneˑ
pał tsẋałsɛmata'pseˑ n'uˈpskił'ałɛta'ₐkẋa'ẋeˑ nɛ'ltuk!ᵘp. k.łaˑ
ẋa'ẋam wa'tak ta'ẋas n'umatsᵢna'mneˑ q!a'peˑ, mɛ'ksa'n
n'ɛse'ᵢneˑ aₐ'kɛłwi'ynam neᵢs kuqᵘa'ka wa'taˑk. tseᵢkatɛ'łne
wa'taˑk. qaq!awats!cˑ'ᵢnmik,[1] oˑk!ᵘqᵤna naₐs kqaoˑẋa'qumˑ-
60 ła'ₐsẋoˑ. kqaqaˈnał'łaqawaˑ'nẋaˑ'm. k.łaqa'keˑka'qoᵘmˈła'ₐsẋo
słaˑ'qaˑqa'pse kqaqawats!ɛ'nˑmeˑk, mɛ'ksa'n nɛ'ltuk!ᵘp n'ɛseˈł-
kikᵤwa'sₐneˑ. neᵢs qa'oˑẋałtu'wuł'ɛtẋo'ᵤmeˑk. qake'ᵢneˑ: "sɛłho-
qᵤna'pᵢneˑ wa'tak." ta'ẋas tsᵤkᵘa'teˑ neᵢs kuqᵘa'ka wa'taˑk.
łats!na'ẋeˑ neᵢ kqaˈnanoqo'yqa łaqawanẋaˑ'mneˑ. ta'ẋas ktsɛł-.
65 miˑ'yɛt.s, ta'ẋas łats!na'ẋeˑ q!a'piłkiłpałneˑnamɛ'sᵢneˑ kma'taps
wa'taks nɛ'ltuk!ᵘp.

Ta'ẋas husłq!apqałpałnᴇmɛ'łneˑ yaₐqałhuqna'mkeˑ wa'takts
nɛ'ltuk!ᵘp neᵢs pɛ'k!aks.

70. THE STAR HUSBAND

Ho'ya's, hutshaqałpałne'ᵢneˑ yaqałsałitɛ'tkeˑ k!o'k!ᵘeˑ
na.u'teˑ aₐˈkɛłno'hoˑs.

Qanit.ła'ₐneˑ pɛk!a'knɛk!. n'a'sₐneˑ na.u'teˑ n'anaẋaˑ'mneˑ.
ta'ẋas ktsẋałq!u'mneˑ nao'k!ᵘeˑ waₐwitskɛ'kᵢneˑ. n'u'pẋₐneˑ
5 yuñałhoho'seˑ. n'u'pẋₐneˑ k!o'k!ᵘeˑs tsaˋqona'seˑ. qake'ᵢneˑ:
"pał sɛłsukuqts!ta'teˑk qoˑaq!aˈniłnoho'skeˑ hułsałɛ'tit." ta'ẋas
n'uma'tsᵢneˑ neᵢ na.u'tekɛ'stik neᵢsts k!aqa'keˑ. ta'ẋas łatᵢna-
ẋaˑ'mneˑ. kq!uˑ'mneˑ. wɛ'łnaˑms naq!ₐmałɛ'ᵢtsᵢneˑ. nakq!ᵢyɛ'tseˑ.
n'u'pẋₐneˑ qa.ɛłkɛ'kseˑ ałakᵢnɛ'k!eˑs. n'o'kᵤnoˑẋaˑ'mneˑ. n'u'pẋₐneˑ
10 qa.o'hᵤneˑ neᵢs aq!sma'kᵢnɛk!s. nułˑak'łe'ᵢseˑ qakɛsna'qₐnema'-
łneˑ. n'u'pẋₐneˑ pał sałitɛ't ᵢneˑ. łaa'k!łaks n'u'pẋₐneˑ yunaqa'-
pseˑ nɛtsta'hałnɛ'nta'keˑs. qałwi'yneˑ: "qa'psin ksɛł'aqa'qa ksɛł-
yuna'qa nɛtsta'hałnɛ'ntik. kqa.ɛ'sᵢniłtsukᵘa'tap? ksɛłhuł'a'k.łe
naₐ kanuł'a'qₐna." qak.ła'pseˑ: "ta'ẋa naₐ hun'ɛ'nˑeˑ neᵢ ktsɛł-
15 miˑ'yit ma kɛnqa'k.łaˑp: ˈkuˋsɛłsukuqts!eta'teˑk heᵢnłsałta'ₐ-
tap.' ta'ẋas husiłtsukᵤatɛ'sᵢncˑ." tseᵢka'teˑ neᵢ kᵤwɛ'łqa aₐ'kiłno'-

---

selves.   Then Antelope stood up. | He laughed at his enemy.   Frog
was lying there.   Then he looked | at Antelope.   They said: "Now
start!"   Then Frog ‖ jumped up.   Antelope laughed. | His enemy   45
looked funny to him.   (Antelope) did not run fast | when Frog gave
his first jump.   Then another Frog lay there and | jumped up, and
all the Frogs did so.   Then | Antelope did not go very fast.   He had
not gone far when he was left behind. ‖ Then Antelope ran more   50
quickly.   He was left far behind. | He ran fast; but even when he
ran fast, the Frogs | were ahead of him.   Then he arrived at the
turning place; | and when he got there, the Frogs lay down in the
opposite direction.   Then | Antelope turned back, but the Frogs
were always ahead of him. ‖ Then Antelope tried hard.   He knew | 55
that he would be beaten.   Antelope was not yet near the starting
point | when Frog arrived.   Then all laughed; but | the people were
sick at heart, because Frog had won.   Frog was looked at. | He was
not out of breath, because he had just given one jump ‖ and then had   60
not moved any more.   He just jumped back from there. | Therefore
he was not out of breath, but Antelope was puffing. | He lay on his
back, and said: | "You beat me, Frog."   Then Frog took what he
had won. | He went back, and those who lay down did not move.‖
In the evening they went back, and it was heard by all that | Frog   65
had beaten Antelope. |

Now I have told how Frog beat | Antelope in olden times. |

70. THE STAR HUSBAND

Well, I'll tell a story of how a girl was married | to a star. |
The people of olden times lived in a tent.   Two girls went out. |
When they were about to go to sleep, one of them looked up.
She saw ‖ many stars.   She saw a small one, and said: | "That is a   5
nice little star [hanging] there.   I'll marry him."   Then | the two
girls laughed when she said so.   They went in again. | After they
had slept, early in the morning she woke up.   There was talking, |
and she knew that those were not the voices of her parents.   She
arose, and she saw ‖ that she did not know the people.   She was sit-   10
ting down next to an old man. | She knew that she was married
to him.   She saw many other | young men.   She thought: "When
there are many | youths, why don't they marry me?   My husband is
old." | He said to her: "Here I am!   The other ‖ night you said to me,   15
'You little nice one! Marry me.' | Now I have taken you."   She looked

hos. taʼχas nʼɛʼnʼeˑ ɛn nɛtstaʼhaɬnɛʼʼnteˑk. neᵢ ktsaquʼnˑa
aₐʼkiɬnoʼhoˑs, nʼɛʼnˑe kuɬʼaʼkˑteˑ. taʼχas nʼiɬaʼnˑeˑ neᵢ na.uʼteˑ,
kǃuʼpχa keᵢmat amˑaʼkǃeˑs. qaoˑsaqaₐneˑ. nʼakakǃoʼᵤneˑ

20 aₐʼkuqɬe its aₐʼkiɬnoʼhoˑs paɬkeᵢnɛʼʼnteˑk. qsamaʼɬneˑ neᵢ
na.uʼteˑ. qakiɬɛʼhneˑ: "at maˑₐtsɛntsomɛtskɛʼnˑeˑ aʼmˑaˑk na
qaʼhanqǃunaₐʼawoᵤk." qaɬwiʼyneˑ neᵢ na.uʼteˑ: "qaʼpsins kǃuʼps-
ki aₐʼkiɬnoʼhoˑs?" qaʼhanqǃunawoʼᵤkseˑ qanaɬʼomɛtskɛʼnˑeˑ
aʼmˑaˑks. pal paʼqtsnanaʼseˑ aʼmˑaˑks. qayaₐqaʼnawɛtskɛʼkᵢneˑ.

25 nʼuʼpχₐneˑ qoᵤs uʼmˑeˑs pal nʼɛʼnˑseˑ amˑaʼkǃeˑs. noʼhᵤneˑ
aₐʼkᵢnɛkǃnamoʼeˑs sɬa:tqǃunaˑχoqᵘaʼₐtseˑ. taʼχas nʼiɬaʼnˑeˑ.
nʼɛtkɛʼnˑeˑ qaʼpsins. nʼitukǃsaʼₐmik, ɬa.unaχaʼmekˑ. ɬa.uʼpχₐ-
neˑmaʼɬneˑ aₐʼkᵢnikǃnamoʼeˑs. qakɬaʼpseˑ: "kaₐ kiₙaqaʼ-
naˑmˀ? kusɛʼisqaˑχₐmitaʼwas." qakeʼᵢneˑ: "neᵢ ma koqᵘaʼkeˑ,

30 huɬsaɬɛʼtit neᵢ ktsaquʼna aₐʼkiɬnoʼhos, taʼχas kuqǃuʼʼmneˑ ku-
haqǃmaʼₐɬeˑts, hunʼuʼpχₐneˑ aₐʼkɛɬnoʼhoˑs. pal nukaˀyaχₐnaʼpᵢneˑ.
husaɬitɛʼtᵢneˑ aₐʼkiɬnoʼhoˑs neᵢ ma ktsaquʼna pal nʼɛʼnˑeˑ kuɬʼaʼkˑteˑ; neᵢ kᵤwɛʼɬqa aₐʼkɛɬnoʼhoˑs pal nʼɛʼnˑeˑ nɛtstaʼhaɬ."
taʼχas qakeʼᵢneˑ yaqaqₐnaʼₐkets ksɛɬaoˑʼkᵘamˑ. nʼuʼpχₐneˑ

35 aₐʼkiɬnoʼhoˑs ɬaqawaʼseˑ neᵢs na.uʼteˑs. tseᵢkaʼteˑ pal ɬaoˑnaʼseˑ.
tsɛɬmiʼyit.s kqǃuʼmneˑʼʼnam, kǃoˑkᵤnuχaʼʼmnam. wɛʼɬnaˑms nʼupχaʼɬneˑ neᵢ na.uʼteˑ qa.oˑkᵤnuχaʼʼmneˑ. wunekɛʼt.se tseᵢkatɛʼɬneˑ.
nʼupχaʼɬneˑ pal nʼɛʼnˑeˑ upnaʼmo. pal nʼupɬaʼpseˑ aₐʼkɛɬnoʼhoˑs
n.eᵢs kˑɬaʼmat pal nukᵘaʼɬaltaʼpseˑ.

40   Taʼχas husɬqǃaʼpqaɬpaɬnemɛʼɬneˑ yaₐqaqₐnaʼₐkeˑ kǃoʼᵤkǃᵘeˑ
na.uʼteˑ.

71. Little Sun

Hoʼyaʼs, hutsaqaɬqǃanuχwaʼteˑ nataʼnɛkǃnaʼna.

Qaₐkˑɬunaʼmneˑ tsǃoᵤtsǃuʼqᵘa. qakeʼᵢneˑ nasoʼᵤkᵘeˑn: "huts-
χalʼanaχakaʼₐneˑ. qaʼɬa nɛtstaʼhaɬnɛʼʼntik yaₐkaɬnɵkuʼpka?"
qakeʼᵢneˑ nataʼnɛkǃnaʼna: "hutsχaɬtsǃɛnaʼχeˑ." taʼχas pɛʼkǃaˑks

5 sɬyukᵘᵢyɛʼtᵢneˑ qatsǃɛnaʼχeˑ. qaɬwiynaʼmneˑ ksɛɬqatsɬɛʼnaˑm.
taʼχas nʼunanuqkᵘaʼnˑeˑ, taʼχas qaiχuktsiyaʼmneˑ. taʼχas kqaˑʼ-
qaskɛʼnʼiˑɬ qoᵤs qanaʼχeˑ nataʼnɛkǃnaʼna. qaɬwiynaʼmneˑ ktsχaɬ-
qaɬaʼχaˑm pal kwuɬeʼet.s. qaˑɬʼat.liʼtɛtnamɛʼsᵢneˑ neᵢsts yaₐqaoˑ-
χaʼmkeˑ kqawaˑʼkₐmɛʼtuk. qaʼhakˑɬunaʼmneˑ kqawaˑʼkₐmɛʼtuk.

10 kǃunanuʼqkᵘa kqaiχuktsiyaʼmneˑ. qaʼkiɬkqaiχuktsiyaʼmneˑ nʼupχaʼɬneˑ nataʼnɛkǃnaʼna neᵢs qakaʼχeˑ ɬa:tᵢnuʼkˑɬatmuʼmeˑk.
qaɬwiynaʼmneˑ waˑɬkᵘaˑs ksiɬtsɬɛʼkaˑm tsǃoᵤtsǃuʼqᵘaˑs. pal qqaₐp-
saₐkaʼteˑ tsaˀqunaʼneˑ. sɛɬqa.upχaɬɛʼsᵢneˑ paˑɬ naɬnuʼkupqaʼₐneˑ.
qakiɬɛʼhneˑ: "qoᵤs snɛt.ɬaʼₐneˑ nasoʼᵤkᵘeˑn." taʼχa neᵢ nasoʼᵤkᵘeˑn

15 qaʼkˑɬeˑk qa.eˑtχaʼmeˑnqaʼmeˑk. tɛnaχaʼʼmneˑ. taʼχas tᵢnaχaʼmnam-
mɛʼsᵢneˑ ktsχaɬtuqǃᵘtsqaʼkeˑ neᵢs yaₐqakχaʼmkeˑ neᵢs nasoᵤ-
kᵘɛʼnʼeˑs nataʼnɛkǃnaʼna qaɬa at.ɬɛʼsᵢneˑ kuˑpɵʼqa tɛɬnaʼmˑu.

at the large stars. | Now, these were the young men. The little | stars were the old ones. Then the girl | cried when she saw that she had [left] been taken away from her country. She staid there. ‖ The star women were digging roots. The girl went along with them. |·20 She was .told: "Don't break the ground where | there is a tree." The girl thought: "What do | the stars mean?" There was a tree, and she dug up | the ground. The ground was just thin. She thought she would look, ‖ and down below she saw this world. She recog- 25 nized | her relatives walking about. Then she cried. | She made something, and tied herself to it, and let herself down. | Then she met her relatives. They said to her: "Where did you go? | We lost you." She said: "When I said ‖ I would marry the little star, then 30 after I had slept, | when I woke up, I saw a star coming down for me. | I married the star. That little one was an |·old man. The large stars were young people." | Then she told what she had done and how she had come down. ‖ The Star noticed that the girl was not 35 coming back. He looked for her. She had gone down again. | At night they slept. The next morning when they got up, | it was noticed that the girl would not rise. They looked at her for a long time. | Then it became known that she was dead. She was killed by the Star | whom she had left. He struck her down. ‖

Now I have told you what a | girl did. | 40

71. LITTLE SUN

Well, I'll tell you about Little Sun. |

There was a town, Chicken Hawk Nest. The chief said: "I'll | go out to fight. Who among the young men can run fast?" | Little Sun said: "I'll start." It was already ‖ noontime, but he did not 5 start. They thought he would start. | When the sun was nearly setting, they began to play ball. | When they had finished, Little Sun went there. They thought he would | not get there, for it was far. The place where he was to go was called | Kqawakmituk ([?] River). There was a town at Kqawakmituk. ‖ When the sun was setting, 10 they played football. The game was going on, | and Little Sun was seen going along dragging his blanket. | They thought: "He must have started from Fish Hawk Nest." | He did not look as though he were strong. He was small. They did not know that he was a fast runner. | They said to him: "There is the tent of the chief." The name of this chief was ‖ Not-sitting-down-Long. He went in. Then 15 they all went in | to hear the news. The chief from whom | Little Sun came was called Crazy Old Woman. |

Ta′ꭗas kuɬna‵k!uktsa′pse· naso′ᵤkᵘe·n qa.etꭗamnaqₐna′ke·s.
qake′ᵢne· naso′ᵤkᵘe·n: "ta′ꭗas he′ᵢtsꭗan′. qa′psin kₑnse′ᵢɬk-
20 qa·ts?" qake′ᵢne· nata‵nₑk!na′na: "a: n′ɖᵤwat!tka′ₐne· naso′ᵤ-
kᵘe·nk.ɬtskaꭗa′me·s k.ɬtsꭗaɬ′anaꭗa′ka· ɫ·′tɖsₑnikₑ′tᵢne·, husɬts!-
ka′ꭗe·." qa·hanqa′me·k naso′ᵤkᵘe·n. qake′ᵢne·: "kts!aqsanmi′′-
yit.s ktsꭗaɬtsₑ′na·m k!anaꭗa′ka?" qake′ᵢne· nata‵nₑk!na′na:
"wₑ′ɬna·ms paɬ kskiɬse′ᵢɬtsꭗa. qake′ᵢne· tsꭗaɬqa‵ɬsanmiyₑ′t.se·.
25 kts!ₑtmase′ᵢte·ɬ a‵k!ᵤwo·ᵤkts aₐ·k.ɬa′ₐkᵤwo, kts!ₑtkaꭗni·′yam.
ta′ꭗas q!aptsꭗaɬo·ɫ′itkᵢnₑ′ɬne·. ta′ꭗas kꭗa·tsa·nmi′yₑt, ta′ꭗas tsꭗaɬts!naꭗa′′mne·." qakiɫₑ′ɬne· nata‵nₑk!na′na: "kₑn′aqaso′ᵤsaɬtsₑ′-
kam!" qake′ᵢne·: "taꭗta naₐ k!unanu′qkᵘa." n′upꭗaɫₑ′sᵢne· paɬ sɖ-
haɬnukupqa′ₐne·. qakiɫₑ′ɬne·: "a′′ₐke· tsꭗaɬqaqa′′ne·. tsꭗaɬqa‵-
30 ɬsanmiyₑ′tᵢne·. ta′ꭗas a′′ₐke· tsꭗaɬts!naꭗa′′mne·. q!a′pe· ɫₑntsu‵-
n·e·kₑ′tᵢne·. kꭗa·tsa·nmi·′yit tsꭗaɬqawu‵ɬiɫ′ɖqa‵nakupmaɬna′mne·
kᵢye·ᵢko·ᵤnmi·′yit ta′ꭗas tsꭗaɫ′u‵pꭗₐnamna′mne· aₐ·k!amₑ′n·a."
Tsɖmi·′yit qa′kᵢyₑksₑ′ɬe·k nata‵nₑk!na′na. kanmi·′yit.s
qao‵saqa′ₐne·. kiyu′kᵢyit qawanaₐkate′ᵢne· nata‵nₑk!na′na.
35 k!unanu′qkᵘa′·s ta′ꭗas sɖ·ats!naꭗe·. ɬatᵢnu‵k.ɬatᵢmu′m·e·k.
ɬa·tiɬ′ₑ′two·kaꭗanₑ′ɬe·k a′′ₐ·k!wo·ᵤks· qa.k.ɬuna′mne· ts!o·ᵤts!u′-
qᵘa. k!unanu′qkᵘa kqaiꭗuktsiya′mne·. qaₐ′ɬe·n sₑ′ɬo·ɬkqaiꭗuktsi-
ya′mne· n′upꭗa′ɬne· nata‵nₑk!na′na neᵢ ɬaka‵nuk.ɬatᵢmume′ke·.
tₑnaꭗa′′mne· naso′ᵤkᵘe·ns aₐ·kₑt.ɬa·ₑ′se·s. n′ₑt!qaoꭗaꭗa′′mne·
40 ktsꭗaɬhuɬpa′ɬniɬ qa′stsꭗaɬaqa′ki·ks naso′ᵤkᵘe·ns. qake′ᵢne·:
"wa′ɬkᵤwa neᵢ ma kutsₑ′n·am qa′ₐɬe·n sɖo·ɬkqai‵ꭗuktsiya′mne·
kuɬa′ꭗam." qakiɫₑ′ɬne·: "kqa′sᵤwo·kts kₑnɬa′ꭗa·m?" qake′ᵢne·:
"tsusɖqake′ᵢne·." qakiɫₑ′ɬne·: "ts!ₑm′ase·ɬkqai‵ꭗuktsiya′mne·
kₑnts!ₑ′na·m." qake′ᵢne·: "tsqa′psints qo·ᵤ ta′ꭗo·ᵧaqao‵ꭗa′m-
45 ke· sɖo·ɬtqaiꭗuktsiya′mne· kuɬa′ꭗam." n′upꭗaɫₑ′sᵢne· paɬ
sɖhaɬnu‵kupqa′′ne·. qakiɫₑ′ɬne·: "qaₐsts k!a‵qa′ke· naso′ᵤ-
kᵘe·n?" qake′ᵢne·: "qaha·′lin he·nyaqakikmₑ′ɬke· a′′ₐke·
qame·ɫₑ′ɬe·k. na ho·sanmiyₑ′tke· ta′ꭗas sɖꭗa·tsᴇqa′pte·k kᵢ-
yu′kᵢyit kints!upꭗₐna′mki·ɬ aₐ·k!amₑ′n·a. tsꭗaɬqats!na′ꭗe·
50 naso′ᵤkᵘe·n. ꭗaɬe′e·s tsꭗaɫ′ₑsᵢniɬts!na′se·. ta′ꭗas husɬoɬ-
tuq!tsqake′ᵢne·." q!a′pe·ɬeheta′mne·.
Ta′ꭗas n′ₑtkinₑ′ɬne· aₐ·k!ts t!a′wu. kꭗa·tsanmi·′yit ta′ꭗas
ts!ₑna‵ɬwats!ꭗakana′mne·.[1] qao‵ꭗaku‵pmaɬna′mne· a′′ₐke· ka-
qawa·kₐmₑ′tuk ts!naꭗa′′mne·. a′′ₐke· qawₑ′ɬi·ɫₑ′ɬqanakup-
55 maɬna′mne·. kanmi·′yₑt aₐ·k!amₑ′n·a, qa′ₐlin kᵢyu′kᵢyit qao‵-
ꭗaɬya‵qꭗaꭗa′mne·. ts!naꭗa′mne· yunaqawu′mne·. qa·na‵-
ꭗa′mne· at ts!ₑna′ꭗe k!e′ᵢtik kaₐke·ns. at qa.upꭗa′ɬne· qa′psin.
qa·naꭗa′mne·. ta′ꭗas nuwasna′mne·.
N′aqa′ₐne· sᵤwᵤ′tᵢmo, nao′k!ᵘe· qa′k.ɬik ktsuku′pꭗa.. pₑ′k!a·ks
60 qakₑ′ɬne· sᵤwu′e·s ktsuku′pꭗa tsꭗaɬyaₐqaqana′ₐke·. q!akpa′kse·

---

[1] Pierre says the modern word would be *ts!ₑnsɫ′a‵naᵧakana′mnc·*.

Then they filled the pipe for Chief Not-sitting-down-Long. | The Chief, said: "Now speak! Why did you come?" ‖ Little Sun said: 20 "The chief made a request | that some one should go on the warpath. Nobody wanted to come, but I came." | The chief was seated. He said: "After how many days | shall the warriors start?" Little Sun said: | "He spoke this morning, and said, 'For three days ‖ work on 25 arrow wood and bow staves. Put feathers on your arrows. | Then, when everything is done, on the fourth day they shall start.'" | They said to Little Sun: "When did you start?" | He said: "This evening." Then it was known that he was a runner. | They said to him: "It shall be so. In three days they ‖ also shall start. They 30 will all be ready. | On the fourth day they will not go far and stop. | On the fifth day they will meet on Low Hills." |

It was dark, and Little Sun staid over night. He staid there in the morning. | At noon Little Sun was not ready to go. ‖ At sun- 35 set he started back, dragging his blanket. | They began to peel their arrow wood. In the town Fish Hawk Nest | they played ball in the evening. Just when they had finished their game, | Little Sun was seen. He came dragging his blanket. | He entered the tent of the chief. They assembled, ‖ and they were going to listen to what the 40 chief would say. He said: | "Yesterday after I started, I reached there just after the game was over." | He was asked: "How high was the sun when you got there?" He said: | "I just said so." He was told: "They were playing ball | when you started." He said: "Why, at the place to which I went ‖ they had just finished their game 45 when I arrived." Then it was known | that he was a runner. He was told: "What did the chief say?" | He said: "He will do just as you said. | Four days from to-day | you will meet at Low Hills. The chief will not go, ‖ but his son will go. Now I have told the news." | 50 And all said: "Yes." |

Then they made arrows and bows. After four days | they went on the warpath. They stopped over night. | The people of Kqawak-mituk started also. They did not go far, and staid over night. ‖ In 55 the morning they went to Low Hills, and just at noon | they met. Many started—a crowd—and they went along. | Scouts went ahead. They did not see | anything. They went on. Now they were hungry. |

There were two friends. One was called Pipe Lighter. Some time before this, ‖ Pipe Lighter had told his friend what he would do   His 60

s_uwu'e·s. ta'xas nuwa'se· swu'e·s ktsuku'pxa. tse·n naqa'ts_i-
ne·kpa'kse· ne_is ma k!aqa'ke·ł. qanaxa'mne·. qałwi'yse·
swu'e·s ktsuku'pxa: "ho'ya's huł'ako'k^ue·n." qanɛts!ła.-
ɛ'n·e· qaha'qkupq!a'nłupxamako'_une·. qakiłɛ'łne· ktsuku'pxa:
65 "ktsuku'pxa." qake'_ine·: "qa'psin?" qakiłɛ'łne·: "nö'pqo·."
qake'_ine·: "ka_as ke'e·n?" qakiłɛ'łne·: "łu'n·u's suwɛtsqa-
nu'n·e·." qakiłamna'mne·. ma'qa·k nałatsukiya'mne· o·'k!^u-
q_una k!oko·'yqa nö'pqo·. sɛ̓'aqałhała'tsu·kkɛlamna'mne·.
łtsxał'oyɛt!axwa'te·ł. tse_ikat.łɛ's_ine· ne_is ya_aqałkɛ'tke·. sq!an-
70 łupxamaku'pse·. ta_xas n'akakɛ'n·e· a'k!e·s ktsuku'pxa.
qao˘xał'atsq_ana'_ane·. qak.łamna'mne·: "qɛ'n·a· tsxałsɛłk!um-
naqa'łalkɛ'n·e·." ta'xas tse_ikatɛ'łne·. ta'xas n'umats_inatɛ'łne·.
qawɛłkiyamɛ's_ine· ne_is k!omats!na'_ate·ł. qao˘xa'xe· ktsuku'p-
xa, at łao'pɛnqana'wɛtskɛ'łne·. ta'xas suk_unułk!o'_une·.
75 ta'xas n'umatsna'mne·. mɛ'txane· sqku'pki·kq!mukupk!o'_une·.
a_a"ke· pɛ'k!aks łao·'q^uwakmɛ'tink!akxo'_une·. ta'xas tsɛma·-
k!ił'omats_ina'mne·, o·'k!^uq_una ksɛłmɛ'txa ło_uk!s. a'_a'ke.
lamɛ'txane· sqkupkikmułupk!o'_une·. sq!ma·'witsłɛnq!a'"ntse·
sqku'pkikwa's·e· nö'pqo·s. n'upxa'łne· ne_i ło_uk! wan·xa'mne·.
80 qałwa·'me·kɛtsqum łasxu'ne· nö'pqo· n'et_uwɛtsq!anu'n·e·. qa'-
xamkikɛ'ł_uwɛtskiłɛ'łne· qa·łski·k_amoxu'n·e· nö'pqo·. pał sɛł'-
ɛlwana'mne·. ta'xas n'ɛt.łuq^ułaxok^ua'_ane· ktsuku'pxa swʋ't_imu.
tsxakxa'łne· nö'pqo·.

    Ko·łatkikx_ani·'yam ła·ts!ɛnaxa'mne·. qa·naxa'mne· nupsła'-
85 t_iyił'qa.upxa'łne· qa'psin; a'_a'ke· łahuwasna'mne·. a'_a'ke·
n'a'sne· swʋ't_imo· a·'nłaa'k!ła·k, n'u'pxane· nao'k!^ue· ma
ya_aqak.ła'pske· swu'e·s. qa·nuxuno'k_une·. xonaxa'mne·.
qak.ła'pse· swu'e·s: "ne_i ma kɛ'ntsxa." (huq^ua.upxamɛ'łne·
ka_as na qa'k.łe·k ne_i swʋ't_imo.) qak.ła'pse· swu'o: "s_uwo'."
90 qakɛ'łne·: "qa'psin?" qakiłɛ'łne·: "ɛs wɛsqa'_ane· to'ho·ł."
qake'_ine·: "ma'qa·k, ta'xa ne_i k_iyuna'q_uwum." qakiłamna'mne·: "ma'qa·k, sawɛsqa'_ane· to'ho·ł." ta'xas tse_ikatɛ'łne·
swʋ't_imo. nao'k!^ue· t!apts!akɛ'n·e· ne_is tsxała_ako'_umo·.
qawo·kałɛ's_ine· at qo_us łaqa'o˘xakqkupkikɛ'ł_uwɛtskɛ'k_ine·
95 wu'o·s. ta'xas qao˘xał'atsq_ana"na. ta'xas n'upxałɛ's_ine·
pał tsxało'_ute· qo_us ło_uk!s. ta'xas n'umatsna'mne· nała'-
tsuk^uya'mne·. ta'xas qu'na·kna'x_ane·. qkupkikmu'łupuqk!o'_u-
ne·. wa'nxa"mne· ne_i ło_uk!^u, n'ɛnqa'pte·k to'ho·ł. n'upkaq-
k!o'_ułne·. ta'xas n'ɛkɛ'łne·. pał ktsaqu'n·a qao˘wumna'mne·
100 pał k_iyuna'q_uwum.

    Ła·ts!ɛnaxa'mne·. ts!ɛna'xe·. k!e·'te_ikka·'kin. ława'xe·.
qa.u'pxane· qa'psin. ta'xas tsɛłmiyɛ't_ine·. qa·naxa'mne· ne_i
tsɛłmiyɛt_ina'mu. ne_i to'x^ua ɛlna'hak tsxana'mne·. qakiya'-
mne·: "ma'qa·k. snɛmsikqa'_ane· aqłsma'k_inɛk!." pał kta-
105 mo'xo. sɛł'aqłu·k!_unatɛ'łne· aqłsma'k_inɛk!. qao˘xaxa'mne·.

friend had forgotten. | Then the friend of Pipe Lighter became hungry.
At once | he remembered what he had been told.   They were going
along, and | the friend of Pipe Lighter thought: "Well, let me try!"
There was a tree, | and there was a burl on it.   Pipe Lighter was
addressed: || "Pipe Lighter!"   He said: "What is it?"   He was told: 65
"A bear." | He said: "Where is it?"   He was told: "Farther on, on
a tree." | They said to one another: "Hold on!"   They whispered, |
because the bear was wild.   Therefore they whispered, | so as not to
scare it away.   They looked at what they referred to. || It was a   70
burl.   Then Pipe Lighter took out his arrow. | He went there softly.
Then they said to one another: "Behold, he will make a mistake!" |
Then they looked at it, and they laughed at him. | They did not make
any noise when they laughed at him.   Pipe Lighter went there | and
looked around to see it.   Then he aimed at it. || The people were   75
laughing.   He shot.   There was a noise of an arrow striking wood, |
but already he had another arrow ready to shoot.   Then they laughed
aloud, | because he was shooting at wood. | He shot again, and hit
something soft.   His arrow stuck out, | and there was the noise of a
bear.   It was seen that the wood was moving. || The bear started to   80
run up the tree.   It stopped; | and while they were looking at it for a
little while, it fell down. | It was killed.   Then Pipe Lighter and his
friend scared the people. | They began to eat the bear. |

  After they had eaten it, they went on.   They went along. || Nothing   85
was seen yet, and they were again hungry.   Now, | there were two
other friends.   The one knew | what his friend had told him.   There
was a brook, and they went to the water. | His friend said to him:
"What did you say?"   (I do not know | the names of the friends.)
The friend said: "Friend!" || He said: "What?"   He was told: 90
"There is a charr." | He said: "Wait, wait!   There are many."   They
said to each other: | "Wait!   There are charrs."   Then the friends
were looked at. | The one put on what he was going to use as a spear. |
He did not look.   He was not looking there at || the water.   Then he   95
went along softly.   Then it was seen | that he was about to spear
wood.   Now they laughed | and whispered.   Then he threw his spear,
and it struck something soft. | It moved and became a charr. | It
was taken out of the water.   It was eaten.   It was small.   They
were not satiated, || because there were many. | 100

  They started again.   They wanted to see what was happening.
They arrived, | and did not see anything.   Then in the evening they
went on. | At night those who were the last talked, and said: | "Wait!
It smells like people." || It was very dark.   Then they smelled the   105

tsu῾kupk!o´ulne·. n'upxa´łne· słqahama´ane· aqłsma´kin⋏k!.
qake´ine· ka´ke·n-k!ayu´kᵘa: "ta´xas hułts!⋏naxa·´ła. na
hutsyaqana´mke· h⋏ntsqanaki´łne·." pał ktamu´xo·. ta´xas
ts!⋏na´xe· ka´ke·n-k!ayu´kᵘa. qa:naxa´mne·. na´nims⋏´kqane·
110 ne₁s aqłsma´kin⋏k!s ka´ken-k!ayu´kᵘa. qa:naxa´mne·. ta´xas
kanmiy⋏´t₁ne·, n'upxa´łne· n'ałm·anma"´ne· k!anaxa´ka. a´ake
pał n'⋏'n·e· k!anaxa´ka tsxałts!⋏na·ł´ana´xane· ktuna´xa·'s.
ts!⋏na´'nmanełⱬ´łne·. qa:naxa´mne·.

   Ts!⋏na´xe· k!e´ite·kka·´ke·ns sw⋄´t₁mo. nao´k!ᵘe· qa´k.łe·k
115 ku´tet!-k!ayu´kᵘa, nao´k!ᵘe· qa´k.łe·k qu´kᵘe·n-k!ayu´kᵘa.
qa·na´xe· s⋏nk!am⋏na´se·. qanałwat!a´xe·. pe·⋏´k!a·ks łayaxawu-
xa´xe·. nao´k!ᵘe· qake´ine·: "hyá·' huła´litqana·´watał⋏´s₁ne·
swu´o." n'u´pxane· pał na·s ⋄´me·'s ske₁kk.h⋲nam⋏´s₁ne·.
sk⋏ke₁ł'ita´qanapa´xaneyam⋏´s₁ne·. k!o´k!ᵘe₁s qa´a⋌e·n qaka·nk!-
120 on⋏´łse·. ta´xas n'⋏t⋄w⋏sqa´ane· ku´tet!-k!ayu´kᵘats qu´kᵘen-
k!ayu´kᵘa. a´ake· n'⋏t⋄w⋏sqa´ane·. ta´xas ne₁ kqa´ka·nk!o·´nił.
ta´xa ne₁ k₁yuna´qa q!a´pe· qakaw⋏tsk⋏´kine·. qa·w⋏sqa´ane·
ku´tet!-k!ayu´kᵘa. qak⋏´łne· swu´e·s: "nił⋏nqa´apske·ł´aaqa-
qa´ane·." łu´qᵘa·łqak.ła´pse· suwu´e·s: "wa's n⋏´nko n⋏´linqa´aps-
125 ke·ł´aaqaqa´ane·." ta´xas tse₁n tse₁kat⋏´łne· ne₁ k!u's´mo-
kᵘaw⋏´sqa. qa·łuqᵘan⋏nm⋏´te·k qa´qxałhuts!⋏nqa·´tse· ku´tet!.
n´⋏nqa´pte·k ku´te·t!s ta´xa n'⋏'n·e· ku´tet!-k!ayu´kᵘa.
ne₁ k!⋌aw⋏´sqa qa·w⋏sqa´ane·. ne₁s qa·nuxu´n·e· to·q!uts-
qa´mna. n'⋏'n·e· e·´qo·ł. qao῾xanoxu´n·e· qo's saw⋏sqa´pske
130 aₐ´k.łam'⋏´se·s. qawaxam⋏´t⋄w⋏tsq!anu´n·e·. łahołnoxu´n·e·.
ta´xa n'⋏'n·e· qu´kᵘen-k!ayu´kᵘa n'⋏nqa´pte·k aₐ´qułu´k!p-
kups., ta´xas n'umats₁na´mne·. k!umnaqałpałne´₁xo· ne₁ t⋏´t-
qa·t! kqa´ke· p⋏´k!aks ks⋏ł´ayaxawa´aka·s aqłsma´kin⋏k!s.
qakił⋏´łne·: "ma ku⋏´siłqa`akiłm⋏txanała´e·s ałak₁n⋏´k!e·s qo
135 ku´te·t! s⋏ł´aqa·ha῾wosa῾qa´ane·. qo⋄ nao´k!ᵘe· s⋏nqułuk!p-
ko´⋄ne·. h⋏n'u´pxane· tuq!tsqa´mna s⋏łqao῾xanoxu´n·e·."
ta´xas, n'umats₁na´mne·. qałwi´yne ne₁ yaqa`s₁nił´upxa´ke·:
"ma ke·'e·n aqłsma´kin⋏k!. qo⋄s łaₐntso´⋄xam ne₁ ku´tet! ta´xas
n'⋏nqa´pte·k t⋏´tqa·t!s. a´ake qo⋄s k.ła⋏tqananu´xo· ne₁ tuq!ts-
140 qa´mna, a´ake· ła⋏nqa´pte·k t⋏´tqa·t!s."

   Ła.upxana´mne· sw⋄´t₁mo kutet!-kayu´kᵘa qu´kᵘen-k!a-
yu´kᵘa. qak.ła´mne·: "pa´me·k hun'a·qaq⋏na´ane·." nao·´k!ᵘe·
qake´ine·: "a´ake· pa·´ me·k hun'a·qaqna´ane·." qakiła´mne·:
"pa·´me·k hułakiłw⋏tskiłna´ła." ta´xas łaqao῾xa´xe·. na`k.ła-
145 tsu´łw⋏tsk⋏´łne· ne₁s ⋏nen⋏´k!e·s. wune·k⋏´t.se n'u´pxane·
ta´xas ła·tsxał⋏´taqnapaxna´kse·. qakiła´mne·: "ta´xas hułats!-
⋏naxa´ła." łats!⋏na´xe·. qa:na´xe·.

   To·´xᵘa s⋏łts⋏łmiy⋏´t.se n'u´pxane· ska´se· ne₁s k₁yuna´-
qa·ps ałswu´e·s. k.łała´xa·m qak⋏´łne·: "hun'upxₐnała´ane.
150 ka·⋏nen⋏k!na´ła. n'upxₐnawa´s₁ne·. pa´me·k hok!umnaqaₐka·'-

people.   They went there, | and started a fire.   Then they saw tracks
of people. | Wolf Hat said: "Let us start, here | where I am going.
You go along."   It was very dark.   Then | Wolf Hat started.   He
went along.   Wolf Hat smelled ‖ the people.   They went along. 110
Then | in the morning the wide trail of the warriors was seen. | There
also were warriors.   They were going to fight against the Kutenai. |
They followed the trail, going along. |

The friends went ahead to see what was going on.   One was named‖
Lamb Hat, the other was named Raven Hat. | They went to a val- 115
ley and went on.   After they reached the other side, | one of them
said: "Go, friend!   I can not do much with you, | friend."   He saw
that down below there was a town. | They were about to put up a
tent.   One man pointed right toward them. ‖ Then Lamb Hat and 120
Raven Hat stopped. | They stood there.   When the one person pointed
their way, | many looked at them. | Lamb Hat was standing there.
He said to his friend: "You might be in some difficulty." | His friend
said to him also: "You might be in some difficulty." ‖ Then the one 125
standing ahead was looked at. | He jumped around, and a lamb
started up the mountain. | Lamb Hat had become a lamb. | Then the
one standing behind stood there.   Then a bird flew that way. | A
small magpie flew that way to the head of the one standing there.‖
It stopped there and flew away again. | Then Raven Hat had turned 130
into a stump. | The people all laughed, because that man had made
a mistake | when he said that people had appeared on the one side. |
They said to him: "We shot the parents of the lamb. ‖ Therefore it 135
is there.   The other one is a stump. | You see, a bird flew to it." |
Then they laughed.   The one who had seen it thought: | "They were
persons.   When the lamb goes behind there, | it will become a man;
and when the bird flies away, ‖ it will also become a man again." | 140

Then the friends Lamb Hat and Raven Hat | saw each other.
They said: "Indeed, I did something."   The other one | said: "In-
deed, I also did something."   They talked together. | "Indeed, let
us watch for a while!"   Then they looked secretly ‖ at their enemies. 145
After a while they saw | that they were beginning again to make
their tents ready.   They said to each other: "Let us | start back!"
Then they started and went along. |

When it was almost dark, their many | friends saw them coming.
When they arrived there, they said: "We saw ‖ our enemies.   They 150

teˑnała'ₐneˑ." ta'χas ts!ₐnaχa'mneˑ. ta'χas tsₑłmiyɛ't¡neˑ,
qaːnaχa'mneˑ. łaχaχa'mneˑ neᵢs yaₐqa'hak.ło'ᵤkeˑ ɛneˑnɛ'k!-
naˑm. pa'ł saˑ'hanłɛɛ't¡neˑ. q!u'ntkałhak!ancłɛ'k!¡ne. qa'tał'-
unaχa'mneˑ. qake'¡neˑ o'k!ₑna'mu ku'tɛt!-k!ayu'kᵘa: "ta'χa
155 ła'nˑa nawɛtsyaₐqana'mkeˑ. qaka'kił." ta'χas ts!ₑna'χeˑ.
qake'¡neˑ ku'tɛt!-k!ayu'kᵘa: "nawɛtsyaˑqaˑoˇχaqanq!ankime'¡-
keˑ, a'ₐ'keˑ qaka'kiˑł." ta'χas ts!ₑnał'una'χeˑ. łₑtkɛk¡noˑkᵘɛ'łneˑ.
mɛ'ka kanχamₑnukna'na qa'tałhaˑk¡noᵤkᵘɛ'łneˑ. ta'χas q!a'-
peˑłqayaqałqatsa'mneˑ. yₑsałso'ᵤkᵘ!akowa'łkeˑ. ta'χas q!u'nt-
160 kałhaqowu'mneˑ neᵢs ˑyaqaˑ'hak.łohu'kᵘeˑ ɛninɛ'k!naˑm. ta'χaˑs
n'ₑtkɛ'kinkla'łeˑχa'łneˑ. qaˑkᵤwu'mneˑ. ta'χas k!atawakan-
mi-'yit, at łaeˑktɛkmeˑtɛ'łneˑ qa'psin. ta'χas su'kᵘiłwoᵤ-
katɛ'łneˑ. qakiya'mneˑː "ta'χas wanaqₐna'kiˑł." ta'χas nała-
t.łokaχaniya'mneˑ ku'stoˑł. ta'χaˑs wanaqₐna'łneˑ ɛnɛnɛ'k!-
165 naˑm.
　　Kopöˇ'qa-tɛłna'mu χałe'eˑs n'ok!ułtsₐquna'seˑ at n'upski-łqa.-
u'pχₐneˑ kᵤwanaqₐnanamna'meˑs. qałwi'yneˑː "kutsχał'a'smaˑł
qa.eˑtχamₑnqa'meˑk naso'ᵤkᵘeˑn kaₐs naˑqa'qₐna kutsχałqa'-
qₐna." ta'χas mɛteˑχałitɛ't¡neˑ qa.eˑtχamₑnqa'meˑk. a'ₐ'keˑ neᵢ
170 nɛtsta'hał qa'k.łeˑk kaˑ'kiyaχa'kukp. ta'χas qapɛsnuła·'ka'teˑ
neᵢs naso'ᵤkᵘeˑns qa.eˑtχamnaqₐna'keˑs. ta'χas nułpałnitɛ't¡neˑ.
ta'χas k!umitskɛ'nłeˑs aₐ'kik.łuna'meˑs, at qakiyamɛ's¡neˑː
"haˑ'heᵢ, ke"nło tɛ'tqaˑt! ko'qᵘaₐqawɛ'tsk!oˑ naso'ᵤkᵘeˑn ka-
k!a'ₐkit! ktsik!eˑnqo'kᵘamłe'¡teˑt." qanakɛ'k¡neˑ swᵥ't¡mo
175 qa.eˑtχamₑnqa'meˑkts kaˑkiyaχa'kukp. pɛ'k!aks wɛłłˑuq!ts-
qana'χeˑ. qatseᵢka'tseˑ sᵤwu'eˑs aₐ'kɛt.łana'meˑs. ta'χas qaya-
qawuχa'χeˑ. sa'nɛt.łanamɛ's¡neˑ qoᵤs qayaqa'woᵤs. a'pkok!ᵘs
qawoχaqu'mˑłasχu'nˑe qa.eˑtχamₑnqa'meˑk. qanał'ako'ᵤneˑ.
qake'¡neˑː "haˑ'heᵢ, ke"nło tɛ'tqaˑt!. ho'paˑks koqᵘaˑ'qa-
180 wɛ'tsk!oˑ naso'ᵤkᵘeˑn kak!a'ₐkiˑt!." ta'χas kaˑ'kiyaχa'kukp
a'ₐ'keˑ tsχa'neˑ. qake'¡neˑː "haˑ'heᵢ, ke"nło tɛ'tqaˑt!. ho'paks
kohek!ₑstɛ'keˑt qa.eˑtχamₑnqa'meˑk naso'ᵤkᵘeˑn." ta'χas łaqaaˑ'kakɛ'nˑe tsuk!oteya'ł'eˑs qa.eˑtχamₑnqa'meˑk. a'ₐ'keˑ kaˑ'-
kiyaχa'kukp a'ₐ'keˑ neᵢs k!a'ₐkoˑ a'ₐ'keˑ łaqaaˑ'kakɛ'nˑe
185 tsuk!oteya'ł'eˑs. ta'χas q!ałuk.łe.ɛ't.seˑ.
　　Ta'χas tsₑmaˑ'k!iˑł'ataˑ'wakanmiyɛ't.seˑ k!oˑ'ktił ɛnenɛ'k!-
nam. sakɛsᵤwisqa'ₐneˑ sᵤwᵥ't¡mo. qaoˇχaχamɛ's¡neˑ. tseᵢkat-
łɛ's¡neˑ. n'upχałɛ's¡neˑ pa'ł sɛł'upɛ'łneˑ naso'ᵤkᵘeˑns qoᵤ swᵥ'-
t¡mo qa.eˑtχamₑnqa'meˑkts kaˑ'kiyaχa'kukp. ta'χas n'upχa'łneˑ
190 ksɛ'ł'eˑn naso'ᵤkᵘeˑns kaˑ'kiyaχa'kukp. ta'χas łats!ₑnaχa'mneˑ.
　　Neᵢ waˑ'łkᵤwaˑs ma k!oˑ'kᵘnaˑk ma k!u'pχa aq!sma'k¡nɛk!s
n'upsa'tᵢyiłqałwi'yneˑː "ma kusɛł'u'pχa aq!sma'k¡nɛk! ma
ktsₑmak!ɛ'łeˑ'n k!aqa'qa k!ₑnqa'pteˑk ku'tɛt!ts toq!tsqa'mna.
maₐts kutsq!u"mneˑ tsₑłmiˑ'yɛt." ta'χas qaqₐna'ₐneˑ. ta'χas
195 ktsₑłmiˑ'yɛt, ta'χas kq!u'mneˑna'mneˑs, n'ₑt.łatsu'nˑe. n'ɛłqana'-

saw us. We tried unsuccessfully | to do something." Then they
started. Now it was night. | They went along, and they arrived at
the town of their enemies. | It was a bad place. There were rough
bowlders around there. They could not | go down. The same one,
Lamb Hat, said: ‖ "Come here, the way I am going!" They went 155
that way, and started. | Lamb Hat said: "When I am going to step, |
come this way also." Then they started, going down. They did not
make any noise on the stones. | Even though there were small stones,
they did not make any noise stepping on them. Then | they all
went down to the place where there was good grass, and ‖ they sur- 160
rounded the place where the enemy was encamped. Then | they
watched for them. They stood there. Early in the morning | they
threw up something. They saw it clearly, | and they said: "Now
fight them!" Then | they blew whistles and fought the ‖ enemy. | 165
Crazy Old Woman's son was the youngest one. He had not seen |
any fighting. He thought: "I'll go with Chief | Not-sitting-down-
Long. Whatever he does, I'll do." | Then Not-sitting-down-Long
began to pursue them, and the ‖ youth named Rattling Claws did not 170
turn his eyes from | the chief, Not-sitting-down-Long. Then he heard |
that the town was being destroyed. They said: | "Ha, he! There is
nobody like me [no man]. I hold Chief Harelip with my knife. | His
clothing is fringed on one side." The two friends, ‖ Not-sitting-down- 175
Long and Rattling Claws, went along. The friends were already |
way in the town. They did not look at the tents. | They went to
the middle. There was a tent there in the middle. | Not-sitting-
down-Long jumped quickly to the head of the tent and stabbed him
there. | He said: "Ha, he! There is nobody like me. I am the first
to hold down with my knife ‖ Chief Harelip." Then Rattling Claws | 180
also spoke, and said: "Ha, he! There is nobody like me. I am the
first | to count coup for Chief Not-sitting-down-Long." Then | Not-
sitting-down-Long did not pull out his spear, and | Rattling Claws
also did not pull out his spear ‖ from the place where he had stabbed 185
him. Then the noise stopped. |
Very early in the morning all the enemies had been killed. | The
two friends stood there. The people went there. | They looked, and
it was seen that | the friends Not-sitting-down-Long and Rattling
Claws had killed the chief. Then it was seen ‖ that it was Chief 190
Harelip. Then they started back. |
The one who had seen the people the day before | always thought:
"I have seen people. | It is sure that they have turned into a lamb
and a bird. | I shall not sleep to-night." Then he did so. ‖ At night 195
when they slept, he hid himself. He went away | higher up. There

xe· ne₁s a·n·a′ₐta·s. qa·łats!łaɛ′nse· qa′o˘xał′ɛtxo′ₐme·k. qa·
q!u′mne″ne·. qao˘saqa′ane·. n′u′pxₐne· ta′xas sɛłkanmiyɛ′t.-
se· nułpałntɛ′t₁ne· k!aqałoₐk.łe′e·t.s. pa·ł sɛłwana′qₐnałɛ′s₁ne·
aₐ′kɛ·k.łu′e·s. qałwi′yne·: "kułɛtk.łɛ′ske·ł?" qa′wɛtsk!a′pałɛ′łe·k

200 ta′xas tsɛma·k!ił′atawaka·′nmiyɛ′t.se· n′u′pxₐne· pa·ł sɛł′o˘-
kᵛiłɛ′s₁ne·. ła.et!qao˘xa′se· ɛnenɛ′k!e·s, ta′xas nawasxuna′kse.
n′ałq!anqało′ₐkse·. ta′xas łats!mas n′iła′n·e·. nułpałnɛ′łne· ne₁s
na′ₐta·′s. qakiłam·namɛ′s₁ne·: "a: maₐts tse₁ka′tki·ł tsxał·a-
ha′łpałne′₁ne· pał ksɛło·k!qa′pe·." qa·qakqa′łiłq!anło′ₐkₐne·.

205 Łats!mxaxa′mne·. naqsa·nmi·′yit łałaxaxa′mne· ne₁ ma
qa·′kiłyaₐkakxaxa′mke·. n′ɛsa′kₐnuna′mne·. ta′xa ne₁ yisan-
miyɛ′tke· kₐwana′qₐnana′mnam. n′upsła′t₁yiłqaki′kse· ałta′t!e·s
ka·′k₁yaxa′kukp: "ha: ka·′k₁yaxa′kukp, kɛ′k!e·stɛ′ke·t
qa.e·txamnaqna′ke·s ka·′k₁yaxa′kukp." ta′xas sɛł′ɛ′n·e· naso′ₐ-

210 kᵘe·ns. ta′xa ne₁ k!ɛsak₁nu′nam ktsxał·ayanqa′ₐtsam, łats-
xa′se· ałta′t!e·s ka·′k₁yaxa′kukp. qakɛ′kse·: "ha: ka·′k₁yaxa′-
kukp kɛk!e·stɛ′kta·ps naso′ₐkᵘe·ns qa.e·txamnaqna′ke·s. qa-
qawɛ′tsk!o· naso′ₐkᵘe·ns kak!a′ₐke·t!s." ta′xas k.łahuwo′kᵘnam.
qake′₁ne· qa.e·txamɛnqa′me·k: "qa′psin kɛnsɛł′aqake′₁ke·ł, mɛ′ka

215 tsɛ′n·e₁s kɛ′k!e·stiłɛ′kta·p. pe.ɛ′k!a·ks hun′itkɛ′n·e· ktsxa′ł′e·n
kanaso′ₐkᵘe·n ka·′k₁yaxa′kukp pał ke′e·n nɛtsta·hałna′na
na·sts k!aqa′qₐna. na ta′xa kɛn′aqake′₁ki·ł ta′xas tsxał·aqa.-
ɛ′n·e· kanaso′ₐkᵘe·n. at qa·waq!wutɛ′łne· k.ła′wła." ta′xas
sa·nke′₁ne· qa.e·txamɛnqa′me·k. ta′xas łaya·nqatsa′mne·.

220 Łałaxaxa′mne· ts!oₐts!u′q!ᵘa. nałq!anq!a′łukna′mne·. n′ana-
xa′mna′mne· ne₁ aₐ′kik.ło″nam. n′upxa′łne· ksɛła′wa·m
k!anaxa′ka. tse₁katɛ′łne· qa′ła ktsxał′ɛ′ne· naso′ₐkᵘe·n. n′up-
xa′łne· ne₁s yaqa·hałhaqwumɛ′ske· a·n′u′sme·ks łaqasosa′xe·
k!u′kᵘe·. n′upxa′łne· qoₐsts ktsxa′ł′e·n naso′ₐkᵘe·n. qaohu′ł-

225 ne·. ta′xas ławaxa′mne·. ta′xas nohu′łne· pał n′ɛ′n·e·
ka·′k₁yaxa′kukp. ta′xas t₁na·xanamɛ′s₁ne· kopˇö′qa-tɛłna′mu.
tsxa′ne· kopˇö′qa-tɛłna′mu: "ho′ya·s, tuq!tsqak.ła′pki·ł kaₐ
k!a′qanɛ′ke·t." tsxa′ne· ne₁ k.ła′wa·m. qake′₁ne·: "kaₐ xₐma ku-
aₐ′qak₁ya′ła·. ka·′k₁yaxa′kukp qa·qawɛtsk!o′ₐne· naso′ₐkᵘe·ns

230 kak!a′ₐkit!s. ktsɛk!ɛ′ke·nqo′kᵘamłe′₁tɛts." ta′xas sukᵘiłq!o′ₐ-
kₐne· kupˇö′qa-tɛłna′mu xałe′e·s. ke′e·ns naso′ₐkᵘe·ns wana-
qₐnanamna′me·s. pał k!upskɛ′ł′ɛn·s nɛtsta·hałna′nas. taxta·′
ktsxałqa′sts!um·qa′qaps. ta′xas łaₐnaxa·′mna′mne·. tsɛłmi·′yit
n′anaxa″mne· naso′ₐkᵘe·n. tsxa′n·e·. qake′₁ne·: "ałkaa·′qa·łt.

235 husukᵘiłq!o′ₐkₐne· na kɛnła′wa·m, kɛnqa′e·p kɛn′anaxa′ka,
kɛn′upiłe′₁te·t. kanmi·′yit hɛntsxałqawanxa″mne·. łu′n·u kan-
mi·′yit ta′xas hɛntsłaqahuk.łu′kₐne·. ta′xas hɛntsxał′ana′xe·.
hɛnts!ana′xₐne· kₐwɛ′łqłe·. tsxałsukₐnɛmse′₁k!aqape·kɛ′me·k
ałtɛłnamu″ne·s. ts!ałamane·′mo kₐwɛ′łqłe·s aₐ′kɛ′nqa·ts."

240 Ta′xas kanmi·′′yit qa·wanxa′n·na′mne·. ka·nmi·′′yit ta′xas

were trees where he lay down. He did not | sleep. Then he staid there. When he saw that it was morning, | he heard some noise. His people were fighting. | He thought: "Didn't I tell you?" Then he listened. ‖ Very early in the morning he saw that they were all 200 killed. | The enemies assembled and sang. | They shouted for joy. When they went back, he cried. He was heard | above. They said to one another: "Don't look at him! | He will carry the news back. He is the only one left." He was left there crying. ‖

They started back. After several days they arrived at | the place 205 from which they had started. They sat down. | During the days when they were fighting, the elder brothers | of Rattling Claws always said: "Oh, Rattling Claws counted coup for | Not-sitting-down-Long." Now he was chief. ‖ Then, when they sat down to separate, | 210 the brothers of Rattling Claws spoke again, and said: "O Rattling Claws! | Chief Not-sitting-down-Long first counted coup for him. | He held down with his spear Chief Harelip." Then they arose again. | Not-sitting-down-Long said: "Why do you say that? He just ‖ counted coup for me. I have made Rattling Claws | my chief, for 215 he did this, although he was a youth. | Now, if you say this, he shall not be | my chief. The grizzly bear will never be taken away from him." Thus | Not-sitting-down-Long spoke badly. Then they separated. ‖

They went home to Fish Hawk Nest. They shouted with joy. | 220 The people of the town went out. The warriors were seen coming home. | They looked to see who was chief. | The file of people was seen, and one was walking far ahead. | It was seen that he was to be the chief. ‖ He was not recognized. When they arrived, it was 225 known that it was | Rattling Claws. Then they entered the tent of Crazy Old Woman. | Crazy Old Woman spoke (and said): "Well, tell the news! | What has been done?" Those who arrived spoke, and said: "What must we say? | Rattling Claws held down with his spear ‖ Chief Harelip. He counted coup." Then | Crazy Old Woman 230 was glad on account of his son, who was chief | warrior, although he was still a boy. | He was going to be clever. Then they went out. At night | the chief went out. He spoke, and said: "My children, ‖ I am glad that you have arrived, that your warriors are not dead, | 235 that you have killed (the enemy). To-morrow you shall not go out. The day after to-morrow | you will not be tired any more, and you may go out hunting. | You will hunt bighorn sheep. It will give good smell | to your wives. They will grease their hair with the tail fat of the bighorn sheep." ‖

On the next day they did not go out. On the following day | one 240 son of Crazy Old Woman went out. | He ran fast. Then the hunter

n'anaxa''mne· ne₁s k!o'k!ᵘe·s xałe'e·s kupö'qa-tₐna'mu.
nałnokupqa'pse·. ta'xas ts!ₑna'xe· k!a'ₐna·m. qałwi'yne· ne₁
kałnoku'pqa ktsxalwa'sił·awa'q!ₐwo.   qa·na'xe· n'u'pxₐne·
kᵤwₑ'łqłe's. mit₁ya'xane·. q!apₑnmatsnu'te·. qała'xan·xo'ᵤne·.
245 ka·'k₁yaxa'kukp n'a·sma'łne· k!o'k!ᵘe·s ta't!e·s.   qa·na'xe·.
qałwi'yse· ne₁s ta't!e·s kaₐs xma n'a·qaka'te· ka·'k₁yaxa'-
kukp. "ho'ya's huł'a'qₐne·ts." qakₑ'łne·: "pₑ'k!a·ks sₑmi-
t₁yaxnawa'sₐne· ·k.ła'wła, ka·'k₁yaxa'kukp." ·nutsₑnqkupe·kₑ'-
me·k. n'umatsₑnata'pse· ta't!e·s. łaha·ts!ₑnakₑ'k₁ne·. n'u'p-
250 xₐne· ne₁ kwₑ'łqa pa·ł pe.ₑ'k!a·ks sₑmit₁yaxₐna'pse·
k.ła'właₐ's. qakₑ'łne· tsa'e·s: "pₑ'k!a·ks sₑmiti'yaxnawa'sₐne·
k.ła'wła." nutsₑnqku'pekₑ'me·k ne₁ kwₑ'łqa. ka·'k₁ya·xkukp
qałwi'yne: "ma ksₑ'aqₐnₑ'tsa·p." qapsła·'tₑqₐna''ne·. tsₑnk₁-
na'pse· k.ła'wła's. n'it!xₐna'pse· ne₁s k!o'k!ᵘe·'s ta't!e·s
255 wat!axu'se·.

Tsₑmi·'yₑt łałaxaxa'mne·. tsxana'mne·: "ka·'k₁yaxa'kukp
n'ₑt!xₐna'pse· k.ła'właₐ's." qawunikₑ't₁ne· tsxana'mne·. qakiya'mne·: "kupö'qa-tₐna'mu xałe'e·s wat!axu'se·." wunikₑ't₁ne·
ktsłmi·'yₑt n'anaxa''mne· kupö'qa-tₐna'mu naso'ᵤkᵘe·n. qa-
260 ke'₁ne·: "ka· k!aqₐnₑ'ke·t? hₑnłₑnqo'qaqₐna'ₐne· ne· kₑn'anaxa'ka. słaqaqa'ₐne· kₑnsa·nwₑtsqu'xa at qaqa'ₐne·." ta'xas
łat₁naxa''mne· aₐ'kit.ła'e·s. t₁naxa''mnamₑ's₁ne·. qakiłₑ'łne·:
"qaqa'ₐne·; qa.e·'txamₑnqa'me·k naso'ᵤkᵘe·n qaqₐwₑtsk!o'ᵤne·
naso'ᵤkᵘe·ns kak!a'ₐke·t!s ktsi·k!ₑ'ke·nqokamłe'₁tits. k.łats!-
265 ka'xa·m ta'xas n'upsła'tiyiłqakiya'mne·: 'qa.e·txamₑnqa'me·k
qa·'qₐwₑtsk!o'ᵤne· naso'ᵤkᵘe·ns.' ta'xas k.ława'xam aₐ'k!a-
mₑ'n·a qa·kiłtsxana'mne·: 'ka·'k₁yaxa'kukp qa·'qₐwₑtsk!o'ᵤne·
naso'ᵤkᵘe·ns kak!a'ₐke·t!s.' qae·'txamₑnqa'me·k nₑk!ₑstiłₑ'kte·
ka·'k₁yaxa'kukps. ta'xas qa·kiłtsxa'ne. qake'₁ne.: 'qawa·q!ₐ-
270 wutₑ'łne· k.ła'wła.'"

Ta'xas hosₑq!a·'pqałq!anuxwa'te·.

72. PINE CONE

Ho'ya, hutsaqałq!anuxᵘa'te· kałqu'pa·ł.

Qa·nałunisna'm·ne·. qao·'xak.łuna'mne· aₐ'kₑkqła·'łak!aq-
łu'nuk. ts!ₑnał'ana'xe· swᵥ't₁mo qał'at.łititna'mne· aₐ'ko'qᵤ-
wit!. łaxa'xe· ne₁ swᵥ't₁mo. qa·kₑłmₑ'txₐne· n'uk!ᵘił'iłwa'ne·
5 nₑ'ł'ya·ps. qa·nukxuna'kse· ławuq!o·'ha·ks. qa·nₑnq!u'kup-
xₐnₑ'łe·k. swᵥ't₁mo. nao'k!ᵘe· qa·k.łek ku'tet!-k!ayu'kᵘa,
nao'k!ᵘe· qa·k.łe·k a'ts!pu-k!ayu'kᵘa. nao'k!ᵘe· sₑ'ₑ'k₁ne·
aₐ'kxa'ska·ks. qa·nqapxa'me·k qakiła'mne·: "a: swu'o
kaₐ xma kₑn'a·qa'qₐna." n'u'pxₐne· ne₁s ksa·hanłe·'et.s ne₁s
10 yaqaka'mke·. qa·qa'sₐmał suk.łe.itₙana'se·. sₑ'aqake·ła'mne·.
qakiła'mne·: "kaₐ xma kₑn'aqa'qₐna hułwanaqₐna·'nała'ₐti·ł."
qake'₁ne· ku'tet!-k!ayu'kᵘa: "há: swu'o. ts xma hun'ₑtkₑ'n·e·

started.   The fast runner thought | he would bring home meat early.
He went along and saw | a bighorn sheep.   He followed it the whole
day, but he could not catch it. ‖ Rattling Claws went with one of his 245
elder brothers.   He went along. | His elder brother thought: "How
is Rattling Claws going to look? | Let me deceive him."   Then he
said to him: | "Grizzly Bear is following us, Rattling Claws."   He
ran away quickly. | Then his elder brother laughed at him.   They
went on. ‖ Now, the elder brother saw that a grizzly bear was follow- 250
ing them. | He said to his younger brother: "A grizzly bear is fol-
lowing us." | The elder one ran away.   Rattling Claws | thought:
"He is deceiving me."   And he did not mind him. | Then the
grizzly bear took him and killed him.   The elder brother ‖ rolled 255
down to the water. |

   At night they came home.   They told: "Rattling Claws | has been
bitten by a grizzly bear."   It was not long before they spoke, | and
said: "Crazy Old Woman's son fell down."   After some time, | late
at night, Chief Crazy Old Woman went out, ‖ and said: "What has 260
happened?   You must have done something when you were out
fighting; | therefore the misfortune happened.   That is the reason."
Then | he went back into his tent.   They went in, and he was told: |
"It is this way: Chief Not-sitting-down-Long held with his spear |
Chief Harelip and counted coup. ‖ When they started back, they 265
always said: 'Not-sitting-down-Long | held down with his spear the
chief.'   Then, when they arrived at | Low Hill, they said: 'Rattling
Claws held down with his spear | Chief Harelip.   Not-sitting-down-
Long counted coup for | Rattling Claws.'   Then (Not-sitting-down-
Long) spoke there, and said: | 'The grizzly bear ‖ will never be taken 270
away from him.'" |

   Now, I have told it. |

72. Pine Cone

Now I'll tell about Pine Cone. |

   There was a party traveling.   They were encamped at Timbered
Hollow. | Two friends went hunting to a place named Bottle. | The
friends went along and shot a mountain goat. ‖ There were rocks in   5
the center of the precipice.   They made a fire to roast the game. |
One of the friends was called Lamb Hat, | the other one was called
Wolverene Hat.   The one was eating | the brisket.   They were sitting
there eating.   They said to each other: "O friend! | what would you
do?"   They knew that the place that they had passed was bad.
The ‖ only good place was narrow.   Therefore they said so to each 10
other. | They said to each other: "What would you do if we should
be attacked?" | Lamb Hat said: "O friend!   I should work my

nöpɛ′k!a.   na·xma huqana′xe· na· nanoqxome′ɪke·.’’ qakiłɛ′lne·
a′ts!pu-k!ayu′kᵘa: ‘‘nɛ′nko· ka_a xma kɪn′aqa′qana?’’ qakɛ′ɪne·:
15 ‘‘a′_ake· xma hun′ɛtkɛ′n·e· nöpɛ′k!a. na· xma hułaqana′xe·
na huyaqakaxała′_ake·.’’

Qawunikɛ′t.se· nao′k!ᵘe· łaqana_awɛtskɛ′kɪne·. n′u′pxₐne· pał
pɛ′k!a·ks sɛdwa·naqna′lne·. ne_is ya·qaka′_amke· pał kqa·qa′s_a-
ma·ł suk.łe′et.s ne_ists qaqa′se· ne_is ɛnenɛ′k!e·s. qakiła′m-
20 ne·: ‘‘ho·wanaqnałatɛ′lne·.’’ nɛt!ɪnkɛ′sɛnmoqkupɪnu‘xon·qa′me·k.
nao′k!ᵘe· na′s ya_aqaha·nukxunakɛ′ske· na_as qa·nałhutsɛn-
qa′_atse·. nao′k!ᵘe· ne_is ya_aqaka′ske· k_uwa·naqna′naps ne_is
łaqana′xe·. ne_is k!u′pxₐna·ps ɛnenɛ′k!e·s ta′xas k!o·h_uwok
qo_us yaqa_akilo·wo′_uke·ste′_ike·, n′upxa′lne· qo_us qakxałutsɛn-
25 qa′_atse· ku′te·t!; qo_us a′_ake· qake_ika′xe· a′ts!pu. nała′xane.
a_akxa·skama′ła·ks ne_i a′ts!pu. ta′xas qatse_ikatɛ′lne· ne_i
a′ts!pu. na_as yaqa·hałyunaq_uwo·mɛ′ske· na słaqa·hałqaya-
qaha′xe·. qałwiyna′mne· ke′e·n a′ts!pu. a′_ake· qałwiy-
na′mne· ke′e·n ku′tet!. ta′xas sɛdqatse_ikatɛ′lne·. ta′xas
30 k.łaxaxa·′me·s qo_us yaqa·′ninq!oku′pske·. ta′xas n′ɛtske·łɛ′lne·.
q!a′pił′itsk.łɛ′lne· pał sɛd·o′_une·. qakiya′mne·: ‘‘łɛntsxał′ɛ′n·e·
ne_i ma kqa′n·am ats!pu, a′_ake· łɛntsxał′ɛ′n·e· ne_i ma
kqa′n·a·m ku′tɛt!.’’ ta′xas łaa·ntsu_uxa′xe· ku′tet!. ne_is
łaqa·hał′una′xe·. ła_ɛnqa′pte·k aqłsma′kɪnɛk!. nao′k!ᵘe· ne_is
35 qa·nał′omona′xe· a_a·kɛnukxona′ke·s. a′_ake· ła_ɛnqa′pte·k
aqłsma′kɪnɛk!. ta′xas łaqa.ɛ′n·e· ku′tet!s, nao′k!ᵘe· a′_ake·
łaqa.ɛ′n·e· a′ts!pu′s. ta′xas ła.upxₐna′mne·. pal tsmak!-
ke′_ine· ktsxał′ɛ′tke·n nöpɛ′k!a·s. ta′xas łats!ɪna′xe·.

Ta′xas ne_is ɛnenɛ′k!e·s sw_ɔ′t_imo n′ɛ′n·se· kuyo′_uk̓ᵘe·s.
40 ta′xas kuyo′_uk̓ᵘe· tse_ikat.łɛ′k!ine· ne_is sw_ɔ′t_imo′s. n′u′pxₐne·
ne_is ku′tet!s pał n′ɛnqapta′kse· aqłsma′kɪnɛk!s. ne_is a′ts!-
pu′s ne_is ma kqa′łwiy ke′e·ns a′ts!pu′s pał n′ɛ′n·se· nao′-
k!ᵘe·′s. •ta′xas su·k̓ᵘiłtse_ikat.łɛ′k!ine·. n′u′pxₐne· qo_us k.łaan-
tso′_uxa·s pał·aqa.ɛ′n·se· ku′tet!sts a′tspu′s. pał xa′tsɛn-
45 ł·aɛ′n·se· tɛtqa·t!s. tse_ikat.łɛ′k!ine·. nanuqka·′nxo′_une·. pał
ta′xas ła.upxₐna′mse·. łats!ɪnakɛ′kse·. ta′xas mit_iya′xane·
yaqanakɛsq!małɛ′kske·.

Łaqana′xe· sw_ɔ′t_imo n′u′pxₐne· sakq!ₐnu′kse·. tunuxa′xe·.
n′u′pxₐne· tɛ′tqa·t!s qo_us a_a·ku′q!ᵘnuks. qao·xa′xe·. no′h_une·
50 pał n′ɛ′n·se· kałqu′pa·ts. kałqu′pa·ł nuł·ak.łe′_ine·. sɛdtskɛ′tse·
ha′nq!o′s. k.ła′xam qakɛ′lne·: ‘‘hosan·oxo·′′nqa·′n. ska′xe·
kwanaqnana′was.’’ qakɛ′_ine· kałqu′pa·ł: ‘‘atu′tske·n ku′t·et!-
k!ayu′k̓ᵘa.’’ qakiłɛ′lne·: ‘‘hutsmak!kiyała′_ane·. kuyo′_uk̓ᵘe· ska′xe·
skanutawa′s_ane·.’’ a′_ake· łaqakɛ′_ine· kałqu′pa·ł: ‘‘atu′tske·n
55 ka_as xma k!a_aqa′kam k_uwa·naqnana′was.’’ ta′xas łaqana·′wɛtsk-
kɛ′k_ine· ne_i sw_ɔ′t_imo ne_is łaya′_aqaka′mke·. n′u′pxₐne·
ta′xas n′e·s a_a·ku′q!nuks tun_uwaka′se· kuyo′_uk̓ᵘe·s. qakiłɛ′lne·

manitou power, | and I should go right up this precipice." | Then
Wolverene Hat was asked: "What would you do?" He said: ‖ "I
should work my manitou power, and I should go back | the same 15
way we came through." |

It was not long before one of them looked, and he saw | that already
they were pursued by enemies. The way they came | was a narrow
ledge (good place). Then the enemies came. They said to each
other: ‖ "We are attacked." Both stood up quickly. | One climbed 20
up the precipice. | The other one, when the attacking party came,
went back. | When the enemies saw them stand up | at the place
where the two stood, a lamb was seen going up, ‖ and a wolverene 25
also came from there. | The wolverene had in its mouth the brisket.
They were not looked at. The | wolverene went past the place where
the crowd was. | They thought it was a wolverene, and they also
thought | it was a lamb, and then they were not looked at. When ‖
they arrived at the place where the fire was, they looked about for 30
them. | They looked all over. There was nothing. They said to
one another: "Maybe | that wolverene that went past us was he, and
maybe | the lamb that went by was he." Then the lamb went out of
sight. It | went around and went down. Then it became a man
again. The other one ‖ went along the bottom, below the precipice, 35
and also became | a person again. Then there was no lamb, and the
other one | was no longer a wolverene. Then they met again. |
They spoke the truth when they said they would work their manitou
power. Then they started. |

Now, the enemies of the friends were Kuyo'kwe. ‖ Then the 40
Kuyo'kwe looked for the tracks of the friends; and they saw | that
the lamb had become a person, and that the | wolverene—what they
thought was a wolverene—was the other one. | They looked carefully
for the tracks. They knew that when | the lamb and the wolverene
had gone out of sight, both had become ‖ men again. They looked for 45
their tracks and followed them. | Then they met again. The two
went back. They were pursued | along their trail. |

The friends went back. They saw a lake. They went out to the
water. | They saw a man on the shore of the lake. They went there.
They knew ‖ it was Pine Cone. Pine Cone was an old man. He was 50
hunting | muskrats. When they arrived, they said to him: "Run
away! They come | in pursuit of us." Pine Cone said: "You tell a
lie, Lamb | Hat." He was told: "We tell the truth. The Kuyo'kwe
come | in pursuit of us." Pine Cone said again: "You tell a lie. ‖
Where should they come from to pursue us?" Then | the friends 55
looked back, and where they had come from they saw them. | The
Kuyo'kwe came out to the lake. Pine Cone was told: | "Look! There

kaĩqu′pa·ł: "tse₁ka′te·n' qo·ᵤs n′ɛ′n·e· kuyo′ᵤkᵘe·. yu‘-
q‵ᵘa‘ḷyunaqa′ₐke·." ta′xas łamatɛ′łne· kałqu′pa·ł. łahats!ɛna-
60 xamɛ′s₁ne·. qanawɛtskɛ′k₁ne·. n′u′pxₐne· pał n′ɛ′se·kate′₁se·
ɛnenɛ′k!e·s. ta′xas ts!ɛnaxa·'me·nłukpqa′ₐne·. ta′xas łaxa′xe·
kuyo′ᵤkᵘe·. n′u′pxₐne· kuyo′ᵤkᵘe· pał n′ɛ′n·se· kuł·a′k.łe·'s.
qakiła′mne·: "maₐts upɛ′łki·ł. pal ksɛłhuł·a′k.łe·."
Kuyo′ᵤkᵘe· qana′xe·. kałqu′pa·ł ło·kᵘɛ′n·e· sɛ′t!e·s. n′ituk!-
65 samu′n·e· ta′na·ĩs. nałak₁nɛ′ktse· sɛ′t!e·s. qałwi′yne·
ktsxałqa′łwiys kuyo′ᵤkᵘe·s ke′e·n. n′upxa′se· tsɛne·'s ke′e·ns
sɛ′t!e·s. qatse₁ka′t.se·. qa·'qawi·słaxₐma′tₐmuna′kse· ta′na·ĩs.
ta′xas k.łaxa″nxo·'ł. tsᵤkᵘa′te· a′ₐk!e·'s. n′a′qtsxₐne· aₐ·kɛnq!a-
qap!ɛ′se·s. mɛ′txₐne· kuyo′ᵤkᵘe·s. qatak!o′ᵤne·. kuyo′ᵤkᵘe·
70 qałwi′yne· tsxał′u′pła·ps ne₁s nuł·a′qₐna·'s. tse₁ka′te· aₐ·k!ɛ′se·s
pał n′aqtsxa′se·. ta′xas ne₁ kqa·'tak!o′ᵤna·ps kałqu′pa·łs.
ta′xas n′umats₁natɛ′łne·. na′qsa·'s a′k!e·s k.ła′qtsxa·
a′ₐkɛnq!aqap!ɛ′se·s at kqata′ₐk!o· kuyo′ᵤkᵘe·s. ta′xas qaₐ-
k.łałɛ′n·q!oyomu′łne· kałqu′pa·ł. pał qałwiyna′me·s ktsxał-
75 qa·up′ɛ′łi·ł. nu·'łk.łɛnq!o·'ymu·ł ta′xas tsxałts!ɛnaxamɛ′s₁ne·
ne₁s łayaqana′mke· swᵤ′t₁mo ku′tet!-k!ayu′kᵘa. ta′xas łaxa-
xa′me·s aₐ·kik.łu′e·s ktsxałwana′qₐna·ł. n′uk!ᵘqape′₁se· a′ₐ·k!e·s
kałqu′pa·ł. łałɛtɛnq!aqa′pse·. mɛ′txₐne· kuyo′ᵤkᵘe·s. tsuk!o′ᵤne·.
n′upɛ′łne· kuyo′ᵤkᵘe·s. kuyo′ᵤkᵘe· k!u′pxa k!u′pła·ps kał-
80 qu′pa·ĩs, qakiła′mne·: "ta′xas upɛ′łki·ł, pał ksɛ′upła′was."
kałqu′pa·ł ne₁sts k.ła′ło·ps a′ₐ·k!e·s. ta′xas ts!ɛna·'nłukpqa′ₐne·.
qałwi′yne· ksɛłqatano·'k!ᵤna·ps kuyo′ᵤkᵘe·s. ta′xas ne₁sts
k.ła′ło·'s a′ₐ·k!e·s. qałwi′yne·: "ta′xas kutsxa′ł'e·p pa·ł
ksił·a′ło ka′a·k!." miti₁xa′łne·. qałwi′yne· kłtsxałmɛ′txa·ł.
85 ta′xas t!awu″e·s aₐ·k.ła′ₐke·s qanałwankɛ′n·e·. sa‵qa‵na′ₐne·
mɛ′txₐna·ps kuyo′ᵤkᵘe·s kts!ɛłqan·mɛ′txo· ak!ɛ′se·s. k.ła-
xa″nxo·'ł qanłałtɛ′łne·. q!akpakitxo‵ᵤłne·. ta′xas n′iła′n·e·
kuyo′ᵤkᵘe· ne₁s k!u′pła·ps kałqu′pa·ĩs. ta′xas łats!ɛna′xe·
am·a′k!e·s.
90   K.łała′xa·m swᵤ′t₁mo ku′tet!-k!ayu′kᵘa aₐ·kɛk.łuna′me·s,
qake′₁ne·: "skɛnutawa′sₐne· kuyo′ᵤkᵘe·. sukᵘakate′₁ne·.
qa·ɛ′n·se· łtsxałqa·upɛ′łił kałqu′pa·ł." qa·witskpaya′mne·
kqa′wa·m kuyo′ᵤkᵘe·. qakiłamna′mne·: "ta′xas hułts!ɛnaxa-
ła′e·s kałqu′pa·ł ɛnsakqa·'nwitsnutɛ′łne·. sɛł'a′qałqawa′se·
95 kuyo′ᵤkᵘe·'s." ta′xas ts!ɛnaxa′mne· ne₁s łayaₐqaka′mke·
swᵤ′t₁mo. łaxaxa′mne· ne₁ aₐ·ku′q!ᵘnu·k. tunuxa′xa·'m.
n′upxa′łne· kałqu′pa·ł sakqa′ₐne·, a′ₐ·ke· n′uk!ᵘe′₁ne· ku-
yo′ᵤkᵘe· sa‵kqa′ₐne·. n′upxałɛ′sₐne· kałqu′pa·ł pał n′upɛ′łne·.
pał·ats!ɛna′xe· kuyo′ᵤkᵘe· ne₁s k!u′pła·ps kałqu′pa·ĩs, ne₁
100 ta′xa aₐ·ku′q!ᵘnuk yaqa·'kqa′ₐke· kałqu′pa·ł naₐ ta′xa
qałaꞏt.łitɛtna′mne· kałqu′pa·ł.
Ta′xas husɛłqlapqałq!anuxwa′te· kałqu′pa·ł.

are the Kuyo'kwe. | They are many." Then Pine Cone was left, and
they went on. ‖ He looked and saw them. The enemies looked   60
terrible. | Then he started to run. The Kuyo'kwe arrived. |
The Kuyo'kwe saw that he was an old man, | and they said to one
another: "Don't kill him, for he is old!" |

The Kuyo'kwe went along. Pine Cone took off his blanket ‖ and   65
tied it with rushes.[1] He tied his blanket over them. He thought |
the Kuyo'kwe would think it was he. They saw that it was only | his
blanket. They did not look at it. The grass was standing there
with the blanket on. | When he was overtaken, he took his pointed
arrow | and shot the Kuyo'kwe. The point did not pierce them. The
Kuyo'kwe ‖ thought that the old man would kill them. They looked   70
at the arrow | which he shot. Then they laughed at him, because Pine
Cone's arrow had not pierced them. | He shot all his arrows, and the
points did not pierce | the Kuyo'kwe. They made fun | of Pine Cone,
and they thought they would not kill him. ‖ After playing with him,   75
they would go on | in the direction where Lamb Hat and his friend
had gone. | After arriving at their camp, they were going to fight with
them. Now, Pine Cone had one arrow | left. There was no point to
it. He shot at a Kuyo'kwe, pierced him, | and killed him. When the
Kuyo'kwe saw that Pine Cone ‖ had killed one of them, they spoke   80
among themselves. "Kill him, for Pine Cone has killed one of us!" |
He had no more arrows. He started to run. | He thought the
Kuyo'kwe could not kill him. Then he | had no more arrows. He
thought: "I must die, for | I have no more arrows." They pursued
him. He thought he would be shot. ‖ Then he moved about his bow   85
on his back. He did this for the purpose | that when the Kuyo'kwe
should shoot him, he would throw off the arrows. | When they reached
him, they struck him and knocked him down. Then the Kuyo'kwe
cried | because Pine Cone had killed one of them. Then they started
back | to their own country. ‖

When Lamb Hat and his friend came back to the town, | they said: 90
"A great number of Kuyo'kwe are pursuing us. | Maybe they have
killed Pine Cone." They were waiting for | the Kuyo'kwe to come.
They talked among themselves: "Now let us go! | Maybe the Kuyo'-
kwe do not come because they are fighting with Pine Cone." ‖ Then   95
they went the way the two friends had come. | They arrived at the
lake. They went out to it, | and they saw Pine Cone lying there and
one Kuyo'kwe lying there. | Then it was known that Pine Cone had
killed him. | The Kuyo'kwe had gone back when Pine Cone had
killed one of them. ‖ That lake where Pine Cone was lying is now | 100
called Pine Cone.[2] |

Now I have told about Pine Cone. |

---

[1] A brittle grass with round stems growing in the lake, softer than reed and larger than rushes.
[2] Alkali Lake, about 20 miles south of Windermere.

73. The Kuyo'ᵤkᵘe

Ho'ya's, hutsχałhaqałq!anuχwa'te· ya̜qał'oᵤkta'pske· tₑłna'-
mo's kuyo'ᵤkᵘe·.

Qa̜kqa·nke·k.łuna'mne·. k!o·kunmi·'yit łaχak.łuna'mne· ya̜-
ksa̜nu·qo qał'at.łetₑtₑna'mne·. kanmi'yₑt nuqunaneya'mne·.
5 n'uk!ᵘqape'ₑne· neₐs ko'o·s tₑłna'm·u. n'aqtsakχo'ᵤne·. sₑł'aqał-
qats!ₑna'χe·. ta'χta kanmi·'yₑt.s tsχałts!ₑna'χe· neₐs ya̜qa-
na'wₑsło·nisnamₑ'ske·. ta'χas ktsₑłmi'yₑt.s nanmo'kᵤne· neₐs
ma·k!s. ktsχałtso'ᵤkᵘat t!ₑna'mo·'s. qałwi'yne·: "kutsχałhan-
mu'ko· q!a'pe· na̜s tsₑłmi'yₑtₑna'mo·'s. kanmi·'yₑt wₑ'łna·m
10 kutsiłts!ₑ'na·m."

Ta'χas na·'nma·nißka'ₐne· kuyo'ᵤkᵘe·. pał ke'e·n wanuyₑtna'-
mo soᵤk!ałukᵘₑ'łne·. łaχa'χe· kuyo'ᵤkᵘe· ya̜ksa̜nu'qus. łaχa'χe·
neₐs ko'o·s. n'u'pχa̜ne· san·ₑnq!oku'pse·. qao·χa'χe· pał ke'e·n
k!anaχa'ka tₑnawₑtsk∕'kₑne· neₐs a̜·kₑt.łana'me·s. n'u'pχa̜ne· pał
15 n'ok!ᵘe'se· tₑłna'mu's. qakiła'mne·: "hułtₑna·χa'mnała'e·s pał
kusiłₑt!kwa·ła·. hułqahak'yₑ'kse·yała'e·s a̜·kₑt.ła'e·s pał ksₑł'-
ₑsqat!łe'et." tₑnaχa·''mne· qa·nqa'me·k. neₐ tₑłna'mo n'u'pχa̜ne·
tkaχa·''mse· kuyo'ᵤkᵘe·s. pał n'u'pχa̜ne· yunaqa'pse· pał n'ₑ'n·se·
k!anaχa'ka·'s. n'onₑ'łne·. ta'χas łuqła'ntₑ'kse· łanₑ'se·s a̜·qa·ti-
20 k.łukᵘn∕'se·s a̜·qa'tᵤwumłat!ₑ'se·s. sₑł'ₑ'tmase'ₑtse·. nowo'ᵤkᵤne·
tₑłna'mu. n'anaχa·''mne·. tkałkₑ'n·e· łoᵤk!ᵘs. ta'χas χuna·''nte·.
ta'χas wₑłₑnq!ku'pse·. ta'χas kuyo'ᵤkᵘe· qake'ₑne·: "pał sₑłso'ᵤ-
kᵤne· tₑłna'mu. k!u'pχa kuₑt!kwała'e·s, k!ₑłkuktsa'was." qao·-
χaχe· tₑłna'mo. a̜·qułuma'e·s n'aqte'ₑte·. n'akakₑ'n·e· a̜·kᵤwu-
25 m·a·'łqaps. tsukᵘa'te· n'a·'se· a̜·kₑnq!a'wo·ks. χunak!o'ᵤne· neₐs
a̜·q!u'ta·łs neₐs ya̜kiłwₑłnq!oku'pske·. ta'χas łuqᵘinku'pse·.
ta'χas n'oma'tsₑne· kuyo'ᵤkᵘe·. qakiła'mne·: "sₑłso'ᵤkᵤne· tₑłna'mu. k!u'pχa kuit!kwała'e·s. k!ₑłkuktsa'was. k!u'pχa kuhu-
wasnała'e·s, k!e·'tke·n ku.ₑ'k¡nała'e·s." ta'χas n'u'pχa̜ne· neₐ
30 tₑłna'mu ktsₑma·'k!ₑłuqᵘₑ'nko·ps neₐs a̜·q!u'ta·łs. qanałwanq-
kupkₑ'n·e·, pał q!a'pe· kuyo'ᵤkᵘe· k.ła'łoᵤs a̜·kuqła·''nt!e·s. k!it-
ma'se̜t neₐts kwanqku'pkin tₑłna'mu. ta'χas n'oᵤkiłhoᵤkᵤna'-
pse· t!ₑna'mo·'s neₐ kuyo'ᵤkᵘe·. nupa·q!ₐłała'nk!a'tek. neₐ tₑłna'mu neₐsts k!u'pχa k!aqa'qₐnaps n'anmuqkup'noχunka'me·k.
35 nutsₑnqku·pekₑ'me·k. neₐsts kanmu'ku ma·k!s, ta'χas ktso'ᵤkᵘat
t!ₑna'mo·'s qaa·ło·qa·witskₑ'n·e· a̜·kₑnoqᵘa'̜kups. nawₑtsnuqᵘa'-
kupk!o'ᵤne·. qao·χakₑ'n·e· a̜·k.ła'm·e·s neₐs a̜·kₑnq!u'kups.
neₐsts k!anaχa·''mktse·k. nutsₑnqkupekₑ'me·k. n'u'pχa̜ne· qakiła'mne· kuyo'ᵤkᵘe·: "mₑtiₐχa'ki·ł. kₑnłq!akpakitχo'ᵤkᵘi·ł."
40 qana'χe· neₐ tₑłna'mu. n'u'pχa̜ne· neₐs ya̜qana'mke·. qana'se·
kuyo'ᵤkᵘe·s pał ktamo'χo·s nupχa'se· ya̜qana'mke·. ta'χta
n'u'pχa̜ne· pał nak!ałmukwa.ₑ't.se·. n'u'pχa̜ne· mₑ'ka ma kqao·-
χa'ke·n a̜·kₑnᵤq!u'ko·ps pał łaqałokᵘₑ'n·e· pał sₑł'aqaqa'pse·

73. THE KUYO'KWE

Now, I'll tell how an old woman killed all the | Kuyo'kwe. |
They were camping about. One day they camped at | Smoky
Place, as it is called. On the following day they moved on. ‖ Only   5
one old woman remained on the village site. She was pounding
(bones). | Therefore she did not go. On the following day she was
going to leave | in the direction where the others had gone. Then at
night she boiled | the bones. She was going to take the fat along.
She thought: "I'll | boil all of them to-night. Early to-morrow morn-
ing I ‖ shall start." | 10
Then the Kuyo'kwe followed the tracks of the people. It was
winter | and good traveling. The Kuyo'kwe arrived at Smoky Place.
When they arrived | at the village site, they saw a fire burning. They
came there, and | the warriors looked into the tent. They saw ‖ one   15
old woman. They said to one another: "Let us go in. | We are
cold. Let us stay here over night in her tent. | It is cold." They
entered. They sat down. The old woman saw | the Kuyo'kwe enter.
She saw that there were many | warriors. She was afraid. They
took off their clothes, ‖ their moccasins, their leggings, and their shirts,   20
and dried them. The old woman arose. | She went out and brought
in fuel. She put it on the fire. | Then there was a great fire. The
Kuyo'kwe said: | "The old woman is good. She knows that we are
cold, and she makes a fire for us." | The old woman went there.
She untied a parflèche and took out lard. ‖ She took two sticks and   25
put | the fat on the fire. Then the fire blazed up. Then it melted. |
The Kuyo'kwe laughed, and said: "That is a good | old woman.
She knows we are cold. She makes a fire for us. She sees | that we
are hungry, and she prepares food for us." Then ‖ the old woman saw   30
that the fat was really melted. | She just stirred it. All the Ku-
yo'kwe were without clothing. | They were drying it. The old
woman moved it about, and then all the grease caught fire. | The
Kuyo'kwe jumped back. When | the old woman saw what they were
doing, she ran out quickly. ‖ She started to run. She took the fat   35
of the bones that she was boiling. | She did not know how to hold
the light. She was holding a torch. | She put it on her head to
serve as a light. | When she ran out, she ran. She noticed | that the
Kuyo'kwe said: "Pursue her! Strike her on the head!" ‖ The old   40
woman went out. She knew which way she was going. | The Ku-
yo'kwe went along. It was very dark. They saw which way she
went. | They began to know it, because she had a light. They knew
that she had just | put a fire on her head. She did not take it off.

k!u'px̣a·'s kuyo'$_{u}$k^{u}e·s ya$_{a}$qana'mke·. tsuk^{u}a'te· ne$_{i}$s a$_{a}$'kɛnq!u'kups. nas sɛn·umu'k!se· qanałwat!ni'te· ne$_{i}$s łu˘q^{u}a'qumłasx̣u'n·e·. n'itq!ankikqa'$_{a}$ne·. ta'x̣as kuyo'$_{u}$k$_{u}$e· k$_{i}$mite'$_{i}$x̣a ne$_{i}$s tɛłna'mu's. ta'x̣as to'x̣^{u}a tsx̣ał·ax̣a'nx̣o'$_{u}$ne·. ne$_{i}$ kałnuku'pqa. qa.u'px̣$_{a}$ne· pɛ'k!a·ks ksɛł·oq!^{u}a'łke·ns ne$_{i}$s a$_{a}$'kɛnq!u'kups. nas kqanałwa't!mɛt.s a$_{a}$'kɛnu'm·o·k!^{u}s. qałwi'yne· k!upsla't$_{i}$yi'ł'ɛn·s ne$_{i}$s tɛłna'mu's ne$_{i}$s ya$_{a}$qa'nmox̣u'ske· a$_{a}$'kɛnq!u'kups. qanałwa't!aqu'młasx̣u'n·e·. qa.u'px̣$_{a}$ne· ne$_{i}$s ksɛn·u'm·o·k!s. ta'x̣as ne$_{i}$ k$_{i}$yuna'qa kuyo'$_{u}$k^{u}e· qanałwa't!aqa'nqum·łasx̣u'n·e·. ta'x̣as q!a'pe· k$_{u}$wat!nɛ'te·k pał k$_{u}$wɛt!nö'mo·k!. ta'x̣as q!a'pe· q!akpakitx̣o'$_{u}$me·k. ta'x̣as tɛłna'mu łaowo'$_{u}$k$_{u}$ne·. nułpa'łne· kuyo'$_{u}$k^{u}e·s ne$_{i}$s u'me·'s nał·uk^{u}a'x̣anmitɛ'tse·. łaqao˘x̣a'x̣e· a$_{a}$'kɛt.ła'e·s. łało'$_{u}$se·; pał sɛł'o·'kte·.

Qałwi'yne·: "ma kqa'e·n naso'$_{u}$k^{u}e·n's kanx̣a'łe·. hułts!ɛna'mił ktsx̣ał'ɛ'kam." ta'x̣as ts!ɛna'x̣e· ne$_{i}$s ya$_{a}$qana'wɛsłonɛsnamɛ'ske·. ta'x̣as łax̣a'x̣e·. t$_{i}$nax̣a''mne· a$_{a}$'kɛt.ła.ɛ'se·s x̣ałe'e·s. qakɛ'łne·: "łu'n·u. ts!ɛ'na·n' ka·kɛ't.ła. hun'o·'kte· kuyo'$_{u}$k^{u}e·. naqa''ne· kqa'e·p. hɛntsx̣ał'upɛ'łne· a'$_{a}$'ke· yunaqa'pse· a$_{a}$'k.łitɛ't!e·s. hɛntstsuk^{u}a'te· ya$_{a}$ke'$_{i}$so·k. ma kɛnqa'e·n naso'$_{u}$k^{u}e·n. ta'x̣as hɛnts!ɛ'n·e· naso'$_{u}$k^{u}e·n." ta'x̣as ts!ɛna'x̣e· ne$_{i}$ nɛtsta'hał. a·nk$_{u}$wunɛ'kit.s ta'x̣as tsx̣anatka'$_{a}$ne· ne$_{i}$ tɛłna'mu. ta'x̣as q!a'pe· ts!ɛnax̣a'mne·. k.łax̣a'x̣am pał pe.ɛ'k!aks n'o·'kte· ne$_{i}$ nɛtsta'hał ne$_{i}$s ya$_{a}$kqa'e·ps, pał n'upɛ'łne·. a'$_{a}$'ke· yake'$_{i}$suks a$_{a}$'k.łe'et.s pał tsuk^{u}a'te·. ta'x̣as n'ɛ'n·e· naso'$_{u}$k^{u}e·n's ne$_{i}$ nɛtsta'hał.

Ta'x̣as husłq!a'pqałq!anax̣wa'te· tɛłna'mu yaqał'o·k^{u}ɛ'tke· kuyo'$_{u}$k^{u}e·s.

74. The Great Epidemic

Ho'ya's, hutsaqałpałne'$_{i}$ne· ne$_{i}$ pɛ'k!ak yaqanekɛ'tke·.

Qa·kit.łaq$_{u}$wu'mne·. n'u'k!^{u}niłsa·nik.łuna'mne·. n'öp$_{i}$na'mne·. n'o·k$_{u}$nukna'mne·. tax̣as kqa$_{a}$tsa'mne· tuq!tsqa'kił·amna'mne· q!a'pe· ktuna'x̣a pał sa·nik.ło'$_{u}$ne·. k.łax̣a'x̣a·'m k!ok!^{u}k.ło'$_{u}$'nam tuq!tsqakiła'mnam pał q!a'pe· qak$_{u}$wu'mne·. tax̣as ne$_{i}$ k!o·'k!k.ło· łaqa˘u'px̣aka'$_{a}$ne·. ta'x̣as q!a'pe· n'upna'mne·. n'o·k!^{u}qape'$_{i}$ne·. naqsanmi·'yit.s, ta'x̣as x̣atk$_{i}$nu'k$_{u}$ne· ne$_{i}$ k!o·k!^{u}qa'pe·, n'ɛ'n·e· tɛ'tqa·t! ne$_{i}$ k!o·k!^{u}qa'pe·. qałwi'yne·: "ho'ya's hułe'$_{i}$kqa·ts na a'm·a·k, na'qa·nqaqó:'qa'ki·łha'qwo·m ku'sił·aqa.upx̣a'ka·. qa.ɛ'n·e· łaha'qwo·m, ksła'qa łaqawa'x̣am." ta'x̣as ts!ɛnaqu'łne· yaqso'mɛ'ł'e·s. sɛłkqa·tsɛmu'ne·. ts!ɛnaqu'łne·. ta'x̣a n'ɛ'n·e· k$_{i}$yapt!akiłha'qa ktuna'x̣a. łax̣a'qo·ł ma n'aqa'$_{a}$kiłhaq$_{u}$wu'm'e·s at łunamɛ's$_{i}$ne·. nɛ''nqa·ts at tsɛn'upna'mu's, at sł'u'px̣$_{a}$ne at łɛ'tikna.ɛ'tse·. n'u'px̣$_{a}$ne· k.łtsᴇma'k!iłałuna'me·s, ksɛł·ɛ'tikna'e·ts. no:'łqa·ts qa.uk^{u}na'k$_{a}$na$_{a}$t wunmana'mu's at ła·ts!ɛnaqu'łne·. k.ła'x̣a·m ma n'a·qa'hak.łuna'me·s nɛ''nqa·ts at

Therefore | the Kuyo'kwe knew where she went. She had taken the fire. ‖ There was a cliff, and she threw the torch down and jumped 45 aside. | She lay down. Then the Kuyo'kwe | followed the old woman. Now the fastest runner had almost overtaken her. | He did not see that she had taken off the torch quickly, | and that she had just thrown it over the cliff. They thought it was still ‖ the old woman. 50 When the fire was falling, he just | jumped down. He did not know that there was a cliff. Then the | many Kuyo'kwe jumped down. | All went down over the high bank. Then they were all | killed. The old woman got up again. She heard the Kuyo'kwe ‖ below groaning. 55 She went back to her tent. | There was nobody there. She had killed them all. |

She thought: "My son is not a chief. I'll go to him. | He shall come." Then she started. She traveled the way they had gone. | Then she arrived, and entered the tent of her son. ‖ She said to him: 60 "Go on; go to my tent. I killed all the Kuyo'kwe. | Some of them are not dead. Kill them. Much is their property. | Take some good clothing. You are not a chief. | Then you will be a chief." Then the youth started. | After a while the old woman told about what had happened. ‖ Then all started. When they got there, the 65 youth had already killed | all those who were not dead. He had killed them and | taken their property. Then the youth became | a chief. |

Now, I have told how the old woman killed all the ‖ Kuyo'kwe. | 70

74. THE GREAT EPIDEMIC

Well, I'll tell a story of what happened long ago. |
The people were living there, and at once they had an epidemic. They died. | All died. Then they went about. They told one another the news. | Among all the Kutenai there was sickness. They arrived at one town, ‖ and told the news to one another. It was 5 everywhere the same. | At one town they did not see anybody. They were all dead. | Only one person was left. One day the one that was left was cured. | He was a man. He was alone. He thought: "Well, | let me go around this world to see if there is any place where there is any one. If there is no one left, ‖ I won't see it 10 again. There is nobody. Nobody ever comes on a visit." Then | he started in his canoe. He went about in it. He started in his canoe, and | came to the last camp of the Kutenai. When he arrived by the water where the people used to be, | there was nobody; and when he went about, he saw only dead ones, | no signs (of a living person). He knew that nobody was left. ‖ There were no signs (of 15 life). After the one who was alive had left, not having seen anything, | he went along in his canoe. He arrived where there had been

tsᴇn upna′mu′s at sᴇk.ɫo′ᵤse· ne̹s aₐ′kᴇk.ɫuna′me·s. at ɫa·-
ts!ᴇna′xo·. ta′xas sᴅqaqa′so·xaɫhaqa′pse· ktuna′xa′s kqa′ₐtse·
ne̹s aₐ′kᴇk.ɫuna′me·s.   q!a′pe·′s sak.ɫᴇnmoxuna′kse· up′na′mu′s·
20 ne̹s a′q!a′s aₐ′kᴇt.lana′me·s. ne̹sts k.ɫa′t̹yiɫkqa′ₐtske·. k!u′pxa
q!a′pe·′s paɫ sᴅ·aɫo′ᵤse· aq!sma′k̹nᴇk!s.   at n′upsɫa′t̹yiɫ′iɫa′n·e·.
qaɫwi′yne·: "kuɫsᴅ′o·k!ᵘqa′pe· na a′m·a·k, o·k!ᵘqᵤna·ts xa′ₐɫ-
tsins at paɫ n′u′pse·."   qoᵤs k.ɫa′xam k̹yapt!a·ki·ɫhaqᵤwu′m′e·s,
ta′xas ke′̹kqa·ts. n′u′pxₐne· naɫᴇ′kse· aq!sma′k̹nᴇk!s, paɫ qani-
25 t.ɫa′ₐase·. ne̹s yaqaha·k.ɫo′ᵤske· up̹na′mo′s. a·n′ᴅqa′haks qoᵤs
qa′hakka′ₐse· ko′o·s. n′u′pxₐne· naqa′n′a·s· naqanqa′ɫsa·s
mᴇ′ksa′n n′u′pxₐne· naɫᴇ′kse· kᵤwᴇ′ɫe·ks a·nktsa′ɫk̹na′nas. qa.u′-
pxₐne· naqanqa′ɫsa·s. n′u′pxₐne· k.ɫa′qaps kxa′tk̹no·ks. ɫa·ts!ᴇna-
qu′ɫne·. qaɫwi′yne·: "ne̹ huɫqana′qo·ɫ ne̹s at ma kqanaɫk.ɫu′-
30 ne·s na ha·′kiɫhaqa′ₐke·; na′pit na′qa tᴇ′tqa·t! na′qanhoqna′-
me·k." ta′xas ts!ᴇnaqu′ɫne·. qa·naqu′ɫne·. n′u′pxₐne· qoᵤs na′ₐtas
n′a′se· nö′pqo. skikᴅ′ᴇkse· ma′xa′s. qaɫwi′yne·: "huɫts!ᴇna′miɫ
kutsmᴇ′txa. hun′ᴇ′lwa kutsxa′ɫ′e·k. kuts!ᴇtma′sit. paɫ kusᴅ′-
u′pxa k.ɫa′qᵤwo·m honuɫ′ᴇtma′se·t. ta′xas kutsɫa.ᴇ′ts!ki·ɫ ne̹
35 kou′pxaɫᴇ′k!e·n aq!sma′k̹nᴇk!. ɫᴇnqa′ₐpskiɫhaqa′ₐne· tᴇ′tqa·t!
k.ɫu′wa·s ne̹ pa′ɫke̹ ktsxa′ɫ′e·k." ta′xas ts!ᴇna′xe·. ɫaxa′xe·
qoᵤs yaqaha·wᴇsa·′qa′pske· nö′pqo′s. ɫaxa′xe·. n′u′pxa paɫ
qa.ᴇ′n·se· nö′pqo·′s paɫ n′ᴇ′n·se· pa′ɫke̹s. n′u′pxₐne· nao·′k!ᵘe·′s
n′ᴇ′n·se· kᵤwᴇ′ɫqa·ps, nao·′k!ᵘe·′s n′ᴇ′n·se· na.u′te·′s.   qaɫwi′y-
40 ne·: "kusᴅsukᵘᴇ′ɫq!o·k kuu′pxa aq!sma′k̹nᴇk!.   ke′e·n pa′ɫke̹
huɫtso′ᵤkᵘat ktsxa′ɫ′e·n katᴅna′mu." ta′xas qona′xe·. tsᴇnkᴇ′n·e·
ne̹s na.u′te·′s. tsxa′ne· ne̹ na.u′te·. qakᴇ′ɫne· ma′′e·s "ka′ma,
hon′u′pxₐne· tᴇ′tqa·t!." tse̹kata′pse· ma′′e·s. n′u′pxₐne· ne̹
pa′ɫke̹ paɫ tsᴇmak!kᴇ′kse· swᴇ′n′e·s.   n′u′pxₐne· tᴇ′tqa·t!s paɫ
45 sᴅtsukᵘa′t.se· swᴇ′n′e·s. ta′xas n′iɫa′n·e· ne̹ pa′ɫke̹ a′ₐ′ke· ne̹
na.u′te·, a′ₐ′ke· ne̹ nᴇtsta′haɫ, o·′k!ᵘqᵤna k!u′pxa q!a′pe·s
ktuna′xa·′s ke′e·ps. ne·′sts k!u′pxₐna·m sɫa·ᵛqa·′qa′psᴇ.
k!o·ᵤkᵘi·ɫ′iɫaxo′′na·m. qake′̹ne· ne̹ kᵤwᴇ′ɫqa pa′ɫke̹: "maₐts
tsᵤkᵘa′te·n′ na kaa′qa·ɫt, n′upski·ɫtsa·ᵛquna′ne·. ᴇ′s̹niɫtsukᵘa′to·.
50 hᴇntsxaɫ′ᴇ′ne· kanuɫ′a′qₐna. taxta·′ wᴇ′ɫqa· na kaa′qa·ɫt tsxaɫ′-
ᴇ′n·e· tᴅnamu′′ne·s. ta′xa·s hᴇntsxaɫ′ᴇtkᴇ′n·e· aₐ′qa′ɫt̹ne·s."
ta′xa·s ne̹ nᴇtsta′haɫ n′ᴇ′n·se· tᴅnamu′′e·s ne̹s kᵤwᴇ′ɫpqa·ps
pa′ɫke̹′s. qawunekᴇ′t.se· qake′̹ne· ne̹ pa′ɫke̹: "ta′xa·s hun′u′p-
xₐne· n′ᴇ′n·e· kᵤwᴇ′ɫqa· na.u′te· na kaa·′qaɫt. ta′xas ɫe′e·n′
55 tᴅnamu′′ne·s. ta′xas tsxaɫso′ᵤkse· kᴇnts!ᴇtkᴇ′nme·ɫ aₐ′qa′ɫt!e·s.
ta′xas tsᴇmak!e′̹se· aₐ′kuɫa′k!e·s." ta′xas ne̹ nᴇtsta′haɫ tsᵤkᵘa′te·
ne̹s na.u′te·′s n′ᴇ′n·se· tᴅnamu′′e·s. ta′xas qake′̹kaɫ′ᴇtᴅxo′′ᵤ-
me·k ktuna′xa.
    Ta′xas husɫq!a′pqaɫne′̹ne· yaqanekᴇ′tke· ne̹ pᴇ′k!ak ta′xas.

a town. He went out, | and there were only dead ones. There was nobody in the town. | He started to go back. Then he came to the last place where Kutenai lived. He went | to the town, and dead bodies were all piled up ‖ inside the tents. He always went about, and 20 he knew | that all the people were gone. He was crying as he went along. | He thought: "I am the only one left in this country, for the dogs | also are dead." When he came to the farthest village, | he went about, and he saw some footprints of people. ‖ They had a tent. 25 There were no dead bodies. Farther away there | was the village site. He knew there must be two or three (alive). | He even saw footprints—large ones and smaller ones. | He did not know if there were three. He knew some one was saved. He went on in his canoe, | and thought: "I'll paddle that way. Those who lived here used to go that way. ‖ If it is a man, he might have moved." | Then he 30 started in his canoe. He went along in his canoe, and saw above there | two black bears eating berries. He thought: "I'll go |.and shoot them. If I shoot them, I'll eat them. I'll dry them. Then I'll | see if any one is left. After I have dried the meat, ‖ I'll look for 35 them. I have seen footprints of people. They might be hungry men | or women. They shall eat." Then he started, and went there | where the bears were. He arrived, and saw | that they were not bears, but women. He saw one older one, | and the other one a girl. He thought: ‖ "I am glad to see people. Let me take that woman | 40 to be my wife." Then he went and took hold of | the girl. The girl spoke, and said to her mother: "Mother, | I see a man." Her mother looked. The woman saw | that her daughter was telling the truth. She saw a man ‖ taking her daughter. Then the woman and | the girl 45 and the youth cried, because they saw that all | the Kutenai were dead. When they saw each other, | they all cried together. The older woman said: "Don't | take my daughter. She is still small. Take me. ‖ You shall be my husband. Later on, when this my 50 daughter is large, | she shall be your wife. Then you shall have children." | Then the youth married the older woman. | It was not long before the woman said: "Now | I see that my daughter is grown up. Now she may be ‖ your wife. It is good if you have children. | 55 Her body is strong now." Then the youth took | the girl for his wife. Then the | Kutenai increased from these. |

Now I have told what happened long ago. Enough. ‖

75. The Giant

60   Qaₐk.łuna′mne·. n′o·kᵘe′ₒne· nɛtsta′hał n′ɛt!xₐna′pse· e′ₒka′s.
ta′xas tɛlna′mu nuł′a′qₐna at n′ɛla′n·e· ke·eps a·qa′łt!e·s. k!o·
kunmi·′yit.s łahutsa′xe· e′ₒka neₒs aₐ′kɛk.łuna′me·s tsɛlmiyɛt
na′mu′s. qoᵤs ahan′ɛlqa′haks qa·nɛt.łanamɛ′sₒne·. qao·xa′xe·.

65 n′u′pxₐne· nuł′a′qₐna′s tɛlna′mu′s pał n′ɛn′se·. qałwi′yne·:
"hułq!u′′mne·. ta′xta kanmi·′yɛt.s kutsxa′ł′ik· na nuł′a′qₐna
tɛlna′mu." ta′xas q!u′mne′ₒne·. wɛlna·m′s n′ɛla′n·e· neₒ
tɛlnamukᵘɛ′ste·k. kuł′e′ₒła n′ukᵤnuxa′′mne· neₒ tɛlna′mu kts
xał′ɛ′łko·. n′u′pxₐne· skɛ′k.łeₒts qa′la·s. tseₒka′te· pał n′ɛn′se·

70 e′ₒka·′s. qakɛ′łne· nuł·aqₐna′′e·s: "tseₒka′te·n′ e′ₒka skɛk.łe′ₒtsₒ
ne· kakɛt.łanała′′e·s." n′ukᵤnoxa′′mne· neₒ nuł′a′qₐna. tsᵤkᵘa′te·
aₐ′ktsama′ł′e·s, lu·łama′′ne· e′ₒka·′s, nałq!a′nqało′ᵤkᵤne·. qaki
ya′mne·: "qa′psins tɛlnamukᵘɛ′ste·k ksɛlsokᵘɛ′łq!o·k. ma ksa·
kił′e′′ła?" qunaxamɛ′sₒne·. sakqa′pse· e′ₒka·′s pał sɛl′opɛ′łne·.

75   Ta′xas husłq!apqałpałnemɛ′łne· yaqa·qa·′na′ₐke· tɛlnamu
kᵘɛ′ste·k neₒs pɛ′k!a·ks.

76. The Giant

Ho′ya′s hutsxałtsxa′n·e· yaₐqaqₐna′ₐke· k!o·′k!ᵘe· pɛk!a′
knɛk! nɛtsta′hałq!łik!a′mał n′ɛnqa′pte·k e′ₒka·′s.

     Qa·k.łuna′mne· n′uk!ᵘe′ₒne· nɛtsta′hałq!łik!a′mał ts!ɛnał′
ana·xe·. ta′xₐ naₐ nɛtsta′hałq!łik!a′mał n′ɛne· kqasts!o′m

5 qa′qa k!a′ₐna·m. (hoqᵘa.u′pxₐne· kaₐs naqa′k.łe·k.) n′ok!ᵘe′ₒse·
k!ɛ′łwa nɛ′łyaps. n′umɛtse′ₒte·. kuł′umɛ′tse·t nowa′sₒne·. qał
wi′yne·: "huł′itₒma′se·t tsxałsɛlɛtxₐma′qa. hułaha′łxo· kanmi′
yit.s pał kwułe′it xₐma kts!anɛ′ke· neₒs hułqa.eₒtₒma′se·t."
ta′xas n′ɛtkɛ′n·e· aₐ′kowask!o′we·s. ta′xas n′ɛtk!anɛ′łne· neₒs

10 aₐ′ku′ła·ks at q!ayakɛ′n·e·. tₐ′xas to′xᵘa q!a′pe·′s tsxałq!a
yakɛ′n·e· neₒs aₐ′kowask!o′we·s n′as qaₐkqa′pse· aₐ′ku′łaks
paqts!nana′se·. qa.u′pxₐne· kaₐs naₐqakeₒkału′xo·′s. pał
ko′wa·s qałwi′yne·: "hułe′e·k." xunakɛ′n·e· neₒs aₐ′ku′łaks.
ku′kups ta′xas n′ɛ′kₒne·. sukᵘaxₐne′ₒse· at qaqa′łaxnɛ′ₒse·

15 neₒs k!ɛ′łwa. qałwi′yne·: "qa′psin ke′e·n ksɛl′a′qałsukᵘa′xₐne·."
qak.ła·′tₒyiłtseₒka′te·, qa.u′pxₐne· kaₐs naₐqakeₒkału′xo·′s.
ta′xas qa·′hanqa′mek tsłemiyɛ′t.se·. nas qaₐkiłɛse′ₒse·, ta′xas
tseₒka′te·. n′u′pxₐne· neₒs aₐ′kuła′k!e·s qa′sił·o′ᵤse·. tseₒ
ka′te·, n′u′pxₐne· aₐ′ktsa′maₐls pał n′uła′se·. ta′xas

20 n′u′pxₐne· pał n′ɛn′se· aₐ′kuła′k!e·s neₒs ma ksukᵘa′xₐne·′s.
qałwi′yne·: "ho′ya′s a′ₐke· hułaqa′sił·u′qᵘa kaₐ′ku′łak." a·′′ke·
łaqa′sił·u′qᵘne·. xunakɛ′n·e· ku′kupsts n′ɛ′kₒne·. n′u′pxₐne·
pał sukᵘaxₐne′ₒse·. ta′xas tsɛmneₒxa′ₐme·k. tsxa′kił·uk!
moxa′me·k aₐ′kuła′k!e·s. mɛ′ka ke′e·k nukuma′nxa′me·k.

25 ta′xas ła·′łɛtq!o·′xᵤmasa′q!ₐne· ta′xas wunekɛ′t.se·. ktsłmi′yɛt

75. THE GIANT

There was a town. All the youths were eaten by a giant. | Then 60
an old woman and her husband cried, for their children were dead. |
Every day the giant went to that town at night. | There, at the far
end, was a tent. He went there, | and he saw an old man and an old
woman. He thought: || "I'll sleep, and in the morning I'll eat the old 65
man and | the old woman." Then he slept. Early in the morning
the old couple cried. | While crying, the old woman arose. She was
about to start a fire, | when she saw some one sleeping. She looked
at him. It was | the giant. She told her husband: "Look at the
giant sleeping || in our tent!" The husband arose, took | his knife, 70
and cut off the giant's head. He shouted. | The people said: "Why
are the old couple glad? | They were crying." They went there, and
the giant was lying there. They had killed him. |

Now I have told what the old couple did || long ago. | 75

76. THE GIANT[1]

Well, I'll tell you what happened to a newly married man | among
the people of olden times who became a giant. |

There was a town. There was a newly married youth. He went
hunting. | The newly married youth was a skillful || hunter. (I do not 5
know his name.) He killed | a mountain sheep. He skinned it. After
skinning it, he felt hungry. | He thought: "I will dry some of it, so
that it may be light. | I will carry it to-morrow. It is far, and it
would be heavy if I should not dry it." | Then he made a place to
dry it. He began to cut up || the meat, and hung it up. He was 10
about to hang almost all | on his drying frame. There were two thin
pieces of meat | lying there. He did not know where they fell off
from. | He was hungry. He thought: "I'll eat it." He put the
meat on the fire; | and when it was done, he ate. It tasted good. ||
What he had killed did not taste that way. He thought: "What 15
may it be, that it tastes so good?" | He looked at it for some time,
but he did not see where it had come from. | Then he sat down.
When it was dark, he felt a pain here. | He looked, and he saw that
his own flesh was missing. | He looked at it, and he saw that a knife
had done it. Then || he knew that it was his own flesh that tasted 20
good. | He thought: "Well, I'll cut off another piece of my flesh." |
He cut it off, put it on the fire, and when it was done he ate it
Then he saw | that it tasted good. He wanted some more. He began
to cook | his flesh on the fire, and, although he had eaten, he wanted.
some more. || Then there was no more flesh on his legs. It was late 25

---

[1] See p. 82.

sakił'ɛ'kₑne· aₐ'kuła'k!e·s. ta'χas kanmiyɛ't.se· sakɛł'ɛ'kₑne·.
nukᵤma'nχa'me·k. qatał·aqa.ɛ'kₑne·. ta'χas pɛ'k!aks a'ₐ'ke
sɛł·awałkwayɛ't.se·. ta'χas q!a'pe·'s aₐ'kuła'k!e·s n'ɛ'kₑne·
q!a'piłkits!χa'me·k. ta'χas tsɛn ma'k!e·s n'ɛnqapta'kse·. aₐ'ka-
30 qłɛ'ł'e·s n'ɛ'kₑne·. tsɛn sqapₑnił·ałaχapa'kin o·'k!ᵘqⁿaₐts wału-
na'k!e·s n'ɛ'kₑne·. q!a'peₑs n'ɛ'kₑne· aₐ'kuła'k!e·s. tsɛn qaₐqap-
ki·kwu'mne· aₐ'quqt!e'e·s mɛ'ksa'n snaχuna'kse· aₐ'k.łuma'e·s.
słaqaqa'pse· kqa'e·k aₐ'quqt!e'e·s aₐ'kwu'm'e·s. tsɛn sqapq!a-
no'ᵤkmała'kₑne·. n'ɛ'nse· kqa'e·k ałqa's'e·s aₐ'kɛnułma'k!e·s;
35 o·'k!ᵘqⁿa lałɛtq!oχᵤmaqa'ₐne· aₐ'k.ła'mała'k!e·s. sanqa'me·k.
ta'χas łaqatseₑka'te· neₑs aₐ'ku'ła·ks nɛ'łyaps. ta'χas qałsa·n-
miyɛ't.se· k.łaqa'wa·m neₑs aₐ'kik.łuna'me·s. ta'χas n'o-
k!ᵘe'ₑse· ta't!e·s ts!ɛnał'ɛts!k.ła'pse· neₑs yaₐqanałɛ'ₑke· ts!ɛ-
na'nuqkanχuna'pse. qana'χe·. n'u'pχₐne· pa·ł qaₐkił'ɛwa'se·
40 nɛ'łyaps tsa''e·s. pa·ł ts!ɛnanoke'ₑt.se· qoᵤs u'me·'s. qa·na'χe·
sɛłqa'noχunu'kse·. n'u'pχₐne· aₐ'kɛnq!o'kups. pa·ł sawɛsaqa'pse·
tsa''e·s pa·ł qaö'pse·. qałwi'yne· na'qanya'qak ksɛł'a'qałaqa-
ts!ɛ'na·m. qaoχa'χe· sɛłtsχa'se·. qakɛ'kse·: "hya' ma kutsła'-
ke·ł ka'tat. kutsχał'aymitɛ'tₑmu." n'u'pχₐne·pałqos naqₐna'k-
45 se·. k!aₐqaqa'pqaps pa·ł tsɛn''ɛnqapta'kse· mak!ɛ'se·s. qakɛ'łne·:
"kaₐ kɛn'aqa'qₐna· kɛ'nsɛł'aqaqa'pqa." qak.ła'pse·: "hołaqa.ɛ'n·e·
aq!sma'kₑnɛk!. ho·n'ɛnqa'pte·k e'ₑka. maₐts qoᵤkᵘa'n' ma
ku·tsła'k.łe·s." ta'χas łaχa'χe· tsɛnkna'pse·. qałwi'yne· pa·ł
tsɛn ke'e·ns ma'k!e·s. k.łqatsma'k!qa. tsɛn·kₑna'pse· n'ɛpła'se·,
50 a'ₐ'ke· n'ɛkₑna'pse·. kanmi'yet.s aₐ'kɛn'ok!ᵘe'ₑse· tsa''e·s.
qakɛ'kse·: "hutsχałts!ɛna'χe·. na'pe·t hołaqa'wamts hutsχał'u'pₑne·." ta'χas ts!ɛna'χe· neₑ nɛtsta'ha·ł, a'ₐ'ke· łaχa'χe·
a'ₐ'ke n'upła'pse·. kanmi'yit.s neₑs k!ukqa'pe·s tsa''e·s.
ts!ɛna'se· qake'ₑne· neₑ nɛtsta'hałna'na: "ta'χas a'ₐ'ke·
55 hutsχał'u'pₑne· ma kutsła'kiₑł ałka'ta·t pa·ł ksił'o'ᵤkⁿuᵤk
a'ₐ'ke· hutsχał'ö'pₑne·." qoᵤs •qana'χe· neₑ nɛtsta'hałna'na.
tsaqᵤna'ne·. qaₐkił'u'pχₐne· nöpɛ'k!a·s qak.ła'pse·: "ts!ɛna-
mɛ'łe·n'. ho'paks ktsɛ'kam ta'tₑne·s saosa·qa'ₐne·. n'oᵤkwa'χₐne·
ałtatₑnɛ'smi·ł. n'ɛnqa'pte·k e'ₑka·'s." ta'χas qaₐki·łsu'kᵘiłtsχa-
60 nata'pse· neₑs nöpɛ'k!a·s neₑ nɛtsta'hałna'na yaₐqa·ł'ɛnqa-
ptakɛ'ske· e'ₑka·'s a'ₐ'ke· neₑs yaₐqa·ł'upɛ'łske· neₑs k.łaχa'ke·ks.
tsχanata'pse· tsχałyaₐqaqa·'na'ₐke·. ta'χas ts!ɛna'χe·. łaχa'χe·.
n'u'pχₐne· saosa·qa'pse· neₑs ta't!e·s. n'ɛsc·katɛ'ₑse·. k!um·-
naqaqa'pse·. qak.ła'pse·: "ka'tsa· ma kɛtsła'k.łe·s. hun'ɛn-
65 qa'pte·k e'ₑka. hutsχał'ɛkₑnɛ'sₑne·." ta'χas n'ɛtkɛ'n·e· neₑs
ma yaₐqak.ła'pske· nöpɛ'k!a·s. ta'χas sɛłqa'tał'upła'pse·.
łatskɛna'χe·. ta'χas n'u'pχₐne·. miti˘yaχna'pse·. łałaχa'χe·
aₐ'kik.łuna'me·s neₑ nɛtsta'hałna'na. qake'ₑne·: "skanuta'pₑne·
e'ₑka. pa·ł n'ɛnqa'pte·k neₑ ka'ta·t e'ₑka·'s. pa·ł n'ɛ't!χₐne·
70 neₑs ma ktsłɛ'na·s ałkata'tmi·ł. qatał'ɛt!χₐna'pₑne·. sɛł·ats!-

at night, | and he was still eating his flesh. Then in the morning he
was still eating. | He wanted more. He could not stop eating. It
was | evening again, and he had eaten all his flesh. | He had gnawed
it off, and only bones remained. ‖ He ate his own eyes, and only the 30
orbits remained. | He even ate his own tongue. He ate his whole
body. Only | his intestines remained lying there. His intestines
remained, and his throat. | It was that way; he did not eat his intes-
tines and his stomach. | Only his bones remained; and he did not
eat his brains and his marrow, ‖ but there was no more flesh on his 35
skull. He was sitting down. | Then he would not look any more at
the mountain sheep. | Three days passed, and he did not return to
his town. Then | one of his elder brothers went to look for him. He
followed his tracks. | He went along, and saw where his younger
brother had killed ‖ the mountain sheep. He could see his tracks 40
below. He went along. | There was a creek. He saw a fire. | His
younger brother was there. He was not dead. He thought: "Maybe
his leg is broken, | and therefore he does not go home." He went
there and spoke to him. He said: "Oh, I love | my elder brother!
I'll keep myself alive for two days with him." (The elder brother)
saw him sitting there. ‖ He looked strange. Only his bones remained. 45
He said to him: | "What did you do, that you look like this?" He
was told: "I am no more | a human being. I have become a giant.
Don't come near me! | I love you." Then (the elder brother) went
there. He was taken hold of. He thought: | "There are only
bones. He is not strong." The giant took hold of him and killed
him ‖ and ate him. On the following day his next younger brother | 50
said: "I'll go. If I do not come back, I shall have died." | Then
the youth started. He also arrived, | and he also was killed. On
the following day the remaining one | started. The boy said: "I
also ‖ may die. I love my elder brothers. They are all dead now, | 55
so I will die, too." The youth went on. | He was small. He saw
a manitou. He was told: | "Go there! Your eldest brother who
went out first is there. He ate all | your elder brothers. He became
a giant." Then the youth was told plainly ‖ by the manitou that 60
(his elder brother) | had been changed into a giant, and how he
had killed the two who went there. | He was told what to do.
Then he started. He arrived, | and saw his elder brother. He looked
terrible. He was pitiable. | He said: "My younger brother, I love
you. ‖ I have become a giant. I'll eat you." Then (the boy) did | 65
what the manitou had told him, and he could not kill him. | (The
boy) went back. He saw that (the giant) followed him. The boy
arrived | at the town. He said: "A giant pursues me. | My brother
has become a giant. He ‖ ate my elder brothers who went there. 70

kanuta′pₐine·.″ ta′ȼas nuqᵤnaneya′mne·. neᵢs tⱬnamu′e·s
e′ᵢka qaosaˇqa′pse·. qake′ᵢne· nei paⱡkeᵢna′na: ″hutsȼaⱡ-
qaosaˇqa′ₐne·. ma kutsⱡa′ke·ⱡ kanuⱡa′qₐna.″ qak.ⱡa′pse·
neᵢs nⱥtsta′haⱡna′nas: ″ⱡaqa.ȼ′n·e· neᵢ at ma ktsⱡa′k.ⱡe·s
75 n′ȼseᵢkate′ᵢne·.″ qaqaⱡwi′yne· nei pa′ⱡkeᵢ. ta′ȼas nuqᵤna-
neya′mne·. qaosaˇqa′ₐne· nei pa′ⱡkeᵢ. qaⱡwi′yne·: ″ma ktsⱡa′-
k.ⱡa·p.″ qawunekⱥ′t.se· nuⱡpa′ⱡne· neᵢs ⱡaya·qaka′ske· neᵢs
nⱥtsta′haⱡna′na′s qak ᵢyamⱥ′sᵢne·: ″Hyâ, ma kutsⱡa′kiⱡ kanȼa-
ⱡena′na kutsȼa′ⱡ′e·k; ma kutsⱡa′kiⱡ katⱥlna′muts kutsȼa′ⱡ′e·k.″
80 ta′ȼas n′u′pȼₐne· la·ska′se·. n′u′pȼₐne· pa·ⱡ n′ȼse·kate′ᵢse·. pa·ⱡ
laqa.ȼ′nse· aqⱡsma′kᵢnⱥk!s. qaⱡwi′yne·: ″maₐts huⱡ′o·′niⱡ paⱡ
ke′e·n kanuⱡ′a′qₐna.″ ta′ȼas qa′wanȼa′′mne·. ta′ȼas wa′se·.
qakⱥ′lne·: ″kanuⱡ′a′qₐna, ma kutsⱡa′k.ⱡe·s. qa′pse·n kⱥnsⱥla-
qaqa′pqa?″ qake′ᵢne· nei tⱥtqa·t! nei e′ᵢka: ″huⱡaqa.ȼ′n·e·
85 aqⱡsma′kᵢnⱥk!.″ ta′ȼas ⱡawa′se· neᵢs aₐ′kit.ⱡa′e·s. n′ȼsakₑnu′se·.
qak.ⱡa′pse·: ″ts!kakⱥ′ne·n′ kanȼa′ⱡe·.″ ta′ȼas namatⱥ′ktse·, naqᵤ-
wiⱡtse′ᵢte·. tsɛmak!wⱥtskⱥ′n·e·. qake′ᵢne· nei e′ᵢka: ″ma kutsⱡa′-
kiⱡ kanȼaⱡna′nats kutsȼa′ⱡ′e·k.″ ta′ȼas pa·ⱡ ktsɛmak!wⱥ′tskin
neᵢs kaqᵘwⱥ′ⱡtseᵢt. ta′ȼas nutsᵢnuq!ᵘkⱥnⱥ′ⱡne·. n′u′pȼₐne· nei
90 pa′ⱡk·eᵢ pa·ⱡ pⱥ′k!a·ks tsȼaⱡsⱥⱡ′upⱥ′ⱡse·. qakⱥ′lne·: ″haq!ama·ⱡ·ats-
kakⱥ′n·e·, hutsȼaⱡts!ⱥnaⱡ′ⱥktoqo′ᵤne·. saha′nse· aₐ′q!uⱡ′e·′s.
taȼta′ₐ huⱡawa′ⱡke·n hⱥntsȼaⱡ′ⱥ′kᵢne·.″ ta′ȼas ⱡapⱥskⱥ′n·e·.
ts!ⱥna′ȼe· nei pa′ⱡkeᵢ. kuⱡ′ⱥktu′qo nutsⱥnqkupekⱥ′me·k neᵢs yaₐ-
qanalu′n′isnamⱥ′ske·. ta′ȼas wune·kⱥ′t.se· ⱡaqawa′se· tⱥⱡna-
95 mu″e·s nei e′ᵢka ta′ȼas ⱡaanaȼa″mne·. tseᵢka′te· tⱥⱡnamu″e·s.
n′u′pȼₐne· paⱡ sⱥⱡ′a·qₐne·tsa′pse·. ta′ȼas ts!ⱥna′ȼe· neᵢs yaₐqa-
nawⱥslunⱥsnamⱥ′ske·. qana′ȼe· nei kᵢyuna′qa aqⱡsma′kᵢnⱥk!.
qakiⱡa′mne·: ″kaₐs kuⱡ′a·qakna′ⱡats kuⱡ′upiⱡna′ⱡa?″ qakᵢya′-
mne·: ″ho′yas huⱡ′akokᵘⱥna′ⱡa hoᵤnaqa′n′tsȼaⱡ′upina′ⱡa.″ qa·-
100 han·mo·′k!ᵘne·. ta′ȼa nei u′me· skikq!anu′kᵤne·. n′oᵤⱡu′ne·
skⱥkq!ano′kᵤne·. n′oᵤⱡu′ne·. ta′ȼas nei aₐ′kⱥn·u′muk!. n′ⱥtk!a-
me′ᵢⱡne·. ta′ȼas qa·hawⱥtsqa′mek k!o·′k!ᵘe· tⱥ′tqa·t!. qake′ᵢne·:
″hutsȼa·ⱡwat!mitⱥkⱥ′ne· e′ᵢka. tsȼaⱡ′upu′qₐne· qoᵤs aₐ′q!a′-
n·o·ks.″ ta′ȼas na aₐqa′t!a·k qa·haqawu′mne·.[1] ta′ȼas
105 n′upȼa′lne· ska′ȼe· nei e′ᵢka. ta′ȼas aₐqa′t!aks qaska′ȼe·
nuⱡpaⱡnⱥ′ⱡne·. paⱡ sⱡa′ti·yiⱡtsȼa′ne·. qake′ᵢne·: ″huⱡaȼa′ₐn-
ȼonⱥ′ske·ⱡ q!a′pe· hutsȼaⱡȼᵢniskⱥ′ⱡne·. sukᵘa′ȼnⱥnaⱡa′pᵢne·
aⱡka′tsa ku′e·k.″ ta′ȼas nei kᵢyuna′qa aₐ′qⱡsma′kᵢnⱥk!
n′oᵤnⱥ′ⱡne· neᵢs k!aqa′kiks ktsȼaⱡ′oᵤka′ȼₐna·ps. qaⱡwiyne·-
110 na′mne· ktsoᵤsan·u′ȼon·a′qᵤwum. qake′ᵢne· nei ktsȼaⱡ′u′piⱡ:
″maₐts wanȼa″mki·ⱡ taȼtâ′ hoqᵘa′taⱡ′u′piⱡ, ta′ȼas hⱥntsoᵤsa-
n·u′ȼoᵤnqapkⱥ′ⱡne·.″ ta′ȼas qaqa′naⱡ·aqawanȼa′mna′mne·.
ta′ȼas wa′ȼe·· e′ᵢkaᵢ neᵢs aₐkⱥn·ü′muk!s aₐq!a′saks qanama-

He could not eat me. | Now he is pursuing me." Then they moved away. The giant's wife | staid behind. The young woman said: "I want | to stay. I love my husband." The youth said to her: | "He is no longer the one who used to love you. ‖ He is terrible." The 75 woman did not want to leave. | Then they moved away. The woman staid behind. She thought: "He loves me." | It was not long before she heard him coming along | the way the boy had come. Some one said: "Oh, I love my little son! | I'll eat him. I love my wife. I'll eat her." ‖ Then she saw him coming. She saw •that he 80 looked terrible. | He was no longer a human being. She thought: "Don't let me be afraid; | he is my husband." Then she did not move, and he arrived. | She said to him: "My husband, I love you. What | makes you like this?" That man the giant said: "I am no longer ‖ a human being." He arrived at his tent. He sat down. | He 85 said to her: "Give me my son!" She gave him to (her husband), | who made him dance. He held him tightly. The giant said: "I love | my little son. I'll eat him." He held him tightly | and made him dance. He made him defecate. Now the woman knew ‖ that he 90 was about to kill him. She said to him: "Give him to me for a little while. | I'll go and wash him. His excrement is bad. | Then when I bring him back you may eat him." He let him go. | The woman started. After she had washed him, she ran away | where the people had gone. After some time, when his wife did not arrive, ‖ the giant went 95 out. He looked for his wife. | He knew that she had deceived him. Then he started | the way they had gone. The many people were going along. | They said: "What shall we do with him? How shall we kill him?" | They said: "Let us try (and see) if we can kill him." ‖ There was a cliff ; and below it was a lake, a deep | lake. It was deep. 100 Then they dug a hole in the cliff, | and one man staid there. He said: | "I'll kick down the giant. He will be drowned in the deep lake." | Then the people staid a little ways off. ‖ The giant was seen coming 105 along. A little ways off he was heard coming. | He was talking. He said: "When I | overtake you, I'll eat all of you. My brother whom I ate tasted good to me." | Then the many people | were afraid when he said that he would eat all of them. They thought ‖ of 110 running away. The one who was about to kill him said: | "Don't move! If I can not kill him, then you may run away." | Then nobody moved. | Then the giant arrived. The trail was close to | the

na'mne·. łak!ɛ'nta· qanamana'mne·. qa·hank!amɛ'ne· yaₐqa'-
115 haosa‸qa'ₐke·¹ neᵢ ktsxał'u'pił. ta'xas wa'xc· e'ᵢka. qana‘qkup-
qłɛkxa'łne· e'ᵢka.   neᵢs k!u'pxa e'ᵢka pɛ'k!a·ks pał tsxałsɛłts!-
qaqłɛkxa'łne·, qałwi'yne· ktsxał'a‘tskałsaq!kɛ'nka·. qawoᵤkᵘɯ-
ka'ₐne·.   nułɯɯmoxu'ne· pał kᵤwɛt!nʋ'm·o·k!. qoᵤs o·'me·'s
qawoxałxunaqu'ne· o'k!ᵘqᵘna tsɯn k!ɯnqapta'ke·s ma'k!e·s qa-
120 tałha'qne·. n'o·k!ᵘniłɛktsᵢnoqu'n·e·. ta'xas tseᵢkatɛ'łne·. wu-
ne·kɛ't.se· łaqa.upxa'łne· pał sɛł'upɛłɛ'łne· e'ᵢka·.

Ta'xas   husɛłq!apqałpałɯɯmɛ'łne·   k!u·'k!ᵘe·   pɛk!a'kᵢnɛk!
yaₐqał'ɯnqaptɛ'ᵢke· e'ᵢka·'s.

77. THE MOTHER-IN-LAW TABOO

Neᵢs pɛ'k!a·ks aqłsma'kᵢnɛk! at nałnu'kpine·ła'mne·. nawaspa'łtᵢmo at qa'tałtłaqta·ła'mne·. at qa‘tałsukᵘiłtseᵢkata'mne
aₐ'kaq!ne'e·s. n'u'pxₐna·m nawaspa'łtᵢmo at n'ɛsɯn·k!ateyxo-
na'mne·. qa'ła qa‘ałnu'kpᵢni·ł nawaspa'ł'e·s at n'upxałɛ'sᵢne·
5 k.łqatsła'ke·ł nawaspa'ł'e·s. qa'ła tsɛma'k!ił'ałnu'kpᵢni·ł nawaspa'ł'e·s at n'upxałɛ'sᵢne k.łtsɛma'k!iłtsła'ki·ł nawaspa'ł'e·s.
ksɛł'a'qał'ałnu'kpᵢni·ł at k.łqa·sa·'niłwi'ynáₐt at k.łqa.ɛ'łki·ł
nawaspa'ł'e·s· qa'ła qa.ałnu'kpᵢni·ł nawaspa'ł'e·s at n'upxałɛ'sᵢ-
ne· at k.ł'upsa‘tᵢyiłsa·niłwi'ynaₐt at k.łupsła'tᵢyiłqa.o'nił ktsxał'-
10 ɛ'łki·ł nawaspa'ł'e·s. nasts qaqa'pse· kᵤwɛ'tske·n neᵢs pɛ'k!a·ks
aqłsma'kᵢnik!. nas ta'xas q!akpa'me·k ma yaqaqa'pske· k!e·'t-
ke·ns ał'ats!mɛ'ł'e·s nuła'se·; neᵢs k!u'pxa kamnu'qło·s aqłsma'kᵢnɛk!s at ya'qakna'mske· nawaspa'łtᵢmo·'s sła‸qa‸qa'pse·
k.łaqa'ałnu'kpᵢne·'łam nawaspa'łtᵢmo.

_____

¹ Pierre Andrew: _yuₐqu'osu‸qa'ₐke·_.

edge of the cliff.   There staid ‖ the one who was going to kill him. 115
Then the giant arrived. | He was kicked hard.   When he saw that he
was about to be kicked, | he tried to take hold of the leg, but he
missed it. | He began to fall.   The cliff was high.   At the bottom | he
fell into the water; and because only his bones remained, ‖ he could not 120
swim, and sank at once.   They looked for him a long time, | but he
was not seen again.   Thus the giant was killed. |

Now I have told you how a person long ago | became quickly
a giant. |

77. The Mother-in-law Taboo

Long ago the people used to be ashamed of each other. | Mother-
in-law and son-in-law could not talk to each other.   They could not
look | at their faces.   When mother-in-law and son-in-law met, they
were afraid of each other. | Those who were not ashamed of the
mother-in-law were known ‖ not to love her.   Whoever was much 5
ashamed of | his mother-in-law was known to love her very much. |
The reason why he is ashamed is that then his mother-in-law will
never get angry at him and never scold him. | Whoever is not
ashamed of his mother-in-law is known | to be always angry at her,
and never afraid to scold ‖ his mother-in-law.   The people held it this 10
way in olden times. | Now they forget how their grandparents used
to do, | because they met white people. | This is the way the mother-
in-law and son-in-law did, | and why they are not ashamed of each
other any more. |

III. ABSTRACTS AND COMPARATIVE NOTES

The folk tales of the Kutenai show intimate relations to the tales of the tribes of the plateaus, as well as to those of the plains east of the mountains. A considerable number of tales are common to the Kutenai and the neighboring Salish tribes, particularly the Okanagon. There are also a considerable number of identical tales found among the Kutenai and the Blackfeet.

It seems that the series of Transformer tales centering around Naɫmu'qtse and Ya.ukᵘe'ᵢka·m are peculiar to the Kutenai, although the tale of the origin of arrows is also known to the Okanagon. These tales are quite distinct from the Transformer tales of the Shuswap and Thompson Indians, and also from the tales of Old One as found among the Blackfoot. In 1891 I was told that when human beings were first created, they arose before they were quite finished, and danced until they fell down dead. Then human beings were created who became the ancestors of the Indians.

So far as the incomplete material allows us to judge, one of the most characteristic traits of Kutenai folk tales is the systematic development of animal society. Frog is the old grandmother of Muskrat, the Chipmunks, and Doe. Her brother, Owl, is hostile to her grandchildren. The fish Kǃ!'k!o·m is the grandfather of Doe, but his relationship to Frog is not stated. The Chipmunks are the wives of Fisher. Chicken Hawk's wife is Grouse. Coyote's wife is Dog. Their children are Misqolo'wum and Qǃota'ptsekǃ. Coyotes' brothers are Moose and Kingfisher. The only animal that is married to various people is Doe, but it is not certain whether the same Doe is meant every time. She is the wife of White Stone. Their child is Ya.ukᵘe'ᵢka·m. Ya.ukᵘe'ᵢka·m's brother is the father of Duck. The Doe is also married to Wolf, and at another place to Lynx. Lynx and Doe have two sons, who are Sun and Moon. The other animals do not seem to be related to this group, but live in the same village, and are either friends or enemies.

It is one of the characteristic traits of Kutenai and Okanagon mythology that the tales are welded together into connected groups. This tendency is not as marked as it is among the Navaho and probably also the Ute tribes, but it sets off the Kutenai tales clearly from the disconnected tales of the Shuswap and Thompson Indians.

In our series one group of tales centers around the creation of the sun. The first part of the story relates to the origin of the brothers who finally become sun and moon. Rabbit finds his sister Doe, whom he hides in the tent of his grandmother Frog. Lynx marries the Doe, and their children are two boys. The couple are deserted;

and when the boys grow up, they come to the place where the sun is being made (see p. 285).

The second part of the story begins with the origin of Ya.uk{u}e'{i}kam, who also goes to the place where the sun is being made and tries his powers. The story of his origin is briefly as follows: Frog's granddaughter, Doe, is taken into the water by White Stone, whom she marries. Their son is Ya.uk{u}e'{i}kam, who in a number of exploits obtains for the use of mankind arrow wood, the arrow straightener, sinew, flint, and the bow stave (see p. 290). Then he goes with Coyote to the place where the sun is being made. They pass a number of dangers—the fat, the giant, and the thunderbirds (see p. 285).

When the various parties meet, one after another tries to act as the Sun, and finally the sons of the Lynx are accepted.

We have no other incidents that are clearly connected with this tale, but I suspect strongly that the tale of the deluge produced by the Chicken Hawk may connect in a similar way with the story of the Sun (see p. 304).

On account of Ya.uk{u}e'{i}ka·m's great powers, the people are afraid of him and drown him. The fish resuscitate him; and he follows the people, finds his brother's wife and her son, and tells them to resist those who maltreat them. He kills the chief, and the people are even more afraid of him (see p. 291). This passage recalls the story of Coyote's son (see MAFLS 11:120). Finally Ya.uk{u}e'{i}ka·m goes to the east end of the world (see p. 291).

The second cycle, apparently independent of the former one, is that of the war against the sky.

Nahmu'qtse crawls about in the country, and his tracks form the rivers (see p. 288). During this period Muskrat kills his sister-in-law and escapes to the sky. The animals make a chain of arrows and climb up, but Wolverene tears the chain. The animals fight with Muskrat. When they find the arrow chain broken, they kill the thunderbird, and with its feathers they fly down. The Bat and the Flying Squirrel, who receive no feathers, sail down. The Sucker jumps down and breaks its bones. The Woodpecker family are not given feathers. They climb down the sky, and reach the earth in the west, passing through the horizon (see p. 288). They meet Nahmu'qtse and try to kill him by throwing into his mouth a red-hot stone wrapped in a goat heart. Nahmu'qtse causes it to fall aside. He warns the woodpeckers not to sleep in wooded places and not to touch a charr floating in the water (see pp. 288, 289). The Woodpeckers disobey; and when they sleep in a wooded place, a toad sticks to the body of one of them. When Flicker touches a charr, he and his wife Duck are swallowed by a water monster. In order to find out where Flicker is, Woodpecker sends out birds to invite the fish to his tent. They come led by their grandfather (a fish with thick head). They smoke, and the fish indicates by signs that Flicker is in the lake. The Woodpeckers try in vain to kill the water monster, which escapes along the Columbia River. At Red Water, near Windermere, it is wounded: therefore the water is red there. It escapes into a cave. Naɫmu'qtse is told to stop up the outlet of the river, and he makes the portage separating Columbia Lakes from Kootenai River by molding the soil with his knees. Fox kills the monster. They cut it up, and Flicker and his wife Duck come out. The flesh of the monster is thrown about to serve as food for the people (see p. 289).

Then Naɫmu'qtse arises, his head touches the sky, his hat falls down, and he himself falls over and dies.

In the Okanagon tales the making of the bow and arrow, which forms a large part of the Ya.uk^ue'ˌka·m tradition, is connected with the war on the sky. The most connected form of the tale has been recorded by Albert S. Gatschet (Globus, vol. 52, p. 137). The animals make war against the sky in order to obtain the fire. They are unable to reach the sky with their arrows. The Wren decides to make a bow and arrow. First he kills an elk (here is introduced the story of Chickadee and Elk, p. 304). The Wolf tries to steal the elk, and Wren throws red-hot stones wrapped in fat into his mouth. He uses the rib of the elk for making his bow. He obtains the feathers for his arrow by allowing the eagle to carry him into his nest. He obtains flint by causing the owners of flint to fight. Then he goes to the place where the animals shoot the arrows up to the sky. He meets Coyote. (Here is introduced a story of the small animal that is able to shoot trees. See Blackfoot, de Josselin de Jong VKAWA 14:73; Uhlenbeck VKAWA 13:182; Pend d'Oreilles, Teit MAFLS 11:114.)

The Wren kills Coyote, and Fox resuscitates him. Coyote meets the Wren a second time. They gamble, and he wins Wren's clothing. He goes on, and meets young Grouse, whom he kills. The old Grouse then scares him so that he falls down a precipice (see p. 293). Wren recovers his arrows, makes the arrow chain, and the animals climb up. When Grizzly Bear climbs up, the chain breaks, owing to his weight. Then Eagle, Beaver, and Turtle are sent to obtain the fire. (See Lillooet, JAFL 25:299, where other references are given.)

The Turtle falls down from the sky and kills a person. Then follows the story of the Turtle who asks to be thrown into the water (see p. 305). The story closes with the return of the animals.

In the following I give brief abstracts of the tales recorded in the present volume and of those published by me in the "Verhandlungen der Berliner Gesellschaft für Anthropologie, Ethnologie und Urgeschichte," 1891. The page references to both series are given in the margin. Those in parentheses refer to the series of Kutenai tales published in the "Verhandlungen der Berliner Gesellschaft für Anthropologie, Ethnologie und Urgeschichte." Comparative notes have been added, which, however, do not claim to be exhaustive. References to the Tahltan and Kaska relate to manuscripts by Mr. James A. Teit to be published in the "Journal of American Folk-Lore." I have used the following abbreviations:

AA......................................"American Anthropologist."
AmAnt.................................."American Antiquarian and Oriental Journal."
BAAS...................................Reports of the British Association for the Advancement of Science.
BAM....................................Bulletin of the American Museum of Natural History.
BArchS.................................Baessler-Archiv, Supplement.
BBAE...................................Bulletin of the Bureau of American Ethnology.
CNAE.................................."Contributions to North American Ethnology" (United States Geographical and Geological Survey of the Rocky Mountain Region, J. W. Powell in charge).
CI.......................................Publications of the Carnegie Institution.
CU.....................................Columbia University Contributions to Anthropology.
FL......................................"Folklore."
FM.....................................Anthropological Publications of the Field (Columbian) Museum.
GSCan.................................Memoirs of the Geological Survey of Canada.
JAFL.................................."Journal of American Folk-Lore."
JAI...................................."Journal of the Anthropological Institute of Great Britain and Ireland."
JE......................................Publications of the Jesup North Pacific Expedition.
MAFLS.................................Memoirs of the American Folk-Lore Society.
PAES...................................Publications of the American Ethnological Society.
PaAM...................................Anthropological Papers, American Museum of Natural History.
RBAE...................................Annual Report of the Bureau of (American) Ethnology.
TRSC...................................Transactions of the Royal Society of Canada.
UCal...................................California Publications in American Archæology and Ethnology.
UPenn..................................Anthropological Publications of the University Museum of the University of Pennsylvania.
VAEU.................................."Verhandlungen der Berliner Gesellschaft für Anthropologie, Ethnologie, und Urgeschichte."
VKAWA................................"Verhandelingen der Koninklijke Akademie van Wetenschappen te Amsterdam."

Boas, Sagen........... ... ...Franz Boas, Indianische Sagen von der
                                                  Nord-Pacifischen Küste Amerikas.
Curtin, Creation Myths.................Jeremiah Curtin, Creation Myths of Primi-
                                                  tive America.
Curtin, Modoc.........................Jeremiah Curtin, Myths of the Modocs.
Curtis, N. A. Indians...................Edward S. Curtis, The North American
                                                  Indians.
Cushing, Folk Tales...................Frank Hamilton Cushing, Zuñi Folk Tales.
Dähnhardt, Natursagen................Oskar Dähnhardt, Natursagen.
Grinnell, Lodge Tales..................George Bird Grinnell, Blackfoot Lodge
                                                  Tales.
Leland...................................Charles G. Leland, The Algonquin Legends
                                                  of New England.
Matthews...............................Washington Matthews, Ethnography and
                                                  Philology of the Hidatsa (Misc. Publ. No.
                                                  7, U. S. Geological Survey, F. V. Hayden
                                                  in charge).   ·
Merriam.................................C. Hart Merriam, The Dawn of the World.
Petitot..................................Emile Petitot, Traditions Indiennes du
                                                · Canada Nord-Ouest.
Rand....................................S. T. Rand, Legends of the Micmacs.
Russell, Expl. in Far North............Frank Russell, Explorations in the Far
                                                  North (University of Iowa, 1898).
Schoolcraft, Hiawatha..................H. R. Schoolcraft, The Myth of Hiawatha
                                                  (Philadelphia, 1856).

1. THE SUN (4 versions: Nos. 33, 48, 54, and VAEU 23:161). *First Version.*—Coyote   49
asks Chicken Hawk to accompany him to the place where the Sun is being made.
Coyote wants to try first to act as the Sun. Chicken Hawk tells him that on their
way they will pass grease, and that in passing he may take one bite. Coyote disobeys, takes more than one bite, and the grease falls down and rolls down a precipice
with Coyote. They reach the place where the Sun is being made.. Coyote walks
along the sky, but is found unsatisfactory. *Chicken Hawk follows, and is found to be a
good Sun.*[1] Coyote is envious and tries to shoot him.[2] His bow and arrows catch
fire, and the earth begins to burn. He lies down on a trail, which does not burn,
and he is saved.[3]

Second Version.—The animals try who is to be the Sun. When Raven acts as the   67
Sun, it is dark. When Chicken Hawk tries, the sky is yellow. When Coyote tries, it
is hot. He tells everything he sees. When he returns, they tell him that he is too
hot and too talkative. A woman has two children, who arrive, and try in their turn.
When the first one goes along the sky, it is comfortable; and when the sun sets, it is   69
cool. *He is selected as Sun. The younger brother is selected to act as the Moon.*[1] Coyote
is envious and shoots the Sun at sunrise.[2] His arrow catches fire, the earth begins to
burn, and he saves himself by lying down on a trail. *For this reason trails do not burn.*[3]

Third Version.—Coyote and Ya.nkⁿe′ₗka·m are traveling along. Ya.nkⁿe′ₗka·m   111
tells Coyote that they will pass a piece of fat, and that he may take one bite. After
they pass, Coyote turns back in order to have another bite, and the fat rolls down.
He runs after it. The fat falls into the water and sinks. When he goes back on his
tracks, all the fat has been transformed into white stone. In order to get the fat that

---

[1] See discussion in Boas RBAE 31:727 (references to Okanagon, Shuswap, Thompson, Tsimshian,
Wasco, Wishram); see also, Coeur d'Alène (Teit MAFLS 11:123).
[2] Shoshoni (Lowie PaAM 2:252, 253).
  Ute (Powell RBAE 1:52).
[3] Thompson (Teit MAFLS 6:39, 74).

has fallen into the water, he heats stones, intending to boil it. Ya.uk^ue′ˌka·m misses Coyote, and finds that the fat is gone. He follows down to the water, and sees Coyote engaged in heating stones. Ya.uk^ue′ˌka·m makes a spear and spears the fat, which

113 breaks up and floats.—They go on, and Ya.uk^ue′ˌka·m tells Coyote not to pay any attention if he should hear a child crying. After they pass the child, Coyote turns back and puts his finger into the child's mouth. The child sucks the finger and pulls in Coyote's arm. When Ya.uk^{u′}ˌka·m notices that the child is silent, he turns back and kills the child with his knife. All the flesh on Coyote's arm has been sucked off. The child was a giant.—They go on, and Ya.uk^ue′ˌka·m tells Coyote not to listen if he should hear birds crying. Coyote disobeys, and finds himself in the nest of the thunderbirds together with Ya.uk^ue′ˌka·m. Ya.uk^ue′ˌka·m asks the young thunderbirds when the old birds come back. They reply that they come back in the evening

115 in the form of a thundercloud. Ya.uk^ue′ˌka·m tells Coyote that the thunderbird will ask whether he is tired, and that he is to reply that his younger brother Ya.uk^ue′ˌka·m is tired. When this happens, Ya.uk^ue′ˌka·m is told by the old thunderbird to stretch out his leg, because the bird wants to suck out the marrow. At this moment Ya.uk^ue′ˌka·m kills the thunderbird with his spear. The same is repeated when the old male thunderbird comes back. When the old birds are dead, Ya.uk^ue′ˌka·m sits on the back of one of the young thunderbirds, which flies up, and then carries him

117 down, while Coyote is shouting. Then Coyote sits on the back of the other thunderbird; and when he shouts, the bird takes him down. Ya.uk^ue′ˌka·m ordains that thunderbirds may only scare people who lie about them.[1] Ya.uk^ue′ˌka·m and Coyote reach the place where the Sun is being made. Ya.uk^ue′ˌka·m is tried; but the day is red because his clothing is painted with ochre. Coyote is tried, but when he acts as the Sun, it is too hot; and he tells what the people are doing, and asks them to leave

119 some food for him. The two sons of the Lynx arrive. They have been brought up by their mother, who had been deserted by Lynx. He had gone to catch salmon for making soup for his wife. The young Lynxes meet him, and he tells them that he is unable to catch salmon. The boys show him how to catch salmon. When the Lynx children arrive at the place where the animals try to make the Sun, *one of them goes*

121 *up and is found a satisfactory sun.*[2] *Then they send the other one up as the Moon.* Coyote is envious and shoots at the rising sun,[3] which sets his arrow on fire. The fire pursues him. He lies down on a trail and covers himself with a blanket. The fire passes over him without hurting him. *Therefore trails do not burn.*[4]

---

[1] Apache, Jicarilla (Russell JAFL 11:257).

Arapaho (Dorsey and Kroeber FM 5:383, 387).

Assiniboin (Lowie PaAM 4:170).

Beaver (Goddard PaAM 10:234).

Chilcotin (Farrand JE 2:12).

Chippewayan (Goddard PaAM 10:48; Lowie *ibid.* 192; Petitot 359; much distorted in Lofthouse, Transactions Canadian Institute 10:46).

Dog-rib (Petitot 323).

Gros Ventre (Kroeber PaAM 1:88).

Hare (Petitot 144).

Kaska (Teit J A F L 30:437).

Okanagon (Gatschet, Globus 52:137).

Ponca (Dorsey CNAE 6:30, 215).

Sanpoil (Gould MAFLS 11:108).

Shoshoni (Lowie PaAM 2:295?).

Shuswap (Teit JE 2:649; Dawson TRSC 32; Boas, Sagen 4).

Sia (Stevenson RBAE 11:48).

Thompson (Teit MAFLS 6:45; also 76; 11:57).

Ute, Uinta (Mason JAFL 23:318).

[2] See discussion in Boas, RBAE 31: 727 (references to Okanagon, Shuswap, Thompson, Tsimshian, Wasco, Wishram).

[3] Shoshoni (Lowie PaAM 2:252, 253).

Ute (Powell RBAE 1:52).

[4] Thompson (Teit MAFLS 6:39, 74).

Fourth Version[1] (VAEU 23).—Hare's wife (a small red bird) has deserted him and (162) lives with a red hawk. Hare finds tracks of elks (not moose, as given in the original), and goes home to make snowshoes. The animals start in pursuit of the elks. When Hare goes to get wood for his snowshoes, he meets Doe. He wishes to marry her. She refuses him. He goes home and tells his grandmother Frog what has happened. She informs him that the Doe is his sister. Hare takes her home, and she lives in the tent. Her presence is unknown to the other people. Hare goes out to pursue the elks. His grandmother tells him to put mittens on his feet in place of his snowshoes. When going out, he meets Raven and other hunters, who are returning empty handed. They maltreat him, but he goes on. He meets Woodpecker, a diver, and Wolf. He passes the game hunters, and meets Hawk and his wife, who pelt him with snow. Only Weasel, Fox, and young Wolf are ahead of him. On the following day he meets them. They return, because they are unable to overtake the elks.

Hare puts on his mittens and soon overtakes the elks. With one arrow he kills (163) one-half of them, and with the second the rest. He butchers them and shakes the fat, which becomes small in size. He fills the stomachs with blood, piles them up, and tells them to burst if any one should carry them. He carries the fat home, shakes it, and it assumes its former size. He feeds his child, and throws some fat into the fire in order to inform his brother Duck, who comes and is given food. He sends his brother to tell the people that they may go to bring in the meat. He wishes that Hawk should select the stomachs. Bear demands the ribs; Wolf, the legs; Raven, the eyes. Hawk loads the stomachs on the back of his wife. Hare follows them, steps on her snowshoes, so that she falls. The blood runs over her, and she freezes to death. The skins are carried into Frog's tent. When within a few days they are ready tanned, the people grow suspicious, and find the tracks of Doe. Lynx finds the place where the girl stopped, tears out four hairs, which he puts on the ground. The hairs impregnate her when she urinates. Doe gives birth to a child. The people hear it crying, and discover the Doe. In order to discover the unknown father of the child, Frog orders the men to take up the child.[2] Coyote, Raven, and others take it, but the child continues to cry. Lynx comes back from hunting. He buries his clothing and strike-a-light under stones. When the people see Lynx coming, the child quiets down; and (164) when he takes it up, it does not cry any more. They maltreat Lynx, extinguish the fires, and desert him, Doe, and their child.[3]

Lynx is a good hunter. After some time Doe has a second son. The people are starving. Lynx's grandmother, Magpie, comes to look after her grandson. He feeds her. In summer Lynx goes to fish salmon. He makes a fish weir. When the boys are grown up, their mother sends them to the place where the sun is being made. She tells them that they will pass their father's fishing-place. The boys start and reach the place where the sun is being made. Raven is the sun; it is dark and cold. Coyote acts as sun; it is very hot, and he tells the people to keep food for him. Because he runs home quickly the day is short. He tells everything he has seen in the daytime. The sons of Lynx are tried, and *one is made the sun, the other the moon*.[4] Coyote is (165) envious, and shoots the sun at sunrise. His arrows catch fire, fall down, and set fire to the grass.[5]

---

[1] Shuswap (Boas, Sagen 9).

Thompson (Teit MAFLS 6:37, 11:11; JE 8:215; Hill-Tout BAAS 65:534).

[2] Lillooet (Teit JAFL 25:328).

Nootka (Boas, Sagen 108).

Shuswap (Boas, Sagen 9; Teit JE 2:684).

Thompson (Teit MAFLS 6:37; JE 8:215; Hill-Tout BAAS 69:534).

[3] See RBAE 31:784.

[4] See discussion in Boas RBAE 31:727 (references to Okanagon, Shuswap, Thompson, Tsimshian, Wasco, Wishram).

[5] Shoshoni (Lowie PaAM 2:252, 253).

Ute (Powell RBAE 1:52).

73   2. The War on the Sky [1] and Naɫmu′qtse (3 versions: Nos. 50, 52, and VAEU 23:165). *First Version.*—Muskrat wants to marry his brother's widow. She refuses him, and he kills her with an arrow which differs in style from the tribal arrows.[2] The people try to find out who killed her, and call in Frog, Muskrat's grandmother. Although she knows what has happened, she declines to tell, and answers by signs. The people think that the Sky people have killed the woman, and decide to make

75 war on the Sky. They shoot arrows up to the Sky and make a chain.[3] Since it is not quite long enough, Raven puts his beak at the lower end. Then it reaches the ground. When the animals are ready to go up, Wolverene asks them to wait for two days because he has to put away his things. When he comes back, he finds the animals have gone. He becomes angry and tears down the chain of arrows. The remaining people pursue Wolverene, who, when almost overtaken, cuts up himself and becomes a squirrel, which he puts under his own belt. When somebody thinks he recognizes him, he says that he is hunting squirrels.—Muskrat has made a large lake in the sky and put up many tents around it. When the people attack the village, a left-handed man comes out. This happens in every tent, and the people recognize that there is only one person, Muskrat. They go back; and when they come to the place where the arrow chain had been, it is gone. They go to the drinking-place of Thunderbird, kill him, and distribute his feathers. While these are being distributed, two bats expect to be given the best feathers, but finally nothing is left for them.

77 They spread out their blankets and sail down. Flying Squirrel pulls out his skin and sails down. The Sucker throws himself down and is broken to pieces. When his brother's widow touches him, he is cured.—The warriors Flicker, the Woodpeckers and their sister (a bird with yellow breast and gray feathers), have been left in the sky. They walk to the place where heaven and earth meet. At Nelson they meet supernatural beings, who tell them never to touch a fish and not to stay over night in the woods. They find a charr which has drifted ashore. Flicker tries to kill it, but is swallowed by it and taken into the lake.[4] They camp in the woods, and a toad crawls under Woodpecker's blanket and sticks to his body. The others go on and meet Naɫmu′qtse, who was crawling along Kootenai River naming the country. He asks the Woodpeckers, his nephews, for some food. They put a red-hot stone into the

79 heart of a mountain goat, and try to throw it into his mouth.[5] They miss, and the place is called Little Heart. Woodpecker sends two water birds to invite in all the Fish, telling them that the lake will be dried up if they should not come. The birds dance at every bay, inviting the Fish. The chief of the Fish, K!ɛ′k!om′, is the last to arrive. He is given a pipe; and Woodpecker, his brothers, and the Fish smoke. The Fish inquires for his grandson; that is, the Flicker that had been swallowed by the water monster; and he moves his eyebrows, showing that Flicker is in the lake. As a reward he is given meat, *which may now be seen as a red spot on each side of the body.* The Woodpeckers make ready to kill the water monster. The first who tries to attack him is Long Legs, who, however, is swallowed. Woodpecker tries next. He intends to kick the monster, but the blow glances off. The monster is chased along Kootenai River and comes back by way of Windermere to Red Water.

81 Woodpecker hits it on the foot. Its blood makes the water red. At Long-Water Bay

[1] Lillooet (JAFL 25:311).
    Okanagon (Hill-Tout JAI 41:146; Gatschet, Globus 52:137; Teit MAFLS 11:85).
    Pend d'Oreilles (Teit MAFLS 11:118).
    Shuswap (Teit JE 2:749).
    Thompson (Teit JE 8:246; Boas, Sagen 17).
    See also Sanpoil (Gould MAFLS 11:107, 108).
[2] Lillooet (Teit JAFL 25:326).
    Shuswap (Teit JE 2:679).
    Thompson (Teit JE 8:361, 362).
[3] See discussion in Boas RBAE 31:864.
[4] See discussion in Boas RBAE 31:611, 659, 687, 718, 868.
[5] See discussion in Boas RBAE 31:682; also Alsea (personal communication from Leo J. Frachtenberg), Hidatsa (Matthews 67).

the monster hides in a cave under water. Flicker takes Woodpecker's war bonnet and spear and tries to chase the monster out of the water. When the monster appears, Flicker is afraid, and drops the spear. Naɫmu'qtse is asked to dam up the end of the lake and to prevent the escape of the monster. He breaks off a piece of the mountain and solidifies it with his knees, *making the portage between Columbia River and Kootenai River*. Woodpecker continues the pursuit; but when the monster looks at him, he becomes afraid and is unable to kill it. The Fox finally takes a tomahawk, kills the monster, and cuts it up. Flicker and Duck come out. *They have become white* in the stomach of the monster. While in its stomach, they made a fire with their canoe. The monster had asked them not to make too large a fire, because it might melt its fat. *The Flicker had been worn down to its present size.*

They cut off the ribs of the monster and throw them down the river, *where they become a cliff*. The body is cut up and scattered about. It becomes the food of the people. They forget the Kutenai, and only a little blood is left, which they scatter over the country. *For this reason the Kutenai are few.*[1]   83

Second Version.—Naɫmu'qtse is called the grandfather of the Kutenai. He is a man   85
of giant size, and never stands up. He knows that he is about to die, and travels over the country, giving names to places. Wherever he crawls, a river flows.[2] He meets   87
the Woodpecker brothers and their sister sitting on a mountain. They have come down from the sky after the animals have made war on Muskrat (as told before). They are angry because they have not been given any feathers to fly down. Woodpecker tries to kill the people; and when he meets his uncle Naɫmu'qtse, he tries to kill him too. He throws a heart containing a red-hot stone at him, pretending that it is food.[3] Naɫmu'qtse nods, and it falls down, and the place is called Little Heart. Naɫmu'qtse warns Woodpecker, telling him not to touch a charr and not to sleep in dense woods. The Woodpeckers disobey, and Flicker is swallowed by a water monster.[4] Naɫmu'qtse crawls along and decides to stand up. When he rises, his war bonnet touches the sky. It falls, and he also falls, saying that the place will be called Ear.   89

Third Version (VAEU 23).—The father of Muskrat[5] has two wives. After his death   (165) Muskrat wants to marry his second wife, who refuses him. He shoots her with an arrow of unknown design. He lies down, pretending to be sick. The people find the dead woman, and inquire for the owner of the arrow. Muskrat smells of it, and says it came from the sky. They make war against the sky. Coyote shoots up an arrow without reaching it. Other animals try in vain. Finally two Hawks shoot. Their first arrow strikes the sky after flying one day and one night. They make a chain of arrows,[6] which Raven completes by putting his beak in the nock of the last arrow. Wolverene asks the other animals to wait, because he wants to look after his traps. They leave before he returns; therefore he is angry and tears down the *arrows, which are transformed into a mountain* (Mount Baker, near Cranbrook, B. C.). Muskrat has climbed up into the sky, where he makes tents along the shore of a lake. The houses are dirty. He shoots from the houses, passing under ground from one to the

[1] Cœur d'Alène (Teit MAFLS 11:122).
  Nez Percé (Mayer-Farrand MAFLS 11:149).
  Shuswap (Teit JE 2:661, 662, 665–667).
  Thompson (Teit MAFLS 6:80; JE 8:255).
[2] Chippewayan (much distorted in Loft house, Transactions Canadian Institute 10:44).
  Dog-Rib (Sir John Franklin, Narrative of a Second Expedition to the Shores of the Polar Sea [London, 1828], p. 293).
  Etheneldeli (Caribou-Eaters), (Samuel Hearne, A Journey from Prince of Wales's Fort in Hudson's Bay, to the Northern Ocean [London, 1795], p. 343).
  Kato (Goddard UCal 5:188).
  Kaska (Teit JAFL 30:444).
[3] See discussion in Boas RBAE 31:682. Also Hidatsa (Matthews 67).
[4] See discussion in Boas RBAE 31:611, 659, 687, 718, 868.
[5] Lillooet (Teit JAFL 25:326).
  Shuswap (Teit JE 2:679).
  Thompson (Teit JE 8:361, 362).
[6] See discussion in Boas RBAE 31:864.

other. Woodpecker discovers that there is only one person, Muskrat, whom they kill.
(166) When they find the arrow chain broken, they snare thunderbird, put on his feathers, and fly down. *Those who receive feathers are transformed into birds; the others, into fish and land mammals.* Coyote sails down, steering with his tail. The Sucker breaks all his bones. He is given new ones: *therefore the sucker's body is now full of bones.*

89   3. YA.UKⁿE′₁KAˑM (No. 53).—Frog warns her granddaughter, Young Doe, not to drink at a water hole. She disobeys,[1] and is pulled down by a man named White Stone, who lives in the water, and marries her. Their son is Ya.ukⁿe′₁kaˑm.—White Stone's brother, Gray Stone, dislikes Ya.ukⁿe′₁kaˑm, who is sent by his mother to visit
91   his great-grandmother Frog. Ya.ukⁿe′₁kaˑm goes; and when he sees the old Frog Woman, he is afraid.[2] He makes her sleep and plays in the tent. He goes back to his mother, who wants him to stay with his great-grandmother. When Frog wakes, she notices that somebody has been there. She makes a small bow and a small basket, and hangs them up. Ya.ukⁿe′₁kaˑm gets back, makes her sleep again, and plays with the bow, which he breaks. When the Frog wakes, she says that her grandchild must have been a boy, because he had been playing with a bow. Next time the Frog captures him.
93   When Ya.ukⁿe′₁kaˑm is growing up, he asks the Frog Woman for arrow wood and service-berry wood.[3] She warns him, but he sets out to obtain the wood from the Grizzly Bear, who owns it. Cranes, Marmots, and Beavers are Grizzly Bear's watchmen, appointed to warn him of the arrival of strangers. The youth bribes them to be quiet until he returns. He takes the service-berry bushes and makes his escape.
95   The animals make a noise; Grizzly Bear assumes his animal form, and pursues Ya.ukⁿe′₁kaˑm. The animals make excuses, but the Bear threatens to kill them after having overtaken Ya.ukⁿe′₁kaˑm, who causes a hill to rise behind him, which detains Grizzly Bear. *Thus arrow wood is obtained.* He goes to his mother's tent, and Gray Stone promises to kill Grizzly Bear. Gray Stone rubs himself with grease and becomes a stone, which is heated by the fire. He orders Ya.ukⁿe′₁kaˑm to stand next to the doorway. Grizzly Bear, when trying to bite him, closes his eyes; Ya.ukⁿe′₁kaˑm steps aside, and the Bear bites the post. Meanwhile Gray Stone becomes so hot, that the
97   stone almost bursts. Just when the Bear opens his mouth, the fragments of the stone fly about; Gray Stone goes right through Grizzly Bear, who dies. *After this the Grizzly Bear remains a bear.* Ya.ukⁿe′₁kaˑm skins the grizzly bear, and drags the skin which is attached to the head into Frog Woman's tent. She is afraid of the grizzly bear. She paints her legs red and stands in the doorway, holding a hammer. She had put up a sharp stone in the doorway. Ya.ukⁿe′₁kaˑm drags the grizzly-bear skin in, and Frog strikes it; but Ya.ukⁿe′₁kaˑm jerks it at that moment, so that she strikes the stone,
99   which she breaks. Ya.ukⁿe′₁kaˑm asks for feathers for his arrow. He is told that ducks on a lake own the feathers. He goes there, wearing ear ornaments. Ya.ukⁿe′₁-kaˑm, who is painted red, asks one of the Ducks to come ashore, asks for his feathers, and promises to pay him with his ear ornaments. The Duck obeys, and becomes
101 very beautiful. When the other Ducks see it, they all go ashore, and he takes their feathers. *He adorns all of them.*[4] *Thus feathers are obtained.*

Ya.ukⁿe′₁kaˑm goes to obtain the arrow straightener from Bighorn Sheep. He goes to Bighorn Sheep, who tells him that the arrow straightener is on the other side of the river. When he is climbing the mountain, Bighorn goes back across the river in his

---

[1] Blackfoot (Uhlenbeck VKAWA 13:156, 158).
  Hidatsa (Matthews 68).
  Shuswap (Teit JE 2:674, 694), etc.
  Takelma (Sapir UPenn 2:125, 157).
[2] Shuswap (Teit JE 2:693).
[3] Beaver (Goddard PaAM 10:235).
  Gros Ventre (Kroeber PaAM 1:88–90).
  Kaska (Teit JAFL 30:437).
  Okanagon (Gatschet, Globus 52:137).
  Thompson (Teit MAFLS 6:76).
[4] See p. 296, No. 18.

canoe. He puts the penis of the Bighorn into the water, by means of which he pro-   103
duces a snowstorm. Ya.uk^ue′_ika·m knows what is coming. He finds a tent, and is
taken care of by his brothers and sisters, (probably animals) that live there. The
house owner counteracts Bighorn's charm by striking his testicles. Bighorn thinks
he hears the bursting of Ya.uk^ue′_ika·m's eyes, and Bighorn causes the cold to stop.
While it is cold, Bighorn is throwing warm things on himself. After some time Bighorn Sheep returns to look for Ya.uk^ue′_ika·m. After the Bighorn has crossed the
river, Ya.uk^ue′_ika·m goes into his canoe, crosses the river, and does the same as the
Bighorn has done. A snowstorm arises, and he goes into Bighorn Sheep's tent and
throws warm things on himself. When he hears the noise of eyes bursting, he says,
"Don't let it be cold any more!" After all this has happened, the old man has been
transformed into a mountain sheep, and Ya.uk^ue′_ika·m takes the arrow straightener.
Thus man obtains the arrow straightener.

In order to obtain sinew, Ya.uk^ue′_ika·m goes to the tent of Mouse, who is afraid of   105
the Bull Moose, which almost breaks the tent. He obtains first a poor bow, then a
good bow, kills the Moose for Mouse, and takes the sinew. *Thus man obtains sinew.*[1]

He goes to obtain Flint.[2] Flint is a man. If a person pays him well, he trans-   107
forms himself into stone, and allows pieces to be broken off. When Ya.uk^ue′_ika·m
arrives, Flint retains the form of a man, because he expects high pay. Ya.uk^ue′_ika·m
tells Flint that Diorite Man claims to be stronger than Flint. By carrying tales from
one to the other he causes them to quarrel and to fight. When they strike each other,
large pieces of flint and diorite fall off, and he is able to obtain the stone he needs.
Thus he produces flint and tough stone for the use of man.

Ya.uk^ue′_ika·m goes to obtain bow wood. Two squirrels as large as grizzly bears   109
stand on each side of a trail. He kills them. *From the body creeps the small squirrel
of our times.* He passes between two moving trees, which crush any one who passes
between them. He keeps them apart by putting his spear across.[3] *Then he scatters
the cedar wood.*

Ya.uk^ue′_ika·.m asks his mother where the sun rises, and he tells her that he is going
there.

4. THE PEOPLE TRY TO KILL YA.UK^uE′_iKA·M (No. 55).—The people kill   121
Ya.uk^ue′_ika·m and throw him into the river. Then they break camp and order Crane
to drag a young tree to cover their tracks. The fish nibble at the drowned man's   123
body, and he awakes. He kicks the fish, but they say that they are restoring him.
He follows the people, meets Crane, whom he kills. He also kills Crane's wife. When
he approaches the people, he sees his sister-in-law, who is lagging behind and who is
crying. She carries her child, Duck, on her back. The child recognizes him and
tells his mother, who, however, disbelieves him. Ya.uk^ue′_ika·m shows himself, and   125
she tells him that the people take away his brother's game, and that Duck has to render
menial services to the chief, that they also take away the tent site that she is preparing.
Ya.uk^ue′_ika·m tells his brother and his sister-in-law to resist the people.[4] The people   127
are afraid when the two act independently. The chief, after defecating, calls Duck
to clean him, and Duck kills him with arrow points that he has attached to his head.[5]
Ya.uk^ue′_ika·m shows himself, and the people are afraid of him.

---

[1] Kaska (Teit JAFL 30:438).
[2] Kalapooya (information given by A. S. Gatschet).
  Shuswap (Teit JE 2: 645; Dawson TRSC 1891 : 35).
  Thompson (Teit MAFLS 6: 76).
  Tillamook (Boas JAFL 11: 144).
  See Boas, RBAE 31: 612, No. 5.
[3] See Boas, RBAE 31: 613, No. 9.
[4] Takelma (Sapir UPenn 2:20).
  Thompson (Teit MAFLS 6:25).
[5] Quinault (Farrand JE 2:100).

191   5. COYOTE AND TREE CHIEF[1] (2 versions: No. 64 and VAEU 23:166).— Coyote passes Tree Chief's tent. Tree Chief's mother likes him, and wishes him to become
193 her son's friend. The two friends go out. When they pass Wolf's trap, Coyote diverts the attention of his friend and pushes him in. He pretends to be unable to pull him out. He induces him to throw out all his clothing, including a hawk, which he carries on his head, and his saliva. Then he leaves him and goes to the town where a chief lives who has two daughters. The chief, Golden Eagle, believes that he is
195 Tree Chief. Wolf and his wife find Tree Chief in the trap. He has taken the form of a young child. Wolf wants to kill him; his wife wants to raise him. They agree that whoever reaches him first shall do with him what he pleases. Wolf's wife digs through the ground very quickly and rescues him.[2]

Tree Chief asks Wolf Woman for sinew, which the boy uses for making a netted ring.
197 He holds it up, and it is full of birds. Next he asks for the leg skin of a yearling buffalo calf. He makes a netted ring, rolls it into the tent, and tells the woman to cover her head. It becomes a buffalo, which he kills. He tells the woman to put the blood and guts behind the tent. On the following day they are transformed into
199 pemmican. Coyote has married one of the daughters of Golden Eagle. Tree Chief takes some pemmican, and goes to the river to draw water. There he meets the chief's daughter, to whom he gives the pemmican. Next the boy asks for the leg part of the skin of a buffalo bull. He obtains a buffalo in the same way as before. He puts the blood in the skin and puts it away. On the next day the blood has been transformed into pemmican; the skin, into a painted blanket. He goes again to draw water, and tells the girl to say that she has received pemmican from the one whom she saw at the river.

Tree Chief hides the buffalo, and the people in the village of Golden Eagle are
201 starving. Golden Eagle throws up a feather of his body, which becomes an eagle, which is perched on a tree. He arranges a contest, and orders every one to try to shoot the eagle. Each is to have one shot. Coyote shoots repeatedly, but does not hit the eagle. Tree Chief appears, and hits the eagle. Coyote pretends that his arrow had hit it; but when he is carrying along the bird on his arrow, it is seen that it
203 is a prairie chicken. The boy goes back to the Wolf. In the evening he meets the girl again, and tells her that on the following day at noon he will show himself. He goes to the village in the same form as he used to have. The people are puzzled, because he himself and Coyote look alike. Tree Chief's saliva turns into shells, which are eaten by the sparrow hawk that sits on the youth's head; while Coyote has lost this art, and his hawk is starving.
205 Tree Chief tells the chief, his father-in-law, to look at his fortune-telling place. The chief sees tracks of buffalo cows, and sends the people to go hunting. Tree Chief goes ahead, piles up buffalo chips, which he transforms into buffaloes. The people kill the buffaloes. Tree Chief takes an old mangy buffalo cow. He is laughed at by
207 Coyote. Tree Chief takes it home. He gives his arrow to his wife, and tells her not

[1] Arapaho (Dorsey and Kroeber FM 5:348, 372).
   Assiniboin (Lowie PaAM 134).
   Blackfoot (Uhlenbeck VKAWA 12:30; 13:160; Wissler PaAM 2:47).
   Cheyenne (Kroeber JAFL 13:170).
   Crow (Simms FM 2:291).
   Hidatsa (Matthews 63).
   Kutenai (Boas VAEU 23:166).
   Nez Percé (Mayer-Farrand MAFLS 11:159).
   Ojibwa (de Josselin de Jong BArchS 5:2; only beginning).
   Okanagon (Teit MAFLS 11:85).
   Omaha (Dorsey CNAE 6:55, 604).
   Pawnee (Dorsey CI 59:159, 161, 280 et seq.).
   Shoshoni (Lowie PaAM 2:274).
   Shuswap (Teit JE 2:695).
   Teton (Curtis, N. A. Indians 3:111).
[2] See Blackfoot (Uhlenbeck VKAWA 13:117).

to touch any one with it. When he is skinning the mangy cow, it turns into a fat buffalo. A dog tries to get some of the meat. The woman touches it with the arrow, and the dog falls down dead. When she touches it again, the dog revives. Coyote also kills a dog, and tries to revive it by touching it with an arrow, but he is unsuccessful. Tree Chief's wife carries the meat in her blanket into her tent. On the   209
following morning the blood is transformed into pemmican; the skin, into a painted blanket. Coyote is unable to imitate this feat. Coyote tries to make buffalo out of   211
buffalo chips, but is unable to do so. Finally Tree Chief gets impatient, and strikes Coyote with a firebrand, intending to kill him.

Coyote runs westward, while Tree Chief goes eastward. Tree Chief says both will   213
come back at the end of the world.

Second Version (VAEU 23).—Tree Chief is Coyote's friend. Golden Eagle asks (166) Tree Chief to marry his daughter. The two young men start, and on the way Coyote throws Tree Chief into a pit. He asks for the bird which Tree Chief carries on his head, for his blanket and saliva. He puts these on, leaves Tree Chief in the pit, and goes to the village of Golden Eagle, where he marries the girl. Tree Chief transforms himself into an infant. The owner of the pit and his wife try who can reach the child first. Tree Chief by magic makes the soil loose where the woman is digging, so that she reaches him first. When the boy is a few years old, he asks for a snare in order to catch birds. He sets it, moves his hands, and the snare is full of birds. He asks for the skin of a buffalo calf and makes a netted ring. He tells the old people to lie down, and rolls the ring against the tent. The ring becomes a buffalo calf, which he kills. The intestines, which the woman puts away according to the boy's orders, are transformed into pemmican. The same happens to the skin of a one-year-old buffalo, which is transformed into a young bull, which he kills. He tells the old people that he is Tree Chief. He goes to the river and meets Golden Eagle's younger daughter, whom he marries. The people are starving because the buffaloes have disappeared. Tree Chief tells the hunters to wait at a buffalo drive. By kicking buffalo chips he transforms them into buffaloes, which are driven to a precipice. There are two buffaloes for each hunter. Tree Chief selects an old lean one for himself. He tells his wife not to strike their dog. When she disobeys, the dog falls down dead. He tells her to strike the dog again, and the dog revives. Coyote is unable to imitate this. Tree Chief drives away Coyote, reminding him that he had tried to kill him.

6. COYOTE AND FOX [1] (No. 1).—Coyote asks Fox for his blanket. They race. (This   1
is probably a reference to the tale of Coyote borrowing Fox's blanket and being carried away by the wind.)   2

7. COYOTE AND LOCUST (No. 2).—Coyote carries Locust. They meet a Grizzly Bear.   3
Coyote puts Locust down at the edge of a cliff. Locust scares the female Grizzly Bear, who falls down the cliff and dies.[2] Coyote and Locust eat the body. Later on they meet the male Grizzly Bear. Coyote is put down and turns into a stump, which the Grizzly Bear tries to bite. Coyote is retransformed and gives fat to the bear to eat. He says it is beaver fat. The bear asks whether they have seen the female   4
Grizzly Bear. After first denying to have seen her, Coyote tells the Bear that he

---

[1] Okanagon (Hill-Tout JAI 41:152).
   Shuswap (Boas, Sagen 6; Teit JE 2:634, 742).
   Thompson (Teit MAFLS 11:8).
[2] The idea of a person being frightened by the sudden flying up of birds or by a sudden movement, and caused to fall down a cliff, is rather widely spread.
   Assiniboin (Lowie PaAM 4:110).
   Lillooet (Teit JAFL 25:305, an incomplete version of the story of Coyote and Grouse).
   Ojibwa ((Jones PAES 7:43, 191, 415).
   Okanagon (Gatschet, Globus 52:138).
   Pawnee (Dorsey CI 59:459).
   Pend d'Oreilles (Teit MAFLS 11:114).
   Sanpoil (Gould MAFLS 11:101).
   Shuswap (Teit JE 2:629, 740).

(the Bear) has eaten his wife's fat. Coyote runs away, pursued by the Bear. Coyote falls, and his hands strike a buffalo horn, with which he scares away the Grizzly Bear.[1]

141   8. COYOTE AND GRIZZLY BEAR [1] (No. 57).—Coyote sees Grizzly Bear feeding, and
143   calls him names.[2] Grizzly Bear pursues him. While they are running, Coyote jumps over the Bear. The Bear chases him around a stone. Coyote falls down and falls on the horns of a buffalo, which stick on his hands. Coyote rises, and with the horns frightens away the Bear. The Bear swims the river, and is hit with the horns.

3   9. COYOTE AND LOCUST [3] (No. 3).—Locust is carrying his leg. Coyote envies him,
4   and breaks his own leg too. The two make friends. Coyote goes ahead, and is kicked by Locust, who kills him. When Magpie picks at Coyote's eyes,[4] Coyote revives.
5   He slaps himself, and the dung tells him [5] that he will become a knife attached to Coyote's foot. Locust goes ahead, and Coyote kills him.

5   10. COYOTE AND GRIZZLY BEAR (No. 4).—Coyote makes fun of Grizzly Bear's dung.[1]
6   In order to catch Coyote, the Bear first creates service berries, then wild cherries,
7   which Coyote does not eat. Then he creates rose hips; when Coyote is eating these, Grizzly Bear catches him, together with the bushes. Coyote pleads that he did not offend Grizzly Bear. When Grizzly Bear tries to hit him, Coyote runs away. He
8   calls for the help of his manitous. One of these becomes a river; another, a log which lies across the river and bobs up and down; a third one becomes a tent. Coyote is told to come out of the tent as soon as the Grizzly Bear appears, and to abuse him. When the Bear reaches the river, he tries to cross on the bobbing log. Coyote holds the log, but lets go of it while the Bear is crossing over it. The Grizzly Bear falls off and is drowned.[6]

8   11. COYOTE GOES VISITING [7] (No. 5).—Coyote's wife is Dog. Coyote sends his chil-
9   dren to visit their uncles. They go to Kingfisher, who stretches his hand back to get his sharp horn. Kingfisher sends his two children to bring two switches. He ties his hair over his forehead, and jumps from the top of the tent into the water through a
10   hole in the ice. He comes back carrying two switches filled with fish. The following day Dog sends her children to visit their uncle Moose. Moose cuts off his wife's nose, throws ashes on the cut, which heals up at once. He sends his children to get roots,
11   which are rolled in the ashes of the wife and become guts. He slaps himself, and camas appears. On the following day Coyote tries in vain to imitate him.

[1] Assiniboin (Lowie PaAM 4:121).
  Blackfoot (Wissler PaAM 2:32; Uhlenbeck VKAWA 12:63).
  Cree (Russell, Expl. in Far North 209).
  Shoshoni (Lowie PaAM 2:277; Lowie-St. Clair JAFL 22:266).
[2] Shuswap (Teit JE 2:654).
  Ute (RBAE 1:54), etc.
[3] Nez Percé (Spinden JAFL 21:23).
  Perhaps Shuswap (Teit JE 2:655).
[4] Nez Percé (MAFLS 11; Mayer-Farrand 151; Spinden 180).
[5] Chilcotin (Farrand JE 2:16).
  Chinook (Boas BBAE 20:92).
  Flathead (Wilson, Trans. Ethn. Soc. of London, 1866, 4:312).
  Kaska (Teit JAFL 30:444).
  Kathlamet (Boas BBAE 26:45).
  Lillooet (Teit JAFL 25:308, 317).
  Nez Percé (Mayer-Farrand MAFLS 11:141).
  Okanagon (Teit MAFLS 11:73-75).
  Shoshoni (Lowie PaAM 2:237, 241, 254).
  Shuswap (Teit JE 2:635).
  Tahltan (Teit MS).
  Takelma (Sapir UPenn 2:65, 83).
  Thompson (Teit MAFLS 6:30, 60; MAFLS 11:2; JE 8:234).
[6] See Waterman JAFL 27:43, "Crane Bridge."
[7] See discussion in Boas RBAE 31:694; also Nez Percé (MAFLS 11; Mayer-Farrand 164; Spinden, 181); Osage (Dorsey FM 7:13, 15); Shoshoni (Lowie-St. Clair JAFL 22:266); Thompson (Teit MAFLS 11:6); Zuñi (Edward S. Handy JAFL 31).
  A number of Californian tales of unsuccessful imitation may perhaps be distantly related to the tale of the bungling host. See Wishosk (Kroeber JAFL 18:102); Yana (Sapir U Cal 9:211).

12. COYOTE AND BUFFALO [1] (2 versions: Nos. 6 and 47). *First Version.*—Coyote finds the skull of a buffalo bull. He kicks it. After a while he hears a noise and sees Buffalo coming in pursuit. His manitous hide him in the stump of a burnt tree, which the Buffalo shatters; next in a stone, which he also shatters; in a pond, which Buffalo drinks; in a rose bush, which Buffalo can not tear to pieces. Coyote asks for peace and offers to smoke with Buffalo. Buffalo says that he lights his pipe by holding it up to the sun. Buffalo's wife had been taken away by other Buffaloes, and he had been killed. Coyote sharpens Buffalo's horns, and the two set out to recover Buffalo's wives. They overcome the other Buffaloes, and Coyote receives the larger Buffalo Cow, which is to be his wife. He sends her ahead, and tries to shoot her in a valley. The arrow does not enter her body. Finally he kills her. After butchering her, he sits on a stone. Wolf comes and eats the Buffalo, and Coyote is unable to get up until the meat has been eaten.[2] He pounds the bones and tries to extract the marrow. A bird tells him that he must not pound them,[3] that Badger is to do so. While Badger is pounding, Coyote is asked to take hold of Badger's tail.

The marrow is put into a bladder. Badger runs away, eats it, and throws back the empty bladder. Coyote intends to break the remaining bones, and is told by a bird that the bird will do it. Coyote is sent away and told to return when he sees smoke. When he returns, the birds have flown away with what remains of the Buffalo.

Second Version.—Coyote finds the head of a Buffalo Bull,[1] passes it three times, and breaks it with a stone. He covers a flat rock with his blanket, and lies down singing. He hears Buffalo coming in pursuit. He runs away. When he is tired, he calls on his manitous. The first one has the form of a stump, in which Coyote hides. Buffalo breaks it in two. The next one is a stone, which Buffalo also breaks in two. The third one is a bush, which Buffalo can not tear. They make peace and smoke together. *Coyote institutes the peace pipe.* Buffalo tells Coyote that other Buffaloes took away his two wives and killed him. Coyote sharpens Buffalo's horns, and they overcome the other Buffaloes and take back the two wives. Buffalo gives to Coyote one of his wives, which Coyote selects because she is not as strong as the other one. Coyote sends his Buffalo wife ahead and kills her. He sits down on a stone and cries for the wife whom he has killed. Wolves come and eat the Cow, while Coyote is unable to get up.[2] After the Wolves have disappeared, the stone lets him go. He is about to break the bones to extract the marrow, when Badger forbids him to break the bones, and offers to break them himself. Coyote holds on to Badger's tail while Badger is pounding the bones. Badger puts the marrow into the bladder and runs away with the marrow, eating it. He throws back the bladder. Coyote intends to pound the remaining bones. Two birds forbid him to do so, and tell him that they themselves will pound them. Coyote is sent to make a spoon. When he comes back, the birds fly away with the chopped bone.

13. COYOTE AND BUTTERFLY (No. 17).—Coyote hears Butterfly singing. (The story is unintelligible.)

14. COYOTE AND GROUSE [4] (No. 8).—While Grouse and husband are away, Coyote enters the tent, puts their children into a bag, and carries them away. The children break the bag and escape.

---

[1] Assiniboin (Lowie PaAM 4:122).
Nez Percé (Spinden MAFLS 11:190).
Okanagon (Teit MAFLS 11:76).
Shoshoni (Lowie PaAM 2:276 [first part only]).
Shuswap (Boas, Sagen 6).
Thompson (Teit JE 8:208; MAFLS 11:32).
See Thompson (Teit MAFLS 6:29).
[2] Assiniboin (Lowie PaAM 9:108, 112).
Shuswap (Teit JE 2:633 [here it is merely said that Coyote is too lazy to rise], 741).
Thompson (Teit MAFLS 11:7).
[3] See Sanpoil (Gould MAFLS 11:104).
[4] Caddo (Dorsey CI 41:102).
Pawnee (Dorsey CI 59:458).
Shoshoni (Lowie PaAM 2:258, 259, 261).

17   15. Coyote and Star (No. 9).—(Unintelligible.)

18   16. Coyote and the Woman [1] (No. 10).—A woman sees Coyote coming. She is afraid and lies down, pretending to be dead. Coyote comes up to examine her, and thinks she has been dead for a long time.

19   17. Coyote and the Manitou with the Hat [2] (No. 11).—Coyote meets a manitou whose hat is made of fat. He eats of it and hurts the manitou.

19   18. Coyote and the Ducks (3 versions: Nos. 12, 59. and VAEU 23:167). *First Version.*—Coyote and his two children reach a lake on which there are many ducks. He tells his children to wail for his brother-in-law. A Mallard Duck comes ashore to hear what is going on. The others follow, and Coyote pulls out their feathers.[3]

161   *Second Version.*—Coyote tells his son to wail for his brother-in-law. The Ducks
163   hear him. One comes ashore, and says that he wants to play with them. They go from one lake to an adjoining one. The Ducks fly; Coyote and his son walk. Coyote stretches a net across the connecting river and induces the Ducks to swim. Then he catches them, takes them home, and dries them. The surviving Ducks
165   discover what he is doing and fly away. Lynx steals Coyote's ducks, and *pulls his face and his tail long.* When Coyote discovers this, and when he overtakes Lynx while asleep, he takes back the ducks and *pushes in his tail and face.*[4]

        Third Version.—In this version the tale forms an incident of the tale of Coyote and Dog. (See p. 299.)

20   19. Coyote and Owl [5] (3 versions: Nos. 13, 24, and 36). *First Version.*—Owl carries away crying children. Coyote pretends to be a child and cries. Owl asks for the child. He is put into the birch-bark basket of Owl, who carries him home. The children dance in Owl's tent. Coyote closes Owl's eyes with gum, and throws him into the fire. The children return.

---

[1] Assiniboin (Lowie PaAM 4:116, 204).
    Blackfoot (Wissler PaAM 2:35; de Josselin de Jong VKAWA 14:18).
    Crow (Simms FM 2:284).
[2] Blackfoot (de Josselin de Jong VKAWA 14:72; Uhlenbeck VKAWA 13:177).
    Caddo (Dorsey CI 41:100).
    Crow (Simms FM 2:285).
    Hupa (Goddard UCal 1:167).
[3] See p. 290, note 4.
[4] Blackfoot (Uhlenbeck VKAWA 13:176).
    Chippewayan (Lofthouse, Transactions Canadian Institute 10:44).
    Nez Percé (Mayer-Farrand MAFLS 11:140, 142).
    Shoshoni (Lowie PaAM 2:276).
    Shuswap (Teit JE 2:678).
    Sia (Stevenson RBAE 11:148).
    Thompson (Teit MAFLS 6:38; JE 8:216).
    Tillamook (Boas JAFL 11:142).
    Ute, Uinta (Mason JAFL 23:301).
[5] Arapaho (Dorsey and Kroeber FM 5:239 [Big Owl]).
    Bellabella (Boas, Sagen 241).
    Bellacoola (Boas, Sagen 249).
    Chilcotin (Farrand JE 2:36).
    Chinook (BBAE 20:110).
    Comox (Boas, Sagen 89).
    Cowichan (Boas, Sagen 49).
    Fraser Delta (Hill-Tout JAI 34:347).
    Hopi (Voth FM 8:173).
    Kato (Goddard UCal 5:236).
    Kutenai (Int. Congr. of Anth., Chicago, 1894, 283, 284; E. F. Wilson, Our Forest Children, 1890, 3:166).
    Lillooet (Teit JAFL 25:314).
    Micmac (Rand 183).
    Nez Percé (MAFLS 11; Mayer-Farrand 176; Spinden 192).
    Osage (Dorsey FM 7:41).
    Rivers Inlet (Boas, Sagen 224).
    Shoshoni (Lowie PaAM 2:288).
    Shuswap (Teit JE 2:698).
    Squamish (Boas, Sagen 57; Hill-Tout BAAS 70:545).
    StsEē'lis (Hill-Tout JAI 34:347).
    Thompson (Teit MAFLS 6:63; 11:26; JE 8:265).
    Ute (Powell RBAE 1:45).

Second Version.—Owl carries the children away in a bark basket, the inside of which   37
is set with awls.   Coyote pretends to be a child, and is carried away by an Owl.   He
sends the children to get gum.   Owl dances; and when he gets hot, Coyote gums up   38
his eyes and burns him.   *The ashes are transformed into owls.*

Third Version.—Coyote transforms himself into a child.   When he cries, he is   51
thrown out of the tent, and Owl carries him along.   He induces Owl to dance, and
kills him.

20. Coyote and Trout (No. 25).—In winter Coyote meets a Trout Woman, marries   38
her, and follows her into the water, which they reach by jumping into a water hole.
The Trout goes to a place where people are fishing, saying that there is much food
there.   Coyote breaks the hook.   The people make a large hook, by means of which   39
they pull him out of the water.   When he is all out, the people club him.   He shouts,
saying that he is not a trout, but Coyote.   He resumes his former shape.

21. Coyote and Caribou (No. 35).—Caribou grows fat by eating young grass.   When   51
he is fat, Coyote kills him and then mourns for him.

22. Coyote and Deer (No. 37).—Coyote intends to kill Deer, and in pursuing him   51
is frightened by the wind.   He kills Deer, who is holding his own head.   He asks
whether he is holding Deer's father's war bonnet.   The story is not by any means clear.

23. Coyote's Contests [1] (No. 49).—The people of several towns have killed   69
Coyote's relatives.   Coyote asks Woodpecker, Flicker, Hawk, Chicken Hawk, and   71

---

[1] The following are parallels of similar matches:
  Climbing:
    Chinook (BBAE 20:57).
    Coos (Frachtenberg CU 1:91).
    Luiseño (Du Bois UCal 8:148).
    Nez Percé (Spinden MAFLS 11:194).
    Quinault (Farrand JE 2:103).
    Shuswap (Boas, Sagen 2; Teit JE 2:645).
    Wishram (PAES 2:87).
  Diving:
    Alsea (personal communication from L. J. Frachtenberg).
    Chinook (BBAE 20:57).
    Comox (Boas, Sagen 79).
    Nez Percé (Spinden MAFLS 11:194).
    Pawnee (Dorsey CI 59:228).
    Quinault (Farrand JE 2:103).
    Shoshoni (Lowie PaAM 2:277).
  Shooting:
    Chinook (Boas, BBAE 20:58).
    Kathlamet (Boas, BBAE 26:67).
    Nootka (Boas, Sagen 107).
    Tlingit (Boas, Sagen 319).
  Wrestling:
    Shoshoni (Lowie PaAM 2:277).
    Wishram (Sapir PAES 2:89).
    See also Kathlamet (Boas, BBAE 26:138); Thompson (Teit JE 8:244, 245, 340; MAFLS 6:67);
      Lillooet (Teit JAFL 25:319).
  Eating:
    Luiseño (Du Bois UCal 8:148).
    Shoshoni (Lowie Pa AM 2:277).
  Sweat house:
    See Boas, RBAE 31:807, 808; also Yana (Sapir UCal 9:69, smoke test).
  Waking:
    Kathlamet (Boas BBAE 26:115); Luiseño (Du Bois UCal 8:149); Quinault (Farrand JE 2:104)
  Harpooning:
    Chinook (Boas BBAE 20:33, 58).
    Tillamook (Boas JAFL 11:25).
    Yana (Sapir UCal 9:71).
  Gambling:
    Chinook (Boas BBAE 20:34).
    Quinault (Farrand JE 2:113).
    Tillamook (Boas JAFL 11:31).
    Wishram (Sapir PAES 2:81, 85).
    See also Boas RBAE 31:812; Yana (Sapir UCal 9:69 *et seq.*); Luiseño (Du Bois UCal 8:148 *et seq.*).

Bluejay to accompany him and to have contests with these people. In the first town they have a diving-contest, in which Duck is matched against Beaver. According to Coyote's instruction, Duck hides under a canoe and breathes through a knot hole. After Beaver has come up, Duck comes up too. In the second town they have a wrestling-match. Flicker wrestles with Kneecap and is almost defeated. Hawk sends his supernatural power to help Flicker. When Kneecap is almost overcome,

73   Flicker finishes the contest alone. In a third town they have an eating-match, which is won by Bluejay. Then Coyote and his friends begin to quarrel, each wanting to go to a different place. Coyote wants to go to swamps, Duck to lakes, Flicker to dry trees, Woodpecker to thick woods, Hawk to scattered trees. They separate accordingly.

127   24. COYOTE AND DOG (2 versions: No. 56 and VAEU 23:167).—Coyote's wife, Dog, and her two children, cut fuel. When the tree falls, a deer jumps out, which Dog holds. The children call Coyote to kill it. When they call him, he spills the rose hips on which they are living, makes a bow, and goes to shoot the deer. He tramps

129   down the snow and tells Dog to let go of the deer. His first arrow passes over the deer, which breaks through the snow. The second one passes under it. The deer escapes. Coyote travels along on his snowshoes, and finds that they are full of shrews, which he roasts. Dog is carrying her daughter on her back. She sees the fire, and

131   thinks that Coyote has killed the deer. Dog and her daughter leave Coyote and his son. Coyote reaches a lake and catches young beavers, which he ties to his son as ear ornaments. While he is away, the beavers revive, and drag the boy into the water.

133   Coyote returns to save the boy, and kills the beavers. He gives the beaver fat to his son, while he eats the meat, but afterwards he exchanges meat and fat. Coyote plays sliding down a hill. While he is doing so, his son freezes to death.[1] On going on, he

135   comes to a town in which he finds a woman and her child. The child knows his thoughts. He discovers that the child is his grandson. He rejoins his wife, the Dog. When the hunters return in the evening with venison, Coyote enters the tent; but

137   they pretend not to see him, and soil his blanket. When he returns, his wife tells him that only hunters are allowed to take part in the evening meal. On the following day he joins them, and says he will kill two bucks and a grizzly bear with seven young ones. When they are out, Coyote sits down at the head of the line of hunters. The people claim that this is improper, because he has not obtained any game. The chief of the hunters, Sun, carries pitchwood for starting a fire. Coyote puts flicker feathers in his moccasin, and when he runs fire starts. He surrounds the deer with

139   fire and kills them. The hunters say that every hunter must carry his own game. Coyote calls his manitous, who tell him that the hunters blow on their game to make it small. He does the same, and carries home seven bears and two bucks. When he kicks the game into the tent, it assumes its natural size. In the evening he does not join tne feasters until his wife tells him that he may go. In the Sun's tent he sees a shield (drying-frame?), which he steals. After walking a long distance, he lies down

141   to sleep, and on the following morning finds that he is back in the Sun's tent. This is repeated until the Sun tells him that he must walk a whole day and a whole night before lying down.[2]

(167)   *Second Version* (VAEU 23).—Coyote's wife, Dog, goes gathering wood and catches a deer. She sends her daughter to Coyote to kill it. Coyote has no arrows, and makes two. He travels slowly because the snow is deep. He tells his wife to let go of the

(168)   deer. He misses it. He tells his wife that they will pursue the deer, and asks her to follow. The woman packs up the tent and follows. Coyote feels that his snowshoes are heavy, and finds that they are full of mice, which he fries. He gives one

---

[1] Blackfoot (Uhlenbeck VKAWA 13:191).

[2] For the attempted theft see:

    Nez Percé (MAFLS 11; Mayer-Farrand 173; Spinden 186).

    Okanagon (Hill-Tout JAI 41:144).

pile to his wife and daughter, and keeps another for himself and son. The dog and her daughter desert him. She goes to the Sun, who marries the daughter. Coyote consoles his son, saying that Dog will come back when she has nothing to eat. He catches beavers, and uses two young beavers as ear ornaments for his son. He goes to get wood. The beavers revive and pull the boy into the water. Coyote rescues him. He goes with his son to a place where two lakes are, connected by a small river. He cries, sitting on the shore of the lake. The Ducks ask him why he is crying. The Ducks offer to play with him. They dive and fly from one lake to the other. In this game Coyote is almost drowned. In order to take revenge, he splits a tree and spreads it. Thus he places it in the river. He tells the ducks to swim from one river to the other, and every day a few are caught in the trap.[1] Coyote takes them to his tent and singes off the feathers. Lynx smells the burning feathers, causes Coyote to sleep, steals the ducks, and pulls out the nose and legs of Coyote and of his son. In return Coyote and his son kick in Lynx's face and break his tail.[2] Lynx is frightened and runs away. Coyote goes to search for his wife, and finds her in the Sun's house. His daughter is holding an ugly child, which hears his thoughts when he thinks that the child is ugly. He wishes to kick the child. The child moves, and thus produces a gale, which starts their fire. The hunters come back, and all the women must leave before they begin to eat. Coyote is also sent away because he has not been out hunting. When he does not go, the hunters soil his blanket and do not give him anything to eat. The woman feeds him. Sun is blind. Wolf tries to restore her eyesight, and after four attempts he succeeds. On the following day Coyote joins the hunters, who go out carrying torches. Coyote does not carry any fire. When he puts feathers into his snowshoes, he produces fire with every step. The chief tests the running-powers of men by letting two run in a circle in opposite directions. Coyote kills seven grizzly bears and two deer. The hunters shake the game in order to make it small, and leave him. Coyote learns from his dung advisers what to do with the (170) animals. He blows on them, and they shrink. He puts them into his belt and runs home. He is allowed to eat with the hunters. One day he leaves in order to visit his son. He steals the Sun's torch. After walking some distance, he lies down to sleep; and when he awakes, he finds he is back in the Sun's house. After this has happened three times, the Sun tells him that he must run for three days and three nights without stopping, and then the Sun will not return to him.

25. COYOTE AND FOX [3] (No. 58).—Coyote and Fox send their sons to obtain super-   143
natural power. Coyote's son returns soon; Fox's son stays away the whole night.   145
The one receives as his power moonlight; the other, darkness.[4] The two boys go to a village in which the people play with a hoop. Young Coyote wants to steal it; Young Fox wants to wait until morning. When Young Fox is ready to start, Young Coyote is asleep. The hoop is in a tent in which two people stand watching the doorway, each holding a hammer.[5] The two pass, take the hoop, which touches the doorway a little and makes a sound. The two old people awake and call the other   147
people, who pursue the boys. Young Coyote carries the hoop. When he becomes tired, he gives it to Young Fox. Young Coyote is caught, and the people say they will not kill him. Young Fox rolls the hoop ahead and sings, saying that Young Coyote has been killed. Old Coyote understands that Young Fox has been killed. The hoop rolls into the tent, and falls down where Coyote is sitting. Then he knows   149
that his own son has been captured. Old Coyote and Fox make war on the people

---

[1] See p. 296, No. 18.
[2] † See p. 296, footnote 4.
[3] Compare the related tales:
    Pawnee (Dorsey CI 59:231).
    Shuswap (Teit JE 2:642).
    Thompson (Teit MAFLS 6:32; JE 8:313; also Teit MAFLS 11:2).
[4] Nez Percé (Mayer-Farrand MAFLS 11:142).
[5] See p. 304, No. 30.

who have captured Young Coyote.   They find the people using Young Coyote in place
151 of their hoop.   Fox makes a sign to him, and Young Coyote runs away and makes
his escape.

Salmon hears about the hoop, and tries to win it by gambling with Coyote.   Coyote
and his partner Young Fox lose the hoop.   Coyote sends Young Fox to Old Fox to
153 borrow his partridge tail.   Fox plays with Young Coyote as partner against Salmon,
and wins back what Coyote has lost.   Salmon loses his daughter, who is then married
to Young Coyote.

The couple have a child.   They travel in their canoe to the Salmon country.   Fox
155 accompanies them.   The woman is seated in the bow of the canoe.   They reach a
dangerous place.   Fox, Coyote, and his son enter a bladder.   Fox has his pipe[1] in
the hole of the bladder.   The canoe upsets above the falls and sinks; but they come
up unharmed below the falls, drifting down in the bladder.   The same happens at
another place.

When they reach the Salmon country, the woman climbs a steep precipice, on which
she hopes to kill Coyote and Fox.   Fox throws tobacco on it, and they are able to
climb it.   The woman asks her elder brother to kill Fox and Coyote.   He throws dog
manure into the fire in order to suffocate them, but Fox saves them in his bladder.[2]
157 They are sent out to fish salmon during the night.   Coyote stays behind in the tent,
and is warned not to fall asleep, because the people will kill him.   He is also told to
come out if he should see a small fire, which would indicate that Fox and Coyote were
fighting with the Salmon people.   Two old persons stand in the doorway; and when
Coyote sees the light of the canoe getting small, he rushes out.   Coyote deceives the
old people, who kill each other with their hammers.   Coyote goes aboard the canoe.
159 The woman's brother transforms himself into a salmon.   A Salmon boy, who accompanies them, moves his torch so that Fox shall not hit the salmon with his spear.
The boy tells Fox to strike the salmon tail.   If he should have done so, the salmon
would have upset the canoe.   Fox knows this, and strikes the stomach of the salmon.
They cut off its head.   Coyote is told not to look back.   He disobeys, and the canoe
can not be moved.   The pursuers are satisfied when Fox throws the salmon head into
161 the water, and the canoe moves on.

The people are sent to dive for the salmon head, and the one who succeeds in getting it is promised the Salmon chief's daughter.[3]   Turtle succeeds, and marries the
girl, who refuses to talk.   When he makes her laugh by tickling her, he finds that her
mouth has a foul smell, and he leaves her.

165   26. COYOTE KILLS PANTHER AND LIBERATES THE SALMON (No. 60).—Coyote's wife,
Dog, sends him to visit Panther.   He finds him engaged in making arrows, while his
167 wife is cleaning skins.   They refuse to give him food.   He sends his wife, telling her
that their meat is hanging close to the doorway.   Panther scolds her.   When she
returns, Coyote makes a bow for himself and his son, and a hammer for his wife and
169 his daughter.   They attack Panther, and eventually kill him and his family.   They
skin them and throw the bodies out of the tent.

Coyote acts as Panther used to do: he calls the game, which appears, and which
he shoots.   Since he shoots too much, the game disappears, except two animals.
The animals suffer, and say that they recognize that it is Coyote who has shot too
many of them.   They send Little Flathorn, who discovers the bodies of the Panthers.
171 The animals make war on Coyote.   They throw stones down from the mountains.
Coyote paints himself and puts on his war dress.   His wife and his children are killed
by the stones, and finally he himself is hit.

---

[1] Shuswap (Teit JE 2:624).
[2] See Boas RBAE 31:808; also Blackfoot (Uhlenbeck VKAWA 13:157).
[3] Okanagon (Hill-Tout JAI 41:160).
     Shuswap (Teit JE 2:676).
     Thompson (Teit MAFLS 6:64, 11:25; JE 8:240).

He transforms himself into a plank [1] and drifts down the river. He lands at a fish trap. Two girls find him and carry him to the tent. When they put fish on the plank, it eats the fish. They recognize that he is Coyote, and throw him into the water.   173

He sees two girls picking berries, and transforms himself into an infant, which they carry home. The girls stay at home, watching the child. Coyote sees that when one of the girls stretches her hand backward, salmon fall down; and that when the other one stretches out her hands, a fawn falls down. When the berries are all eaten, they deliberate whether they may leave the child alone and tell him to put out the fire. Since he is able to do so, they go out. When the girls are gone, he discovers the salmon and fawns behind the tent. He digs a ditch to the river. On the following   175 day he completes the ditch and drives the salmon into the river. He throws the fawn into the fire and leaves it. He sets fire to the house. When the girls come back, they find the salmon gone. They think that the bones in the fireplace are those of the child. Finally they recognize that they have been fooled by Coyote, and ask him to leave some food. He shakes his blanket, and a few of the salmon turn back.

He meets Wolverene, who is fishing. Wolverene's sister announces his arrival; and Wolverene says that the visitor is Coyote, and asks her not to look at him. For this reason Coyote does not give them salmon. He meets Sparrow, who is fishing.   177 When his arrival is announced, Sparrow accepts him, and his daughter marries him. Therefore he leaves salmon there. On the following morning he tells the salmon to go into the fish trap, first one, then two, then three, and finally many. Coyote leaves   179 his wife, and *closes the passage between Columbia Lakes and Kootenai River.*

27. ORIGIN OF THE SEASONS [2] (No. 61).—Coyote goes to Squirrel to ask for food. She has no more, and tells him that spring is still far away. He tells her what to do.   181 Squirrel cries, and says there will be no food until spring. The seasons are kept in another town; and after twelve months of winter, the owners untie the bag containing spring, summer, and fall. The people start to steal the summer season. They go to a town in the sky, and Lynx is sent ahead to enter the tent. The people are placed outside at intervals, the strongest one farthest away from the tent.[3] The Lynx boy goes into the tent, and two old women tell him where the springtime is hanging. He heats some gum by the fire; and when it is melted, he sticks it on the mouths of the old women. Then he takes down the bag containing the spring. The women can not speak, but finally the people discover that the bag containing the spring is being

---

[1] For the second part see:

Cœur d'Alène (Teit MAFLS 11:121).
Flathead (Wilson, Trans. Ethn. Soc. of London. 1866, 4:313).
Hupa (Goddard UCal 1:124).
Lillooet (Teit JAFL 25:303).
Nez Percé (Spinden JAFL 21:15; Mayer-Farrand MAFLS 11:139).
Okanagon (Hill-Tout JAI 41:146; Teit MAFLS 11:67, 70).
Sanpoil (Gould MAFLS 11:101).
Seshelt (Hill-Tout JAI 34:43).
Shoshoni (Lowie PaAM 2:275, 278).
Shuswap (Teit JE 2:629, 741).
Thompson (Teit MAFLS 6:27, 28; 11:7; JE 8:205, 301; Hill-Tout BAAS 1899:559; FL 10:207; Boas, Sagen 18).
Wishram (Sapir PAES 2:3).
Also Caddo (Dorsey CI 41:61, 108).

[2] Assiniboin (Lowie PaAM 4:101).
Chippewayan (Petitot 373; a much-distorted version, Lofthouse, Transactions Canadian Institute 10:43).
Crow (Simms FM 2:283).
Gros Ventre (Kroeber PaAM 1:65).
Ojibwa (Carson JAFL 30:492; Jones PAES 7, pt. 2, 469).
Shoshoni (Lowie-St. Clair JAFL 22:279).
Shuswap (Teit JE 2:624; see also 671).
Slavey (Bell JAFL 14:26).
Thompson (Teit MAFLS 11:3).
Yana (Sapir UCal 9:211).
See also Chilcotin (Farrand JE 2:25).

[3] Kaska (Teit JAFL 30:443).
Shoshoni (Lowie PaAM 2:245).
Thompson (Teit MAFLS 6:33, 11:2).

carried away.   The animals throw it from one to another, and at last to the grizzly bear, who tears the bag; then *the heat comes out*, and the snow melts.

183   28. COYOTE JUGGLES WITH HIS EYES [1] (No. 62).—Coyote sees a man, Snipe, who takes his eyes out of their sockets and throws them up.   Then they fall back.   Coyote steals the eyes.   He puts his fingers into the eyes of Snipe, who finally catches him,

185   tears out Coyote's eyes, puts them into his own eye sockets, and takes Coyote's eyes to his tent.   Coyote finds some gum and puts it into his orbits; but when it is hot, the gum melts.   He puts some foam into his orbits; it bursts, and he is blind again.   He picks huckleberries, which he uses for eyes.   Then he meets two children who are picking huckleberries, takes out the eyes of one of them, and uses them for his own. On his way to the town he hears that the people are using Coyote's eyes to obtain good luck.   He kills the old woman who gives him this information, shakes her body

187   out of her skin, and assumes her shape. [2]   When the granddaughters of the old woman come, he asks them to take him to the place where the people are playing with Coyote's eyes.   Then he dances, and during the dance he takes away the eyes.

189   29. COYOTE AND DEER [3] (No. 63).—The deer kills the people.   Coyote resolves to pull out its teeth.   When the deer gets his scent, it pursues him.   Coyote catches

---

[1] Apache, Jicarilla (Mooney AA 11:197).
   Arapaho (Dorsey and Kroeber FM 5:52).
   Assiniboin (Lowie PaAM 4:117).
   Blackfoot (Wissler PaAM 29; Grinnell, Lodge Tales 153; Uhlenbeck VKAWA 13:195).
   Caddo (Dorsey CI 41:103).
   Cheyenne (Kroeber JAFL 13:168).
   Comanche (Lowie-St. Clair JAFL 22:278).
   Cree (Russell, Expl. in Far North 215).
   Gros Ventre (Kroeber PaAM 1:70).
   Hopi (Voth FM 8:194).
   Navaho (Matthews MAFLS 5:90).
   Nez Percé (Spinden JAFL 21:19; Mayer-Farrand MAFLS 11:155).
   Shoshoni (Lowie-St. Clair JAFL 22:269; PaAM 2:272).
   Shuswap (Boas, Sagen 7; Teit JE 2:632).
   Sia (Stevenson RBAE 11:153).
   Thompson (Teit JE 8:212).
   Ute, Uinta (Mason JAFL 23:315).
   Zuñi (Cushing, Folk Tales 262, 268; Handy JAFL 31).
[2] Alsea (personal communication from L. J. Frachtenberg).
   Assiniboin (Lowie PaAM 4:147, 157).
   Blackfoot (Wissler PaAM 2:152).
   Chippewayan (Lofthouse Transactions Canadian Institute 10:44).
   Chukchee (Bogoras JE 8:45).
   Coos (Frachtenberg CU 1:151, [169]).
   Cree (John McLean, Canadian Savage Folk, 74).
   Eskimo (Boas BAM 15:185).
   Fox (Jones PAES 1:355).
   Haida (Swanton BBAE 29:110, 118, 136, 160).
   Menominee (Hoffman 133).
   Nez Percé (Spinden JAFL 21:211; Mayer-Farrand MAFLS 11:156, 173).
   Ojibwa (Jones PAES 7:117, 263, 401; Schoolcraft, Hiawatha 40; de Josselin de Jong BArch S 5:14; Speck
      GSCan 71:34).
   Omaha (Dorsey CNAE 6:241).
   Pawnee (Dorsey CI 59:170, 442, 506; see also MAFLS 8:250).
   Shoshoni (Lowie PaAM 2:241, 243, 260).
   Shuswap (Teit JE 2:676, 694).
   Stseē'lis (Hill-Tout JAI 34:349).
   Takelma (Sapir UPenn 161).
   Thompson (Teit JE 8:[213], 239, 242, 266, 309; MAFLS 6:63).
   Tillamook (Boas JAFL 11:137).
   Wishram (Sapir PAES 2:111).
   Yana (Sapir UCal 9:158, 216; Curtin, Creation Myths, 318, 359).
   Zuñi (Cushing, Folk Tales 461).
[3] Blackfoot (Grinnell, Lodge Tales 140).
   Caddo (Dorsey CI 41:50).
   Cheyenne (Kroeber JAFL 13:161).
   Menominee (Skinner PaAM 13:411).
   Pawnee (Dorsey CI 59:67).
   Shuswap (Teit JE 2:653).
   Tahltan (Teit MS).
   Thompson (Teit MAFLS 11:3).

the deer and pulls out its teeth and makes a tail of grass for it. He tells the deer to snort when it sees people. He kills two deer and comes to the town, and people are scared when they see him carrying the deer.

30. RAVEN (No. 65).—A chief wishes that *everybody shall die* twice. Everybody 213 agrees except Raven, who wants to eat the eyes of corpses. His decision is accepted. The people kill Raven's two children, and he wishes in vain to have the previous decision reversed.[1]

Ant tightens his belt in order to bury the dead. *For that reason the ant has a narrow waist.*[2]

Raven is hungry and hides the buffalo.[3] The people are starving. They ask 215 Beaver to pretend to be dead. Raven appears and wants to eat Beaver's eyes. Beaver holds him, and the people capture him. Raven is taken into the tent where the people are assembled. Coyote sits on top of the smoke hole. Raven refuses to tell where he has hidden the game. Finally he shouts and frightens Coyote, who falls down. Then Raven flies away through the smoke hole. Magpie has good eyes, and sees in what direction Raven is flying. This makes Coyote angry, and he throws dust

---

[1] Apache, Jicarilla (Goddard PaAM 8:194; Russell JAFL 11:258).
Arapaho (Dorsey and Kroeber FM 5:17, 81).
Assiniboin (Lowie PaAM 4:104).
Blackfoot (Wissler PaAM 2:20, 21; de Josselin de Jong VKAWA 14:29; Grinnell, Lodge Tales 138, 272).
Caddo (Dorsey CI 41:14, 15).
Cheyenne (Kroeber JAFL 13:161).
Cœur d'Alène (Teit MAFLS 11:125).
Comanche (Lowie-St. Clair JAFL 22:279).
Coos (Frachtenberg CU 1:43; also 4:41).
Diegueño (Du Bois JAFL 14:183).
Dog-Rib (Sir John Franklin, Narrative of a Second Expedition to the Shores of the Polar Sea [London, 1828], p. 293).
Eskimo (David Crantz, Historie von Grönland 262).
Hare (Petitot 115).
Kaska (Teit JAFL 30:444).
Klamath (Gatschet CNAE 2:103).
Lillooet (Teit JAFL 25:356).
Maidu (Dixon BAM 17:43, 46, 47; PAES 4:29, 51; Merriam 55).
Miwok (Merriam 55, 132).
Navaho (MAFLS 5:77).
Pawnee (Dorsey CI 59:44, MAFLS 8:17).
Pomo (Merriam 213).
Quinault (Farrand JE 2:111).
Sanpoil (Gould MAFLS 11:106).
Shasta (Dixon JAFL 23:19; Frachtenberg-Farrand JAFL 28:209).
Shoshoni (Lowie PaAM 2:239).
Shuswap (Teit JE 2:746).
Tahltan (Teit MS).
Takelma (Sapir UPenn 2:99).
Thompson (Teit JE 8:329, 330; Teit MAFLS 11:1).
Ute (Powell RBAE 1:45).
Wintun (Curtin, Creation Myths, 163, 174).
Wishosk (Kroeber JAFL 18:96, 99).
Yana (Sapir UCal 9:91).
See also Luiseño (Du Bois UCal 8:134, 146).
[2] Thompson (Teit MAFLS 6:25).
[3] Apache, Jicarilla (Goddard PaAM 8:212; Russell JAFL 11:259).
Arapaho (FM 5:275).
Beaver (Goddard PaAM 10:250).
Blackfoot (Wissler PaAM 2:50; Uhlenbeck VKAWA 13:164; Grinnell, Lodge Tales 145).
Chippewayan (Petitot 379; Lowie PaAM 10:184).
Comanche (Lowie-St. Clair JAFL 22:280).
Gros Ventre (Kroeber PaAM 1:65).
Kaska (Teit JAFL 30:441).
Nez Percé (Mayer-Farrand MAFLS 11:162).
Pawnee (Dorsey CI 59:43).
Thompson (Teit JE 8:241).
See also Caddo (Dorsey CI 41:10).

217   into Magpie's eyes. *Therefore magpies' eyes water.* The people send Jack Rabbit (Dog?) and Hare to look for game. They reach a tent inhabited by two old women. They see the tracks of buffaloes. The one transforms herself into a pup; the other one, into a stone. The dog lies down near a water hole. One of the old women wants to throw the pup into the water; the other one pities the pup and takes it home. The other woman takes the stone home in order to use it as an anvil. A bladder and a bunch of claws are hanging in the doorway. When the buffaloes come in, these two give notice by their noise. At night the one boy breaks the bladder with a stick; the other one steals the claws. When the boys are some distance away, they shake the

219   claws and sing, calling the buffaloes. The game runs out of the tent. The women find that the bladder is broken and the rattle taken away. The women with lifted hammers stand by the side of the trail of the game. The two youths hang on with their teeth to the testicles of a buffalo bull. The women strike it, and *make its sides flat.* All the pemmican in the house rolls out. Thus the game is secured by the people.

41   31. The Deluge (2 versions: Nos. 27 and 66). *First Version.*—Chicken Hawk's wife picks huckleberries. A sea monster abducts her.[1] Chicken Hawk shoots the monster, which drinks all the water.[2] When Chicken Hawk pulls out his arrow, the water streams out,[3] and there is a deluge. Chicken Hawk takes off his tail and puts it up, saying that if the water rises higher than the stripes on his tail the people will die. The water stops before reaching the last stripe, and then goes down again.[4]

219   *Second Version.*—Chicken Hawk's wife, Grouse, picks huckleberries. When swim-
221   ming in a lake, the water monster threatens to kill her. She pours the huckleberries into its mouth. When she goes home, she pretends to have been unable to pick huckleberries because she felt ill. When she goes out again, she meets the sea monster, who becomes her lover. When going home, she pretends to be sick. Finally Chicken

223   Hawk goes out to watch her. He sees her with the sea monster. When his wife comes home, he tells her that the huckleberries are bad, and asks her to wash them. On the following day Chicken Hawk follows her, and shoots the water monster with one of his two arrows. With the other one he shoots his wife, *whom he transforms into a grouse.* The water monster goes back into the lake and drinks lake and rivers.

225   Then he dies. The people almost die of thirst. Chicken Hawk pulls out the arrow, and the people are able to drink again. The water rises, and the people climb the mountains. He places his tail upright, and says that if the water should pass the third stripe of the tail the world would come to an end. The water stops rising before reaching the last stripe, and goes down again.

---

[1] Assiniboin (Lowie PaAM 4:177).
  Bellacoola (Boas, Sagen 247).
  Caddo (Dorsey CI 41:66).
  Cheyenne (Kroeber JAFL 13:184).
  Chippewayan (Petitot 407; Lowie PaAM 1:187).
  Chukchee (Bogoras JE 8:26).
  Cree (Russell, Expl. in Far North 202).
  Lillooet (Teit JAFL 25:334).
  Ojibwa (Jones JAFL 29:379, 387; Schoolcraft, Hiawatha 265).
  Passamaquoddy (Leland 273).
  Shuswap (Teit JE 2:724, 725).
  Sioux (Wissler JAFL 20:195).
  Thompson (Teit MAFLS 6:83; JE 8:372).
  Ts!Ets!a'ut (Boas JAFL 9:259).
  Tungus (A. Schiefner, Baron Gerhard von Maydell's Tungusische Sprachproben [Mélanges asiatiques tires du Bulletin de l'académie impériale des sciences St. Petersburg, 7:349]).
  Yana (distantly related) (Sapir UCal 9:156).
[2] Chilula (Goddard UCal 10:361).
  Huron (Hale JAFL 1:181).
  Luiseño (Du Bois UCal 8:156).
  Micmac (Speck JAFL 28:62 [frog keeps water in bladders]).
[3] Kaska (Teit JAFL 30:439).
[4] A Beaver story (Goddard PaAM 10:237) may refer to a similar deluge.

32. CHICKADEE AND ELK [1] (No. 14).—Chickadee wishes to cross a river, and asks   21
Elk to take him across. While Elk is carrying him, Chickadee kills him.

33. FROG AND PARTRIDGE (No. 15).—Frog Woman marries Partridge. After a while
Partridge finds his first wife, and they go back to their children.

34. BEAVER AND TURTLE [2] (No. 16).—Turtle goes after the head of a chief while   22
he is asleep. He is captured the next morning. The people threaten to cut off his
head: Turtle says he does not fear a knife. They threaten to shoot him: he says he
does not fear a bow. They threaten to chop him up: he says he does not fear an ax.   23
They threaten to drown him, and he asks them not to do it. When he is thrown into
the water, he swims away, shaking the head of the chief. The people try to pursue
him; but Beaver gnaws through their bows, and the pursuers go back.

35. SKUNK AND PANTHER [3] (3 versions: Nos. 17, 26, and 34). *First Version.*—   23
Panther sees Skunk coming, and pretends to be dead. Skunk carries him on his back.
Skunk puts Panther down and covers him with his bucket, which Panther breaks.
When Skunk comes back, he sees Panther's tracks. Panther climbs a tree. Skunk

---

[1] Apache, Jicarilla (Goddard PaAM 8:228; Russell JAFL 11:263).
Assiniboin (Lowie PaAM 4:202).
Chilcotin (Farrand JE 2:40).
Nez Percé (Spinden JAFL 21:21).
Okanagon (Gatschet, Globus 52:137).
Osage (Dorsey FM 7:15, 16).
Pawnee (Dorsey CI 59:453).
Sanpoil (Gould MAFLS 11:107).
Shoshoni (Lowie PaAM 2:267).
Shuswap (Teit JE 2:751).
Thompson (Teit MAFLS 6:76).
Ute (Kroeber JAFL 14:270).
Ute, Uinta (Mason JAFL 23:316).
Wichita (Dorsey CI 21:271).
Zuñi (Cushing, Folk Tales 243).
See also Caddo (Dorsey CI 41:99); Maidu (Dixon BAM 17:83).
[2] Biloxi (J. O. Dorsey JAFL 6:49).
Blackfoot (Wissler PaAM 2:160).
Cherokee (Mooney RBAE 19:278).
Cheyenne (Kroeber JAFL 13:189).
Dakota (Wissler JAFL 20:126).
Hopi (Voth FM 8:182).
Kickapoo (Jones PAES 9:39).
Laguna (Parsons Pueblo-Indian Folk-Tales, No. X, JAFL 31).
Menominee (Skinner PaAM 13:392).
Micmac and Passamaquoddy (Leland 56).
Natchez (Swanton JAFL 26:193).
Ojibwa (Jones JAFL 29:368; PAES 7 [pt. 2]: 117, 343; Radin GSCan 48:61).
Okanagon (Gatschet, Globus 52:138).
Osage (Dorsey FM 7:16).
Pawnee (Dorsey MAFLS 8:275; CI 59:469).
Ponca (Dorsey CNAE 6:275; JAFL 1:207).
See also Celebes (Revue des traditions populaires 14: 547); Philippine I. (Bayliss JAFL 21:47); Visayan
    (Millington and Maxfield JAFL 20:316); Ceylon (Jātaka No. 543, ed. Fausböll, 6.161, 12); Burmah
    (Journal Royal Asiatic Society n. s. 24); China (Stanislas Julien, Les Avadânas 1.201); Angola
    (Chatelain MAFLS 1:154; A. Seidel, Geschichten und Lieder der Afrikaner 153); North American
    negroes (Harris, Uncle Remus 53; Parsons JAFL 30:171, 181, 225, where other references to Ameri-
    can negro versions will be found).
Compare the corresponding tale of the crayfish (Schildbürgerbuch, edited by Bobertag 41) and of Brer
    Rabbit (JAFL 1:148; Harris, Uncle Remus 25; Fortier MAFLS 2:35; Parsons MAFLS 13:15); Brazil
    (Herbert Smith, Brazil, The Amazons and the Coast 551). (Quoted after Dähnhardt, Natursagen 4:44.)
See also Chinook (Boas BBAE 20:121); Quinault (Farrand JE 2:91); Snohomish (Haeberlin, personal
    information).
[3] Okanagon (Hill-Tout JAI 41:148).
Sanpoil (Gould MAFLS 11:106).
Shoshoni (Lowie PaAM 2:271).

sees Panther's reflection in the water.[1]   He tries to hit him in the water with his fluid.
When he is unable to do so, he lies down and sees Panther in the tree.   He turns to
shoot him; but Panther kills him with his arrow, which he points with his claw.

41   *Second Version.*—Panther sees Skunk coming, and pretends to be dead.   Skunk puts
him into a bucket and carries him along.   Skunk says he is afraid only of whistling.
Somebody whistles.   Skunk is scared, puts down Panther, who breaks the bucket.
Skunk finds Panther's tracks.   Panther climbs a tree.   When Skunk drinks, he sees
Panther's reflection, and tries to kill him in the water by means of his fluid.   When he
is tired, he lies down and sees Panther in the tree.   He shoots him and kills him.

48   *Third Version.*—Skunk finds Fox, whom he puts into a pot.   He says that he is
afraid of whistling.   Somebody whistles.   Skunk runs away.   Fox breaks the pot
and escapes.   Skunk pursues Fox, who hides in a tree.   Skunk sees Fox's reflection
in the water,[2] and tries to kill him.   When Skunk is tired, Fox shoots him.

43   36. CHICKEN HAWK AND TOAD (No. 28).—(This story is almost unintelligible.)
Chicken Hawk and Blue Hawk are hunters.   Toad and Golden Eagle (?) marry them.
Chicken Hawk kills Toad.   Toad's parents find her, and try to kill Chicken Hawk.
They capture him and put him over the fire.   Blue Hawk knows what is happening
to his brother, and rescues him.

46   37. CHIPMUNK AND OWL [3] (2 versions: Nos. 32 and 46).   *First Version.*—Frog is the
grandmother of Chipmunk.   She sends her to the river, where she gathers rose hips.
She meets Owl, who pretends that Chipmunk's mother wishes her to accompany Owl.
Chipmunk asks Owl to cover his eyes, and runs away.   She runs back to her grandmother, and asks her to hide her.   Frog puts her into a kettle of soup, in which Chipmunk is drowned.

50   *Second Version.*—Frog warns her granddaughter, Chipmunk, not to go to the river.
She disobeys, and meets Owl, who tries to seduce her by saying that her relatives
want her to accompany him.   She always replies that the particular relative is dead.
Chipmunk asks Owl to cover his eyes, and escapes.   Owl just succeeds in *scratching
Chipmunk's back.*   Chipmunk asks her grandmother to hide her.   When she puts her
into a basket, Chipmunk makes a noise.   When she puts her into her mouth, she can
not hold her.   She puts her into a kettle with soup.   Owl arrives.   Frog says that she
has not seen Chipmunk.   Owl asks for a drink, discovers the soup, drinks it, and

61   finds Chipmunk in the bottom.   He kills her.   Frog washes the bones of Chipmunk,
and revives her.

25   38. MOSQUITO [4] (No. 18).—Mosquito is invited to eat choke cherries and service
berries, but declines.   He is offered blood, and drinks a great deal.   He is killed,
and *small mosquitoes fly out of his body.*

[1] Assiniboin (Lowie PaAM 4:109).
   Bellacoola (Boas, Sagen 253; JE 1:84).
   Blackfoot (Uhlenbeck VKAWA 12:64; Wissler PaAM 2:29; Grinnell, Lodge Tales 157).
   Caddo (Dorsey CI 41:97).
   Chilcotin (Farrand JE 2:28).
   Comox (Boas, Sagen 66, 80).
   Haida (Swanton BBAE 29:329; JE 5:265).
   Kaska (Teit JAFL 30:433).
   Kwakiutl (Boas, Sagen 168; Rep. U. S. Nat. Mus. 1895:373).
   Nootka (Boas, Sagen 114).
   Ojibwa (Jones PAES 7:117, 179).
   Osage (Dorsey FM 7:17).
   Quinault (Farrand JE 2:100, 123).
   Shuswap (Teit JE 2:753).
   Tahltan (Teit MS).
   Thompson (Teit MAFLS 6:45).
   Tsimshian (Boas RBAE 31:741).
   See also Dähnhardt, Natursagen 4:230; Pochutla, México (Boas JAFL 25:206); Chatino, México.
      (Boas JAFL 25:237); Bahama Islands (Parsons MAFLS 13:106).
[2] See note 1, above.
[3] Okanagon (Hill-Tout JAI 41:143); Sanpoil (Gould MAFLS 11:105).
[4] Lillooet (Teit JAFL 25:311).
   Shuswap (Teit JE 2:709).
   Thompson (Teit MAFLS 6:56; JE 2:229, 335).

39. RACE OF FROG AND ANTELOPE [1] (2 versions: Nos. 29 and 69). *First Version.*— **43**
Frog and his friends go to Antelope's tent in order to play. They stake their clothing.
Frog makes his people lie down along the race course. When Antelope is running,
one Frog after another appears ahead of him.

Second Version.—Chief Frog goes with his people to Fish Hawk Nest, the town of **245**
Antelope, in order to race with him. They stake their property. The men and
women Frogs lie down along the race track. Frog stakes his blue clothing. Antelope **217**
laughs at Frog. In the beginning Antelope does not run fast; but when he finds that
Frogs are always ahead of him, he runs faster and faster until he is exhausted.

40. THE TWO TSA'KAP (No. 31).—There are a brother and sister Tsa'kap. The boy **45**
bathes in a lake, and is swallowed by a charr. His sister catches the charr on the
hook, and cuts it open. The brother speaks inside, and comes out.[2] They go back to
their tent. The sister warns him not to shoot a squirrel. He disobeys. When he
shoots, his arrow falls down in a tent, in which he finds a woman, who compels him
to undergo a swinging-contest. When the Tsa'kap swings, the rope does not break.
When the woman swings, it breaks and she is killed.[3] The sister warns him not to
go in a certain direction. He disobeys, and kills a beaver. The supernatural people
say that he stole it from them. He returns home and asks his sister for their father.
The sister first prevaricates, and then tells him that their father has been killed by a **47**
grizzly bear. The brother goes to kill the grizzly bear. He shows his strength by
shooting at a tree, which falls over. He kills the grizzly bear with his arrow, skins
it, and takes his father's scalp. He returns, and he and his sister move camp.

41. THE MINK (VAEU 23).—Mink has three brothers. He is the lover of the Grizzly- **(170)**
Bear woman, and Grizzly Bear tries to kill the brothers. He gives them a basket
which he said contains berries. As soon as Bear is gone, Mink opens the basket

---

[1] Algonquin (E. R. Young, Algonquin Indian Tales, p. 246).
Apache, Jicarilla (Goddard PaAM 8:237).
Arikara (Dorsey CI 17:143).
Caddo (Dorsey CI 41:104).
Cherokee (Mooney RBAE 19:271).
Cora (K. T. Preuss, Die Nayarit-Expedition, Leipzig, 1912, p. 209).
Eskimo, Asiatic (Bogoras BBAE 68).
Natchez (Swanton JAFL 26:202 [No. 10]).
Oaxaca (P. Radin and A. Espinosa, El Folklore de Oaxaca, pp. 124, 193; Boas JAFL 25:214).
Ojibwa (Radin GSCan 43, 44).
Piegan (Michelson JAFL 29:409).
Sanpoil (Gould MAFLS 11:111).
Tarahumare (Lumholtz, Unknown Mexico, 1:302).
Thompson (Teit JE 8:395; JAFL 29:326).
Zuñi (Cushing, Zuñi Folk-Tales, p. 277).
See Dähnhardt, Natursagen 4:54; Araucanian, Brazil, Cherokee, NANegro, Tupi; for North American
    negroes, also Parsons JAFL 30:174, 225; also Kamerun, Cross River (Alfred Mansfeld, Urwald
    Dokumente, Berlin, 1908, p. 224); Hottentot (Leonhard Schultze, Aus Namaland und Kalahari,
    Jena, 1907, p. 528); Visayan (Millington and Maxfield JAFL 20:315).
[2] See discussion Boas RBAE 31:611, 659, 687, 718, 868.
[3] Apache, Jicarilla (Mooney AA 11:210).
Arapaho (Dorsey and Kroeber FM 5:11).
Assiniboin (Lowie PaAM 4:157).
Blackfoot (Wissler PaAM 2:57).
Chinook (Boas BBAE 20:21).
Cree (Russell, Expl. in Far North 205).
Fox (Jones PAES 1:103).
Gros Ventre (Kroeber PaAM 1:87).
Hupa (Goddard UCal 1:128 [sea-saw]).
Lillooet (Teit JAFL 25:370).
Modoc (Curtin 154).
Osage (Dorsey FM 7:26).
Pawnee (Dorsey CI 59:179, 474, also 235 [slide]).
Ponca (Dorsey CNAE 6:161; JAFL 1:74; Am Ant 9:97).
Quinault (Farrand JE 2:82).
Seshelt (Hill-Tout JAI 34:49).
Shoshoni (Lowie PaAM 2:260, 262).
Thompson (Teit JE 8:252).
Yana (Sapir UCal 9:234 [elastic tree]).

and finds it contains bear hair with which he was to be poisoned. Bear sees this and rushes after them. He kills the brothers. Only Mink survives. Mink makes a small pit and throws something into it, which is transformed into a girl. He throws (171) her away. He repeats this experiment, and finds a boy, whom he raises. When he sees the Bear on the other side of the river, he jumps into the water. The Bear tries to get him, makes a raft, drifts down the river. Here Mink kills him. He meets Bear's brothers, transforms himself into a fly, but is seen by the Bears. Then he transforms himself into a very small fly, which the Bear swallows without noticing it. He kills the Bear with his knife.[1] At Bonner's Ferry he builds a salmon weir under an overhanging rock. Every day the weirs are found empty, except that of Mink. The people see a meteor coming down, which empties the weirs. The meteor is a basket. The thieves leave the basket and carry the fish back. The animals discover that the rope by which the meteor is let down is a snake. Owl and Lynx cut the snake. They find that in the basket there are a buffalo, a mountain goat, a frog, and a turtle. These are transformed into stones. The people try to kill the frog by striking it with sticks, but they are unable to do so. For this reason the place is named Strong Belly.

225   42. WOLF (No. 67).—Wolf is married to Doe. He does not like the moccasins that 227 his wife makes, and therefore goes to fight his brothers-in-law. The Buck hides his wife and son in a hole, and transforms himself into a deer. He goes up a mountain. The Wolves kill the people, but can not find Wolf's brother-in-law. Wolf follows the tracks of his brother-in-law; but whenever he reaches one mountain, Buck is on the following one. Finally Buck goes to his father's father, the fish K!ɛ́k!om', who is 229 smoking. The Fish throws his mittens on the Buck, and thus hides him. Wolf enters Fish's tent, but does not see his brother-in-law. He asks for him, but the Fish denies having seen him. Fish makes the figure of a deer of grass, throws it out of the smoke hole, and it becomes a deer, which stands on the other side of the river. When Wolf sees it, he swims across the river in order to get it. Then the Fish launches his 231 canoe and goes aboard with Buck. They catch up with Wolf and kill him.

43. SKUNK[2] (No. 68).—Skunk and his younger brother Fisher live in one tent; Frog and his granddaughters Chipmunk and Big Chipmunk, in another one. The Chipmunks want to get meat; and Frog sends them to Fisher, but warns them to beware of Skunk. She tells them that Fisher always gets home in the evening. The girls wait at some distance from the tent. Skunk causes his guardian spirit to pound bones in the tent, while he himself goes out dressed like Fisher. Big Chipmunk 233 insists that the person who came out is Fisher, and finally persuades her elder sister to go in with her. When Fisher comes home, he sends Skunk for water. Skunk is afraid to go far away, and goes to his own spring. Fisher sends him back to get water from his spring[3] and to bring in the game. He gives him a tump-line made of entrails.[4] 235 Skunk is afraid that Fisher may take the girls, but has to go. Fisher causes a gale to overtake Skunk. The tump-line breaks repeatedly, and he is almost frozen to death. Meanwhile Fisher finds the girls, and with them leaves the tent. He tells them to

[1] See discussion in Boas RBAE 31:611, 659, 687, 718, 868.
[2] Achomawi (Dixon JAFL 21:163).
  Coos (Frachtenberg-St. Clair JAFL 22:35).
  Kathlamet (Boas, BBAE 26:129).
  Shuswap (Teit JE 2:752).
  Takelma (Sapir UPenn 2:65).
  Ute, Uinta (Mason JAFL 23:311).
  Yana (Sapir UCal 9:133).
  See also Lillooet (Teit JAFL 25:318); Shuswap (Teit JE 2:684); Thompson (Teit MAFLS 6:67; JE 8:243, 345).
[3] Shoshoni (Lowie PaAM 2:238, 239).
  Shuswap (Teit JE 2:718).
[4] Lillooet (Teit JAFL 25:309).
  Thompson (Teit MAFLS 6:26; JE 8:297; Boas, Sagen 18).
  Ute, Uinta (Mason JAFL 23:321).

remove all the rotten bones, because one of these is Skunk's guardian. They go
first to Chipmunk's hole, then to Big Chipmunk's, but both are too small. They
climb a tree at the place where Fisher lives. When Skunk succeeds in getting home,
he finds the tent empty. and after searching finds a single rotten bone that Big Chipmunk had left. Then he pursues the fugitives. By means of the bone, which is   237
his guardian spirit, he finds the tree. He shoots it with his fluid, and it falls.[1] Fisher
and his wife jump to another tree, but finally they fall down and are killed. Skunk
restores the sisters, and they go to Big Chipmunk's tent. It is too small, but by
shooting his fluid into it he enlarges it. They sleep in the tent. When Skunk is
sound asleep, the women leave him and go to search for Fisher. They reduce the   239
size of the tent by means of their supernatural power, so that it becomes as small as
before. They restore Fisher to life and move away. When Skunk is awakened, he
finds himself in the narrow hole, unable to move. He succeeds in enlarging it a
little by means of his fluid, and sees an opening. He pushes out his musk bag at the
end of his bow; and Raven, who happens to fly by, takes it away. Skunk cuts off   241
his legs and his arms.[2] and puts one part of his body after another out of the hole. When
outside, he puts himself together, but parts of his entrails have been lost. He puts
leaves in their place. Raven takes the musk bag to his village. He transforms it   243
into a pup, and they play with it. Skunk reaches the village and is given food, which,
however. falls right through him. He goes out, and sees the children playing with
the pup. He makes signs to it, and the pup runs towards him. It is retransformed
into his musk bag, which he takes away.[3]

44. THE STAR HUSBAND [4] (No. 70).—Two girls sleep outside and see many stars.   247
One of them says that she wants to marry a small star that she sees there. When she
wakes, she finds herself sitting next to an old man, who tells her that he is the star.
The large stars are young men; the small stars, old ones. She goes out digging roots,   249
and against the commands of the people breaks the ground near a tree. She can look
down, and sees her relatives walking about. She makes a rope and lets herself down.
At home she tells what has happened, and on the following morning she is found dead,
killed by the star.

45. THE WOMAN AND THE GIANT [5] (2 versions: No. 30 and VAEU 23:171).   *First*   43
Version.—A woman who is traveling with her child meets a Giant. The Giant asks

---

[1] Shuswap (Teit JE 2:636).
  Takelma (Sapir U Penn 2:53).
  Thompson (Teit MAFLS 6:35, 82; JE 8:208, 253).
  See also JAFL 25:259.
[2] Takelma (Sapir U Penn 2:93).
  Yana (Sapir U Cal 9:124).
[3] See Boas R BAE 31:569, No. 38; 706.
[4] Arikara (Dorsey CI 17:14).
  Assiniboin (Lowie PaAM 4:171).
  Blackfoot (Wissler PaAM 2:58; W. McClintock, The Old North Trail 491).
  Caddo (Dorsey CI 41:27, 29).
  Chilcotin (Farrand JE 2:28).
  Dakota (Riggs CNAE 9:90).
  Gros Ventre (Kroeber PaAM 1:100).
  Kaska (Teit JAFL 30:457).
  Koasati (personal information from Dr. J. R. Swanton).
  Micmac (Rand 160, 306).
  Otoe (Kercheval JAFL 6:199).
  Pawnee (Dorsey CI 59: 56; Grinnell JAFL 2:197).
  Quinault (Farrand JE 2:108).
  Shuswap (Teit JE 2:687).
  Songish (Boas, Sagen 62).
  Tahltan (Teit MS).
  Thompson (Teit MAFLS 11:7).
  Ts'ets'aut (Boas JAFL 10:39).
  Wichita (Dorsey CI 21:298).
  See also Arapaho (Dorsey and Kroeber FM 5:321); Crow (Simms FM 2:301).
[5] See discussion in Boas R BAE 31:762 *et seq.*; also Chippewayan (Lofthouse, Transactions Canadian
Institute 10:50).
  Sanpoil (Gould MAFLS 11:105).

her how it happens that her son is so white. She tells him that she cooked him in
45 order to make him white. He asks to be treated in the same way, and is killed.

(171) *Second Version.*—A woman has gone out berrying, and puts her child down in the grass. A giant steps up to her and asks why the child, whom he calls his brother, is so white. The woman says that this is the result of roasting. The giant asks to
(172) be roasted too. The woman puts him into an oven, covers him over with stones, lights the fire, and kills him.—A giant who sits on the bank of a river is overtaken by some boys, who kill him by shooting him from behind.

83   46. THE GIANT (2 versions: Nos. 51 and 76). *First Version.*—Two brothers go out hunting. The elder one shoots a bighorn sheep. He starts a fire, and dries the meat over the fire. He roasts a piece of the meat, and does not like the taste. Then he cuts a piece of flesh from his body, roasts it, and likes the taste. He eats himself entirely. The younger brother goes out to search after him. He sees a fire, and hears his brother saying, "I love my brother, and it will take me two days to eat him." The transformed brother pursues him, strikes him with his intestines, and kills him. The elder brother's wife goes out to search for her husband. Something tells her to
85 put sharp stones on her clothing. She does so. The man strikes her with his intestines, but tears them. She runs home and tells the people what has happened. They move camp. The man's wife and his son alone remain. Crane stays near by. The transformed man comes. He takes the child and tears it in two. The woman offers to wash it, goes out, and runs away. She tells the people what has happened. Crane hides in a hole near a steep bank. When the man pursues his wife, he passes this place, and Crane kicks him into the water, where he is drowned.

273   *Second Version.*—A young man goes hunting sheep and dries the meat. Suddenly he sees two slices of meat, which he eats and which he likes. When he sits down, he feels a pain, and sees that he has eaten of his own flesh. He cuts one piece after
275 another from his body until only bones and intestines remain. After three days one of his elder brothers goes to look for him. When he finds him, the transformed brother says that he loves him, but kills and eats him. Thus he kills all his brothers. The
277 youngest one is warned by his guardian spirit. The boy makes his escape, and tells the people to leave. The hunter's wife stays behind with her son. When the man arrives, he holds his son tightly and makes him dance. The woman pretends that she wants to wash the child, and runs away. When she reaches the people, they make
279 a hole next to a cliff, and one of them kicks him into the water, where he is drowned.

55   47. RABBIT, COYOTE, WOLF, AND GRIZZLY BEAR (No. 45).—Rabbit runs past Coyote,
56 saying that he has been scared. Coyote follows, passes Wolf, and tells him that he has been scared. Wolf passes Grizzly Bear and scares him. They all reach a prairie,
57 where they sit down and ask one another what frightened them. One accuses the other, while Rabbit finally says that snow fell from the trees and frightened him. They laugh and separate.

26   48. LAME KNEE [1] (No. 20).—The chief orders the people to break camp in order to plant tobacco. The young men tell Lame Knee to take away the chief's wife. He
27 holds her when she comes to draw water. The chief is told that Lame Knee is holding his wife. He sends repeatedly, ordering him to let her go, but Lame Knee refuses.
28 Then the chief cuts off Lame Knee's head, which rolls away smiling. He cuts off his arms and his legs. When the people are asleep, they hear the voice of Lame Knee, who has come back to life. He kills the chief and marries his wives.

28   49. THE YOUTH WHO KILLED THE CHIEFS [2] (No. 21).—The daughter of an old man is married to a chief, who kills all her sons, while he allows her daughters to live.
29 The chief hunts buffaloes, but is stingy, and does not give any food to his parents-in-law. The woman has a son, but conceals the fact from her husband.[3] When the

---

[1] Blackfoot (Wissler PaAM 2:143).
[2] Arapaho (FM 5:298).
  Blackfoot (Wissler PaAM 2:53; Grinnell, Lodge Tales 29).
  See also Dakota (Riggs CNAE 9:101); Omaha (Dorsey CNAE 6:48).
[3] See RBAE 31:857.

boy grows up, the woman tells her father to shoot a buffalo cow. The chief demands it,
but the woman's father refuses to give it up. When the chief tries to kill the woman's 30
father, her son shoots him. The youth enters the chief's tent, kills his wives,
and gives the tent to his mother. He goes traveling, and reaches a village in which
the people are hungry. A woman gives him a little to eat; and when he is not satis- 31
fied, she tells him that the chief is rich but stingy. The youth goes into his tent.
The chief becomes a rattlesnake, which he kills. Then he gives meat to the people.
He goes down the river to another village, where the same happens with the Grizzly- 32
Bear chief. He goes on down the river, and the same happens to the Buffalo chief. 33

50. Little Sun (No. 71).—The chief at Fish Hawk Nest, Crazy Old Woman, wants 249
to go to war, and calls for a runner. Little Sun offers to go. He starts when the people
begin to play ball in the afternoon. He arrives at the place to which he had been sent,
which is far distant, before the people stop playing ball in the evening. He arrives
dragging his blanket. He tells Chief Not Sitting Down Long what is wanted. He tells 251
the chief that his people are to work for three days preparing bows and arrows, and
then to start. They are to meet at Low Hills. In the afternoon Little Sun starts
back, dragging his blanket, and arrives at Fish Hawk Nest in the evening. After
four days they start, and meet at Low Hills at noon. Among the warriors are Pipe
Lighter and his friend. They are hungry. Pipe Lighter shoots at a burl on a tree, 253
which is transformed into a bear. The first time his arrow strikes, it sounds like wood.
The second time he kills the bear. The people are afraid of him. When the people
are hungry again, his friend spears a piece of wood in the water, which is transformed
into a charr. The first time he strikes it, it is wood; the second time, it is a fish. In the
evening they reach the village of their enemies. Two scouts, Lamb Hat and Raven 255
Hat, go out and see the village of the enemy. The people (except one man, who is
suspicious) think they are animals. Lamb Hat transforms himself into a lamb, and 257
is able, with the other warriors, to go down a slope of loose stones without making
any noise. Crazy Old Woman's son, Rattling Claws, goes with Not Sitting Down Long,
who captures Chief Hare Lip, and shouts that he is holding him. Rattling Claws
counts coup for the chief. Early in the morning all the enemies have been killed.
The one man, who had been suspicious, keeps away. In the morning he sees that 259
the village has been destroyed. The warriors spare him and let him carry the news
back to his people. While the warriors are going back, Rattling Claws brags, and
says that Chief Not Sitting Down Long counted coup for him. The chief becomes
angry, and wishes him to be killed by a grizzly bear. They arrive at Fish Hawk Nest,
Rattling Claws going ahead, indicating that he is chief warrior. Chief Crazy Old
Woman tells them to rest and then to go out hunting. Rattling Claws and one of his 261
elder brothers go hunting bighorn sheep. The elder brother tries to frighten him,
saying that he is being pursued by a bear. When a grizzly bear is really coming, and
the elder brother warns Rattling Claws, he does not believe him, and is killed by the
bear. This is due to the wish of Chief Not Sitting Down Long, whom he had offended.

51. Pine Cone (No. 72).—Two friends, Lamb Hat and Wolverene Hat, are hunting 261
mountain goat. When enemies come, the one transforms himself into a mountain 263
goat, which climbs the steep mountain. The other one becomes a wolverene, and
runs back along a ledge upon which they are standing. The enemies pursue them,
and the friends reach an old man named Pine Cone, who is hunting muskrats. They
warn him, but he disbelieves them. When he sees the enemies coming, he hides, and 265
puts his blanket over a figure made of rushes, intending to deceive the enemies. The
enemies find him, and he tries to shoot them. His arrows hit them, but do not pierce
them. His last arrow has no point, and with it he kills one of the enemies, who then
attack him. He tries to ward off their arrows with his bow, but is killed. The enemies go back. When the people of the two friends reach the lake, they find the body
of Pine Cone.

267   52. THE KUYO'KWE (No. 73).—The people are moving camp, and a woman is left behind boiling bones. The Kuyo'kwe arrive and look into the tent. They enter, take off their clothing, and the woman makes a fire for them and gives them to eat. She throws melting fat into the fire, which startles the Kuyo'kwe. She takes this
269 opportunity to run away. She carries a torch. The Kuyo'kwe pursue her. She reaches a cliff and throws down the torch, while she herself jumps aside.[1] The Kuyo'kwe believe that they are still following her, and fall down the precipice. The woman follows the people, and tells her son to take the property of the dead enemies. Thus the boy becomes a chief.

269   53. THE GREAT EPIDEMIC (No. 74).—During an epidemic all the people die. One man only is left. He travels from one camp to another, trying to find survivors.
271 He sees some tracks, and thinks that some people must have survived. He notices what he believes to be two black bears, follows them, and finds a woman and her daughter. He marries first the woman, then her daughter, and the present Kutenai are their descendants.

273   54. THE GIANT (No. 75).—The people in a village are eaten by a Giant. An old couple live at the end of the village. The Giant enters their tent, and says that he will eat them in the morning. The old woman wakes up. She calls her husband, who cuts off the Giant's head.

26   55. THE MAN AND THE WASPS (No. 19).

33   56. THE WHITE MAN (No. 22).—A white man is chopping off a branch on which he is sitting. He is warned, but continues until he falls down.

34   57. THE FRENCHMAN AND HIS DAUGHTERS [2] (No. 23).—A Frenchman has three daughters. When walking in the woods, he finds a stump, which is the home of the Grizzly Bear. The Grizzly Bear demands to marry the Frenchman's daughter. He
35 takes the eldest daughter to the stump. She marries the Grizzly Bear, but runs away in the evening because she is afraid. The same happens with the next daughter.
36 The third daughter goes to the Grizzly Bear and stays with him. The young woman's mother goes to see how she fares. During the night the Grizzly Bear is invisible. In the morning she sees him again.

279   58. THE MOTHER-IN-LAW TABOO (No. 77).—The men were ashamed to talk to their mothers-in-law. Only those who disliked their mothers-in-law talked to them.

---

[1] Blackfoot (Uhlenbeck VKAWA 13:171, 197).
  Kaska (Teit JAFL 30:431).
  Shoshoni (Lowie Pa AM 2:273).
  Ts'ets'aut (Boas JAFL 10:45).
  Ute, Uinta (Mason JAFL 23:316).
[2] See Bolte und Polivka, Anmerkungen zu den Kinder- u. Hausmärchen der Brüder Grimm, 2: 229.

IV. VOCABULARY

The following vocabulary contains a selection of the more important stem-words, prefixes, and suffixes, together with examples showing the use of these stems. So far as possible, these examples have been taken from the texts. The Kutenai-English vocabulary has been arranged in such order that sounds which are closely related stand near together. The order selected is, vowels, labials, dentals, palatals, velars, laterals. This results in the following order of sounds:

a	y	p	t	k	l
$\iota,\ i$	w	$p!$	$t!$	$k!$	
$o,\ u,\ \upsilon$	h	m	s	q	
			ts	$q!$	
			$ts!$	x	
			n		

The long lists of nouns beginning with $a_a{}'k$- have been placed together. I have embodied in this list a long list of nouns collected by Dr. Chamberlain, which I have not checked. I have kept these separate, because it is impossible to distinguish between $a_a{}'k$-, $a_a{}'k!$-, $a_a{}'q$-, $a_a{}'q!$-.

In the verbal forms I have generally given the stem without ending and without prefix. This is indicated by hyphens at the beginning and at the end of the word. Prefixes have been marked by a following hyphen and the abbreviation pr., although they may also take verbal prefixes. Suffixes have been marked by a preceding hyphen and the abbreviation suff. References are to page and line of the preceding texts; 256.161, for instance, means p. 256, line 161. Words marked Kel. were obtained from a young Lower Kutenai named James Keluwat; those marked Aitken were collected by Mr. Robert T. Aitken, who accompanied me part of the time I spent among the Kutenai.

Kutenai-English

$a{}^{\cdot}$ oh!

a- pr. out of. (See an-, ak-)

-a- verbal stem 256.182

-ai- $>$ -$as+n$ (see -as- two)

$(n')ao{}^{\cdot\prime}k!^ue{}^{\cdot}$ the one, the other 64.120. (See $ok!u$-)

-ay- to steal, to cheat 38.8; 244.7

313

-awut- to shout for joy 188.44

-apak!ın- to pin, to stick into 138.244; 170.105

-apıs- to be straight 174.224

apko·k!u head of tent 134.174

am·a·k land, country 76.73

(a·ma′le·t post 94.157 [perhaps a$_a$·-male·t])

at but, however

-at- to name 122.56

ata- pr. above 256.161. (See na′$_a$ta)

-as- to be two 236.129

ats- pr. stealthily, secretly 180.32

atsa′wats! husband's brother 122.44

a′tse· brother's wife

a′tso pottery dish, kettle, bucket 32.12

(a$_a$′tsu·′la bag 17.5 [perhaps a$_a$·k-tsula])

-atskup- to break wind 48.40

ats!po· wolverene 74.19

ats!mił great-grandfather 278.12

an- pr. out of (away from speaker) 178.13

a·n- pr. more 56.10

a·′na necklace 214.61

a′n·an magpie 4.15

-anaxa′m- to go out 90.59

-anaxaka- to go to war (= to go out for something?) 76.72

-anaxe· to hunt (= to go out?) 124.67

-anık!e·· to be heavy 128.45

-antsa- to practice witchcraft 76.82

antsu- pr. behind 202.274

-a′nxo- to reach, to overtake

ak- pr. out of (toward speaker) 180.37

akamın- pr. around 136.231

a$_a$·k- prefix of noun[1]

  a$_a$′ma′le·t tent pole, post

  a$_a$′tsu·′la bag 17.5

  a$_a$·ka′wu tent cover

  a$_a$·kawu′k!o· parting of hair

  a$_a$·ka′mał corral (-kamal)

  (akamın- around. [See in alphabetical order preceding this group])

  a′$_a$·ka·mt belt 74.27 (-ka·mt)

  a′$_a$·ka·k water hole 38.9

  a$_a$·ka′k!o· trap 162.42

  a$_a$·kaqł·′łna·m eye 4.14 (-qłił)

  a$_a$·ka′q!ne· face 72.5 (-q!ne·)

  a$_a$·kaxapa′kna·m orbit 182.20 (-xapak). (See a$_a$·kın·ł·alaxapa′kna·m)

  a$_a$·kaxa′pqle· rapids, cascade 154.226, 235 (-xapqle·)

  a$_a$·kaxmała′na·m flesh 42.37 (-xma-la)

  a$_a$·ka·ł bag

  a$_a$·key hand 142.36 (-hey)

  a$_a$·kıt.la′na·m tent 11.4 (-t.la)

  a$_a$·kıts tent pole, stick 14.14 (-[ı]ts)

  a$_a$·kıtsk!a′la·k branch of a tree 33.9 (-tsk!a·-lak)

  a$_a$·kı′tsqa fish trap 176.253 (-kıts-)

---

[1] All nouns of this group have been entered here, because in many cases the exact form of the stem has not been ascertained.

$a_a\cdot k$- prefix of noun

$a_a\cdot k\imath tsq!ahe'yna\cdot m$ finger (-ts-q!a-hey)

$a_a\cdot k\imath tsq!ackama'lak$ talons of birds (-ts-q!a-hey[?]-ka-malak)

$a_a\cdot k\imath tsq!a'kna\cdot m$ toe (-ts-q!a-k) Kel.

$a_a\cdot k\imath tsq!a'kam$ a root found in swamps (Aitken)

$a_a\cdot k\imath tsq!alu'pta\cdot k$ hoof of deer or cattle

$a_a\cdot k\imath tsla'_ame\cdot$ plain

$a_a\cdot k\imath tslaq!o''na$ berry cake (Aitken)

$a_a\cdot k\imath'ts!qa\cdot l$ bark of tree (-ts!qal)

$a_a\cdot k\imath ts!ka'k\imath\cdot l$ coal (-ts!kakil)

$a_a\cdot k\imath ts!la'e\cdot n$ tree 3.9 (-ts!lae·n)

$a_a\cdot k\imath n\imath'k!na\cdot m$ thigh, parents 98.244

$a_a\cdot k\imath nd\cdot alaxapa'kna\cdot m$ orbit 274.30. (See $a_a\cdot kaxapa'kna\cdot m$)

$a_a\cdot k\imath no\cdot malnoka\cdot'kna\cdot m$ embroidered vest (Aitken)

$a_a\cdot k\imath nu'm\cdot o\cdot k!$ cliff 2.4 (-nom·ok!)

$a_a\cdot k\imath noka'kna\cdot m$ rib 80.189 (-nokak)

$a_a\cdot k\imath nusu'k!po\cdot n$ place with scattered trees 72.74 (-nusuk!po·n)

$a_a\cdot k\imath nu'kwe_it$ pitfall 190.33

$a_a\cdot knukxume\cdot k$ it is rock 112.80

$a_a\cdot k\imath noq^ua'_ako$ pitchwood, torch 136.221; 266.36 (-nuq^ua-ko)

$a_a\cdot k\imath nuqo'yka\cdot k$ fist (-n[u]-qoyka-k). (See $a_a\cdot qo'ytka\cdot k$ wrist)

$a_a\cdot k\imath nu'qle\cdot$ tomahawk 80.173

$a_a\cdot k\imath nuqle'et$ prairie 192.60 (-nuq-leet)

$a_a\cdot k\imath noq!ota'tit$ a small hawk

$a_a\cdot k\imath nu'q!yuk$ $ya'q!e\cdot t$ tobacco seeds ($a_a\cdot k\imath nu'q!yuk$ flower Kel.)

$a_a\cdot k\imath nuq!ma'_ana$ bird's tail 152.181

$a_a\cdot k\imath nuq!la'nuk$ flat stones 170.117 (-nuq!la-nuk). (See $a_a\cdot k\imath ts!la'nuk$)

$a_a\cdot k\imath nuq!la\cdot nu'k!^{u}e\cdot n$ sharp, flat stones

$a_a\cdot k\imath nuq!^ula\cdot k!a'_ako\cdot$ plank, board 170.125

$a_a\cdot k\imath nuq!^uloxona\cdot'tit$ a small, gray bird

$a_a\cdot k\imath nuqlo'la\cdot m$ bald-headed eagle

$a_a\cdot k\imath nuxo'_unuk$ brook 162.37 (-nuxonuk)

$a_a\cdot k\imath nu'la\cdot m$ snake 52.10

$a_a\cdot k\imath nu'lma\cdot k$ marrow 15.14 (-nulmak)

$a_a\cdot k\imath nmi'tuk$ river 30.8 (-nmit-uk)

$a_a\cdot k\imath nku'ma\cdot l$ (buffalo) calf

$a_a\cdot k\imath nk!a'_alik$ toe (probably $a_a\cdot k\imath nq!a'l\imath k$ [-nq!a point; -l\imath k foot])

$a_a\cdot k\imath nk!u'ma\cdot l$ cradle 112.43 (-nk!umal)

$a_a\cdot k\imath'nqa\cdot t$ fat on top of tail of bighorn sheep 258.239

$a_a\cdot k\imath'nqa\cdot n$ ($a_a\cdot k\imath'nq!a\cdot n$? Kel.) top

  $a_a\cdot k\imath nqanu'qla\cdot m$ crown of head

$a_a\cdot k\imath nqa\cdot'lna\cdot m$ forehead

$a_a\cdot k\imath'nqo\cdot$ frame of tent

$a_a\cdot k\imath nqo\cdot'wa$ wing, feather 74.49 (-nqowa)

$a_a\cdot k\imath nqu'm'yu$ shoulder

$a_a\cdot k\imath'nqo\cdot l$ stem of tobacco plant

$a_a\cdot k\imath nq!a'wo\cdot k$ stick 118.192 (-nq!a-wok)

$a_a\cdot k\imath nq!a'qa$ arrow point 264.68 (-nq!a-qa)

$a_a\cdot k\imath nq!a'qa\cdot t$ fish tail (-nq!a-qat)

$a_a\cdot k\imath nq!a'lqa$ sinew 74.26

$a_a\cdot k\imath nq!u'ts\cdot ak$ fawn 172.165

$a_a\cdot k\imath nq!u'ko\cdot$ fire 38.4 (-nq!u-ko·)

$a_a\cdot k\imath nxamulu'la\cdot k$ a piece of dried meat 230.11

$a_a\cdot k\imath nlu'm\imath n$ arm above elbow

$a_a\cdot k\imath nlqa'yka\cdot k$ whirlpool

a_a'k- prefix of noun

(-$ak\iota k$- see in alphabetical order following this group)

a_a'$k\iota k\iota nqowax̣oniyi'e\cdot s$ flapping of wings (-k-$nqowa\cdot x̣o$-$me\cdot k$)

a_a'$k\iota'kpuk!$ backside 18.7 (-$kpuk!$)

a_a'$k\iota kts!la'nuk$ flat stone 64.84 (-k-$tsl!a$-nuk). (See a_a'$k\iota nuq!la'nuk$)

a_a'$k\iota kne'la\cdot m$ hair rings made of brass spirals

a_a'$k\iota kqapx̣oniyi'e\cdot s$ flapping of wings (-k-$qa[p]$-$x̣o$-$me\cdot k$)

a_a'$k\iota kq!alanmi'tuk$ bend in river (Aitken) (-k-$q!ala$-$nmit$-uk)

a_a'$k\iota kq!a\backslash lale'\iota t$ hollow place in ground (-k-$q!ala$-$le\iota t$)

a_a'$k\iota kq!a\backslash lawuq!e'\iota t$ hollow place in mountain side (-k-$q!ala$-wuq-$le\iota t$)

a_a'$k\iota kq!a\backslash lak!aq!u'nuk$ hollow place with dry timber 260.2 (-k-$q!ala$-$k!aq!unuk$)

a_a'$k\iota k.le'yam$ name 76.101 (-$k.l$-$e\cdot yam$)

a_a'$k\iota k.lite'yam$ noise 148.99 (-$k.l\iota t$-$e\cdot yam$)

a_a'$k\iota k.lu'na\cdot m$ village, town 31.10 (-$k.lu$)

a_a'$k\iota q!ye\cdot t$ talking 138.275

a_a'$k\iota lalaqu'no\cdot k$ cave under water 80.152 (probably a_a'$k\iota q!alaqʊ'nok$, from a_a'$k[\iota]$-$q!ala$-qu-nuk)

a_a'$k\iota l\iota'nqan$ cyclone, dust storm

a_a'$k\iota'lwey$ heart, mind, innermost part 62.49 (-$lwey$)

a_a'$k\iota'lma\cdot k!$ cherry (Prunus demissa) 6.11 (-$lma\cdot k!$)

a_a'$k\iota lmi'y\iota t$ sky 72.12 (-$lmiy\iota t$)

a_a'$k\iota lno'hos$ star 17.9 (-$lnohos$)

a_a'$k\iota lk!aku'ko\cdot t$ season 180.23 (-$lk!aku$-kut)

a_a'$k\iota lq!a'n\iota l$ song Kel.

a_a'$k\iota lq!an\cdot otsa'ko$ $ma_ak!$ burnt bone. (See a_a'$q!ono'\mathrm{u}ko\cdot$)

a_a'$k\iota lq!aku'pk!o\cdot$ fence post, rail

a_a'$k\iota lq!a'lukp$ bunch of dew hoofs of deer 216.111 (-$lq!al$-ukp). (See a'_a'$kukp$ claw, finger nail)

a_a'$k\iota lq!aluq!pwaq!$ (a_a'$k\iota lkalu'kwak$) a black bird with white spots, size of a robin (Aitken)

a_a'$k\iota'lxo\cdot$ body Kel

(-ako_u- see in alphabetical list following this group)

a_a'$kowa'sk!o\cdot$ place for drying meat 272.9 (-was-$k!o$)

a_a'$ko\cdot'wal$ onion

a_a'$kowa'lwo\cdot k$ birch (-$wo\cdot k$ tree, wood)

a_a'$kuwuk.le'\iota t$ mountain 76.97 (-wuk-$le\iota t$)

a_a'$kumaql\iota'lna\cdot m$ eyelashes (-$q!il$ eye)

a_a'$ku'me\cdot$ wind

a_a'$ko'mo\cdot$ fruit of Viburnus opulus

a_a'$kumle'\iota t$ frost (-$le\iota t$ country, weather)

a_a'$ko'\mathrm{u}nal$ three-pointed fish spear

a_a'$ko'\mathrm{u}ka\cdot k$ neck

a'_a'$kukp$ claw, finger nail 58.20 (-ukp)

a_a'$kukts\iota'ke\cdot n$ bladder 64.100

a_a'$kuk.lako'wum$ locust 1.7

a_a'$kok!\mathrm{u}ats\iota'nko\cdot$ hair ribbon, worn in front 126.15

a_a'$kok!\mathrm{u}a'tsʋum$ cinch (-wum belly)

a_a'$kok!\mathrm{u}atsk!a'k!o\cdot$ ear ornament 130.103

a_a'$kok!\mathrm{u}ats\iota tsq!a'yna\cdot m$ finger ring (-ιts-$q!a$-hey)

a_a'$kok!\mathrm{u}atska'lma$ bridle, halter

a_a'$ko_\mathrm{u}k!ala'_akna\cdot m$ back (-$k!a$-lak)

a_a'$kok!uplo\cdot'lal$ red cedar

a_a'$ku'k!pa\cdot k$ heel (-$k!p$-$a\cdot k$)

a_a'$kuk!pax̣ma'ko\cdot$ firebrand 210.454

$a_a\cdot k$- prefix of noun

$a_a\cdot kuk!p^\varepsilon'ka\cdot m$ root 10.12

$a_a\cdot ku'k!pma\cdot k!$ ear ornament 98.214 (-$k!p$-$ma\cdot k!$)

$a_a\cdot kuk!pla'^ymka\cdot'kna\cdot m$ nape of neck 114.99 (-$k!p$-$la'm$-$ka\cdot k$)

$a_a\cdot kuk!ple'\iota t$ foot of mountain 224.131 (-$k!p$-$le\iota t$)

$a_a\cdot ku'qwa\cdot t!$ ear (-$qwa\cdot t!$)

$a_a\cdot ko'q_uwit!$ bottle (also place name) 260.3

$a_a\cdot ko'q^uma\cdot l$ rattle

$a_a\cdot kuqmo\cdot'ko\cdot$ ashes Kel

$a_a\cdot ku'qtna\cdot m$ intestines 11.14

$a_a\cdot kuqsala'na\cdot m$ nose 11.11 (-$qsala$)

$a_a\cdot ku'qla$ skin 210.448 (-qla)

  $a_a\cdot ku'qla'nt$ clothing 9.3

$a_a\cdot kuqla'wo$ fish line, fish hook 38.14; 39.2

$a_a\cdot ku'qla\cdot'm$ hair (-ql[?]-$la'm$)

$a_a\cdot kuqla'la_ak\cdot$ buffalo drive (-$qlala$ hollow in ground) 204.307

$a_a\cdot ku'qle\cdot$ horn 3.10 (-$qle\cdot$)

$a_a\cdot kuqle'et$ an edible root (?) 248.20. (See $a_a\cdot kuq!le'et$)

$a_a\cdot kuql\iota k!a'lna\cdot m$ calf of leg 190.9 (-$ql\iota k!al$)

$a_a\cdot kuqlu'pe\cdot n$ young tree 188.19 (-$qlup\iota n$)

$a_a\cdot kuqlo\cdot laxa'na\cdot m$ beard Kel.

$a_a\cdot ku'q!ua\cdot l$ rice ($a_a\cdot q!u'qa\cdot l$?)

$a_a\cdot ku'q!o\cdot$ strawberry ($a_a\cdot q!u'ko\cdot$?)

$a_a\cdot kuq!yum\iota'n\cdot a$ side hill 204.320 (-$q!yu$-$m\iota n\cdot a$)

$a_a\cdot kuq!yu'muk!$ cliff 102.323 (-$q!yu$-$muk!$). (See $a_a\cdot k\iota n\jmath'm\cdot o\cdot k!$)

$a_a\cdot kuq!yuk!alaxwe'et$ doorway 94.147 (-$q!yu$-$k!a$-$laxweet$)

$a_a\cdot koq!yule'et$ mountain 46.7 (-$q!yu$-$leet$)

$a_a\cdot kuq!mö'ko\cdot$ ashes 10.10 (-$q!mö$-ko)

$a_a\cdot kuq!no'k^uat$ nest 114.101 (-$q!nok^uat$). (See $a_a\cdot qo\cdot'q^ua$

$a_a\cdot ku'q!nuk$ lake 44.12 (-$q!nuk$)

$a_a\cdot kuq!lay\cdot'tlin$ corpse 5.3

$a_a\cdot kuq!la\cdot'm$ hair. (See $a_a\cdot ku'qla\cdot'm$)

$a_a\cdot kuq!le'et$ berry, fruit 172.170 (-$q!$-$lcet$?)

$a_a\cdot ku'q!li\cdot l$ stripe, painting, writing 224.124 (-$q!lil$)

$a_a\cdot koxni'yam$ firewood 124.102

$a_a\cdot ko'la$ pipe stem 78.124

  $a_a\cdot kula'wo\cdot k$ pipe-stem wood (Alnus incana)

$a_a\cdot ku'lats$ penis 102.325

$a_a\cdot ku'lak$ body, meat 2.7

$a_a\cdot ku'la\cdot l$ leaf of pine; green boughs 16.6; 240.235

$a_a\cdot k\iota yu'kwa$ war bonnet 192.50

$a_a\cdot kwi'yat!$ side 142.22 (-$wiyat!$)

$a_a\cdot kw\iota t!$ wing, shoulder 98.251

$a_a\cdot kwi\cdot t!$ ice

$a_a\cdot kwi'tsa\cdot k$ elbow, ankle, wrist, knuckle

$a'_a\cdot kwum$ belly (-wum)

$a'_a\cdot kwo\cdot k$ bark for canoe

$a_a\cdot kwak^ua(\iota'se\cdot s)$ its bushes 92.112

$a_a\cdot kwo'q!la$ dried skin

$a_a\cdot kp\iota'tsna\cdot m$ food (-$p\iota ts$)

$a_a\cdot kma'na\cdot m$ trail 68.68 (-ma)

  $a_a\cdot kma'e\cdot s$ $xa'_alts\iota n$ (=dog's trail) Milky Way

$a_a\cdot kma'k!tsuk$ yellow fluid 220.28 (-$mak!ts$-uk)

$a_a\cdot kma'q!a\cdot n$ egg, testicle 102.300 (-$maq!an$)

$a_a{}^{\cdot}k$- prefix of noun

(-*akme*- see in alphabetical order following this group)

$a_a{}^{\cdot}km\varepsilon nuq\hbar u'nuk$ white stone 88.13 (-*mɛnqłu-nuk*)

$a_a{}^{\cdot}kmoq!o{\cdot}'ma{\cdot}l$ tobacco 62.44

$a_a{}^{\cdot}kmoxo'na{\cdot}m$ seat 192.66 (-*mo-xo*)

$a_a{}^{\cdot}kmölu'pu{\cdot}q$ lungs

$a_a{}^{\cdot}ktaptse'{}_ikna{\cdot}m$ forearm 7.11 (-*taptse_ik*)

  $a_a{}^{\cdot}k\varepsilon nuqtaptsɛ'k_ina{\cdot}m$ elbow

  $a_a{}^{\cdot}k\varepsilon nkataptsɛ'k_ina{\cdot}m$ wrist

$a_a{}^{\cdot}kte'{}_imo{\cdot}$ whetstone, strike-a-light 76.105 (-*te*)

$a'_a{}^{\cdot}ksaq!$ leg 3.13 (-*saq!*)

$a_a{}^{\cdot}ktsa'mał$ knife 106.383

$a_a{}^{\cdot}ktsłɛ'ka$ rawhide strap 96.193

$a_a{}^{\cdot}knenmo'xo$ act of falling 170.124 (-*nɛn-mo-xo*)

(*ak_inɛk!* see in alphabetical order following this group)

$a_a{}^{\cdot}knu'łma{\cdot}k$ marrow 15.12 (-*nułmak*). (See $a_a{}^{\cdot}k\varepsilon nu'łma{\cdot}k$)

$a_a{}^{\cdot}kxa'ska{\cdot}k$ breast piece of game 260.8

$a'_a{}^{\cdot}k.la{\cdot}'m$ head 192.73 (-*la{\cdot}'m*)

$a'_a{}^{\cdot}k.la{\cdot}t!$ arm 180.55 (-*lat!*)

$a'_a{}^{\cdot}k.lak$ back 264.85

$a_a{}^{\cdot}k.laqpɛ'sqap$ tripe 15.12

$a_a{}^{\cdot}k.la'xwe{\cdot}$ valley

$a_a{}^{\cdot}k.la'xwe{\cdot}k!$ pit for cooking 44.2 (-*łaxwe{\cdot}k!*)

$a_a{}^{\cdot}k.le'_ite{\cdot}t$ property 90.38

$a_a{}^{\cdot}k.letsate'yam$ dream (-*le_its-at-eyam*)

$a_a{}^{\cdot}k.lɛ'kna{\cdot}m$ foot, tracks 142.38 (-*lɛk*)

(-*ak.le{\cdot}l* see in alphabetical order following this group)

$a'_a{}^{\cdot}k.lo{\cdot}$ snow 126.22 (-*łu*)

$a'_a{}^{\cdot}k.to{\cdot}m'$ bat 74.51

$a_a{}^{\cdot}k.luma'na{\cdot}m$ throat 274.32 (-*luma*)

$a_a{}^{\cdot}k.lu'ma{\cdot}k$ cottonwood

$a_a{}^{\cdot}k.luk.le'et$ noise 168.81 (-*luk-leet*)

$a_a{}^{\cdot}k.luktsum{\cdot}o'ɛn$ wound 224.107

$a_a{}^{\cdot}k.to'_ukłwa$ shadow 116.144

$a_a{}^{\cdot}k!$ arrow 72.3

  $a'_a{}^{\cdot}k!wo{\cdot}k$ arrow wood, service-berry wood 92.85

$a_a{}^{\cdot}k!ayukwa'_ana{\cdot}m$ hat 88.54 (-*k!ayukwa*)

$a_a{}^{\cdot}k!awatsłe'_iko{\cdot}$ graveyard

$a_a{}^{\cdot}k!a'_ame{\cdot}$ hole, pit 192.37 (-*k!ame{\cdot}*)

$a_a{}^{\cdot}kamɛ'n{\cdot}a$ valley 14.13

$a_a{}^{\cdot}kasłaka'kna{\cdot}m$ nostril

$a_a{}^{\cdot}k!ano'_uko{\cdot}$ sharp stones 82.25

$a_a{}^{\cdot}k!anu'le{\cdot}k$ rough, sharp stone (-*k!anu'lek*)

$a_a{}^{\cdot}k!a'nqo{\cdot}(t)$ smoke hole 9.12

$a_a{}^{\cdot}k!aku'xa$ drinking-place 74.48

$a_a{}^{\cdot}k!a'_akpo{\cdot}k!$ hips

$a_a{}^{\cdot}k!ak.lu'nuk$ place with dry trees 72.69 (-*k!a-k.lunuk*)

$a_a{}^{\cdot}k!aq$ hole in ice 88.5. (See $a'_a{}^{\cdot}ka{\cdot}k$)

$a_a{}^{\cdot}k!a'qayt$ snowshoes 128.45

$a_a{}^{\cdot}k!aqła'ha{\cdot}l$ swamp

$a_a{}^{\cdot}k!a'_aq!yu$ leg part of skin 196.123

$a_a{}^{\cdot}k!a'lak$ shore

$a_a{}^{\cdot}k!ałaka'kna{\cdot}m$ navel

$a_a{}^{\cdot}k!ała'xɛkp$ anus 96.169

$a_a\cdot k$- prefix of noun

$a_a\cdot k\!alax̣uwe'et$ doorway 96.191

$a_a\cdot k\!ale'et$ largest rivers

$a_a\cdot k\!alu'k^vil$ tracks in snow 122.13

$a_a\cdot k\!alu'ko$ trail in snow 218.133

$a_a'k\!alma'na\cdot m$ mouth 64.102 ($k\!a$-lum)

$a_a\cdot k\!a'_almo\cdot k$ hoop 146.57

$a_a\cdot k\!almok^ua'et$ light 156.279

$a_a\cdot k\!o'ne_is$ saddle

$a_a\cdot k\!u'nka\cdot k$ nose, beak 164.82 (-$k\!un$-$ka\cdot k$)

$a_a\cdot k\!watsq\!a'yna\cdot m$ finger ring (-$k\!wa$-$tsq\!a$-hey)

$a_a\cdot k\!ma'ma\cdot l$ cheek

$(ak\!lan)$ } (see in alphabetical order at end of this group)
(aqa)

$a_a\cdot qa'ox̣al$ otter

$a_a\cdot qay\!'nme\cdot k$ wave

$a'_a\cdot qat$ tail (-qat) 164.82

$a_a\cdot qa\grave{}tik.lu'k^ua$ leggings 266.19

$a_a\cdot qatwu'mlat$ coat 1.8 (-qat-wum-tat)

($a_aqa't\!$- see in alphabetical order at end of this group)

$a_a\cdot qatskana'mke\cdot$ joint

$a_a\cdot qa'tsko\cdot$ flint 104.371

$a_a\cdot qanq\!yum\!'n\cdot a$ hillside (a place name) 94.135 (-qan-$q\!yu$-$m\!n\cdot a$)

$a_a\cdot qank̇knat\!tx̣ai'yam$ bed

$a_a\cdot qax̣apk.la't\!na\cdot m$ armpit (-$qax̣a$-pk-$lat\!$)

(aqa [l]- see in alphabetical order at end of this group)

$a'_a\cdot qal$ cloud

$a_a\cdot qala''mla$ scalp (-qa-$la'm$-la)

$a_a\cdot qalwi'yat\!$ side of body

$a_a\cdot qalpalne'yam$ historical tale 126.117 (-qal-pal-$me\cdot k$)

$a_a\cdot qalq\!anox̣wa'te\cdot$ myth 142.1 (-qal-$q\!anox̣wate$)

$a_a\cdot qeya'mlapskak.le\!'tske\cdot$ name of place near Nelson

$a_a\cdot qo'ytka\cdot k$ wrist (?). (See $a_a\cdot k̇nuqo'yka\cdot k$ fist)

$a_a\cdot qo'wat$ fur, hair 208.410 (-q_uwat)

$a_a\cdot qu'pa\cdot t\!$ bud

$a_a\cdot qo'pal$ cone of pine or larch 264.101

$a_a\cdot qu'ta\cdot l$ ax 15.10

$a_a\cdot qonak\!'lmak\!$ limb (-$mak\!$ bone)

$a_a\cdot qunk\!a'la\cdot k$ fog

$a_a\cdot qoka'pma\cdot l$ infant (until the time when it is taken off the cradle board)

$a_a\cdot qu'kam$ fringes (-$qukam$)

$a_a\cdot qoku'wum$ housefly

$a_a\cdot qok.la\cdot'k\!o$ saddlebag

$a_a\cdot qo'k\!a\cdot m$ beaver holes in water 130.91 (-$k\!am$)

$a_a\cdot qo\cdot'qol$ bark rope

$a_a\cdot qu'q\!wuk$ spruce-bark basket

$a_a\cdot qo\cdot'q^uat$ nest. (See $a_a\cdot kuq\!no\cdot'^uat$)

$a_a\cdot qu'qwat\!$ (or $a_a\cdot ku'qwa\cdot t\!$) ear

$a'_a\cdot quqt$ entrails 232.66

$a_a\cdot qo_uq\!k'lup$ foam 184.45

$a_a\cdot qo_uq\!k̇luṗnqo'wa$ insides of quills

$a_a\cdot qux̣ma'nuk$ gray stone 94.138 (-$qux̣ma$-nuk

$a_a\cdot qo\cdot l$ calf of leg (-$qo\cdot l$)

$a_a\cdot qo\cdot la'_aka\cdot$ a place name 104.353

a_a·k- prefix of noun

  a_a·qo_ula'qp$ɩ$k leaf 222.69

    a_a·$qoɫa$'qpe·s Apocynum cannabinum

    a_a·qo_ula'kpe·kna'na Salix desertorum

  a_a·qu'ɫum parflèche 128.42

  a_a·qulu'k!pko· stump 2.11 (-qulu-k!p-ko)

  a_a·qwatq!aɫka'kna·m eyebrow

  (-aqte· see in alphabetical order at end of this group)

  a'qto· black bear, one year old

  $\left.\begin{array}{l}(-aqtuq!^u)\\(aqsa-)\end{array}\right\}$ (see in alphabetical order at end of this group)

  a_a·qsu`k!uitna'mu summer 100.268

  $\left.\begin{array}{l}(aqts-)\\(aqts!ɩxmala-ɩ\\(-aqnɩts-)\end{array}\right\}$ (see in alphabetical order at end of this group)

  a'$_a$'qanuk anvil 216.99 (-qa-nuk ?)

  $\left.\begin{array}{l}(a'qla)\\(-aqluk!-)\\(aq!a)\end{array}\right\}$ (see in alphabetical order at end of this group)

  a_a·q!asak edge (see also aq!as in alphabetical order at end of this group) 98.220

  a'$_a$·q!a·n handle

  a_a·q!a'na·k knee 80.170; remains of broken bones 64.109

  a_a·q!a'nuk deep water

  a_a·q!anuk.le'et prairie on side of hill 182.62 (-q!an-uk-leet)

  a_a·q!a'nkme· island

  a_a·q!ankɩ'tsqa beaver dam 130.96

  a_a·q!anqats!la'e·n place with thick trees 72.72 (-q!an-qa-ɩts!lae·n)

  a_a·q!a'nq!ak notch of arrow 72.16

  a_a·q!a'nq!me·wae·k throat (?) (a_a·q!$_u$wa'e·k windpipe [?])

  a_a·q!a'nɫup milt of fish

    a_a·q!anɫup$x_a$ma'ko· lump, wart

  (a_a·qakou- see in alphabetical order at end of this group)

  a'$_a$·q!a·ɫ gloves

  a_a·q!a'le· antlers 124.99

  a_a·q!aɫka'kna·m eyebrows 78.130 (-q!aɫk[ak]). (Also a_a·q!watq!a`ɫka'kna·m)

  a_a·q!o·'wuk! thigh

  a_a·q!u'ta·ɫ fat 2.7

  a_a·q!utsa'ne·k passer-by (not used in modern speech) 60.15

  a_a·q!utsk!a'lakna'na little twig 222.69. (See a_a·kɩtsk!a'la·k)

  a_a·q!uma'$_a$wo·k willow

  a_a·q!u'na·n' tooth 188.16

  a_a·q!onakɩ'lma·k! (or a_a·qɔnakɩ'lma·k!) limbs 240.227

  a_a·q!u'na·q white blanket 174.222 (a_a·q!u'nal)

  a_a·q!uka'ma·ɫ travois 29.2

  a_a·q!ono'$_u$ko· no'$_u$k$_u$cy burnt stones 236.125. (See a_a·q!a'na·k)

  a_a·q!u'ko· strawberry, raspberry

  a_a·q!ok.lu'pqa small feathers, bird's down 86.19

  a_a·q!uk.lu'mna·m saliva 192.53 (-q!-uk-lum)

  a_a·q!o$x_u$male'et bow and arrows; "plant standing up," used for arrowshafts 190.1

  a'$_a$·q!uɫ canoe calking

  a_a·q!u'le· excrement 276.91

  a_a·q!uɫu'mko· grave

  a_a·q!u'ɫka vein, sinew

  a_a·q!u'ɫukp backside 238.197

a_aʻk- prefix of noun

WORDS in a_aʻk- RECORDED BY CHAMBERLAIN [1]

a_aʻ$kauma′kso·k$ Skukum Chuck (below Finlay Creek)
a_aʻ$kapmate·s yu·′wat!$ hornet. (See $yu·′wat!$)
$a′_a$ʻ$ka·m$ white pine, bark used for making canoes
a_aʻ$kamo·kin$ a fish, sp (?)
a_aʻ$kamtsınka·′k(na·m)$ lower jaw. (See a_aʻ$kınkamtsınka·′k[na·m]$ chin)
a_aʻ$ka′tak$ Sand Creek, Warren Creek
a_aʻ$kanakalmu′ko·$ field
a_aʻ$kanu′xo·$ Tobacco River
a_aʻ$kanu′k.le·l$ Missoula, a place about four miles from Sand Point, Idaho
a_aʻ$kanka′wok$ stick
a_aʻ$kankaʻnuk.lulmukna′e·t$ window
a_aʻ$kankaltsı′ka$ noose (in rope)
a_aʻ$kankome′ıka$ fireweed (Epilobium angustifolium)
a_aʻ$kanlixuna′e·t$ lightning
a_aʻ$kako·′wo·k$ region inhabited by the Lower Kutenai
a_aʻ$ka′k!o·s$ Finlay Creek
a_aʻ$kakolmite′yuk$ region of a camping-place on the trail to the Lower Kutenai
a_aʻ$kak.lu′lal$ (also a_aʻ$kok.lu′lal$) juniper (Juniper communis)
a_aʻ$kalat.la′tna·m$ ·old lodge
a_aʻ$kalaʻlaa′al$ sack-cloth, also name of a man
a_aʻ$kalı′kna·m$ stockings, socks
a_aʻ$kalme′et$ eye of needle
a_aʻ$kalnolatako·′ko·$ steam
a_aʻ$kiye′nık!$ Kutenai of Pend d'Oreille and St. Ignace
a_aʻ$kıskak.le′et$ Joseph's Prairie, at Cranbrook, B.C.
a_aʻ$kıtslak.lu′lal$ gum tree
a_aʻ$kıno·mukna′na$ crackers, biscuit
a_aʻ$kenı′lxal$ gunpowder
a_aʻ$ke′nuk$ thigh of bird
a_aʻ$kınukota′te·k$ a medium-sized, gray bird
a_aʻ$kınu′kmak$ three-pointed fish spear
a_aʻ$kınu′k·luk$ Kicking Horse River
a_aʻ$kınuk.luxona′ka$ Artemisia discolor; A. frigida; Bigelovia graveolens. (See a_aʻ$ku·o·k.laixuna′_ate·t$)
 a_aʻ$kınuk.luxokona′_aka awı′mo$ medicine made of Artemisia discolor
a_aʻ$kınuk.lohona′te·t$ a small, gray bird
a_aʻ$kınuxle·etna′na$ Hot Springs, Ainsworth, B.C.
a_aʻ$kı′nhas$ breast of bird
a_aʻ$kı′nskwal$ Carex scoparia
a_aʻ$kınka′ma·k$ dragon fly
a_aʻ$kınkamtsınka·′k(na·m)$ chin
a_aʻ$kınko′ko·l$ sand
a_aʻ$kınku′la·l$ wheat (Lower Kutenai a_aʻ$kinkowa′la·l$)
a_aʻ$kınqai kaxlukᵘa′tse·s$ handle of tin cup
a_aʻ$kikaku·kwi′et$ a small, gray bird
a_aʻ$kı′k.luk$ longitudinal strips on sides and bottom of canoe
a_aʻ$kila′ktsu$ (also a_aʻ$kola′ktsu$) thread
 a_aʻ$kilaktsumu·′in$ seam

---

[1] The following words have been entered as a group by themselves, because it is impossible to distinguish from the collector's orthography the sounds k, $k!$, q, $q!$.

$a_a\dot{}k$- prefix of noun

$a_a\dot{}kilalaqai$ eye of potato

$a_a\dot{}kilu\backslash k^uatspu\dot{}kna\dot{}m$ braces, suspenders. (See $a_a\dot{}kuk.lu\backslash k^uatskpu\dot{}k[na\dot{}m]$)

$a_a\dot{}kilkanoskowo\dot{}k$ Cherry Creek

$a_a\dot{}kilkaxnilko\dot{}lom$ strings for tying up parflèche

$a\prime_a\dot{}ko\dot{}$ points of bark canoe

$a_a\dot{}koa\prime pla$ stomach of partridge

$a_a\dot{}komu\prime na\dot{}m$ lower lip

$a_a\dot{}kutskakilukpo\prime xal$ small ornamental pieces on border of root kettle ($y\varepsilon\prime tske\dot{}$)

$a_a\dot{}ko\dot{}\prime nak$ apple peel, rind

$a_a\dot{}ku\prime\prime no\dot{}k$ Barnard, B.C.; also sluice box

$a_a\dot{}kuno\prime\prime kyo\dot{}k$ berries of Philadelphus Lewisii

$a_a\dot{}kunwo\dot{}k$ binding strips at pointed ends of canoe

$a_a\dot{}kunle\prime et$ frost, rime

$a_a\dot{}ko\prime u\dot{}k$ Aralia nudicaulis

$a_a\dot{}ku\prime kmat$ bladder of fish

$a_a\dot{}ko\prime kna\dot{}m$ shin

$a_a\dot{}ko\dot{}\prime kyu$ bent side strips on top of canoe

$a_a\dot{}kukwat\varepsilon\prime lil$ wad of gun

$a_a\dot{}koka\dot{}yuk!alm\varepsilon(na\dot{}m)$ (also $a_a\dot{}kokwiyok!al\varepsilon ma$) upper lip

$a_a\dot{}ko\dot{}\prime ko\dot{}$ bridge

   $huts\varepsilon tkokopk\varepsilon\prime n\dot{}e\dot{}$ I shall make a bridge (hu-ts-εt-$koko[p]$-$k\varepsilon n$-$ne\dot{}$)

$a_a\dot{}kuk!pwu$ stock of gun ($a_a\dot{}k[u]$-kp-wu)

$a_a\dot{}kukpanmitu\prime kxo\dot{}$ Bonner's Ferry ($a_a\dot{}k[u]$-$kp[a]$-$nmituk$-$xo\dot{}$)

$a_a\dot{}kukp\varepsilon tskla\prime la\dot{}k$ knot in tree ($a_a\dot{}k[u]$-kp-$[\varepsilon]tsk!alak$ butt end of branch)

$a_a\dot{}ku\prime kple\dot{}$ quill end of feather

$a_a\dot{}kukplu\prime lal$ pepper

$a_a\dot{}kuk.la\prime_i(na\dot{}m)$ palm of hand ($a_a\dot{}k[u]$-$k\dot{}la[?]$-hey-$na\dot{}m$)

$a_a\dot{}kuk.lak.l\varepsilon\prime k(na\dot{}m)$ sole of foot ($a_a\dot{}k[u]$-$k.lak[?]$-$l\varepsilon k$-$na\dot{}m$)

$a_a\dot{}ku\dot{}o\dot{}k.laixuna\prime_ate\dot{}t$ Artemisia discolor, used for headache

$a_a\dot{}kuk.la\prime xal$ Lower Kootenay River

$a_a\dot{}kuk.lu\prime k^ua$ stalk

$a_a\dot{}kuk.lu\backslash k^uatskpu\prime k(na\dot{}m)$ suspenders

$a_a\dot{}kuk.luka\prime tslo\dot{}$ moccasin string, lacings

$a_a\dot{}koq^uatse\prime qa$ gills (of fish)

$a_a\dot{}kolawite\prime yal$ moss (Lillagenilla rupestris)

$a_a\dot{}ko\prime la\dot{}m$ eel

$a_a\dot{}kolamka\prime k(na\dot{}m)$ hair of head

$a_a\dot{}kola\prime na\dot{}m$ palate

$a_a\dot{}kola\prime_anak$ moss (Lillagenilla rupestris)

$a_a\dot{}kula\prime ko$ bag, pouch, pocket

$a_a\dot{}kole\prime kam$ powder flask

$a_a\dot{}kolu\prime q^uats$ handle (of tin pail). (See $a_a\dot{}kuk.luka\prime tslo\dot{}$ and $a_a\dot{}kuluqa\prime tslum$)

$a_a\dot{}kuluqa\prime tslum$ shoe lacing

$a_a\dot{}kolu\prime xpe\dot{}$ fence post

$a_a\dot{}kya\prime mlu\dot{}p$ Nelson

$a_a\dot{}kw\varepsilon\prime tsko\dot{}$ screw, buckle of belt

$a_a\dot{}kwu\prime kxo\dot{}$ wicker fish weir

$a_a\dot{}kwitsle\prime et$ hill

$a_a\dot{}ktsa\prime k.le\dot{}$ Wild Horse Creek

$a_a\dot{}k.la\prime xa$ fish spear

$a_a\dot{}k.l\varepsilon malak(na\dot{}m)$ turnip

$a_a\dot{}k.la\prime ixo\dot{}$ square pieces forming border of root basket

$a_a\dot{}k.lilkaku\prime pko\dot{}$ hoe (?)

$a_a\dot{}k$- prefix of noun

   $a'_a\dot{}k!am$ region of Fort Steele and St. Eugène Mission

      $a'_a\dot{}k!am$ $a_a\dot{}ku'q!nuk$ St. Mary's Lake

      $a'_a\dot{}k!am$ $a_a\dot{}kinmi'tuk$ St. Mary's River

   $a'_a\dot{}k!ne\cdot s$ Wasa

      $a'_a\dot{}k!ne\cdot s$ $a_a\dot{}ku'q!nuk$ Hanson's Lake

      $a'_a\dot{}k!ne\cdot s$ $a_a\dot{}kinuxo'_unuk$ Hanson's Creek

-$akik$- to go (dual) 34.11

-ako_u- to stab 108.442

-ako_uk^un- to try 252.63

-$akme$- to call guardian spirit 8.1

$ak_inek!$ relatives, parents 96.188

-$ak.lel$- to question 180.17

$ak!la(n)$ different 72.15

aqa fat 80.187

$aqa(l)$- pr. therefore 92.84

$aqat!$- pr. a little ways off 276.104

-a_aqa- to be strange 90.45

-$aqte$- to untie 2.16

-$aqtuq!^u$- in mouth 220.25

$aqsa$- pr. under blanket, under cover 102.298

-$aqts$- to break 64.117

$aqts!i(xmala)$- white (skin) 42.37 ($aqts!$-$xmala$)

-$aqnits$- to fool 228.83

$a'qla$ inside 90.45

-$aqluk!$- to smell

$aq!a$ thicket 188.21

$aq!an$- pr. into (woods)

$aq!as$ edge 276.113

-$aq!ako_u$- to be on fire; to perspire 120.207

-$axe\cdot$ to go

   $ts!ina'xe\cdot$ he starts 1.1

   $wa'xe\cdot$ he arrives 2.4

   $skaxe\cdot$ he goes along 2.9

-$axne\cdot$ to taste 82.7

-al suff. grass 256.159

-al- thick, stout, wide 39.3

$al\cdot a$ moss 190.8

ala friend (used by women to designate a woman friend) 170.135

-ala- verbal stem

   -$alakin$- to put on with hand 230.24

   -$alaxo_u$- to put on back 232.77

-$alas$- to divide 232.48

$ali'tskei l$ reciprocal term used by brother and sister 44.8

-$alikwa.i't(ne\cdot)$ burning food 162.47

-$alsin(t)$- to endeavor, to try hard 70.37

$alqa$ brain

$alqan$- pr. across 21.3

e oh 86.39

-$eya(kin)$- to put up 224.123

$iya'mu$ game, cattle, buffalo 212.23

-ip- dead 70.18. (See -up-)

-$i'mqot$- to swallow 80.174

ɛt- to make, to do
  -ɛtaqna- to get ready 78.136
  -ɛtctɛl to bury 212.19
  -ɛtetɛʼl(eˑk) to bet 152.198
  -ɛtɛt.la- to make a house 74.34
  -ɛteˑk to act 66.34
  -ɛtelxo- to increase 82.204
  -ɛtkɛn- to make with hand 1.5
  -ɛtkʼlo_u- to do with a point (*i. e.*, to kill with arrow) 86.18
  -ɛtqa- to stop
  -ɛtxoʼ_umeˑk to lie down 60.9
-eˑtax- to sharpen [1]
-ituk!sa- to tie 2.8
-ɛtwas(k!o)- to dry meat 82.5
-ɛtwɛs(qa)-, -ɛtwɛts- to stop, to stay 46.7; 158.350
-ɛtmo(k!o)- to sow 26.5
-ɛtnumoˑts(te)- to make a law 76.96
ɛtkɛk- pr. up (?) 4.10
-ɛtk!an- to butcher 196.144
-itqana(qa)- to pick up 204.310
-ɛtq!an(kɛk)- to lay down 268.46
-ɛtq!aʼnxam- to come back to life 4.16
-ɛtq!anxo- to tan skin 208.409
(-eˑtxamɛn-)
  qa.eˑtxaʻmeˑnqaʼmeˑk not sitting down a long time 248.15
-(ɛ)t.la tent, house, lodge 1.5; 9.6
-ɛt.latsu- to hide 42.13
-ɛt.lɛkɪnatɛt- to propose a plan 232.39
-ɛt!(qa)- to be full 46.23
-ɛt!_uwoˑ- to be ten 180.23
  ɛt!_uwuʼnwo one hundred
-ɛt!na- to stretch out 114.96
ɛt!na- pr. over 60.9
-ɛt!k!o- cold 126.105. (Also -ɛsqat!-)
-ɛt!qao(xa)- to come together, to put together, to pile up 66.18; 134.168
-ɛt!(xa)- to bite 3.6 (perhaps ɛt-xa to do with teeth)
-ɛs- to own 198.168
-ɛs(k!o)- to shoot 44.23
-ɛsakɪnu- to sit down 62.79
-ɛseˑ- to hurt, to wound 182.26
-ɛse(qa)- sharp 62.57
-ɛseˑ(kaʼteˑ)- to look terrible 80.163
-ɛseˑl- pr. very 98.252
-ɛsɛn- pr. self
-ɛsnɛ- pr. self
-ɛskaxₐmete- to lose 52.7
-ɛsqawɛts- to stand holding 50.18
-ɛsqaq!anaq!neˑʼnɛl- to nod 78.109
ɛtskɛl- to look for or at something 24.6
  (-wɛtskɛk- to look, intr.) 180.57
-(ɛ)tfk!alaˑk branch of tree 57.8
-ɛtsqawaˑqaˑ(l)- to walk along shore (?) 76.83

---

[1] Many of the verbs beginning with *t-*, *ɛt-*, are derived from *t-* TO DO; but in many cases the derivation is uncertain.

ı́ts!na·t! cedar 108.449

-(*ı*)*ts!la′e·n* tree 3.9

-*ın*- to be 62.69

   -*ınqa′pte·k* to become 74.24

-*ın·a·ke·sınqame′ıke·* they two sat down 114.104 (-*kıs*- two)

-*ınalaqa′a_ake·* those who are in line 130.71

(*ts′*)*ınalqana′′nte·* he had something to put in 78.134

ıne′nık! enemy 256.186

ıne′si·n horsefly

inı′stin molar and canine teeth

ını′tska gopher

inu′t!ke· grouse

(-*ınmak*) to pay

   -*ıtınmak*- to pay 106.384

-*ın·mısa*- to be six 180.28

ı́nta edge, shore 2.4

ı́ntsuk! mouse

-*ıntse*- to mind 76.93

-*ınk!at*-
   ta′nta oxakısınk!a′te·k the two jumped to the back of the tent 92.116 (*lanta-oxa-kıs-ınk!a-te·k*)

-(*ı*)*nqowa* wing 74.49

ı́nla·k chicken hawk 42.2

-*ık*- to eat 2.6

-*ıkıyıksı′te·k* to camp over night 76.91

e·′ka monster, giant 42.33

-*ıkı(me·k)* to run 3.4

(-*ıkıt!_uwo*, see -*ı′t!_uwo·*- to be ten)
   qa·ıkı·t!_uwo nine 136.208

-*ıkın* suff. with foot 8.9

(-*ıkpak*[*te*]), -*ukpak*- to be disposed
   sa·nlıkpakta′pse· he hated him 86.27; he disliked it 216.91 (*sahan-l-*)
   -*ukpak*-
   sa′hanlukpa′kte· he hated him 76.104
   suk.lukpa′kte· he likes it
   k!umna′nlukpakitmu′!ne· he pitied it 242.276

ıktık- pr. up 256.162

-*ıktxone(mu)*- to rub (with) 124.70

-*ıktoqo*- to wash 80.182

-*ıksıa(t)*- to scratch 58.19

-*ıktsın(uq)*- to sink 78.141

-*ıktsık*- to catch 52.10

-*ıkınatıt*- to lay out place for tent 124.95

-(*ı*)*k.ley* name 84.5

(*ı*)*k!na′mu* relative 168.93

e·qo·l a small magpie (?) 64.113

il- pr. behind 4.8; 254.125

-*ıl(kın)*- to come (?) 78.116

-*ila*- to cry 20.2

-*ilala* cave 80.152

ılın- pr. may be 86.30

-*ılınk!oma′te·k* to cover head with blanket 196.130

-*e·le_ik* out of the top of something

-*ilıkt* to mean 152.182

-*ılwa*- to shoot 82.3

-ʿłwa· gum 20.9

-ɛlwatl- to work 66.1; 250.20

-(ɛ)lwey- mind, heart 76.106

　qałwe′yne· he thought thus 122.52

-ɛlwɛtsk- to watch 92.89. (See -ɛtskɛl-)

-e·lma·k! cherry 6.11

-ɛlta(xa)- to lick off 16.1

-(ɛ)lno′hos star 17.9

-ɛlkɛl- to scold, to quarrel 72.64

-ɛlk-

　-ɛlkɛlwey- wise 214.35 (-ɛlk-ɛlwey)

-(ɛl)ke· to say 218.128

-ɛlko- to make a fire 272.9

ɛlqa- pr. some distance back 92.88

-ɛlqawɛsqokᵘ- to float 98.240

-ɛlq!okᵘ- to be in danger 60.26

-ɛlxo- to feel 66.30

u- pr. down (always with -n if away from speaker, or with -k if towards speaker). (See un-, uk-)

o·u white goose

-o·ya- to be warm 102.300

-oyɛt!axwa(t)- to scare 252.69

uwa′ha no!

-uwokᵤ- to arise 24.2

-oho- (oᵤ-) to know 72.9

up- pr. from water to land 178.266

-up- to die 8.10. (See -ip-)

　-upɛl- to kill 4.9

　-upʊqᵤ- to drown 8.10

o·pa·t! whitefish 150.341

-upɛ(qa)- to be foolish

-upᵢyɛt!eᵢ- stingy 164.5

upɛn- pr. sideways, about 74.29

-upt!ɛnmit-

　n′upt!ɛnmɛtɛlwe′yxome·k he trembled for fear 80.162 (-[ɛ]lwey mind)

-ups(t)- to take one's own 190.7

(n′)upsawɛtsaₐkɛnxa′ₐne· he stood ready to spear 80.155 (ups-awɛtsa-kɛn-xa-ne·)

upskɛl- pr. still 144.33

-upxa- to know, to see 64.115

ʊm(e·) pr. below 254.118

-umats- to laugh 5.12

-umɛts- to break 26.6

-omo- to walk 76.77

(n′)umnaqałpalne′ᵢxo·- he makes a mistake 254.132

-u′mqol- to swallow 222.87. (See -ɛ′mqol-)

-ute- to want, desire 62.107

-utᵢme·- to be warm 37.13

-us- first 4.7

-utspat!- to be helpful

un- pr. down (away from speaker) 184.43

one·k last 210.469

(n′)un·aqało·qniya′xᵤne· he helps 60.20

-onɛl- to be afraid 50.17

uk- pr. down (towards speaker)

-*uk* suff. fluid 82.197

  aₐ'kɛnmi'tuk river

-*oko* ashes 10.10

-*okoy(qa)-* wild 190.55

-*(u)kot* season 180.19

-*o·kᵤ(e·)-* to be all 66.31

-*ukp* claw 58.20

-*uktuk-* to smell bad 160.377

-*uktman(qa)-* to be crazy, foolish

-*ukts(qa)-* to be slim 240.223

-*(u)ktsɛken* bladder 64.100

-*ukᵘnak-* to see at a distance indistinctly 256.191

-*uknu-* to rise 60.13; 138.275

-*ok!ᵘ(e·)-* to be one 72.65

  ok!ᵤɛl- pr. at once 30.6

  ok!ᵤɛnl- pr. at once 55.1

  uk!ᵘnɛl- pr. at once 180.40

(n')uk!en(axe·) he walks about 62.77

-*uk!u(n)-* to open 34.3

-*uq* suff. in water 8.10; 21.3

-*(u)k!puka·m* root 10.12

o'k!qᵤna because 60.15

-*oᵤqa-* short 164.80, 83

-*oqᵘaₐko* pitchwood 136.221 (-*ko* fire)

oqo- pr. in 152.218

  o'qoᵤks inside 136.233

(n)uqo'kxamu'me·k he went out of himself 70.46

-*oqoq!u'ko·l-* to be black

-*uqtaptse·k!* elbow 7.11

-*uqᵤna(me·k)* to move camp 46.18

-*uqɫawo·* (-*uk!awo-* ?) to fish 38.12; 39.2

-*uqɫa'nt* clothing 9.4

-*uq!yu(leet)* mountain 46.7

-*uq!wiya-* to swallow 76.88

(n')uxte·k to defecate 124.69

-*uɫa* pipe stem

-*uɫa-* to do 68.73

-*uɫu-* to be deep 110.12

-*uɫaks* meat, flesh, body 2.7

-*uɫa·l* green boughs 16.6

ya- pr. on each side 62.73

ya——ke· (verbal noun) where there is 84.56

ya.ukᵘe'ᵢka·m name of a culture hero 112.43

ya'wo below water 48.39; below 122.14

yawo'ᵤnek! bright red; water monster 80.161

-*yapt!a-* to be farthest, last 268.12

-*yaptsa(kɛn)-* to push in (?) 164.79

yama'kpa·l red-headed woodpecker 80.152

yam·u smoke 16.4, 7

ya't!aps curdled blood 196.143

yusul- (?) 94.153

-*yanxu-* to starve 192.75

yaₐkwu'la·k Longwater Bay 78.151

-*yaq(lɛ'et)-* to be steep 110.9

-yaq-   to break (a stick) 14.14 (*yaq!*- 64.94)

ya'qa   fish trap 170.136

yaqa'nla·lt   flying squirrel 76.63

yaqso''mil   canoe 70.13

-yaq!-   to break. (See -yaq-)

   ya'q!e$_i$t   tobacco 154.249

-yax̣-   to come into contact, to reach, to get

   -qunyax̣$_a$-   to touch 19.2

   -ts!ɪnyax̣$_a$-   to go to get back 62.60

   -ts!ɪnyax̣ak!o-   to dip water 196.162 (*ts!ɪn-yax̣-ha-k!o*)

   -mɪtyax̣$_a$-   to pursue 7.13

-yɪt-   suff. time

   wanuyɪtna'm·u   winter time 178.4

   walkwa.ɪyɪtne·   evening 36.10

yɪs—ke·   entirety

   yɪ'ske·   size 108.437

   yɪsa'ske·   number 168.78

   yɪslɪɪ'tke·   world 92.82

yɪ'tske·   cooking-basket

   yɪtske'ɪme·   pottery vessel

-ye'$_i$ku-   to be five (from *hey* hand ?)

   kye$_i$ko$_u$nmi·'yɪt   the fifth day 250.31

   ye$_i$ku'nwo   fifty

-yɪksɪ'le·k   to stay over night 76.81

-yɪk!ta-   to be spilled 196.142

-yɪlna'nts(te·)   to be pleased with something, to wish for something 222.74

yu·-   pr.   up 20.9

yu·'wa   go ahead!

yu·''wat!   yellow-jacket, hornet, wasp 26.1

-yuna(qa)-   to be many, much 60.15; 74.34

-yuk^{u}a   war bonnet 80.153

-yuk!k^{u}aka(te·)   to miss, to fail to obtain 78.149

   -yuk!k$_u$akatɪl-   to be saved 214.71

w-   pr.   to arrive

   wa'xe·   he arrives 184.67

   walkɪ'n·e·   he brings it 184.35

wa·-   pr.   up (*waha*- 166.28)

   wa·wɪtskɪ'k$_i$ne·   he looked up 16.9

   wa·mɪtak!o'$_u$ne·   he shot upward 72.14

waha·'   no! 134.193

wa'ma·t!   buck 136.204

-wa·mɪlnilkɪt-   snowstorm 234.102

wa'ta·k   frog 88.3

wat!-   pr.   across (over a high object)

   wat!mɪ·'te·kɪ'n·e·   he kicked him across 84.61

   qanalwat!a'xe·   he went across 254.116

was-   pr.   quickly

   wasaq$_a$na'$_a$ne·   he hurried 194.102

   wa`sɪt·axa'xe·   he comes back quickly 62.78

wasa'q$_a$na·n   tobacco 13.12

wa'tsk$_a$na   dried meat 216.100

-wats!-   to dive 70.9

-wats!-   to play 72.55

-wan- to move 8.7

  wanla'ṭ!ne· he moved his arm 180.55

  wanuqkɪ'n·e he moved it in the water 100.289

wanakate'ᵢ(ne·) he is ready to go 250.34

-*wanaqₐ(na)*- to go to war 226.14

wanu(yɪtna'm·o) winter 178.4

  wanuyɪ'tᵢne it is winter time

wa''nmo blood 206.358

-*wa(k)*- to take away

  wakaltɪ'lne· his wife is taken away from him 62.51

  wakᵢnɪ'lne· it is taken from him 166.54

wa'kuks a bird sp.? 64.120

-*waq(e'ᵢne·)* to be thick

-*waq!ₐwu*- to carry meat 104.362

waq!o·'pe·s rose hips 7.2

-*walɪnk!alalu'ne·* it is snowing

walu·'nak tongue 274.30

-*walne*- to vomit 220.28

waloq!kᵘku'tᵢ(ne·) (waluxko·ku'tᵢne·) it is raining 114.86, 106

wa'lkwa yesterday 250.41

  walkwayɪ'tᵢne· it is evening 76.90

wɪ- (?)

  wɪst!a·'la seven 136.207

  wuxa'ₐtsa eight

-*wiyat!*- side of body 142.22

wɪt!- to be deep 192.44; 278.118

-*wɪt!* wing, shoulder 98.251

wɪt!qkupqo·q!am·akɪ'n·e a blow glances off from head 78.144 (-*qkup-qo·q-la'm-a-kɪn-ne·*)

-*wɪs*- to stand

  n'ɪtwɪsqa'ₐne· he stood still 82.13

  la·awa·kmɑwɪsu'kᵤne· he emerges again 70.26 (*la-a-wa·-k-me-wɪs-uk-ne·*)

  qa·wɪsqa'ₐne· he stands thus 254.122

  wɪsqu'le·k it floats

-*wɪs(e·k)* to sweat in sweat lodge

  wɪsi'al sweat lodge

wɪ'suk!ᵘ a small bird, yellow at tip of feathers, with tip on head 194.118

-*wɪts*-

  tunwakakɪswɪts·a'q!ₐne· legs stick out 228.58 (*tunwa-k-a-kɪs-wɪts-saq!-ne'*)

  nawɪtskpayatɪ'lne· he was waited for 78.123

wɪtswe·ts a small, gray bird living on lake shore 78.113

-*wɪtskɪk*- to look 166.28

  -*wɪtskil*- to watch for something 82.22

-*wɪtsq!nu(ne·)* to climb 64.120

-*wɪl(qa)*- large 58.16

  kwɪ'lqle· bighorn sheep 82.3

wɪlma'pe·s rectum 232.68

wɪ'lma·l rattlesnake 31.5

wɪ'lna·m early 36.2; 66.39

-*wo·* bow

  aₐ·k.lakwo'ᵤte·s his bow stave 15.7

  swu'ᵤte· he has a bow 52.10

  n'ɪt'wukᵘnɪ'le̜k he made a bow for himself 68.59

-wu- to touch

  wuqkupxo'ₐne· he touched him roughly 192.42

  wuk!o'ₐne· he hits it 60.34

wu(qa)- to be long 164.66

  wu'saq! long-leg 78.139

  qawule·'tₐne· not far 64.83

  yɩsɩnwosa'q!ke· the length of his legs 84.53

wu'u water 70.12

-wup- to be new 208.406

-wum belly, stomach 80.185

  wɩlwu'mne· his belly is big 25.11

wʋ'm'a·l wild rhubarb 5.12

wʋ'ne· gambling-bone 152.195

wʋnmana'mu alive 268.15

-woₐkᵘ wood 60.33

-wukᵘ(at)- to see 226.21 (*woₐ-ka-t*)

  -wukᵘqₐ- to find 72.5

wu'qt!e· fisher 230.2

wo'q!ka· soup 46.35. (See *ho'q!ka*)

há· oh! 86.31

hai oh! 86.30

hao'm· (exclamation) 230.6

-ha- to have; to be 70.37;

  -haqa'ₐne· to have 148.121; to be born 92.84

  -hate· to have

    huna'ₐte· I have it

    naka'ₐne· he has an arrow

  -(yu)ha(kɩ'ne·) he rubs it on 20.9

ha—ke· place 80.185

hank!amₐnake· place where there is a hole in a mountain 14.12

-ha- demonstrative verbal prefix.[1]

  -hanɩmsɩqqₐ- to smell 254.109

  -hakʋmsɩkeᵢ(te·) to smell of 238.204

  -hanokᵘeᵢ(te·) to drag 96.184.193

  hakunkɩ'n(·e·) to pull 44.17

  -halukme- noise 60.13

  -halukwaxniyam to whistle 40.9

  -hawɩsqa'ₐne· he stands

  -hawɩskaxu'ktse· to swing 44.26

  -hawɩsk!akanɑ'na·m to dance squatting 52.8

  -hawɩtskɩ'n·e· he stands holding

  nawɩtsqatkɩ'n·e· it holds it by the tail 15.13 (*qat-* tail)

  nawɩ'tsxane· he stands biting 94.157

  -hawɩ'tsno·t- to coax 228.65

  qanawɩtso''me· wind blows a certain way 168.85

-hayaxₐ- to go and get 92.90

-hawasxo- to sing 16.12

ha`phohe'ha (exclamation) 238.207

ham- prefix of color terms

  -hamqoq!uku·lakat.le·tɩtₐne·- blackish sky 66.9

  namqok!oko'ₐlne· it is black

-hamat- to give 206.353

---

[1] Many of the following verbs in *ha* contain presumably this prefix.

-ha·m:luqkat:'le·k to slide on snow 132.126
-hamaxu'k^ue· to fall 88.56
ha'tsa mother's brother and sister's child (reciprocal term) 76.104
-hatsl:t- it is a well-hidden place 192.38 (ha-ats-le:t)
-hats!ala(qa)- to be sleepy 90.55
-han-
  -hanuq!^uya'_a(te·) to swallow (-uq!wiya-)
  -hanuxo- to fly
  -hanmuko- to boil 134.170 (-huko- to boil)
  -hanquxol- sun dance 50.24
  -hanq!o·ko- fire 64.115
  -hanlukp(qa)- to run 48.25
-hanaq-, -hanqa- to sit down
  ya·qaha'nqame·'ke· where he was seated 136.211
  sanaqna'kse· sitting there 132.140
-hanil-
  nanilwok^u:nxa'lne· they waited 74.48
-(ha)nohos red 128.59. (See 78.135)
-han·u'qo.i·xo'^u(ne·) she broke it 96.204
ha'nq!o muskrat 74.33
hak:il- pr. (See -k:l)
  nak:lw:tsqa'_ane· it stands in it 37.4
-hako- to butt 60.23
-hakup(malna'mne·) to stop over night 250.53
-hakumal- to be bloody 58.20
hako·l- to get (milk) 118.169
-hakwa- to howl 140.20
  (n)hakwase'kme·k to pant 140.20
ha·'ksa (exclamation) 90.47; 230.7
-haq!alikwa.:t- to catch fire 120.229
-hakq!y:t- to talk, to discuss 66.2; 216.79. (See -uq!wiya-)
-hakq!_uwasxo'_ume·k to cough
-hakq!me·- to burst 104.339
-hak.latsulw:tsk:l- to look secretly 254.144
-hak.le:t- noise 168.69
-hak.luq!^uwiyax_a- to wish
-hak!ak.lonuk-· dry trees 72.69.
(qa)hak!o_u- to pass (?) 238.200
-haq_a- to swim 218.8
  la.u'pkaqk:n:'lne· it was taken ashore 170.136 (la-up-k-haq-k:n-l-ne·)
  na'qtse·k he washes his body, bathes
-haqai- to roll 240.226
-haqanak!aqla'ha·l swamp 72.65
-haq_an:l to drive game 29.1. (See -halaq_an:l-)
-haqan(ke)- to call 130.106 (haqan-ke)
-haqal-
  naqalpalne·'ne· he talks 72.59. (See -pal-)
-haqosa- (?)
  naqo_usaq!maxo'_ume·k he sat down on top 12.9
-haqoka'm- fringed 202.276
-haqul- to travel by canoe 150.158
-haqwil- to dance 37.11
(qa)haqowu'm'ne· they were assembled 138.279
-haqtuq!^ua- to put in 112.50

-*haqts!ɛqkɛl*- to have clear eyes 214.74 (-*qkɛl* eye)

-*haqloyɛt*(*qa*)- green

-*haq!awu*- to carry meat 188.47

-*haq!a-ko*·- to be on fire 174.182 (*aq!a-ko*· ?); to perspire 120.207

-*haq!a·naq!neᵢ*- to nod 194.102

-*haq!ank!o·*'(*te·k*) limping 26.9

  q!o·matq!a'n·ko· Wounded-Knee 26.9

-*haq!anqots!lae·n* place with thick trees, forest 76.81; 86.43 (-*ha-q!anqo-ts!lae·n*)

-*haq!anqoqᵘat*(*qa*)- round (-*ha-q!anqo-qᵘat-ne·*)

-*haq!axo'ᵤxᵤ*(*ne·*) to shoot 166.47

-*haq!alɛkwaɛtᵢ*(*ne·*) to be on fire 68.65; (172.171)

-*haq!ma*- to do suddenly

  -*haq!maxo*- to scare 116.130

  nukᵘhaq!ma·kɛkqa'ₐne· suddenly he entered 12.13

  naq!male'ᵢtsne· he awoke 138.274

  qanaq!mak.lɛnq!oku'pse· fire started 136.226

-*haq!nuk*- lake (*ha-q!nuk*)

  n'a·qa·nałhoq!nukna'na little lakes 72.67

-*haq!lɛsak*- to cut hair 148.129

-*hal*-

  nałxo'ᵤne· he carries on back 4.2

  nałkɛ'n·e· he carries in hand 80.173

  n'atskałkɛ'n·e· he takes it 134.182

  nal'ana'xe· he goes hunting 82.2

  nalumɛ'n·e· wind blows 164.61

  kałnuku'pqa swift

  -*halqok!almaxₐ*- to kiss (-*k!a-lma* mouth)

  -*hałuk.litᵢya'xₐ*(*ne·*) to shout 210.437

  -*hałatsukᵘiya'm*(*ne·*) to whisper 252.67 (-*ats*- secretly)

  -*halaqₐnɛl*- to drive game 134.167. (See -*haqₐnɛl*)

  -*hałnuqᵘ*- to carry torches 156.266

  -*hałkɛ'kwas*- to pant

  -*hałkoᵤ*- to carry water 134.173

  yu·hałhaq!aku'n·e· it is burnt on top (-*haq!a-ku*-)

-*hala'ₐ*(*ne·*) to faint 130.67

-*hal·axwat*(*e·k*) to be proud 78.140

-*halitɛt*- to marry (*hałalitɛ'tᵢ*[*ne·*] to be married 152.208)

-*halɛnq!oyło·kᵘa'ₐ*(*me·k*) to utter war cry 166.37

-*halikinaₐtɛ'tᵢ*(*ne·*) there is evidence of some one having been present 90.49

-*halonɛs*- to go away 128.42

-*haluqkᵢnɛlxneᵢnɛ'*(*n·e·*) to use a spoon 64.114

hał·ya· oh! 12.6

-*halwats!* to gamble 70.32

-*hałnukup*(*qa*)- to run 244.4. (See -*hanłukp*- under -*han*-)

-*hałnukuxᵤ*- to bleed from mouth 130.96

-*hałnukp*· to be ashamed 208.424

-*halqo·ma·t*- to surround 148.128

-*halq!at!eᵢ*- to pick berries 88.4

-*halq!ahalt*- lehal 150.161

hê oh! 94.140

heᵢ yes

he he ha burden of song 100.291

-*hey*- hand
   mane′ᵢne· he covers it with his hand
   la′ntaqahe′ᵢne· he put his hand back 9.7
   aₐ′ke′ᵢe·s his hand 72.11
heyâ (exclamation) 82.17
he′m·o pine
-*hɩs*- to give food 29.3; 174.208
hesan- pr. away. (See *hosan*-)
-*henehe*- a game, dancing in circle 52.8
-*hɩk!ɩst*- to count coup 256.182
-*hɩle·kxaqkɩn*- to put into water 100.289 (-*hɩle·kxa-qᵘ-kɩn*-)
-*hɩluk*- to be dry 78.116 (*hɩl-uk*-)
-*hɩlke·*- to make noise 82.16
--*hɩlkupxoᵤ*- to blow 138.245
-*hu*- to finish
   -*hukᵘɩn*- to finish something (-*hu-kɩn*-)
   -*hul′e·k*- to finish eating 130.86
   kulatɩ′qna ready 96.195
   -*hul·ak.le·* to be full grown 92.119
   -*hunmeᵢtak.le·*- to be full grown 102.305
hu-te· to use
ho′ya well! go on! let me go on! 84.1
-*hoyɩt!t*- to drive 174.202 ·
-*huwas*- to be hungry 82.4
-*hupa*- to be first 74.37
-*hupö(qa)*- to be crazy 256.166
-*hupumak(ne·)* snow falls from trees 57.7
-*humas*- to be dry 222.100 (-*hu-mas*-)
-*huto·qsa*- to tie hair in knot (?)
-*hutkawumako*- belly swells up (-*wum* belly)
-*hut!*- to freeze 234.103
   hosan- pr. away. (See *hesan*-)
   no·sanoxunqa′ₐne· he ran away 68.65
   hosanmiyɩ′tke· to-day 250.48
-*huts*- pr. towards
   nutsa′xe· he approaches 124.90
   nutsu′kᵘne· water rises 118.189
-*huts*- to lie
   nutske′ᵢne· he lies, speaks untruth 86.16
-*hutsqan*- to be lengthwise 170.104. (See -*maqan*- crosswise)
   kutsqa′nq!le·l striped lengthwise
-*hutsɩn*- to start
   no·tsɩnqkupekɩ′me·k he started running 58.18
-*hunuq!me·*- to skin 15.4
-*huko*- red-hot 68.75; to boil; cooked, done 272.14
-*hukuya(kateᵢ)*- to be dangerous 224.103
   -*hukoyɩlxoneᵢ*- to feel uneasy 220.41 (-*ilxo* body)
   -*hukᵘeᵢ(qapqa)*- to be wild 190.55
-*hukᵤnu*- to raise. (See -*uknu*-)
-*huk.luk*- tired 60.19
   huk.lukpa(me·k) lonesome 148.122
-*huk!ᵘe·n*- to be open 144.52
   ŏk!ᵘɩnkɩ′ne·n′ open it! 148.102

-*huk!ukyɛtᵢ-* it is (day) light 68.52; -*hoq!ukᵢyɛt-* to shine 120.217

-*huk!nuq!ɫuma* thirsty 42.29

-*hoq-* to win 72.63

-*huqaxo-* to fall 110.8

-*huqna(me·k)* to break camp 84.40

   nuqᵤnaneya'mne· they broke camp 276.71

-*huq!utsko-* to extinguish fire 172.173

-*huq!yu'k!oᵤ̯-* to grasp with beak 240.209

ho'q!ka rotten bone 234.87. (See *wo'q!ka.*)

-*hoq!ko·-* it melts 80.187

huɫ- pr. from land towards water 100.263; 240.209

   -*huɫuqᵘ-* to swim 142.43 (-*huɫ-uq-*)

-*huɫpaɫ-* to hear, to listen 92.107 (-*huɫ-paɫ*). (See *paɫ*)

-*huɫnak!o-* ·to fill pipe 62.39, 46

hya· (exclamation) 148.95

pa· brother's daughter

-*payo·t-*

   q!akpayotɛ'tne· it is forgotten 82.196

pa'pa grandmother (said by male), grandfather, grandson 88.27

papa'la·'m leaves of tobacco plant

pa·mɛk nevertheless 86.41

pa·ts- pr. apart

   pa·tsɛnmɛ't- to scatter 106.418

paɫ! nephew 64.94

-*paqts-* to be thin 272.12

-*paq!ₐme·-* to burst 184.47

pa·ɫ weak disjunctive, but 78.125

-*paɫ-*

   -*haqaɫpaɫnɛᵢ-* to talk 72.60

   -*k!apaɫ(tɛle·k)* to listen 102.316

   -*huɫpaɫ(ne·)* to hear, to listen 66.24; 92.107

   wɛɫka'nɛɫpaɫnexu'n·e· he made big noise 98.219; 220.54

pa'ɫ'ya mittens 228.57

pa'ɫkeᵢ woman 26.12

-*pɛs-* to let go

   pɛsɛk!'n·e· he let it go with hand 90.51 (-*kɛn-*)

-*pɛtsqa-* to be afraid

   pɛtsqaɫwɛ'ync· he is afraid 174.185 (*pɛtsqa-ɫwɛy-nc·*)

-*pɛts* food

   aₐ'kpɛ'tsna·m food

   pɛ'tsa·k spoon

   pɛtsɛk!'meᵢk he eats while going 198.187

-*pɛts-*

   pɛtsxo'ᵤne· he chops off 104.343

pɛ'k!a·ks long ago 88.2

po'po hammer 128.35

pɔ'stɪn American (=Boston)

p!e·q!s night hawk 172.152

ma mother 94.138

ma but 94.138

-*ma* trail

   aₐ'kma'na·m a trail 62.51

   n'aɫmamaₐ'nc· trail is wide 254.111

   wuɪnana'mne· it is a long trail

-ma- (long objects)

k!almanmi′tuk a wide river 86.10

-may*t* season

ɫuma′y*t* spring of year 100.258

ma′yo·k weasel

-mat-

matqɫaxwa′*a*te· he spits it out 6.8, 12

-mate· to leave 134.172

ma′te*i*t!· whitefish

-mas(e*i*)- to be dry 64.117

ma*a*ts don't! 58.3

-mats to be dirty 194.84

-matsqak

k!a‵le·matsqakɛma′ak big toe (-*al*- wide)

man- pr. past

manq!ank*ɛ*′me·k he went past 84.60

man- pr. back

ɫamanw*ɛ*tskik*ɛ*′ɫne· he looks back 158.343

-man- to cover 58.17

ma′*a*ka flicker 80.180

ma·k! bone 84.31

-maqan- crosswise

ma′qak later on 126.106

-maq!an egg, testicle 102.300

-maq!ne·(xo)- to slap

ma′xa a berry, sp. (?) 270.32

maɫ(u)- pr. sideways 150.170

maɫu′q!ɫiɫ striped sideways 150.170

-maɫ suff. together, with 130.85; 166.42

-maɫ*ɛ*n- to open

maɫ*ɛ*nk!aɫma′n·e· he opened his mouth 220.51

-maɫak bone

a*a*‵k.ɫam·aɫa·k skull (a*a*′k-ɫa′m-maɫak)

-me· suffix

a*a*‵k!a′*a*me· hole

y*ɛ*ts!ke·′me· pot

-miy*ɛ*t day

y*ɛ*s*ɛ*nwunmiy*ɛ*′tke· the whole night 144.9

naqsanmi′y*ɛ*t several days 88.6

a*a*‵k*ɛ*lmi′y*ɛ*t sky 86.51

ts*ɛ*lmi′y*ɛ*t evening 68.52

kts*ɛ*lmet*ɛ*lnu′qka going at night (=moon) 68.50

-m*ɛ*t- to throw 68.65

m*ɛ*txa- to shoot 74.32

m*ɛ*squɫo′*u*wo·m name of Coyote's daughter 60.11

m*ɛ*′tsu·k a small water fowl, long, slender neck, white belly, dark back 98.246

m*ɛ*tsqo‵ko·*ɛ*′ɫna· a bush with white berries, not edible 126.14

m*ɛ*ts!qa′qas chickadee 176.231

-m*ɛ*nxo·qa- to jump 96.168; 246.45

-me·k reflexive ending of verbs in -ne·

m*ɛ*′ka even 66.25

m*ɛ*′ksa'n but 98.219

-mu(w*ɛ*su′q)- to emerge

n′awak!mosu′q*u*ne· it emerges 110.39 (n-a-wa-k-mo-w*ɛ*s-uq-ne·)

-mu suff. by means of

  kmιtҳa′m·u shooting with it 72.3

-moҳun·e· to fall into, to hit 192.39

  ksa$_a$kmu′ҳo‘ while he was away 232.64

  sanmuҳo′me·k to pile up 168.87

    sanmolkι′n·e· he had a pile 136.237

moqkupnoҳunqa′me·k he runs 60.18

mo′q!$_u$ne· young beaver 130.92

-mnuqka-, mɛnuqka-

  yaqa\naɩwat!mɛnuqka′ske· where the sun sets 86.21 (*ya-qanɩ-wat!-mɛnuqka-s-ke·*)

t- pr. into, always with *n* GOING, or with *k* COMING. (See *tιn-, tιk-*)

ta$_a$q oh if!

-taptse·k forearm, elbow 7.11

-tamoҳu(n·e·) it is dark 266.41

tat! elder brother 68.53

ta′naɩ reed (?), rushes (?) 264.65

-takҳaҳo$_u$(ne·) to fall 132.124

ta·k!a·ts squirrel 74.27

ta′ҳa then 1.5

ta′ҳta later on 3.7

taɩ- pr. can

-t$_i$mo suff. mutually, together with

  swι′t$_i$mo friends 1.2

  aɩa·qaltι′t$_i$mo parents and children

tι′tc· granddaughter of woman; grandmother of girl; mother-in-law 184.67; 58.22

tι′tu father of male

tι′tqa·t! man 166.42

tιn- pr. going into 88.32; 90.61

  ɩatnaɩkι′n·e· he carried it back into 90.61

tιk- pr. coming into 92.116

  tιkιmι′tҳ$_a$ne· he pulled it in 96.203

-te·k reflexive suffix of transitive verbs in *-tc·*

tι′lle·t! father's sister (said by woman) 58.14

tι′lna old woman 3.4

  tιlna′mu wife, old woman 26.6; 62.55

tιlna′ako hare (?) 216.81

tuw- pr. back

  tuwuɩ′ιtҳo′$_u$me·k he lay on his back 246.62

  tuwunιnmuҳu′n·e· he fell back 96.170

tuwukҳo′naɩ diorite 106.394

to′hoɩ charr 44.14

tu′ts!a·k! thumb

-tunak- to be lean 216.95

tunwa- pr. out of, out of woods (Lower Kutenai *tun-*)

  tunwakakιswιts·aq!a′$_a$ne· his two legs stuck out 228.58

  ktuna′ҳa Kutenai 254.112

-tuk!ҳo(ɩne·) (tent) is covered 214.53

-tuq!ts- news 78.132

  tuq!tsqake′$_i$nc· to tell news 250.50

tuq!tsqa′mna bird, small animal 196.121

tu′ҳ$_u$a almost 66.30

-t.la tent, house

  a$_a$·kιt.la′na·m tent 8.5

  n′ιtιt.la′$_a$te·k he made a tent for himself 74.34

  sa·nιt.la′$_a$ne· there is a tent 9.5

-*t!a*- to knock

  t!axo'une· to knock at door 202.291

  t!amuxo- to drum

  t!awo gun 90.50 (*t!a-wu*)

    t!a˅wu'mka bowstring 128.27

t!a˅pɛs(wukna'na) a little bush 60.33

t!aptslɛ'nwa·s cricket

-*t!apts*- to stick on 98.234; 252.93

t!a'tka uvula

-*t!ats!anel·(ɛkɛ'n·e)* to tramp on something 126.20

-*t!anoko'u(ne·)* to burst by heat 96.168

-*t!anukqlo'uku(ne·)* to snort 168.89

t!a'n·qu·ts partridge 152.181

t!aqu'mo· netted ring 194.117

t!aqta·la'mne· they talk together 278.2

-*t!aqts*- to hurt

  t!aqtseyxo'ume·k he hurt his hand 26.3 (*taqts-hey-xou-me·k*)

-*t!alo'uku(ne·)* to make noise 92.92 (*t!a-louku-ne·*)

t!ɛna'mu grease 110.2

t!uk.lun·maku'lɪne· two seasons

s- pr. along

  sakqa'ane· it lies here

  saq!a'n·e· it hangs

  sa·nɛt.la'mne· there is a house

sao-, *saw*- pr. there (demonstrative)

  sa·usaqa'ane· he staid there 2.14

-*sahan*-, -*sa·n*- to be bad

  saha'n·e· it is bad 58.25

  sa˅hanlɛɪ'tne· it is a bad place 256.153

  sa˅hanlukpa'kte· he hated him 76.104

  sa˅kɛlsa·nɛlwe'yne· he is still angry 86.26

  sa'nla Piegans 52.13

-*sa'n(qa)*- to be tired 204.316

sak (exclamation) 226.43

-*sak*-

  ksakɛ'me·k tired walking 114.109

sakɛl- pr. still

  sa˅kɛlsa·nɛlwe'yne· he is still angry 86.26

-*sakno·'ktse·k* he is starving 176.251

  ksano·˅ktsɪyɛnkɛ'tsqa starving, although having a fish trap 176.251

-*sɛn*- there stands (*s-n*-)

  sɛnk!ala·xwiɛ'tsne· there is a door 34.4

-*saq*- to lie

  saq(qaa)- to lie down

-*saqxal*- there 96.201; 98.240; 130.105

-*saq!*- leg

  aa˅ksa'q!na·m leg 3.13

  wu'saq! long leg 78.139

  lusaq!a'lne· leg is cut off 28.3

-*salilɛt*- to marry 164.2. (See -*halitɛt*-)

seɪt! blanket 1.2; 154.260

sɛ'n·a· beaver 70.11

-*sɛn·akpa'me·k* he wants to act his own way 74.30

-s*ɪ*k- fat 50.4

-s*ɪ*l- pr. continuative 35.9; 40.5

su father of girl

soya′pe Englishman 33.8

-so$_u$k- . to be good 58.39

  suk.le*ʹ*t*ɪ*ne· it is a good place 100.260

  ksuk^{u}aka′te· plenty 168.80

  suk^{u}nohu′se· bright red 90.71

  suk^{u}xo′$_u$me·k he took a good seat 68.62

  suk^u*ɪ*l′upx$_a$ne· he sees well 128.53

swa' panther 164.8

swa′q!$_a$mo salmon 176.252

-sw*ɪ*ts- there stands

  sw*ɪ*lsle.*ɪ*′t*ɪ*ne· there is a hill 12.2

  sw*ɪ*tsnu′k^{u}ne· there is a stone 26.3

sw*ɪ*n daughter 270.44

  swina′le·l sister's daughter (said by woman)

sw*ʋ* friend (used by man to designate male friend) 222.85

-st*ɪ*l(e·k) to stake in gambling 150.180

st!u′k^{u}al female

-(stsu′m- always with qa- NOT)

  qastsu′mqaqa′$_a$ne· he is wise, skillful 70.38

-sn*ɪ*msik(qa$_a$)- it smells of 252.104

skat relation between sister's husband and wife's brother 224.9

sk*ɪ*′n·ku·ts coyote 1.1

  s*ɪ*lsk*ɪ*n·ku·′tste·k to act foolishly 210.434

-sk*ɪ*k- a flat object is somewhere 12.1

  sk*ɪ*kts!la′nuqle!*ɪ*t flat country (=prairie) (see under *flat*)

-sk*ɪ*kil- a flat object is still there 82.197

sq!u′m·o· service berry 92.104

-ts and 2.5

ts- pr. future 1.8

-tsa- to be small

  hutsat.lanana′ne· I have a small house

  ktsaqu′na small 50.4

  tsale.*ɪ*t*ɪ*nana′ne· a place is small 234.93

tsa· younger brother 70.39

tsa′hal grass 50.4

-tsamal knife 10.9

tsa′$_a$tsa grass figure representing deer 90.60

tsa′kap a spirit (?) 44.8

-tsak*ɪ*l- to refuse 72.2

tsa′qa partridge berry 58.8

tsaqan- pr. into a pile of things; up river

  tsaqa·natsq!ahe′*ɪ*ne· he stretched his hand into it 18.8

  ts!*ɪ*naltsaqana′xe· he started up river 216.83

  ts$_a$qa′haks source of river 216.119

-ts*ɛ*ma·k! very, strongly

  ts*ɛ*ma′k!ke′*ɪ*ne· to speak the truth 98.215

  ts*ɛ*mak!qa′$_a$ne· he is strong 180.41

  ts*ɛ*ma·k!e·l′ut*ɪ*mile.*ɪ*′t*ɪ*ne· it was really hot 116.152

  ts*ɛ*ma·k!*ɪ*lwu′qt!e· the real fisher 234.98

tsiya younger brother 184.61

ts*ɪ*mne·xa′$_a$me·k he wants to eat more 272.23

ts*ɪ*t!(na′na) pup (of dog) 216.92

-tse̜ite· suff. to cause 164.76

tse̜'tsqo·m water ousel 78.113

tsle̜n only 74.24

-tse̜n- to catch, to hold

  tse̜nke̜'n·e· he catches it

  tse̜nxu'n·e· it squeezes him

tse̜nmaɫ(qa'ₐne·) something happens 55.4

tse̜'nɫa shrew 128.46

tse̜ns(ke'ₑne·) he did not mean it 192.44 (*-keᵢ-* to say)

tse̜nɫa(kate'ₑne·) it looks nice 188.29

tseᵢ(ka'te·) he sees it 58.20

-tse̜k!- to destroy

  tse̜'k!xₐne· to break with teeth

  tse̜k!ke̜'n·e· to split with hand 44.19

tse̜k!e·n- pr. on one side 256.174

-tse̜k!maɫe̜n(ke̜'n·e·) he makes a mistake 128.55

-tse̜ɫ- to be dark 66.30

tsu sister of girl 58.11

tsu'u milk 118.170; breast 166.33

tsu'wak! fish hook 39.3

tsu'm(o·kᵘ) bubble (*-ukᵘ* water) 70.25

tsoᵤɫ name of a dog 242.255

-tsutiɫ- to suck 112.51

(k)tsquna'ₐke̜nxa'm·u spear 80.165

-tsunok!oᵤ- to open (rock) 238.193

tsu(k!o'ᵤne·) to pierce 264.78

tsukᵘ(a'te·) to take 2.7

  tsukokuₑ'n·e· to take with hand 106.411

  tsukuqkuₑ'n·e· to take with hand out of water 98.212

  tsukᵘatu'maɫ slave

tsuk(ɫa'ma'ne·) to comb (*-ɫa·'m* head)

-tsuku- to start a fire 136.221

  tsuku'pxₐne· to light a pipe 13.13

tsuk!na'ₐ(ne·) to invite to a feast 78.115

tsuk!oti'yaɫ spear 80.153

-tsuɫa bag

  aₐ'tsu·'ɫa bag 17.5

-tspuq!ueᵢ- to be soft 184.47

-iska(ke̜n)- to give 104.361

-tsk!aɫak branch. (See [*-e̜*]*tsk!aɫa·k*)

  pe̜tstsk!aɫakxo'ᵤne· he chops off a branch

-tsq!ahe̜y finger (*-he̜y* hand)

-tsxa(n·e·) to talk 66.3

  tsxa·maɫktsaɫa'mne· to shake hands 62.73

-tsɫakeᵢɫ- to like 206.371

(k)ts!ak!ɫana'ke· a different way. (See *ak!ɫa*)

-ts!aqₐ- to rub, to oil 94.143

ts!axu'na ant 212.18

ts!e̜n- pr. to start away from speaker 2.2

ts!ema'k!- hard

-ts!e̜nak- to run

ts!e̜k- pr. to start towards speaker 152.189

ts!e̜lq!e̜nku'pse· it burnt quickly 68.64

-ts!upna- to shut 46.29; 94.157

ts!up'na'kot autumn 100.257

ts!o'ᵤts!o· fish hawk

   ts!oᵤts!u'q!ua fish-hawk nest 244.3

-ts!kakɩl- coal

   yu·nats!kakɩ'lne· there is much coal

-ts!qaₐl bark of tree

   hututs!qalxo'ᵤne· I tear off bark

-ts!la- pr. flat

   aₐ'kɩkts!la'noᵤk flat stone 64.84

   skɩkts!la`nuqle'ɩt prairie 204.309

-ts!lae·n tree

   qa`ₐkilhaq!a`nqu·ts!la'in there is a forest 86.43

n- prefix of indicative forms of all verbs beginning with an h

n'- prefix of indicative forms of all verbs beginning with a vowel

na this 60.21

na.u'te· girl 126.11

nao·'k!ue· the other one 68.48 (See o!k!u-)

nawa'spal son-in-law, father-in-law 29.3, 4; 200.236

na''he·k birch-bark basket 58.25; 90.51

na'pit if 90.52; 226.37

-nam suff. some one (indefinite subject)

namɩ't·a red paint 96.190

-nam'te·xa (?)

   l'apko·k!ᵤna'm'te·xa he might jump to the head of the tent 96.200

na'mlat! a species of chipmunk 230.4

na'ₐta above 204.330; 212.30. (See ata-)

nata'ne·k! sun, moon 13.13; 120.224

naso'ᵤkᵘe·n chief 29.4

na'na younger sister of girl 58.14, 15

   alna'na sisters 78.126

   nana'ₐlɩmo sisters 230.17

-nana suff. small 44.13; 55.6; 76.92

na''nka orphan

   kana'nka·'qal orphan adopted by me

na''ka young gopher

na'ksaq master 50.25

na·'k!ₐyo fox 1.1

-naq- to swim 58.27

naqa- some one 268.61; 270.30

naqan- pr. probably, about 36.3; 62.71; 270.26

   naqanqa'lsa about three 270.26

   naqa'ₐl- pr. 62.71

na'qpoᵤk soup 58.26, 34

a'qsa- pr. several 4.13; 88.6; 144.12, 19. (See naqa-, ṅaqan-

naq!an- pr. into woods

na'xₐne· caribou 50.1

-na·l- to continue

nalaqlɩ'lɩk golden eagle 74.52

na'lme·t! badger 64.96, 100

nalmü'qtse· name of a hero 80.166; 84.1

nalmuxna'yi·t (nalmcxna'yct) a small woodpecker 80.153, 159, 161

ne· that one 8.12; 9.13; 86.9

nɩlsta'hal youth 30.1; 126.11

   nɩlsta`halq!lik!a'ma·l youth about to marry

nɛtsna'pku   moose 10.7; 11.5

nɛ''nha·ks   there is water 86.9

nɛ'nko   thou 44.28; thine 29.14

-*neyaχ*-   to send for some one 72.6

nɛ'le·   shade 66.26, 41; 116.152

nilo'uqʷat   doe 88.3

nɛ'lya·p   mountain sheep 168.72

nɛ'ltuk!ᵘp   antelope 244.2

nɛ'lse·k   buffalo bull 60.1, 5, 17

nɛ'lko   iron, money 52.6

   nɛlko'ᵤts!ap   arrow point of metal 106.383

nɛ'lksaq   porcupine

nɛlxamyu·'wat!   snail

nüpɛ'k!a   manitou 5.1; 94.134; 224.9

nu'm·a   thunder 74.48

-*nɛ'm·ok!*   cliff 2.4; 84.52; 278.118

-*nut*-   to pursue 15.15; 26.8; 58.22; 60.19

-*not*-

   skɛkɛnotxonɛ'le·k   there is a rattling noise 146.74, 75

-(*nohos*)-, *nos*-   red 78.135, 147; 90.71; 96.190

-*nusu'k!po·n*   place with scattered trees 72.74

   aₐ·kɛnusu'k!po·n

nu'kᵘ(ey)   stone 60.7, 27; 94.142

   -*nukᵘ*-   in compounds 60.8; 64.83; 88.19

-*no·kak*   rib 80.189

-(*nokᵘi*)-

   ts!ɛnawɛs'nokᵘe'ɛte·   they dragged them 168.59 (also 248.11; 250.35, 38)

nuktsa'qleₑl   hummingbird

   (*k!uktsa'qleₑl*   pointed eye)

nuktsnaq!a''nka·m   snipe 184.31

nu'k.loᵤkᵘ   elk fawn

-(*nuk!ᵘ*)-

   hun'onyilnu'k!ᵤne·   I know how to get it. (See 98.217)

-(*nok!ᵘɛn*)-   to get out (to open) 76.72

-*nuqa'koᵤ*   pitchwood 168.69; 266.36

-*nuq*-

   aₐ·kɛnuqle'et   prairie 55.6; 180.39

-*nuqᵤ*-   to smoke 266.3

   -*ɛknoqukᵤ*-   to smoke a pipe (= to eat smoke) 62.40

-*nuqka*-   to go up, to rise 66.21; 68.43

   ktsɛlme·tilnu'qka   moon (= the one going up at night) 68.55

   yu·wa·kmnuqka'n·e·   he went up on high 66.8

-*nuqlum*-   white

  aₐ·kmɛnuqlu'nuk   white stone 88.13

  kianuqlu'mna   rabbit

  kianuqlo·q!u'lo·kp   bumblebee (= white end)

  nuqlu'k!ᵘe·n   loon

-*noq!ᵘm*-   to break 90.60, 63

-*nuq!*-   (?)

  knu'q!lam'   long-haired one (Chinaman)

-*nuq!la*-

  aₐ·kɛnuq!la·nu'k!ᵘe·n   sharp, flat stones 96.191

-*nuχu*-   to fly 212.29; 214.70; to run away 80.165

  kɛlnuχu'kna·m   a race 1.6

-nul-

  -nulk!o- to aim, to stab 68.63; 80.159

  nawₑtsnulxo'ₐne· he stood ready to pound 96.192

nu'·la old man

  nu·l'a'qₐna husband 84.32; Frenchman 34.1

-nulmak marrow 64.101

-nma- to carry

  qalsanma'xo· one who carried three

  la·aimaxo'ₐne· he carried two 188.40 (aim < as-nm)

-nmakut year

-nmiyₑt day

-nmituk river 8.3; 80.190; 86.10

-nmukₐ- to boil something 266.7, 8

-nmok! cliff. (See -nₐm·ok!)

-nmu(xo)- to pile; to throw many things 82.201; 118.195; 130.68

-nk!un- to point

  qa`nank!unₑ'lne· it was pointed that way 180.55, 56

-nqo· (?) frame of tent

-nqowa feathers 86.18; 98.208

  k·lunqowa'·xo· feathers coming off 98.213

-nq!a- point 9.7; 14.3; 62.56, 57

-nq!oko- fire 80.186; 128.57; 136.233; 266.13

-nlₑ'kxo·

  kianlₑ'kxo· woodchuck

k- prefix of participle and interrogative 5.4

k- pr. coming, motion towards speaker. (See ₑak-, ts!ₑk-)

ka- pr. my 58.14

-ka- to take

  la·upkak!o'ₐne· he took it out of fire 2.7

  k!upka'ₐnqo·l what he had taken out of water 130.98

-ka suff. some one (indefinite object) 92.92

  tsxanatka'ₐne· she told some one 268.64

-ka- arrow 15.6

  n'aimaka'ₐne· he had two arrows 68.59 (< n-as-nma-ka-ne·)

kaá (exclamation) 228.92

kaₐ where 96.186; ka'a 78.129

-kamal corral

  skₑkₑska'ma·l there are two corrals

ka'min I 44.37, 38; 78.139. (See ka- my)

  kamina'la we, our 70.11

-ka·mt- belt

  aₐ`ka'mta·m somebody's belt

-kat(e·) to look

  tseₑka'te· he sees

  n'ₑse·kate'ₑne· it looks terrible 90.42

  koa`qaka'te· how do I look? 92.117

  namak!tsa`ₐkat.le·tₑtₑne·'ne· it looks yellowish 66.15

  sukʷakate'ₑne· plenty 92.100

kat!kak!'lsaq! Blackfoot Indians

ka'tska·ts a bird, yellow breast and gray wings 78.126

kanq!usqwe'ₑkak mallard duck 19.8, 10

ka·kiyaxa'kukp Rattling-Claws (a name) 256.175

ka'ₐke·n wolf 194.81

kak!a'ₐkit! Hare Lip (a name) 256.173

kaq!a'le· bull moose 104.350. (See kₑlq!a'le· bull elk)

ka′χaχ turtle 160.362

-*ka*(*χu*)- to fall

   n′o·niłkaχu′n·e· it fell down 96.196

kaχu′lo·k goose 17.10

kała′wo·k thorn bush (?)

ka′łta·t shrew 130.68, 86

ka′ₐlka ghost

-*keᵢ*- to say

   qake′ᵢne· he said so 1.1

   słutske′ɪne· he lied 23.2; 58.38

kia′wa·ts fool hen, grouse (?) 17.1; 218.3

kiapt!aha‵nɪtsq!ahai′na·m little finger

   kiapt!aha′nłukp claw 25.2

kianu′kχo goat 86.23

kianuqłu′mna rabbit 55.1

kianuq!u′łupq bumblebee

kianq!ał(*na′na*) two-year-old buck 226.11

kianlɪ′k!χo· woodchuck 92.96

kiakqa′loᵤk a hawk, sp. (?) 70.5 (*kiaqka′loᵤk* 42.3)

kiakχa′χu·l something tied together (?)

kia′kχo· fish 118.182

kiaq!nu′kᵘa·′t golden eagle 42.1 198.207

kiaq!aku′tats sparrow hawk 192.54, 76

kia′q!la duck 98.210 (*kia′qła* 19.13)

kiyu′kmuł digging-stick 52.11

kɪ′tᵢmuk! white clay

-*k s*- dual

   łkamukᵘɪ′ste·k two children 9.10,13

   n′anakɪsχa′mne· they two went out 9.9

   hɪnwɪlkɪsqlɪ′łne· you have big eyes (*hɪn-wɪl-kɪs-qlɪl-ne·*)

-*kɪts*-

   n′ɪntakitsχo′ᵤne· he chopped it off close to edge 33.9

   qaₐnkitsχo′ᵤne· he chopped along 33.11

-*kits* tent pole

   a′ₐ‵kɪts tent pole

-*kɪtsqa* fish trap 176.253

-*kɪts!χₐ* to gnaw (-*χₐ* with teeth) 274.39

   ksano‵ktsᵢyɪnkɪ′tsqa they are starving with their fish trap 176.251

-*kɪn* suff. with hand 188.11, 16

   t!apts!akɪ′n·e· he stuck it on 188.26

   ksaₐna′ₐki·n bad gambler 150.157

kɪndzodz (King George) Canadian

-*kn*(*ɪlwiy*)- to think about something

   kinełwi′ytik he thinks about it 68.1

   siłkᵢniłwiyteya′ₐte· he is thinking about it 68.2

-*keᵢk*- to cook 42.37, 38

-*kik*- to make noise, to puff, to howl 146.55, 64; 218.125 (-*kak*- 146.57)

   n′anmuqkupnoχo‵ne·łkɪkwakɪ′me·k she ran out howling 11.8 (*n-an-mu-qkup-noχone-l-kɪk-wa-kɪme·k*)

   lɪtkɪkᵢnokᵘɪ′łne· without noise of stones 256.157 (*lɪt-kɪk-nokᵘ-ɪl-ne·*)

-*kik*-

   naqa‵nkikqa′me·k he jumped sideways 170.106

-*kɪl*- (with demonstratives *yakɪl*-, *hakɪl*-, *sakɪl*-, *qakɪl*-)

   -*kɪlhaq!anqots!la′e·n* thicket 76.81, 90 (-*ts!lae·n* tree)

   ya′ₐkɪl′ana′mke· when they had been hunting 82.12

-kɛl- plural

   hunakɪlwɛsqawala'ₐne· we stand

kɪlku'lka pemmican 196.146; 208.396, 397

kɪlq!a'le· bull elk. (See *kaq!a'lc·* bull moose)

-ko- suff. fire

   q!apku'pse· everything is burnt 174.195

   naq!ₐko'ᵤne· it is burning 174.194

   t!anoko'ᵤ(ne·) it burst by heat 96.168

ko'o tent site 122.29; 266.5

-kup- raw

   ke'ᵢko·p raw, purple

ku'peᵢ owl 58.7, 9

ku'po·k! black woodpecker

-kumal- to be bloody 208.403, 405

ko·'s pipe 154.230

ku'sto·l whistle 256.164

ko'uko· toad 76.92

ko·kt mother's sister 58.13

ko·dli'dlus butterfly 16.13

-kul-

   kulwiya't!ne· left-handed 74.37

kwɛ'se· food 134.185; 166.22

-kᵢyukpuktse(te·) to initiate, to send a boy to get manitou power 146.91

-kpa(me·k) to wait

   nawɛtskpayatɛ'lne· he was waited for 116.141 (*n-hawits-kpa[ya]-tɛl-ne·*)

-kpuk! backside 18.7; 64.87

ktuna'χa Kutenai (perhaps *k-tuɹun-aχe* going out to valley; modern Kutenai would be *ktu'na·m*)

ktsɛ'tsqa·l spruce

kts!ɛ'q!la prairie chicken 200.239

kq!a'laχa'ₐltsin horse 52.5, 14 (= elk dog)

-kq!owas(χo)- to cough

   laqa'oχalkɪkq!owasχoneyik'me·k he came back there coughing 166.12 (*la-qaoχal-k-kq!owas-χo-ney-kɪ-me·k*)

-kq!u- to laugh

   qakq!u'n·e· he laughed thus 156.301

   wɪlkɪkq!u'n·e· he laughed aloud 132.127

k.la'wla grizzly bear 2.9, 12

-k.laqₐnan- to fight 106.407

-k.le· name 74.30; 226.16

-k.lɪnq!o- to play, toy 52.9; 90.71; 98.219

-k.lu town, village 62.59; 74.24

   haₐk.lo'ᵤkᵘe· those in the town 70.11, 39

-k.luk- to divine

   sa'kɪlk.lu'kmul used for divination 184.66

-ku water, fluid (compare -qᵘ IN WATER)

   n'utᵢme'ᵢkᵤne· water is warm 66.28

   ya·knosc'ᵤkᵘe· where there is red water 78.150

k!ayu'kᵘa hat 254.107; 260.12

-k!apal- to listen 170.122; 182.30

   k!apaltɛ'le·k he listened 160.13

-k!a(me·) hole 23.10, opening. (See words beginning with -k!a and -k!ala)

   n'ɛtk!amɛ'ᵢne· he made a hole 226.12

-k!a·mɪna valley 14.12, 13; 254.116

-$k!asla'_akak$ nostril

-$k!a(no'_uko{\cdot})$ sharp (stones) 82.25

-$k!anqo{\cdot}t$ smoke hole 9.12

-$k!a_ak$ lair of a deer, hole (?) 126.4, 5

-$k!aqayt$ snowshoes 128.45

-$k!aqlahal$ swamp 72.65

-$k!a\chi(me{\cdot}k)$

   $ts!{\iota}nha{\grave{}}q!mak!a\chi ne'kse{\cdot}$ he struck him suddenly 70.47

-$k!olakak$ navel

   $a_a{\cdot}k!_alaka'kna{\cdot}m$ navel

   $a_a{\cdot}ko_uk!ala'ak!e{\cdot}s$ his back 240.230

-$k!ala\chi apak$-   berry patch

   $sk{\iota}{\grave{}}k{\iota}l'w{\iota}lk!ala\chi apa'kse{\cdot}$ there is a large berry patch 184.50

-$k!ala\chi ekp$ anus 25.1; 26.2

-$k!ala\chi awuet$ doorway 144.48; 166.26 (-$k!ala\chi weet$ 34.4)

-$k!alcet$ large river

   $a_ak!ale'et$ Kootenay River

-($k!a)lma$ mouth 96.167, 168

-$k!almukwa'e{\cdot}t$ light 186.86; 266.42

   $tsa_ak!a_almi{\grave{}}yitna'na$ a little light (shining) through a hole 238.192

-$k!a_almo{\cdot}k$ hoop 146.58, 59

$k!{\iota}'k!o_um'$ a fish with large head and thin tail 78.123; 226.33

-$k!o$- suff.   with point 2.7; 72.16

$k!u''mtsak(s)$ shell 192.53

-$k!umna$-   to be poor

   $k!umnaqaqa'_ane{\cdot}$ he is poor 42.15, 16; 110.33

$k!u'sti{\cdot}t!$ larch

-$k!on$ nose (of man)

-$k!unkak$ bill, beak, nose (of an animal) 70.16; 96.197; 164.84

$k!u'q_une{\cdot}$ lynx (= short face)

-$k!p{\nu}'kam$ root 11.12

-$q(a)$ suff.   with knife

   $lu{\cdot}q^ual{\iota}'sne{\cdot}$ it was cut off 28.1 (= it was deprived of it with a knife)

   $lusaq!qa'lne{\cdot}$ his leg was cut off 28.3 (lu-$saq!$-qa-l-$ne{\cdot}$)

qa-   not 3.3, 5.11; 144.33, 35

qa-   thus

   $qake'{\iota}ne{\cdot}$ he said thus 1.1

   $qaqa'_ane{\cdot}$ he is thus 4.5

   $qalo'_uk_une{\cdot}$ he cried thus 19.7

   $qalwe'yne{\cdot}$ he thought so 62.69

qa- pr.   along

   $qaosaqa'_ane{\cdot}$ he staid 5.14; 9.15

   $qaka{\cdot}nk!on{\iota}'lne{\cdot}$ he pointed at them hither 254.119

   $laqa{\grave{}}nank!on{\iota}'lne{\cdot}$ he pointed at them thither 192.41

   $ya_aqanak{\iota}lhaqwu'mke{\cdot}$ generations 68.2

   $qanalwa'ts!ne{\cdot}$ they play along 70.19

   $qaknu'te{\cdot}$ he came pursuing her 64.105

   $qakal'akano\chi onu'k_une{\cdot}$ it came flying out 224.107

   $qa{\grave{}}k{\iota}lhaqa'_ane{\cdot}$ it is right along there 92.88

-qa-   to be

   $yunaqa'_ane{\cdot}$ there are many 1.5

   $tsEmak!qa'_ane{\cdot}$ he is strong 180.41

-$qa.ik{\iota}t!_uwu$- (see also [=${\iota}k{\iota}t!_uwo$])   to be nine

$qai\chi o'ktse{\cdot}k$ he plays ball with bat. (See qay- to roll)

qao-, qaw- pr.　there (demonstrative) 48.8

  quosaqa'ₐne·　he staid there 2.4; 6.6; 14.13

  qaoxa'xe·　he arrived there 2.6; 15.8

  qooxal'ɩtk'n·e·　just there he made it 6.11

  qawakalɩ'kᵢne·　he comes to his own tracks

-(ha)qay-　to roll 196.130; 210.466

  tsxalhaqayeqa'me·k　he will roll himself 52.2 (*ts-xal-ha-qay[e]-qa-me·k*)

qayaqa- pr.　through 7.15; 74.59

  qayaqa'wo　half, middle 8.8

  qayaₐqa'la·m　yearling buffalo calf 196.124

qaha- pr.　along

-qaps- pr.　like

  qapsqaqa'ₐne·　it is like (it) 198.204

  sɩlqa`psqakɩsqlɩ'lne·　his eyes were like — 194.90 (*sɩl-qaps-qa-kɩs-qlɩl-ne·*)

qa'psin　something, what 66.35 90.34

-qat　tail 126.7

  qalyuwa·kaq!alqa'tₗne·　he put the tail up quickly 188.29 (*qal-yu-wa·-kaq!al-qat-ne·*)

qatal- pr.　can not.　(See *qa-* not, *tal-* can)

  qataltsxa'n·e·　he can not speak 70.38

-qa·twumlaₐl　shirt 82.25

qas- pr.　alongside of 80.175

-qas-　to break to pieces

  qa'sxₐne·　he bit a piece off 48.10 (*qas-x-ne·*)

  qasnɩnqa'me·k　he cut himself to pieces 74.26 (*qas-nɩn-qa-me·k*)

qaspɩ'l'o·kᵘ　crane 84.37

qa'snal　shield 192.57; 202.277

qa'sk!o　male

-qasl'oq!wek　to be disappointed 130.74

-qa·ts-　to come from a place 66.35; 86.8

qa'lsuk　fresh meat 230.12

qan- pr.　along there

  qa·na'xe·　he went along 60.2

  qanla'lte·　he struck it 3.11

-qan-　plural 222.98

  wuqanmitu'kᵤne·　rivers are long (*wu-qan-nmituk-ne·*)

  tɩnaqanxa''mne·　they went in 72.58

-qa'k.lɩk-　he was named thus 88.13.　(See *-k.le·*)

-qaqas-　to stop 62.36, 66

  qaqask'n·e·　he stops

-qa·noxunuk-　a creek is somewhere 274.41.　(See *qa-* along)

-qal-

  qalqa'ₐtse·　he went around in a circle 60.3

  kuqa˘ha'ₐlkqaₐts　I who walk about 240.220

qa'la　somebody 60.20, 92.90; who? 72.57, 248.3

  qa'la·n·　whoever 70.34

qala'k'ne·s　straight upward 214.73

qa'ₐlɩn　just 76.86, 87 (*qa'hₐlɩn* 44.12)

(qalt)　child 136.235; 160.358

  aqa''ltle·s　his child 42.34

  alaqa'ltle·s　his children 70.35; 92.111

  n'asqa'lte·　she had two children 66.33

-qalsa-　to be three 60.5; 250.24

  qalsaqa'lte·　he has three children 34.1

qe·'na (qɛ'n·a) behold 98.242; 170.135; 252.71

qo· there, that 14.12, 13; 15.11

-qᵘ suff. in water. (See *-uq*)

   nonaqᵥ'n·e· he fell into the water 8.10

-qupaɫ spruce cone 260.1

   aₐ'qu'paɫ spruce cone

-qumɫas(χo)- to jump 126.6; 156.285, 291

-quta·ɫ ax 15.10

   aₐ'qu'ta·ɫ ax

qu'stɛt! trout 39.1, 6

qun- pr. contact

   qunya'xₐne· he touched it 60.1; 76.67

   qo·na'xe· he visits 74.57

   qunatsa'ₐxₐne· he poked him 122.48

   quna·kɛnxamu'n·e· he stabbed him with it 114.99

qo'ᵤka·n' come! 60.21, 27

-qok!am beaver's house 130.91, 104, 105. (See *-k!a[me·]* hole)

qo'kᵘᵉ·n raven 74.17; (*qu'kᵘᵉ·n*) 212.1

-qoqᵘat nest

qu'qoᵤq swan

qoqu'ske· bluejay ˍ72.59

-qoqu'n(te·) to do something on purpose 192.44

-qoqᵘts!aɫa-

   skɛkqoqᵘts!aɫa'ɛne· it lay there wet 134.190

-qoq!okuɫ- black

   kamqoq!o'kuɫ black

(*-quxma-*) gray

   aₐ'quxma'nuk gray stone 88.19

-quɫuk!pko stump 126.3, 4 (in derivatives *-quɫuk!pkup-*)

-qᵤwaₐ(te·)

   sukqᵤwa'ₐte· it has good hair 204.327

-qᵤwat ear

   kᵤwɛ'ɫqᵤwa't!e·'s mule (= his big-ears) 190.7

-qsa- to go, to move (?)

   qsama'ɫne· to go together 126.2; 134.154

   qsaklo'ᵤne· to dip

-qsaɫa nose 11.7, 9

   aₐ'kuqsa'ɫa nose 11.11

-qₐnuks- to crawl 86.25

-qkup- quickly 3.4; 12.3, 10; 70.41

-qqa'ₐtse· he goes about 58.2, 3. (See *-qa·ts-*)

-qxa- (perhaps better *-kxa*, from *-k-* towards speaker)

   ɫao·'niɫ·a'qxaqku\plaɫtɛ'ɫne· he struck again from underneath 70.44 (*ɫa-o·n-ɫ(a)-qxa-qkup-ɫaɫ-tɛ-ɫ-ne·*)

   tsxalyaqxa·\ɫaɫta'pse· will strike from each side 156.278 (*tsxal-ya-qxa-ɫaɫ-tapse·*)

-qɫa(te·), qɫa(kɛn)- to skin 168.58, 59

-qɫa·ɫ-

   n'ɛtkɛkqɫa·\ɫaɫqa·'tse· he went way around 4.10; 7.14

-qɫe· horn 3.10⸗ 14.3

   aₐ'ku'qɫe· horn 3.10; 62.56

-qɫɛl eye 46.29; 94.153, 158

   aₐ'kaqlɛ'l'eᵢs his eye 58.18

-qɫupin young tree 120.11; 126.14; 166.38; 188.19

-q!a- plural

 ats!m:lq!aluk!puka′m′e·s his grandfathers 72.60

 kaq!ak!o·′n:st my saddles

 koq!aka′ko· my traps

 kaq!aka′ma·lt my corrals

q!awa·ts!:′nme·k he was out of breath 60.19, 25; 74.25; 94.136

-q!awuka- to scrape, to cut tobacco

 kq!awu′ₐka·l plug tobacco

-q!aha- q!a- to hang, 180.35, 45

-q!a- to break

 q!axo′ₐne· it is broken 126.3

 q!axomu′n·e· he chopped with it 128.35

-q!ap- all, entire (before suffixes)

 q!a′pe· all 20.10

 q!apku′ₐne· he was burnt entirely 20.10

 q!apxa′me·k he ate himself entirely 82.10 (q!ap-xa-me·k)

 q!apil- all, entire (before independent verbs) 84.7; 94.143

q!a′pqa·l kingfisher 9.5, 7, 8

-q!an- to hang 166.29. (See -q!aha-)

-q!an- flat, spread out

 qa`oxal′:tq!ank:kqa′ₐne· he lay down there quietly 120.232

 aₐ·q!ana′kₐna·m knee

 yu·w:sq!a′na·k Knee-Cap (a name) 70.40

 sk:kq!ano′ₐkₐne· it is flooded

 haq!an·uqle·′:′tke· where there is a level place (on a hill) 16.3

 ga·q!a`nmoqts!:nu′kₐne· there was a flat prairie 154.245

 aₐ·q!anquts!la′e·n thickly-wooded place 72.71; 76.81

 qayaₐqawaₐq!anq!l:′lne· he made a mark in the center 198.183

 -q!anququat- round

 naq!anququatqa′ₐne· it is round

-q!anlupxamako- there is a lump, excrescence, on surface 252.64, 69

-q!akpa(me·k) to forget 50.19; 82.196; 114.89; 206.356

-q!akpa(kit) to kill by striking 70.34; 74.25; 250.60

-q!ax- to tie up (for shamanistic performance)

 kq!axna′mnam some one who is tied up 52.1

-q!al- to stretch out 3.9

 qal′:t!naqkupq!alsa′q!ne· he stretched his leg out quickly 84.61

 n′a`kaq!alk:′n·e· he stretched it out 200.234 (n-a·-ka-q!al-k:n-ne·)

-q!al·:kak- eyebrows 78.128, 130

q!aluk.le·′t:ne· noise stopped 256.185 (-luk-le.:l-ne·)

-q!ey:t

 nakq!ey:′t:ne· they talked 74.41

-q!o·mal to be dirty 27.6 (?)

 sk:kq!uma′lne· he lay (there) dirty 134.190

q!u′me a fish sp. 76.65

-q!u′mne·- to sleep 66.21

q!u′tsaₐts chipmunk 46.20; 58.1

-q!utse′:(le·) to tickle 160.377; 236.156

q!oₐkoxa′me·k he made a fire 80.186, 187

q!untka- pr. around 256.159

 q!untkathawasxo′me·k he sings going around 52.13

-q!uxma fleshy 190.7. (See -xma)

 la`l:tq!o`xₐmasa′q!ₐne· he also had no flesh on legs 272.25

 k!a`k!lan·aq!o`xₐmale′:l different kind of tree (?) 190.1

q!u'lwa_a rose hip 7.1

-*q!yu*- top (?)

　a_a'kuq!yuk!alaxwe'et doorway 94.147

　a_a'qanq!yumɛ'n·a hillside 94.135

　wa'kaq!yule.ɛ'tke· end of mountain 136.217

　qa·witsq!ayule.ɛ't_ine· top of mountain 226.16

-*q!wiya(te·)* to swallow

　k!unuq!^uwiya'_ate· he swallowed him 86.46

-*q!ma*- lightly

　wu'q!maxo'_une· he touched it lightly 146.55

　wo·q!^uma_ane·kɛ'l_ine· a little while

　sq!ma·'wi·tslɛnq!a·''ntse· it stuck out a little 252.78

-*q!nu*- to climb

　wa·q!_anu'n·e· he climbed up 214.55

　nu·lqanka·qoq!^unu'ne· he climbed across the water 8.8

-*q!nuk* lake

　a_a'ku'q!nuk 76.99; 78.112

　kwɛ'lq!nok a big lake 74.33

-*q!nuk^ua·t* golden eagle 17.10

　kiaq!nu'k_uat golden eagle 198.170

-*q!le_il* stripe, mark 208.406

　kqayaqa·wuha'q!lil middle stripe 224.125

-*x̣a*- suff. with teeth, with mouth

　q!a'px̣_ane· he ate all 64.89; 84.32

　kawɛ'tsx̣a standing biting 94.158

　suk^uax̣_ane'_ise· it tastes good 272.14

-*x̣a*- to put, to place

　n'oqox̣akɛ'n·e· he put it into it 76.106

　łao·qox̣ax̣a''mne· he went back aboard 152.218

x̣a uncle (father's brother) 88.25; 94.138

x̣a'pe_i camas 11.1

-*x̣_ama*- light (?)

　lɛtx̣_amaqa'_ane· it is heavy 272.7

-*x̣at(kɛnuk^u)*- to save

　x̣atkɛ'n·e· he saved himself 214.50

　x̣atknu'k_une· he was saved 68.71

　x̣atk_inuk^uɛ'n·e· he saves him

-*atkax̣'niyatu'mal* reciprocal relation between parents-in-law and children-in-law, intermediate relative dead

x̣a'tsa uncle (mother's brother)

-*x̣a'_atsa*- to be four 62.66

　kx̣a·tsa·nmi'yɛt four days 250.26

x̣atsɛn- pr. both

　x̣atsɛnqawa'l!ne· both ears

　x̣a'tsɛnɛltsuk^ua'te· he took both 28.9

-*x̣anx̣o (-a'nx̣o ?)* to overtake 3.10

x̣a'x̣as skunk 23.12; 230.2

-*x̣a(x̣e·)* to reach

　kyu·x̣a'x̣a·m one who reached the top 74.32

　qaox̣ax̣a''mne· they reached there 76.71

-*x̣al*- pr. future, always with *ts*- (*tsx̣al*-) 76.75; 84.33

-*x̣al*- suff. with saw

x̣a'l(e·) child 84.33

　x̣ale'_ine· O child! 102.332

　x̣alna'le_il nephew, niece (sister's child, said by woman)

xa′aⁱtsin dog 60.11; 164.2; horse 190.14

-*xo*- suff. with back, with body, by striking

  pɩsxo′ᵤnu put me off! 2.4

  naⁱxo′ᵤne· he carried him 2.2

-*xoᵤ*-

  qanaⁱtsɛqan′mɩ`nxoᵤqa′ₐne· he flew into it 96.168

  qakiⁱaq!maxoka′ₐne· he scared them 136.227

xun- pr. into fire (*xun*—*qᵘ* into water)

  xunakinɩ′ⁱne· he was thrown into fire 37.13

  xunmɩtqu′ⁱne· he throws it into water

  xunmɩtquⁱɩ′ⁱne· it was thrown into water 23.5

xma ought 26.8; 76.85, 93

-*xma* flesh 42.37; 96.171

  aₐ`kaxmaⁱa′na·m flesh

-*ⁱ*- suff. passive

  pɩsxo′ⁱne· he was put off 2.4

-*ⁱ*- suff. object

  qakɩ′ⁱne· he said to him (*qa-ke-l-ne·*)

ⁱ- pr. evidently, must be

  k.lsa′kq!nuk it must be a lake 72.12

ⁱa- pr. again, also

  ⁱaⁱo′ᵤsc· again there is nothing 64.90

  ⁱao·k!ᵘe.ɩ′sc· one more 88.56

-*ⁱa·-* back, in turn 2.10

ⁱa′a outside 226.51. (See *ⁱa′ⁱa·k*)

  k.ⁱaⁱaha′qᵤwom they were outside 200.226

ⁱawi·′ya·ⁱ huckleberries 184.51

ⁱa′wo female elk 21.1

ⁱaps- pr., *ⁱapsiⁱ-* pr. again 60.25, 31; 148.117

ⁱa·m′ a switch for stringing fish, twig (?) 9.9, 10

-*ⁱa·′m* head

  aₐ`k. ⁱa′′ma·m head 78.143

-*ⁱa(maⁱ)* blanket 264.67

  sⁱama′ⁱne· it is a blanket 204.342

  n′anuxo·′nⁱatɩmo′me·k he shook his blanket 174.209

-*ⁱatᵢyiⁱ-* pr. always

  n′o`k!ᵘɩnⁱa`ₐtᵢy`ⁱtsha`qaiyɩmo`xona`titmo′ⁱne· at once he was always rolling about 70.42

  n′upsⁱa`tᵢyiⁱ′ɩ′kᵢne· he was always eating

-*ⁱatᵢqkat(kɩn)-* to go to get

  n′uk!ⁱatᵢqkatkɩ′n·e· he went to get one 118.194

-*ⁱat!* arm 180.55

ⁱa′tuq! duck 70.6; 80.180

ⁱa′tsᵢne· the other side 162.28; 236.131

ⁱa·n′ moccasin 224.5

ⁱa′n·a come! 62.38; 240.220

ⁱa′′nta rear part of tent, back of fire; outer side of tent, at bottom, all around 97

  sⁱa`tᵢyiⁱ·a`n·ⁱaqanaqna′ksc· he always sat with back to fire 88.32

ⁱa′q!a part of tent near door

  ⁱaq!anxo′ᵤna·ⁱ door 94.146; 96.196

ⁱaⁱaq!aqa′ne· he choked while eating

-*ⁱax-* to complete

  ⁱaxa′qo·ⁱ he arrived at water 268.12

  k.ⁱaⁱaxa′ⁱkin one who carried it back 194.111

ⁱa′xa bed 198.199

laxlo·'mał widow. widower

la'ła·k outside

-*łał(te·)* to strike

  qanła'łte· he struck it 15.5

  qaoxała'łte· he hit it there

-*łehι'(te·)* to say "yes"

-*łe.ιt* weather, country 16.3

  yιsle.ι't.se· there is a mountain 46.2

  sahanłe.ι'ține· it is bad weather 66.18

łιt- pr. without

  łιtqawu'mne· it is empty 72.62

  łιtu'kᵘne· there is no water

  łιtkuma'łne· it is not bloody

-*łitιt* clothing

  aₐ·k.litι'ține·s your clothing 244.20

  suk.litι'ține· good clothing 244.39

-*łitιt-*

  tse·kalitι'ține· he looked around 60.13

  hun'oᵤlitι'ține· I know a place

l̦'se· paddle 228.96

-*łe̦ts-* to sleep

  kᵤwι'l·e·ts sound asleep 144.44

  skιk.le'̦itsne· he lay asleep 144.42

  n'askik.le'̦itse· two were asleep 216.106

-*łιn* pr. may 250.30

  hιnłιn'o'ᵤte· you may want it 64.107

le'̦ine· on the other side 100.281; 226.34

-*łιk* foot

  aₐ·k.lι'kna·m foot, tracks 24.8

  qanaqlι'kxₐne· he kicked it 24.3

-*łιk-* noise (?)

  qa·atskιk.lιknatι'ține· he made noise inside 58.24

ło'u awl 37.4

loᵘ fir

lu- nothing

  lu'n·e· nothing 3.2

  lu''nte· he made it nothing 98.233

  luqkιpqsała'ₐte· quickly he cut off the nose 11.7

-*lu* snow

  a'ₐ·k·lu snow

łu- other side, far side

  k.łuha'kq!nuk lake on other side 162.56

  k.łohanιts!ła'e·n tree on other side 236.131

  łu'n·o beyond, far away 72.61

  łoa'q!mawιsqa'ₐne· he jumped a little to the other side 94.155

luma'yιt springtime 100.258; 180.45

luna'tłe· brother-in-law, sister-in-law (all kinds), intermediate relative dead, 72.1; 76.69

lu'kpu· buffalo cow 29.2, 7

łoᵤk!ᵘ wood 128.35; 130.99

-*łuk!puk-*

  ats!mιdq!ałuk!puka'm'e·s his great-grandfather 72.60

-*łuk!mo-* .to roast 128.50

  łuk!moxa'me·k he roasted it 82.7

łuqᵘa- (see *łu-* other side, far side)

  łuqᵘalitxo'ᵘme·k he lay down the other way 94.151

łuquꞏnꞏko- to melt 184.42

  tsɛmaꞏkꞏlⁱꞏloquꞏnkuꞌpseꞏ it melted strongly by heat

-łwey mind, heart 60.14; 132.144

  kꞏlupxɑluⁱꞌyteꞏ one who knows mind 132.144

-łnohoᵤs star 17.9

  kꞏlaqsaꞏłnoꞌhoꞏs how many stars?

łkaꞌmꞏu child 17.9

  łkamnɛꞌntik children 188.45

-łqꞏokᵘ- (-ɩlqꞏokᵘ-) to be in danger (?) 60.26

  nułqꞏoꞌkᵤneꞏ he is wise

ENGLISH–KUTENAI

aboard, he went back *laoꞏqoxaxaꞌꞌmneꞏ* (see *-xa-*)

about, probably *upɩn-* pr. *naqan-* pr.

  about three *naqanqaꞌlsa*

above *ata-* pr., *naꞌₐta*

across *alqan-* pr.

  (over a high object) *watꞏ-* pr.

  he climbed across the water *nuꞏlqankaꞏqoqꞏlᵘnuꞌneꞏ* (see *-qꞏnu-*)

  he kicked him across *watꞏmɛꞏteꞏkɩꞌnꞏeꞏ* (see *watꞏ-*)

  he went across *qanałwatꞏlaꞌxeꞏ* (see *watꞏ-*)

act, to *-iteꞏk* (see *-ɩt-*)

  to act foolishly *sɩlskɩnꞏkuꞏꞌtsteꞏk* (see *skɩꞌnꞏkuꞏts*)

  he wants to act his own way *-sɩnꞏakpaꞌmeꞏk*

afraid, to be *-onɩl-*, *-pɩtsqa-*

  he is afraid *pɩtsqałweꞌyneꞏ* (see *-pɩtsqa-*)

again *la-*, *laps-*, *lapsil-*, pr.

  again there is nothing *lałoꞌᵤseꞏ* (see *la-*)

aim, to *-nułkꞏo-* (see *-nuł-*)

alive *wunmanaꞌmu*

all, to be *-oꞏkᵤ(eꞏ)-*

all (before independent verbs) *qꞏlapil-* (see *-qꞏlap-*); (before suffixes) *-qꞏlap-*; *qꞏlaꞌpeꞏ* (see *-qꞏlap-*)

almost *tuꞌxᵤa*

along *s-*, *qa-*, *qaha-*, pr

  along there *qan-* pr.

  he went along *qaꞏnaꞌxeꞏ* (see *qan-*)

  it is right along there *qaꞏkɩlhaqaꞌₐneꞏ* (see *qa-* pr.)

  they play along *qanałwaꞌtsꞏneꞏ* (see *qa-* pr.)

alongside of *qas-* pr.

also *la-* pr.

always *-latᵢyil-* pr.

  he was always eating *nꞌupstaꞏtᵢyilɛꞌkᵢneꞏ* (see *-latᵢyil-*)

  at once he was always rolling about *nꞌoꞏkꞏlᵘꞏnlaꞏatᵢyꞏꞏltshaꞏqaiyɩlmoꞏxonaꞏtitmoꞏłne* (see *-latᵢyil-*)

American (= Boston) *pɔꞌstɩn*

and *-ts*

angry, he is still *saꞏkɩlsaꞏnɩlweꞌyneꞏ* (see *-sahan-*, *-sakɩl-*)

animal, small *tuqꞏltsqaꞌmna*

ankle *aₐꞏkuⁱꞌtsaꞏk*

ant *tsꞏlaxuꞌna*

antelope *nɛꞌłtukꞏlᵘp*

antlers *aₐꞏqꞏlaꞌlɛꞏ*

anus *-kꞏlalaxekp*, *aₐꞏkꞏlalaꞌxɩkp*

anvil *aꞌₐꞏqaⁿuk*

apart *pa·ts-* pr.

Apocynum cannabinum *a_a'qoła'qpe·s* (see *a_a'qoula'qp:k*)

approaches, he *nutsa'xe·* (see -*huts-*)

Aralia nudicaulis *a_a'ko'u·k* C

arise, to · -*uwok_u-*

arm *a'_a'k.la·t!, -lat!*

　he moved his arm *wanla't!ne·* (see -*wan-*)

arm above elbow *a_a'k:nlu'm:n* (see also FOREARM)

armpit *a_a'qaxapk.la't!na·m*

around *q!untka-, akam:n-, qal-,* pr.

arrive, to *w-* pr.

　he arrived at water *łaxa'qo·l* (see -*lax-*)

　he arrived there *qaoxa'xe·* (see *qao-*)

　he arrives *wa'xe·* (see *w-* pr. and -*axe·*)

arrow -*ka-, a_a'k!*

　he has an arrow *naka_a'ne·* (see -*ha-*)

　he had two arrows *n'aimaka_a'ne·* (see -*ka-*)

arrow point *a_a'k:nq!a'qa*

　(of metal) *n:lko'_uts!ap* (see *n:'lko*)

arrow wood *a'_a'k!wo·k* (see *a_ak!*)

Artemisia discolor, frigida *a_a'k:nuk.luxona'ka* C; used for headache *a_a'ku·o·k.lai-*
　xuna'_ate·t C

　medicine made of *a_a'k:nuk.luxokona'_aka awu'mo* C (see *a_a'k:nuk.luxona'ka*)

ashamed, to be -*hałnukp-*

ashes *a_a'kuqmo·'ko·, a_a'kuq!mü'ko·, -oko*

ashore *up-* pr.

asleep, sound *k_uw:'ł·e·ts* (see -*le_its-*)

　he lay asleep *sk:k.le'_itsne·* (see -*le_its-*)

　two were asleep *n'askik.le'_itse·* (see -*le_its-*)

assembled, they were *(qa)haqowu'm'ne·*

autumn *ts!up'na'kot*

away *hosan- (hesan-), ts!:n-,* pr.

　he ran away *no·sanoxunqa'_ane·* (see *hosan-*)

awl *lo'u*

awoke, he *naq!małe'_itsne·* (see -*haq!ma-*)

ax *a_a'qu'ta·l, -quta·ł*

back *tuw-, man-* pr.; -*la·-*

　he fell back *tuwun:nmuxu'n·e·* (see *tuw-*)

　he lay on his back *tuwuł':txo'_ume·k* (see *tuw-*)

　he looks back *lamanw:tskik:'łne·* (see *man-*)

back *a'_a'k.łak, -k!ałakak, a'ko_uk!ała'_akna·m*

　with back -*xo-* suff.

backside *a_a'q!u'lukp, a_a'k:'kpuk!, -kpuk!*

bad, to be -*sahan-*

　it is bad *saha'n·e·*

　it is a bad place *sa'hanle:'tne·* (see -*sahan-*)

badger *na'łme·t!*

bag *a_a'tsu·'ła, tsuła, a_a'ka·ł, a_a'kuła'ko* (?) C

ball, he plays — with bat -*qaixo'ktse·k*

bark of tree *a_a'k:'ts!qa·l, -ts!qa_ał*

　I tear off bark *hułuts!qalxo'_une·* (see -*ts!qa_ał*)

bark for canoe *a'_a'kwo·k, a'_a'ka·m* C

Barnard, B.C. *a_a'ku·'no·k* C

basket, birch-bark *na′ʻheˑk*
  spruce-bark *aₐ‛qu′q!wuk*
bat *a′ₐˑk.toˑm′*
bathe, to *na′qtseˑk* (see *-haqₐ-*)
be, to *-qa-, -ha-, -ɩn-*
  there are many *yunaqa′ₐncˑ* (see *-qa-*)
beak *aₐˑk!u′nkaˑk, -k!unkak*
bear, black, one year old *a′qtoˑ*
beard *aₐˑkuqloˑłaxa′naˑm*
beaver *sɩ′nˑaˑ*
  young beaver *mo′q!ᵤneˑ*
beaver dam *aₐˑq!ankɩ′tsqa*
beaver holes in water, beaver's house *aₐˑqo′k!aˑm, -qok!am*
because *o′k!qᵤna*
become, to *-ɩnqa′pteˑk* (see *-ɩn-*)
bed *ła′xa, aₐˑqanłknatɩtxai′yam*
behind *antsu-, ił-,* pr.
behold! *qeˑ′na*
belly *a′ₐˑkwum, -wum*
  belly swells up *-hutkawumako-*
  his belly is big *wɩłwu′mncˑ* (see *-wum*)
below *ʋm(eˑ)* pr., *ya′wo*
belt *a′ₐˑkaˑmt, -kaˑmt-*
bend in river *aₐˑkɩkqłalanmi′tuk*
berry *aₐˑkuq!łe′ɩt* (see also service berry, strawberry, etc.)
  partridge berry *tsa′qa*
  berries of Philadelphus Lewisii *aₐˑkuno‛′kyoˑk* C
  berry, a, sp. (?) *ma′xa*
  berry cake *aₐˑkɩtsłaq!o′ʻna*
  berry patch *-k!ałaxapak-*
    there is a large berry patch *skɩʻkɩl′wɩlk!ałaxapa′kseˑ* (see *-k!ałaxapak-*)
bet, to *-ɩtetɩ′l(eˑk)* (see *-ɩt-*)
beyond *lu′ʻnˑo* (see *lu*)-
big, large *-wɩl(qa-) -wił(qa)-*
  his belly is large *wɩłwu′mneˑ* (see *-wum*)
Bigelovia graveolens *aₐˑkɩnuk.luxona′ka* C
bill, beak *-k!unkak*
birch *aₐˑkowa′łwoˑk*
bird *tuq!tsqa′mna*
  a small bird, yellow at tip of feathers, with tip on head *wɩ′suk!ᵘ*
  a bird, yellow breast and gray wings *ka′tskaˑts*
  a small, gray bird, living on lake shore *wɩtsweˑts*
  a small, gray bird *aₐˑkikakuˑkwi′ɩt* C
  a small, gray bird *aₐˑkɩnuq!ᵘloxonaˑ′tɩt, aₐˑkɩnuk.lohona′teˑt* C
  a medium-sized, gray bird *aₐˑkɩnukota′teˑk* C
  a black bird with white spots, size of a robin *aₐˑkɩlq!ałuq!pwaq!*
  a bird, sp. (?) *wa′kuks*
biscuit *aₐˑkɩno‛mukna′na* C
bite *-ɩt!(xa)-* (perhaps *ɩt-xa* to do with teeth, see *-xₐ*)
  he bit a piece off *qa′sxₐncˑ* (see *-qas-*)
black, to be *-oqoq!u′koˑt-*
  black *kɩmqoq!o′kuł* (see *-qoq!okuł-*)
  it is black *namqok!oko′ᵤlneˑ* (see *ham-*)
Blackfoot Indians *katᵢkakɩ′tsaq!*

bladder a_aʻ$kukts$ʻkeʻn, -(u)ktsᵢken
  (of fish) a_aʻkuʹ$kmat$ C
blanket seʹᵢ$t!$, -la(mal)
  white blanket a_aʻ$q!u$ʹnaʻq
  it is a blanket $slama$ʹlneʻ (see -la[mal])
bleed from mouth, to -$halnukux_u$-
blood waʹʹnmo
  curdled blood yaʹ$t!aps$
  to be bloody -$hakumal$-, -$kumal$-
  it is not bloody lᵢ$tkuma$ʹlneʻ (see lᵢt-)
blow, to -hᵢ$lkupxo_u$-
  wind blows $nalum$ᵢ$$ʹnʻeʻʻ (see -hal-)
  wind blows a certain way $qanaw$ᵢtsoʹʹmeʻ (see -ha-)
bluejay $qoqu$ʹskeʻ
board a_aʻkᵢ$nuq!$ᵘlaʻ$k!a$ʹ$_ako$ʻ
body -$ulaks$, a_aʻkᵢ$ʹlxo$ʻ, a_aʻkuʹlak
  with body -xo- suff.
boil, to -$hanmuko$- (see -$hanuxo$-), -$huko$-
  to boil something -$nmuk_u$-
bone -$malak$, maʻ$k!$
  burnt bone a_aʻkᵢ$lq!an$ʻ$otsa$ʹko $ma_ak!$
  rotten bone hoʹ$q!ka$
  remains of broken bones a_aʻ$q!a$ʹnaʻk
Bonner's Ferry a_aʻ$kukpanmitu$ʹkxoʻ C
bonnet, war -yukᵘa, a_aʻk_iyuʹkwa
border, square pieces forming — of root basket a_aʻ$k.la$ʹlxoʻ C
  small ornamental pieces on border of root kettle a_aʻ$kutskakilukpo$ʹxal C
born, to be -$haqa$ʹaneʻ (see -ha-)
both $xats$ᵢn- pr.
  both ears $xats$ᵢ$nqawa$ʹ$t!ne$ʻ (see $xats$ᵢn-)
  he took both xaʻtsᵢnᵢ$ltsuk$ᵘaʹteʻ (see $xats$ᵢn-)
bottle a_aʻkoʹ$q_uwit!$
boughs, green -ulaʻl, a_aʻkuʹlaʻl
bow -woʻ
  he made a — for himself nʹᵢtʹwukᵘnᵢ$ʹ$le_ik$ (see -woʻ)
  bow stave, his a_aʻ$k.lakwo$ʹᵤteʻs (see -woʻ)
bow and arrows a_aʻ$q!ox_umale$ʹet
bowstring $t!a$ʻwuʹmka (see -$t!a$-)
braces a_aʻ$kilu$ʻkᵘ$atspu$ʹknaʻm C
brain $alqa$
branch (of tree) -a_aʻkᵢ$tsk!a$ʹlaʻk, -($ᵢ$)$tsk!ala$ʻk, -$tsk!alak$,
  he chops off a branch pᵢ$tstsk!alakxo$ʹᵤneʻ (see -$tsk!a$ʻ-lak)
break, to -$q!a$-, -umᵢts-, -$aqts$-, -$yaq!$-, -$noq!$ᵘm-
  (a stick) -yaq-
  (camp) -$huqna$(meʻk)
  (to pieces) -qas-
  (wind) -$atskup$-
  (with teeth) tsᵢ$ʹ$k!x_ane$ʻ (see -$ts$ᵢ$k!$-)
  she broke it -hanʻuʻ$qo.i$ʻxoʹᵘ(neʻ)
  it is broken $q!axo$ʹᵤneʻ (see -$q!a$-)
breast tsuʹu
  (of bird) a_aʻkᵢ$ʹ$nhas$ C
breast pieces of game a_aʻkxaʹskaʻk
breath, he was out of $q!awa$ʻ$ts!$ᵢ$ʹ$nme$ʻ$k$
bridge a_aʻkoʻʹkoʻ C
  I shall make a bridge $huts$ᵢ$tkokopk$ᵢnʻeʻ (see a_aʻkoʻʹkoʻ) C

bridle *aₐ'kok!ᵘatska'lma*
bright red *sukᵘnohu'se·* (see -*soᵤk*-), *yawo'ᵤnek!*
brings, he — it *walkɪ'n·e·* (see *w*- pr.)
brook *aₐ'kɪnuxo'ᵤnuk*
brother (said by sister) *alɪ'tskeᵢt*
brother, elder, *tat!*
brother, younger *tsa·*, *tsiya*
brother's daughter *pa·*
brother's wife *a'tse·*
brother-in-law (all kinds), intermediate relative dead *tuna't!e·*
bubble *tsu'm(o·kᵘ)*
buck *wa'ma·t!*
  two-year-old buck *kianq!at(na'na)*
bucket *a'tso*
buckle of belt *aₐ'kwɪ'tsko·* C
bud *aₐ'qu'pa·t!*
buffalo *iya'mu*
  buffalo bull *nɪ'tse·k*
  buffalo calf *aₐ'kɪnku'ma·t*
  yearling buffalo calf *qayaₐqa'la·m* (see *qayaqa*-)
  buffalo cow *tu'kpu·*
  buffalo drive *aₐ'kuqla'laₐk·*
bumblebee *kianuq!u'lupq*, (= white end) *kianuqlo·q!u'lo·kp* (see -*nuqlum*-)
burden of song *he he ha*
burning, it is *naq!ₐko'ᵤne·* (see -*ko*-)
  burning food -*atikwa.ɪ't*ᵢ*(ne·)*
  it is burnt on top *yu·halhaq!aku'n·e·* (see -*hal*-)
  it burnt quickly *ts!ɪlq!anku'pse·*
  he was burnt entirely *q!apku'ᵤne·* (see -*q!ap*-)
  everything is burnt *q!apku'pse·* (see -*ko*-)
burst, to -*paq!ₐme·*-, -*hakq!me·*
  to burst by heat -*t!anoko'ᵤ(ne·)* (see also -*ko*-)
bury, to -*ɪtetɪl* (see -*ɪt*-)
bush, a — with white berries, not edible *mɪtsqo·ko·lɪ'lna·*
  a little bush *t!a·pɪs(wukna'na)*
  its bushes *aₐ'kwakᵘa(ɪ'se·s)*
but *at*, *mɪ'ksa'n*, *ma*, (weak disjunctive) *pa·t*
butcher, to -*ɪtk!an*-
butt, to -*hako*-
butt end of branch (see *aₐ'kukpɪtsk!a'la·k*) C
butterfly *ko·dli'dlus*
calf of leg *aₐ'kuqlɪk!a'lna·m*, *aₐ'qo·l*
call, to -*haqan(ke)*-
  to call guardian spirit -*akme*-
camas *xa'pɛᵢ*
camp, to, over night -*ɪkᵢyɪksɪ'le·k*
can *tal*- pr.
Canadian *kɪndzɛrdz* (King George)
can not *qatal*- pr.
  he can not speak *qataltsxa'n·e·* (see *qatal*-)
canoe *yaqso''mit*
canoe calking *a'ₐqut* (?)
canoe, longitudinal strips on sides and bottom of *aₐ'kɪ'k.tuk* C
canoe, side strips on top of, bent *aₐ'ko·'kyu* C
canoe, binding strips at pointed ends of *aₐ'kunwo·k* C

Carex scoparia a_a'k$_i$'nskwal

caribou na'x$_a$ne·

carry, to -nma-

 to carry meat -haq!awu-, -waq!$_a$wu-

 to carry torches -halnuq^u- (see -hal-)

 to carry water -halko$_u$- (see -hal-)

 he carried him nalxo'$_u$ne· (see -hal- -xo- suff.)

 he carried two la.aimaxo'$_u$ne· (see -nma-)

 he carried it back into latnalk$_i$'n·e· (see t$_i$n-)

 one who carried it back k.lalaxa'lkin (see -lax-)

 one who carried three qalsanma'xo· (see -nma-)

 he carries in hand ṅalk$_i$'n·e· (see -hal-)

cascade a_a'kaxa'pqle·

catch, to -ts$_i$n-, -$_i$kts$_i$k-

 he catches it ts$_i$nk$_i$'n·e· (see -ts$_i$n-)

cattle iya'mu

 hoof of a_a'k$_i$tsq!alu'pta·k.

cause -tse$_i$te· suff.

cave -ilala (?)

 cave under water a_a'k$_i$lalaqu'no·k

cedar $_i$'is!na·t!

 red cedar a_a'kok!uplo·'lal

charr to'hol

cheat, to -ay-

cheek a_a'k!ma'ma·l

cherry a_a'k$_i$'lma·k!, -e·lma·k!

Cherry Creek a_a'kilkanoskowo·k C

chickadee m$_i$ts!qa'qas

chicken hawk $_i$'nla·k

chief naso'$_u$k^{u}e·n

child (qalt), xa'l(e·), lka'm·u

 O child! xale'$_i$ne· (see xa'l[e·])

 she had two children n'asqa'lte· (see [qalt])

 he has three children qalsaqa'lte· (see -qalsa-)

chin a_a'k$_i$nkamts$_i$nka·'k(na·m) C

Chinaman knu'q!lam' (=long-haired one) (see -nuq!-)

chipmunk q!u'tsa$_a$ts

 a species of chipmunk na'mlat!

choked, he — while eating lalaq!aqa'ne·

chopped, he — along qa$_a$nkitsxo'$_u$ne· (see -kits-)

 he chopped it off close to edge n'$_i$ntakitsxo'$_u$ne· (see -kits-)

 he chopped with it q!axomu'n·e· (see -q!a-)

 he chops off p$_i$tsxo'$_u$ne· (see -p$_i$ts-)

 he chops off a branch p$_i$tstsk!alakxo'$_u$ne· (see -tsk!alak)

cinch a_a'kok!^{u}a'tswim

claw -ukp, a'$_a$'kukp, kiapt!aha'nlukp (see kiapt!aha·n$_i$tsq!ahai'na·m)

clay, white k$_i$'t$_i$muk!

cliff -nmok!, -n$_i$'m·ok!, a_a'kn$_i$'m·o·k!, a_a'kuq!yu'muk!

climb, to -q!nu-, -w$_i$tsq!nu(ne·)

 he climbed across the water nu·lqanka·qoq!^{u}nu'ne· (see -q!nu-)

 he climbed up wa·q!$_a$nu'n·e· (see -q!nu-)

clothing -uqla'nt, a_a'ku'qla·nt (see a_a'ku'qla). -lit$_i$t

 good clothing suk.lit$_i$'t$_i$ne· (see -lit$_i$t)

 your clothing a_a'k.lit$_i$'t$_i$ne·s (see -lit$_i$t)

cloud a'$_a$'qal

coal $a_a\dot{k}\iota ts!ka'ki\cdot l$, -ts!kak\iota t-
    there is much coal $yu\dot{}nats!kak\iota'lne\cdot$ (see -ts!kak\iota t-)
coat $a_a\dot{q}atwu'mlat$
coax, to -haw\iota'tsno\dot t- (see -ha-)
cold -\iota t!k!o-
color terms, prefix of ham-
comb, to tsuk(la'ma'ne\dot{})
come! la'n\dot a, qo'\u uka\dot n'
    to come (?) -\iota l(k\iota n)- (see il-)
    to come back to life -\iota tq!a'nxam-
    he came back there coughing laqa\dot{}oxalk\iota kq!owasxoneyik\iota'me\dot k (see -kq!owas[xo]-)
    he comes back quickly wa\dot{}s\iota l\dot ax a'xe\dot{} (see was-)
    to come from a place -qa\dot ts-
    to come together -\iota t!qao(xa)-
    he comes to his own tracks qawakal\iota'k_ine\dot{} (see qao-)
    coming, motion towards speaker k- pr.
    feathers coming off k.lunqowa''xo\dot{} (see -nqowa)
complete, to -lax-
cone of pine, larch, spruce $a_a\dot{q}u'pal$, -qupal
contact qun- pr.
    to come into contact -yax-
continuative -s\iota l- pr.
continue, to -na\dot l-
cook, to -ke_ik-
    cooked, to boil -huko-
    cooking-basket y\iota'tske\dot{}
corpse $a_a\dot kuq!lay\iota't!in$
corral -kamal, $a_a\dot ka'mal$
    my corrals kaq!aka'ma\dot lt (see -q!a-)
    there are two corrals sk\iota k\iota ska'ma\dot l (see -kama\dot l)
cottonwood $a_a\dot k.lu'ma\dot k$
cough, to -kq!owas(xo)-, -hakq!_uwasxo'_ume\dot k
    he came back there coughing laqa\dot{}oxalk\iota kq!owasxoneyik\iota'me\dot k (see -kq!owas[xo]-)
country am\dot a\dot k, -le\iota t
coup, to count -h\iota k!\iota st-
cover, to -man-
    to cover head with blanket -\iota lnk!oma'te\dot k
    he covers it with his hand mane'_ine\dot{} (see -hey-)
    (tent) is covered tuk!xo(lne\dot{})
coyote sk\iota'n\dot ku\dot ts
cracker $a_a\dot k\iota no\dot{}mukna'na$ C
cradle $a_a\dot k\iota nk!u'ma\dot l$
crane qasp\iota'l'o\dot k^u
crawl, to -qa^nuks-
crazy, to be -uktman(qa)-, -hupü(qa)-
creek, a — is somewhere -qa\dot noxunuk-
cricket t!aptsl\iota'nwa\dot s
crosswise -maqan-
crown of head $a_a\dot k\iota nqanu'qla\dot m$ (see $a_a\dot k\iota'nqa\dot n$)
cry, to -ila-
    he cried thus qalo'_uk_une\dot{} (see qa-)
cut, to — hair -haq!l\iota sak-
    to cut tobacco -q!awuka-
    he cut himself to pieces qasn\iota nqa'me\dot k (see -qas-)

cut, to
  his leg is cut off *lusaq!qa'lne·* (see *-saq!-, -q[a]*)
  it was cut off *lu·qᵘalɛ'sne·* (see *-q[a]*)
  quickly he cut off the nose *luqkupqsala'ₐte·* (see *lu-*)
cyclone *aₐ'kɛk'nqan*
dance, to *-haqwil-*
  dance squatting, to *-hawɛsk!akana'na·m* (see *-ha-*)
  sun dance *-hanquxol-* (see *-hanuxo-*)
danger, to be in *-ɛlq!okᵘ-, (-lq!okᵘ-)*
dangerous, to be *-hukuya(kateᵢ)-*
dark, to be *-tsɛl-*
  it is dark *-tamoxu(n·e·)*
daughter *swɛn*
day *-nmiyɛt, -miyɛt*
(day)light, it is *-huk!ukyɛtᵢ-*
dead *-ip-*
deep, to be *-ulu-, -wɛt!-*
deer hoof *aₐ'kɛtsq!alu'pta·k*
  bunch of dew hoofs of deer *aₐ'kɛlq!a'lukp*
defecate, to *(n')uxᵢte·k*
desire, to *-ute-*
destroy, to *-tsɛk!-*
die, to *-up-*
different *ak!la(n)*
  a different way *(k)ts!ak!lana'ke·*
digging-stick *kiyu'kmul*
diorite *tuwukxo'nal*
dip, to *qsak!o'ₐne·* (see *-qsa-*)
  to dip water *-ts!ɛnyaxak!o-* (see *-yax-*)
dirty, to be *-mats, -q!o·mal*
  he lay (there) dirty *skɛkq!ₐma'lne·* (see *-q!o·mal*)
disappointed, to be *-qasl'oq!wek*
discuss, to *-hakq!yɛt-*
dish of pottery *a'tso*
disliked, he — it *sa·nlɛkpakta'pse·* (see *-ɛkpak[te]*)
disposed, to be *(-ɛkpak[te])*
distance, some — back *ɛlqa-* pr.
dive, to *-wats!-*
divide, to *-alas-*
divination, used for *sa'kɛlk.lu'kmul* (see *-k.luk-*)
divine, to *-k.luk-*
do, to *-ula-, -ɛt-*
  to do something on purpose *-qoqu'n(tc·)*
  to do with a point (*i. e.*, kill with arrow) *-ɛtk!oᵤ-* (see *-ɛt-*)
doe *nilo'ᵤqᵘat*
dog *xa'ₐltsin*
done, cooked, to boil *-huko-*
don't! *maₐts*
door *łaq!anxo'ᵤna·l* (see *la'q!a*)
  there is a door *sɛnk!ala·xwiɛ'tsne·* (see *-sɛn-*)
doorway *aₐ'kuq!yuk!alaxwe'et* (see *-q!yu-, -k!alaxawuet, aₐ'k!alaxuwe'et*)
down (away from speaker) *un-* pr.
  'towards speaker) *uk-* pr.

down, bird's $a_a{}^\cdot q!ok.lu'pqa$

drag, to *-hanok^{u}e$_i$(te·)* (see *-ha-*)

   they dragged them *ts!ɛnawɛs'nok^{u}e'$_i$te·* (see [*-nok^{u}i*]-)

dragon fly $a_a{}^\cdot k\imath nka'ma\cdot k$ C

dream $a_a{}^\cdot k.letsate'yam$

drinking-place $a_a{}^\cdot k!aku'\chi a$

drive, to *-hóyɛl!t-*

   to drive game *-halaq$_a$nil-* (see *-hal-*), *-haq$_a$nɛl*

drown, to *-upɔq$_u$-* (see *-up-*)

drum, to *t!amuχo-* (see *-t!a-*)

dry, to be *-mas(e$_i$)-*, *-hɛluk-*, *-humas-*

   to dry meat *-ɛlwas(k!o)-*

     dried meat *wa'tsk$_a$na*

     a piece of dried meat $a_a{}^\cdot k\imath n\chi amulu'la\cdot k$

dual *-kɨs-*

duck *kia'q!la, la'tuq!*

dust storm $a_a{}^\cdot k\imath l\imath'nqan$

eagle, bald-headed $a_a{}^\cdot k\imath nuqlo'la\cdot m$

eagle, golden *nalaqlɨ'lɨk.* See *-q!nuk^{u}a·t, kiaq!nu'k^{u}a·'t*

ear $a_a{}^\cdot ku'qwa\cdot t!, a_a{}^\cdot qu'qwat!, -quwat$

   both ears *χatsɛnqawa't!ne·* (see *χatsɛn-*)

   ear ornament $a_a{}^\cdot kok!^uatsk!a'k!o\cdot, a_a{}^\cdot ku'k!pma\cdot k!$

early *wɨ'lna·m*

eat, to *-ɛk-*

   he was always eating *n'upsla$^\backprime$t$_i$yil'ɛ'k$_i$ne·* (see *-lat$_i$yil-*)

   he eats while going *pɛtsekɛ'me$_i$k* (see *-pɛts*)

   he ate all *q!a'px$_a$ne·* (see *-χa-* suff.)

   he ate himself entirely *q!apχa'me·k* (see *-q!ap-*)

edge *ɛ'nta, aq!as, $a_a{}^\cdot q!asak$*

eel $a_a{}^\cdot ko'la\cdot m$ C

egg $a_a{}^\cdot kma'q!a\cdot n$, *-maq!an*

eight *wuχa'$_a$tsa* (see *wɛ-*)

elbow *-uqtaptse·k!, -taptse·k, $a_a{}^\cdot kwi'tsa\cdot k, a_a{}^\cdot k\imath nuqtaptsɛ'k$_i$na·m$* (see $a_a{}^\cdot ktaptsɛ'_iknam$)

elder brother *tat!*

elk, bull *kɨlq!a'le·*

   fawn *nu'k.lo$_u$k^u*

   female *la'wo*

emerges, he — again *la·awa·kmewɛsu'k$_u$ne·* (see *-wɛs-*)

   it emerges *n'awak!mosu'q$_u$ne·* (see *-mu[wɛsu!q]-*)

empty, it is *lɛtqawu'mne·* (see *lɛl-*)

endeavor, to *-alsɛn(t)-*

enemy *ɛne'nɛk!*

Englishman *soya'pe*

entered, suddenly he *nuk^{u}haq!ma·kɛkqa'$_a$ne·* (see *-haq!ma-*)

entire (before independent verbs) *q!apil-* (see *qa!p-*), (before suffixes) *-q!ap*

   he was burnt entirely *q!apku'$_u$ne·* (see *-q!ap-*)

   he ate himself entirely *q!apχa'me·k* (see *-q!ap-*)

entirety *yɛs—ke·*

   the whole night *yɛsɛnwunmiyɛ'tke·* (see *-miyɛt*)

   world, the *yɛslɛ·'tke·* (see *yɛs—ke·*), *yɛsle.ɛ'tske·* (see *-le.ɛt*)

entrails *a'$_a$quqt*

Epilobium angustifolium, fireweed $a_a{}^\cdot kankome'_ika$ C

even *mɛ'ka*

evening *tsɛlmi'yɛt* (see *-miyɛt*), *walkwa.ɛyɛtne·* (see *-yɛt-, wa'lkwa*)

evidence, there is — of some one having been present -halikina_at̮ʼt_i(ne·)
evidently t̮- pr.
(exclamations) sak, ha`phohcʼha, hoo'm·, ha·'ksa, kaá, heyá, hya·, hat·ya·, hê
excrement a_aʼq!uʼlc·
excrescence on surface, there is a -q!anlupxamako-
extinguish fire, to -hug!utsko-
eye a_aʼkaql̮ʼlna·m, -ql̮t
  his eyes were like s̮ilqa`psqak̮sql̮ʼlne· (see -qaps-)
  of needle a_aʼkalmeʼt C
  of potato a_aʼkilala'qai C
eyebrow a_aʼqwatq!al̮ka'kna·m
  eyebrows a_aʼq!al̮ka'kna·m, -q!al·ckak-
eyelashes a_aʼkumaql̮ʼlna·m
face a_aʼka'q!ne·
fail, to — to obtain -yuk!kᵘaka(tc·)
faint, to -hala'_a(ne·)
fall, to -ka(xu)-, -huqaxo-, takxaxoʼu(ne·), -hamaxuʼkᵘc· (?)
  he fell back tuwun̮nmuxuʼn·e· (see tuw-)
  it fell down n'o·nilkaxuʼn·e· (see -ka[xu]-)
  to fall into -moxun·e·
  he fell into the water nonaqⱴʼn·c· (see -qᵘ)
  act of falling a_aʼknenmo'xo
  snow falls from trees -hupumak(ne·)
far away luʼn·o (see lu-)
  far side lu-, luqᵘa-
  not far qawulcʼt̮ne· (see -wu[qa]-)
farthest, to be -yapt!a-
father (of girl). su, (of male) t̮ʼtu
  father's brother xa
  father's sister (said by woman) t̮ʼlte·t!
  father-in-law nawa'spal
fat -s̮k-, a_aʼq!uʼta·l, aqa
  fat on top of tail of bighorn sheep a_aʼk̮ʼnqa·t
fawn a_aʼk̮nq!uʼts·ak
feather a_aʼk̮nqo·'wa, -nqowa
  quill end of feather a_aʼkuʼkpl̮· C
  small feathers a_aʼq!ok.luʼpqa
  feathers coming off k.lunqowaʼ'xo· (see -nqowa)
feel, to -dxo, -ukpak-, -ckpak-
female st!uʼkᵘal
fence post a_aʼk̮lq!akuʼpk!o·, a_aʼkoluʼxpe· C
field a_aʼkanakalmuʼko· C
fifth, the — day kyc̮iko_unmi·'y̮t (see -yc'_iku-)
fifty yc̮iku'nwo (see -yeʼ_iku-)
fight, to -k.laq_anan-
figure, grass — representing deer tsa'_atsa
fill pipe, to -hulnak!o-
find, to -wukᵘq_a- (see -wukᵘ[at]-)
finger a_aʼk̮tsq!aheʼyna·m, -tsq!ahey
  little finger kiapt!aha`n̮tsq!ahai'na·m
finger nail aʼ_aʼkukp
finger ring a_aʼk!watsq!a'yna·m, a_aʼkok!ᵘats̮tsq!a'yna·m
finish, to -hu-
  to finish eating -hul'e·k- (see -hu-)
  to finish something -hukᵘ̮n- (see -hu-)

Finlay Creek a_a'ka'k!o·s C
fir lo^u
fire a_a·k$_ı$nq!u'ko·, -hanq!o·ko- (see -hanuxo-), -ko- suff., -nq!oko-
   to be on fire -aq!ako$_u$-, -haq!a-ko·-, -haq!al$_ı$kwa$_ı$t$_ı$(ne·)
   to extinguish fire -huq!utsko-
   to make a fire -$_ı$lko-
   into fire xun- pr.
   he was thrown into fire xunakin$_ı$'lne· (see xun-)
   to start a fire -tsuk^u-
firebrand a_a·kuk!paxma'ko·
fireweed (Epilobium angustifolium) a_a·kankomc′$_ı$ka
firewood · a_a·koxni'yam
first (to be) -hupa-, -us-
fish kia'kxo·
   a species of fish (?) a_a·kamo·kin C
   a species of fish, q!u'me
   a fish with large head and thin tail k!$_ı$′k!o$_u$m'
   to fish -uq!awo·-
fisher wu'qt!e·
   the real fisher ts$_E$ma'k!$_ı$lwu'qt!e· (see -ts$_E$ma·k!)
fish hawk ts!o'$_u$ts!o·
fish line a_a·kuq!a'wo
fish trap a_a·k$_ı$′tsqa, -k$_ı$tsqa, ya'qa
fish weir, wicker a_a·kwu'kxo· C
fist a_a·k$_ı$nuqo'yka·k
five, to be -ye'$_ı$ku-
flapping of wings a_a·k$_ı$$_ı$nqowaxoniyi′e·s, a_a·k$_ı$kqapxoniyi′e·s
flat -q!an-, -ts!la- pr.
   a flat object is still there -sk$_ı$kil-
   flat stones a_a·k$_ı$nuq!la'$_a$nuk, a_a·k$_ı$ts!la'no$_u$k
   a flat object is somewhere -sk$_ı$k-
   flat country (= prairie) sk$_ı$kts!la'nuq!e'$_ı$t (see ts!la-)
flesh a_a·kaxmalu'na·m (see also -xma), -ulaks, -xma
   he also had no flesh on legs la'k$_ı$tq!o'x$_u$masa'q!$_a$ne· (see -q!uxma)
fleshy -q!uxma
flicker ma'$_a$ka
flint a_a·qa'tsko·
float, to -$_ı$lqaw$_ı$sqoku- (?)
   it floats w$_ı$squ'le·k (see -w$_ı$s-)
flooded, it is sk$_ı$kq!ano'$_u$ku$_n$e· (see -q!an-)
flower a_a·k$_ı$nu'q!yuk Kel.
fluid -uk suff., -ku.
   yellow fluid a_a·kma'k!tsuk
fly, to -nuxu-, -hanuxo-
   he flew into it qanaltsEqan'm$_ı$'nxo$_u$qa'$_a$nc· (see -xo$_u$-)
   it came flying out qakal'akanoxonu'k$_u$ne· (see qa- pr.)
flying squirrel yaqa'nla·lt
foam a_a·qo$_u$q!l$_ı$'lup
fog a_a·qunk!a'la·k
food -p$_ı$ts, a_a·kp$_ı$'tsna·m (see -p$_ı$ts), kw$_ı$'se·
fool, to -aqn$_ı$ts-
fool hen kia'wa·ts
foolish, to be -up$_ı$(qa)-, -uktman(qa)-
   to act foolishly s$_ı$lsk$_ı$n·ku·'tste·k (see sk$_ı$′n·ku·ts)

foot -lɛk, aₐ'k.lɛ'knam
  with foot -ɛkɛn suff.
  foot of mountain aₐ'kuk!ple'ɛt
forearm -taptse·k, aₐ'ktaptsɛ'ɛkna·m
forehead ˀaₐ'kɛnqa·'lna·m
forest -haq!anqots!lae·n
  there is a forest qaˋₐkɩlhaq!a'nqu·ts!la'in (see -ts!lae·n)
forget, to -q!akpa(me·k)
  forgotten, it is q!akpayotɛ'lne· (see -payo·t-)
four, to be -ẋa'ₐtsa-
  four days kẋa·tsa·nmi'yɛt (see -ẋa'ₐtsa-)
fox na·'k!ₐyo
freeze, to -hut!-
Frenchman nu·l'a'qₐna (see nu''la)
fresh meat qa'tsuk
friend (used by women to designate a woman friend) -ala
  friend (used by man to designate male friend) swʋ
  friends swʋ't¡mo (see -t¡mo)
fringed -haqoka'm-
  fringes aₐ'qu'kam
frog wa'ta·k
from land towards water hul- pr.
  from water to land up- pr.
frost aₐ'kumle'ɛt, aₐ'kunle'et C
fruit aₐ'kuq!le'ɛt
fruit of Viburnus opulus aₐ'ko'mo·
full, to be -ɛt!(qa)-
fur aₐ'qo'wat
future ts-, tsẋal-, pr.
gamble, to -halwats!
gambler, bad ksaₐna'ₐki·n (see -kɛn)
gambling-bone wʋ'ne·
game iya'mu
game, dancing in circle -henche-
generations yaₐqanakɛlhaqwu'mke· (see qa- pr.)
get, to -yaẋ-
  to get (milk) -hako·l-
  to get out -(nok!ʋɛn)-
ghost ka'ₐlka
giant e·'ka
gills (of fish) aₐ'koqᵘatsɛ'qa C
girl na.u'te·
give, to -tska(kɛn)-, -hamat-
  to give food -hɛs-
glances, a blow — off from head wɛt!qkupqo·q!am·akɛ'n·e·
gloves aˈₐ'q!a·l
gnaw, to -kɛts!ẋₐ-
go, to -aẋe·, -qsa-, dual -akɛk-
  he goes about -qqa'ₐtse·
  he goes along skaẋe· (see -aẋe·)
  go ahead! yu''wa
  to go away -halonɛs-
  go on! ho'ya
  to go out -anaẋa'm-

go, to
   go along, to   qa·na′xe·   (se -qan-)
   they two went out   n'anakɩsxa′mne·   (see -kɩs-)
   to go together   qsama′lnc·   (see -qsa-)
   to go up   -nuqka-
   he went up on high   yu·wa·kmnuqka′n·c·   (see -nuqka-)
   to go and get   -hayaxₐ-
   to go to get   -latɩqkat(kɩn)-
      he went to get one   n'uk!latɩqkatkɩ′n·c·   (see -latɩqkat[kɩn]-)
   to go to get back   -tslɩnyaxₐ-   (see -yax-)
   to go to war   -wanaqₐna-, -anaxaka-   (= to go out for something?)
   going at night (= moon)   ktsɩlmetɩlnu′qka   (see -miyɩt)
   going into   tɩn- pr.
   he went across   qanalwat!a′xe·   (see wat!-)
   he went back aboard   lao·qoxaxa′'mne·   (see -xa-)
   they went in   tɩnaqanxa′'mne·   (see -qan-)
   he went out of himself   (n)uqo`kxamu′me·k
   he went way around   n'ɩtkɩkqla·'lalqa·′tse·   (see -qla·l-)
   he went around in a circle   qalqa′ₐtse·   (see -qal-)
goat   kianu′kxo
good, to be   -soᵤk-
   it has good hair   sukqᵤwa′ₐte·   (see -qᵤwaₐ[te·])
   it is a good place   suk.leɩ′tɩne·   (see -soᵤk-)
   he took a good seat   sukᵤxo′ᵤme·k   (see -soᵤk-)
goose   kaxu′lo·k
   white goose   o·u
gopher   ɩnɩ′tska
   young gopher   na′'ka
granddaughter (of woman)   tɩ′te·
grandfather   pa′pa
   his grandfathers   ats!mɩlq!aluk!puka′m'e·s   (see -q!a-, -luk!puk-)
   great-grandfather   ats!mil
grandmother (said by male)   pa′pa
   (of girl)   tɩ′te·
grandson   pa′pa
grasp, to — with beak   -huq!yu'k!oᵤ-
grass   tsa′hal, -al suff.
   grass figure representing deer   tsa′ₐtsa
grave   aₐ`q!ulu′mko·
   graveyard   aₐ`k!awats!e′ɩko·
gray   (-quxma-)
grease   t!ɩna′mu
green   -haqloyɩt(qa)-
grizzly bear   k.la′wla
grouse (?)   kia′wa·ts, inu′t!ke·
grown, to be full   -hul·ak.le·-, -hunmeɩlak.lc·-   (see -hu-)
gum   -ɩ′lwa·
gum tree   aₐ`kɩtslak.lu′lal   C
gun   t!a′wo   (see -t!a-)
gunpowder   aₐ`kenɩ′lxal   C
hair   aₐ`qo′wat, aₐ`ku′qla·′m, aₐ`kuq!la·'m (?)
   hair of head   aₐ`kolamka′k(na·m)   C
   it has good hair   sukqᵤwa′ₐte·   (see -qᵤwaₐ[tc·])
   long-haired one (Chinaman)   knu′q!lam'   (see -nuq!-)

half *qayaqa′wo* (see *qayaqa-*)
halter *a̱a·kok!ᵘatska′lma*
hammer *po′po*
hand *a̱a·kcy, -hcy-*
  his hand *a̱a·ke′ᵢe·s* (see *-hey-*)
  he put his hand back *la′ntaqahe′ᵢne·* (see *-hey-*)
  he covers it with his hand *mane′ᵢne·* (see *-hey-*)
  with hand *-kɪn* suff.
  to make with hand *-ɪtkɪn-* (see *-ɪt-*)
handle *a′a·q!a·n*
  (of tin pail) *a̱a·kolu′qᵘats* C
  (of tin cup) *a̱a·kɪnqai kaxlukᵘa′tse·s* C
hang, to *-q!an-, -q!aha-*
  it hangs *saq!a′n·e·* (see *s-*)
Hanson's Creek *a′a·k!ne·s a̱a·kɪnuxo′ᵤnuk* C
Hanson's Lake *a′a·k!ne·s a̱a·ku′q!nuk* C
happens, something *tsɪnmal(qal̲a̲ne·*
hard *ts!ɛma′k!-*
hare (?) *tɪlna′ako*
Hare Lip (a name) *kak!a′a̱kit!*
hat *a̱a·k!ayukwa′a̲na·m, k!ayu′kᵘa*
hated, he —— him *sa·nlɪkpakta′pse·* (see *-ɪkpak[te]*), *sa\hanlukpa′kte·* (= he felt bad)
  (see *-sahan-, -ɪkpak [te]*)
have, to *-ha-, -haqa′a̲ne·, -hate·* (see *-ha-*)
  I have it *huna′a̲te·* (see *-ha-*)
  he has an arrow *naka′a̲ne·* (see *-ha-*)
  he had two arrows *n'aimaka′a̲ne·* (see *-ka-*)
  he has a bow *swu′ᵤte·* (see *-wo·*)
  you have big eyes *hɪnwɪlkɪsqlɪ′lne·* (see *-kɪs-*)
  to have clear eyes *-haqts!ɪqlɪl-*
hawk, a species of (?) *kiakqo′loᵤk*
  a small hawk *a̱a·kɪnoq!ota′tit*
head *a′a·k.la·'m, -la·'m*
  of tent *apko·k!ᵘ*
hear, to *-hul̲pal(ne·)-* (see *-pal-*)
heart *a̱a·kɪ′lwey, -lwcy, -(ɪ)lwey-*
heavy, to be *-anɪk!e·-*
  it is heavy *lɪtx̲a̲maqa′a̲nc·* (see *-x̲a̲ma-*)
heel *a̱a·ku′k!pa·k*
helps, he *(n')un·aqato·qniya′x̲ᵤne·*
helpful, to be *-ɪtspat!-*
hide, to *-ɪt.latsu-*
hill *a̱a·kwitsle′et* (?) C
hill *a̱a·qanq!ɪyumɪ′n·a* (see *-q!yu-*)
  Hillside (a place name) *a̱a·qanq!yumɪ′n·a*
hips *a̱a·k!a′a̲kpo·k!* C
hit, to *-moxun·e·*
  he hit it there *qaoxala′lte·* (see *-lal[te·]*)
  he hits it *wuk!o′ᵤne·* (see· *-wu-*)
hoe (?) *a̱a·k.lɪtkaku′pko·* C
hold, to *-tsɪn-*
  it holds it by the tail *nawɪtsqatkɪ′n·e·* (see *-ha·*)

hole (?) -k!a_ak, -k!a(me·), a_aˋk!a′_ame· (see also -me·)
  he made a hole n′ɪtk!ame′ɪne· (see -k!a[me·])
  hole in ice, water hole a′_aˋka·k, a_aˋk!aq
  where there is a hole in a mountain hank!amɹnake· (see ha—ke·)
hollow place in ground a_aˋkɪkqla`lale′ɪt
  hollow place in mountain side a_aˋkɪkqla`lawuqle′'t
  hollow place with dry timber a_aˋkɪkqla`lak!aqlu′nuk
hoof of deer or cattle ·a_aˋkɪtsq!alu′pta·k
hook a_aˋkuqla′wo, tsu′wak!
hoop a_aˋk!a′_almo·k, -k!a_almo·k
horn a_aˋku′qle·, -qle·
hornet a_aˋkapmate·s yu·′wat! C
horse xa′_altsin, kq!a`laxa′_altsin (= elk dog).
horsefly ɪne′si·n
hot, it was really tsɛma`k!e·l′utɪmɪ·le.ɪ′tɹne· (see -tsɛma·k!)
Hot Springs, Ainsworth, B.C. a_aˋkɪnuxle`etna′na C
house, tent -t.la, -(ɪ)t.la
  to make a house, tent -ɪtɪt.la- (see ·-ɪt-)
  there is a house, tent sa·nɪt.la′mne· (see s-)
housefly a_aˋqoku′wum
however at
howl, to -hakwa-, -kik-
  she ran out howling n′anmuqkupnoxo·`ne·lkɪkwakɹ′me·k (see -kik-)
huckleberries lawi·′ya·l
hummingbird nukɪtsa′qleɪl
hundred ɪt!_uwu′nmo (see ɪt!_uwo)
hungry, to be -huwas-
hunt, to -anaxe· (= to go out?)
  he goes hunting nal′ana′xe· (see -hal-)
  when they had been hunting ya′_akɪl′ana′mke· (see -kɪl-)
hurried, he wasaq_ana′_ane· (see was-)
hurt, to -ɪse·-, -t!aqts-
  he hurt his hand t!aqtseyxo′_ume·k (see -t!aqts-)
husband nu·l′a′q_ana (see nu·′la)
  husband's brother atsa·′wats!
I ka′min
ice a_aˋkwi·t!
if na′pit
in oqo- pr.
in water -q^u, -uq, suff.
increase, to -ɪtclxo- (see -ɪt-)
indicative forms of all verbs beginning with an h, prefix of n-
  of all verbs beginning with a vowel n′-
infant (until the time when it is taken off the cradle board) a_aˋqoka′pma·l
initiate, to (see manitou) -kɪyukpuktse (te·)
innermost part a_aˋkɪ′lwey
inside o′qo_uks (see oqo-), a′qla
  (of water) ya′wo
  (of quills) a_aˋqo_uq!ɪɪlupɪnqo′wa (see a_aˋqo_uq!ɪ′lup)
interrogative and participle, of verbs beginning with h, w, y, prefix k-
  of verbs beginning with vowel k!,-
  of monosyllabic verbs kɪ-
intestines a_aˋku′qtna·m
into t-, (away from speaker) tɪn- pr.
  (towards speaker) tɪk- pr.
  (a pile of things) tsaqan- pr.

into fire *xun-* pr.
into water *xun—qᵘ*
into woods *aq!an-, naq!an-,* pr.
invite to a feast, to *tsuk!na′ₐ(ne·)*
iron *nɩ′lko*
island *aₐ·q!a′nkme·*
jaw, lower *aₐʿkamtsɩnka·′k(na·m)* C
joint *aₐ·qatskana′mke·*
Joseph's Prairie, at Cranbrook, B.C. *aₐʿkɩskak.le′et* C
jump, to *-mɩnxo·qa-, -qumlas(xo)-*
    he might jump to the head of the tent *l′apko·k!ₐna′m′te·xa* (see *-nam′te·xa* [?])
    he jumped sideways *naqaˋnkikqa′me·k* (see *-kik-*)
    he jumped a little to the other side *loaˋq!mawɩsqa′ₐne*
    the two jumped to the back of the tent *laˋnta oxakɩsɩnk!a′te·k* (see *-ɩnk!at-*)
juniper *aₐʿkak.lu′lal* C, *also aₐʿkok.lu′lal*
just *qa′ₐlɩn*
kettle of pottery *a′tso*
kicked, he — him across *wat!mɩˋte·kɩ′n·e·* (see *wat!-*)
    he kicked it *qanaql′ɩkxₐne·* (see *-lɩk*)
Kicking Horse River *aₐʿkɩnu′k.luk* C
kill, to *-upɩl-* (see *-up-*)
    by striking *-q!akpa(kit)*
kingfisher *q!a′pqa·l*
kiss, to *-halqok!almaxₐ-* (see *-hal-*)
knee *aₐ·q!a′na·k, aₐ·q!ana′kₐna·m* (see *-q!an-*)
Knee-Cap (a name) *yu·wɩsq!a′na·k* (see *-q!an-*)
knife *aₐʿkɩtsa′mal, -tsamal*
    with knife *-q(a)* suff.
knock, to *-t!a-*
    (at door) *t!axo′ₐne·* (see *-t!a-*)
knot in tree *aₐʿkukpɩtsk!a′la·k* C
know, to *-upxa-, -oho-*
    I know how to get it *hun′onyilnu′k!ₐne·* (see *-[nuk!ᵘ]-*)
    I know a place *hun′oₐlitɩ′tɩne·* (see *-litɩt-*)
    one who knows mind *k!upxalwi′yte·* (see *-lwey*)
knuckle *aₐʿkwi′tsa·k*
Kootenay River *aₐk!ale′et* (see *-k!aleet*)
    Kootenay River, Lower *aₐʿkuk.la′xal* C
Kutenai *ktuna′xa*
Kutenai of Pend d'Oreille and St. Ignace *aₐʿkiye′nɩk!*
lacings *aₐʿkuk.luka′tslo·* C
lair of a deer *-k!aₐk*
lake *-haq!nuk-, aₐʿku′q!nuk, -q!nuk*
    a big lake *kwɩ′lq!nok* (see *-q!nuk*)
    it must be a lake *k.lsa′kq!nuk* (see *l-* pr.)
    lake on other side *k.luha′kq!nuk* (see *lu-*)
    little lakes *n′a·qaˋnalhoq!nukna′na* (see *-haq!nuk-*)
land *am·a·k*
larch *aₐ·qo′pal, k!u′sti·t!*
large *-wɩl(qa)-*
last, to be *-yapt!a-*
    last one *one·k*
later on *ma′qak, ta′xta*

laugh, to *-kq!u-*, *-umats-*
  he laughed aloud *wɪtkɪkq!u′n·e·* (see *-kq!u-*)
  he laughed thus *qakq!u′n·e·* (see *-kq!u-*)
law, to make a *-ɪtnumo·ts(te)-*
lay down, to *-ɪtq!an(kɪk)-*
lay out place for tent, to *-ɪkɪnatɪt-*
leaf *aₐ‘qouₗla′qpɪk*
  leaf of pine *aₐ‘ku′la·l*
  leaves of tobacco plant *papa′la·′m*
lean, to be *-tunak-*
leave, to *-mate·*
left-handed *kutwiya′t!ne·* (see *-kut-*)
leg *a′ₐ‘ksaq!*, *-saq!-*, *aₐ‘ksa′q!na·m* (see *-saq!-*)
  leg is cut off *tusaq!a′lne·* (see *-saq!-*, *-q[a]*)
  long leg *wu′saq!* (see *-saq!-*, *-wu[qa]-*)
  leg part of skin *aₐ‘k!a′ₐq!yu*
  length of his legs, the *yɪsɪnwosa′q!ke·* (see *-wuq[a]-*)
leggings *aₐ‘qa‘tik.lu′kᵘa*
lehal *-halq!ahalt-*
lengthwise, to be *-hutsqan-*
  striped lengthwise *kutsqa′nq!le·l* (see *-hutsqan-*)
let go, to *-pɪs-*
  let me go on! *ho′ya*
  he let it go with hand *pɪsɪkɪ′n·e·* (see *-pɪs-*)
level place (on a hill), where there is a *haq!an·uqle·ɪ′tke·* (see *-q!an-*)
lick off, to *-ɪlta(ᵡa)-*
lie, to (to recline) *-saq-*,
  it lies here *sakqa′ₐne·* (see *s-* pr.)
  to lie down *saq(qaₐ)-* (see *-saq-*), *-ɪtᵡo′ᵤme·k* (see *-ɪt-*)
  he lay on his back *tuwul′ɪtᵡo′ᵤme·k* (see *tuw-*)
  he lay (there) dirty *skɪkq!ᵤma′lne·* (see *-q!o·mal*)
  it lay there wet *skɪkqoqᵘts!ala′ᵢne·* (see *-qoqᵘts!ala-*)
  he lay down there quietly *qa‘oᵡal′ɪtq!ankɪkqa′ₐne·* (see *-q!an-*)
  he lay down the other way *luqᵘalitᵡo′ᵘme·k* (see *luqᵘa-*)
lie, to (to speak untruth) *-huts-* (see *-keᵢ-*)
light (not heavy) *-ᵡₐma-*
light (?) *aₐ‘k!almokᵘa′et*, *-k!almukwa′e·t*
  a little light (shining) through a hole *tsaₐk!aₐlmi‘yitna′na* (see *-k!almukwa′e·t*)
light a pipe, to *tsuku′pᵡₐne·* (see *-tsukᵘ-*)
lightly *-q!ma-*
  he touched it lightly *wu‘q!maᵡo′ᵤne·* (see *-q!ma-*)
lightning *aₐ‘kanliᵡuna′e·t* C
like, to *-tslakcᵢt-*
  he likes it *suk.lukpa′kte·* (see *-ɪkpak[te]*)
like *-qaps-* pr.
  it is like (it) *qapsqaqa′ₐne·* (see *-qaps-*)
  his eyes were like *sɪlqa‘psqakɪsqlɪ′lne·* (see *-qaps-*)
limb *aₐ‘qonakɪ′lmak!*
limping *-haq!ank!o·′(te·k)*
line, those who are in *-ɪnataqa′aₐke·*
lip, lower *aₐ‘komu′na·m* C
  upper lip *aₐ‘koka·yuk!almE(na·m)*, also *aₐ‘kokwiyok!alEma* C
listen, to *-k!apal-*, *-hutpal(ne·)* (see *-pal-*)
  he listened *k!apaltɪ′le·k* (see *-k!apal-*)

little, it stuck out a *sq!ma·ˋwitslᵻnq!a·ˊˊntse·* (see -*q!ma*-)
　a little while *wo·q!ᵘma̜ne·kᵻˊtᵢne·* (see -*q!ma*-)
locust *a̜·kuk.lako'wum*
lodge, tent, house -(ᵻ)*t.la*
　old lodge *o̜·kalat.la'tna·m* C
lonesome *huk.lukpa(me·k)* (see -*huk.luk*-)
long, to be -*wu(qa)*-
long ago *pᵻ'k!a·ks*
(long objects) -*ma*-
long-haired one (Chinaman) *knu'q!am'* (see -*nuq!*-)
Longwater Bay *ya̜kwu'la·k*
look, to -*kat(e·)*, -*wᵻtskᵻk*-
　to look for or at something -*ᵻtskᵻl*-
　how do I look? *koa·ˋqaka'te·* (see -*kat*[*e·*])
　to look secretly -*hak.latsulwᵻtskᵻl*-
　to look terrible -*ᵻse·(ka'te·)*
　it looks terrible *n'ᵻse·kate'ᵢne·* (see -*kat*[*e·*])
　he looked around *tse·kalitᵻ'tᵢne·* (see -*litᵻt*-)
　he looked up *wa·wᵻtskᵻ'kᵢne·* (see *wa·*- pr.)
　he looks back *lamanwᵻtskikᵻ'lne·* (see *man*-)
　it looks nice *tsᵻnla(kate'ᵢne·)*
　it looks yellowish *namak!tsaˋ̜kat.le·tᵻtine·ˊne·* (see -*kat*[*e·*])
loon *nuqlu'k!ᵘe·n* (see -*nuqlum*-)
lose, to -*ᵻskax̜mele*-
lump *a̜·q!anlupx̜ama'ko·* (see *a̜·q!a'nlup*)
　there is a lump, excrescence, on surface -*q!anlupx̜amako*- (see -*q!an*-)
lungs *a̜·kmölu'pu·q*
lynx *k!u'q̜ne·* (= short face)
magpie *a'n'an*
　a small magpie (?) *e·qo·l*
make, to -*ᵻt*-
　I shall make a bridge *hutsᵻtkokopkᵻ'n·e·* (see *a̜·ko·'ko·* C)
　to make a fire -*ᵻtko*-
　he made a fire *q!o̜koxa'me·k*
　to make a house, tent -*ᵻtᵻt.la*- (see -*ᵻt*-)
　he made a tent for himself *n'ᵻtᵻt.la'̜te·k* (see -*t.la*)
　to make a law -*ᵻtnumo·ts(te)*-
　to make with hand -*ᵻtkᵻn*- (see -*ᵻt*-)
　he made a bow for himself *n'ᵻt'wuk̜nᵻ'lᵢk* (see -*wo·*)
　he made a hole *n'ᵻtk!ame'ᵢne·* (see -*k!a*[*me·*])
　just there he made it *qooxal'ᵻtkᵻ'n·e·* (see *qao*-)
　he made a mark in the center *qaya̜qawa̜q!anq!lᵻ'lne·* (see -*q!an*-)
　he made it nothing *lu''nte·* (see *lu*-)
male *qa'sk!o*
mallard duck *kanq!usqwe'ᵢkak*
man *tᵻ'tqa·t!*
manitou *nöpᵻ'k!a*
　to send a boy to get manitou power -*kᵢyukpuktse(te·)*
many, to be -*yuna(qa)*-
　there are many *yunaqa'̜ne·* (see -*qa··*)
mark -*q!leᵢl*
　he made a mark in the center *qaya̜qawa̜q!anq!lᵻ'lne·* (see -*q!an*-)
marrow *a̜·kᵻnu'lma·k*, -*nulmak*
marry, to -*halitᵻt*-, -*salitᵻt*-

married, to be -halalit!'t_i(ne·)

master na'ksaq

may -k_in pr.

  may be i̯l_in- pr.

mean, to -il_ikt

  he did not mean it ts_ins(ke'_ine·)

means, by — of -mu suff.

meat -ulaks, a_a`ku'lak

  to dry meat -_itwas(k!o)-

  dried meat wa'tsk_ana

  a piece of dried meat a_a`k_inxamulu'la·k

  fresh meat qa'tsuk

medicine made of Artemisia discolor u_a`k<sub>i</sub>nuk.luxona'<sub>a</sub>ka aw<sub>v</sub>'mo (see  a<sub>a</sub>`k_inuk.-
  luxona'ka) C

melt, to luqu·_in`ko·

  it melted strongly by heat ts_Ema`k!il·oqu_ink_u'pse· (see luqu·_in·ko-)

  it melts -hoq!ko·-

middle qayaqa'wo (see qayaqa-)

milk tsu'u

Milky Way (= dog's trail) a_a`kma'e·s xa'<sub>a</sub>lts<sub>i</sub>n (see  a<sub>a</sub>`kma'na·m)

milt of fish a_a`q!a'nlup

mind a_a`k_i'lwey, -(_i)lwey-, -lwey

mind, to -_intse-

miss, to -yuk!k^uaka(te·)

Missoula, a place about 4 m. from Sand Point, Idaho a_a`kanu'k.le·l C

mistake, he makes a (n')umnaqalpalne'_ixo·-, -ts_ik!mal_in(k_i'n·e·)

mittens pa'l'ya

moccasin la·n'

money n_i'lko

monster, giant c·'ka

moon nata'ne·k!

  moon (=the one going up at night) kts_ilme`tilnu'qka (see -nuqka-, -miy_it)

moose n_itsna'pku

  bull moose kaq!a'le·

more a·n- pr.

  one more lao·k!^ue._i'se· (see la-)

moss a_a`kola'<sub>a</sub>nak C, al·a,  (Lillagenilla rupestris)  a<sub>a</sub>`kolawite'yal C

mother ma

mother-in-law t_i'te·

mother's brother ha'tsa, xa'tsa

mother's sister ko·kt

motion towards speaker k- pr.

mountain -uq!yu(leet), a_a`kuwuk.le'<sub>i</sub>t, a<sub>a</sub>`koq!yulc'et

  end of mountain wa`kaq!yule._i'tke· (see -q!yu-)

  foot of mountain a_a`kuk!pie'_it

  there is a mountain y_isle._i't.se· (see -le._it), sakq!yule_i't.s· (see -le._it)

mouse _i'ntsuk!

mouth a'_ak!alma'na·m, (-k!a)lma

  in mouth -aqtuq!^u-

  with mouth -xa- suff.

move, to -wan-, (?) -qsa-

  he moved his arm wanla't!ne· (see -wan-)

  he moved it in the water wanuqk_i'n·e (see -wan-)

  to move camp -uq_una(m_i·k)

much *-yuna(qa)-*
　much coal, there is *yu·nats!kak.ʻl̦e·* (see *-ts!kak.l-*)
mule (=his big-ears) *k_uwɪʻlq_uwa'tle·'s* (see *-q_uwal*)
muskrat *ha'nq!o*
must be *l-*
　must be a lake, it *k.lsa'kq!nuk* (see *l-* pr.)
mutually *-t_imo* suff.
my *ka-* pr.
myth *a_a'qalq!anoxwa'te·*
name *a_a'k_ık.le'yam, -(ɪ)k.ley -k.le·*
　he was named thus *-qa'k.l̦ık-*
name, to *-at-*
　(names of culture heroes) *ya.uk^ue'_ıka·m, nalmö'qtse·*)
　(name of a dog) *tso_ul*
　(of Coyote's daughter) *mısqulo'_uwo·m*
　(of a man) *a_a'kala`laa'al* C
　(of place near Nelson) *a_a'qeya'mlapskak.le.ʻtske·*
　(place name) *a_aqo·la'_aka·, a_a'ko'q_uwit!*
　(of region inhabited by Lower Kutenai) *a_a'kako·'wo·k* C
　(of region of a camping place on the trail to the Lower Kutenai) *a_a'kakolmitɪ'yuk* C
　(of region of Fort Steele and St. Eugène Mission) *a'_a'k!am* C
　(St. Mary's Lake) *a'_a'k!am a_a'ku'q!nuk* C (see *a'_a'k!am*) C
　(St. Mary's River) *a'_a'k!am a_a'kɪnmi'tuk* (see *a'_a'k!am*) C
　(Wild Horse Creek) *a_a'ktsa'k.le·* C
　(Skukum Chuck, below Finlay Creek) *a_a'kauma'kso·k* C
navel *a_a'k!alaka'kna·m, -k!alakak*
neck *a_a'ko'_uka·k*
　nape of neck *a_a'kuk!pla`'mka·'kna·m*
necklace *a·'na*
Nelson *a_a'kya'mlu·p* C
nephew *pat!,* (sister's child, said by woman) *xalna`le_il* (see *xa'l̦[e·]*)
nest *a_a'kuq!no'k^uat, a·qo·'q^uat, -qoq^uat*
　fish-hawk nest *ts!o_uts!u'q!^ua* (see *ts!o'_uts!o·*)
nevertheless *pa·mɪk*
new, to be *-wup-*
news *-tuq!ts-*
　to tell news *tuq!tsqake'_ıne·* (see *-tuq!ts-*)
niece (sister's child, said by woman) *xalna`le_il* (see *xa'l̦[e·]*)
　(brother's daughter) *pa·*
　sister's daughter (said by woman) *swina'le·l* (see *swyn*)
night hawk *p!e·q!s*
nine, to be *-qa.ikɪtl_uwo-* (see *[-ɪkɪt!_uwo]*), *qa.ɪkɪ'tl_uwo* (see *-qa-*)
no! *waha·', uwa'ha*
　there is no water *lɪtu'k^une·* (see *lɪt-*)
nock of arrow *a_a'q!a'nq!ak* C
nod, to *-haq!a·naq!ne_ı-, -ɪsqaq!anaq!ne·'nɪl-*
noise *a_a'k.luk.le'et, a_a'kɪk.lite'yam, -hak.leɪt-, -halukme-* (see *-ha-, -lɪk-* [?])
　to make noise *-hɪlke·-, -t!alo'_uk^u(ne·), -kik-*
　he made noise inside *qa·atskɪk.lɪknatɪ't_ıne·* (see *-lɪk-*)
　he made big noise *wɪlka`nilpalnexu'n·e·* (see *-pal-*)
　without noise of stones *lɪtkɪkɪnok^uɪ'lne·* (see *-kik-*)
noose (on rope) *a_a'kankaltsɪ'ka* C
nose *a_a'k!u'nka·k, -k!unkak; -k!on, a_a'kuqsala'na·m, -qsala*

nostril -k!asla'ₐkak, aₐ'k!aslaka'knaˑm (?)

not qa-

  not far qawuleˑ'tᵢneˑ (see -wu[qa]-)

nothing lu-, lu'nˑeˑ (see lu-)

  he made it nothing lu''ntcˑ (see lu-)

  again there is nothing lalo'ₐseˑ (see la-)

number yₑsa'skeˑ (see yₑs—keˑ)

object -l- suff.

off, a little ways aqat!- pr.

oh ę, aˑ

  .oh! hê, hal'yaˑ, hai, háˑ

  oh if! taₐq

oil, to -ts!aqₐ-

old man nu''la

old woman tₑ'lna, tₑlna'mu

once, at ok!uₑl-, ok!uₑnl-, uk!unₑl-, pr. (see -ok!u[eˑ]-)

one, to be -ok!u(eˑ)-

  the one (n')aoˑ'k!uc·

  one hundred ₑt!ᵤwu'nwo (see -ₑt!ᵤwoˑ-)

onion aₐ'koˑ'wal

only ts!ₑn

open, to -malₑn-, -uk!u(n)-, -(nok!uₑn)-

  to open (rock) -tsunok!oᵤ-

  to be open -huk!ᵘeˑn- (?)

  he opened his mouth malₑnk!alma'n·eˑ (see -malₑn-)

  opening, hole -k!a(mₑˑ)

orbit aₐ'kₑnₑl·alaχapa'knaˑm, aₐ'kaχapa'knaˑm

ornamental pieces on border of root kettle, small aₐ'kutskakᵢlukpo'χal C

orphan na''nka

  orphan adopted by me kana'nkaˑ'qal (see na''nka)

other, the (n')aoˑ'k!ueˑ

  the other one naoˑ'k!uc·

  the other side la'tsᵢneˑ, on the other side leˑ'ᵢneˑ

  other side lu-, luqᵘa-

  lake on other side kₑluha'kq!nuk (see lu-)

  he lay down the other way luqᵘalitχoᵘmeˑk (see luqᵘa-)

otter aₐ'qa'oχal

ought χma

our kamina'la (see ka'min)

out of a- pr.

  out of (away from speaker) an- pr.

  out of (towards speaker) ak- pr.

  out of woods tunwa- pr. (Lower Kutenai tun-)

  his two legs stuck out tunwakakₑswiˑts·a'q!ncˑ (see tunwa-)

  out of the top of something -eˑleᵢk-

outer side of tent, at bottom, all around la''nta

outside la'a, la'laˑk

  they were outside kₑlalaha'qᵤwom (see la'a)

over ₑt!na- pr.

overtake, to -χanχo, (?) -a'nχo-

owl ku'peᵢ

own, to -ₑs-

own way, he wants to act his sₑn·akpa'meˑk

paddle k!scˑ

paint, red namₑ't·a

painting $a_a{}^{\cdot}ku'q!li{}^{\cdot}l$
palate $a_a{}^{\cdot}kola'na{}^{\cdot}m$ C
palm of hand $a_a{}^{\cdot}kuk.la'_i(na{}^{\cdot}m)$ C
pant, to *-halkɛkwas-* (see *-hal-*), *(n)hakwase'kme·k* (see *-hakwa-*)
panther *swa'*
parents $ak_ínek!$, $a_a{}^{\cdot}k_{ín}{}_{ɛ}'k!na{}^{\cdot}m$
    parents and children $ala{}^{\cdot}qall_{ɛ}'t_imo$ (see *-t_imo*)
parflèche $a_a{}^{\cdot}qu'lum$
(participle and interrogative pr.) *k-*
parting of hair $a_a{}^{\cdot}kawu'k!o{}^{\cdot}$
partridge *t!a'n·qu·ts*
pass (?), to $(qa)hak!o_u$-
passer-by $a_a{}^{\cdot}q!utsa'ne{}^{\cdot}k$ (not used in modern speech)
passive *-l-* suff.
past *man-* pr.
    he went past *manq!ankɛ'me·k* (see *man-*)
pay, to (*-ɛnmak*), *-ɛt_ɛnmak-* (see [*-ɛnmak*])
peel, apple $a_a{}^{\cdot}ko{}^{\cdot\prime}nak$ C
pemmican *kɛlku'lka*
penis $a_a{}^{\cdot}ku'lats$
pepper $a_a{}^{\cdot}kukplu'lal$ C
perspire, to *-haq!a-ko·-*, $-aq!ako_u$-
Philadelphus Lewisii, berries of $a_a{}^{\cdot}kuno{}^{\cdot\prime}kyo{}^{\cdot}k$ C
pick berries, to $-halq!at!e_i$-
pick up, to *-itqana(qa)-*
piece he bit off, a $qa'sx_ane{}^{\cdot}$ (see *-qas-*)
    to break to pieces *-qas-*
    he cut himself to pieces *qasnɛnqa'me·k* (see *-qas-*)
Piegan *sa'nla* (see *-sahan-*)
pierce, to $tsu(k!o'_une{}^{\cdot})$
pile, to *-nmu(xo)-*
    he had a pile *sanmolkɛ'n·e·* (see *-moxun·e·*)
    to pile up *sanmuxo'me·k* (see *-moxun·e·*), *-ɛt!qao(xa)-*
pin, to *-apak!ɛn-*
pine *he'm·o*
    white pine $a'_a{}^{\cdot}ka{}^{\cdot}m$ C
pipe *ko·'s*
    to fill pipe *-hulnak!o-*
pipe stem $a_a{}^{\cdot}ko'la$, *-ula*
    pipe-stem wood (Alnus incana) $a_a{}^{\cdot}kula'wo{}^{\cdot}k$ (see $a_a{}^{\cdot}ko'la$)
pit $a_a{}^{\cdot}k!a'_ame{}^{\cdot}$ '
    (for cooking) $a_a{}^{\cdot}k.la'xwe{}^{\cdot}k!$
pitchwood $-nuqa'ko_u$, $a_a{}^{\cdot}k_{ɛ}noq{}^ua'_ako$, $-oq{}^ua_ako$
pitfall $a_a{}^{\cdot}k_{ɛ}nu'kwe_ɛt$
pitied, he — it *k!umna'nlukpakilmu'lne·* (see *-ɛkpak[le]*)
place *ha—ke·*
    place for drying meat $a_a{}^{\cdot}kowa'sk!o{}^{\cdot}$
    place with thick trees $a_a{}^{\cdot}q!anqats!la'e{}^{\cdot}n$, *-haq!anqots!lae·n*
    thickly-wooded place $a_a{}^{\cdot}q!anquts!la'e{}^{\cdot}n$ (see *-q!an-*)
    place with dry trees $a_a{}^{\cdot}k!ak.lu'nuk$
    place with scattered trees $a_a{}^{\cdot}k_{ɛ}nusu'k!po{}^{\cdot}n$, *-nusu'k!po·n*
    it is a bad place *sa'hanlɛɛ'tne·* (see *-sahan-*)
    it is a good place $suk.le_ɛ't_ɛne{}^{\cdot}$ (see *-so_uk-*)
    it is a well-hidden place *-hatslɛɛt-*
    to place *-xa-*

plain $a_a\dot{k}itsla'_ame\dot{}$

plank $a_a\dot{k}inuq!^ula\dot{}k!a'_ako\dot{}$

"plant standing up," used for arrowshafts $a_a\dot{q}!ox_umalc'et$

play, to $-k.linq!o-,$ $-wats!-$

　　they play along $qanalwa'ts!ne\dot{}$ (see qa- pr.)

　　he plays ball with bat $-qaixo'ktse\dot{}k$

pleased with something, to be $-yitna'nts(te\dot{})$

plenty $suk^uakate'_ine\dot{}$ (see -kat[e·]); $ksuk^uaka'tc\dot{}$ (see -so_uk-)

plural $-kil-,$ $-q!a-,$ $-qan-$

pocket $a_a\dot{k}ula'ko$ (?) C

point, to $-nk!un-$

　　point $-nq!a-$

　　with point $-k!o-$ suff.

　　(pointed eye) $k!uktsa'qle_il$ (see $nuktsa'qle_il$)

　　he pointed at them hither $qaka\dot{}nk!onc'lne\dot{}$ (see qa- pr.)

　　he pointed at them thither $laqa\dot{}nank!onc'lne\dot{}$ (see qa- pr.)

　　it was pointed that way $qa\dot{}nank!unc'lne\dot{}$ (see -nk!un-)

points of bark canoe $a'_a\dot{k}o\dot{}$ C

poked him, he $qunatsa'_ax_anc\dot{}$ (see qun-)

poor, to be $-k!umna-$

　　he is poor $k!umnaqaqa'_ane\dot{}$ (see -k!umna-)

porcupine $nc'lksaq$

post $a\dot{}ma'le\dot{}t$

pot $yits!ke\dot{}'me\dot{}$ (see -me·)

pouch $a_a\dot{k}ula'ko$ (?) C

powder flask $a_{ı}\dot{k}ole'kam$ C

prairie $a_a\dot{k}inuqle'et$ (see -nuq-), $skikts!la\dot{}nuqle'it$ (see -ts!la-)

　　there was a flat prairie $qa\dot{}q!a\dot{}nmoqts!inu'k_une\dot{}$ (see -q!an-)

　　prairie on side of hill $a_a\dot{q}!anuk.le'et$

prairie chicken $kts!c'q!la$

probably $naqan-$ pr.

property $a_a\dot{k}.le'_ile\dot{}t$

propose a plan, to $-it.likinatit-$

proud, to be $-hal\dot{}ax wat(e\dot{}k)$

puff, to $-kik-$

pull, to $hakunkc'n(\dot{}e\dot{})$ (see -ha-)

　　he pulled it in $tik_imc'tx_ane\dot{}$ (see tik-)

pup (of dog) $tsit!(na'na)$

purple $ke'_iko\dot{}p$ (see -kup-)

pursue, to $-mityax_a-$ (see -yax-), $-nut-$

　　he came pursuing her $qaknu'te\dot{}$ (see qa- pr.)

push in, to (?) $-yaptsa(kin)-$

put, to $-xa-$

　　he put his hand back $la'ntaqahe'_ine\dot{}$ (see -hey-)

　　to put in $-haqtuq!^ua-$

　　to put into water $-hile\dot{}kxaqkin-$

　　to put on back $-alax o_u-$ (see -ala-)

　　to put on with hand $-alakin-$ (see -ala-)

　　to put together $-it!qao(xa)-$

　　to put up $-eya(kin)-$

　　he had something to put in (?) $(ts')inalqana''nte\dot{}$

　　he put it into it $n'oqoxakc'n\dot{}e\dot{}$ (see -xa-)

put, to *-xa-*
  put me off! *pısxo'ₐnu* (see *-xo-* suff.)
  he was put off *pısxo'lne·* (see *-l-* suff.)
quarrel, to *-ılkıl-*
question, to *-ak.lel-*
quickly *-qkup-, was-* pr.
  quickly he cut off the nose *luqkupqsala'ₐte·* (see *lu-*)
  he comes back quickly *wa\sıl·axa'xe·* (see *was-*)
  it burnt quickly *ts!ılq!anku'pse·*
  he stretched his leg out quickly *qal'ıt!naqkupq!alsa'q!ne·* (see *-q!al-*)
quietly he lay down there *qa\oxal'ıtq!ankıkqa'ₐne·* (see *-q!an-*)
quill end of feather *aₐ'ku'kplc·* C
quills, insides of *aₐ'qoₐq!lılupınqo'wa*
rabbit *kianuqlu'mna* (see also *-nuqlum-*)
race, a *kalnuxu'kna·m* (see *-nuxu-*)
rail *aₐ'kılq!aku'pk!o·*
raining, it is *waloq!kᵘku't_i(ne·)*
raise, to *-hukₐnu-*
rapids *aₐ'kaxa'pqle·*
raspberry *aₐ'q!u'ko·*
rattle *aₐ'ko'qᵘma·l*
  bunch of dew hoofs of deer *aₐ'kılq!a'lukp*
rattlesnake *wı'lma·l*
Rattling-Claws (a name) *ka·kiyaxa'kukp*
rattling noise, there is a *skıkınotxonı'le·k* (see *-not-*)
raven *qo'kᵘe·n*
raw *-kup-, ke'ᵢko·p* (see *-kup-*)
reach, to *-xa(xe·), -a'nxo-, -yax-*
  one who reached the top *kyu·xa'xa·m* (see *-xa[xe·]*)
  they reached there *qaoxaxa''mne·* (see *-xa[xe·]*)
ready *kutatı'qna* (see *-hu-*)
  to get ready *-ıtaqna-* (see *-ıt-*)
  he is ready to go *wanakate'ᵢ(ne·)*
  he stood ready to spear *(n')upsawıtsaₐkınxa'ₐne·*
rear part of tent, back of fire *la''nta*
rectum *wılma'pe·s*
red *-(nohos)-, nos-, -(ha)nohos*
  bright red *sukᵘnohu'se·* (see *-soₐk-*), *yawo'ₐnek!*
red-hot *-huko-*
reed (?) *ta'nal*
reflexive ending of verbs in *-ne· -me·k*
  suffix of transitive verbs in *-te· -te·k*
refuse, to *-tsakıl-*
relation between sister's husband and wife's brother *skat*
relation, reciprocal, between parents-in-law and children-in-law, intermediate relative dead *xatkax'niyatu'mal*
relation, reciprocal, between brother and sister *alı'tskeᵢl*
relative *(ı)k!na'mu*
relatives *akᵢnek!*
remains of broken bones *aₐ'q!a'na·k*
rhubarb, wild *wⱱ'm'a·l*
rib *-no·kak, aₐ'knoka'kna·m*
ribbon, hair, worn in front *aₐ'kok!ᵘatsı'nko·*
rice *aₐ'ku'q!ᵘa·l*

rime a_a'$kunle'et$ C

rind a_a'ko'nak C

ring, netted t!$aqu'mo$·

   finger ring a_u'kok!$uats\textit{\i}tsq$!$a'yna$·m

   hair rings made of brass spirals a_a'$k\textit{\i}kne'la$·m

rise, to -$nuqka$-, -$uknu$-

   water rises $nutsu'k^une$· (see -$huts$-)

river -$nmituk$, a_a'$k\textit{\i}nmi'tuk$ (see -uk)

  ·a wide river k!$almanmi'tuk$ (see -ma-)

   rivers are long $wuqanmitu'k_une$· (see -qan-)

   largest rivers a_a'k!$ale'et$, -k!$aleet$

roast, to -luk!mo-

   he roasted it luk!$mo\chi a'me$·k (see -luk!mo-)

rock, it is a_a'$knuk\chi u'me$·k

roll, to -$haqai$-, -(ha)qay-

   he will roll himself $ts\chi alhaqayeqa'me$·k (see -[ha]qay-)

   at once he was always rolling about n'o`$k$!$u\textit{\i}nla$`$_at_iy\textit{\i}$`$ltsha$`$qaiy\textit{\i}lmo$`$\chi ona$`$titmo'lne$.

    (see -lat_iyil-)

root -k!$pu'kam$, a_a'kuk!$pu'ka$·m, -(u)k!$puka$·m

   an edible root (?) a_a'$kuqle'et$

   a root found in swamps a_a'$k\textit{\i}tsq$!$a'kam$

rope, bark a_a'qo'qol

rose hip waq!o'pe·s, q!$u'lwa_a$

round -haq!$anqoq^uat$(qa)-, -q!$anquqwat$- (see -q!an-)

   it is round naq!$anquqwatqa'_ane$· (see -q!an-)

rub, to -ts!aq_a-

   rub (with), to -$\textit{\i}kt\chi one$(mu)-

   he rubs it on -$yuhak\textit{\i}'ne$· (see -ha[$k\textit{\i}'nc$]-)

run, to -$halnukup$(qa)-, -$hanlukp$(qa)- (see -$hanu\chi o$-), -$\textit{\i}k\textit{\i}$(me·k), -ts!$\textit{\i}nak$-

   to run away -$nu\chi u$-

   he ran away no·$sano\chi unqa'_une$· (see $hosan$-)

   she ran out howling n'$anmuqkupno\chi o$`ne·$lk\textit{\i}kwak\textit{\i}'me$·$k$, (see -$kik$-)

   he runs $moqkupno\chi unqa'me$·k

rushes (?) $ta'nal$

sack-cloth a_a'$kala$`$laa'al$ C

saddle a_a'k!$o'ne_is$

   my saddles kaq!ak!o'$n\textit{\i}st$ (see -q!a-)

saddlebag a_a'$qok.la$·'k!o

saliva a_a'q!$uk.lu'mna$·m

Salix desertorum a_a'$qo_ula'kpe$·$kna'na$ (see a_a'$qo_ula'qp\textit{\i}k$)

salmon $swa'q$!$_amo$

sand a_a'$k\textit{\i}nko'ko$·l C

Sand Creek a_a'$ka'tak$ C

save, to -$\dot{\chi}at$($k\textit{\i}nuk^u$)-

   to be saved -yuk!$k_uakat\textit{\i}l$- (see -yuk!k^uaka[te·])

   he saved himself $\chi atk\textit{\i}'n$·e· see -χat[$k\textit{\i}nuk^u$]-)

   he was saved $\chi atknu'k_une$· (see -χat[$k\textit{\i}nuk^u$]-)

   he saves him $\chi atk\textit{\i}nuk^u\textit{\i}'n$·$e$· (see -$\chi at$[$k\textit{\i}nuk^u$]-)

saw, with -χal suff.

say, to -ke_i-, -($\textit{\i}l$)ke·

   he said so $qake'_ine$· (see -ke_i-)

   he said thus $qake'_ine$· (see qa-)

   he said to him $qak\textit{\i}'lne$· (see -l-)

   to say "yes" -$lch\textit{\i}'$(te·)

scalp a_a'$qala$'mla

scare, to -haq!maxo- (see -haq!ma-), -oyɛt!axwa(t)-
    he scared them qakiłaq!maxoka'ₐne· (see -xoᵤ-)
scatter, to pa·tsɛnmɛ't- (see pa·ts-)
scold, to -ɛlkɛl-
scrape, to -q!awuka-
scratch, to -ɛksɛa(t)-
screw aₐ·kwɛ'tsko· C
seam aₐ·kiłɑktsumu·'in (see aₐ·kiła'ktsu) C
season aₐ·kɛlk!aku'ko·t, -mayɛt, -(u)kot
    two seasons t!uk.lun·maku'tₗne·
seat aₐ·kmoxo'na·m
    where he was seated ya·qaha`nqame·'ke· (see -hanaq-)
secretly ats- pr.
    to look secretly -hak.latsulwɛtskɛl-
see, to -wukᵘ(at)-, -upxa-
    to see at a distance indistinctly -ukᵘnak-
    he sees tseᵢka'te· (see -kat[e·])
    he sees it tseᵢ(ka'te·)
seeds, tobacco aₐ·kɛnu'q!yuk ya'q!e·t
self -ɛsɛn-, -ɛsnɛ-, pr.
send for some one, to -neyax-
service berry sq!u'm·o·
    service-berry wood a'ₐ·k!wo·k (see aₐk!)
sets, where the sun yaqa`nałwat!mɛnuₐqka'ske· (see -mnuqka-)
seven wɛst!a·'la (see wɛ-)
several na'qsa- pr.
    several days naqsanmi'yɛt (see -miyɛt)
shade nɛ'le·
shadow aₐ·k.lo'ᵤk!wa
shake hands, to tsxa·małktsala'mne· (see -tsxa [n·e·])
    shook his blanket, he n'anuxo·'nlatₗmo'me·k (see -la[mał])
sharp -ɛse(qa)-
    sharp (stones) -k!a(no'ᵤko·)
sharpen, to -e·tax-
sheep, bighorn kwɛ'lqle· (see -wɛl[qa]-)
    mountain sheep nɛ'lya·p
shell k!u·'mtsak(s)
shield qa'snał
shin aₐ·ko'kna·m C
shine, to -hoq!ukₗyɛt- (see -huk!ukyₗtₗ-)
shirt -qa·twumlaₐt
shoe lacing aₐ·kułuqa'tslum C
shoot, to -ɛs(k!o)-, -ɛlwa-, mɛtxa- (see -mɛt-), -haq!axo'ᵤxᵤ(ne·)
    he shot upward wa·mɛtak!o'ᵤne· (see wa·-)
    shooting with it kmɛtxa'm·u (see -mu)
shore ɛ'nta, aₐ·k!a'lak
short, -oᵤqa-
shoulder aₐ·kɛnqu'm'yu, aₐ·kwɛt!, -wɛt!
shout, to -haluk.litₗya'xₐ(ne·) (see -hal-)
    to shout for joy -awut-
shrew tsɛ'nla, ka'lta·t
shut, to -ts!upna-
side aₐ·kwi'yat!
    side of body aₐ·qałwi'yat!, -wiyat!-

side a_{ι}‘kwi′yat!
  on each side ya- pr.
  on one side tsιk!e·n- pr.
  on the other side le′$_\iota$ne·
  the other side la′ts$_\iota$ne·
sideways upιn-, mal(u)- pr.
  striped sideways malu′q!lil (see mal[u]-)
sinew a_a‘q!u′lka, a_a‘kιnq!a′lqa
sing, to -hawasxo-
  he sings going around q!untkalhawasxo′me·k (see q!untka-)
sink, to -ιktsιn(uq)-
sister (said by brother) al′tske$_\iota$l
  sister (of girl) tsu
  younger sister (of girl) na′na
  sisters nana′$_a$t$_\iota$mo (see na′na)
  sister-in-law (all kinds), intermediate relative dead luna′t!e·
  sister's child ha′tsa, (said by woman) xalna′le$_\iota$l (see xa′l[e·])
  sister's daughter (said by woman) swina′le·l (see swιn)
sit down, to -ιsak$_\iota$nu-, -hanaq-, -hanqa-
  they two sat down -ιn·a·ke·sιnqame′$_\iota$ke·
  he sat down on top naqo$_u$saq!maxo′$_u$me·k (see -haqosa-)
  he always sat with back to fire sla·‘t$_\iota$yil·a‘n·taqanaqna′kse· (see la′nta)
  not sitting down a long time qa.e·txa·me·nqa′me·k (see -[e·txamιn]-)
  sitting there sanaqna′kse· (see -hanaq-)
six, to be -ιn·mιsa-
size yι′ske· (see yιs—ke·)
skillful qastsu′mqaqa′$_a$ne· (see -stsu′m-)
skin, to -q!a(te·), -hunuq!me·-
  skin a_a‘ku′q!a
  dried skin a_a‘kwo′q!la
  tan skin, to -ιtq!anxo-
  white (skin) aqts!ι(xmala)-
skull a_a‘k.lam·ala·k (see -malak)
skunk xa′xas
sky a_a‘kιlmi′yιt (see -miyιt), a_a‘kιl.mi′yιt
  blackish sky hamqoq!uku·lakat.le·tιt$_\iota$ne·- (see ham-)
slap, to -maq!ne·(xo)-
slave tsuk^{u}atu′mal (see tsuk^u[a′te·])
sleep, to -q!u′mne·-, -le$_\iota$ts-
sleepy, to be -hats!ala(qa)-
slide on snow, to -ha·mιluqkatι′le·k
slim, to be -ukts(qa)-
sluice box a_a‘ku·′no·k C
small, to be -tsa-
small ktsaqu′na (see -tsa-), -nana
  I have a small house (or tent) hutsat.lanana′ne· (see -tsa-)
  a place is small tsale·ιt$_\iota$nana′ne· (see -tsa-)
smell, to -aqluk!-, -hanιmsιqq$_a$- (see -ha-)
  to smell of -hakυmsιke$_\iota$(te·) (see -ha-)
  it smells of -snιmsik(qa$_a$)-
  to smell bad -uktuk-
smoke, to -nuq$_u$-
  to smoke a pipe (= eat smoke) -ιknoquk$_u$- (see -nuq$_u$-)

smoke *yam·u*
  smoke hole *-k!anqo·t, a_a·k!a'nqo·(t)*
snail *nɛlxamyu·'wat!*
snake *a_a·kɛnu'la·m*
snipe *nuktsnaq!a''nka·m*
snort, to *-t!anukqlo'_uk^u(ne·)*
snow *-lu, a'_a·k·lu* (see *-lu*), *a'_a·k.lo·*
snow falls from trees *-hupumak(ne·)*
  it is snowing *-walɛnk!alalu'ne·*
snowshoes *-k!aqayt, a_a·k!a'qayt*
snowstorm *-wa'milnilkɛt-*
so, he thought *qalwi'yne·* (see *qa-*)
socks *a_a·kat·ɛ'kna·m* C
soft, to be *-tspuq!uɛį-*
sole of foot *a_a·kuk.lak.lɛ'k(na·m)* C
some one *na'qa,* (indefinite object) *-ka* suff., (indefinite subject) *-nam* suff.
somebody *qa'la*
something *qa'psin*
son-in-law *nawa'spal*
song *a_a·kɛlq!a'nil*
soup *na'qpo^uk, wo'q!ka·*
source of river *ts_aqa'haks* (see *tsaqan-*)
sow, to *-ɛtmo(k!o)-*
sparrow hawk *kiaq!aku'tats*
speak the truth, to *tsɛma'k!ke'įne·* (see *-tsɛma·k!*)
  he can not speak *qataltsxa'n·e·* (see *qatal-*)
spear *(k)tsquna'_akɛnxa'm·u, tsuk!oti'yal*
  fish spear *a_a·k.la'xa* C
  three-pointed fish spear *a_a·ko'_unal, a_a·kɛnu'kmak* C
spilled, to be *-yɛk!ta-*
spirit (?), a *tsa'kap*
spits it out, he *matqlaxwa'_ate·* (see *-mat-*)
split with hand, to *tsɛk!kɛ'n·e·* (see *-tsɛk!-*)
spoon *pɛ'tsa·k* (see *-pɛts;* see also *-haluqkįnɛlxneįmv'[n·e·]*)
spread out *-q!an-*
spring of year, springtime *luma'yɛl* (see also *-mayɛl*)
spruce *ktsɛ'tsqa·l*
squeezes him, it *tsɛnxu'n·e·* (see *-tsɛn-*)
squirrel *ta·k!a·ts*
stab, to *-nulk!o-* (see *-nul-*), *-ako_u-*
  he stabbed him with it *quna·kɛnxamu'n·e·* (see *qun-*)
stake in gambling, to *-stɛl(e·k)*
stalk *a_a·kuk.lu'k^ua* C
stand, to *-wɛs-*
  he stands *hawɛsqa'_ane·* (see *-ha-*)
  he stands thus *qa·wɛsqa'_ane·* (see *-wɛs-*)
  we stand *hunakɛlwɛsqawala'_ane·* (see *-kɛl-*)
  there stands *-swɛts-, -sɛn-*
  it stands in it *nakɛlwɛtsqa'_ane·* (see *hakil-*)
  he stands biting *nawɛ'tsxane·* (see *-ha-*)
  standing biting *kawɛ'tsxa* (see *-xa-* suff.)
  to stand holding *-ɛsqawɛts-*
  he stands holding *-hawɛtskɛ'n·e·* (see *-ha-*)

stand, to -wɛs-
  he stood ready to pound nawɛtsnulxo′ᵤneˑ (see -nul-)
  he stood still n′ɛtwɛsqa′ₐneˑ (see -wɛs-)
star aₐ′nɛlno′hos, -(ɩ)lno′hos, -lnohoᵤs
  how many stars? k!aqsaˑlno′hoˑs (see -lnohoᵤs)
start, to ts!ɛna′xeˑ (see -axeˑ), -hutsɛn-
  to start away from speaker ts!ɛn- pr.
  to start towards speaker ts!ɛk- pr.
  to start a fire -tsukᵘ-
  fire started qanaq!mak.lɛnq!oku′pseˑ (see -haq!ma-)
  he started running noˑtsɛnqkupek!′meˑk (see -hutsɛn-)
  he started up river ts!ɛnaltsaqana′xeˑ (see tsaqan-)
starve, to -yanxu-
  he is starving -sakno′′ktseˑk
  starving, although having a fish trap ksano′′ktsᵢyɛnkɛ′tsqa (see -sakno′′ktseˑk,
    -kɛtsqa)
stay, to -ɛtwɛs(qa)-, -ɛtwɛts-
  to stay over night -yᵢksɩ′leˑk, -hakup(malna′mneˑ)
  he staid qaosaqa′ₐneˑ (see qa- pr.)
  he staid there sa.osaqa′ₐneˑ (see sao-), qaosaqa′ₐneˑ (see qao-)
steal, to -ay-
stealthily ats- pr.
steam aₐ′kalnolatako′′koˑ C
steep, to be -yaq(le′et)-
stem of tobacco plant aₐ′kɩ′nqoˑl
stick aₐ′kɩnq!a′woˑk, aₐ′kanka′wok, a′ₐ′kɛts
  stick into, to -apak!ɛn-
  to stick on -t!apts-
  he stuck it on t!apts!akɛ′nˑeˑ (see -kɛn)
  legs stick out tunwakakɛswɛtsˑa′q!ₐneˑ (see -wɛts-)
  his two legs stuck out tunwakakɛswiˑtsˑa′q!neˑ (see tunwa-,
  it stuck out a little sq!maˑ′wiˑtslɩnq!a′′′ntseˑ (see -q!ma-)
still upskɩl-, sakɛl-, pr.
  he is still angry saˋkɛlsaˑnɛlwe′yneˑ (see sahan-, sakɛl-)
stingy -upᵢyɛt!eᵢ-
stock of gun aₐ′kuk!pwu C
stockings aₐ′kalɛ′knaˑm C
stomach -wum
  of partridge aₐ′koa′pla C
stone nu′kᵘ(ey), -nukᵘ-
  flat stone aₐ′kɛkts!la′nuk (see -ts!la-)
  gray stone aₐ′quxma′nuk (see [-quxma-])
  rough, sharp stone aₐ′k!anu′leˑk
  white stone aₐ′kmɛnuqlu′nuk (see -nuqlum-)
  burnt stones aₐ′q!ono′ᵤkoˑ no′ᵤkᵤey
  flat stones aₐ′kɛnuq!laᵤnuk
  sharp stones aₐ′k!ano′ᵤkoˑ, -k!a(no′ᵤkoˑ)
  sharp, flat stones aₐ′kɛnuq!laˑnu′k!ᵘeˑn (see -nuq!la-)
stop (intransitive), to ɛtwɛs(qa)-, -ɛtwɛts-, -ɛtqa- (see -ɛl-), -qaqas-
  he stops qaqaskɛ′nˑeˑ (see -qaqas-)
stopped, noise q!aluk.le.ɛ′tᵢneˑ
stout -al-
straight, to be -apɛs-

straight upward *qala'k·ne·s*
strange, to be *-aₐqa-*
strap, rawhide *aₐ·kts!ɪ'ka*
strawberry *aₐ·q!u'ko·, aₐ·ku'q!o·*
stretch out, to *-ɪt!na-, -q!al-*
   he stretched his leg out quickly *qal'ɪt!naqkupq!alsa'q!ne·* (see *-q!al-*)
   he stretched it out *n'a`kaq!alkɪ'n·e·* (see *-q!al-*)
   he stretched his hand into it *tsaqa·natsq!ahc'ɪne·* (see *tsaqan-*)
strike, to *-lal(te·)*
   he struck it *qanla'lte·* (see *qan-*, *-lal[te·]*)
   will strike from each side *tsxalyaqxa·`lalta'pse·* (see *-qxa-*)
   he struck again from underneath *lao·'nil·a`qxaqku`plaltc'lne·* (see *-qxa-*)
   he struck him suddenly *ts!ɪnha`q!mak!axne'kse·* (see *-k!ax[me·k]*)
   by striking *-xo-* suff.
strike-a-light *aₐ·kete'ɪmo·*
string, moccasin *aₐ·kuk.luka'tslo·* C
   strings for tying up parflèche *aₐ·kilkaxnilko'lom* C
stripe *-q!leᵢl, aₐ·ku'q!li·l*
   middle stripe *kqayaqa`wuha'q!lil* (see *-q!leᵢl*)
   striped sideways *malu'q!lil* (see *mal[u]-*)
strong, he is *tsɛmak!qa'ₐne·* (see *-qa-*, *-tsɛma·k!*)
   strongly *-tsɛma·k!-*
stump *-qutuk!pko, aₐ·qulu'k!pko·*
suck, to *-tsutil-*
suddenly, to do *-haq!ma-*
   suddenly he entered *nukᵘhaq!ma·kɪkqa'ₐne·* (see *-haq!ma-*)
summer *aₐ·qsu`k!ᵘitna'mu*
sun *nata'ne·k!*
sun dance *-haquxol-* (see *-hanuxo-*)
surround, to *-halqo·ma·t-*
suspenders *aₐ·kuk.lu`kᵘatskpu'k(na·m), aₐ·kilu`kᵘatspu'kna·m* C
swallow, to *-u'mqol-, -ɪ'mqol-, -hanuq!ᵘyo'ₐ(te·)* (see *-han-*), *-uq!wiya-, -q!wiya(te·)*
   he swallowed him *k!unuq!ᵘwiya'ₐte·* (see *-q!wiya[te·]*)
swamp *aₐ·k!aqla'ha·l, -k!aqlahal, -haqanak!aqla'ha·l*
swan *qu'qouq*
sweat in sweat lodge, to *-wɪs(e·k)*
   sweat lodge *wɪsi'al* (see *-wɪs[e·k]*)
swells up, belly *-hutkawumako-*
swift *kalnuku'pqa* (see *-hal-*)
swim, to *-naq-, -haqₐ-, -huluqᵘ-* (see *hul-*)
swing, to *-hawɪskaxu'ktse·* (see *-ha-*)
switch for stringing fish *la·m'*
tail *-qat, a'ₐ·qat*
   bird's tail *aₐ·kɪnuq!ma'ₐna*
   fish tail *aₐ·kɪnq!a'qa·t*
   he put the tail up quickly *qalyuwa·kaq!alqa'tɪnc* (see *-qat*)
take, to *tsukᵘ(a'te·), -ka-*
   to take away (?) *-wa-*
   to take one's own *-ups(t)-*
   to take with hand *tsukokuɪ'n·e·* (see *tsukᵘ[a'te·]*)
   to take with hand out of water *tsukuqkuɪ'n·e·* (see *tsukᵘ[a'te·]*)
   it was taken ashore *la.u`pkaqkɪnɪ'lne·* (see *-haqₐ-*)
   his wife is taken away from him *wakaltɪ'lne·* (see *-wak-*)
   it is taken from him *wakɪnɪ'lne·* (see *-wak-*)

take, to *tsuku(a′te·)*, *-ka-*
   what he had taken out of water *k!upka′ₐnqo·l* (see *-ka-*)
   he took a good seat *sukᵘxo′ᵤme·k* (see *-soᵤk-*)
   he took both *xa`tsɪnɪltsukᵘa′te·* (?) (see *xatsɪn-*)
   he took it out of fire *la·upkak!o′ᵤne·* (see *-ka-*)
   he takes it *n′atskalkɪ′n·e·* (see *-hal-*)
tale, historical *aₐ′qalpalne′yam*
talk, to *-tsxa(n·e·)*, *-haqalpalneᵢ-* (see *-pal-*), *-hakq!yɪt-*
   he talks *naqalpalne·′ne·* (see *-haqal-*)
   they talk together *t!aqta·la′mne·*
   they talked *nakq!eyɪ′tᵢne·* (see *-q!eyɪt*)
   talking *aₐ′kɪq!ye·t*
talons of birds *aₐ′kɪtsq!aekama′lak*
taste, to *-axne·*
   it tastes good *sukᵘaxₐne′ɪse·* (see *-xa-* suff.)
tear off bark, I *huluts!qalxo′ᵤne·* (see *-ts!qaₐl*)
teeth, with *-xa-* suff.
   molar and canine teeth *inɪ′stin*
tell news, to *tuq!tsqake′ᵢne·* (see *-tuq!ts-*)
   she told some one *tsxanatka′ₐne·* (see *-ka*)
ten, to be *-ɪt!ᵤwo·-*
tent *-t.la*, *-(ɪ)t.la*, *aₐ′kɪt.la′na·m* (see *-t.la*)
   part of tent near door *la′q!a*
   he made a tent for himself *n′ɪtɪt.la′ₐte·k* (see *-t.la*)
   (tent) is covered *-tuk!xo(lne·)*
   tent cover *aₐ′ka′wu*
   tent frame *-nqo·*, *aₐ′kɪ′nqo·*
   outer side of tent, at bottom, all around *la′′nta*
   rear part of tent, back of fire *la′′nta*
   tent pole *aₐ′kɪts; aₐ′ma′le·t; -kits, -[ɪ]ts*
   tent site *ko′o*
terrible, it looks *n′ɪse·(kate)ᵢ*
testicle *-maq!an*, *aₐ′kma′q!a·n*
that *qo·*
   that one *ne·*
then *ta′xa*
there (demonstrative) *sao-*, *saw-* pr., *-saqxal-*, *qao-*, *qaw-* pr., *qo·*
   along there *qan-* pr.
   it is right along there *qa`kɪlhaqa′ₐne·* (see *qa-* pr.)
   he arrived there *qaoxa′xe·* (see *qao-*)
   he staid there *sa·usaqa′ₐne·* (see *sao-*), *qaosaqa′ₐne·* (see *qao-*)
   just there he made it *qooxal′ɪtkɪ′n·e·* (see *qao-*)
there stands *-swɪts-*, *-sɪn-*
   there is a hill *swɪtslɪ·ɪ′tᵢne·* (see *-swɪts-*)
   there is a stone *swɪtsnu′kᵘne·* (see *-swɪts-*)
therefore *aqa(l)-* pr.
thick, to be *-waq(c′ɪne·)*
thick *-al-*
thicket *-kɪlhaq!anqots!la′e·n* (see *-kɪl-*), *aq!a*
thigh *aₐ′kɪnɪ′k!na·m*, *aₐ′q!o·′wuk!*
   (of bird) *aₐ′ke′nuk* C
thin, to be *-paqts-*
thine *nɪ′nko*

think about something, to -kn(ɩlwiy)-
  he is thinking about it silkᵢnilwiyteya'ₐt·e, kinelwi'ytik (see -kn[ɩlwiy]-)
  he thought thus or so qalwe'yne· (see qa-, -[ɩ]lwey-)
thirsty -huk!nuq!luma
this na
thorn bush (?) kala'wo·k
thou nɩ'nko
thread aₐ·kila'ktsu (also aₐ·kola'ktsu) C
three, to be -qalsa-
  he has three children qalsaqa'lte· (see -qalsa-)
throat aₐ·k.luma'na·m, aₐ·q!a'nq!me·wae·k
through qayaqa- pr.
throw, to -mɩt-
  to throw many things -nmu(ẋo)-
  he was thrown into fire ẋunakinɩ'lne· (see ẋun-)
thumb tu'ts!a·k!
thunder nu'm·a
thus qa-
  he said thus qake'ᵢne· (see qa-)
  he cried thus qalo'ᵤkᵤne· (see qa-)
  he is thus qaqa'ₐne· (see qa-)
tickle, to -q!utse'ᵢ(te·)
tie, to -ituk!sa-
  to tie hair in knot (?) -huto·qsa-
  to tie up (for shamanistic performance) -q!aẋ-
  some one who is tied up kq!aẋna'mnam (see -q!aẋ-)
  something tied together (?) kiakẋa'ẋa·l
time -yɩt- suff.
tired -huk.luk-
  to be tired -sa'n(qa)-
  tired walking ksakɩ'me·k (see -sak-)
toad ko'uko·
tobacco ya'q!eᵢt (see -yaq!-), wasa'qₐnɩ·n, aₐ·kmoq!o·'ma·l
  plug tobacco kq!awu'ᵤka·l (see -q!awuka-)
  stem of tobacco plant aₐ·kɩ'nqo·l
  tobacco seeds aₐ·kɩnu'q!yuk ya'q!e·t
  Tobacco River aₐ·kanu'ẋo· C
  to cut tobacco -q!awuka-
to-day hosanmiyɩ'tke·
toe aₐ·kɩtsq!a'kna·m, aₐ·kɩnk!a'ₐlik
  big toe k!a·le·matsqakɛma'ak (see -matsqȧk)
together -mal suff.
  together with -tᵢmo suff.
tomahawk aₐ·kɩnu'q!e·
tongue walu·'nak
tooth aₐ·q!u'na·n'
top aₐ·kɩ'nqa·n (aₐ·kɩ'nq!a·n), (?) -q!yu-
  to be on top of water -mu(wɩsu'q)-
torch aₐ·kɩnoqᵘa'ₐko
touch, to -qunyaẋₐ- (see -yaẋ-), -wu-
  he touched him roughly wuqkupẋo'ᵤne· (see -wu-)
  he touched it qunya'ẋₐne· (see qun-)
  he touched it lightly wu·q!maẋo'ᵤne· (see -q!ma-)

towards -*huts*- pr.
  motion towards speaker *k*- pr.
  towards speaker and out of *ak*- pr.
  towards speaker and into *tɪk*-
town a_a'*kɪk.lu'na·m*, -*k.lu*
  those in the town *ha$_a$k.lo'$_u$ku^c·* (see -*k.lu*)
toy -*k.lɪnq!o*-
tracks a_a'*k.lɪ'knam*
  (in snow) a_a'*k!alu'ku^{i}l*
  his tracks a_a'*k.lɪ'k!e·s* (see -*lɪk*)
trail a_a'*kma'na·m*, -*ma*
  it is a long trail *wumana'mne·* (see -*ma*)
  (in snow) a_a'*k!alu'ko* (see a_a'*k!alu'ku^{i}l*)
  trail is wide *n'almama'$_a$ne·* (?) (see -*ma*)
tramp on something, to -*t!ats!aane·*(*ɪkɪ'n·e*)
trap a_a'*ka'k!o·*
  fish trap a_a'*kɪ'tsqa*, -*kɪtsqa*, *ya'qa*
  my traps *kaq!oka'ko·* (see -*q!a*-)
travel by canoe, to -*haqul*-
travois a_a'*q!$_u$ka'ma·l*
tree -*ts!lae·n*, -(ɪ)*ts!la'e·n*, a_a'*kɪts!la'e·n* (see *place*, *thicket*)
  young tree -*qlupin*, a_a'*kuqlu'pe·n*
  different kind of tree (?) *k!a'k!lan·aq!o'x$_u$male'et* (see -*q!uxm̀a*)
  tree on other side *k.lohanɪts!la'e·n* (see *lu*-)
  dry trees -*hak!ak.lonuk*-
trembled for fear, he *n'upt!ɪnmɪtɪlwe'yxome·k* (see -*upt!ɪnmit*-)
tripe a_a'*k.laqpɪ'sqap*
trout *qu'stɪt!*
try, to -*ako$_u$ku$_ɪn$*-
  to try hard -*alsɪn*(*t*)-
turn, in -*la·*-
turnip a_a'*k.lɛmala'k*(*na·m*) C
turtle *ka'xax̣*
twig *la·m'*
  little twig a_a'*q!utsk!a'lakna'na*
two -*as*, -*ɑi*- $>$ -*as+n* (see -*as*)
  to be two -*as*-   .
  two children *lkamuku$_ɪ$'ste·k* (see -*kɪs*-)
  she had two children *n'asqa'lte·* (see [*qalt*])
  two seasons *t!uk.lun·maku'tɪne·*
uncle (father's brother) *x̣a*
  (mother's brother) *x̣a'tsa*, *ha'tsa*
under blanket, under cover *aqsa*- pr.
uneasy, to feel -*hukoyɪlx̣oneɪ*- (see -*hukuya*[*kateɪ*])
untie, to -*aqte*-
up -*ɪktɪk*-, *ɪtkɪk*- pr., *yu·*-, *wa·*-
up river *tsaqan*- pr.
use, to -*hu—te·*
  to use a spoon -*haluqkɪnɪlx̣neɪmʋ*(*n·e·*)
uvula *t!a'tka*
valley a_a'*kamɪ'n·a*, -*k!a·mɪna*, a_a'*k.la'x̣we·*
vein a_a'*q!u'lka*
verbal stem -*a*-, -*ala*-
very -*tsɛma·k!*, -*ɪsc·l* pr.
vessel, pottery *a'tso*, *yɪtske'ɪme·* (see *yɪ'tske·*)
vest, embroidered a_a'*kɪno·malnoka'kna·m* C

Viburnus opulus, fruit of $a_a \cdot ko'mo \cdot$

village $-k.lu$, $a_a \cdot k_\epsilon k.lu'na \cdot m$

visits, he $qo \cdot na'xe \cdot$ (see qun -)

vomit, to (?) $-walne$ -

wad of gun $a_a \cdot kukwat_\epsilon'lil$ C

wait, to $-kpa(me \cdot k)$

  they waited $nanilwok^{u_\epsilon}nxa'lne$ (see $-hanil$ -)

  he was waited for $naw_\epsilon tskpayat_\epsilon'lne \cdot$ (see $-kpa[me \cdot k]$, $-w_\epsilon ts$ -)

walk, to $-omo$ -

  I who walk about $kuqa \smile ha'_a lkqa_a ts$ (see $-qal$ -)

  to walk along shore (?) $-\epsilon tsqawa \cdot qa \cdot (l)$ -

  he walks about $(n')uk!en(axe \cdot)$

want, to $-ute$ -

  you may want it $h_\epsilon nl_\epsilon n'o'_u te \cdot$ (see $-lin$)

  he wants to act his own way $-s_\epsilon n \cdot akpa'me \cdot k$

  he wants to eat more $ts_\epsilon mne \cdot xa'_a me \cdot k$

war, to go to $-wanaq_a na$ -, $-anaxaka$ -

war cry, to utter $-hal_\epsilon nq!oylo \cdot k^ua'_a (me \cdot k)$

warm, to be $-ut_i me \cdot$ -, $-o \cdot ya$ -

Warren Creek $a_a \cdot ka'tak$ C

wart $a_a \cdot q!anlupx_a ma'ko \cdot$ (see $a_a \cdot q!a'nlup$)

Wasa $a'_a k!ne \cdot s$

wash, to $-\epsilon ktoqo$ -

  he washes his body $na'qtse \cdot k$ (see $-haq_a$ -)

watch, to $-\epsilon tw_\epsilon tsk$ -

  to watch for something $-w_\epsilon tskil$ - (see $-w_\epsilon tsk_\epsilon k$ -)

water $-ku$, $wu'u$

  water is warm $n'ut_i me'_i k_u ne \cdot$ (see $-ku$)

  there is no water $l_\epsilon tu'k^u ne \cdot$ (see $l_\epsilon t$ -)

  he arrived at water $laxa'qo \cdot l$ (see $-lax$ -)

  deep water $a_a \cdot q!a'nuk$

  there is water $n_\epsilon''nha \cdot ks$

  it was thrown into water $xunm_\epsilon tqu'lne \cdot$ (see xun -)

  he throws it into water $xunm_\epsilon tqu'lne \cdot$ (see xun -)

  where there is red water $ya \cdot knoso'_u k^u e \cdot$ (see $-ku$)

water fowl, a small (long, slender neck, white belly, dark back) $m_\epsilon'tsu \cdot k$

water hole $a'_a ka \cdot k$

water monster $yawo'_u nek!$

water ousel $ts_\epsilon'tsqo \cdot m$

wave $a_a \cdot qay_\epsilon'nme \cdot k$

we $kamina'la$ (see $ka'min$)

weasel $ma'yo \cdot k$

weather $-le.\epsilon t$

 it is bad weather $sahanle.\epsilon't_i ne \cdot$ (see $-le.\epsilon t$)

weir, fish $a_a \cdot kwu'kxo \cdot$ C

well! $ho'ya$

well, he sees $suk^{u_\epsilon}l'upx_a ne \cdot$ (see $-so_u k$ -)

wet, it lay there $sk_\epsilon kqoq^u ts!ala'_i ne \cdot$ (see $-qoq^u ts!ala$ -)

what $qa'psin$

wheat $a_a \cdot k_\epsilon nku'la \cdot l$, $a_a \cdot k_\epsilon nkowa'la \cdot l$ (Lower Kutenai) C

where ka_a

  where there is (verbal noun) $ya-ke \cdot$

  where there is a hole in a mountain $hank!am_i nake \cdot$ (see $ha-ke \cdot$)

  where there is a level place (on a hill) $haq!an \cdot uqle \cdot \epsilon'tke \cdot$ (see $-q!an$ -)

whetstone $a_a \cdot kte'_i mo \cdot$

while he was away $ksc_a kmu' \chi o \cdot$ (see -$mo\chi un \cdot e \cdot$)

whirlpool $a_a \cdot k\iota n\iota qa' yka \cdot k$

whisper, to -$halatsuk^u iya' m(ne \cdot)$ (see -hal-)

whistle $ku'sto \cdot l$

  whistle to -$halukwa\chi niyam$ (see -ha-)

white -$nuqlum$-

whitefish $ma'te_i t!, o \cdot pa \cdot t!$

who? $qa'la$

whoever $qa'la \cdot n \cdot$ (see $qa'la$)

whole night, the $y_\iota \iota nwunmiy_\iota' tk_\varepsilon \cdot$ (see -$miy_\varepsilon t$). (See *entirety*)

wide -al-

widow, widower $la\chi lo \cdot' mal$

wife $t\iota'lna$

wild -$okoy(qa)$-

  to be wild -$huk^u e_i (qapqa)$- (see -$hukuya[kate_i]$-)

willow $a_a \cdot q!uma'_a wo \cdot k$

win, to -hoq-

wind $a_a \cdot ku'me \cdot$

  wind blows $nalum_\iota' n \cdot e \cdot$ (see -hal-)

  wind blows a certain way $qanaw_\iota tso'' me \cdot$ (see -ha-)

window $a_a \cdot kanka \cdot nuk.lulmukna' e \cdot t$ C

windpipe $o_a \cdot q!uwa' e \cdot k$ (see $a_a \cdot q!a'nq!me \cdot wa \cdot k$)

wing -$(\iota)nqowa, a_a \cdot k\iota nqo \cdot' wa, -w\iota t!, a'_a \cdot kw\iota t!$

winter $wanu(y_\iota tna'm \cdot o)$ (see -$y_\iota t$-)

  it is winter time $wanuy_\iota' t_i ne$ (see $wanu[y_\iota tna'm \cdot o]$)
  (see -$y_\iota t$-)

wise -$\iota lk\iota lwey$- (see -ιlk-)

  he is wise $qastsu'mqaqa'_a ne \cdot$ (see -$stsu'm$-), $nulq!o'k_u ne \cdot$ (see -$lq!ok$-)

wish, to -$hak.luq!^u wiya\chi_a$-

  to wish for something -$y_\iota lna'nts(te \cdot)$

witchcraft, to practice -$antsa$-

with -mal suff.

  shooting with it $km\iota t\chi a'm \cdot u$ (see -mu)

  with body or back -χo- suff.

  with foot -$\iota k\iota n$ suff.

  with hand -$k\iota n$ suff.

  with knife, -$q(a)$ suff.

  with mouth, with teeth, -χa- suff.

  with point -$k!o$- suff.

  with saw -χal suff.

without $l\iota t$- pr.

wolf $ka'_a ke \cdot n$

wolverene $ats!po$

woman $pa'lke_i$

wood $lo_u k!u, -wo_u k^u$

woodchuck $kianl\iota' k!\chi o \cdot, kianl\iota' k\chi o \cdot$ (see -$nl\iota' k\chi o \cdot$)

woodpecker, black $ku'po \cdot k!$

  red-headed woodpecker $yama'kpa \cdot l$

  a small woodpecker $nalmu\chi na'yi \cdot t$

work, to -$\iota lwat!$-

world $y_\iota sle_\iota' tke \cdot$ (see $y_\iota s$—$ke \cdot$), $y_\iota sle.\iota' tske \cdot$ (?)

wound $a_a \cdot k.luktsum \cdot o'\iota n$

  to wound -$\iota se \cdot$-

  Wounded Knee $q!o \cdot malq!a'n \cdot ko \cdot$ (see -$haq!ank!o \cdot'[le \cdot k]$)

wrist a_a'$qo'ytka\cdot k$; a_a'$kwi'tsa\cdot k$; a_a'$kınkataptsı'k_ına\cdot m$ (see a_a'$ktaptse'_ıkna\cdot m$),

writing a_a'$ku'q!li\cdot l$

year   -$nmakut$

yellow fluid a_a'$kma'k!tsuk$

yellowish, it looks $namak!tsa$'$_akat.le\cdot tıt_ıne$'$ne\cdot$ (see -kat [$e\cdot$])

yellow-jacket $yu\cdot$''$wat!$

yes he_i

yesterday $wa'lkwa$

youth $nıtsta'hal$

   youth about to marry $nıtsta$'$halq!lik!a'ma\cdot l$ (see $nıtsta'hal$)

Reprint Publishing

FOR PEOPLE WHO GO FOR ORIGINALS.

This book is a facsimile reprint of the original edition. The term refers to the facsimile with an original in size and design exactly matching simulation as photographic or scanned reproduction.

Facsimile editions offer us the chance to join in the library of historical, cultural and scientific history of mankind, and to rediscover.

The books of the facsimile edition may have marks, notations and other marginalia and pages with errors contained in the original volume. These traces of the past refers to the historical journey that has covered the book.

ISBN 978-3-95940-199-9

www.reprintpublishing.com